REAL ESTATE
FINANCE

NINTH EDITION

SHERRY SHINDLER PRICE

LEIGH CONWAY

ALLIED
REAL ESTATE SCHOOLS
A Division of Allied Business Schools

This publication is designed to provide accurate and current information regarding the subject matter covered. The principles and conclusions presented are subject to local, state and federal laws and regulations, court cases and revisions of same. If legal advice or other expert assistance is required, the reader is urged to consult a competent professional in the field.

Real Estate Publisher
Leigh Conway

Academic Information Analyst
Laura King

Writers
Nicole Thome, Senior Technical Writer
Sue Carlson, Technical Writer

Editor
Emily Kazmierski

Production Designer
Susan Mackessy Richmond

©2017 by Allied Real Estate Schools, a division of Allied Business Schools, Inc.
Ninth Edition

Published by:
Allied Real Estate Schools
22952 Alcalde Drive
Laguna Hills, California 92653

Printed in the United States of America

ISBN: 978-0-934772-15-0

TABLE OF CONTENTS

PREFACE

This comprehensive text is written primarily for real estate students; however, inquiring consumers and investors will also find answers to their real estate finance questions.

Each unit has been divided into topics. Topic content is reinforced through real-life examples, photographs, illustrations, charts, and tables. Important terms are highlighted in **bold type** in each unit. Each unit ends with a summary.

Review exercises have been designed for each unit. The quiz exercises features real estate finance terms and multiple choice questions. The multiple choice questions at the end of each unit will help the student prepare for the real estate exam. These questions were designed to test higher-level concepts and will often require the student to combine information they have learned in different units.

After completing a quiz exercise, students can check their answers by reviewing the Answer Key in the Appendix. Students should be encouraged to review their work often to make sure they understand what they have read.

ABOUT THE AUTHORS

SHERRY SHINDLER PRICE

Sherry Shindler Price has been a California Community College real estate instructor since 1986. She has over twenty-five years of experience in the real estate profession, including eight years of specialization in investment properties and residential sales. She has authored *California Real Estate Principles* and *Escrow Principles and Practices*. In addition, Ms. Shindler Price has reviewed numerous real estate textbooks for major publishers and has written a series of continuing education courses for private real estate schools. Her extensive knowledge in real estate was used to write test questions for state licensing examinations in Nevada, Wisconsin, Minnesota, Maryland, and Iowa. Ms. Shindler Price has a Bachelor of Science degree in Education from Long Beach State College.

LEIGH CONWAY

Leigh Conway brings a rich background in real estate to the creation and production of this textbook. She is a licensed real estate broker in California with experience in commercial brokerage, residential and commercial property management, syndication, and real estate development. With over ten years of experience in real estate education, she has taught various statutory and continuing education courses. In addition, she co-authored a number of real estate textbooks and wrote several continuing education courses for private real estate schools. Ms. Conway has a Bachelor's Degree from the University of California at Los Angeles.

ACKNOWLEDGMENTS

The authors would like to thank the following reviewers for their feedback and suggestions. Their experience and expertise assisted in the creation of this text.

Rick Boone – Santa Ana, California
Licensed California Real Estate Salesperson
Adjunct Real Estate Instructor for Orange Coast Community College

Steven David – Fort Lauderdale, Florida
Licensed Florida Real Estate Broker
Licensed Florida Real Estate Instructor
CRB, CRS, GRI, MBA, LCAM
Senior Faculty Member of the Florida Graduate REALTOR® Institute (GRI)
program since 1988
Author of CE courses for the Florida Association of REALTORS®

Gary Frimann – Gilroy, California
Licensed California Real Estate Broker
GRI, GRI-MASTERS, ALHS, SRES, ABR, CIPS, CRS, CCIM, e-PRO, CRB ABRM
Approved Broker for U.S. Department of Housing and Urban Development

Ignacio Gonzales – Ukiah, California
Licensed California Real Estate Broker
Real Estate Coordinator and Adjunct Real Estate Instructor for Mendocino
Community College
Instructor for the GRI and serves as a faculty member
Author of California Real Estate Economics

Alexander Robertson – Richmond, Texas
Certified Mortgage Planning Specialist™ (Member CMPS® Institute)

Ronald J. Roth, Jr. – Ridgefield, Connecticut
Licensed New York Real Estate Broker
Past Director – Real Estate Finance Association of Connecticut (Hartford and
Fairfield Chapters)

The Nature & Cycle of the Economy and Real Estate Finance

Unit 1

INTRODUCTION

Financing is an important and even necessary part of most real estate deals. What is finance? Finance is a branch of economics concerned with resource allocation as well as resource management, acquisition, and investment. Simply, finance deals with matters related to money and the markets.

The purchase of real estate generally is the largest acquisition consumers make in their lifetime. Most people cannot pay "all cash" for a property and must obtain some type of financing—conventional or government-backed loans, hard money loans, HELOCs, seller financing, or some other form of financing. This course describes the importance of financing when buying real estate.

Learning Objectives

After completing this Unit, you should be able to:

1A   recall the importance of finance to the economy and its categories.

1B   indicate typical mortgage lending activities.

1C   identify characteristics of business and real estate cycles.

1D   recall the interaction of markets and the economy.

1E   identify information resources used in this Unit.

THE NATURE OF REAL ESTATE FINANCE

Finance can be defined as the commercial activity of providing funds and capital to a borrower. Finance describes the management, creation and study of money, banking, credit, investments, assets, and liabilities that make up financial systems, as well as the study of financial instruments.

Broad Categories of Finance

Some people prefer to divide finance into three distinct categories: public finance, corporate finance, and personal finance.

Public Finance

Public finance includes tax systems, government expenditures, budget procedures, stabilization instruments, debt issues, and other government concerns. The government helps prevent market failure by overseeing allocation of resources, distribution of income and stabilization of the economy. Regular funding for these programs is secured mostly through taxation. Borrowing from banks, insurance companies and governments; receiving grants and aid; and earning dividends from its companies also help finance the government. In addition, user charges from ports, airport services and other facilities; fines resulting from breaking laws; revenues from licenses and fees, such as for driving; and sales of government securities are also sources of public finance.

Corporate Finance

Corporate finance involves managing assets and debt for a business. Businesses obtain financing through equity investments and credit arrangements, and by purchasing securities. Startup businesses may receive money from venture capitalists, and established companies may obtain money by selling stocks or bonds. Businesses may purchase dividend-paying stocks, blue-chip bonds, or interest-bearing bank deposits. Acquiring and managing debt properly can help a company expand and become more profitable.

Personal Finance

Personal finance includes proper management of an individual's income and expenses so enough money is left over for savings. Earning more money and spending less money is the basis of personal finance.

Real estate is the single largest component of wealth for individuals. Because of its magnitude, it plays a key role in shaping the economic condition of individuals and families. For example, it can substantially influence a family's ability to finance education for their children. Changes in the value of real estate can dramatically affect the personal wealth of individuals and families as many experienced in the Great Recession (2007-2009).

Real Estate Finance

Finance has many subcategories, one of which is real estate finance. **Real estate finance** provides the flow of money and credit needed to complete transactions for the purchase and/or development of real property. The study of real estate finance includes the markets, institutions, and instruments necessary for those transactions.

Finance affects the way the market buys and sells real estate. Finance, as applied economics, deals with matters related to money and the markets. A brief overview of the markets is presented later in the Unit; money is discussed in Unit 2.

MORTGAGE LENDING ACTIVITIES

Due to the millions of dollars in mortgage lending activity, retail lenders—banks, thrifts, and credit unions—play a crucial role in the national economy. The mortgage lending industry is highly competitive and involves many types of firms, including commercial banks, investment banks, savings associations, mortgage bankers, mortgage brokers, and loan correspondents. Some of these firms are small and local, while others are large and national. Banks and their subsidiaries and affiliates make up a large and growing proportion of the mortgage lending industry.

Mortgage lending activity generally involves loan originations as well as purchases and sales of loans through the secondary mortgage market. When retail lenders originate mortgage loans, they create two commodities: a loan and the right to service the loan. The lender may retain or sell loans it originates or purchases from affiliates, brokers, or correspondents. Additionally, the lender may also retain or sell the servicing on the loans.

For most retail lenders, loans are the primary use of their funds and the principal way in which they earn income. A mortgage lender's key function is to provide funds for the purchase or refinancing of residential properties. This function is carried out in the primary mortgage market, in which lenders originate mortgages by lending to homeowners and purchasers. In the secondary mortgage market, lenders and investors buy and sell loans that were originated in the primary mortgage market.

Sources of Funds to Loan

As financial intermediaries, retail lenders stand between depositors who supply capital (money) and borrowers who demand capital (money). Retail lenders generally lend money for mortgages, auto loans, and consumer-finance loans.

At the most basic level, retail lenders accept deposits from customers or raise capital from investors, and then use that money to make loans and provide other financial services to customers.

Deposits

Deposits are the primary source of funds for retail lenders. Generally referred to as "core deposits", these are typically the checking and savings accounts. In most cases, these deposits have very short terms because customers have the right to withdraw the full amount at any time. Because of this, many retail lenders pay no interest at all on checking account balances, or at least pay very little, and pay interest rates for savings accounts that are well below U.S. Treasury bond rates.

Obviously, the financial intermediaries (banks, credit unions, and thrifts) encourage customers to make deposits into their institutions. However, if customers think they can make more money in a different investment, they may withdraw their funds. This is known as **disintermediation**—the withdrawal of funds from intermediary financial institutions, such as banks, credit unions, and thrifts, to invest the funds directly in other investments.

Non-Interest Income

There has been a general shift by commercial banks from activities that produce interest income to ones that produce non-interest income and fees. Non-interest income has become a key component of the profits of many commercial retail lenders.

Fees on Deposits and Loans

Customers may dislike service fees, but service fees provide a large amount of revenue for many retail lenders. Retail lenders can charge fees for allowing a customer to have an account open, for using ATMs, or overdraft fees for overdrawing an account. Retail lenders also earn income from fees for services like cashier's checks and safe deposit boxes.

Loan Sales

In some cases, lenders are not well equipped to manage the back office tasks that go into servicing loans. So, they sell the rights to service the loans (**mortgage-servicing rights**)—collecting and forwarding payments, handling escrow accounts, and responding to borrower questions to another financial institution. Although this can be done for almost any kind of loan, it is most common with mortgages and student loans.

Other Sources of Income

Many retail lenders have expanded into offering various investment and retirement products to their customers. In many cases, they offer an array of products like mutual funds, annuities, and portfolio advice. Larger retail lenders may actually operate these funds themselves, through a subsidiary, but others will simply act as a broker.

Although the deposit guarantees that cover bank deposits do not extend to retirement accounts, many investors are under the misconception that they do, and will buy securities from retail lenders under the misconception that they are less risky.

Sources of Income

Making loans generates fee income. Consumer lending makes up the bulk of retail lender lending activity, and of this, **residential mortgages** make up by far the largest share. Mortgages are used to buy residences and the homes themselves are most often the security that collateralizes the loan. **Collateral** is something of value given as security for a debt. Mortgages are typically written for 30-year repayment periods and interest rates may be fixed, adjustable, or variable.

Automobile lending is another significant category of secured lending for many retail lenders. Compared to mortgage lending, auto loans are typically for shorter terms and higher rates. Retail lenders face extensive competition in auto lending from other financial institutions, like auto financing operations run by automobile manufacturers and dealers.

Prior to the collapse of the housing bubble, home equity lending was a fast-growing segment of consumer lending for many retail lenders. **Home equity lending** involves lending money to consumers, for whatever purposes they wish, with the equity in their home. **Equity** is the difference between the appraised value of the home and any outstanding mortgage.

Credit cards are another significant lending type and an interesting case. Credit cards are, in essence, **personal lines of credit** that can be drawn down at any time. Although Visa and MasterCard are well-known names in credit cards, they do not actually underwrite any of the lending. Visa and MasterCard simply run the proprietary networks through which money (debits and credits) is moved between the shopper's bank and the merchant's bank, after a transaction. Not all retail lenders engage in credit card lending because the rates of default are traditionally much higher than in mortgage lending or other types of secured lending. However, credit card lending delivers lucrative fees for retail lenders.

BUSINESS AND REAL ESTATE CYCLES

The financial and real estate markets are driven by the business climate and activity in the economy, which are continuously changing. The changes occur as trends, cycles, or short-term fluctuations. **Trends** are changes in the market in a consistent direction that occur over a long-term period. **Cycles** are periodic, irregular up-and-down movements in economic activity that take place over a period of two to six years. **Short-term fluctuations** are changes in business and economic activity that occur within the year. Typical economic cycles include the business and real estate cycles, which experience expansion followed by contraction—called recession.

Tracking the Economic Cycles

The unofficial beginning and ending dates of national economic expansions and contractions have been defined by the **National Bureau of Economic Research** (NBER), a private nonprofit research organization. The NBER defines an **expansion** as "a period when economic activity rises substantially, spreads across the economy, and typically lasts for several years." The NBER defines a **recession** as "a significant decline in economic activity spread across the economy, lasting more than two quarters, which is 6 months, normally visible in real gross domestic product (GDP), real income, employment, industrial production, and wholesale-retail sales." The NBER dates expansions and recession on a monthly basis. Remember, expansions follow recessions in a continuous cycle.

Expansions

From the end of World War II in 1945 until 2007, there have been ten periods of expansion. Some were short (2 years) others lasting five years or longer. The 1960s experienced increased employment and growth, but at the cost of rising inflation. The expansion of 1975-1980 was marked by even higher inflation. In fact, home mortgage interest rates hit a high of 17.5% in 1981. The years (1965 to 1982) are called the **Great Inflation** due to runaway inflation and high interest rates. The **Great Moderation** (1982 to 2007) was a long period of economic expansion broken by a mild recession in 1991. Currently, the economy is in another expansionary phase.

Recessions

Since the **Great Depression** (1929–1933), there were 12 recessions prior to the **Great Recession** (2007–June 2009). The Great Depression lasted nearly 4 years—banks collapsed, stock markets crashed, and unemployment rose to 24.9%. Just 4 years later, the Recession of 1937 devastated the economy again with unemployment rising to 19%. During the years between 1945 and 2001, there were several recessions—some mild, some steep.

Prior to the 2007-2009 recession, the 1981-82 recession was the worst economic downturn in the United States since the Great Depression, with a nearly 11% unemployment rate. It was triggered by tight monetary policy in an effort to fight mounting inflation incurred during the Great Inflation.

Then in 2007, the subprime mortgage meltdown led to the collapse of the housing bubble and ushered in the Great Recession.

Business Cycles

Business cycles are the ups and downs in economic activity, defined in terms of periods of expansion followed by periods of contraction. Business cycles, i.e., short-run economic fluctuations, occur because disturbances to the economic activity above or below full employment. **Full employment** means that all eligible people who want to work can find employment at prevailing wage rates. Deviations from full employment are often the result of monetary policy. For example, low interest rates and easy money partly fueled the inflationary booms of the 1960s and 1970s. Conversely, the severe recessions of both the early 1970s and the early 1980s were directly attributable to decisions by the Federal Reserve to raise interest rates. Monetary policy is discussed in the next Unit.

Many economists identify a business cycle as a sequence of four phases: (1) expansion, (2) peak, (3) contraction, and (4) trough. However, the National Bureau of Economic Research defines the business cycle as two phases and two turning points. The two phases are expansion (recovery or boom) and contraction (recession or bust). The two turning points are peaks and troughs. An **expansion** is an increase in the pace of economic activity. Conversely, a **contraction** is a slowdown in the pace of economic activity. The **peak** is the upper turning point of a business cycle, and the **trough** is the lower turning point of a business cycle.

Turning Points

The Dating Committee of the National Bureau of Economic Research (NBER), established in 1920, determines the official dates for the business cycles in the United States. The date determined by the Dating Committee as peak date identifies the end of expansion and the beginning of contraction. Conversely, the trough date identifies the end of contraction and beginning of expansion. When determining the dates for peaks and troughs, the Committee acts only on actual indicators and does not rely on forecasts.

The Dating Committee has determined that the U.S. economy has experienced 10 complete business cycles from 1948 through 2001, and that another contraction began in December 2007. The Committee assigned June 2009 as the technical "trough date" to the 2007-2009 recession because the economy is growing, although extremely slowly. Due to this nearly imperceptible growth, many people feel that the economy still is in a recession. Some economists call this a "shadow recession" and give mixed messages on when to expect the economy to improve.

During the period from 1948 through 2001, the average business cycle lasted approximately five years and nine months; the average expansion lasted about five years, whereas the average recession lasted just under one year.

U.S. Business Cycles from 1948 to 2010

Contraction Phase Turning Point	Duration	> < Turning Point	Expansion Phase Turning Point Duration		Business Cycle Duration
Peak	No. Months	Trough	No. Months	Peak	No. Months
Nov-48	11	Oct-49	45	Jul-53	56
Jul-53	10	May-54	39	Aug-57	49
Aug-57	8	Apr-58	24	Apr-60	32
Apr-60	10	Feb-61	106	Dec-69	116
Dec-69	11	Nov-70	36	Nov-73	47
Nov-73	16	Mar-75	58	Jan-80	74
Jan-80	6	Jul-80	12	Jul-81	18
Jul-81	16	Nov-82	92	Jul-90	108
Jul-90	8	Mar-91	120	Mar-01	128
Mar-01	8	Nov-01	73	Dec-07	81
Dec-07	18	June-09			

Business Cycle Indicators

The economic indicators that the government publishes every month help economists to determine which phase of the business cycle the economy might be entering. Some of the indicators are **leading indicators** because they tend to predict where the economy is going. Others are considered **lagging indicators** as they tend to show up after a change from one phase to another has occurred. Lagging indicators also tend to give economists important clues as to the duration of economic upturns or downturns. Others are considered **coincident indicators** since they coincide with a change in the economy from one phase to another.

Business Phases

The long-term growth trend in the economy fluctuates between expansion and contraction. However, the upswings and downswings in economic activity are not regular. In fact, they are irregular in both timing and duration. Since 1948, the shortest duration of a recession is 6 months with the longest being the recent 2007-2009 recession with 18 months. The shortest recovery was 12 months in the 1980s and the longest expansion lasted from March of 1991 through March of 2001.

Expansion Cycle

The economy speeds up during **expansion cycles** and then peaks. During expansions, the economy, measured by indicators like jobs, industrial production, and retail sales, is growing. During an expansion output rises, new construction increases, employment rises, and unemployment falls. Unfortunately, if the economic activity is too fast, inflation may rise.

Inflation

Inflation is defined as a rise in the general level of prices caused by excessive money creation. Inflation reduces the value of money, forcing consumers to spend more money for the same goods and services they were previously able to purchase at lower prices. When general price levels increase, purchasing power falls, and this situation translates into a lower standard of living. The Consumer Price Index (CPI) and the Producer Price Index (PPI) are two of the most common measures of inflation. These measure, respectively, the price increases (or decreases) of basic consumer goods and services and selling prices received by producers for their goods.

Causes of Inflation

It is generally accepted that inflation is caused by increases in the supply of money. Too much money will drive up prices and, consequently, inflation. In addition, a rise in production costs leads to an increase in the price of the final product.

Effects of Inflation

A **modest inflation rate**, between 2% to 4% annually, is considered acceptable and actually good for business. However, **runaway inflation** erodes purchasing power and can be devastating to those living on a fixed income, such as retirees. The dollars that they expect to retire with will be worth less as time passes and inflation rises. Savings will be worth less if the inflation rate exceeds the interest rate savings earn.

When wages do not keep up with inflation, the dollars do not buy the same amount of goods and services. The choices are to buy less of the goods and services, purchase a substitute, or do without the goods or services. Oftentimes, buyers change their spending habits as they meet their purchasing thresholds. This forces producers to reduce output, which could lead to reduced hours or layoffs.

If an excessive amount of currency is printed, its purchasing power is diminished and prices rise, which could lead to hyperinflation. **Hyperinflation** is an extremely rapid or out of control rate of inflation. As inflation continues to rise, more money is printed leading to a self-reinforcing vicious cycle of printing money, leading to inflation, leading to printing money, and so on. Famous examples of hyperinflation include Germany (1922 to 1923) and Zimbabwe (1999 to 2009). In 1923, a wheelbarrow full of German Marks was insufficient to purchase a single loaf of bread, and in 2008, a Zimbabwean Ten Million Dollar bill could not purchase a hamburger—its price was 15 million Zimbabwe dollars. This is one reason why inflation is feared.

Contraction Cycle

During the **contraction phase**, the output of goods and services declines, employment falls, unemployment rises, and new construction declines. Clearly, a key feature of contractions is that they are times of rising unemployment. Sharply reduced economic activity causes extensive job losses. As demand for goods and services weakens, businesses lay off workers during periods of contraction.

Deflation

If inflation is allowed to rise at an unsustainable rate, the reactionary deflation can be severe. **Deflation** is a sustained decrease in the general level of prices—a negative inflation rate. Deflation can cause a severe business downturn; i.e., a recession.

> Example 1: Between 1998 and 2000, the Internet euphoria led to rapid acceleration in stock prices. This eventually became unsustainable and led to a disastrous fall.
>
> Example 2: From 1991 to 2001, Japan experienced a disastrous decade of economic deflation and stagnation after bubbles in its stock market and land market collapsed. Equity prices plunged 63% by 1992 and by 2001, land values had dropped by 70%. This period of Japanese economic history is referred to as the lost decade.

A current example of a severe deflationary cycle is the housing bubble that burst with the ensuing mortgage meltdown.

> Example 3: From 2002 to 2005, home prices increased at an astonishingly rapid rate, fueled by easy financing. As long as there were more buyers to feed the spiral, the housing bubble expanded until it peaked in 2005. It finally reached the point where the prices became too high.
> Even with the "easy money" provided by the financial institutions, buyers met their purchasing thresholds. After the peak of 2005, prices for single-family homes and condominiums fell 5% to 40% or more, depending on the area. States that were largely affected include Arizona, California, Florida, and Nevada. During the housing market's accelerated growth, speculative activity was rampant in these areas, causing prices to surge much higher than other regions. Prices dropped to the late 2003 levels and the country experienced the worst housing recession since the 1940s.

Recession

When does a period of contraction become a recession? The common definition of a **recession** is a period when real gross domestic product (GDP) declines for two consecutive quarters. The NBER defines recession and expansion as follows:

> "A recession is a significant decline in activity spread across the economy that lasts more than a few months and is visible in industrial production, employment, real income, and wholesale-retail sales. A recession begins just after the economy reaches a peak of activity and ends as the economy reaches its trough. Between trough and peak, the economy is in an expansion."

The most recent recession started in December 2007. That is when production peaked and the economy started to slow. The date for the end of this recession was June 2009—based on economic indicators.

Depression

When does a recession become a depression? A **depression** may be defined as an economic downturn that is more severe compared to a recession or an economic downturn where real GDP declines by more than 10%. By this definition, the Great Depression of the 1930s can be seen as two separate events. The first was an incredibly severe depression lasting from August 1929 to March 1933 when real GDP declined by almost 33%. The second was less severe, from May 1937 to June 1938, when real GDP declined by 18.2 percent. In the last 60 years, the worst recession was from November 1973 to March 1975, when real GDP fell by 4.9%.

Real Estate Cycles

Many people think that real estate cycles mirror the economy; others think they drive the economy. Regardless, real estate markets are cyclical due to the relationship between demand and supply for particular types of property. As a reminder, cycles are periodic, irregular up and down movements of economic activity that take place over a period of 2 to 6 years.

There are national real estate cycles, city and neighborhood market cycles, and cycles for individual property types within a city. Real estate cycles exist in both the residential and commercial property markets and their submarkets. In addition, each market and submarket is impacted by different economic, financial, and demographic factors. People  want to know where the real estate market is heading, which submarket is hot, which submarket is losing market share, and where new supply will appear over the next few years.

Phases and Turning Points of a Real Estate Cycle

The real estate cycle, just like the business cycle, has two turning points and two phases. The two turning points are peaks and troughs. The **peak** is the upper turning point of a business cycle, and the **trough** is the lower turning point of a business cycle. The two phases are expansion (recovery or boom) and contraction (recession or bust). An **expansion** is an increase in the pace of economic activity. Conversely, a **contraction** is a slowdown in the pace of economic activity. Example: In 1986 and again in 2007, real estate prices peaked and oversupply coupled with negative demand sent real estate prices spiraling downward.

Peak

The **peak** of the market occurs when real estate supply growth slowly begins to exceed demand growth. Real estate prices enter a period of stabilization after a period of expansion. At this time, new construction must compete for fewer buyers in the marketplace since the majority of potential buyers have purchased homes or are priced out of the market. Typically, most real estate participants do not recognize when a peak occurs because transactions are at their highest level of activity.

> A prime example of a peak occurring was in the years prior to the financial crisis that took place in 2007. Before the crisis, home values reached all-time highs preceded by exponential gains in appreciation.

Contraction

As more homes are delivered to the market with less demand, the market contracts and sales growth slows. Eventually, market participants realize that the market has turned down, which causes commitments for new construction to slow down or completely stop.

As the **contraction phase** progresses, the market continues to exhibit high supply and low or negative demand. The extent of the contraction-cycle is determined by the difference between the excess market supply and demand. Market liquidity is low or nonexistent in this phase since the listing-offer spread in property prices is too wide. Property owners quickly realize that they will not be able to sell their properties if they do not lower their asking prices. As a result, the average prices of homes begin to fall in the overall market. During contraction, the entire region can experience bad loans, foreclosures, unemployment, and even recession.

> Example: The financial crisis in 2007 caused a sharp contraction in the real estate market due to a number of factors. The list starts with borrowers who purchased or refinanced homes with loans for which they did not fundamentally qualify. A number of these loans also included adjustable interest rates, which caused a higher risk of default when interest rates reset to a higher rate. Next in line were mortgage brokers who provided inappropriate loans to borrowers in order to collect very lucrative fees. Other contributors include the mortgage lenders who acknowledged the potential risks in the subprime market, but chose to make loans available to almost anybody with a pulse. Their risk ended when they sold these loans to issuers

in the secondary mortgage market to be packaged into debt instruments, such as mortgage-backed securities, and then sold to investors. Furthermore, pension fund and financial portfolio managers were also hungry for higher yields and may have been blind to problems with debt instruments backed by subprime mortgages. This exposure to system risk eventually resulted in a sharp contraction in the real estate market, which negatively affected the entire economy.

Trough

At the **trough**, the real estate market experiences an oversupply of unsold homes, allowing buyers to choose from a wide variety of properties. Sales prices are no longer sharply declining, but maintaining a steady average. The trough gives buyers the best opportunity to purchase real estate, allowing absorption of oversupply to take place. An abundance of alternatives exists for bargain hunters who were unable to purchase a home at the peak or speculators and investors looking to profit in the next real estate cycle.

Although the market oversupply may consist of property owners voluntarily selling their homes, many owners are forced into short sales or foreclosure due to the economic hardships experienced in the trough.

> Example: In 2008 and 2009, the Mortgage Bankers Association reported that over 2 million foreclosures were filed. This is the highest level reported since the Mortgage Bankers Association started this survey 37 years ago.

As the trough of the real estate cycle passes, demand growth slowly begins to exceed the existing oversupply, which allows recovery to begin.

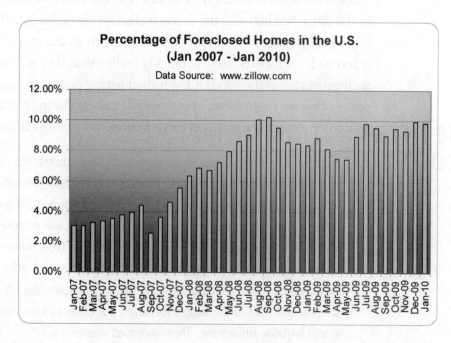

Expansion

The **expansion phase** of a real estate market is marked by speculation and expansion of credit, which stimulates the local, regional, and even national economy. Demand continues to increase, creating a need for more properties. As the supply of available property tightens in the marketplace, prices begin to rise rapidly. Expansion continues as long as demand growth rates are higher than supply growth rates. This phase peaks when demand and supply grow at the same rate (reach equilibrium). Before equilibrium, demand grows faster than supply; after equilibrium, supply grows faster than demand.

The Existing Home Sales Report is a monthly report published by the National Association of REALTORS®, which provides data on the number of closed sales during a specific month. The report also includes existing inventory levels and the time necessary to absorb the existing inventory measured during a specific period. This is a key economic indicator because decreasing inventory levels show signs that an expansion phase is under way.

Example: Just before the financial crisis in 2007, rapid expansion occurred that led to an explosive increase in the number of homes sold. Due to the availability of credit and lax underwriting standards, the demand for real estate continued to climb. The number of total homes sold reached unforeseen levels and beat previously set records.

After the expansion phase, the real estate market will once again reach a peak and restart the cycle. Economists cannot predict exactly when a cycle will begin or end, but they can make educated assumptions based on the level of market activity occurring in the present.

For more information about the median and average sale price of houses sold, visit the U.S. Census Bureau website at www.census.gov.

THE INTERACTION OF MARKETS AND THE ECONOMY

Any major changes in the economy affect financial and real estate markets and vice versa. Mortgage lending activity is affected by changing economic conditions and new legislation, regulations, accounting principles, regulatory guidance, examination efforts, and legal actions.

The real estate industry has a significant role in the U.S. economy by contributing wealth to the economy, generating significant banking activity, and strongly affecting the job market. The real estate industry provides employment for a large segment of the population, including those in finance, development, construction, brokerage, and management. It accounts for billions of dollars in national income.

The state of the national economy is of vital importance to the financial and real estate markets because the real estate sector constitutes a very large segment of our economic profile, particularly when combined with the other industries and businesses that service and depend on real estate.

A market is any marketplace where buyers and sellers trade assets. A market can be as simple as a country fair where people meet to trade produce and handicrafts or as sophisticated as an online auction with bids from all over the world and the buyer and seller never meet. A **market** may be defined as trade in a specified commodity. Markets work by bringing interested buyers and sellers together and making it easier to complete transactions.

In general, markets are described as perfect or imperfect. A **perfect market** is an economic model in which the products are homogenous, there is complete information, and no single buyer or seller can influence the market. An **imperfect market** is a market that cannot meet the requirements for a perfect market. Due to the nature of real estate, the real estate market is imperfect.

Even though a market is not truly perfect, it can be efficient and organized. In fact, most commodities are bought and sold in markets that are efficient and organized. An **efficient market** is one with a large number of buyers and sellers in which easily produced goods and services are readily transferable, and market prices adjust rapidly to reflect new information. An **organized market** is one in which participants operate under recognized rules for the purpose of buying and selling a particular commodity.

Although there are markets for virtually every known commodity and service, this unit provides a brief overview of financial, mortgage, and real estate markets.

Financial Markets

A **financial market** allows people to buy and sell financial securities and commodities with relative ease. The three major financial markets in the world are New York, London, and Tokyo. These take care of the American, European, and Asian money and capital markets.

Financial markets are further subdivided into money, capital, commodity, and mortgage markets.

Money Markets

The **money market** is the interaction of buyers and sellers of short-term money market instruments such as short-term financing and securities. These short-term market instruments may have low or high interest rates, which is part of their risk. An **interest rate** is the amount charged, expressed as a percentage of principal, by a lender to a borrower for the use of assets.

The interest rate on a money market instrument is usually set on the date the money is borrowed. While the interest rate is negotiable, it is usually based on some type of index that matures in 1 year or less, such as the federal funds rate or the interest rate paid on certificates of deposit (CDs).

The major money market securities include T-bills, certificates of deposit, commercial paper, banker's acceptances, Eurodollars, and repurchase agreements.

Capital Markets

Capital is the money needed to start, expand, and continue a business. In the early days of capitalism, raising money meant contacting friends and family members. This approach was effective for small amounts of capital, but as capital needs grew larger, an organized capital market developed.

The **capital market** is the market in which long-term or intermediate-term securities are traded. The creation of the capital markets is one of the key ingredients to the industrialization of Europe and the United States. Capital markets have developed into complex institutions that are integral in the functioning of our economic system. The capital market includes the stock market and the bond market.

Stock Markets

Stock markets provide financing through the issuance and trading of shares or common stock. A **share of stock** is an instrument that represents a claim on a proportionate share of a corporation's assets and profits. Stock is traded on stock exchanges such as the New York Stock Exchange, the National Association of Securities Dealers Automated Quotations, the Tokyo Stock Exchange, and the London Stock Exchange.

Bond Markets

Bond markets provide financing through the issuance and trading of bonds. A **bond** is a debt instrument in which the issuer guarantees the payment of interest and principal on the money borrowed at a specified date. **Interest** is the charge for use of money and **principal** is the amount borrowed and still owed on the debt. A bond is similar to a loan—the issuer is the borrower and the holder is the lender. The issuer is equivalent to the borrower, the bondholder to the lender, and the coupon to the interest.

Commodity Markets

A **commodity market** is a market where commodities are traded or exchanged. Traded commodities include a wide variety of products, such as grains, energy sources, foods and fibers, livestock, and even carbon offsets. Commodities are traded on regulated exchanges, such as the Chicago Board of Trade, Chicago Mercantile Exchange, New York Board of Trade, EUREX, or the London Metal Exchange.

Mortgage Markets

The mortgage markets are made up of the institutions that originate loans (primary mortgage market) and the markets in which they are transferred (secondary mortgage market). The interaction between the primary and secondary mortgage markets is the foundation of the mortgage lending process and is an essential part of our national economic health. These markets facilitate the flow of funds for residential financing. The mortgage markets are discussed later in the course.

Real Estate Markets

The real estate industry is so large that it influences local, state, and even the national economies. Real estate creates net worth, increases cash flow, and creates new jobs. Real estate in the form of land and improvements makes up a very large portion of the total net worth of the United States as a nation (not to be confused with the Government). **Net worth** is the value of all assets minus all liabilities.

Real Estate as an Economic Multiplier

How is the economic impact of a home sale measured?

Each home sale results in additional expenditures for remodeling, appliances, services, and furnishings. In addition, as the supply of homes for sales declines, home builders respond by adding new inventory. The employees of building companies and material suppliers in turn spend their incomes thereby expanding the economy, a process referred to as an **economic multiplier**. Furthermore, rising home values have a strong wealth effect where consumers will spend more of their income if they feel confident that rising home prices are expanding their personal wealth.

Source of Economic Contributions

- Home construction
- Real estate brokerage
- Mortgage lending
- Title insurance
- Rental and Leasing
- Home appraisal
- Moving truck service
- Other related activities

Real estate markets are unique when compared to other assets. There is no single real estate market such as the New York Stock Exchange or the Chicago Mercantile Exchange.

Characteristics of Real Estate

The two primary characteristics of real estate assets are their heterogeneity and immobility. Because of these two factors, the market for buying, selling, and leasing real estate tends to be illiquid, localized, and highly segmented, with privately negotiated transactions and high transaction costs.

Heterogeneous Products

Real estate tends to be **heterogeneous**, meaning that each property has unique features—age, building design, and especially location combine to give each property distinctive characteristics. Even in residential neighborhoods with very similar houses, the locations differ.

Immobile Products

Real estate is **immobile**. The land cannot be moved. Although it is sometimes physically possible to move a building from one location to another, this is generally not financially feasible. The vast majority of structures removed from the land are demolished rather than moved.

Localized Markets

Real estate markets tend to be **localized**. By this we mean that the potential users of a property, and competing sites, generally lie within a short distance of each other. For example, competing apartment properties may lie within 15 minutes, or less, in driving time from each other, while competing properties of single-family residences may tend to be within a single elementary school district or even within a small number of similar subdivisions.

Segmented Markets

Real estate markets tend to be **highly segmented** due to the heterogeneous nature of the products. In fact, the real estate market consists of four specific (individual) markets, each with several submarkets. The specific markets for real estate are residential, commercial, agricultural, and special purpose markets.

The **residential market** includes property used for residential purposes. For example, households that search for single-family detached units in the market will generally not consider other residential product types such as an attached townhouse unit or condominium. Real property zoned and intended for commercial and business purposes (retail space, office space, hospitality property, and industrial property) is part of the **commercial market**. The **agricultural market** includes properties dedicated to an agricultural purpose, such as farms and ranches. The **special purpose market** is a "catch all" market and is comprised of the properties that do not fit into the other broad categories.

Because the real estate market is segmented into a variety of sub-markets that are localized, different parts of the economy may be affected by over- or under-supply of available property, tight money, or other factors; whereas, others may not.

Case Study: Texas Banking Crisis (1980-1989)

Between 1980 and 1989, 349 Texas commercial banks failed, and an additional 76 required assistance from the FDIC. The number of failed and assisted Texas banks rose from 3 in 1983 to 134 in 1989.

In 1988 and 1989, the failed and assisted banks in the state comprised over 80% of total U.S. failed-bank assets, and over 80% of total FDIC reserves for losses on failed banks. In addition, both the domestic energy and local commercial real estate markets, in which Texas banks invested heavily, experienced dramatic declines after 1985.

Case Study: Texas Banking Crisis (1980-1989) - Continued

According to a report prepared by the Federal Deposit Insurance Corporation (FDIC) in 1990, the high failure rates among Texas commercial banks appear to be attributable to a combination of several developments.

Reasons for the High Bank-Failure Rates

1. **Drop in Oil Prices.** The first was the trend in crude oil prices (and related products). The OPEC oil embargo of 1973 contributed to large increases in domestic crude oil prices between January 1973 and June 1981. Crude oil prices subsequently declined at a moderate rate from midyear 1981 to December 1985, then fell dramatically in 1986. Texas crude oil prices fell 45% in 1986.

2. **Overbuilding.** The second important development was the boom and bust in Texas real estate, especially office and land development projects. Following the late 1970s boom in the energy markets, Texas office real estate grew rapidly, as did office employment. However, after the drop in oil prices in 1982, the expansion in office space outpaced the growth in office employment and continued to do so until 1987. Overbuilding in Texas eventually led a 30% office vacancy rate by 1987 for the combined Austin, Dallas, Houston, and San Antonio areas.

3. **Non-performing Loans.** The changes in the composition of the loan portfolios of Texas commercial banks appears to be the third factor contributing to the high failure rates of the late 1980s. Concentrations in construction and land development projects among Texas banks grew from 3.5% of bank assets in 1978 to 8.3% of assets in 1984, and remained at high levels through 1986. Over this same period, non-performing real estate loans grew steadily among Texas banks. Concentrations in commercial and industrial loans (which include energy loans) followed oil price movements, rising from 20.7% of Texas bank assets in 1978 to 27.8 percent in 1982.

Privately Negotiated Transactions with High Transaction Costs

A final distinctive feature of real estate is the complexity of property and transactions. The property interest to be conveyed cannot be standardized and therefore must be carefully assessed to determine what rights it actually contains. Further, because real estate has a history of ownership, the current claims of ownership must be confirmed by examining the past history of the property. Finally, property parcels are contiguous, so the problem of accurate description requires unique and elaborate systems of delineation. All these special issues in real estate are sufficient to compel unique laws, institutions, and procedures for the conveyance of real estate.

Moreover, real estate agents, mortgage lenders, attorneys, appraisers, property inspectors, and others are usually involved in the transaction. The negotiation process between buyers and sellers can be lengthy, and the final transaction price and other important details such as lease terms are not usually observable. Thus, in almost every transaction involving real estate, there are time requirements and costs not present in most non-real estate transactions.

Investors and lenders seem to get into trouble most commonly when they lose sight of these unique characteristics of real estate. The latest, graphic example of this is the recent sub-prime meltdown. The creation and dissemination of sub-prime mortgage securities became detached from any thoughtful assessment of the underlying borrowers, housing values, or market depth.

INFORMATION RESOURCES

Please refer to the following information resources for further information:

- U.S. Census Bureau website at (www.census.gov)
- Article – "How to Use Real Estate Trends to Predict the Next Housing Bubble", Harvard Extension School. https://www.extension.harvard.edu/inside-extension/how-use-real-estate-trends-predict-next-housing-bubble
- Mortgage Banking, Office of the Comptroller of the Currency. https://www.occ.gov/publications/publications-by-type/comptrollers-handbook/ch-mortgage-banking.pdf
- National Bureau of Economic Research at (www.nber.org)
- CoreLogic at (www.corelogic.com/)

SUMMARY

Almost all real estate transactions involve some kind of financing. Financial and real estate markets are driven by economic changes, such as trends, cycles, or short-term fluctuations. The real estate cycle undergoes various phases that reveal the level of market activity. The peak of the market occurs when real estate supply growth slowly begins to exceed demand growth. As more homes are delivered to the market with less demand, the market contracts and sales growth slows. At the trough, the real estate market experiences an oversupply of unsold homes, allowing buyers to choose from a wide variety of properties. The expansion stage of a real estate market is marked by speculation and expansion of credit, which stimulates the local, regional, and even national economy. The cyclic nature of the real estate market allows economists to identify the phases and turning points as they occur.

Markets work by bringing interested buyers and sellers together and making it easier to complete transactions. The real estate lending industry is comprised of two distinct markets—the primary mortgage market and the secondary mortgage market. The real estate market consists of four specific markets (residential, commercial, agricultural, and special purpose markets), each with several submarkets.

UNIT 1 REVIEW

Matching Exercise

Instructions: Write the letter of the matching term on the blank line before its definition. Answers are in Appendix A.

Terms

A. business cycles	P. imperfect market
B. capital	Q. inflation
C. capital markets	R. market
D. collateral	S. money market
E. contraction	T. mortgage market
F. cycles	U. mortgage-servicing rights
G. deflation	V. net worth
H. depression	W. organized market
I. disintermediation	X. peak
J. efficient market	Y. perfect market
K. expansion	Z. public finance
L. finance	AA. real estate finance
M. financial market	BB. recession
N. heterogeneous	CC. trends
O. hyperinflation	DD. trough

Definitions

1. _____ Commercial activity of providing funds and capital

2. _____ Category of finance that includes tax systems, government expenditures, budget procedures, stabilization instruments, debt issues, and other government concerns

3. _____ Category of finance that provides the flow of money and credit needed to complete transactions for the purchase and/or development of real property

4. _____ The withdrawal of funds from intermediary financial institutions, such as banks, credit unions, and thrifts, to invest the funds directly in other investments

5. _____ The right collect and forward payments, handle escrow accounts, and respond to borrower questions to another financial institution

6. _____ Something of value given as security for a debt

7. _____ Periodic, irregular up and down movements in economic activity that take place over a period of 2 to 6 years

8. _____ Changes in the market in a consistent direction that occur over a long-term period

9. _____ Period when real gross domestic product declines for two consecutive quarters

10. _____ Ups and downs in economic activity, defined in terms of periods of expansion followed by periods of contraction

11. _____ Upper turning point of a business cycle

12. _____ Lower turning point of a business cycle

13. _____ Rise in the general level of prices caused by excessive money creation

14. _____ Extremely rapid or out of control rate of inflation

15. _____ Sustained decrease in the general level of prices—a negative inflation rate

16. _____ Economic downturn that is more severe compared to a recession or an economic downturn where real GDP declines by more than 10%

17. _____ Increase in the pace of economic activity

18. _____ Slowdown in the pace of economic activity

19. _____ Economic model in which the products are homogenous, there is complete information, and no buyers or sellers may influence the market

20. _____ Market that cannot meet the requirements for a perfect market

21. _____ Market with a large number of buyers and sellers in which easily produced goods and services are readily transferable, and market prices adjust rapidly to reflect new information

22. _____ Market in which participants operate under recognized rules for the purpose of buying and selling a particular commodity

23. _____ Trade in a specified commodity

24. _____ Market in which long-term or intermediate-term securities are traded by buyers and sellers

25. _____ Market that allows people to buy and sell financial securities and commodities with relative ease

26. _____ Interaction of buyers and sellers of short-term (less than one year) money market instruments and securities

27. _____ Money needed to start, expand, and continue a business and something that every business needs

28. _____ The market that facilitates the flow of funds for residential financing

29. _____ Value of all assets minus all liabilities

30. _____ Unique and distinctive

Multiple Choice Questions

Instructions: Circle your response and go to Appendix A to read the complete explanation for each question.

1. The single largest component of wealth for individuals is:
   a. earned income.
   b. real estate.
   c. savings.
   d. stocks and bonds.

2. A mortgage lender's key function is to provide funds for the purchase or refinancing of residential properties. This function is carried out in the:
   a. bond market.
   b. commodities market.
   c. primary mortgage market.
   d. stock market.

3. All of the following occur during an expansion, except:
    a. retail sales grow.
    b. industrial production increases.
    c. inflation occurs.
    d. deflation occurs.

4. What defines a recession according to the National Bureau of Economic Research?
    a. A significant decline in economic activity lasting more than 6 months
    b. A sharp decline in economic activity lasting less than a few months
    c. A sharp decline in economic activity lasting less than a few weeks
    d. A sharp decline in economic activity lasting more than one month

5. Which real estate cycle is occurring when housing supply begins to exceed demand and prices stabilize after expanding?
    a. Retraction
    b. Contraction
    c. Expansion
    d. Peak

6. Which of the following statements regarding cycles is correct?
    a. Cycles are periodic, regular up and down movements.
    b. Cycles take place over a period of 1 to 3 years.
    c. Real estate cycles are linear due to the relationship between demand and supply.
    d. None of the above.

7. The real estate cycle has two phases and two turning points. In order, they are:
    a. peak, contraction, expansion, and trough.
    b. expansion, panic, contraction, and recovery.
    c. extraction, peak, contraction, and revitalization.
    d. expansion, peak, contraction, and trough.

8. The National Bureau of Economic Research defines business cycles as:
    a. two phases and one turning point.
    b. two phases and two turning points.
    c. two phases and three turning points.
    d. four phases.

9. All of the following are characteristics of an efficient market, except:
    a. a large number of buyers and sellers.
    b. easily produced goods and services are readily available.
    c. market prices adjust quickly to new information.
    d. market prices respond slowly to new information.

10. Which of the following is not a subtype of the financial market?
    a. Money markets
    b. Capital markets
    c. Commodities markets
    d. Free trade markets

Money & The Monetary System

Unit **2**

INTRODUCTION

At the center of nearly all real estate transactions is some type of financing. Without an understanding of how real property is financed, the developer, contractor, real estate professional, and property manager will find themselves out of a job. Most sellers will not be able to sell because most buyers will be financially unable to pay cash or unwilling to purchase unless a large part of the purchase price can be borrowed.

It should be no surprise that nearly every economic decision at the federal level has a real impact on real estate activity and economic well-being. Unless the United States has a healthy national economy, there will be few, if any, economically healthy real estate markets. Any federal policies that have substantial impact on fiscal or monetary policy or that adversely affect inflationary or employment trends have a real and measurable impact upon the level of real estate activity in the nation.

Learning Objectives

After completing this Unit, you should be able to:

2A   recall characteristics of the money supply and the purpose of capital equity, and debt.

2B   indicate how fiscal policy regulates economic activity.

2C   specify how monetary policy stabilizes the economy and controls inflation.

2D   recognize functions of the Federal Reserve System.

2E   specify functions of the Department of the Treasury.

2F   identify the Federal Deposit Insurance Corporation's major programs.

2G   recognize functions of the Federal Housing Finance Agency and the Federal Home Loan Bank System.

2H   identify information resources used in this Unit.

MONEY

One definition of **money** is any generally accepted medium of exchange and unit of account. The key is the fact that money is a medium of exchange. Money means nothing if it cannot buy something. People exchange money for the goods and services they want and need—they do not barter for them. In a real estate transaction, a purchaser gives up money to the seller and, in exchange, receives a house. The seller gives up the house and, in exchange, receives money. Consideration is the act of giving up something to get something in return. Money, as an accepted medium between a buyer and seller, facilitates exchange.

In common usage, money refers to currency. **Currency** refers to a country's official unit of monetary exchange. It is the minted coins and paper money issued by a government for legal exchange or tender.

Characteristics of Money

- Money is a medium of exchange and functions as an intermediary of trade.

- Money acts as a standard unit of measurement, which is used to measure the market value of various commodities and services and other dealings.

- Money functions as a store of value because the forms of money can be stored and recovered and used for any future purpose.

- Money has the highest degree of liquidity because money is universally accepted and recognized as a basic form of currency.

In addition, money also functions as a standard of value and a store of value because with the help of money, the value of various goods and services can be measured. Money, as an accepted medium between a buyer and seller, facilitates exchange. A synonym for money is capital.

Capital: Equity and Debt

Capital consists of equity (one's own money) and debt (borrowed money). In other words, if you are going to purchase a home, typically you use some of your own money and a lot of the bank's money.

Equity

Equity is an owner's financial interest in real or personal property at a specific moment in time. In real estate, it is the difference between what a property is worth and what the owner owes against that property. At purchase, the equity is equal to the amount of the down payment. If the property is encumbered with a loan, the equity is the difference between the appraised market value of the property and the balance of any outstanding loans.

Example: Robert purchased his home 3 years ago for $150,000 with a 10% down payment. At that time, his equity was $15,000 and the debt was $135,000. After making payments for 3 years, the mortgage is $130,000 and the current market value of his home is $175,000. Therefore, his equity in the property is $45,000.

In finance, equity also refers to the stock ownership interest (common or preferred) in a corporation. Shares of stock are proof of ownership (equity) in a company. If a shareholder owns stock and the stock goes up in value, the value of the shareholder's equity goes up. If it goes down in value, the value of the shareholder's equity goes down. While he or she owns stock, assuming the company makes enough profit, the shareholder will earn a dividend based on the number of shares owned and the quantity of profits available to shareholders. The stock market is the market for buying and selling stock.

Debt

Debt is a dollar amount that is borrowed from another party, usually under specific terms. It can be secured or unsecured. **Secured debt** is a debt owed to a creditor that is secured by collateral. **Collateral** is something of value given as security for a debt. A good example of this is mortgage debt or a car loan. The opposite of secured debt is **unsecured debt**, which is a debt that is not connected to any specific piece of property. Instead, the creditor may satisfy the debt against the borrower rather than just the collateral.

Because it has a value, debt can be traded just as money can be traded. The financial section of the newspaper talks about the sale and purchase of paper. This means the purchase and sale (at a discount) of debt. While there are variations, debt normally consists of bonds and mortgages.

Bonds

A **bond** is a debt instrument. When you buy a bond, you lend someone money at a fixed interest rate for a fixed period of time. While your money is out you receive interest on it. At a specific time in the future, you receive your principal back. Thus, the interest the bond issuer pays you before the bond matures is the return *on* capital and, when you get your money back, you receive the return *of* your capital. The bond market is the market for buying and selling bonds.

Mortgages

Mortgages and deeds of trust are security instruments. Because mortgages bear interest and give a periodic cash flow to the mortgage owner, there is an informal market for them and they are bought and sold regularly. Remember, if you have surplus funds, you can invest in mortgages and earn interest.

Money Supply

The **money supply**, or money stock, is the total amount of money available for transactions and investment in the economy. The exact amount cannot be calculated because the amount varies with changes in demand. In macroeconomic terms, supply of money is the amount of currency and money held in bank accounts along with the money circulating to purchase goods, services, and securities.

The money supply consists of currency in circulation, money in checking accounts, deposits in savings, and other liquid assets. **Liquid assets** are securities and financial instruments that are converted easily and quickly into cash. Liquid assets include certificates of deposit (CDs), stocks, bonds, mortgage-backed securities, and a variety of other financial assets. Real estate is not considered liquid and, as a result, is not part of the money supply.

Categories of the Money Supply

The money supply is categorized by how quickly the asset can be converted into cash. Currently, it is measured two different ways–M_1 and M_2—with M_1 being the most liquid. The two money supply measures track slightly different views of the money supply. The categories frequently are referred to as **monetary aggregates**.

Categories of the Money Supply	
M_1	Currency, checking accounts, demand deposits, credit union share drafts, travelers' checks, NOW accounts, and ATS accounts
M_2	All M_1 plus savings accounts, small CDs, shares in money market mutual funds, overnight Eurodollars, and repurchase agreements

For more information about the money supply, visit the Federal Reserve website at www.federalreserve.gov.

The Fed and economists monitor the growth of the money supply because of its influence on economic activity and on the price levels. An increase in the money supply usually leads to an increase in inflation. **Inflation** is a sustained increase in the general level of prices, which is equivalent to a decline in the value or purchasing power of money. Money supply growth, although important for gauging economic and financial conditions, is not the sole benchmark used by the Fed to conduct monetary policy. Currently, the analysts at the Federal Reserve rely on different measures to determine whether monetary policy should be tighter or looser, such as comparing the actual and potential growth rates of the economy. Potential growth is presumed to equal the sum of the growth in the labor force plus any gains in productivity, or output per worker. If the actual growth is in excess of the long-term potential growth, there is a danger of inflation, which would require a tighter monetary policy. Another measure used is the non-accelerating inflation rate of unemployment (NAIRU).

Currently, the Money Supply Report is a component of the Index of Leading Economic Indicators, and many market analysts rely on the M2 as a reasonably good signal of pending recessions and recoveries.

Supply of and Demand for Money

Money must circulate to have value. That is, it must leave one person's hands and arrive in someone else's hands.

> Example: Kate purchases a new 52" TV. Her money goes to the retailer. The retailer pays its employees, who then start the cycle over again. The money returns to the banks to be lent once again in the form of savings and checking accounts, IRAs, certificates of deposit (CDs), and so forth. If money were to stop circulating, the economy would crash to a halt within a very short period.

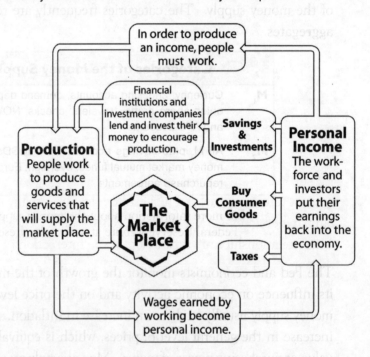

One of the major ways money circulates is through the purchase and sale of real estate. It takes a lot of money to purchase and sell real estate. That money also employs developers, architects, carpenters, lawyers, accountants, real estate brokers, real estate appraisers, title companies, and home inspectors.

The amount of money in the economy at any given time is a function of both supply and demand. As we review the interaction of supply and demand, remember that money is an asset or commodity that is purchased and sold in the world's marketplaces every day.

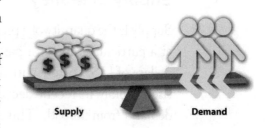

Supply   Demand

Supply

Demand

If the economy is booming, there is demand for money.

When the economy is slow, there is less demand for money.

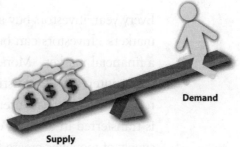

Demand

Supply

Too much money in relation to the output of goods tends to push interest rates down and push inflation up. If there is too little money, interest rates are pushed up and prices go down.

It is important for real estate agents to understand how interest rates affect the way people in the market buy and sell real estate. It is no great secret that as interest rates increase, the real estate prices eventually decrease. On the other hand, when interest rates decrease, real estate prices tend to increase over time. These relationships are a function of the interaction of supply and demand, or the supply/demand dynamic.

Lower interest rates tend to encourage higher home prices. If a buyer can afford a $1,000 per month mortgage payment (principal and interest, at 5% interest), a larger proportion of that $1,000 goes toward paying off the loan than paying interest. If interest rates are 7%, more of the $1,000 will go toward paying interest and less toward paying the loan. In general, when interest rates are high, homes are less affordable.

Supply of Money

Supply is the quantity of a product on the market that is available for consumption at a particular time at a particular price. Currently, there is over $930 billion dollars of U.S. currency in circulation. The amount of cash in circulation has risen rapidly in recent decades and much of the increase has been caused by demand from abroad. This supply comes from governments, private investors, banks, and other similar sources. Their job is to fund the money supply. They do this by putting cash in banks or by purchasing debt.

> Example: If a government wants to borrow money to fund its operations, one option it has is to sell bonds. A bond is a debt instrument or, essentially, a loan. Investors buy bonds, and this puts money in the hands of the government. The government uses the money to purchase the goods and services it needs to operate.

Every year, investors buy and sell these debt instruments in the major financial markets. Investors can buy them anywhere, but the transaction goes through a financial market. Money that is put into an IRA or savings account is lent out at interest by the institution holding it to those who need it. The investor receives part of that interest as the rent on his or her money. When money is transferred in and out of the hands of banks, investors, and consumers, the supply of money is created.

Demand for Money

Demand is the desire to possess plus the ability to buy. The demand for something is the number of consumers in the marketplace at any given time who can afford to pay for that item. It is measured by interest or yield rates.

> Example: Steve has $100,000 to loan his friend Pam for purchasing a house. Pam tells Steve that she will pay 4% interest on the money. However, Steve's neighbor Fred comes along and tells Steve he will pay 6% interest. Both Fred and Pam can afford to pay for Steve's money; but, all other things being equal, Steve wants to lend his money to the highest bidder. In this case, Fred gets the money and pays Steve interest for the privilege of renting it.

Note that demand has two components: (1) the desire for something and (2) the ability to pay for it. Both components must be present before one unit of demand exists, but the latter is more important than the former.

FISCAL AND MONETARY POLICIES

The role of the federal government in the national economy is to manage the overall pace of economic activity to avoid wild swings in the financial markets, while maintaining high levels of employment and stable prices. It has two main tools for achieving these objectives: fiscal policy and monetary policy.

> Fiscal policy is the means by which a government adjusts its spending levels and tax rates to monitor and influence a nation's economy. It is the sister strategy to monetary policy through which a central bank influences a nation's money supply. These two policies are used in various combinations to direct a country's economic goals.

The **fiscal policy** is the government policy on taxes and government spending and affects demand. Fiscal policy is determined by the executive and legislative branches of the federal government. The **monetary policy** influences the cost and availability of credit to promote economic growth, full employment, and price stability. It works by affecting demand across the economy—that is, people's and firms' willingness to spend on goods and services. The Federal Reserve Board, established by Congress in 1913, is responsible for determining monetary policy.

Since then, the economic policy in the United States has involved a continuing effort by the government to find a mix of fiscal and monetary policies that will allow sustained growth and stable prices.

Fiscal Policy

The government uses fiscal policy to regulate the total level of economic activity within the nation. Determining the fiscal policy for the country is the federal government's responsibility, which involves preparing a budget and implementing a financial strategy for the country. The term "**fiscal policy**" refers to the government's financial strategy with respect to government spending, taxation, and debt management.

Goals of Fiscal Policy

The primary goal of fiscal policy is to achieve economic growth, which is an indicator of the overall health of the economy. **Economic growth** includes the nation's macroeconomic goals, particularly with respect to gross domestic product (GDP), full employment, price level stability, and equilibrium in balance of payments. Fiscal policy can directly alter the growth rate of the gross domestic product (GDP) by changing the level of government spending and tax rates. Implementing sound fiscal policy can help control the pace of economic growth and ensure that the economy is not growing too slow or too fast. For example, economists may feel that the economy is growing at an unsustainable pace, causing uncontrollable inflation. The government can implement fiscal policy to slow down economic growth and tame inflation. Conversely, if economic growth slows down and contracts considerably, fiscal policy can help ease problems associated with slow economic growth, such as deflation.

Maintain Real GDP

Most economists prefer to have a 3% annual growth in GDP. This growth rate is sufficient to keep the unemployment rate at a level consistent with the full-employment level. **Full-employment** is not zero unemployment, but a level where all those who are in the labor force seeking work can find a job quickly. A non-inflationary growth rate also keeps price levels stable.

Calculating GDP

The two main ways to calculate gross domestic product (GDP) are the expenditure approach and the income approach. The **expenditure approach** focuses on total expenditures on goods and services produced in the period, whereas the **income approach** focuses on the payments to the factors of production involved in those production activities within the period.

Tools of Fiscal Policy

The tools of fiscal policy include government spending and taxation.

Government Spending

The first tool is government spending, i.e., subsidies, transfer payments including welfare programs, public works projects, and government salaries. Whoever receives the funds has more money to spend. That increases demand and economic growth.

The amount of government spending is determined annually by the President and Congress when they develop and pass the federal budget. The **federal budget** shows fiscal policy and budget priorities not only for the coming year but also for the next five years or more. Developing fiscal policy and the federal budget follows specific steps and procedures described in the Congressional Budget Act of 1974.

Every February, the President proposes a detailed budget, or spending plan, to Congress. The Secretary of the U.S. Treasury serves as a major policy advisor to the President and has primary responsibility for participating in the formulation of broad fiscal policies that have general significance for the economy. The Treasury Department was created in 1789 to manage the government finances, with Alexander Hamilton as the first Secretary of the Treasury. The Department of the Treasury operates and maintains systems that are critical to the nation's financial infrastructure, such as the production of coin and currency, the disbursement of payments to the American public, revenue collection, and the borrowing of funds necessary to run the federal government.

Purpose of the Budget Request

- It states the President's recommendations for federal fiscal policy.
  1. Amount of money that should be spent on public purposes
  2. Amount of money that should be collected as tax revenues
  3. Size of the deficit (or surplus) the federal government should run

- It states the President's relative priorities for federal programs; i.e., the amount that should be spent on defense, agriculture, education, health, and so on.

- It states the President's recommendations for changes to spending and tax policies.

Congressional lawmakers consider the President's proposals in several steps. First, they develop a congressional budget resolution that states the overall level of spending and taxation. Next, they divide that overall figure into 19 broad categories, such as national defense, social security, health and human services, interest on the debt, and transportation. Finally, Congress considers individual appropriations bills and allocates money for each category.

> Example: Assume that in a fiscal year the federal government is projected to spend $3.5 trillion, amounting to 40% of the nation's Gross Domestic Product (GDP). Of that $3.5 trillion, approximately two-thirds is financed by federal tax revenues. The remaining one-third is financed by borrowing. This deficit will be repaid by future taxpayers.

The congressional budget resolution is supposed to be passed by April 15, but often the budget process takes an entire session of Congress. If Congress does not pass a budget resolution, the previous year's resolution stays in effect. In order to take effect, each appropriations bill must be signed by the President.

Levy and Collect Taxes

The federal government levies and collects taxes in order to finance various public services. The federal government's chief source of funds to cover its expenses is the income tax on individuals. Other revenue sources include payroll taxes, taxes on corporate profits, and other miscellaneous taxes. In contrast, local governments generally collect most of their tax revenues from property taxes, and state governments depend on sales and excise taxes.

Levy Taxes

Because the federal government relies so heavily on income taxes for its operation, taxation levels on income are as much a political issue as an economic issue. Most income tax disputes revolve around the tax rate, its progressivity, and its use to redistribute wealth and promote social objectives.

Since Congress sets tax policy, many politicians have used tax policy to promote their political agendas by initiating tax reforms, such as decreasing (or increasing) tax rates or granting tax breaks to certain groups.

> Example: The top marginal federal tax bracket for married couples filing jointly during the 1950s was 91%. In 1964, President Johnson and Congress dropped the top marginal rate to 70% to stimulate economic growth and reduce unemployment. Again, the rate dropped to 50% in the early 1980s and from 1988 through 1990, it dropped sharply to 28%. From 2003 to 2012, the top marginal tax rate was 35% for married, single, and head of household taxpayers. Beginning in 2013, the top marginal tax rate was increased to 39.6%.

The U.S. tax system income tax is a progressive levy—the percentage of income an individual pays in taxes increases with increasing income. Not only do those with higher incomes pay more in total taxes, but they also have a higher tax rate.

> Example: A person making a $100,000 annual salary might have a 25% tax rate and pay $25,000 in taxes. Whereas, someone with an income of $30,000 might have a 10% tax rate and pay only $3,000 in taxes.

Many politicians and their constituents support a progressive tax as a way to address economic inequalities in our society. They believe that taxing high-income households at a higher rate is an appropriate and effective way to lessen societal inequalities. However, a steeply progressive rate structure is counterproductive because it discourages people from working and investing, and therefore hurts the overall economy. No one is entirely satisfied with the current tax structure, so periodically, the idea of a uniform or "flat" tax rate is raised. Some economists propose that the income tax should be eliminated and be replaced with a consumption tax. A consumption tax would tax people on what they buy rather than on what they earn.

Collect Taxes

Collecting money (usually taxes) to pay the government's bills is the Treasury Department's key priority for managing the government's finances. On a typical day, the Treasury Department's cash transactions average in excess of $58 billion. Therefore, one of the most important functions the Treasury Department performs is tax collection to fund the operation of the federal government and pay for its programs. The Internal Revenue Service collects income taxes and the Alcohol and Tobacco Tax and

Trade Bureau collects excise taxes on the sale of alcohol, tobacco, and firearms. A taxpayer's voluntary compliance with the tax laws reduces the cost of tax administration, increases revenue, lessens the need to borrow, and ultimately lowers the cost of government. The Internal Revenue Service's voluntary compliance program combined with effective targeted enforcement is expected to increase tax revenues.

Debt Management

The Treasury Department forecasts receipts and payments, determines borrowing needs, and executes the borrowing strategy to meet the financial needs of the federal government. When the total operating cost of the federal government exceeds available funds, the Treasury Department's Bureau of the Public Debt borrows money by selling U.S. Treasury Securities (treasuries) to the public, institutional investors, and authorized government agencies. Treasuries are marketable and non-marketable. Marketable treasuries include Treasury bills, Treasury notes, Treasury bonds, and Treasury Inflation Protected Securities. Non-marketable treasury securities include State and Local Government Series (SLGS), Government Account Series debt issued to government-managed trust funds, and savings bonds. Because the marketable Treasury securities are liquid, they are traded on the secondary market.

In January 2000, the federal debt was only $5.7 trillion ($5,751,743,092,605.50). Since then, it has more than tripled so that currently it is nearly $20 trillion. The national debt currently increases on average more than $2 billion per day.

Fiscal Policy Positions

The primary debate within this field is how active a government should be in manipulating the economy. Proponents of a tight fiscal policy argue that government acts best when it acts least; they promote low taxes and spending and ideally limit government involvement to the setting of prevailing interest rates. Proponents of a loose fiscal policy believe that government has a larger role in promoting economic well-being, such as spending money to stimulate the economy.

Neutral Fiscal Policy

A **neutral fiscal policy** describes a balanced budget in which government spending equals tax revenue. Since government spending is fully funded by tax revenue, a neutral fiscal policy neither stimulates nor restricts economic activity.

Expansionary Fiscal Policy

An **expansionary fiscal policy** expands the amount of money available for consumers and businesses to spend and speeds up the rate of GDP growth. The purpose of an expansionary fiscal policy is to reduce unemployment, increase consumer demand, and avoid a recession. If a recession has already occurred, then it seeks to end the recession and prevent a depression.

To stimulate economic activity and lower unemployment rates, the government would implement a combination of tax cuts and/or increase government spending. However, these policies will lead to higher federal budget deficits. The theory is that deficit spending replaces some of the demand lost during a recession and prevents the waste of economic resources idled by a lack of demand.

However, when the federal government spends more than it receives from taxes and other income—known as **deficit spending**—a budget deficit is created. The difference is made up for by borrowing from the public through the issuance of debt. A deficit is considered a transfer of income between generations. Current living standards are promoted at the expense of the economic welfare of future generations. The federal budget deficit is the yearly amount by which spending exceeds revenue. The sum of all annual federal deficits is the national debt.

On January 1, 1791, the national debt was just $75 million. Except for a rise at the end of World War II, the debt remained remarkably constant for nearly forty years at slightly less than $2 trillion (corrected for inflation). However, since 1983 the trend has been upward even when inflation is taken into account. On October 18, 2005, the national debt rose to above $8 trillion. Currently, the national debt is approaching $20 trillion.

Economists typically expect budget deficits to stimulate economic growth and budget surpluses to slow economic growth. Stimulating the economy with budget deficits is often recommended during and immediately after recessions when economic growth is negative or weak. However, many economists believe that large government deficits tend to crowd out private sector investment and place upward pressure on interest rates.

A direct result of record deficit spending is a sharp increase in the amount of borrowing the U.S. Treasury must undertake to finance the large annual deficits. Of course, as the deficit rises, so do the net interest payments the government must pay each year.

Another concern is the potential impact that deficits might have on interest rates and on the supply and demand for loanable funds. When the government runs a budget deficit, the interest rate rises and investment falls. Because investment is important for long-run economic growth, government budget deficits reduce the economy's growth rate. The estimated effects of government debt and deficits on interest rates are statistically and economically significant: a one-percentage point increase in the projected deficit-to-GDP ratio is estimated to raise long-term interest rates by roughly 25 basis points (or 0.25 percentage point).

How It Works

With an expansionary fiscal policy, the government increases spending, puts more money into consumers' hands with subsidies and transfer payments, or implements tax cuts. It usually uses a combination of all three.

Implementing Expansionary Fiscal Policy

1. The government can increase discretionary spending, including military expenditures. It reduces unemployment by contracting public works or hiring new government workers.

2. The government puts more money into consumers' hands by increasing payments in mandatory programs such as Social Security, Medicare, or welfare programs. Sometimes these payments are called **transfer payments** because they reallocate funds from taxpayers to targeted demographic groups. A transfer payment that is not a mandatory program is expanded unemployment benefits.

3. The government can cut any or all of the following taxes: income, capital gains taxes, taxes on small businesses, payroll taxes, and corporate income taxes.

Pros and Cons of Expansionary Fiscal Policy

Expansionary fiscal policy works fast because it can put money into the hands of consumers. It can create jobs and immediately lower unemployment. Most important, it restores the consumer and business confidence. That is critical for them to start spending again. Without that leadership, a recession could turn into a depression. Everyone would just stuff their money under their mattress.

However, tax cuts decrease revenue that can create a budget deficit that is added to the debt. The tax cuts must be reversed when the economy recovers to pay down the debt. Otherwise, it grows to unsustainable levels. Unfortunately, the U.S. federal government has no limitation because it prints money and can pay for the deficit by issuing new Treasury bills, notes, and bonds. As a result, the national debt is now approaching $20 trillion.

Examples

Example: The Obama Administration used expansionary policy with the Economic Stimulus Act. It cut taxes, extended unemployment benefits, and funded public works projects. In 2010, he continued many of these benefits with the Obama tax cuts. He also increased defense spending. All this occurred while tax receipts dropped thanks to the 2008 financial crisis.

Example: The Bush Administration correctly used expansive fiscal policy to end the 2001 recession. It cut income taxes with EGTRRA, and the tax rebates were mailed out. However, the 9/11 terrorist attacks sent the economy back into a downturn. Bush boosted government defense spending with the War on Terror and cut business taxes in 2003 with JGTRRA. By 2004, the economy was in good shape, with unemployment at just 5.4%. However, Bush continued the expansionary policy, boosting defense spending with the War in Iraq.

Example: President John F. Kennedy used expansionary policy to stimulate the economy out of the 1960 recession. He was one of the first advocates of sustaining the policy until the recession was over, regardless of the impact on the debt.

Example: President Franklin D. Roosevelt used expansionary policy to end the Great Depression. He then cut back spending on the New Deal in response to pressure to cut the debt. As a result, the Depression reappeared in 1932. FDR returned to expansionary policy to gear up for World War II. That massive spending finally ended the Depression.

Contractionary Fiscal Policy

A **contractionary fiscal policy** involves raising taxes or cutting government spending in an attempt to slow growth in the GDP and lower inflationary pressures. Contractionary fiscal policy is so named because it contracts the economy. It reduces the amount of money available for businesses and consumers to spend. An economy that is growing too fast is an **overheated economy** that may have several negative repercussions.

Negative Aspects of Overheated Economy

First, it usually creates an asset bubble, like what happened to housing in 2006.

Second, it lowers unemployment to below the natural rate of unemployment. That makes it difficult for employers to find enough workers to meet market demand.

Third, it can create inflation. High inflation can destroy savings and the standard of living.

Fourth, an economy that is growing too fast will burn out, leading to a recession.

How It Works

Increasing spending or cutting taxes puts more money into consumers' hands— giving them more purchasing power. The government provides subsidies, transfer payments including welfare programs, contracts for public works, and hiring new government employees. That increases demand, boosting business profit and allowing them to increase employment.

Example: President Bill Clinton used contractionary policy by cutting spending in several key areas. First, he required welfare recipients to work within two years of getting benefits. After five years, benefits were cut off. He raised the top income tax rate from 28% to 39.6%

Example: President Franklin D. Roosevelt used contractionary policy too soon after the Depression. He was reacting to political pressure to cut the debt. The Depression came roaring back in 1932 and did not end until FDR geared up spending for World War II. That was a massive return to expansionary policy.

Monetary Policy

Monetary policy is a term used to refer to the actions of the Federal Reserve System (commonly known as the Fed) to achieve macroeconomic policy objectives such as price stability, full employment, and stable economic growth. By influencing the effective cost of money, the Federal Reserve can affect the amount of money that is available to consumers and businesses.

If the Fed puts too much liquidity into the banking system, it risks triggering **inflation**. The Fed sets a 2% inflation target. When inflation gets higher than 2-3%, consumers start stocking up to avoid higher prices later. That drives demand faster, which triggers businesses to produce more, and hire more workers. The additional income allows people to spend more, stimulating more demand. Sometimes businesses start raising prices because they know they cannot produce enough. Other times, they raise prices because their costs are rising. If it spirals out of control, it can create hyperinflation. **Hyperinflation** occurs when prices rise 50% or more. To stop inflation, the Fed puts on the brakes by implementing contractionary or restrictive monetary policy. The Fed raises interest rates and sells its holdings of Treasuries and other bonds. That reduces the money supply, restricts liquidity and cools economic growth. The Fed's goal is to keep inflation near its 2% target while keeping unemployment low as well.

Goals of Monetary Policy

The goals of monetary policy are to promote maximum employment, stable prices and moderate long-term interest rates. By implementing effective monetary policy, the Fed can maintain stable prices, thereby supporting conditions for long-term economic growth and maximum employment.

Tools the Fed Uses to Implement Monetary Policy

In carrying out its monetary policy, the Fed uses three tools—the discount rate, open market operations, and reserve requirements.

The Discount Rate

Federal Reserve member banks are permitted to borrow money from the Reserve Banks to increase their lending capabilities. The interest rate the banks pay for the federal funds is called the discount rate. The **discount rate** is the interest rate that is charged by the Federal Reserve to its member banks for borrowing money.

The Fed is a major player in the supply of money. The Fed can raise and lower the discount rate that it charges to its member banks. Essentially, it can stimulate or hinder the economy. A decrease in the discount rate allows more bank borrowing from the Fed. Bank borrowing increases money available for lending to the consumer. When the Fed lowers interest rates to member banks, those banks usually charge the consumer lower interest rates on everything from credit cards to home mortgages. This stimulates the economy and prompts more consumers to buy.

However, if the Fed thinks the economy is increasing too quickly (i.e., pushing up the price of merchandise by purchasing so much of it), it raises the discount rate. Raising the discount rate will result in less borrowing from the Fed. The decrease in bank borrowing reduces the amount of money available for lending to the consumer and the economy slows down. The prime rate, which is the rate the bank charges its strongest customers (those with the highest credit ratings), is heavily influenced by the discount rate.

Open Market Operations

The open market operations process is the Fed's most flexible, widely used monetary policy tool for expanding or slowing the economy. **Open market operations** refer to the purchases and sales of U.S. Government securities carried out through the trading desk of the Federal Reserve Bank of New York as directed by the Federal Open Market Committee. The **Federal Open Market Committee** (FOMC) consists of twelve members—seven members from the Board of Governors, the president of the Federal Reserve Bank of New York, and four of the other eleven Reserve Bank presidents. The purpose of the **FOMC** is to set the nation's monetary policy. It does this by overseeing the open market operations.

Each year, the FOMC holds eight regularly scheduled meetings to review economic and financial conditions and set monetary policy. Their decisions influence the availability and cost of money and credit, which affect a range of economic variables, including output, employment, and the prices of goods and services. The committee also decides whether to change its target for the federal funds rate and, if so, by how much. The fed funds rate is the rate at which depository institutions trade balances at the Federal Reserve.

When implementing open market operations, the Fed buys and sells government securities to influence the amount of available credit. When the Fed **buys government securities,** the banks have more money to lend, interest rates may fall, and consumer and business spending may increase, encouraging economic expansion.

To tighten money and credit in the economy, the FOMC directs the New York trading desk to **sell government securities**, collecting payments from banks by reducing their reserve accounts. With less money in these reserve accounts, banks have less money to lend, interest rates may increase, consumer and business spending may decrease, and economic activity may slow down.

Many economists think that total spending (**aggregate demand**) is determined more by monetary policy than by fiscal policy. In other words, the effects of tax or spending legislation intended to affect total spending can be fully offset or outweighed by changes in monetary policy. In fact, the fiscal policy of altering budget deficits to manage economic activity or aggregate demand is not considered desirable. However, economists tend to agree that changes in monetary policy do have predictable and potent effects on spending and economic activity.

Reserve Requirements

The Fed sets reserve requirements for all commercial banks, savings banks, savings and loans, credit unions, and U.S. branches and agencies of foreign banks. **Reserve requirements** refer to a certain percentage of each deposit in a bank that must be set aside either as a reserve to be held as cash on hand or as a reserve account balance at a Reserve Bank.

The Fed increases or decreases the amount of money in circulation by raising or lowering reserve requirements for member banks. When the Fed requires a larger reserve, the banks have less to lend, so interest rates increase while borrowing and spending decrease. If the Fed lowers the reserve requirement, the banks have more money to lend, interest rates may decrease, and borrowing and spending increase.

The Fed's influence affects key interest-rate sensitive sectors of the economy, such as housing, autos, and investment. **Short-term rates** are more directly influenced by Federal policy because its reserve operations involve purchases and sales of short-term government securities, which influence bank reserves. Nonetheless, **long-term rates** are also influenced by monetary policy. The only way monetary policy can sustain lower long-term rates is to promote price stability, thereby removing the uncertainty of inflationary expectations.

Altering reserve requirements is rarely used as a monetary policy tool. However, reserve requirements support the implementation of monetary policy by providing a more predictable demand for bank reserves, which increases the Fed's influence over short-term interest rate changes when implementing open market operations.

A bank that is unable to meet **overnight reserve requirements** borrows from fed funds deposited to regional Federal Reserve Banks by commercial banks, including funds in excess of reserve requirements. These non-interest bearing deposits are lent out at the fed funds rate to other banks unable to meet overnight reserve requirements.

Types of Monetary Policies

There are two types of monetary policy—expansionary and contractionary; however, in recent years the Fed has used some alternative policies.

Expansionary Monetary Policy

An **expansionary monetary policy** is used by the Fed to **stimulate the economy**—increase the money supply, lower interest rates, and increase aggregate demand. Expansionary monetary policy increases the money supply in order to lower unemployment, boost private-sector borrowing and consumer spending, and stimulate economic growth.

This action boosts growth as measured by Gross Domestic Product (GDP). It usually diminishes the value of the currency, thereby decreasing the exchange rate. It is the opposite of contractionary monetary policy.

Contractionary Monetary Policy

A **contractionary monetary policy** is used by the Fed to slow the rate of growth in the money supply or outright decrease the money supply in order to **control inflation**. The Fed must do this without pushing the economy into a recession. Although sometimes necessary, contractionary monetary policy can slow economic growth, increase unemployment and depress borrowing and spending by consumers and businesses.

> Example: The Federal Reserve intervened in the early 1980s in order to curb inflation of nearly 15%. The Fed raised its benchmark interest rate to 20%. This hike resulted in a recession, but did keep spiraling inflation in check.

The Fed's target for inflation is 2% for the core inflation rate. That is year-over-year price increases except volatile food and oil prices. The Fed prefers to use the Personal Consumption Expenditures Price Index rather than the Consumer Price Index even though it is the most popular inflation indicator.

Alternative Monetary Policies

In recent years, alternative monetary policies have become more common, such as quantitative easing, credit easing, and signaling.

Quantitative easing is the purchase of varying financial assets from commercial banks. In the U.S., the Fed loaded its balance sheet with trillions of dollars in Treasury notes and mortgage-backed securities between 2008 and 2013. The effect of quantitative easing is to raise the price of securities, therefore lowering their yields, as well as to increase total money supply.

Credit easing is a related unconventional monetary policy tool, involving the purchase of private-sector assets to boost liquidity.

Signaling is the use of public communication to ease markets' worries about policy changes. An example would be a promise not to raise interest rates for a given number of quarters.

Which is Better: Fiscal or Monetary Policy?

Although there are a variety of opinions regarding what constitutes appropriate fiscal and monetary policies, the importance of monetary policy in economic stabilization efforts is growing and the role played by fiscal policy is diminishing. The widespread agreement is that monetary policy is the primary instrument for macroeconomic stabilization and fiscal policy plays a supporting stabilizing role, particularly in relatively severe downturns and in periods when inflation is very low.

This delineation of their roles in managing the economy may reflect both political and economic realities. Fiscal policy may be more suited to fighting unemployment, whereas monetary policy may be more effective in fighting inflation. This is because fighting inflation requires the government to reduce spending or raise taxes, which is unpopular. Whereas, traditional fiscal policy solutions to fighting unemployment tend to be more popular since they require increasing spending or cutting taxes. Monetary policy has a bigger role during times of inflation.

THE FEDERAL RESERVE SYSTEM

The Panic of 1907, known as the 1907 Bankers' Panic, was a financial crisis that started when the New York Stock Exchange fell almost 50% from its peak the previous year. People panicked and quickly withdrew their funds from banks and trust companies that led to a severe monetary contraction. The fallout from the panic encouraged Congress to create the **Federal Reserve System**. Congress established the Federal Reserve System in 1913 to provide the nation with a stable monetary and financial system.

Currently, the Federal Reserve System **(the Fed)**—our **Central Bank** (or monetary authority)—is one of the country's most powerful economic institutions. The Federal Reserve affects the economic and financial decisions of virtually everyone—from a family buying a house, to a business expanding its operations, to a consumer choosing a sound financial institution. In the global economy, the Federal Reserve's actions have significant economic and financial effects around the world.

Functions of the Federal Reserve

The goal of the Federal Reserve is to maintain the stability of the nation's financial systems. To achieve that goal, the Fed has several functions.

Functions of the Federal Reserve System

- Acts as the banker for the U.S. Treasury
- Supervises and regulates banking institutions and certain consumer protection laws
- Acts as lender of last resort to nation's banks
- Determines monetary policy

Acts as the Government's Banker

The Federal Reserve acts as the banker for the U.S. government by maintaining the checking account for the U.S. Treasury Department and clearing U.S. Treasury checks. The Fed processes a wide range of electronic payments for the government, such as Social Security and payroll checks. The Fed also issues, transfers, and redeems U.S. Treasury securities and conducts Treasury securities auctions.

Regulates Financial Institutions

The Federal Reserve helps supervise and regulate the nation's financial institutions to ensure their financial soundness and compliance with banking, consumer, and other applicable laws. Specifically, the Fed monitors bank holding companies, state-chartered banks that are members of the Federal Reserve System, and various international banking operations. **National banks**, which by law must be members of the Federal Reserve System, are supervised by the Office of the Comptroller of the Currency (OCC) in the U.S. Treasury Department. **State-chartered banks** that are not members of the Federal Reserve System are supervised by the Federal Deposit Insurance Corporation (FDIC) and state authorities.

The Fed also writes rules and enforces a number of laws that offer consumers protection in their financial dealings, such as the Electronic Fund Transfer Act and the Community Reinvestment Act.

Acts as the Lender-of-Last-Resort

The Federal Reserve provides credit to depository institutions to help them adjust to temporary, unexpected changes in their deposits or loan portfolios. The Fed also helps institutions that have seasonal or emergency needs for credit.

During financial crises, the Central Bank is the **lender-of-last-resort** to the nation's banks to stabilize the financial system. During business downturns, the Fed may assist banks that are healthy but need help to see them through temporary credit problems. Failure to provide this function, for example, as occurred in the Great Depression of the 1930s, can be disastrous. On the other hand, this liquidity provision helped prevent a serious financial system failure in the late 1980s and again in 2008-2010. The Federal Reserve has the responsibility to ensure that lender-of-last-resort safeguards are adequate and in place in case of unforeseen financial shocks. If banks or other federally insured depository institutions are forced to close, depositors are protected by the FDIC up to the legal limit of $250,000 per depositor.

Determines Monetary Policy

Although the Federal Reserve has many functions, its most critical role is to keep the economy healthy through the proper application of monetary policy. The country's economic performance is influenced by fiscal policy determined by the legislative and executive branches of government and by monetary policy carried out by the Federal Reserve.

The objective of monetary policy is to influence the country's economic performance to promote stable prices, maximum sustainable employment, and steady economic growth. Congress set forth this objective in the Federal Reserve Act of 1913, the Employment Act of 1946, and the Full Employment and Balanced Growth (Humphrey-Hawkins) Act of 1978.

The importance of the Federal Reserve cannot be overemphasized. The Fed implements **monetary policy** to manage the flow of money and credit in the economy. If money and credit expand too rapidly, businesses cannot produce enough goods and services to keep up with increased spending. Prices may rise, causing inflation. **Inflation** is the upward price movement of goods and services in an economy, usually measured by the Consumer Price Index. Inflation adversely affects savings and distorts investment decisions. Higher inflation is associated with lower economic growth. Therefore, a key objective of monetary policy should be to promote price stability to foster long-term economic growth.

If the contraction of money and credit is too great, spending and business activity may dwindle, workers may lose their jobs, and a **recession** may result. The Fed sets the monetary policy to attempt to balance these two extremes to keep prices steady, workers employed, and factories productive.

Changes in the monetary policy are often a major factor in movements of the business cycle. In fact, many booms and recessions are directly related to changes in monetary policy. Conversely, stable economic activity is often the result of appropriate, stable monetary policy. For example, when the Fed institutes a non-inflationary policy, it helps to stabilize the economic cycles as well as most financial markets.

Structure of the Federal Reserve System

The Federal Reserve System was created as an independent agency of the United States government to provide a safer, more flexible banking and monetary system. To ensure autonomy and to insulate the central bank from short-term partisan political pressures, the founders stipulated that the Fed's operations would be financed from its own resources.

There are three key entities in the Federal Reserve System: (1) the Board of Governors, (2) the Federal Reserve Banks (Reserve Banks), and (3) the Federal Open Market Committee (FOMC).

Board of Governors

The **Board of Governors (BOG)** is an independent agency of the federal government that reports to and is directly accountable to Congress. The BOG oversees the Federal Reserve System. It is made up of seven members who are appointed by the President and confirmed by the Senate. Although they periodically must report on their actions to Congress, the governors are independent from the President and from Congress. Board members serve 14-year terms, which are arranged so that one expires in every even-numbered year. The terms were designed to be long enough to prevent day-to-day political pressures from influencing the formulation of monetary policy and the supervision of the operations of the 12 regional Reserve Banks.

The BOG guides the operation of the Federal Reserve System to promote the goals and fulfill the responsibilities given to the Federal Reserve by the Federal Reserve Act.

Federal Reserve Banks

The **Federal Reserve System** consists of twelve **Federal Reserve Banks** (Reserve Banks) located in major cities throughout the United States. These banks are under the supervision of the Board of Governors in Washington, D.C. In establishing the Federal Reserve System, the United States was divided geographically into 12 Districts, each with a separately incorporated Reserve Bank. District boundaries were based on prevailing trade regions that existed in 1913 and related economic considerations, so they do not necessarily coincide with state lines.

The twelve Federal Reserve Banks are the operating arms of the Federal Reserve System. The Federal Reserve Banks handle the Treasury's payments, assist with the Treasury's cash management and investment activities, and sell government securities. They supervise member banks, holding companies, and international organizations that do banking business in the United States. Often called the banker's bank, a Federal Reserve Bank (**Reserve Bank**) stores currency and coin, processes checks and electronic payments, and operates a nationwide payments system to distribute the nation's currency and coin.

The Twelve Federal Reserve Districts

Each of the Federal Reserve Banks is responsible for a particular geographic area or district of the United States. Each Reserve District is identified by a number. In addition to administering nationwide banking and credit policies, each Reserve Bank acts as a depository for the banks in its own District.

The Twelve Federal Reserve Districts

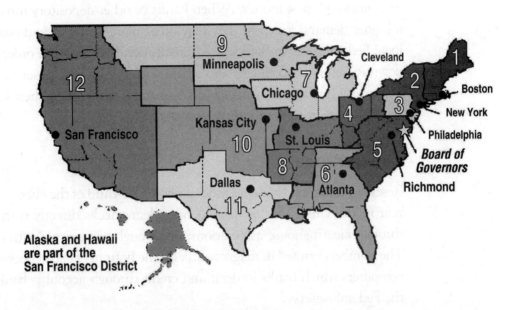

Alaska and Hawaii
are part of the
San Francisco District

Reserve Bank Responsibilities

In its role providing key financial services, the Reserve Bank acts as a financial institution for the banks, thrifts, and credit unions in its District. In essence, each Reserve Bank acts as a "bank for banks". In that capacity, it offers (and charges for) services to these depository institutions similar to those that ordinary banks provide their customers.

Reserve Bank Services

Reserve Banks provide certain financial services, such as distributing coin and paper money, processing and clearing checks, and transferring electronic funds and payments. They help regulate the flow of money and credit and provide a safe and efficient method of transferring funds throughout the banking system.

Currency and Coin

Reserve Banks are responsible for meeting public demand for currency and coin within their districts. New currency and coin are shipped to Federal Reserve Banks and Branches across the country where the money is stored. Currency is printed by the U.S. Bureau of Engraving and Printing in Washington, D.C., and Fort Worth, Texas. Coins are produced at U.S. Mints in Philadelphia and Denver.

Reserve Banks store coin and reusable paper notes in their vaults until depository institutions request money. When banks or other depository institutions have a higher demand for cash, they may order more currency and coin from their local Federal Reserve Banks. Each institution pays for these orders by drawing down its reserve account balances held with the Federal Reserve. Conversely, depository institutions with excess cash may return it to their local Reserve Banks for credit to their reserve accounts.

Check Processing

Reserve Banks and Branches process about one-third of the checks written each year in the United States. Banks may clear checks directly with each other, through clearinghouse associations, or through agreements with other banks. The numbers printed in magnetic ink on the bottom of each check tell the Fed's computers which banks to debit and credit through accounts banks hold with the Federal Reserve.

Funds Transfer

The Reserve Banks provide two electronic payment services: Fedwire and the automated clearinghouse. Fedwire, a highly sophisticated, computerized communications system, transfers funds almost instantly from one depository institution to another anywhere in the country. The **automated clearinghouse** (ACH) provides a nationwide network to exchange paperless payments among financial institutions and government agencies. The ACH accommodates a wide range of recurring corporate and consumer transactions, such as payroll deposits, electronic bill payments, insurance payments, and Social Security disbursements.

Federal Open Market Committee

The **Federal Open Market Committee (FOMC)** consists of voting twelve members—the seven members of the Board of Governors, the president of the Federal Reserve Bank of New York, and four of the other eleven Reserve Bank presidents. The purpose of the FOMC is to set the nation's monetary policy.

FOMC Responsibilities

The FOMC makes all decisions regarding the conduct of open market operations, the principal tool by which the Federal Reserve executes U.S. monetary policy.

These operations affect the federal funds rate, which in turn influence overall monetary and credit conditions, aggregate demand, and the entire economy. The federal funds rate **(fed funds)** is the interest rate at which depository institutions lend to each other. The FOMC also directs operations undertaken by the Federal Reserve in foreign exchange markets and, in recent years, has authorized currency swap programs with foreign central banks.

> For more information on the Federal Reserve System, visit www.federalreserve.gov.

Tools of the Federal Reserve System

The Federal Reserve implements monetary policy through its control over the Federal Reserve funds. **Federal Reserve funds** are overnight loans banks use to meet the reserve requirement at the end of each day. The Federal Reserve uses the Fed funds to control the nation's interest rates. That is because banks borrow Fed funds from each other. The interest rate they pay is called the **Fed funds rate**. The Fed influences the supply of money and credit available by raising and lowering the amount of reserves that banks are required to hold and the discount rate at which they can borrow money from the Fed. The Fed also trades government securities (called repurchase agreements) to take money out of or put it into the system. This is called open market operations.

Reserve Requirements

The Fed increases or decreases the amount of money in circulation by raising or lowering reserve requirements for member banks. **Reserve requirements** refer to a certain percentage of each deposit in a bank that must be set aside as a reserve. When the Fed requires a larger reserve, the banks have less to lend, so interest rates increase while borrowing and spending decrease. If the Fed lowers the reserve requirement, the banks have more money to lend, interest rates may decrease, and borrowing and spending increase.

Discount Rates

Federal Reserve member banks are permitted to borrow money from the Reserve Banks to increase their lending capabilities. The interest rate the banks pay for the federal funds is called the discount rate. The **discount rate** is the interest rate that is charged by the Federal Reserve to its member banks for borrowing money. A decrease in the discount rate allows more bank borrowing from the Fed. Bank borrowing increases money available for lending to the consumer.

Raising the discount rate results in less borrowing from the Fed. The decrease in bank borrowing reduces the amount of money available for lending to the consumer. The **prime rate**, which is the rate the bank charges its strongest customers (those with the highest credit ratings), is heavily influenced by the discount rate.

The Fed is a major player in the supply of money. The Fed can raise and lower the interest rates that it charges to its member banks. Essentially, it can stimulate or hinder the economy. When the Fed lowers interest rates to member banks, those banks usually charge the consumer lower interest rates on everything from credit cards to home mortgages. This stimulates the economy and prompts more consumers to buy. However, if the Fed thinks the economy is being irrationally exuberant (i.e., pushing up the price of merchandise by purchasing so much of it), it raises interest rates and the economy slows down; thus, consumers purchase less.

Open Market Operations

Each year, the **FOMC** holds eight regularly scheduled meetings to review economic and financial conditions and set monetary policy. Its decisions influence the availability and cost of money and credit, which affect a range of economic variables, including output, employment, and the prices of goods and services. The committee also decides whether to change its target for the federal funds rate and, if so, by how much.

When implementing open market operations, the Fed buys and sells government securities to influence the amount of available credit. When the **Fed buys securities**, the banks have more money to lend. When the **Fed sells securities**, the opposite is true. The open market operations process is the most flexible and widely used technique for expanding or slowing the economy.

U.S. DEPARTMENT OF THE TREASURY

On September 2, 1789, Congress created the **U.S. Department of the Treasury** for the management of government finances and Alexander Hamilton became the first Secretary of the Treasury.

> "Be it enacted by the Senate and House of Representatives of the United States of America in Congress assembled, That there shall be a Department of Treasury, in which shall be the following officers, namely: a Secretary of the Treasury, to be deemed head of the department; a Comptroller, an Auditor, a Treasurer, a Register, and an Assistant to the Secretary of the Treasury, which assistant shall be appointed by the said Secretary."

The U.S. Department of the Treasury (**Treasury Department**) is a cabinet-level agency that manages Federal finances by collecting taxes and paying bills and by managing currency, government accounts, and public debt. The Treasury Department also enforces finance and tax laws.

The Secretary of the Treasury serves as a major policy advisor to the President and has primary responsibility for participating in the formulation of broad fiscal policies that have general significance for the economy. The government uses fiscal policy to regulate the total level of economic activity within a nation. Examples of fiscal policy include setting the level of government expenditures and the level of taxation.

In addition, the Secretary helps formulate domestic and international financial, economic, and tax policies and helps manage the public debt.

The Treasury Department's responsibilities vary from printing and minting all paper currency and coins in circulation (United States Mint) to collecting all federal taxes (Internal Revenue Service).

Duties & Functions of the Treasury Department

The Treasury Department is the executive agency responsible for promoting economic prosperity and ensuring the financial security of the United States. The Treasury Department is responsible for a wide range of activities such as advising the President on economic and financial issues, encouraging sustainable economic growth, and fostering improved governance in financial institutions. It analyzes and reports on current and prospective economic developments in the U.S. and world economies and assists in the determination of appropriate economic policies.

The Treasury Department operates and maintains systems that are critical to the nation's financial infrastructure, such as the production of coin and currency, the disbursement of payments to the American public, revenue collection, and the borrowing of funds necessary to run the federal government.

The Treasury Department works with other federal agencies, foreign governments, and international financial institutions to encourage global economic growth, raise standards of living, and to the extent possible, predict and prevent economic and financial crises.

The Treasury Department also performs a critical and far-reaching role in enhancing national security by implementing **economic sanctions** against foreign threats to the U.S., identifying and targeting the financial support networks of national security threats, and improving the safeguards of our financial systems.

Basic Functions of the Department of the Treasury

- Managing Federal finances
- Collecting taxes, duties, and monies paid to and due to the U.S. and paying all bills of the U.S.
- Printing all currency and postage and minting coins
- Managing government accounts and the United States public debt
- Supervising national banks and thrift institutions
- Advising on domestic and international financial, monetary, economic, trade and tax policy (fiscal policy being the sum of these)
- Enforcing Federal finance and tax laws
- Investigating and prosecuting tax evaders, counterfeiters, and forgers

Organization

The Department of the Treasury is organized into two major components the Treasury Offices and the Operating Bureaus. The Departmental Offices are primarily responsible for the formulation of policy and management of the Department as a whole, while the Operating Bureaus carry out the specific operations assigned to the Department.

Treasury Offices

The Treasury Department has several **Treasury Offices** that are primarily responsible for policy formulation and overall management of the Treasury Department. Some of the Offices are described below.

The **Office of Domestic Finance** advises and assists the Secretary of the Treasury Department on the domestic financial system, fiscal policy and operations, governmental assets and liabilities, and related economic and financial matters.

The **Office of Economic Policy** monitors key economic indicators to report on current and prospective economic developments and assist in the determination of appropriate economic policies. The office is responsible for the review and analysis of both domestic and international economic issues and developments in the financial markets.

The **Office of Debt Management** is responsible for providing the Assistant Secretary for Financial Markets with advice and analysis on matters related to the Treasury's debt management policy, the issuance of Treasury and federally related securities, and financial markets. The Treasury Department's primary goal in debt management is to finance government-borrowing needs at the lowest cost over time.

The **Treasurer of the United States** oversees the Bureau of Engraving and Printing and the United States Mint. In addition, the Treasurer serves as a senior advisor and representative of the Treasury on behalf of the Secretary in the areas of community development and public engagement.

Treasury Bureaus

The **Treasury Bureaus** are responsible for carrying out specific operations assigned to the Treasury Department.

Current Treasury Bureaus
- United States Mint
- Bureau of Engraving and Printing
- Office of the Comptroller of the Currency
- Financial Crimes Enforcement Network (FinCEN)
- Internal Revenue Service
- Alcohol and Tobacco Tax and Trade Bureau
- Bureau of the Fiscal Service
- Community Development Financial Institutions Fund

U.S. Mint

The framers of the U.S. Constitution realized the critical need for a respected monetary system for the country.

> "The Congress shall have the Power . . . To coin Money."
> — *Constitution of the United States, Article I, Section 8*

Soon after the Constitution's ratification, Secretary of the Treasury Alexander Hamilton personally prepared plans for a national Mint. On April 2, 1792, Congress passed The Coinage Act, which created the Mint and authorized construction of a Mint building in the nation's capital, Philadelphia. This was the first federal building erected under the Constitution.

The **United States Mint** (Mint) became part of the Department of the Treasury in 1873. The primary mission of the Mint is to manufacture, distribute, and circulate precious metal and collectible coins and national medals. It is the sole manufacturer of legal tender coinage for the United States. The  Mint also produces numismatic products, including proof, uncirculated, and commemorative coins; Congressional Gold Medals; and silver and gold bullion coins. The United States Mint's numismatic programs are self-sustaining and operate at no cost to the taxpayer.

The United States Mint operates six facilities across the United States with each facility performing unique functions. Current facilities include the Headquarters in Washington, DC; production facilities in Philadelphia, West Point, Denver, and San Francisco; and the United States Bullion Depository at Fort Knox, KY.

Bureau of Engraving and Printing

The **Bureau of Engraving and Printing** (BEP) prints billions of dollars, referred to as **Federal Reserve notes**, each year for delivery to the Federal Reserve System. The Federal Reserve operates as the nation's central bank and serves to ensure that adequate amounts of currency and coin are in circulation. In addition, the BEP processes claims for the redemption of mutilated currency. The BEP does not produce coins. All U.S. coinage is minted by the United States Mint.

Office of the Comptroller of the Currency

The **Office of the Comptroller of the Currency** (OCC) charters, regulates, and supervises all national banks and federal savings associations as well as federal branches and agencies of foreign banks. The OCC is an independent bureau of the U.S. Department of the Treasury.

The Financial Crimes Enforcement Network (FinCEN)

The **Financial Crimes Enforcement Network** (FinCEN) supports law enforcement investigative efforts and fosters interagency and global cooperation against domestic and international financial crimes. It also provides U.S. policy makers with strategic analyses of domestic and worldwide trends and patterns.

The Internal Revenue Service (IRS)

The **Internal Revenue Service** (IRS) is the largest of Treasury's bureaus. It is responsible for determining, assessing, and collecting taxes.

The Alcohol and Tobacco Tax and Trade Bureau

The **Alcohol and Tobacco Tax and Trade Bureau** (TTB) is responsible for enforcing and administering laws covering the production, use, and distribution of alcohol and tobacco products. TTB also collects excise taxes for firearms and ammunition.

To learn more about the functions of the U.S. Department of the Treasury, go to www.ustreas.gov.

FEDERAL DEPOSIT INSURANCE CORPORATION

The **Federal Deposit Insurance Corporation** (FDIC) is an independent agency of the federal government responsible for insuring deposits made by individuals and companies in banks and other thrift institutions. The Federal Deposit Insurance Company (FDIC) was created in 1933 when President Roosevelt signed the Banking Act (also known as the Glass-Steagall Act) and was placed under the jurisdiction of the Federal Reserve. The FDIC began extending its coverage for deposits on January 1, 1934.

The FDIC protects depositors against the loss of their insured deposits if an FDIC-insured bank or thrift fails. FDIC insurance is backed by the full faith and credit of the United States Government. Deposit insurance is a fundamental component of the FDIC's role in maintaining stability and public confidence in the U.S. financial system. By promoting industry and consumer awareness of deposit insurance, the FDIC protects depositors at banks and savings associations of all sizes. When banks fail, the FDIC ensures that the financial institution's customers have timely access to their insured deposits and other services.

The FDIC's Major Programs

The **FDIC** has three major program areas or lines of business: insurance, supervision of financial institutions, and receivership management.

Insurance Program

The Federal Deposit Insurance Company (FDIC) mitigates any potential damage to the United States economy by **insuring deposits** made to banks and other financial institutions. Savings, checking, individual retirement accounts (IRAs) and other deposit accounts (when combined) are insured up to $250,000 per depositor. The deposits are fully insured if a depositor's accounts at one FDIC-insured bank or thrift total $250,000 or less. Deposits in separate branches of an insured bank are not separately insured. Deposits maintained in different categories of legal ownership at the same bank can be separately insured. Therefore, it is possible to have deposits totaling more than $250,000 at one insured bank and still be fully insured.

> For example, if a person had a CD account in her name alone with a principal balance of $195,000 and $3,000 in accrued interest, the full $198,000 would be insured, since principal plus interest did not exceed the $250,000 insurance limit for single ownership accounts.

The FDIC does not insure securities, mutual funds, or similar investments, such as stocks, money market accounts, and bonds. It does not cover investments backed by the U.S. Government, such as U.S. Treasury securities, contents of safe deposit boxes, accounting errors, or losses due to theft or fraud at an institution.

Supervision Program

In addition to its role as insurer, the FDIC is the primary **federal regulator** of federally insured state-chartered banks that are not members of the Federal Reserve System. The FDIC promotes safe and sound financial institution practices through regular risk management examinations, publication of guidance and policy, ongoing communication with industry officials, and the review of applications submitted by FDIC-supervised institutions to expand their activities or locations. When appropriate, the FDIC has a range of informal and formal enforcement options available to resolve safety-and-soundness problems identified at these institutions. The FDIC also has staff dedicated to administering off-site monitoring programs and to enhancing the Corporation's ability to timely identify emerging safety-and-soundness issues.

Red Flag Rules - Section 114 of FACTA

In 2007, several agencies (Federal Deposit Insurance Corporation, Office of the Comptroller of the Currency, Federal Reserve Board, Office of Thrift Supervision, National Credit Union Administration, and Federal Trade Commission) passed the **Interagency Guidelines on Identity Theft Detection, Prevention, and Mitigation** as Section 114 of the Fair and Accurate Credit Transactions Act (FACTA) of 2003. This law is known as the **Red Flag Rules**.

Under the Red Flags Rules, financial institutions and creditors must develop a written "**Identity Theft Prevention Program**" to detect, prevent, and mitigate identity theft in covered accounts. A **covered account** is any personal account, such as checking and savings accounts, credit card accounts, mortgage loans, automobile loans, margin accounts, and cell phone or utility accounts.

Each creditor's Identity Theft Prevention Program must create a list of warning signs—"red flags"—for possible identity theft. **Red flags** are suspicious patterns or practices or specific activities that indicate the possibility of identity theft. The law lists five categories of warning signs.

Categories of Red Flags

Alerts, Notifications, & Warnings from a Credit Reporting Agency

- Fraud or active duty alert on a credit report
- Notice of credit freeze in response to a request for a credit report
- Notice of address discrepancy provided by a credit reporting agency
- Credit report indicating activity inconsistent with the person's history.
  - Big increase in inquiries or credit use, especially on new accounts
  - Unusual number of recently established credit relationships
  - Account that was closed because of an abuse of account privileges

Suspicious Documents

- Identification that looks altered or forged
- Person presenting the id does not match the photo or the physical description
- Identification information that does not match with other information, like a signature card or recent check
- Application that looks altered, forged, or torn up and reassembled

Suspicious Personal Identifying Information

- Inconsistencies with known facts
  - An address that does not match the credit report
  - Social security number that is listed on the social security administration death master file, or a number that has not been issued
  - Date of birth that does not correlate to the number range on the social security administration's issuance tables
- Social security number used by someone else opening an account
- Address, phone number, or other personal information that has been used on an account known to be fraudulent
- Bogus address, such as an address for a mail drop or prison
- Invalid phone number
- Address or telephone number used by other people opening accounts
- Required information omitted on an application and applicant does not respond to notices that the application is incomplete

Suspicious Account Activity

- After being notified of a change of address, the creditor is asked for new or additional credit cards, cell phones, etc., or to add users to the account
- New account that is used in ways associated with fraud
- Customer does not make the first payment, or makes only an initial payment
- Available credit is used for cash advances or for jewelry, electronics, or other merchandise easily converted to cash
- Existing account used inconsistent with established patterns
- Big increase in the use of available credit
- Major change in buying or spending patterns or transfers
- Noticeable change in calling patterns for a cell phone account
- Inactive account suddenly being used again
- Mail sent to the customer that's returned repeatedly as undeliverable although transactions continue to be conducted on the account
- Information that the customer is not receiving his or her account statements in the mail
- Information about unauthorized charges on the account

Notice from Other Sources

- Information provided by a customer, a victim of identity theft, a law enforcement authority, or someone else.

Receivership Management Program

When an insured depository institution fails, the FDIC is ordinarily appointed receiver. In that capacity, it assumes responsibility for efficiently recovering the maximum amount possible from the disposition of the receivership's assets and the pursuit of the receivership's claims. Funds that are collected from the sale of assets and the disposition of valid claims are distributed to the receivership's creditors according to priorities set by law.

For more information about the FDIC, go to www.fdic.gov.

FEDERAL HOUSING FINANCE AGENCY

The **Federal Housing Finance Agency (FHFA)** is an independent regulatory agency created in 2008 when the Housing and Economic Recovery Act was signed into law. FHFA was created by merging three existing agencies—the Federal Housing Finance Board (FHFB), the Office of Federal Housing Enterprise Oversight (OFHEO), and the GSE mission office at HUD. FHFA assumed the regulatory powers of all three agencies, and gained expanded authority as well.

The Federal Housing Finance Agency is responsible for the oversight of the housing Government Sponsored Enterprises. A **government-sponsored enterprise** (GSE) is a financial services corporation created by the United States Congress. The **housing GSEs** are Fannie Mae (Federal National Mortgage Association), Freddie Mac (Federal Home Loan Mortgage Corporation), and the Federal Home Loan Bank System (System), which currently consists of 11 Federal Home Loan Banks (FHLBanks). The housing GSEs are critical in providing liquidity, stability, and affordability to the mortgage market, particularly for long-term, fixed-rate mortgages.

Fannie Mae and Freddie Mac are among the most active participants in the secondary mortgage market by investing in and selling mortgage-backed securities (MBS) to a wide variety of investors in the capital markets. The FHLBs provide advances and other financial products to support their members' affordable housing activities.

The housing GSEs are regulated by the **Federal Housing Finance Agency** (FHFA), an independent regulatory agency that was established by the Federal Housing Finance Reform Act of 2007. FHFA is committed to ensuring that qualified, eligible borrowers have fair and equitable access to finance and the services offered by the housing GSEs.

The GSEs are mandated to devote a percentage of their business to three specific affordable housing goals each year. This started in 1996, when HUD began setting annual goals for the proportion of low- and moderate-income family mortgages that Fannie Mae and Freddie Mac were required to buy. The goal was increased each year, rising from 40% in 1996 to 57% by 2008. Eventually, over time, this mandate promoted subprime and other nontraditional mortgages and degraded mortgage underwriting standards.

Currently, FHFA establishes, monitors, and enforces the affordable housing goals for Fannie Mae and Freddie Mac that are mandated by the Housing and Economic Recovery Act of 2008 (HERA).

FHFA Single-Family Owner-Occupied Purchase Goals

1. **Low-Income Housing Goal** (24%). This targets families with incomes no grater than 80% of the area median income. (**Area median income** is defined as the median income of the metropolitan area, or for properties outside of metropolitan areas, the median income of the county or the statewide nonmetropolitan area, whichever is greater.)

2. **Very Low-Income Housing Goal** (6%). This targets families with incomes no grater than 50% of the area median income.

3. **Families That Reside In Low-Income Areas Housing Goal** (14%). Three categories of home purchase mortgages qualify for the low-income areas housing goal:
   a. Low-income census tracts (tracts with median family income no greater than 80% of AMI)
   b. Minority census tracts (tracts with minority population of at least 30% and a median family income less than 100% of AMI)
   c. Federally-declared disaster areas (regardless of the minority share of the population in the tract or the ratio of tract median family income to AMI).

As the conservator of Fannie Mae and Freddie Mac, FHFA will continue to improve their condition by restricting new risk-taking, strengthening underwriting practices, and reducing assets from their pre-conservatorship book of business.

Each year FHFA sets the limit of the size of a conforming loan, which is based on the October-to-October changes in mean home price.

> Go to http://www.fhfa.gov/ for more information about the FHFA.

Fannie Mae & Freddie Mac

FHFA is responsible for ensuring that Fannie Mae and Freddie Mac operate in a safe manner. This is done through prudential supervision and regulation. Fannie Mae and Freddie Mac are the popular names for the Federal National Mortgage Association, chartered by Congress in 1938, and the Federal Home Loan Mortgage Corporation, chartered in 1970.

Although both Fannie Mae and Freddie Mac currently have similar charters, congressional mandates and regulatory structure, they were originally formed with different focuses. **Fannie Mae** was formed to support the secondary market for Federal Housing Administration (FHA) loans after the Great Depression, whereas **Freddie Mac** was created to provide a secondary market for conventional mortgages during the severe credit crunch of 1969–70 in the thrift industry. Today both Fannie Mae and Freddie Mac deal with all types of depository institutions and conventional as well as government-insured or guaranteed mortgage loans.

Even though Fannie Mae and Freddie Mac are both publicly traded companies, they receive explicit and implicit government subsidies. Although Fannie Mae and Freddie Mac securities are not backed by the full faith and credit of the federal government, investors have indicated that they believe the government would provide any support necessary to keep these companies solvent because of their implicit public sponsorship.

Both Fannie Mae and Freddie Mac are discussed later in the course. Please reference the Oversight of Fannie Mae & Freddie Mac chart as listed in the course.

Federal Home Loan Bank System

The **Federal Home Loan Bank System** (System) was created by the Federal Home Loan Bank Act as a government sponsored enterprise to support mortgage lending and related community investment. It is composed of 11 regional **Federal Home Loan Banks (FHLBanks)** and more than 7,400 member financial institutions.

FHFA is responsible for ensuring that the Federal Home Loan Banks operate in a financially safe fashion, remain adequately capitalized and able to raise funds in the capital markets, and operate in a manner consistent with their housing finance mission. To carry out these statutory duties, FHFA has implemented a program of FHLBank supervision to conduct on-site annual examinations and off-site monitoring of the FHLBanks and the Office of Finance.

Please reference the Oversight of the Federal Home Loan Bank System chart as listed in the course.

Federal Home Loan Banks

The 11 **regional FHLBanks** are located in Atlanta, Boston, Chicago, Cincinnati, Dallas, Des Moines, Indianapolis, New York, Pittsburgh, San Francisco, and Topeka. Each FHLBank is a separate, government-chartered, member-owned corporation that lending institutions use to finance housing and economic development in their communities. Created by Congress, the FHLBanks have been one of the largest, private sources of funding for community lending in the U.S. for more than eight decades. They provide stable, on-demand, low-cost funding to financial institutions (not individuals) for home mortgage loans, small business, rural, agricultural, and economic development lending.

Each regional Bank is an individual corporate entity, which must meet strict management and capitalization criteria befitting its status as a government-sponsored enterprise. Federal oversight, in conjunction with normal bank regulation and shareholder vigilance, assures that the 11 regional Banks remain conservatively managed and well capitalized.

Because the FHLBanks are regionally focused and controlled, each FHLBank is responsive to the specific community credit needs in its geography. At the same time, the FHLBanks collectively use their combined size and strength to obtain funding at the lowest possible cost for their members. This means that the members can advance credit to their local communities at competitive rates.

Approximately 7,400 lenders are members of the FHLBanks. Banks, thrifts, credit unions, community development financial institutions and insurance companies are all eligible for membership. Members, ranging in size from some of the largest financial institutions in the world to banks with just a single branch, do business throughout the United States.

With their members, the FHLBanks represents the largest collective source of home mortgage and community credit in the United States.

> For more information about the Federal Home Loan Banks, go to http://www.fhlbanks.com.

INFORMATION RESOURCES

Please refer to the following information resources for further information:

- Federal Reserve System (www.federalreserve.gov)
- U.S. Department of the Treasury (www.ustreas.gov)
- Federal Deposit Insurance Corporation (FDIC) (www.fdic.gov)
- Federal Housing Finance Agency (FHFA) (www.fhfa.gov)
- Federal Home Loan Banks (www.fhlbanks.com)

SUMMARY

Financing involves money, interest, and debt. Money is any generally accepted medium of exchange and unit of account. Interest is the charge for the use of money. Debt is a dollar amount that is borrowed from another party, usually under specific terms.

In the U.S., the money supply consists of currency in circulation, money in checking accounts, deposits in savings, and other liquid assets. Liquid assets are securities and financial instruments that are converted easily and quickly into cash. Money and capital markets are short- and long-term markets in which money instruments are traded by buyers and sellers.

The federal government's role in the national economy is to manage the overall pace of economic activity to avoid wild swings in the financial markets, while maintaining high levels of employment and stable prices. It has two main tools for achieving these objectives: fiscal policy and monetary policy. The fiscal policy is the government policy on government spending and taxation. The monetary policy controls the supply of money and influences the cost and availability of credit to promote economic growth, full employment, and price stability.

The government uses fiscal policy to regulate the total level of economic activity within a nation. The term fiscal policy refers to the government's financial strategy with respect to government spending, taxation, and debt management.

The primary goal of fiscal policy is to achieve economic growth, which is an indicator of the overall health of the economy. Implementing sound fiscal policy can help control the pace of economic growth and ensure that the economy is not growing too slow or too fast.

Monetary policy is the regulation of the money supply and interest rates by a central bank to stabilize the economy and control inflation. In the United States, monetary policy is the province of the Federal Reserve System, commonly known as the Fed. By influencing the effective cost of money, the Federal Reserve can affect the amount of money that is available to consumers and businesses. The amount of money in the economy at any given time is a function of both supply and demand. If the economy is booming, there is demand for money. When the economy is slow, there is less demand for money. Too much money in relation to the output of goods tends to push interest rates down and push inflation up. If there is too little money, interest rates are pushed up and prices go down.

Congress established the Federal Reserve System in 1913 to provide the nation with a stable monetary and financial system. Currently, the Federal Reserve System (the Fed)—our Central Bank (or monetary authority)—is one of the country's most powerful economic institutions. The goal of the Federal Reserve is to maintain the stability of the nation's financial systems. To achieve that goal, the Fed acts as the banker for the U.S. Treasury, supervises and regulates banking institutions and certain consumer protection laws, acts as lender of last resort to nation's banks, and determines monetary policy.

Although there are a variety of opinions regarding what constitutes appropriate fiscal and monetary policies, the importance of monetary policy in economic stabilization efforts is growing and the role played by fiscal policy is diminishing. The widespread agreement is that monetary policy is the primary instrument for macroeconomic stabilization and fiscal policy plays a supporting stabilizing role, particularly in relatively severe downturns and in periods when inflation is very low.

UNIT 2 REVIEW

Matching Exercise

Instructions: Write the letter of the matching term on the blank line before its definition.
Answers are in Appendix A.

Terms

A. automated clearinghouse

B. contractionary fiscal policy

C. debt

D. discount rate

E. expansionary fiscal policy

F. fed funds rate

G. Federal Deposit Insurance Corporation

H. Federal Home Loan Bank System

I. Federal Reserve System

J. fiscal policy

K. government-sponsored enterprise

L. liquid assets

M. monetary policy

N. money

O. money supply

P. Office of Economic Policy

Q. open market operations

R. supply

S. Treasury Department

T. United States Mint

Definitions

1. _____ Any generally accepted medium of exchange and unit of account

2. _____ Dollar amount borrowed from another party, usually under specific terms

3. _____ Total amount of money available for transactions and investment in the economy

4. _____ Securities and financial instruments that are easily and quickly converted into cash

5. _____ Quantity of a product on the market that is available for consumption at a particular time at a particular price

6. _____ Influences the cost and availability of credit to promote economic growth, full employment, and price stability

7. _____ Government policy on taxes and government spending

8. _____ Fiscal policy that aims to expand the amount of money available for consumers and businesses to spend and speed up the rate of GDP growth

9. _____ Fiscal policy that involves raising taxes or cutting government spending in an attempt to slow growth in the GDP and lower inflationary pressures

10. _____ Interest rate charged by the Federal Reserve to its member banks for borrowing money

11. _____ Purchases and sales of U.S. Government and federal agency securities

12. _____ Nation's central bank

13. _____ Provides a nationwide network to exchange paperless payments among financial institutions and government agencies

14. _____ Rate at which depository institutions trade balances at the Federal Reserve

15. _____ The cabinet-level agency that manages Federal finances by collecting taxes and paying bills and by managing currency, government accounts, and public debt

16. _____ Office of the Treasury that monitors key economic indicators to report on current and prospective economic developments and assist in the determination of appropriate economic policies

17. _____ The Treasury Bureau that is responsible for the manufacture of legal tender coinage for the United States

18. _____ The independent agency that is responsible for insuring deposits made by individuals and companies in banks and other thrift institutions

19. _____ A financial services corporation created by the United States Congress

20. _____ The government sponsored enterprise composed of 11 regional banks that was created to support mortgage lending and related community investment

Multiple Choice Questions

Instructions: Circle your response and go to Appendix A to read the complete explanation for each question.

1. Collateral is:
    a. a debt owed to the creditor that is secured by collateral.
    b. something of value given as security for a debt.
    c. a debt that is not connected to any specific piece of property.
    d. a dollar amount that is borrowed from another party, usually under specific terms.

2. The supply of money comes from:
    a. governments.
    b. private investors.
    c. banks.
    d. all of the above.

3. The desire for something combined with the ability to pay for it is called:
    a. demand.
    b. supply.
    c. yield.
    d. collateral.

4. The level of government spending affects the development of fiscal policy. The _____ shows the fiscal policy and budget priorities for upcoming years.
    a. federal revenue statement
    b. federal budget
    c. consumption tax
    d. progressive levy

5. How is GDP calculated?
    a. Through the income approach only
    b. Through the expenditure approach only
    c. Through the rental income approach only
    d. Through the income or expenditure approach

6. What happens when the total operating cost of the federal government exceeds available funds?
    a. The Treasury Department's Bureau of the Public Debt borrows money by selling U.S. Treasury Securities (treasuries).
    b. The Treasury Department's Bureau of the Public Debt imposes an excise tax on the public.
    c. The Treasury Department's Bureau of the Public Debt borrows money from a local bank.
    d. The Treasury Department's Bureau of the Public Debt begins selling common stock in the U.S. Treasury.

7. Tight fiscal policy is based on the idea that:
    a. increased government involvement is necessary.
    b. decreased government involvement is necessary.
    c. when government acts least, it promotes higher taxes.
    d. when government is more involved, it promotes lower taxes.

8. In order to expand the amount of money available for consumers and businesses to spend and speed up the rate of GDP growth, the government can implement:
    a. higher tax rates.
    b. higher unemployment.
    c. mandatory job cuts to slow down economic growth.
    d. expansionary fiscal policies.

9. _____ involves regulating the money supply and interest rates through a central bank in order to provide economic stability.
    a. Fiscal policy
    b. Monetary policy
    c. Deficit spending
    d. National income

10. In carrying out its monetary policy, the Fed uses three tools. Which of the following is not one of those tools?
    a. Discount rate
    b. Open market operations
    c. Debt management
    d. Reserve requirements

11. The Federal Reserve System increases or decreases the amount of money in circulation by:

    a. raising or lowering reserve requirements for member banks.

    b. offering loans directly to consumers.

    c. allowing banks to set their own reserve requirements.

    d. selling mortgage-backed securities to the public.

12. Which of the following is not one of the functions of the Federal Reserve?

    a. It supervises and regulates banking institutions.

    b. It acts as a lender of last resort to banks.

    c. It accepts deposits from consumers.

    d. It determines monetary policy.

13. The Board of Governors:

    a. supervises the twelve Federal Reserve Banks.

    b. is made up of eight members who are appointed by the President.

    c. is made up of eight members who are confirmed by the Senate.

    d. None of the above

14. Which of the following statements is true regarding the Federal Reserve?

    a. There are 10 Federal Reserve Districts.

    b. There are 12 Federal Reserve Districts.

    c. A Federal Reserve Bank is located in Phoenix, Arizona.

    d. A Federal Reserve Bank is located in Denver, Colorado.

15. The automated clearinghouse:

    a. provides a communications link among financial institutions and government agencies.

    b. provides a nationwide network to exchange paperless payments among financial institutions and government agencies.

    c. accommodates a wide range of recurring corporate and consumer transactions.

    d. does both (b) and (c).

16. The first Secretary of the Treasury was _____.

    a. Benjamin Franklin

    b. Alexander Hamilton

    c. Thomas Jefferson

    d. George Washington Carver

17. The Secretary of the Treasury has primary responsibility for participating in the formulation of broad _____ policies that have general significance for the economy.

    a. fiscal

    b. financial

    c. frugal

    d. federal

18. Which of the following is not included in the FDIC's major program areas?

    a. Insurance

    b. Management of interest rate

    c. Supervision of financial institutions

    d. Receivership management

19. The _____ establishes, monitors, and enforces the affordable housing goals for Fannie Mae and Freddie Mac that are mandated by the Housing and Economic Recovery Act of 2008 (HERA).

    a. Federal Reserve System

    b. U.S. Department of the Treasury

    c. Federal Deposit Insurance Corporation

    d. Federal Housing Finance Agency

20. FHLBanks provide stable, on-demand, low-cost funding to financial institutions for which of the following?

    a. Small business

    b. Rural

    c. Economic development lending

    d. All of the above

Government Influence on Lending

Unit **3**

INTRODUCTION

The real estate finance industry is subject to a wide variety of laws, regulations, and government oversight. Lending is a for-profit business, which puts the borrowers and the lenders in opposition. Through the years, laws have been passed and programs instituted to put the borrower in a less challenging position *vis-a-vis* the lender.

Additionally, it seems that whenever there is a disruption to the economy that leads to financial upheaval, the federal lawmakers get busy passing laws aimed to correct the problem. Sometimes, the laws are effective, whereas other times, the law needs to be adjusted due to unintended consequences of the initial legislation.

This Unit discusses some additional governmental influences on the lending industry.

Learning Objectives

After completing this Unit, you should be able to:

3A   recall laws regarding financial reform, including the Community Reinvestment Act, the SAFE Act, and the Dodd-Frank Act.

3B   recall the purpose of the USDA and identify types of rural and agricultural lending programs.

3C   indicate the key HUD offices and recall the enforcement of the Fair Housing Act and the Americans with Disabilities Act.

3D   recall the significance of the Consumer Financial Protection Bureau and the laws under the CFPB's authority—including TILA and RESPA.

3E   clarify the purpose of the TILA-RESPA Integrated Disclosures.

3F   differentiate between the Loan Estimate and the Closing Disclosure.

REGULATION AND REFORM

As we learned earlier in the course, the economy is cyclical with periods of expansion followed by periods of contraction. Some of the contractions are catastrophic to the financial industry and the economy as a whole. It seems that lawmakers respond to the downturns in the economy by passing new legislation.

Example: The **Panic of 1907** led to the passage of the Federal Reserve Act of 1913 that established the Federal Reserve System.

Example: The Federal Trade Commission (FTC) was created in 1914 in an attempt to "bust up" trusts and break apart monopolies that discouraged competition from smaller and less powerful businesses. The two **anti-trust laws** in 1914 were the Federal Trade Commission Act and the Clayton Act.

A classic example of regulation following a catastrophe is the plethora of legislation that followed the **Stock Market Crash of 1929**. The "Crash" ended the epic boom of the "Roaring Twenties" and began the economic downturn that led to the Banking Panics of 1930 and 1931 and ultimately to the Great Depression.

"New Deal" Legislation – 1932 - 1940

By 1932, at least one-quarter of the American workforce was unemployed. When President Roosevelt took office in 1933, he tried to stabilize the economy and create jobs. Between 1932 and 1940, the legislature passed several laws and the government instituted a series of projects and programs, known collectively as the **New Deal**.

In 1932, two emergency laws were passed to address the banking panics—the Reconstruction Finance Corporation Act and the Banking Act of 1932. Then in March 1933, President Roosevelt suspended all banking transactions for a week by declaring a Banking Holiday. It was immediately followed up with the 1933 Emergency Banking Act.

In 1933, the Banking Act of 1933 (**Glass-Steagall Act**) was passed that separated commercial banking from investment banking. Basically, commercial banks, which took in deposits and made loans, were no longer allowed to underwrite or deal in securities, whereas investment banks, which underwrote and dealt in securities, were no longer allowed to have close connections to commercial banks, such as overlapping directorships or common ownership. Following the passage of the act, institutions were given a year to decide whether they would specialize in commercial or investment banking. Another important provision of the act created the Federal Deposit Insurance Corporation (FDIC), which insures bank deposits with a pool of money collected from banks.

The **National Housing Act of 1934** was passed to make housing and home mortgages more affordable. It created the **Federal Housing Administration** (FHA) and the Federal Savings and Loan Insurance Corporation (FSLIC). It also created the United States Housing Authority to make low-interest, long term loans to local public agencies for slum clearance and construction of low-income dwellings. Additionally, it led to the 1937 creation of Fannie Mae.

The **Banking Act of 1935** completed the restructuring of the Federal Reserve and financial system. The purpose of the Banking Act of 1935 was "to provide for the sound, effective, and uninterrupted operation of the banking system."

The **U.S. Housing Act of 1937** (Wagner-Steagall Act or the **Low-Rent Housing Act**) built on the National Housing Act of 1934. Under the programs of the Act, the federal government, through the Department of Housing and Urban Development (HUD), provides subsidies to local public housing agencies (PHAs) that rent housing to low-income families.

Basically, the stated purpose of each new law revolves around safety, sound practices, stability, confidence, etc. in the financial system being regulated.

Regulation 1965-1989

The **Great Inflation** (1965-1982) was the defining macroeconomic event of the second half of the twentieth century. The origins of the Great Inflation were Federal Reserve policies that allowed for an excessive growth in the supply of money. In 1964, inflation measured a little more than 1% per year. It had been in this vicinity over the preceding six years. Inflation began ratcheting upward in the mid-1960s and reached more than 14% in 1980. In part, the inflationary trend was created by the mandate to create more jobs and lower unemployment (Employment Act of 1978). Then, in an effort to fight the mounting inflation, the Fed tightened monetary policy, which led to the Recession of 1981-1982. Prior to the Great Recession (2007-2009), the 1981-82 recession was the worst economic downturn in the United States since the Great Depression. Unemployment was widespread with an 11% unemployment rate.

1977 - Community Reinvestment Act

Passed by congress in 1977, the **Community Reinvestment Act** (CRA) encourages regulated financial institutions to serve their immediate community's needs. Prior to the CRA, lenders tended to avoid lending in high-risk communities and neighborhoods in a practice known as **redlining**. The CRA requires that lenders meet their local communities' needs first by lending to low to moderate income families for housing, small business, and farming.

When a lending institution is recognized by the Federal Reserve, there are three basic requirements that must be met. First, the institution must draw a map that defines the community in which it does business and post it visibly within its facilities. This area most likely will overlap with the areas served by other institutions. The institution must also list the types of credit it offers and make this list of loans available to the public. Finally, the lender must post notice within its facilities that federal regulators are evaluating the institution. This notice must provide a forum for public comment on the institution's performance.

Deregulation

The inflation and interest rates rose dramatically in the late 1970s and early 1980s. The first indication of a problem came in the late 1970s, when savers began to take their money out of S&Ls and put it into investments that paid a higher rate of interest. This process, called **disintermediation**, began as a result of uncontrolled inflation, causing interest rates to soar to heights unseen in any market at any time. The regulated S&Ls were restricted by law from offering competitive interest rates, so depositors moved their money out of the S&Ls and put it into government securities, corporate bonds, and money market funds. The reason was that customers could get a higher interest rate on their savings from the unregulated institutions than the regulated lenders were allowed to pay under the law. The S&Ls had to pay a higher interest rate to their depositors than they were getting on their long-term loans. Since S&Ls could not compete with the higher returns from other sources, depositors began to drift away along with their money.

Many people felt that the government should remove the strict banking regulations and let them compete on the open market. In fact, this was the belief during both the Carter and Reagan administrations.

The financial deregulation was designed to benefit depository institutions, especially the thrift industry. **Deregulation** is the process of removing or reducing government regulations, typically in the economic sphere. However, deregulation allowed financial institutions to offer products with more risk.

1980 - Depository Institution's Deregulation & Monetary Control Act

The **Depository Institutions Deregulation and Monetary Control Act** (DIDMCA) of 1980 had sweeping changes, one of which was to raise deposit insurance from $40,000 to $100,000. It also permitted Savings and Loans (S&Ls) to offer a much wider range of services than ever before. The deregulatory measures allowed savings and loan associations to enter the business of commercial lending, trust services, and non-mortgage consumer lending. Although the S&Ls had many of the capabilities of banks, they did not have the same regulations as banks or FDIC oversight.

1982 - Garn-St Germaine Depository Institutions Act

The Garn-St Germain Depository Institutions Act (Garn Act) was designed to complete the process of giving expanded powers to federally chartered S&Ls and to enable them to diversify their activities with the view of increasing profits. Major provisions included elimination of deposit interest rate ceilings and elimination of the previous statutory limit on loan to value ratio.

Title II of the Garn Act enforced the **due-on-sale provisions** in mortgage contracts that forced property sellers to repay their loans. In the absence of due-on-sale provisions, sellers could pass their low-rate mortgages to buyers, thus preventing the lender from earning a higher market rate on its repaid funds. The due-on-sale clause is triggered by sales and by any transfer of real property by assumptions, installment land sales contracts, wraparound loans, contracts for deed, transfers subject to the mortgage or similar lien, and other like transfers. However, the law does not apply to transfers between family members to to a living trust. [12 CFR §591].

Title VIII of the Garn Act is the **Alternative Mortgage Transaction Parity Act of 1982.** The AMTPA allowed lenders to originate adjustable-rate mortgages, and mortgages with balloon payments and negative amortization.

The S&Ls moved away from their traditional low-risk residential lending practices and began making higher-risk loans on undeveloped land, real estate development, and joint ventures. Some S&Ls engaged in large-scale real estate speculation leading to the financial failure of over 500 institutions during the 1980s. Finally in 1989, the Federal Savings and Loan Insurance Corporation (FSLIC), the insurer who provided a recovery fund for depositors in the event of an S&L failure, did not have enough funds to bail out the failing S&Ls, became insolvent and also failed. Currently, the AMTPA is regulated by the Consumer Financial Protection Bureau and implemented by **Regulation D**.

Savings and Loan Crisis

Once regulations were loosened, Savings & Loans (S&Ls) began engaging in high-risk activities, such as commercial real estate lending and investments in junk bonds. Depositors in S&Ls continued to funnel money into these risky endeavors because their deposits were insured by the Federal Savings and Loan Insurance Corporation (FSLIC).

The S&L Crisis was the greatest bank collapse since the Great Depression. By 1989, more than 1,000 of the nation's S&Ls had failed, thus ending one of the most secure sources of home mortgages.

Widespread corruption and other factors led to the insolvency of the FSLIC, the $124 billion bailout of junk bond investments, and the liquidation of more than 700 S&Ls by the Resolution Trust Corporation.

1989 - Financial Institutions Reform, Recovery, and Enforcement Act

The inevitable legislative backlash to the behavior of the savings and loan industry was the enactment by Congress of the **Financial Institutions Reform, Recovery, and Enforcement Act** (FIRREA). This was an attempt to rebuild an industry that had disgraced itself by disregarding the welfare of consumers and nurturing greed and profiteering within the banking business.

Under FIRREA, the Office of Thrift Supervision (OTS) and the Housing Finance Board were authorized to oversee the savings and loan regulation responsibilities. The Federal Deposit Insurance Corporation (FDIC) now insures deposits in all federally chartered banks and savings institutions up to $250,000 per account for commercial and savings banks. The FDIC supervises the Deposit Insurance Fund.

Continued Deregulation 1990-2007

The economy seemed back on track and the increase in home prices that began in the late 1990s continued, fueling employment growth in construction, financial services, and other sectors related to housing.

1999 – Gramm-Leach-Bliley Act

The **Gramm-Leach-Bliley Act** (GLBA) repealed part of the Glass–Steagall Act prohibiting banks from affiliating with securities firms. This allowed commercial banks, investment banks, insurance companies, and securities firms to consolidate. Additionally, it created a new "**financial holding company**" that could engage in insurance and securities underwriting and agency activities, merchant banking, and insurance company portfolio investment activities.

Under GLBA, protections were put in place to safeguard consumers' non-public personal information—the Financial Privacy Rule, the Safeguards Rule, and Pretexting Protection. The **Privacy Rule** requires clear disclosure by all financial institutions of their privacy policy regarding the sharing of non-public personal information with both affiliates and third parties. Consumers must be given a notice to "opt-out" of sharing of non-public personal information with nonaffiliated third parties. The **Safeguards Rule** requires financial institutions to develop a written information security plan that describes how the company is prepared for, and plans to continue to protect clients' nonpublic personal information. The **Pretexting Protection** requires financial institutions to have a plan in place to prevent unauthorized people from accessing non-public personal information based on some *pretext*.

Currently, the Consumer Financial Protection Bureau regulates sections 502 through 509 of the Gramm-Leach-Bliley Act.

In the same year, 1999, Fannie Mae eased the credit requirements to encourage banks to make home loans to borrowers whose credit was not good enough to qualify for conventional loans. Before the changes in government policy were made to encourage affordable housing, most borrowers obtained conventional fixed-rate mortgages with 10 to 20% down, for 15 to 30 years. Alternatively, they obtained FHA or VA loans. However, these borrowers had verifiable employment history, steady income, and a good credit record.

And in 2000, Fannie Mae was required by the Department of Housing and Urban Development **(HUD)** to allocate 50% of its business to low- and moderate-income families, with a goal of financing over $500 billion in Community Reinvestment Act related business by 2010.

Subprime Mortgage Meltdown (2007-2009)

The perfect storm of record low interest rates, abandonment of mortgage underwriting standards, subprime loans, and out-right mortgage fraud combined to create a housing bubble that burst in 2006.

Many lenders and loan originators did not care about the quality of the loans as long as the loans could be sold to the secondary market. So, the risky loans were sold off in bulk to securitization firms that packaged the loans into mortgage–backed securities, which were sold to investors. Most of these securities were given triple-A ratings by the credit rating companies so investors believed the securities were safe. Often, the securities were repackaged again into even riskier collateralized debt obligations (CDOs) that were sold to different investors. Unfortunately, these securities, based on such poor quality mortgages, were toxic because the securitization process actually turned a bad mortgage into a worse security.

Because of the ease of obtaining financing, a new term was coined: **"I'll be gone, you'll be gone"** (IBGYBG). It refered to the attitude of the players in this money machine—borrowers, originators, securitizers, and rating agencies. They did not care if the loans ultimately went bad because by the time they did, the loans were in the hands of unwitting investors. Each step in the mortgage securitization pipeline depended on the next step to keep it going. The borrowers, mortgage brokers, lenders, securitizers, and credit rating agencies all believed they could off-load their risks to the next person in line. They miscalculated.

When borrowers stopped making mortgage payments, the losses (amplified by the securitization of the mortgages) created a domino effect that precipitated the collapse of large financial institutions and contributed to the economic crisis.

The plunge in home sales led to a huge increase in foreclosures of subprime mortgages. By the middle of 2007, there were approximately 27 million subprime and Alt-A mortgages in the U.S. financial system (about one-half of all outstanding mortgages) that were ready to default when the housing bubble began to deflate.

Many subprime lenders filed for chapter 11 bankruptcy or closed. Even large mortgage lenders, such as Countrywide Financial, and investment banks, such as Bear Sterns were not immune to the meltdown. The economy plunged into a steep recession known as the Great Recession (2007-2009).

Bailouts

By the summer of 2008, the financial institutions were in a state of chaos and reported billions of dollars in losses. The government responded with an unprecedented $700 billion bank bailout and $787 billion fiscal stimulus package.

2008 - Housing and Economic Recovery Act

On July 30, 2008, President Bush signed the **Housing and Economic Recovery Act** (HERA), known as the **Housing Stimulus Bill**. It authorized temporary measures to stimulate the housing market—homebuyer tax credits, additional property tax deductions, seller-funded down payment assistance programs, and neighborhood revitalization funds for communities to purchase foreclosed homes. It also established the **Federal Housing Finance Agency** (FHFA).

On September 7, 2008, Fannie Mae and Freddie Mac came under the conservatorship of the FHFA in a attempt to stabilize the floundering mortgage markets.

SAFE Act

The **Secure and Fair Enforcement for Mortgage Licensing Act** of 2008 (**SAFE Act**) is found in Title V of the Housing and Economic Recovery Act. [12 CFR 1007]. The SAFE Act required all states to have a loan originator licensing and registration system in place by August 1, 2010. The SAFE Act provides uniform national licensing standards, including minimum licensing and education. Additionally, it created a comprehensive national licensing database to enable government and consumers to track loan originators and help prevent fraud. Loan originators registered in the national database are provided with a Unique Identifier number. A **loan originator** is defined as an individual who "takes a residential mortgage loan application and also offers or negotiates terms of a residential mortgage loan for compensation or gain." Additionally, HUD considers the definition of loan originator to encompass any individual who, for compensation or gain, offers or negotiates pursuant to a request from and based on the information provided by the borrower. A person who performs only administrative or clerical tasks in connection with loan origination is not considered a loan originator. The SAFE Act's definition of "**residential mortgage loan**" includes a loan secured by a consensual security interest on a dwelling as defined by the Truth in Lending Act. A **dwelling** is "a residential structure that contains 1 to 4 units, whether or not that structure is attached to real property. The term includes an individual condominium unit, cooperative unit, mobile home, and trailer, if it is used as a residence." Currently the SAFE Act is regulated by the Consumer Financial Protection Bureau and implemented by Regulations G and H.

2008 - Emergency Economic Stabilization Act

In 2008, the Emergency Economic Stabilization Act was passed, creating a $700 billion **Troubled Assets Relief Program** (TARP). TARP was established to stabilize the United States financial system and prevent a systemic collapse. The U.S. Treasury established several Financial Stability Programs, such as the Making Home Affordable Program, Asset Guarantee Program, and the Targeted Investment Program to stop further deterioration of financial institutions.

Dodd-Frank Act of 2010

On July 21, 2010, the federal **Dodd-Frank Wall Street Reform and Consumer Protection Act** (Dodd-Frank Act) was enacted into law as a response to the financial turbulence and recession in the late 2000s. It made sweeping changes to financial regulatory agencies that affected almost every aspect of the nation's financial services industry.

The Dodd-Frank Act has sixteen titles, two of which—Title X-Bureau of Consumer Financial Protection (CFPB) and Title XIV-Mortgage Reform and Anti-Predatory Lending Act—directly impact on the mortgage industry.

Title X - Consumer Financial Protection Bureau

Title X of the Dodd-Frank Act established the **Consumer Financial Protection Bureau** (CFPB or Bureau) as an independent bureau within the Federal Reserve Board. The CFPB is headed by a Director appointed by the President and confirmed by the Senate for a five-year term. The Bureau is comprised of six Divisions that enforce the federal consumer financial laws, promote consumer financial education, and handle consumer complaints and inquiries. The CFPB is discussed later in the Unit.

Title XIV - Mortgage Reform and Anti-Predatory Lending Act

Title XIV of the Dodd-Frank Act established the **Mortgage Reform and Anti-Predatory Lending Act** (Reform Act). The provisions of the Reform Act are designated as designated consumer laws, which are the laws that will come under the authority of the CFPB. The CFPB issued new rules and regulations regarding how mortgage loan originators and brokers may be compensated and how that compensation must be disclosed. The Reform Act took effect July 21, 2011.

Applicability

The Reform Act defines a **mortgage originator** as a person who, for compensation or gain, does any of the following:

(i)   takes a residential mortgage loan application;

(ii) assists a consumer in obtaining or applying for such a loan (inclusive of advising on loan terms, preparing loan packages, or collecting information); or

(iii) offers or negotiates the terms of the loan.

The definition also encompasses any person who represents to the public that he or she provides such services.

Office staff who performing administrative or clerical tasks are not mortgage originators. Real estate licensees are not considered mortgage originators, unless they are compensated by a lender or mortgage broker.

Prohibited Practices

The Reform Act bans the payment of yield spread premiums (YSPs) or other originator compensation that is based on the interest rate or other terms of the loans. In general, a mortgage originator may not receive any origination fee, except from the consumer. Any person who knows that a consumer is directly compensating a mortgage originator may not pay an origination fee.

Mortgage originators are prohibited from:

- steering a consumer to obtain a loan that the consumer lacks a reasonable ability to repay;
- steering a consumer to obtain a loan that has predatory characteristics (such as equity stripping, excessive fees, or abusive terms);
- steering a consumer from a "qualified mortgage" loan for which the consumer is qualified to a loan that is not a qualified mortgage;
- participating in abusive or unfair lending practices that promote "disparities" among equally creditworthy consumers based on race, ethnicity, gender, or age;
- mischaracterizing a consumer's credit history or the available loans or mischaracterizing or suborning the mischaracterizing of the appraised value of the property securing the loan; and
- discouraging a consumer from seeking a loan from another mortgage originator.

Required Practices

Subtitle B of the Reform Act establishes national underwriting standards for residential loans. Loan originators must make a reasonable effort based on verified and documented information that "at the time the loan is consummated, the consumer has a reasonable ability to repay the loan, according to the terms, and all applicable taxes, insurance (including mortgage guarantee insurance), and other assessments." Loan originators must verify a borrower's income for residential mortgages.

U.S. DEPARTMENT OF AGRICULTURE (USDA)

On May 15, 1862, President Abraham Lincoln signed legislation to establish the United States Department of Agriculture. The **U.S. Department of Agriculture (USDA)** is a cabinet-level agency that oversees the American farming industry. Obviously, it has undergone many changes since its creation.

The USDA administers programs to help American farmers and ensure food safety for consumers. USDA aid includes distributing price supports and other subsidies to farmers, inspecting food processed at agricultural facilities, working to expand overseas markets for U.S. agricultural products, providing financing to expand job opportunities and improve housing, utilities, and infrastructure in rural America, and providing food assistance and nutrition education.

USDA Agencies and Offices

The USDA is made up of 17 agencies and several offices with nearly 100,000 employees who serve the American people at more than 4,500 locations across the country and abroad.

Some of the USDA Agencies and Offices

Farm and Foreign Agricultural Services

- Farm Service Agency
- Foreign Agricultural Service
- Risk Management Agency

Food, Nutrition, and Consumer Services

- Food and Nutrition Service
- Center for Nutrition Policy and Promotion

Food Safety

- Food Safety and Inspection Service

Marketing and Regulatory Programs

- Agricultural Marketing Service
- Animal and Plant Health Inspection Service
- Grain Inspection, Packers and Stockyards Administration

Natural Resources

- United States Forest Service
- National Resources Conservation Service

Research, Education, and Economics
- Agricultural Research Service
- Economic Research Service
- Research, Education, and Economics
- National Agricultural Library
- National Institute of Food and Agriculture
- National Agricultural Statistics Service
- Office of the Chief Scientist

Rural Development
- Rural Development

Farm Service Agency

The **Farm Service Agency** (FSA) was formed to support farmers in times of need with loans, commodity price supports, conservation payments, and disaster relief assistance. The aid is meant to protect farmers from the risks that come with growing food that relies on market, food preferences, and the weather. The FSA also provides credit to agricultural producers who are unable to receive private commercial credit, in addition to giving grants to those that qualify. The FSA also works with farmers and their debtors to try to arbitrate agreements and head off foreclosure.

Farm Loan Programs

The FSA makes direct and guaranteed farm ownership and operating loans to family-size farmers and ranchers who cannot obtain commercial credit from a bank, Farm Credit System institution, or other lender. FSA loans can be used to purchase land, livestock, equipment, feed, seed, and supplies. Loans can also be used to construct buildings or make farm improvements.

Loans Made by the Farm Service Agency
- Farm Operating Loans
- Farm Ownership Loans
- Guaranteed Farm Loans

Rural Development Division

The USDA's **Rural Development** (RD) Division has been called the venture capitalist for rural America. The division includes a number of agencies created in the Great Depression that were successful in supporting the agriculture industry, electrifying rural America, and building community resources. The division operates more than 40 rural development programs focusing on housing, community facilities, water and waste management, and business and technological development.

The Rural Development Division provides direct loans and grants. Additionally, if offers Rural Development loan guarantees through participating intermediaries such as approved banks, mortgage companies, etc. There are three agencies in the Rural Development Division—Rural Housing Service, Rural Business-Cooperative Service, and Rural Utilities Service.

Rural Housing Service

The **Rural Housing Service** (RHS), also known as the Rural Development Housing and Community Facilities Programs (RDHCFP), is an agency within Rural Development that administers aid to rural communities in the form of direct loans, loan guarantees, and grants for housing and community facilities.

Programs focus on home ownership and restoration, farm worker housing, multi-family housing projects, community facilities, and rental assistance. According to a 2014 CRS Report to Congress, rural areas account for a "disproportionate share of the nation's substandard housing." In rural areas, homeownership is the principal form of housing, but residents are faced with higher development costs, limited access to mortgage credit, and pay more of their household income for housing than urban residents.

Rural Business-Cooperative Service

The **Rural Business-Cooperative Service** (RBCS) offers programs to support business development and job training opportunities for rural residents. The programs help provide the capital, technical support, educational opportunities and entrepreneurial skills that can help rural residents start and grow businesses or access jobs in agricultural markets and in the bio-based economy.

Rural Utilities Service

The **Rural Utilities Service** (RUS) is an agency within Rural Development responsible for providing public utilities—including water, waste, telephone and electricity—to rural areas through public-private partnerships. The agency administers loan, loan guarantee and grant programs to eligible populations.

Types of USDA Loans for Rural Property

The USDA is a source of financing for rural properties. **Rural property** is property located in the outlying region of an urban center. Obtaining financing for rural property can be a challenge, because most traditional lenders do not specialize in these types of properties.

See the USDA **Summary of Major Programs** chart at www.rd.usda.gov for a review of the loans, grants, and guarantees available to rural renters, homeowners, and business owners.

USDA Guaranteed Loan

A **USDA Guaranteed Loan** is a government-insured 100% purchase loan for properties in rural areas. Under the USDA, the Housing and Community Facilities Programs guarantees loans made by private-sector lenders.

According to the terms of the program, an individual or family may borrow up to 100% of the appraised value of the home, which eliminates the need for a down payment. Mortgages are 30-year fixed-rate loans at market interest rates. Loans may include funds for closing costs, the guarantee fee, legal fees, title services, and other prepaid items, if the appraised value is higher than the sales price.

To be eligible, applicants must have an adequate and dependable income, and be a U.S. Citizen, qualified alien, or legally admitted to the United States for permanent residence.

Income and Credit Guidelines

Income. The borrower(s) must have an adjusted annual household income that does not exceed the moderate-income limit established for the area. A family's income includes the total gross income of the applicant, co-applicant, and any other adults in the household. Applicants may be eligible to make certain adjustments to gross income—such as annual childcare expenses and $480 for each minor child—in order to qualify. USDA Rural Development field offices can provide information on the moderate-income limits for the areas that fall within their jurisdiction, and can provide further guidance on calculating household income.

Credit History. The borrower(s) must have a credit history that indicates a reasonable willingness to meet obligations as they become due.

Repayment Ability. The borrower(s) must have the ability to repay the loan. The USDA uses a 29/41 ratio. The principle, interest, taxes, and insurance (PITI) divided by gross monthly income must be equal to or less than 29%. Total monthly debt divided by gross monthly income must be equal to or less than 41%.

Property Guidelines

Guaranteed loans can be made on either new or existing homes. Existing homes must be structurally sound, functionally adequate, and in good repair. There are no restrictions on the size or design of the home financed. The home must be owner-occupied and not used for income-producing purposes.

The home must be located in a rural area. **Rural areas** include open country and places with a population of 10,000 or less and—under certain conditions—towns and cities with between 10,000 and 25,000 residents. USDA Rural Development field offices can determine eligible areas.

Housing Assistance

The USDA provides homeownership opportunities to low- and moderate-income rural Americans through several loan, grant, and loan guarantee programs.

Housing for Individuals

The USDA provides homeownership opportunities to rural Americans, and home renovation and repair programs. The programs also make funding available to individuals to finance vital improvements necessary to make their homes decent, safe, and sanitary.

USDA Multi-Family Housing Programs offer Rural Rental Housing Loans to provide affordable multi-family rental housing for very low-, low-, and moderate-income families; the elderly; and persons with disabilities. In addition, rental assistance is available to eligible families.

Housing Assistance Programs for Individuals
- Single Family Housing Direct Home Loans
- Single Family Housing Guaranteed Loan Program
- Multi-Family Housing Rental Assistance

Housing Development Opportunities

The USDA works with public and nonprofit organizations to provide housing developers with loans and grants to construct and renovate rural multi-family housing complexes. Eligible organizations include local and state governments, nonprofit groups, associations, nonprofit private corporations and cooperatives, and Native American groups.

Housing Development Programs

- Single-Family Housing Repair Loans and Grants
- Mutual Self-Help Housing Technical Assistance Grants
- Multi-Family Housing Direct Loans
- Farm Labor Housing Direct Loans and Grants
- Housing Preservation Grants
- Rural Housing Site Loans

Rural Development Loan and Grant Assistance

USDA Rural Development forges partnerships with rural communities, funding projects that bring housing, community facilities, business guarantees, utilities, and other services to rural America. USDA provides technical assistance and financial backing for rural businesses and cooperatives to create quality jobs in rural areas. Rural Development works with low-income individuals, State, local and Indian tribal governments, as well as private and nonprofit organizations and user-owned cooperatives.

Beginning Farmers and Ranchers

USDA, through the Farm Service Agency, provides direct and guaranteed loans to beginning farmers and ranchers who are unable to obtain financing from commercial credit sources. Each fiscal year, the Agency targets a portion of its direct and guaranteed farm ownership (FO) and operating loan (OL) funds to beginning farmers and ranchers.

U.S. DEPARTMENT OF HOUSING AND URBAN DEVELOPMENT (HUD)

The precursor agency to the U.S. Department of Housing and Urban Development was the Housing and Home Finance Agency (HHFA) that was created in 1947 to oversee all federal housing and urban development programs. In 1965, the HHFA became the U.S. Department of Housing and Urban Development (HUD) a few weeks prior to the passage of the **Housing and Urban Development Act of 1965**, which instituted several major expansions in federal housing programs.

The **Department of Housing and Urban Development** (HUD) is a cabinet-level agency that oversees federal programs designed to help Americans with their housing needs. HUD seeks to increase homeownership, support community development, and increase access to affordable housing free from discrimination. The agency enforces numerous federal housing laws, operates mortgage-supportive initiatives, and distributes millions of dollars in federal grants.

Key HUD Offices

HUD oversees several mortgage, grant, assistance, and regulatory programs. This course presents an overview of a few of the programs, but for a complete list, go to the HUD website at: https://portal.hud.gov/hudportal/HUD.

Federal Housing Administration

The **Federal Housing Administration** (FHA) was originally the forerunner of HUD. The FHA was founded in 1934 to revive a housing industry leveled by the Great Depression, FHA sought to stimulate homeownership by providing mortgage insurance and regulating interest rates. The agency was incorporated into HUD when HUD became a cabinet-level agency in 1965. As FHA experienced a significant loss of market share in the last several years, attention turned toward reform measures to "modernize" its programs, making them more flexible and accessible to a wider range of buyers—while simultaneously providing stability and a safe alternative to sub-prime lending.

Office of Public and Indian Housing

The **Office of Public and Indian Housing** (PIH) was created in 1937 when the Housing Act of 1937 (Wagner-Steagall Act) was signed into law. PIH manages a large number of programs that provide funding through grants that are designed to help residents of affordable housing become more self-sufficient and economic independent.

The Five Public and Indian Housing Offices
- Office of Native American Programs
- Office of Community Relations and Involvement
- Office of Public and Assisted Housing Operations
- Office of Public Housing Investments
- Office of Policy, Program and Legislative Initiatives

Government National Mortgage Association

Congress established the Government National Mortgage Association (**Ginnie Mae**) in 1968 as a government-owned corporation within the Department of Housing and Urban Development. Ginnie Mae is designed to support the government's housing programs by facilitating a secondary market to buy and sell residential mortgages. Ginnie Mae provides guarantees for mortgage-backed securities (MBS), most of which are federally insured loans issued by the FHA and other federal housing offices. As a result, Ginnie Mae operations have directly helped low- and moderate-income potential homeowners.

Office of Fair Housing and Equal Opportunity

The **Office of Fair Housing and Equal Opportunity** (FHEO) seeks to prevent discrimination in housing on the basis of race, sex, family status and other grounds. As one of the largest federal civil rights agencies, FHEO administers federal laws and makes policy regarding equal access to housing. The office administers funding, processes discrimination complaints, and oversees enforcement and compliance with federal laws.

The agency is responsible for implementing and enforcing the Fair Housing Act and other civil rights laws—including Title VI of the Civil Rights Act of 1964, the Architectural Barriers Act of 1968, Title IX of the Education Amendments Act of 1972, Section 504 of the Rehabilitation Act of 1973, Section 109 of the Housing and Community Development Act of 1974, the Age Discrimination Act of 1975, and Title II of the Americans with Disabilities Act of 1990.

Enforcing Fair Housing Legislation

Although home ownership has become a reality for many Americans over the last 140 years, the process has not always been fair to everyone. Over the years, laws have been created to make the housing market equitable to level the playing field for all Americans. Many of these laws have been aimed at discriminatory practices in the sale, financing, and rental of homes. The federal government has taken an active role in the prohibition of discriminatory housing practices.

The HUD Office of Fair Housing and Equal Opportunity (FHEO) is responsible for enforcing federal fair housing policies and laws and for handling fair housing and equal access discrimination complaints.

Federal Fair Housing Act

The **Fair Housing Act** protects against illegal discrimination in the financing, leasing, or selling of residential property. Title VIII of the Civil Rights Act of 1968 and the Fair Housing Amendments Act of 1988, taken together, constitute the Fair Housing Act.

Protected Classes

The Fair Housing Act protects specific groups of people. The Fair Housing Amendments Act of 1988 added disability and familial status to bring the total to seven protected classes. A **protected class** is a group of people given legal protection from discrimination under federal or state law.

The 7 Protected Classes under the Federal Fair Housing Act

- Race (1968)
- Color (1968)
- Religion (1968)
- Sex (1968)
- National origin (1968)
- Disability (1988)
- Familial status (1988)

Many state and local communities have passed laws that add "sexual preference or orientation" to this list of seven categories.

Included or Exempt Property

The Fair Housing Act prevents discrimination in specific types of housing.

Types of Housing Covered by the Fair Housing Act

- All residential property owned or operated by the Federal Government
- Single-family homes owned by private persons, including corporations or partnerships, even if a broker is not used to sell or rent the home
- Multi-family dwellings with four or more units, including rooming houses
- Multi-family dwellings with four or less units, if the owner does not live in one of the units

Types of Property Exempt from the Fair Housing Act
- Commercial and industrial properties
- Unimproved land, unless the land is specifically offered for construction for residential purposes

Practices Prohibited by the Federal Fair Housing Act

One of the most noteworthy features of the Fair Housing Act is that it specifically prohibits a number of common practices that amounted to unfair discrimination when renting, selling, or financing property.

Illegal Discriminatory Housing Practices

The Fair Housing Act makes it unlawful to deny or discriminate against persons of a protected class who are seeking housing, including imposing different terms for purchasing, constructing, improving, repairing, or maintaining a residence.

- Refusing to rent housing
- Refusing to sell housing
- Treating applicants differently from one another for housing
- Treating residents differently from one another in connection with terms and conditions
- Advertising a discriminatory housing preference or limitation
- Providing false information about the availability of housing
- Harassing, coercing, or intimidating people from enjoying or exercising their rights under the act
- Blockbusting or Steering
- Denying use of, or participation in, real estate services, such as brokers' organizations or multiple-listing services.

Blockbusting

Blockbusting is a tactic used by some real estate brokers to induce panic selling by making property owners believe that the "character" of a neighborhood is likely to change because one or two properties are acquired by members of a minority group, usually African-American. The tactics included supposedly mistaken phone calls for "the black family that just moved in." Sometimes, a business card was left on properties adjacent to a house that had recently been sold to a member of a minority group. Another tactic was to contact a non-minority family stating that a nearby home had recently been sold to a non-white family, and then attempting to induce a sale by the non-minority owners, sometimes at less than fair market value.

> ## Zuch v. Hussey
>
> In *Zuch v. Hussey*, 394 F.Supp. 1028 (D.Mich, 1975), the various real estate firms conducted campaigns to solicit business involving door-to-door canvassing, fliers, and telephone calls. The fliers contained such statements as "We think you may want a friend for a neighbor" and "Know Your Neighbors." A mailing addressed to "Resident" supposedly contained "neighborhood news."
>
> It informed the recipients that the real estate agency had purchased a home in the recipient's neighborhood, that the firm had paid cash, and that the recipients of the mailing might receive the same service.
>
> Because residents would have been aware that the racial character of the neighborhood had been changing and that black families had been moving into the area, the implication was that white families worried about the changes could "cash out" quickly if they were willing to accept the firm's offer. The federal district court concluded that this conduct amounted to blockbusting.

Steering

Steering is the practice of directing members of certain racial or ethnic groups to certain neighborhoods and directing members of other groups to different neighborhoods. Steering is based on assumptions that persons of a given ethnic background will only want to live in neighborhoods with persons of the same ethnic background. Conversely, people of one ethnic background prefer not to live in neighborhoods where the predominant group has a different background.

In a chicken-and-egg kind of way, of course, steering may itself create the very situation that its practitioners claim to be the justification for their action. Because a given agent or broker may assume, for example, that people of a Hispanic background prefer to live only around people who are also Hispanic, the agent's or broker's actions in steering people to certain neighborhoods reinforces those very patterns *because of* their actions, and not the other way around.

United States v. Real Estate One, Inc.

One of the most notorious steering cases of all time was *United States v. Real Estate One, Inc.*, 433 F.Supp. 1140 (E.D. Mich, 1977). A brokerage in the Detroit area assigned new sales agents to its field offices based solely on whether they were white or black. Certain offices were essentially all white or all black depending on the neighborhoods where these agents would be showing housing.

Furthermore, houses in certain neighborhoods that were mostly black were only advertised in certain publications that had a mostly black readership. A separate phone number was used for the advertisements in these newspapers, so that when the call came in, the person answering the phone would know that it was coming on the "black" line and could assume that the call was coming from someone who was black. If the call did come in on that line, it was assigned to a black sales agent.

The court ordered that Real Estate One conduct an educational program and to make no assignments to agents on the basis of race or the composition of the neighborhood where a house was to be sold. The court also ordered that the company change its practices of advertising to ensure that advertising was not based solely on the racial composition of the target readership of the newspaper or of the neighborhoods where particular houses were located.

Example: Maria was born in Mexico and legally immigrated to the United States some twenty-five years ago. She asks her agent to show her houses in areas where large numbers of Hispanics live. Now Maria's agent knows of two neighborhoods with large Hispanic populations. Can the agent direct Maria to these neighborhoods?

Answer: No. The agent is now being asked to steer the buyer to houses based upon the racial and ethnic make-up of a neighborhood. This would be in violation of fair housing laws. In this situation the agent can explain to Maria that under our fair housing laws, agents cannot steer clients to neighborhoods based upon the national origin of the residents therein or, for that matter, any other protected class.

Remember, steering occurs when the agent directs the buyer to a particular neighborhood. It does not occur when the buyer asks only to see homes in a given city or neighborhood.

Illegal Discriminatory Lending Practices

The Fair Housing Act makes it unlawful to deny or discriminate in the terms and conditions of a mortgage or loan modification based on a protected class, including imposing different application or qualification criteria.

Illegal Discriminatory Lending Practices

- Refusing to make a mortgage loan
- Refusing to provide information regarding loans
- Imposing different terms or conditions on a loan, such as different interest rates, points, or fees
- Discriminating when appraising property
- Refusing to purchase a loan
- Setting different terms or conditions for purchasing a loan
- Redlining

"Persons with disabilities should not have to meet higher mortgage qualification standards because they rely on disability insurance payments as a source of income," said Bryan Greene, HUD's Acting Assistant Secretary for Fair Housing and Equal Opportunity. "Banks and mortgage companies may verify income and have eligibility standards, but they may not single out homebuyers with disabilities or deny financing when they are otherwise qualified."

> Example: HUD charges Fifth Third Bank, Mortgage Broker with discrimination against couple with disabilities. Washington (August 22, 2013). The U.S. Department of Housing and Urban Development (HUD) announced today that it is charging Fifth Third Bank, Fifth Third Mortgage Company and Cranbrook Mortgage Corporation with discriminating against a couple with disabilities who were attempting to refinance their home mortgage. HUD's charge alleges that the Cincinnati, Ohio-based mortgage lender and the Clinton Township, Michigan-based mortgage broker required unnecessary medical documentation in order to qualify the couple for an FHA loan.

Redlining

Redlining is the practice of designating, usually although not exclusively on a map, certain neighborhoods as areas where loans will not be made, or at least will not be made to members of certain minority groups. The term "redlining" comes from a practice that originated in the 1930s, when lenders would sometimes rate various parts of a city according to whether it was desirable to make loans within each area. The least desirable areas were either colored in red or had a red line around them, hence the term.

Redlining is not so much a problem in the sale of real estate as it is in the practices of lenders. There is a related kind of redlining that involves the reluctance of insurance carriers to make loans within certain neighborhoods, once again making it difficult for homeowners or business owners to acquire property and

casualty insurance. Without such insurance, home and business owners face increased risks that a fire or similar calamity will cost them the equity in their property.

Because property insurance usually is required as a condition of obtaining financing for a home loan, the lack of property insurance makes a purchase-money loan, as a practical matter, unavailable.

Harrison v. Otto G. Heinzeroth Mortgage Co.

In *Harrison v. Otto G. Heinzeroth Mortg. Co.*, 414 F.Supp. 66 (D.Ohio, 1976), the plaintiffs were white persons who attempted to purchase a home in an integrated or predominantly black neighborhood. They alleged that they were refused a mortgage loan with terms and conditions equal to those of loans on homes in predominantly white neighborhoods solely because of the racial composition of their intended neighborhood. In other words, the plaintiffs alleged not that they were denied a loan because they were being discriminated against because of their race, but rather because the company did not want to make loans based on the company's perception of the "character" of the neighborhood where they wanted to live.

The defendant company tried to dismiss the case, arguing that the Fair Housing Act only applied if the plaintiff alleged discrimination based on the plaintiff's race. The district court disagreed. The court

found that nothing in the Fair Housing Act limited its applicability to discrimination on the basis of the complainant's race. Rather, it was enough that the plaintiff could demonstrate a denial of housing opportunities solely based on racial considerations—here, the racial composition of the neighborhood, or what would today be called redlining. The case was allowed to proceed forward to trial.

Fair Housing Poster

Under the laws of the Fair Housing Act, it is mandatory that all offices dealing with real estate transactions display the Fair Housing poster.

"Any business, real estate broker, agent, salesman, or person in the business of residential real estate or related real estate transactions shall post the fair housing poster. Failure to post the fair housing poster as required by law, might be considered as a discriminatory housing practice."

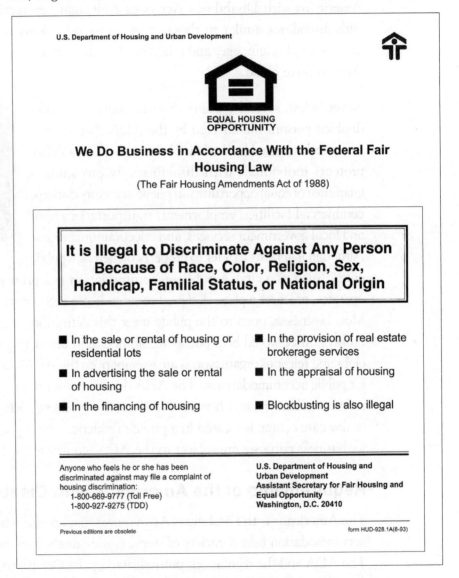

Americans with Disabilities Act of 1990

Congress passed the **Americans with Disabilities Act of 1990** (ADA) to provide a clear, enforceable, and comprehensive national mandate for the elimination of discrimination against individuals with disabilities. A **disability** is "any physical or mental impairment that substantially limits one or more of an individual's major life activities."

With respect to fair housing, however, the Fair Housing Act Amendments of 1988 had already added handicapped individuals as one of the protected classes. Consequently, a person who alleges discrimination based on handicap with respect to the sale or rental of real property would probably rely on the Fair Housing Act and would not have need of the ADA.

The ADA was designed so that the federal government would play a central role in enforcing these standards on behalf of individuals with disabilities. The Americans with Disabilities Act gives civil rights protections to individuals with disabilities similar to those provided to individuals based on race, color, sex, national origin, age, and religion. The definition of a disability under the ADA is quite broad.

Nevertheless, several types of discrimination involving disabled persons are covered by the ADA that are not necessarily covered by the Fair Housing Act. The ADA protects individuals with disabilities by providing a guarantee of equal opportunity in public accommodations, commercial facilities, employment, transportation, state and local government services, and telecommunications. Although it appears to refer to property owned by a public entity (such as a city), a **public accommodation** is a private entity that owns, operates, or leases a place designed to provide products or services to the public. Most businesses open to the public meet this definition, and thus, a real estate broker's office would be a public accommodation under this definition. Private clubs and religious organizations are exempt from the ADA's Title III requirements for public accommodations. The ADA does not cover the majority of residential private apartments and homes. However, if a business, such as a doctor's office or day care center, is located in a private residence, those portions that are used for business purposes are subject to the ADA requirements.

Requirements of the Americans with Disabilities Act

The Americans with Disabilities Act requires that anyone who operates a public accommodation take a variety of steps, as long as they are **readily achievable**. The ADA and the regulations promulgated by the Department of Justice define "readily achievable" to mean something "easily accomplishable and able to be carried out without much difficulty or expense."

The ADA prohibits discrimination on the basis of disability in the full and equal enjoyment of goods, services, facilities, privileges, advantages, or accommodations of any place of public accommodation by any private entity that owns, leases or leases to, or operates a place of public accommodation. A public accommodation must make **reasonable modifications**—in other words, change its policies, practices, or procedures—if they are necessary to afford persons with disabilities the enjoyment of goods, services, or accommodations provided by that business. The only exception is if the owner of the public accommodation (business) can demonstrate that making the modifications would fundamentally alter the nature of the goods, services, facilities or accommodations it provides.

Fortyune v. American Multi-Cinema, Inc.

In *Fortyune v. American Multi-Cinema, Inc.*, 364 F.3d 1075 (9th Cir. 2004), a quadriplegic movie patron and his wife attempted to view the defendant's sold-out screening of a film. They were unable to do so when a man and his son refused to vacate the wheelchair companion seats they occupied. The theater's manager informed the Fortyunes that, under company policy concerning the use of wheelchair companion seats at sold-out screenings, he could not require the man and his son to change seats.

The Fortyunes sued, arguing that the theater chain's policy violated the ADA. The trial court issued a court order directing the theater chain to modify its policies regarding companion seating, and the Ninth Circuit affirmed. The court order directed that wheelchair-bound patrons should receive priority in the use of companion seats.

Because there were only four such seats in the theater, patrons in wheelchairs had limited opportunities for alternative seating in a full theater. The court order directed the company to ensure that the companion seat was made available to the wheelchair-bound patron and his or her companion if they arrived at least 10 minutes prior to show time.

When a broker is involved in the leasing or sale of commercial real property, knowledge of ADA standards is important. If an existing commercial building does not satisfy ADA requirements, needed alterations to accommodate the client's use of the building may be a consideration of the purchase or lease. The broker or sales agent salesperson should counsel the buyer to seek bids from contractors to determine costs associated with any needed remodel or alteration.

CONSUMER FINANCIAL PROTECTION BUREAU

The **Consumer Financial Protection Bureau** (CFPB or Bureau) is an independent bureau within the Federal Reserve Board. The CFPB is headed by a Director appointed by the President and confirmed by the Senate for a five-year term. The Bureau is comprised of six Divisions that enforce the federal consumer financial laws, promote consumer financial education, and handle consumer complaints and inquiries.

The Supervision, Enforcement, and Fair Lending Division provides oversight and enforcement of federal fair lending laws, including the Equal Credit Opportunity Act (ECOA) and the Home Mortgage Disclosure Act (HMDA), coordinates fair lending efforts of the Bureau with other Federal agencies and with state regulators, and works with financial institutions and consumer groups on the promotion of fair lending compliance.

The Bureau has expansive authority to adopt and enforce new regulations that will apply to covered persons or service providers offering any consumer financial product or service. A **covered person** is any person (or its affiliate) that engages in offering or providing a consumer financial product or service. [12 USC 5481(6)]. The Bureau may take action to prevent a covered person or a service provider from committing or engaging in an unfair, deceptive, or abusive act or practice under Federal law in connection with a consumer financial product.

Supervisory Authority

The Bureau has primary supervisory and examination authority over certain nondepository and FDIC-insured depository institutions or insured credit unions with assets over $10 billion. Nondepository covered persons include mortgage originators, brokers, and servicers, lenders offering consumer financial products, private education lenders, and payday lenders.

Exemptions from Supervisory Authority of the Bureau
- Accountants and tax preparers
- Legal practitioners
- Manufactured home retailers and modular home retailers
- Motor vehicle dealers,
- Persons regulated by the SEC, state securities commissions or insurance regulators, or the Farm Credit Administration
- Real estate brokerage activities
- Retailers and other sellers of nonfinancial goods or services

Rulemaking Authority

On July 21, 2011, the CFPB took over the authority from many existing agencies. It has the responsibility to regulate consumer financial products and services and enforce certain designated consumer protection laws.

As part of the Dodd-Frank Act, the CFPB recodified and republished the inherited regulations under Chapter X of Title 12 of the Code of Federal Regulations. For example, RESPA (24 CFR 3500) no longer belongs to HUD and is now 12 CFR 1024. The CFPB also implemented a new numbering system in the 1000 series. Now, all regulations correspond with the number of the alphabet, e.g., Reg. B is 12 CFR 1002, Reg. C is 12 CFR 1003, and Reg. Z is 12 CFR 1026.

Designated Consumer Protection Laws & Implementing Regulations

- Alternative Mortgage Transaction Parity Act of 1982 - Reg. D
- Consumer Leasing Act of 1976 – Reg. M
- Electronic Fund Transfer Act (EFTA) – Reg. E
- Equal Credit Opportunity Act (ECOA) – Reg. B
- Fair Credit Billing Act of 1974 (FCBA) – Reg. Z
- Fair Credit Reporting Act (FCRA) (with certain exceptions) Reg. V
- Fair Debt Collection Practices Act – Reg. F
- Federal Deposit Insurance Act (only section 43(b)-(f)) – Reg. I
- Gramm-Leach-Bliley Act (only section 502 through 509, except section 505 as it applies to section 501(b)) – Reg. P
- Home Mortgage Disclosure Act (HMDA) Reg. C
- Home Owners Protection Act (PMI Cancellation Act) of 1998
- Home Ownership and Equity Protection Act of 1994 (HOEPA) – Reg. Z
- Interstate Land Sales Full Disclosure Act - Reg. J
- Mortgage Acts and Practices–Advertising Rule - Reg. N
- Omnibus Appropriations Act of 2009 (§1015) – Reg. O
- Real Estate Settlement Procedures Act (RESPA) – Reg. X
- S.A.F.E. Mortgage Licensing Act of 2008 (SAFE Act) - Regs. G & H
- Truth in Lending Act – Reg. Z

Laws Under CFPB Authority

As we have seen, since the 1960s, laws that protect consumers in real estate financial transactions have multiplied rapidly. The concepts of fair and equal financing have been written into lending laws that prohibit unfair discrimination, protect consumers' credit rights, and clarify settlement procedures. Together, these laws set a standard of how individuals should be treated in their financial dealings. The CFPB enforces many of these laws to protect consumers from unethical and/or illegal lending and credit practices.

Equal Credit Opportunity Act (ECOA)

The **Equal Credit Opportunity Act (ECOA)** of 1976 ensures that all consumers are given an equal chance to obtain credit. This does not mean that all consumers who apply for credit receive it, because lenders use factors such as income, expenses, debt, and credit history to determine creditworthiness. [15 USC §1691 et seq.]. The CFPB implements the Equal Credit Opportunity Act through **Regulation B**.

The law protects a borrower when he or she deals with any creditor who regularly extends credit, including banks, small loan and finance companies, retail and department stores, credit card companies, and credit unions. The law covers anyone involved in granting credit, such as mortgage brokers who arrange financing. The law also protects businesses applying for credit.

The Equal Credit Opportunity Act covers a borrower's application for a home loan or home improvement loan. The Act bars discrimination based on characteristics such as the borrower's race, color, gender, or the race or national origin of the people in the neighborhood in which a borrower lives or wants to buy a home. Creditors may not use any appraisal of the value of the property that considers the race of the people in the neighborhood.

Prohibited Basis under ECOA
- Race or color
- Religion
- Sex
- National origin
- Marital status
- Age (provided the applicant has the capacity to contract)
- The applicant's receipt of income derived from any public assistance program
- The applicant's exercise, in good faith, of any right under the Consumer Credit Protection Act

ECOA requires lenders to notify applicant of the result of their application within certain time limits. This applies to approvals as well as disapprovals. They must also state the specific reasons for disapproval.

In addition, a borrower is entitled to receive a copy of an appraisal report that he or she paid for in connection with an application for credit by submitting a written request for the report. The creditor must provide a copy of the appraisal report promptly (generally within 30 days). [§1002.14].

Regulation B

Regulation B implements the provisions of the Equal Credit Opportunity Act (ECOA). [12 CFR §1002]. In 1974, the Act made it unlawful for creditors to discriminate in any aspect of a credit transaction based on sex or marital status. In 1976, amendments to the Act made it unlawful to discriminate based on race, color, religion, national origin, age, and receipt of public assistance. In addition, a consumer may exercise his or her rights under the Consumer Credit Protection Act without fear of discrimination.

The primary purpose of the ECOA is to prevent banks and other creditors from discriminating when granting credit by requiring them to make extensions of credit equally available to all creditworthy applicants with fairness, impartiality, and without discrimination on any prohibited basis. The regulation applies to consumer and other types of credit transactions.

Handling Borrowers' Applications

Creditors must treat all potential borrowers equally and fairly when handling loan applications. Therefore, it is inappropriate and illegal to question potential borrowers about their age, gender, marital status, national origin, religion, race, sexual orientation, or because they receive public assistance income.

Creditors may ask borrowers to disclose information voluntarily regarding their ethnicity, race, and sex if the borrower is applying for a real estate loan. If a borrower chooses not to provide the information or any part of it, that fact shall be noted on the form, and the lender is required to note the information of the basis of visual observation or surname provided. This information helps federal agencies enforce anti-discrimination laws. [§1002.13]. The creditor may ask a borrower about his or her residence or immigration status.

Usually, creditors may not ask a borrower's gender on an application form (one exception is on a loan to buy or build a home). A female borrower does not have to use Miss, Mrs., or Ms. with her name on a credit application.

When permitted to ask marital status, a creditor may use only the terms married, unmarried, or separated. Unmarried includes single, divorced, or widowed. A creditor may ask the borrower to provide this information if the borrower lives in a community property state. These states are Arizona, California, Idaho, Louisiana, Nevada, New Mexico, Texas, Washington, and Wisconsin. A creditor in any state may ask for this information if the borrower is applying for a joint account or one secured by property.

Creditors must not ask about the borrower's plans for having or raising children. Even though a creditor may not ask if the borrower receives alimony, child support, or separate maintenance payments, the creditor may ask if the borrower pays any of them.

Extending Credit

Creditors must act fairly and cannot refuse loans to qualified, creditworthy borrowers. Creditors cannot lend borrowers money on terms that differ from those granted to others with similar income, expenses, credit history, and collateral.

The race of people in the neighborhood in which the borrower wants to buy or refinance a house cannot be used in consideration for a loan.

The borrower's age is immaterial unless he or she is too young to sign contracts (generally under 18 years). If the borrower is 62 or older, a creditor can use the borrower's age to determine if income might drop because of retirement.

Evaluating Borrowers' Income

Creditors must evaluate the source of income objectively. Creditors may not refuse to consider or discount income from alimony, child support, part-time employment, pensions, social security, or public assistance. Income from child support and alimony payments does not have to be disclosed unless the borrower wants the creditor to include it as income. A creditor may ask the borrower to provide proof of consistent payment.

The amount of income cannot be discounted because of the borrower's sex or marital status. For example, a creditor cannot count a man's salary at 100% and a woman's at 75%. A creditor may not assume a woman of childbearing age will stop working to raise children.

Credit Application Denial

A creditor must tell the applicant if the application was accepted or rejected within 30 days of having received a complete application. After analyzing the risk factors of the borrower and the property, a creditor may deny the loan. This is legal as long as all potential borrowers are assessed according to the same underwriting guidelines.

If the application is rejected, the applicant must be given the reasons for the rejection. Acceptable reasons include inadequate income, length of employment, or a low credit score. Indefinite or vague reasons are illegal so the lender should be specific.

Creditors must give borrowers a notice of the rejection. It must state the specific reason(s) for the rejection or tell the borrower he or she has the right to learn the reason within 60 days of receipt of the letter.

Home Mortgage Disclosure Act (HMDA)

The federal **Home Mortgage Disclosure Act** of 1975 (HMDA) is enforced by the CFPB's **Regulation C** [12 CFR 1003]. HMDA requires most mortgage lenders in metropolitan areas to gather data from their borrowers when they apply for a loan. The purpose of HMDA is to determine whether financial institutions are serving the housing needs of their communities and to identify any possible discriminatory lending patterns. Mortgage and consumer finance companies may have to report HMDA data, depending on their asset size, whether they have an office in a metropolitan statistical area, and the extent of their housing-related lending activity.

The loans subject to the provisions of HMDA include loans made to purchase residential dwellings, home improvement loans, and loans to refinance a home previously covered by HMDA. The act does not apply to vacant land or new construction.

The data tracked include the type and amount of the loan, the type of property with its location and the borrower's ethnicity, race, sex, and income. The financial institution must state whether the application was approved or denied. The financial institutions submit annual reports, called a Loan Application Register (LAR), every March to the Federal Financial Institutions Examination Council (FFIEC).

Regulation C

Regulation C requires a lending institution to post a general notice about the availability of HMDA data in the lobby of its home office and of each branch office located in a metropolitan area. The following is suggested, not required, wording. Insert an address at the end, or if HMDA data is available at branch offices, omit the last sentence.

> ## HOME MORTGAGE DISCLOSURE ACT NOTICE
>
> The HMDA data about our residential mortgage lending are available for review. The data show geographic distribution of loans and applications, ethnicity, race, sex and information about loan approvals and denials. Inquire at the office regarding the locations where HMDA data may be inspected. To receive a copy of this data, send a written request to ...

Fair Credit Reporting Act (FCRA)

The **Fair Credit Reporting Act (FCRA)** of 1970 is one of the most important laws that protects consumer identity and credit information. It is designed to promote the accuracy, fairness, and privacy of the information collected and maintained by credit reporting agencies. The CFPB implements the Fair Credit Reporting Act through **Regulation V**.

The Fair Credit Reporting Act establishes procedures for correcting mistakes on a person's credit record and requires that a consumer's record only be provided for legitimate business needs. It also requires that the record be kept confidential. A credit record for judgments, liens, suits, and other adverse information may be retained for 7 years. The exception is bankruptcies, for which the record may be retained for 10 years.

A consumer may sue any credit reporting agency or creditor for breaking the rules regarding who may see his or her credit records or for failing to correct errors in a credit file. If the violation is proved to have been intentional, a consumer may be entitled to actual damages plus punitive damages allowed by the court, as well as court costs and attorney's fees. Any person who obtains a credit report without proper authorization, or a credit reporting agency employee who gives a credit report to an unauthorized person, may be fined up to $5,000 or imprisoned for 1 year, or both.

Consumers must be told if personal credit information is used against them. If a consumer is denied credit, employment, or insurance because of information in the credit report, the denying party must alert the consumer and provide the name, address, and phone number of the credit reporting agency used to support the denial.

A consumer has access to his or her file. Upon request, a credit reporting agency must give a consumer the information in the file and a list of everyone who has requested it within a certain time period. There is no charge for the credit report if the consumer has been denied credit, employment, or insurance because of items in the file (if a request is made within 60 days). [§612(b)]. Additionally, a consumer is entitled to one free credit report from each of the three credit bureaus every 12 months. [§612(a)].

A consumer can dispute inaccurate information and a credit reporting agency must investigate those items reported as inaccurate by the consumer. The consumer should receive a full copy of the investigation report. If the dispute is not settled to his or her satisfaction, the consumer may add a statement to the report. Inaccurate information must be corrected or deleted. Credit reporting agencies are required to remove or correct inaccurate or unverified information. They are not required to remove accurate data unless it is outdated.

Access to a consumer's file is limited. Only people and institutions with needs recognized by the FCRA may legally access a credit file. This normally includes creditors, government agencies, insurers, employers, landlords, and some businesses.

A consumer can remove his or her name from credit reporting agency lists used for unsolicited credit and insurance offers. Unsolicited offers must include a toll-free phone number the consumer can call to be removed from credit reporting agency lists.

The FACTA Amendment to the FCRA

The **Fair and Accurate Credit Transactions Act (FACTA)** of 2003 amends the FCRA. FACTA gives borrowers the right to see what is in their credit file and to have any errors corrected.

If a lender refuses credit to a borrower because of unfavorable information in his or her credit report, a borrower has a right to get the name and address of the agency that keeps the report. A borrower may request information from the credit bureau by mail or in person. The law also says that the credit bureau must help a borrower interpret the data in the report because the raw data may be difficult for the average person to analyze. If a borrower is questioning a credit refusal made within the past 60 days, the credit bureau cannot charge a fee for explaining the report.

If a borrower notifies the credit bureau about an error, generally the credit bureau must investigate and resolve the dispute within 30 days after receiving the notice. The credit bureau contacts the creditor who supplied the data and removes any information that is incomplete or inaccurate from the credit file. If a borrower disagrees with the findings, he or she can file a short statement (100 words) in the record that gives the borrower's side of the story. All future reports to creditors must include this statement or a summary of its contents.

Free Credit Report Every 12 Months

The Fair and Accurate Credit Transactions Act of 2003 allows consumers to request and obtain a free credit report once every 12 months from each of the three nationwide consumer-credit reporting companies—Equifax®, Experian®, and TransUnion™. The three major credit reporting agencies maintain a website (www.annualcreditreport.com) that provides free access to annual credit reports.

Real Estate Settlement Procedures Act (RESPA)

The federal **Real Estate Settlement Procedures Act (RESPA)** of 1974 requires lenders, mortgage brokers, or servicers of home loans to provide borrowers with pertinent and timely disclosures regarding the nature and costs of the real estate settlement process. **Settlement**, which is known as closing in some states, is the process by which ownership of real property or title to the property is passed from seller to buyer. Certain disclosures protecting consumers from unfair lending practices are required at various times during loan transactions and settlement. Congress has amended RESPA significantly since its enactment. Currently the CFPB implements RESPA through **Regulation X**.

RESPA applies to all **federally related home loans** used to purchase or refinance real property or improved real property of one-to-four units, provided the property includes the principal residence of the borrower. These include most purchase loans, assumptions, refinances, property improvement loans, and equity lines of credit.

> **RESPA's Purposes**
> - To help consumers get fair settlement services by requiring that key service costs be disclosed in advance
> - To protect consumers by eliminating kickbacks and referral fees that will unnecessarily increase the costs of settlement services
> - To further protect consumers by prohibiting certain practices that increase the cost of settlement services

RESPA requires lenders or servicers to provide a disclosure statement, give proper notice when the loan servicing is going to be transferred, grant a grace period during the transfer of the loan servicing, and respond promptly to written inquiries.

RESPA requires that borrowers receive disclosures at various times. Some disclosures spell out the costs associated with the settlement, outline lender servicing and escrow account practices, and describe business relationships between settlement service providers.

Prohibited Practices Under RESPA

RESPA was also designed to prohibit abusive practices such as kickbacks and referral fees, seller-required title insurance, and imposes limitations on the use of escrow accounts.

Kickbacks, Fee Splitting, and Unearned Fees

The Act prohibits anyone from giving or accepting a fee, kickback, or anything of value in exchange for referrals of settlement service business involving federally related mortgage loans. A **kickback** is an illegal payment made in return for a referral that results in a transaction. This applies to almost every loan made for residential property. RESPA also prohibits fee splitting and receiving fees for services not actually performed. Violation of these RESPA provisions can be punished with criminal and civil penalties.

Seller-Required Title Insurance

A seller is prohibited from requiring a homebuyer to use a particular title insurance company. A buyer can bring a lawsuit against a seller who violates this provision.

Unlimited Deposits into Escrow Accounts

A limit is set on the amount that a lender may require a borrower to put into an escrow account to pay taxes, hazard insurance, and other property charges. RESPA does not require lenders to impose an escrow account on borrowers, but some government loan programs or lenders do require an escrow account. During the loan term, RESPA prohibits a lender from charging excessive amounts for the escrow account. The lender must notify the borrower annually of any escrow account shortage and return any excesses of $50 or more.

Truth in Lending Act (TILA)

The federal **Truth in Lending Act (TILA)** is Title 1 of the **Consumer Credit Protection Act of 1968**. The Truth in Lending Act is aimed at promoting the informed use of consumer credit by requiring disclosures about its terms and costs. The CFPB implements TILA through **Regulation Z**.

This legislation requires creditors to state the cost of borrowing in a common language so that consumers can figure out what the charges are, compare the costs of loans, and shop for the best credit deal.

A **creditor** is a lender (person or company) who regularly extends consumer credit, such as real estate loans that are secured by a dwelling. A **dwelling** is a residential structure that contains one-to-four units, whether or not that structure is attached to real property. The term includes an individual condominium unit, cooperative unit, mobile home, and trailer, if it is used as a residence. These loans are subject to a finance charge or are payable in more than four installments, excluding the down payment. [12 CFR §1026.2(a)(17)]. **Consumer credit** means credit offered or extended to a consumer primarily for personal, family, or household purposes. [12 CFR §1026.2(a)(12)].

The law also requires the lender to state a maximum interest rate in variable rate contracts secured by a borrower's dwelling. It imposes limitations on home equity plans subject to the requirements of certain sections of the Act. Finally, it requires the lender to inform the consumer of the maximum interest rate that may apply during the term of a mortgage loan.

The law also establishes disclosure standards for advertisements that refer to certain credit terms. It requires disclosure of the finance charge, the annual percentage rate, and certain other costs and terms of credit. This allows a consumer to compare the prices of credit from different sources.

Regulation Z

The purpose of **Regulation Z** is to promote the informed use of consumer credit by requiring disclosures about its terms and cost. The regulation also gives consumers the right to cancel certain credit transactions that involve a lien on any dwelling of a consumer—even a second home. If credit is extended for business, commercial, or agricultural purposes, Regulation Z does not apply. For more detailed information, go to ecfr.gpoaccess.gov. [12 CFR §1026].

Since its passage, the Truth in Lending Act and Regulation Z have been amended many times.

In 2008, Regulation Z was amended by the **Mortgage Disclosure Improvement Act** (MDIA). The purpose of the MDIA is to ensure that consumers receive disclosures earlier in the mortgage process and to clarify the mandatory waiting periods.

In 2010, Title XIV of the Dodd-Frank Act—**Mortgage Reform and Anti-Predatory Lending Act** was signed into law. It included several provisions affecting Reg. Z including originator compensation, the integrity of the appraisal process, underwriting requirements, and qualified mortgage provisions, to name a few. Most of the provisions took effect on January 21, 2013.

The **TILA-RESPA Integrated Disclosure Rule** (TRID) rule further amended Regulation Z as well as Regulation X in 2013.

Disclosure Timing – 3/7/3 Rule

According to the MDIA, the disclosures are classified as early disclosures, re-disclosures, and final disclosures and the timing of the disclosures can be remembered by the 3/7/3 rule.

Early Disclosure

With an **early disclosure**, creditors are required to give the Loan Estimate (or Good Faith Estimate) to disclose mortgage loan costs at the time the borrower completes the application for a mortgage loan or within 3 business days after receiving an application.

According to TILA, for purposes of rescission and the 3-day or 7-day waiting period, a **business day** is defined as all calendar days except Sundays and legal public holidays. Legal public holidays include New Year's Day, the Birthday of Martin Luther King, Jr., Washington's Birthday, Memorial Day, Independence Day, Labor Day, Columbus Day, Veterans Day, Thanksgiving Day, and Christmas Day.

Neither the lender nor anyone else may charge a fee, other than a reasonable fee for obtaining the consumer's credit history, until after the borrower has received this disclosure. In addition, creditors must wait 7 business days after they provide the early disclosures before closing the loan. A consumer can waive the 7-day waiting period if the consumer can show that it is a bona fide personal financial emergency.

Re-Disclosure

A **re-disclosure** will be required if the annual percentage rate (APR) provided in the Loan Estimate (or Good Faith Estimate) changes beyond a specified tolerance for accuracy since the last disclosure. A re-disclosure is required if the APR changes by more than .125% for a regular transaction (fixed mortgages) or more than .25% for an irregular transaction, such as an adjustable rate mortgage. If the borrower is re-disclosed, the transaction cannot be closed for 3 business days from last disclosure. If the APR changes, then the borrower must be re-disclosed.

Final Disclosure

The **final disclosure** of the APR is found in the Closing Disclosure (effective 10/3/2015) or in the final Truth in Lending statement.

The MDIA requires that the following language is clearly written on both the initial and the final Truth in Lending statements (TIL): "You are not required to complete this agreement merely because you have received these disclosures or signed a loan application."

Disclosure Statement

For each transaction other than most closed-end mortgage loans (e.g., a mortgage transaction subject to §1026.19(e) and (f), TILA requires lenders to disclose the important terms and costs of their loans, including the annual percentage rate, finance charge, the payment terms, and information about any variable rate feature.

The **finance charge** is the dollar amount the credit will cost, and, as a condition to obtaining credit, is composed of any direct or indirect charges. Those include interest, loan fees, finder fees, credit report fees, insurance fees, and mortgage insurance fees. [§1026.4(b)] IN REAL ESTATE, the finance charge does NOT include fees for appraisals or credit reports, title insurance, notary services, or for preparing loan-related documents, such as deeds or mortgages. [§1026.4(c)(7)].

The **annual percentage rate (APR)** is the relative cost of credit expressed as a yearly rate. Expressed as a percentage, it is the relationship of the total finance charge to the total amount financed.

Regulation Z requires that the first four disclosure, called **material disclosures**, must be displayed in a certain way to allow consumers ease of comparison.

- **Amount financed** - *The amount of credit provided to you or on your behalf*
- **Finance charge** - *The dollar amount the credit will cost you*
- **Annual Percentage Rate** - *The cost of your credit expressed as a yearly rate*
- **Total of payments** - *The amount you will have paid when you have made all the scheduled payments*

- **Payment schedule** - The number, amount, and timing of payments
- **Interest Rate** - Variable interest rate and discounted variable rate disclosures, including limitations and effects of a rate increase and an example of payment terms resulting from the increase. This may be accomplished by giving the consumer the Consumer Handbook on Adjustable-Rate Mortgages or a suitable substitute.
- **Name of the lender** - Creditor making the disclosure
- **Written itemization** - Written itemization of the amount financed, or a statement that the consumer has a right to receive a written itemization, and a space in the statement for the consumer to indicate whether the itemization is requested

In addition to the above-mentioned disclosure, the regulation also requires disclosures regarding due-on-sale clauses, prepayment penalties, late payment charges, description of the property, insurance requirements, and loan assumptions.

The penalties for failure to comply with the Truth in Lending Act can be substantial. A creditor who violates the disclosure requirements may be sued for twice the amount of the finance charge. In the case of a consumer lease, the amount is 25% of the total of the monthly payments under the lease, with a minimum of $100 and a maximum of $1,000. Costs and attorney's fees may also be awarded to the consumer. The consumer must begin a lawsuit within a year of the violation.

Adjustable-Rate Loan Disclosure

If a residential mortgage loan transaction has a variable interest rate and an APR that is scheduled to increase secured by the consumer's principal dwelling with a term greater than one year, the lender must provide certain disclosures at the time an application form is provided or before the consumer pays a non-refundable fee, whichever is earlier. [12 CFR §§1026.18(f)(1) and 1026.19(b)].

Required Disclosures

- The **CHARM Booklet** published by the CFPB, or a suitable substitute.
- A loan program disclosure consistent with the applicable model forms for each variable-rate program in which the consumer/borrower expresses an interest. [12 CFR §§1026.19(b)(1-2)].

The **Consumer Handbook On Adjustable-Rate Mortgages** (CHARM Booklet) is an informational booklet containing general information on Adjustable Rate Mortgages (ARM's) that is provided by the lender to the loan applicant at the time of application for certain adjustable mortgage loans. The booklet is intended to make the borrower aware of the basics of an ARM product.

Closed-End and Open-End Loan Disclosure

Open-end credit includes types of credit arrangements such as revolving credit cards and home equity lines of credit. Home equity plans require that disclosures and a brochure also be given to the consumer along with the application.

Closed-end credit includes any credit arrangement that does not fall within the definition of an open-end credit transaction, such as a real estate loan. Closed-end credit has a stated maturity date. Usually, disclosure is required before any closed-end credit transaction is completed.

The type and timing of disclosures required under Regulation Z for closed-end and open-end loans are provided at the website of the Consumer Financial Protection Bureau (CFPB) at www.consumerfinance.gov.

Right of Rescission

The **right to rescind** (cancel) a real estate loan applies to most consumer credit loans (hard money loans) or refinance loans. Loans used for the purchase or construction of the borrower's personal residence (purchase money loans) have no right of rescission. The lender must provide a written rescission disclosure to every borrower who is entitled to rescind. When the right of rescission applies, the borrower has a right to rescind the agreement until midnight of the 3rd business day after the promissory note is signed.

Advertising

The Truth in Lending Act establishes disclosure standards for advertisements that refer to certain credit terms, called triggering terms. **Triggering terms** include the amount or percentage of any downpayment, the number of payments or period of repayment, the amount of any payment, and the amount of any finance charge. [12 CFR §1026.24]. If the annual percentage rate (APR) is disclosed in the advertisement, no other disclosures are required.

For example, if the APR is not stated, then the specifics of all credit terms must be disclosed. An advertisement that discloses the number of payments must also disclose the amount or percentage of the down payment, amount of any payment, finance charge, interest rate, property description, and so forth. In

fact, if the advertisement states the interest rate, it must also disclose the APR. For example, ads that require complete disclosure include *No money down* or *100% financing.*

Advertising Guidelines

The questions and answers below illustrate some aspects of advertising regulations under Regulation Z. Advertising includes newspapers, electronic media, signs, handouts, brochures, and other similar mediums.

1. *Can the advertisement include only the interest rate?* No.
2. *Can the annual percentage rate be advertised without disclosure of other terms?* Yes, but if the rate varies, that must be disclosed.
3. *Is using APR in place of the term annual percentage rate allowed in advertising?* No, use the annual percentage rate.
4. *Is advertising $10,000.00 down without disclosing other terms allowed?* No, the annual percentage rate and other terms must be disclosed.
5. *Is advertising no closing costs without disclosing other terms permitted?* Yes.
6. *Is advertising that mentions a small down payment without disclosing other terms allowed?* Yes.
7. *Can advertising disclose liberal rates without disclosing other terms?* Yes.
8. *Can terms be advertised without disclosing other terms?* Yes.
9. *Can the deferred payment price or the total of loan payments be disclosed in any residential real estate advertisement?* No.
10. *If only the sales price or loan amount and the annual percentage rate are advertised, must the advertisement include other terms?* No, but if the rate is advertised, the advertisement must expressly state whether it is an annual percentage rate or a variable rate.
11. *Can a $350.00 monthly payment be advertised?* Yes, but the additional disclosure requirements must be met.
12. *Can an advertisement state, "Assume a 9% loan." or "11.9% Financing is available."?* Yes, but ALL additional disclosure requirements must be met.
13. *Can MLS sheets be used as credit advertising?* No.

Reg. Z - Home Ownership and Equity Protection Act of 1994

The **Home Ownership and Equity Protection Act of 1994** (**HOEPA**) deals with high-rate, high-fee home loans that are refinance or home equity installment loans. The law addresses certain deceptive and unfair practices in home equity lending. It amends the Truth in Lending Act (TILA) and establishes requirements for certain loans with high rates and/or high fees. Since the rules for these loans are contained in **Section 32 of Regulation Z**, they are called **Section 32 Mortgages**.

A **high-cost mortgage** is a consumer credit transaction secured by a consumer's 1-4 unit principal dwelling, including purchase and non-purchase money closed-end credit transactions and HELOCs that meets certain thresholds.

The rules primarily affect refinancing and home equity installment loans involving the borrower's primary residence that meet the definition of a high-cost loan. The rules do not cover the following loans. [12 CFR §1026.32(a)(1-2)].

Loans Exempt from HOEPA Coverage

- Reverse mortgages
- Transactions to finance the initial construction of a dwelling
- Transaction originated by a Housing Finance Agency as lender
- USDA Rural Development Section 502 Direct Loan Program
- Business purpose loans not governed by Regulation Z

Section 32 Triggers

Coverage is triggered when a loan's **average prime offer rate** (APOR) exceeds comparable Treasury securities by specified thresholds for particular loan types, or where **points and fees** exceed a specified percentage of the total loan amount or a dollar threshold. [12 CFR §1026.32(a)]. The **average prime offer rate** is an estimate of the rate that people with good credit pay for a similar first mortgage.

High-Cost Mortgage Disclosures

If a loan meets the specified requirements, a borrower must receive several disclosures at least 3 business days before the loan is finalized. These disclosures must be given in addition to the other TILA disclosures that the borrower must receive no later than the closing of the loan.

As part of the additional disclosures, the lender must give borrowers a written notice stating that the loan need not be completed even though they have signed the loan application and received the required disclosures.

Borrowers have 3 business days after receiving the special Section 32 disclosures to decide if they will sign the loan agreement.

The notice must warn borrowers that the lender will place a lien on their home and, if the borrowers fail to make payments, they can lose the residence and any money put into it.

In addition, the lender must disclose the APR, the regular payment amount (including any balloon payment when the law permits balloon payments), and the loan amount. If the borrowed amount includes credit insurance premiums, that fact must be stated. For variable rate loans, the lender must disclose that the rate and monthly payment may increase and state the amount of the maximum monthly payment. [12 CFR §1026.32(c)].

High-Cost Mortgage Restrictions

Once a transaction is determined to be a high cost mortgage, several restrictions apply. [§§1026.32, 1026.34].

Additional Requirements for High-Cost Mortgages

- Balloon payments are generally prohibited.
- Prepayment penalties are prohibited.
- Financing points and fees are prohibited.
- Late fees cannot exceed 4%t of the past due payment or be imposed until after 15 days past due.
- Payoff statement must be provided within 5 days of request and fees are restricted.
- Fees for loan modification or loan deferral are prohibited.
- Ability-to-repay assessment is required for HELOCs.
- Closed-end loans must meet the 2013 Ability-to-Repay Final Rule requirements.
  - Lenders and mortgage brokers are prohibited from encouraging borrowers to default on debts to be refinanced with a high-cost mortgage loan.

Mortgage Counseling Requirements

The revisions to HOEPA made by the Consumer Financial Protection Bureau (CFPB) require potential borrowers to receive mortgage counseling for high-cost mortgages and mortgages with negative amortization.

High-Cost Mortgage Counseling Requirements

Lenders are required to provide to consumer borrowers a list of federally certified or approved homeownership counselors or organizations (List) within 3 business days after receiving an application for a mortgage loan. The list is to be obtained by the lender from the CFPB or from the Department of Housing and Urban Development (HUD). A lender does not need to provide the List if before the end of the 3 business days, the application is denied or withdrawn, or the application is for a reverse mortgage or loan secured by a timeshare. [§12 CFR 1026.20].

Before making a high-cost mortgage loan, lenders are required to obtain written **Certification of Counseling** from a HUD-certified or approved homeownership counselor that the consumer has received counseling on the advisability of the loan. [§1026.34(a)(5)].

Negative Amortization Counseling Requirements

Before making a closed-end loan secured by a 1-4 unit dwelling that may result in negative amortization, lenders must obtain confirmation that a first-time borrower received counseling on the risks of negative amortization from a HUD-certified or -approved counselor or counseling organization. A creditor cannot direct a consumer to choose a particular counselor or organization. Although a creditor cannot make the loan prior to receiving this confirmation, a creditor may engage in other activities, such as processing the application or ordering the appraisal or title search. This requirement does not apply to reverse mortgages or loans secured by a timeshare. [§1026.36(k)].

In addition, creditors cannot make loans based on the collateral value of the secured property regardless of the borrower's ability to repay the loan. They cannot refinance a HOEPA loan into another HOEPA loan in the first 12 months of origination unless the new loan is in the borrower's best interest. Creditors cannot document a closed-end, high-cost loan as an open-end loan. For example, a high-cost loan may not be structured as a home equity line of credit if there is no reasonable expectation that repeat transactions will occur.

Lenders may be sued if they violate these requirements. Additionally, a violation of the high-rate, high-fee requirements of TILA may enable the borrower to rescind the loan for up to 3 years.

Reg. Z - Higher-Priced Mortgage Loans - 2008

The Housing and Economic Recovery Act (HERA) amended TILA and Regulation Z, defining a new type of mortgage called a higher-priced mortgage loan. According to TILA, §1026.35(a)(1), a **higher-priced mortgage loan** is a closed-end mortgage loan secured by the consumer's principal dwelling with an APR that exceeds the average prime offer rate for a comparable transaction. The threshold is 1.5 or more percentage points for first lien loans or 3.5 or more percentage points for junior lien loans. This definition pertains to home purchase loans.

TILA-RESPA INTEGRATED DISCLOSURES (TRID)

In 2013, the **TILA-RESPA Integrated Disclosure** (TRID) rule further amended Regulation Z as well as Regulation X. **Regulation Z** implements the Truth in Lending Act (TILA) and **Regulation X** implements the Real Estate Settlement Procedures Act (RESPA).

The TRID rule created new **integrated disclosure forms** for most closed-end mortgage loan transactions by consolidating four existing disclosures required under TILA and RESPA into two disclosure forms. The new integrated mortgage disclosure forms are the Loan Estimate and the Closing Disclosure.

> The **Loan Estimate** replaces the Good Faith Estimate (GFE) and the "early" Truth-in-Lending disclosure. The Loan Estimate provides borrowers with good-faith estimates of credit costs and transaction terms.

> The **Closing Disclosure** integrates and replaces the existing HUD-1 and the final TILA disclosure. For loans that require a Loan Estimate and that go to closing, lenders must provide borrowers with the Closing Disclosure reflecting the actual terms of the transaction.

Mortgages Covered by the TRID Rule

Beginning October 3, 2015, lenders must use the Loan Estimate and Closing Disclosure for most closed-end federally related residential mortgages that are covered by RESPA. Additionally, the integrated disclosure requirements apply to construction-only loans, vacant-land loans, and 25-acre loans, all of which are currently exempt from RESPA coverage.

However, some home loans (reverse mortgages, HELOCs, and manufactured home loans) are exempt from the TRID rule. Lenders originating these types of mortgages must continue to use, as applicable, the GFE, HUD-1, and Truth-in-Lending disclosures required under current law. To see examples of a GFE or HUD-1 Settlement Statement, click on the form name.

FICUS BANK
4321 Random Boulevard • Somecity, ST 12340

Save this Loan Estimate to compare with your Closing Disclosure.

Loan Estimate

DATE ISSUED	2/15/2013	**LOAN TERM**	30 years
APPLICANTS	Michael Jones and Mary Stone	**PURPOSE**	Purchase
	123 Anywhere Street	**PRODUCT**	Fixed Rate
	Anytown, ST 12345	**LOAN TYPE**	☒ Conventional ☐FHA ☐VA ☐ _____
PROPERTY	456 Somewhere Avenue	**LOAN ID #**	123456789
	Anytown, ST 12345	**RATE LOCK**	☐ NO ☒ YES, until 4/16/2013 at 5:00 p.m. EDT
SALE PRICE	$180,000		

*Before closing, your interest rate, points, and lender credits can change unless you lock the interest rate. All other estimated closing costs expire on **3/4/2013** at 5:00 p.m. EDT*

Loan Terms

		Can this amount increase after closing?
Loan Amount	$162,000	**NO**
Interest Rate	3.875%	**NO**
Monthly Principal & Interest *See Projected Payments below for your Estimated Total Monthly Payment*	$761.78	**NO**

		Does the loan have these features?
Prepayment Penalty		**YES** • As high as **$3,240** if you pay off the loan during the first 2 years
Balloon Payment		**NO**

Projected Payments

Payment Calculation	Years 1-7	Years 8-30
Principal & Interest	$761.78	$761.78
Mortgage Insurance	+ 82	+ —
Estimated Escrow *Amount can increase over time*	+ 206	+ 206
Estimated Total Monthly Payment	**$1,050**	**$968**

		This estimate includes	In escrow?
Estimated Taxes, Insurance & Assessments *Amount can increase over time*	$206 a month	☒ Property Taxes ☒ Homeowner's Insurance ☐ Other: *See Section G on page 2 for escrowed property costs. You must pay for other property costs separately.*	**YES** **YES**

Costs at Closing

Estimated Closing Costs	$8,054	Includes $5,672 in Loan Costs + $2,382 in Other Costs – $0 in Lender Credits. *See page 2 for details.*
Estimated Cash to Close	$16,054	Includes Closing Costs. *See Calculating Cash to Close on page 2 for details.*

Visit **www.consumerfinance.gov/mortgage-estimate** for general information and tools.

Closing Cost Details

Loan Costs

A. Origination Charges	$1,802
.25 % of Loan Amount (Points)	$405
Application Fee	$300
Underwriting Fee	$1,097

B. Services You Cannot Shop For	$672
Appraisal Fee	$405
Credit Report Fee	$30
Flood Determination Fee	$20
Flood Monitoring Fee	$32
Tax Monitoring Fee	$75
Tax Status Research Fee	$110

C. Services You Can Shop For	$3,198
Pest Inspection Fee	$135
Survey Fee	$65
Title – Insurance Binder	$700
Title – Lender's Title Policy	$535
Title – Settlement Agent Fee	$502
Title – Title Search	$1,261

D. TOTAL LOAN COSTS (A + B + C)	$5,672

Other Costs

E. Taxes and Other Government Fees	$85
Recording Fees and Other Taxes	$85
Transfer Taxes	

F. Prepaids	$867
Homeowner's Insurance Premium (6 months)	$605
Mortgage Insurance Premium (months)	
Prepaid Interest ($17.44 per day for 15 days @ 3.875%)	$262
Property Taxes (months)	

G. Initial Escrow Payment at Closing		$413
Homeowner's Insurance $100.83 per month for 2 mo.		$202
Mortgage Insurance per month for mo.		
Property Taxes $105.30 per month for 2 mo.		$211

H. Other	$1,017
Title – Owner's Title Policy (optional)	$1,017

I. TOTAL OTHER COSTS (E + F + G + H)	$2,382

J. TOTAL CLOSING COSTS	$8,054
D + I	$8,054
Lender Credits	

Calculating Cash to Close

Total Closing Costs (J)	$8,054
Closing Costs Financed (Paid from your Loan Amount)	$0
Down Payment/Funds from Borrower	$18,000
Deposit	– $10,000
Funds for Borrower	$0
Seller Credits	$0
Adjustments and Other Credits	$0
Estimated Cash to Close	$16,054

Additional Information About This Loan

LENDER	Ficus Bank	MORTGAGE BROKER	
NMLS/__ LICENSE ID		NMLS/__ LICENSE ID	
LOAN OFFICER	Joe Smith	LOAN OFFICER	
NMLS/__ LICENSE ID	12345	NMLS/__ LICENSE ID	
EMAIL	joesmith@ficusbank.com	EMAIL	
PHONE	123-456-7890	PHONE	

Comparisons — Use these measures to compare this loan with other loans.

In 5 Years	$56,582	Total you will have paid in principal, interest, mortgage insurance, and loan costs.
	$15,773	Principal you will have paid off.
Annual Percentage Rate (APR)	4.274%	Your costs over the loan term expressed as a rate. This is not your interest rate.
Total Interest Percentage (TIP)	69.45%	The total amount of interest that you will pay over the loan term as a percentage of your loan amount.

Other Considerations

Appraisal
We may order an appraisal to determine the property's value and charge you for this appraisal. We will promptly give you a copy of any appraisal, even if your loan does not close. You can pay for an additional appraisal for your own use at your own cost.

Assumption
If you sell or transfer this property to another person, we
☐ will allow, under certain conditions, this person to assume this loan on the original terms.
☒ will not allow assumption of this loan on the original terms.

Homeowner's Insurance
This loan requires homeowner's insurance on the property, which you may obtain from a company of your choice that we find acceptable.

Late Payment
If your payment is more than *15* days late, we will charge a late fee of *5% of the monthly principal and interest payment.*

Refinance
Refinancing this loan will depend on your future financial situation, the property value, and market conditions. You may not be able to refinance this loan.

Servicing
We intend
☐ to service your loan. If so, you will make your payments to us.
☒ to transfer servicing of your loan.

Confirm Receipt

By signing, you are only confirming that you have received this form. You do not have to accept this loan because you have signed or received this form.

_____   _____   _____   _____
Applicant Signature   Date   Co-Applicant Signature   Date

Closing Disclosure

This form is a statement of final loan terms and closing costs. Compare this document with your Loan Estimate.

Closing Information

Date Issued	4/15/2013
Closing Date	4/15/2013
Disbursement Date	4/15/2013
Settlement Agent	Epsilon Title Co.
File #	12-3456
Property	456 Somewhere Ave
	Anytown, ST 12345
Sale Price	$180,000

Transaction Information

Borrower	Michael Jones and Mary Stone
	123 Anywhere Street
	Anytown, ST 12345
Seller	Steve Cole and Amy Doe
	321 Somewhere Drive
	Anytown, ST 12345
Lender	Ficus Bank

Loan Information

Loan Term	30 years
Purpose	Purchase
Product	Fixed Rate
Loan Type	☒ Conventional ☐ FHA
	☐ VA ☐ _____
Loan ID #	123456789
MIC #	000654321

Loan Terms

		Can this amount increase after closing?
Loan Amount	$162,000	**NO**
Interest Rate	3.875%	**NO**
Monthly Principal & Interest *See Projected Payments below for your Estimated Total Monthly Payment*	$761.78	**NO**
		Does the loan have these features?
Prepayment Penalty		**YES** • As high as **$3,240** if you pay off the loan during the first 2 years
Balloon Payment		**NO**

Projected Payments

Payment Calculation	Years 1-7	Years 8-30
Principal & Interest	$761.78	$761.78
Mortgage Insurance	+ 82.35	+ —
Estimated Escrow *Amount can increase over time*	+ 206.13	+ 206.13
Estimated Total Monthly Payment	**$1,050.26**	**$967.91**

Estimated Taxes, Insurance & Assessments *Amount can increase over time* *See page 4 for details*	$356.13 a month	This estimate includes	In escrow?
		☒ Property Taxes	YES
		☒ Homeowner's Insurance	YES
		☒ Other: Homeowner's Association Dues	NO
		See Escrow Account on page 4 for details. You must pay for other property costs separately.	

Costs at Closing

Closing Costs	$9,712.10	Includes $4,694.05 in Loan Costs + $5,018.05 in Other Costs – $0 in Lender Credits. *See page 2 for details.*
Cash to Close	$14,147.26	Includes Closing Costs. *See Calculating Cash to Close on page 3 for details.*

Closing Cost Details

Loan Costs		Borrower-Paid		Seller-Paid		Paid by Others
		At Closing	Before Closing	At Closing	Before Closing	
A. Origination Charges		**$1,802.00**				
01 0.25 % of Loan Amount (Points)		$405.00				
02 Application Fee		$300.00				
03 Underwriting Fee		$1,097.00				
04						
05						
06						
07						
08						
B. Services Borrower Did Not Shop For		**$236.55**				
01 Appraisal Fee	to John Smith Appraisers Inc.					$405.00
02 Credit Report Fee	to Information Inc.		$29.80			
03 Flood Determination Fee	to Info Co.	$20.00				
04 Flood Monitoring Fee	to Info Co.	$31.75				
05 Tax Monitoring Fee	to Info Co.	$75.00				
06 Tax Status Research Fee	to Info Co.	$80.00				
07						
08						
09						
10						
C. Services Borrower Did Shop For		**$2,655.50**				
01 Pest Inspection Fee	to Pests Co.	$120.50				
02 Survey Fee	to Surveys Co.	$85.00				
03 Title – Insurance Binder	to Epsilon Title Co.	$650.00				
04 Title – Lender's Title Insurance	to Epsilon Title Co.	$500.00				
05 Title – Settlement Agent Fee	to Epsilon Title Co.	$500.00				
06 Title – Title Search	to Epsilon Title Co.	$800.00				
07						
08						
D. TOTAL LOAN COSTS (Borrower-Paid)		**$4,694.05**				
Loan Costs Subtotals (A + B + C)		$4,664.25	$29.80			

Other Costs		Borrower-Paid		Seller-Paid		Paid by Others
		At Closing	Before Closing	At Closing	Before Closing	
E. Taxes and Other Government Fees		**$85.00**				
01 Recording Fees	Deed: $40.00 Mortgage: $45.00	$85.00				
02 Transfer Tax	to Any State			$950.00		
F. Prepaids		**$2,120.80**				
01 Homeowner's Insurance Premium (12 mo.) to Insurance Co.		$1,209.96				
02 Mortgage Insurance Premium (mo.)						
03 Prepaid Interest ($17.44 per day from 4/15/13 to 5/1/13)		$279.04				
04 Property Taxes (6 mo.) to Any County USA		$631.80				
05						
G. Initial Escrow Payment at Closing		**$412.25**				
01 Homeowner's Insurance $100.83 per month for 2 mo.		$201.66				
02 Mortgage Insurance per month for mo.						
03 Property Taxes $105.30 per month for 2 mo.		$210.60				
04						
05						
06						
07						
08 Aggregate Adjustment		− 0.01				
H. Other		**$2,400.00**				
01 HOA Capital Contribution	to HOA Acre Inc.	$500.00				
02 HOA Processing Fee	to HOA Acre Inc.	$150.00				
03 Home Inspection Fee	to Engineers Inc.	$750.00			$750.00	
04 Home Warranty Fee	to XYZ Warranty Inc.			$450.00		
05 Real Estate Commission	to Alpha Real Estate Broker			$5,700.00		
06 Real Estate Commission	to Omega Real Estate Broker			$5,700.00		
07 Title – Owner's Title Insurance (optional) to Epsilon Title Co.		$1,000.00				
08						
I. TOTAL OTHER COSTS (Borrower-Paid)		**$5,018.05**				
Other Costs Subtotals (E + F + G + H)		$5,018.05				

		Borrower-Paid		Seller-Paid		Paid by Others
J. TOTAL CLOSING COSTS (Borrower-Paid)		**$9,712.10**				
Closing Costs Subtotals (D + I)		$9,682.30	$29.80	$12,800.00	$750.00	$405.00
Lender Credits						

Calculating Cash to Close

Use this table to see what has changed from your Loan Estimate.

	Loan Estimate	Final	Did this change?
Total Closing Costs (J)	$8,054.00	$9,712.10	YES · See **Total Loan Costs (D)** and **Total Other Costs (I)**
Closing Costs Paid Before Closing	$0	– $29.80	YES · You paid these Closing Costs **before closing**
Closing Costs Financed (Paid from your Loan Amount)	$0	$0	NO
Down Payment/Funds from Borrower	$18,000.00	$18,000.00	NO
Deposit	– $10,000.00	– $10,000.00	NO
Funds for Borrower	$0	$0	NO
Seller Credits	$0	– $2,500.00	YES · See Seller Credits in **Section L**
Adjustments and Other Credits	$0	– $1,035.04	YES · See details in **Sections K and L**
Cash to Close	$16,054.00	$14,147.26	

Summaries of Transactions

Use this table to see a summary of your transaction.

BORROWER'S TRANSACTION

K. Due from Borrower at Closing	$189,762.30
01 Sale Price of Property	$180,000.00
02 Sale Price of Any Personal Property Included in Sale	
03 Closing Costs Paid at Closing (J)	$9,682.30
04	
Adjustments	
05	
06	
07	
Adjustments for Items Paid by Seller in Advance	
08 City/Town Taxes to	
09 County Taxes to	
10 Assessments to	
11 HOA Dues 4/15/13 to 4/30/13	$80.00
12	
13	
14	
15	

L. Paid Already by or on Behalf of Borrower at Closing	$175,615.04
01 Deposit	$10,000.00
02 Loan Amount	$162,000.00
03 Existing Loan(s) Assumed or Taken Subject to	
04	
05 Seller Credit	$2,500.00
Other Credits	
06 Rebate from Epsilon Title Co.	$750.00
07	
Adjustments	
08	
09	
10	
11	
Adjustments for Items Unpaid by Seller	
12 City/Town Taxes 1/1/13 to 4/14/13	$365.04
13 County Taxes to	
14 Assessments to	
15	
16	
17	

CALCULATION	
Total Due from Borrower at Closing (K)	$189,762.30
Total Paid Already by or on Behalf of Borrower at Closing (L)	– $175,615.04
Cash to Close ☒ From ☐ To Borrower	**$14,147.26**

SELLER'S TRANSACTION

M. Due to Seller at Closing	$180,080.00
01 Sale Price of Property	$180,000.00
02 Sale Price of Any Personal Property Included in Sale	
03	
04	
05	
06	
07	
08	
Adjustments for Items Paid by Seller in Advance	
09 City/Town Taxes to	
10 County Taxes to	
11 Assessments to	
12 HOA Dues 4/15/13 to 4/30/13	$80.00
13	
14	
15	
16	

N. Due from Seller at Closing	$115,665.04
01 Excess Deposit	
02 Closing Costs Paid at Closing (J)	$12,800.00
03 Existing Loan(s) Assumed or Taken Subject to	
04 Payoff of First Mortgage Loan	$100,000.00
05 Payoff of Second Mortgage Loan	
06	
07	
08 Seller Credit	$2,500.00
09	
10	
11	
12	
13	
Adjustments for Items Unpaid by Seller	
14 City/Town Taxes 1/1/13 to 4/14/13	$365.04
15 County Taxes to	
16 Assessments to	
17	
18	
19	

CALCULATION	
Total Due to Seller at Closing (M)	$180,080.00
Total Due from Seller at Closing (N)	– $115,665.04
Cash ☐ From ☒ To Seller	**$64,414.96**

Additional Information About This Loan

Loan Disclosures

Assumption
If you sell or transfer this property to another person, your lender
- ☐ will allow, under certain conditions, this person to assume this loan on the original terms.
- ☒ will not allow assumption of this loan on the original terms.

Demand Feature
Your loan
- ☐ has a demand feature, which permits your lender to require early repayment of the loan. You should review your note for details.
- ☒ does not have a demand feature.

Late Payment
If your payment is more than *15* days late, your lender will charge a late fee of *5% of the monthly principal and interest payment.*

Negative Amortization (Increase in Loan Amount)
Under your loan terms, you
- ☐ are scheduled to make monthly payments that do not pay all of the interest due that month. As a result, your loan amount will increase (negatively amortize), and your loan amount will likely become larger than your original loan amount. Increases in your loan amount lower the equity you have in this property.
- ☐ may have monthly payments that do not pay all of the interest due that month. If you do, your loan amount will increase (negatively amortize), and, as a result, your loan amount may become larger than your original loan amount. Increases in your loan amount lower the equity you have in this property.
- ☒ do not have a negative amortization feature.

Partial Payments
Your lender
- ☒ may accept payments that are less than the full amount due (partial payments) and apply them to your loan.
- ☐ may hold them in a separate account until you pay the rest of the payment, and then apply the full payment to your loan.
- ☐ does not accept any partial payments.
If this loan is sold, your new lender may have a different policy.

Security Interest
You are granting a security interest in
456 Somewhere Ave., Anytown, ST 12345

You may lose this property if you do not make your payments or satisfy other obligations for this loan.

Escrow Account
For now, your loan
- ☒ will have an escrow account (also called an "impound" or "trust" account) to pay the property costs listed below. Without an escrow account, you would pay them directly, possibly in one or two large payments a year. Your lender may be liable for penalties and interest for failing to make a payment.

Escrow		
Escrowed Property Costs over Year 1	$2,473.56	Estimated total amount over year 1 for your escrowed property costs: *Homeowner's Insurance Property Taxes*
Non-Escrowed Property Costs over Year 1	$1,800.00	Estimated total amount over year 1 for your non-escrowed property costs: *Homeowner's Association Dues* You may have other property costs.
Initial Escrow Payment	$412.25	A cushion for the escrow account you pay at closing. See Section G on page 2.
Monthly Escrow Payment	$206.13	The amount included in your total monthly payment.

- ☐ will not have an escrow account because ☐ you declined it ☐ your lender does not offer one. You must directly pay your property costs, such as taxes and homeowner's insurance. Contact your lender to ask if your loan can have an escrow account.

No Escrow	
Estimated Property Costs over Year 1	Estimated total amount over year 1. You must pay these costs directly, possibly in one or two large payments a year.
Escrow Waiver Fee	

In the future,
Your property costs may change and, as a result, your escrow payment may change. You may be able to cancel your escrow account, but if you do, you must pay your property costs directly. If you fail to pay your property taxes, your state or local government may (1) impose fines and penalties or (2) place a tax lien on this property. If you fail to pay any of your property costs, your lender may (1) add the amounts to your loan balance, (2) add an escrow account to your loan, or (3) require you to pay for property insurance that the lender buys on your behalf, which likely would cost more and provide fewer benefits than what you could buy on your own.

Loan Calculations

Total of Payments. Total you will have paid after you make all payments of principal, interest, mortgage insurance, and loan costs, as scheduled.	$285,803.36
Finance Charge. The dollar amount the loan will cost you.	$118,830.27
Amount Financed. The loan amount available after paying your upfront finance charge.	$162,000.00
Annual Percentage Rate (APR). Your costs over the loan term expressed as a rate. This is not your interest rate.	4.174%
Total Interest Percentage (TIP). The total amount of interest that you will pay over the loan term as a percentage of your loan amount.	69.46%

Questions? If you have questions about the loan terms or costs on this form, use the contact information below. To get more information or make a complaint, contact the Consumer Financial Protection Bureau at **www.consumerfinance.gov/mortgage-closing**

Other Disclosures

Appraisal
If the property was appraised for your loan, your lender is required to give you a copy at no additional cost at least 3 days before closing. If you have not yet received it, please contact your lender at the information listed below.

Contract Details
See your note and security instrument for information about
• what happens if you fail to make your payments,
• what is a default on the loan,
• situations in which your lender can require early repayment of the loan, and
• the rules for making payments before they are due.

Liability after Foreclosure
If your lender forecloses on this property and the foreclosure does not cover the amount of unpaid balance on this loan,

☒ state law may protect you from liability for the unpaid balance. If you refinance or take on any additional debt on this property, you may lose this protection and have to pay any debt remaining even after foreclosure. You may want to consult a lawyer for more information.

☐ state law does not protect you from liability for the unpaid balance.

Refinance
Refinancing this loan will depend on your future financial situation, the property value, and market conditions. You may not be able to refinance this loan.

Tax Deductions
If you borrow more than this property is worth, the interest on the loan amount above this property's fair market value is not deductible from your federal income taxes. You should consult a tax advisor for more information.

Contact Information

	Lender	Mortgage Broker	Real Estate Broker (B)	Real Estate Broker (S)	Settlement Agent
Name	Ficus Bank		Omega Real Estate Broker Inc.	Alpha Real Estate Broker Co.	Epsilon Title Co.
Address	4321 Random Blvd. Somecity, ST 12340		789 Local Lane Sometown, ST 12345	987 Suburb Ct. Someplace, ST 12340	123 Commerce Pl. Somecity, ST 12344
NMLS ID					
ST License ID			Z765416	Z61456	Z61616
Contact	Joe Smith		Samuel Green	Joseph Cain	Sarah Arnold
Contact NMLS ID	12345				
Contact ST License ID			P16415	P51461	PT1234
Email	joesmith@ ficusbank.com		sam@omegare.biz	joe@alphare.biz	sarah@ epsilontitle.com
Phone	123-456-7890		123-555-1717	321-555-7171	987-555-4321

Confirm Receipt

By signing, you are only confirming that you have received this form. You do not have to accept this loan because you have signed or received this form.

_____ _____   _____ _____
Applicant Signature   Date   Co-Applicant Signature   Date

Loans That Continue to Use the GFE and the HUD-1 Statement
- Home-equity lines of credit (HELOCs)
- Reverse mortgages
- Mortgages secured by a mobile home or a dwelling that is not attached to real property

As a side note, if the transaction is an all-cash sale, a commercial sale, or an investment sale not subject to RESPA, then the buyer, seller, and settlement agent are not required to use the integrated disclosure forms. In general, the HUD-1, Closing Disclosure, or any other settlement statement can be used in cash transactions. [12 CFR §1026.19(e)(f)].

Timing of the Disclosures

RESPA requires that borrowers receive disclosures at various times—when a borrower submits a loan application, before the closing, during settlement, and after the closing. These disclosures spell out the costs associated with the settlement, outline lender servicing and escrow account practices, and describe business relationships between settlement service providers.

Disclosures at the Time of Loan Application

When a potential homebuyer applies for a home loan, the lender must give the buyer a special information booklet, the Loan Estimate, and a Mortgage Servicing Disclosure Statement.

The disclosures must be provided at the time a written application is submitted, or no later than 3 business days after the application is received. However, if the application is denied before the end of the 3-business day period (or the application is withdrawn), the loan originator is not required to provide the disclosures.

Special Information Booklet

Lenders must provide a copy of a **Special Information Booklet** to borrowers who apply for a purchase loan secured by real property. Beginning October 3, 2015 the CFPB booklet "*Your Home Loan Toolkit*" (Toolkit) must be provided. The Toolkit is designed for use in connection with the Loan Estimate and Closing Disclosure forms. However, the Toolkit booklet does not need to be provided for refinancing transactions, a closed-end loan secured by a subordinate lien, or a reverse mortgage.

If the borrower is applying for a Home Equity Line of Credit (HELOC), the lender can instead provide a copy of the brochure entitled, "*When Your Home is On the Line: Lines of Credit.*"

The Special Information Booklet must be provided to the borrower at the time a written application is submitted, or no later than 3 business days after the application is received. The booklet does not need to be provided if the lender denies the application or the application is withdrawn. For multiple applicants, the lender may provide a copy of the special information booklet to just one of them. If used, the mortgage broker must provide the special information booklet instead of the lender.

Loan Estimate

The Loan Estimate replaces the early Truth in Lending statement and the Good Faith Estimate. It summarizes key loan terms and gives an estimate of loan and closing costs. The lender is generally required to provide the Loan Estimate within 3 business days of the receipt of the borrower's loan application. Lenders must allow applicants to have a **7-business day waiting period** after mailing or delivering the Loan Estimate prior to closing the loan.

Borrowers may modify or waive the 7-day waiting period if they can show that it is a bona fide personal financial emergency. Lenders are advised to follow strict procedures for proper documentation and borrower signatures. For purchase transactions that a "time is of the essence" clause, the closing date should be amended to accommodate the full waiver requirements.

Mortgage Servicing Disclosure Statement

The **Mortgage Servicing Disclosure Statement** states whether the lender intends to sell the real estate loan servicing immediately, if the loan servicing can be sold at any time during the life of the loan, and the percentage of loans the lender has sold previously. The lender must also provide information about servicing procedures, transfer practices, and complaint resolution. The borrower may file a complaint with the CFPB at www.consumerfinance.gov/complaint/process.

Disclosures Before Closing Occurs

If information in the Loan Estimate substantially changes, the lender must provide the borrower with a **revised Loan Estimate**.

Reasons Lenders Revise Loan Estimates

- Changed circumstances affecting the settlement charges.
- Changed circumstances affecting eligibility of the borrower.
- Revision is requested by the borrower.
- Interest rate dependent charges. The points can change because the interest rate is not locked.
- Expiration. The borrower expresses the intent to proceed with the transaction more than 10 business days after the original disclosures.

The general rule is that the lender must deliver or mail the revised Loan Estimate to the borrower no later than 3 business days after receiving the information that required the revision in the Loan Estimate. [12 CFR §1026.19(e)(4)(i-)].

Example: ABC Mortgage requires pest inspections before making loans. The pest inspection company (unaffiliated) hired to inspect the property informs ABC Mortgage on Tuesday that the subject property contains evidence of termite damage, requiring a further inspection. The cost of the additional inspection will cause an increase in estimated settlement charges by more than 10%. Because of this increase, ABC Mortgage must provide revised disclosures to the borrower by Friday to meet the 3-business day requirement.

An **Affiliated Business Arrangement Disclosure** is required whenever a settlement service refers a buyer to a firm with which the service has any kind of business connection, such as common ownership. Usually, the service cannot require the buyer to use a connected firm.

Delivering the Closing Disclosure

The Closing Disclosure has the final settlement charges that need to be paid by both the buyer and the seller.

Lenders must ensure that BORROWERS receive the Closing Disclosure at least **3 business days before consummation** (the day the loan closes). [12 CFR §1026.19(f)(1)(ii)(A)].

Consummation occurs when the borrower becomes contractually obligated to the lender on the loan, not, for example, when the borrower becomes contractually obligated to a seller on a real estate transaction. [12 CFR §1026.2(a)(13)].

The seller's Closing Disclosure must be provided to the seller **at or before consummation.**

Disclosures During Settlement

The **Closing Disclosure** must show the actual charges at settlement. In addition, an **Initial Escrow Statement** is required at closing or within 45 days of closing. This statement itemizes estimated taxes, insurance premiums, and other charges to be paid from the escrow account during the first year of the loan.

Disclosures After the Closing

The servicer must deliver an **Annual Escrow Loan Statement** to the borrower. This statement summarizes all escrow account deposits and payments during the past year. It also notifies the borrower of any shortages or surpluses in the account and tells the borrower how these can be paid or refunded. A **Servicing Transfer Statement** is required if the servicer transfers the servicing rights for a loan to another servicer.

Overview of the Loan Estimate

For closed-end credit transactions secured by real property (other than reverse mortgages), the lender is required to provide the borrower with good-faith estimates of credit costs and transaction terms on the **Loan Estimate**.

Requirements for Loan Estimates

- Loan Estimate must be in writing.
- Loan Estimate must contain a good faith estimate of credit costs and transaction terms.
- The lender must deliver the Loan Estimate or place it in the mail no later than the third business day after receiving the application.
- If a mortgage broker receives a borrower's application, either the lender or the mortgage broker may provide the Loan Estimate. A lender can rely on a mortgage broker to deliver the Loan Estimate; but the lender remains responsible for its accuracy.
- Lenders generally may not issue revisions to Loan Estimates because they later discover technical errors, miscalculations, or underestimations of charges. Lenders can issue revised Loan Estimates only in certain situations such as when changed circumstances result in increased charges.

Model Loan Estimate Forms

The CFPB published model Loan Estimate Forms for different types of closed-end mortgage products, including fixed-rate loans, interest only adjustable-rate loans, loan refinances, and loans with balloon payments and negative amortization. The new three-page Loan Estimate integrates at least seven pages of disclosures currently required under various federal laws. The format of the Loan Estimate and the required content and disclosures are described in 12 CFR §1026.37.

Page 1 of the Loan Estimate

The top of page 1 of the Loan Estimate includes the name and address of the lender. It also includes the title "Loan Estimate" and the statement "Save this Loan Estimate to compare with your Closing Disclosure."

The applicant's name, property address, and sales price are written in the upper left side of the form. The upper right side has space to state the type of loan, its term, purpose, ID number, and whether it has a rate lock.

Main Sections of Page 1 of the Loan Estimate

- Loan Terms table
- Projected Payments table
- Costs at Closing table

Page 2 of the Loan Estimate

Page 2 of the Loan Estimate includes closing cost details. For transactions with adjustable payments or adjustable interest rates, an Adjustable Payment (AP) table or an Adjustable Interest Rate (AIR) table is provided.

Main Sections of Page 2 of the Loan Estimate

- Loan Costs table
- Other Costs table
- Calculating Cash to Close table
- Adjustable Payment (AP) table
- Adjustable Interest Rate (AIR) table

Page 3 of the Loan Estimate

Page 3 of the Loan Estimate provides additional information about the loan.

Main Sections of Page 3 of the Loan Estimate

- Contact information
- Comparisons table
- Other Considerations table
- Confirmation Receipt of the Form

Overview of the Closing Disclosure

For loans that require a Loan Estimate and that go to closing, lenders must provide borrowers with a final disclosure reflecting the actual terms of the transaction called the **Closing Disclosure**. The Closing Disclosure contains general requirements, integrates sample disclosure forms, and contains additional disclosure information.

General Requirements

Under the TRID rule's general requirements, the lender must provide the borrower with the Closing Disclosure Form at least 3 business days before consummation of the loan.

> Consummation may occur at the same time as settlement (closing), but it is a legally distinct event.

When a borrower becomes contractually obligated to the lender on the loan depends on state law. Therefore, lenders and settlement agents should verify the applicable state laws to determine when consummation actually will occur, and make sure delivery of the Closing Disclosure occurs at least 3 business days before this event.

The Closing Disclosure generally must contain the **actual terms and costs of the transaction**. Lenders may estimate disclosures using the best information reasonably available when the actual term or cost is not reasonably available to the lender at the time the disclosure is made. However, lenders must act in good faith and use due diligence in obtaining the information.

Model Closing Disclosure Forms

As is the case for the Loan Estimate, the CFPB created sample Closing Disclosure Forms for different mortgage transaction scenarios, including closing on a fixed-rate loan, closing with funds from a simultaneous second-lien loan, closing on a refinance transaction, and closing on transactions with various changes in closing costs.

The five-page Closing Disclosure Form integrates at least nine pages of new and existing disclosures under RESPA, TILA, and Dodd-Frank amendments to TILA. The Closing Disclosure must be in writing and contain the information prescribed in 12 CFR §1026.38(a) through (s) as shown in **Model Form H-25**.

Page 1 of the Closing Disclosure

The top of page 1 of the Closing Disclosure includes general information about the transaction—closing information, transaction information, and loan information. It also includes the statement "This form is a statement of final loan terms and closing costs. Compare this document with your Loan Estimate."

Main Sections of Page 1 of the Closing Disclosure
- Loan Terms table
- Projected Payments table
- Costs at Closing table

Page 2 of the Closing Disclosure
- Loan Costs table
- Other Costs table

NOTE: The number of items in the Loan Costs and Other Costs tables can be expanded and deleted to accommodate the disclosure of additional line items. Items that must be disclosed, even if they are not charged to the borrower, cannot be deleted. Loan costs and other costs tables can be disclosed on two separate pages if the page cannot accommodate all the costs required to be disclosed on one page.

Page 3 of the Closing Disclosure
- The Calculating Cash to Close table
- Summaries of Transactions Tables.

NOTE: For transactions without a seller, a Payoffs and Payments table may substitute for the Summaries of Transactions table and be placed before the alternative Calculating Cash to Close table.

Page 4 of the Closing Disclosure

Page 4 has additional information about the loan.

- Loan Disclosures
- The Adjustable Payment table (if applicable)
- Adjustable Interest Rate table (if applicable)

Page 5 of the Closing Disclosure

- The Loan Calculations table
- Other Disclosures
- Contact Information

NOTE: The Contact Information provides space for the name, address, ID number, email, and phone number for the lender, mortgage broker, real estate broker(s), and settlement agent.

SUMMARY

These laws set a standard for how individuals are to be treated in their financial dealings, including real estate.

Fair Housing

Fair housing laws make the housing market equitable. The Fair Housing Act provides anti-discriminatory protection in education, housing, and employment for 7 classes—race, color, religion, sex, national origin, familial status, and disability.

Credit

Since 1968, the number of credit protection laws has multiplied rapidly. Some of these laws are the Truth in Lending Act, the Equal Credit Opportunity Act, the Fair Credit Reporting Act, and the Fair and Accurate Credit Transaction Act. The concepts of fair and equal credit have been written into laws that prohibit unfair discrimination in credit transactions, require that consumers be told the reason credit is denied, give borrowers access to their credit records, and set up ways for consumers to settle billing disputes.

Settlement Issues

Settlement (closing) is the process by which ownership of real property or title to the property is passed from seller to buyer. The federal Real Estate Settlement

Procedures Act (RESPA) applies to all federally related home loans used to purchase or refinance real property or improved real property of one-to-four units. Certain practices are prohibited under RESPA, such as kickbacks, fee splitting, unearned fees, seller-required title insurance, and unlimited deposits into escrow accounts. Borrowers may file a complaint with the lender if they believe the lender has violated RESPA.

UNIT 3 REVIEW

Matching Exercise

Instructions: Write the letter of the matching term on the blank line before its definition. Answers are in Appendix A.

Terms

A. Americans with Disabilities Act

B. closing disclosure

C. Community Reinvestment Act

D. Consumer Financial Protection Bureau

E. covered person

F. Department of Housing and Urban Development

G. deregulation

H. Equal Credit Opportunity Act

I. Fair Credit Reporting Act

J. Fair Housing Act

K. loan estimate

L. Office of Fair Housing and Equal Opportunity

M. protected class

N. redlining

O. Regulation Z

P. Rural Development

Q. SAFE Act

R. settlement

S. TRID rule

T. U.S. Department of Agriculture

Definitions

1. _____ Act passed by congress in 1977 that encourages regulated financial institutions to serve their immediate community's needs

2. _____ The process of removing or reducing government regulations, typically in the economic sphere

3. _____ The federal act passed in 2008 that required all states to have a loan originator licensing and registration system in place by August 1, 2010

4. _____ Bureau established under Title X of the Dodd-Frank Act as an independent bureau to enforce the federal consumer financial laws, promote consumer financial education, and handle consumer complaints and inquiries

5. _____ A cabinet-level agency established in 1862 by Abraham Lincoln to oversee the American farming industry

6. _____   Division of the USDA that has been called the venture capitalist for rural America

7. _____   A cabinet-level agency designed to help Americans with their housing needs by overseeing several mortgage, grant, assistance, and regulatory programs

8. _____   The office within HUD that seeks to prevent discrimination in housing on the basis of race, sex, family status and other grounds

9. _____   Act that protects against discriminatory housing practices based on race, sex, religion, color, handicap, familial status, or national origin

10. _____   Group that is given legal protection from discrimination under federal or state law

11. _____   Illegal use of a property location to deny financing or insurance

12. _____   The act that protects individuals with disabilities by providing a guarantee of equal opportunity in public accommodations, commercial facilities, employment, transportation, state and local government services, and telecommunications

13. _____   According to the CFPB, any person (or its affiliate) that engages in offering or providing a consumer financial product or service

14. _____   Act ensuring that consumers have an equal chance to obtain credit

15. _____   Act promoting the accuracy of information collected by credit reporting agencies

16. _____   Known in some states as closing, it is the process by which ownership of real property or title to the property is passed from seller to buyer

17. _____   Regulation that implements the Truth in Lending Act

18. _____   The rule that in 2013 further amended Regulation Z as well as Regulation X and created integrated disclosures

19. _____   The document that provides borrowers with good-faith estimates of credit costs and transaction terms

20. _____   The document used at closing that lenders must provide borrowers reflecting the actual terms of the transaction

Multiple Choice Questions

Instructions: Circle your response and go to Appendix A to read the complete explanation for each question.

1. Which federal law allowed savings and loan associations to enter the business of commercial lending, trust services, and non-mortgage consumer lending?
   a. Depository Institutions Deregulation and Monetary Control Act
   b. Emergency Economic Stabilization Act
   c. Glass-Steagall Act
   d. Gramm-Leach-Bliley Act

2. Under the SAFE Act, which person would not be considered a loan originator?
   a. Mortgage loan broker who takes applications
   b. Loan officer who calls prospective borrowers to discuss loan terms
   c. Loan processor who also negotiates the terms of loans
   d. Office manager of a mortgage company

3. The Equal Credit Opportunity Act (ECOA) is implemented by:
   a. the Board of Governors.
   b. Regulation Z.
   c. Regulation B.
   d. the Board of Directors of NAR.

4. The _____ establishes procedures for correcting mistakes on a person's credit record and requires that a consumer's record only be provided for legitimate business needs.
   a. Rights to Financial Privacy Act
   b. Fair Trade Commission Act
   c. Fair Credit Reporting Act
   d. Home Equity Loan Consumer Protection Act

5. Which statement is not a purpose of the Real Estate Settlement Procedures Act?
   a. Help consumers get fair settlement services by requiring that key service costs be disclosed in advance
   b. Protect consumers by prohibiting certain practices that increase the cost of settlement services
   c. Protect consumers by eliminating kickbacks and referral fees that unnecessarily increase the costs of settlement services
   d. Disclose the APR for a loan

6. The federal Truth in Lending Act (TILA) is Title 1 of the:
   a. Consumer Credit Protection Act.
   b. Real Estate Settlement Procedures Act (RESPA).
   c. Equal Credit Opportunity Act (ECOA).
   d. Community Reinvestment Act.

7. Under TILA, which of the following is not included in the finance charge for a real estate loan?
   a. Loan fees
   b. Mortgage insurance fees
   c. Credit report fees
   d. Finder fees

8. Which of the following mortgages is covered by the TRID rule and must use the loan estimate or closing disclosure?
   a. Closed-end federally related residential mortgage
   b. HELOC
   c. Manufactured home loan
   d. Reverse mortgage

9. The lender is generally required to provide the Loan Estimate within how many business days of the receipt of the borrower's loan application?
   a. 1
   b. 3
   c. 7
   d. 10

10. Lenders must ensure that borrowers receive the Closing Disclosure:
    a. at or before consummation.
    b. at least 3 business days before consummation
    c. at least 3 business days before closing the transaction.
    d. at least 1 business days before closing the transaction.

The Mortgage Markets

Unit 4

INTRODUCTION

A **market** is a medium that allows buyers and sellers of specific assets or services to interact in order to facilitate an exchange. In any discussion of markets, it is helpful to distinguish primary markets from secondary markets. **Primary markets** are markets where buyers and sellers negotiate and transact business directly, without any intermediary such as resellers. **Secondary markets** are markets in which previously issued financial instruments are bought and sold. A robust secondary market increases the liquidity and ultimately the value of the underlying assets being traded. There are secondary markets for stocks, bonds, mortgages, and other types of debt such as auto loans, credit card debt, and corporate debt.

Simply put, real estate loans are originated in the primary mortgage market and then bought and sold in the secondary mortgage market. The interaction between the primary and secondary mortgage markets is the foundation of the mortgage lending process and is an essential part of our national economic health. Because of the mortgage markets, the real estate lending industry has expanded to over $9 trillion in residential mortgage debt outstanding (MDO). [Federal Reserve]. In fact, the total real estate debt in the country is the largest in the world, second only to the debt of the United States government.

The mortgage markets are made up of the institutions that originate loans (primary mortgage market) and the markets in which they are transferred (secondary mortgage market). The secondary mortgage market's main function is to get money to lenders in the primary market so they can loan it to consumers. These markets facilitate the flow of funds for residential financing.

Learning Objectives

After completing this Unit, you should be able to:

4A   specify the purpose of the mortgage markets.

4B   identify the participants in the mortgage markets.

4C   recognize the types of mortgage-backed securities.

4D   indicate how REMICs are structured.

4E   recall the functions of the housing GSEs - Fannie Mae and Freddie Mac.

4F   recall the functions of Ginnie Mae.

4G   recall the purpose of Farmer Mac and identify its programs.

INTRODUCTION TO THE MORTGAGE MARKETS

The real estate lending industry is comprised of two distinct markets—the primary mortgage market and the secondary mortgage market. The **primary mortgage market** is the market in which mortgage originators provide loans to borrowers. The **secondary mortgage market** channels liquidity into the primary market by purchasing loans from the lenders.

Purpose of the Mortgage Markets

Why is there a secondary mortgage market? Historically, the loan origination, underwriting, and loan servicing were handled under one roof.

> For example, the lender advertised its loan terms, and a loan officer would meet with a loan applicant and "underwrite" the risk of making the loan. The lender (bank or thrift) would lend savings deposit dollars so the borrower could buy a house, make improvements, or refinance an existing loan. Then the institution's staff would monitor the borrower's payment activity and take action if payments were missed.

The existence of an active secondary mortgage market allows an organization to specialize in one of these areas, toward becoming more efficient and producing greater value for mortgage borrowers.

The purpose of the mortgage markets is to create a continuous flow of money to borrowers. This stimulates the real estate industry and financial markets.

Overview of the Primary Mortgage Market

The **primary mortgage market** is the market in which lenders originate real estate loans directly to borrowers. Participants in the primary mortgage market include commercial banks, thrifts, mortgage companies, and other financial intermediaries. These lenders are discussed in the next unit.

These institutions provide money to qualified borrowers. The borrower is seeking financing in order to make a purchase or to refinance an existing loan. Lenders help consumers by identifying the appropriate loan for the borrower, helping to complete the loan application, and gathering the necessary documentation required to underwrite the loan. A loan that meets the lender's criteria is closed and funded.

Depository institutions, such as commercial banks and credit unions, make their money by lending at a higher interest rate than the interest rate paid to their depositors or paid to borrow from the Fed. The goal of all lenders is to make a profit. The lender is looking for a loan that is an investment that can be held or sold.

Lenders earn income on the loans they originate in several ways—up-front finance charges, loan fees, interest from the loan, servicing fees, and selling the loan. Up-front finance charges, such as points and fees, increase the lender's yield on the loan. **Points**, or discount points, are calculated as a percentage of the loan amount. One point equals one percentage point. Therefore, 2 points on a $100,000 loan is $2,000. **Loan origination fees** or funding fees are typically one or two points of the amount of the loan. The income the lender derives from this source is called the mortgage yield. **Mortgage yield** is the amount received or returned from real estate loan portfolios expressed as a percentage.

Much of the lenders' income is from the loan fees. Some lenders sell their loans as soon as possible to the secondary mortgage market to obtain more money. This enables the lender to make more loans and collect more loan fees.

Loan servicing lenders receive fees for collecting payments from the borrower on behalf of the loan originator or subsequent noteholder. A **loan servicer** collects payments from borrowers, subtracts fees, and sends the balance of the money to investors who own the loans. The servicer is in charge of collecting payments, handling escrows for taxes and insurance, making payments to the mortgage investor, and administering a loan after it has been made.

Overview of the Secondary Mortgage Market

The **secondary mortgage market** is the the market where mortgage loans and servicing rights are bought and sold between mortgage originators, mortgage aggregators (securitizers), and investors. In contrast to the primary mortgage market, in which lending institutions make mortgage loans directly to borrowers, the secondary mortgage market can be seen as a resale marketplace for loans, in which existing loans are bought and sold. Participants in the secondary mortgage market do not originate loans.

The secondary mortgage market connects lenders, homebuyers, and investors in a single, efficient system that benefits homebuyers in many ways.

Benefits to Homebuyers

- Keeping mortgage rates lower.
- Enabling interest rates for mortgage loans to be similar across the country, in good times and bad.
- Making mortgage loans with longer terms, such as 15 and 30 years, available to borrowers.
- Putting homeownership within reach of more of America's qualified homebuyers.
- Allowing borrowers to refinance at any time without penalty, in most cases.

Without a secondary market, the only institutions originating mortgage loans are those with the capacity to hold them permanently, called **portfolio lenders**. Because portfolio lenders hold the loans, they generally restrict their loans to "A-quality" borrowers, in large part because of regulatory concerns about their safety and soundness.

Before the secondary mortgage market was established, only larger banks had sufficient funds to keep a mortgage for the life of the loan, typically 15 or 30 years. In small cities, borrowers could obtain mortgage loans from a few local banks or savings and loan associations. As a result, potential homebuyers had a more difficult time finding mortgage lenders. Since there was less competition between lenders, they could charge higher interest rates.

The secondary mortgage market exists because commercial banks and thrifts needed to be able to sell their assets quickly when they needed more money, particularly in a market in which consumers are demanding more home loans. In the past, the bulk of a financial institution's resources consisted of depositor's funds, which were tied up in long-term mortgage loans. These funds were not particularly convenient as a source of quick money because of the perceived risk of default or unsoundness by creditors who might be located a continent away from the collateral of the loan in question. To make matters worse, there were areas of the country with a greater supply of capital in the form of deposits, which resulted in excess money with nowhere to spend it. Another area of the country would have a greater demand for mortgage loans but no money to lend because of lack of deposits. Because lending institutions were unable to buy and sell mortgages easily, the supply and demand for money was always uncoordinated.

The solution was to create a mortgage market in which loans could be bought and sold without difficulty. This allowed funds to be moved from capital-surplus areas to capital-needy areas and created a stable market.

America has a secondary mortgage market that attracts capital from around the world to finance a wide range of mortgage products designed specifically to make homeownership affordable and accessible. No other country has a comparable secondary mortgage market.

Participants in the Mortgage Markets

The participants in the mortgage markets are the mortgage loan originators, aggregators, securities dealers (brokerage firms and investment banks), and investors. The participants will be introduced here and explained more fully later in the unit.

Residential Loan Originators

Residential mortgage lenders (loan originators) are part of the primary mortgage market. They originate and fund loans to borrowers. Primary mortgage market lenders include commercial banks, thrifts, mortgage bankers, credit unions, and others. A **mortgage banker** is a direct lender that lends its own money, whose principal business is the origination and funding of loans secured by real property. Once a loan is originated, lenders have a choice. Either they can hold the mortgage in their own portfolios or they can sell the mortgages to secondary market issuers. A **portfolio lender** is a lender that not only originates mortgage loans, but also holds a portfolio of their loans instead of selling them off in the secondary mortgage market. About half of all new single-family mortgages originated today are sold to secondary market issuers. When lenders sell their mortgages, they replenish their funds so they can turn around and lend more money to home buyers.

Depending on the size and sophistication of the originator, it might aggregate mortgages for a certain period of time before selling the whole package, or it might sell individual loans as they are originated.

In contrast, a **mortgage broker** originates loans with the intention of brokering them to lending institutions. Both mortgage bankers and mortgage brokers are **loan originators** who take residential mortgage loan applications and offer or negotiate terms of a residential mortgage loan for compensation or gain.

In general, mortgage originators make money through the fees that are charged to originate a mortgage and the difference between the interest rate given to a borrower and the premium a secondary market investor will pay for that interest rate.

Aggregators (Issuers)

An **aggregator** (issuer) is a party involved within the secondary mortgage market that purchases mortgages from financial institutions and then securitizes them into mortgage-backed securities (MBS).

> **Securitization** is the process of creating securities by pooling together various cash flow producing financial assets. These securities are then sold to investors.

Aggregators are large mortgage originators with ties to Wall Street firms and Government-Sponsored Enterprises (GSEs), like Fannie Mae and Freddie Mac. Aggregators purchase newly originated mortgages from smaller originators, and along with their own originations, form pools of mortgages that they either securitize into private label mortgage-backed securities (by working with Wall Street firms) or into Fannie Mae/Freddie Mac mortgage-backed securities (by working through the GSEs).

Aggregators earn a profit by the difference in the price that they pay for mortgages and the price for which they can sell the MBSs backed by those mortgages.

Securities Dealers

After mortgage-backed securities (MBSs) are formed, they are sold to a securities dealer. Most Wall Street securities brokerage firms have MBS trading desks. Dealers do all kinds of creative things with MBS and mortgage whole loans. The end goal is to sell securities to investors. Dealers frequently use MBSs to structure collaterized mortgage obligations (CMO) investments. The CMOs can be structured to have different and somewhat definite prepayment characteristics and enhanced credit ratings compared to the underlying MBS or whole loans. Securities dealers make a spread in the price at which they buy and sell MBS, and look to make profits in the way they structure CMOs.

Investors

Investors are the end users of mortgages. Hedge funds, pension funds, investment funds, commercial banks, life insurance companies, foreign goventments, and GSEs invest in mortgage-backed securities. Foreign governments, pension funds, insurance companies, and banks typically invest in high-credit rated mortgage products. Hedge funds are typically big investors in low-credit rated mortgage products and structured mortgage products that have greater interest rate risk. Of all the mortgage investors, the GSEs have the largest portfolios. The type of mortgage product they can invest in is largely regulated by the Federal Housing Finance Agency. These investors supply the capital needed to make loans that, otherwise, might not be available.

Products Offered in the Secondary Mortgage Market

The investment that is bought and sold in the secondary mortgage market is an asset called a mortgage-backed security. Mortgage-backed securities (MBS) or mortgage-related securities (MRS) are debt issues collateralized by the mortgages. A **mortgage-backed security (MBS)** is a type of asset-backed security that is protected by a collection of mortgages usually with similar characteristics. The mortgages are pooled and secured against the issue of bonds. MBS carry the guarantee of the issuing organization to pay interest and principal payments on their mortgage-backed securities.

> For example, an aggregator making home mortgages might pool $10 million worth of the mortgages into MBSs and sell them to a federal government agency like Ginnie Mae or a government sponsored-enterprise (GSE) such as Fannie Mae or Freddie Mac, or to a securities firm to be used as the collateral for the new MBS.

The majority of MBSs are issued or guaranteed by an agency of the U.S. government such as Ginnie Mae, or by GSEs, including Fannie Mae and Freddie Mac. Although Ginnie Mae's guarantee is backed by the "full faith and credit" of the U.S. government, those issued by GSEs are not.

A third group of MBSs is issued by private firms. These "private label" MBS are issued by subsidiaries of investment banks and financial institutions whose credit-worthiness and rating may be much lower than that of Ginnie Mae or the GSEs.

Most bonds backed by mortgages are classified as mortgage-backed securities (MBS). This can be confusing because some securities derived from MBS are also called MBS. The qualifier pass-through is used to distinguish the basic MBS bond from other mortgage-backed instruments. The value of MBS is based on the underlying pool of residential mortgages.

Securitization provides liquidity to originators of real estate loans. Securitization is the pooling and repackaging of cash flow that turns financial assets into securities that are then sold to investors. Any asset that has a cash flow can be securitized.

Before securitization became prevalent, banks funded real estate loans with their customers' deposits (savings). The availability of credit was dictated, in part, by the amount of bank deposits. Banks were essentially portfolio lenders. They held loans until they matured or were paid off. However, after World War II, depository institutions simply could not keep pace with the rising demand for housing credit. Asset securitization began with the structured financing of mortgage pools in the 1970s, which are called mortgage-backed securities (MBS).

Today, banks and other lenders have the option of retaining the real estate loans they originate or purchase, or they may sell them to issuers in the secondary market where loans are pooled. These pools can be used to back bond issues, package as mortgage-backed securities, or retain as an investment.

Types of Mortgage-Backed Securities

The two most common types of mortgage-backed securities are pass-through securities and collateralized-mortgage obligations.

Pass-Through Securities

The simplest mortgage-backed securities are **pass-through securities**. The pass-through or participation certificate represents direct ownership in a pool of mortgages. They are called pass-throughs because the principal and interest of the underlying loans are passed directly through to investors. Each investor owns a pro-rata share of all principal and interest payments made into the pool as the issuer receives monthly payments from borrowers. Pass-through securities are comprised of mortgages with the same maturity and interest rate.

A residential mortgage-backed security (RMBS) is a pass-through MBS that is backed by mortgages on residential property. A commercial mortgage-backed security (CMBS) is a pass-through MBS that is backed by mortgages on commercial property.

Collateralized Mortgage Obligations

Collateralized mortgage obligations (CMOs), a type of MBS, are bonds that represent claims to specific cash flows from large pools of home mortgages. The streams of principal and interest payments on the mortgages are distributed to the different classes of CMO interests, known as tranches. Some CMOs are backed by pools of mortgage-backed securities that are issued by another agency such as Fannie Mae, instead of a mortgage pool.

REMICs

As a result of a change in the 1986 Tax Reform Act, most CMOs are issued in **REMIC** (Real Estate Mortgage Investment Conduit) form to create certain tax advantages for the issuer. A **Real Estate Mortgage Investment Conduit (REMIC)** is a mortgage securities vehicle authorized by the Tax Reform Act of 1986 that holds commercial and residential mortgages in trust, and issues securities representing an undivided interest in these mortgages. A REMIC, which can be a corporation, trust, association, or partnership, assembles mortgages into pools and issues pass-through certificates, multiclass bonds similar to a Collateralized Mortgage Obligation (CMO), or other securities to investors in the secondary mortgage market. To qualify as a REMIC, an organization makes an "election" to do so by filing a Form 1066 with the Internal Revenue Service, and by meeting certain other requirements. The federal income taxation of REMICs is governed primarily under 26 U.S.C. §§860A–860G of Part IV of Subchapter M of Chapter 1 of Subtitle A of the Internal Revenue Code (26 U.S.C.). They were introduced in 1987 as the typical vehicle for the securitization of residential mortgages.

In a REMIC, the cash flow from the underlying mortgage-related collateral is directed to several classes, wherein each class may have a different pass-through rate, average life, prepayment sensitivity, and final maturity from other classes in the same REMIC. Investors with different investment strategies can invest in a class that satisfies their investment and portfolio needs. Classes are distinguished by their sensitivity to the prepayment risk of the underlying mortgage-related collateral.

Collateral for REMICs includes single-family or multi-family mortgage-backed securities (MBSs), stripped mortgage- backed securities (SMBS), classes from other REMICs, and whole loans (single-family or multifamily).

Sequential Pay CMO

In a sequential pay CMO, issuers distribute cash flow to bondholders from a series of classes, called tranches. A **tranche** is a part or segment of a structured security. A security may have more than one tranche, each with different risks and maturities. Each tranche consists of MBS with similar maturity dates or interest rates and is different from the other tranches within the CMO. For example, a CMO can have three tranches with MBS that mature in five, seven, and 20 years each.

Stripped Mortgage-Backed Security

Stripped Mortgage-Backed Securities (SMBS) are pass-through securities that are created by separating—or stripping apart—the principal and interest payments from underlying mortgage assets that back standard mortgage-backed securities, REMIC certificates, previously issued SMBS certificates, or other mortgage-related assets.

A **principal-only stripped mortgage-backed security (PO)** is a bond with cash flows that are backed by the principal repayment component of a property owner's mortgage payments. Because principal-only bonds sell at a discount, they are zero coupon bonds. A **zero coupon bond** is a bond that pays no coupons, is sold at a deep discount to its face value, and matures to its face value. These bonds satisfy investors who are worried that mortgage prepayments might force them to re-invest their money when interest rates are lower.

An **interest-only stripped mortgage-backed security (IO)** is a bond with cash flows that are backed by the interest component of the property owner's mortgage payments. IO bonds change in value based on interest rate movements.

Default Risk

The risk of mortgage-backed securities depends on the likelihood that the borrower will pay the promised cash flows (principal and interest) on time. Pooling many mortgages with similar characteristics creates a bond with a low risk of default. **Default risk** is the borrower's inability to meet interest payment obligations on time. Lenders pool mortgages by their interest rate and date of maturity. Additionally, mortgages are pooled by the initial credit quality of the borrower. Pools are comprised of prime, Alt-A, and subprime loans.

> **Prime**: Conforming mortgages, prime borrowers, full documentation (such as verification of income and assets), and strong credit scores

> **Alt-A**: Non-conforming mortgage (such as vacation home), generally prime borrowers, less documentation

> **Subprime**: Non-conforming mortgage, borrowers with weaker credit scores, and no documentation

Some mortgage-backed securities have guarantees against the risk of borrower default. Mortgage-backed securities guaranteed by Ginnie Mae are backed with the full faith and credit of the U.S. Federal government. Fannie Mae and Freddie Mac use lines of credit with the U.S. Treasury Department to guarantee the MBS they issue.

Process

The original lender makes loans to borrowers. Rather than keep the loans, the lender sells them to one of the aggregators. This gives the original lender more money to make loans to more borrowers while decreasing borrowing costs.

Issuers purchase existing mortgages with funds they have acquired by issuing bonds or other types of debt instruments. Through securitization, the mortgages they buy are formed into mortgage pools and used as security for those debt instruments. A **mortgage pool** is a group of mortgages that usually have the same interest rate and term. The **debt instruments**, which are known as mortgage-backed securities, are collateralized by the mortgage pool.

MBS that represent shares in these pooled mortgages are sold to investors in the capital market by the issuer, securities dealers, or investment bankers. The large companies that deal in mortgage-backed securities include Cantor Fitzgerald & Co., Citigroup Global Markets Inc., Credit Suisse, and Morgan Stanley, among others.

Originating lenders use the proceeds secured from selling loans to secondary mortgage market to fund new mortgages. This continuously replenishes the funds available for lending to home buyers. Just as the stock market has put investor capital to work for corporations, the secondary mortgage market puts private investor capital to work for home buyers. Repeating this cycle increases the availability, accessibility, and affordability of mortgage funds for low- and middle-income Americans. This mortgage market cycle is illustrated in the following graphic.

Secondary Money Market Cash Flow

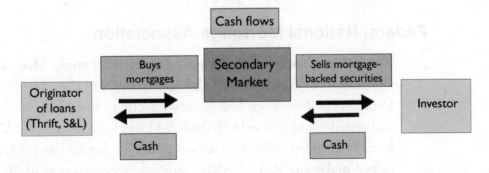

PARTICIPANTS IN THE SECONDARY MORTGAGE MARKET

The major participants in the secondary mortgage market are the Federal National Mortgage Association (Fannie Mae) and the Federal Home Loan Mortgage Corporation (Freddie Mac). Fannie Mae and Freddie Mac dominate the secondary mortgage market because the government provides them with both implicit and explicit subsidies, helping these organizations to reduce their funding costs. Both Fannie Mae and Freddie Mac are congressionally chartered, shareholder-owned corporations commonly known as government-sponsored enterprises (GSEs). They provide stability, liquidity, and affordability to the nation's housing finance system under all economic conditions. They stimulate the housing market, which comprises 10% of the economy. Low and moderate-income families are able to get a higher standard of living in the form of home ownership.

Housing GSEs

The housing GSEs are Fannie Mae (Federal National Mortgage Association), Freddie Mac (Federal Home Loan Mortgage Corporation), and the Federal Home Loan Bank System (FHLBank System), which currently consists of 11 Federal Home Loan Banks (FHLBanks). The
housing GSEs are critical in providing liquidity, stability, and affordability to the mortgage market, particularly for long-term, fixed-rate mortgages. The Federal Home Loan Bank System was discussed previously. This unit discusses the role of Fannie Mae and Freddie Mac in the secondary mortgage market.

Federal National Mortgage Association

The **Federal National Mortgage Association (Fannie Mae)** was created by Congress in 1938 to bolster the housing industry in the aftermath of the Great Depression. It does not lend money directly to home buyers. Initially, it was authorized to buy and sell FHA-insured loans from lenders, but VA-guaranteed loans were added in 1944. This secondary market for the FHA and VA loans helped make sure that affordable mortgage money was available for people in communities all across America and helped fuel the housing boom in the 1950s. Its role was expanded in 1972, when Fannie Mae was permitted to buy and sell conventional mortgages. This made Fannie Mae the largest investor in the secondary mortgage market.

In 1968, the Federal National Mortgage Association was divided into two entities—the Federal National Mortgage Association and the Government Housing Mortgage Association (Ginnie Mae). Fannie Mae became a stockholder company that operated with private capital on a self-sustaining basis, but Ginnie Mae) remained a government agency.

Through the years, Fannie Mae has consistently been one of the nation's largest sources of financing for home mortgages. Fannie Mae's common and preferred stock trades on the OTC Bulletin Board under FNMA. Fannie Mae is committed to make the American dream of homeownership possible by expanding opportunities for homeownership and by helping lenders reach out and serve more first-time homebuyers.

Fannie Mae supports the secondary mortgage market by issuing mortgage-related securities and purchasing mortgages. Fannie Mae buys loans from lenders who conform to their guidelines and, by doing so, puts mortgage money back into the system so lenders can make more loans. For more information about Fannie Mae go to http:/www.fanniemae.com.

Overview of Products

Fannie Mae pools loans that generally conform to Fannie Mae standards and issues mortgage backed securities (MBSs) backed by those loans. When a MBS is issued, Fannie Mae guarantees to the MBS trust that Fannie Mae will supplement amounts received by the trust as required to permit timely payment of principal and interest on the MBS certificates.

Single-Family Mortgage-Backed Securities (MBS)

Fannie Mae creates MBS that represent beneficial ownership interests in a pool of mortgage loans secured by single-family (1-4 units) residential properties. An individual Single-Family MBS pool may hold mortgage loans that are either fixed-rate or adjustable-rate loans but will not hold both fixed-rate and adjustable-rate loans.

Creating a Single-Family MBS begins with a mortgage loan. The loan is made by a financial institution or other lender to a borrower to finance or refinance the purchase of a home or other property with 1 to 4 residential units. These loans are made to borrowers under varying terms (e.g., 15-year, 30-year, fixed-rate, adjustable-rate, etc.); during the life of the loan, the balance is generally amortized, or reduced, until it is paid off. The borrower usually repays the loan in monthly installments that typically include both principal and interest.

Single-Family MBS may be placed into Megas, REMICs, SMBS, or other Structured Transactions mortgage-related securities.

Multifamily Mortgage-Backed Securities (MBS)

Fannie Mae creates MBS that represent beneficial ownership interests in a pool of mortgage loans secured by multifamily (5 or more units) residential properties. An individual Multifamily MBS pool may hold one or more mortgage loans that are either fixed-rate or adjustable-rate loans but will not hold both fixed-rate and adjustable-rate loans.

Creating a Multifamily MBS begins with a mortgage loan made by a financial institution or other lender to a borrower to finance or refinance the purchase of a multifamily property (e.g., an apartment building, seniors housing facility, manufactured housing community, cooperative property). Many multifamily properties qualify as affordable housing properties.

Multifamily loans are made to borrowers under varying terms (e.g., 10-year, 7-year, fixed-rate, adjustable-rate, full or partial interest only, etc.). During the life of a multifamily loan, the balance is generally amortized over an amortization term that is significantly longer than the term of the loan. As a result, there is little amortization of principal, resulting in a balloon payment at maturity. The borrower usually repays the loan in monthly installments that may include only interest for the entire term of the loan, only interest for a portion of the term and then both principal and interest, or principal and interest for the entire term of the loan.

In addition to typical MBS, Fannie Mae issues Discount Mortgage-Backed Securities (DMBS), which are non-interest bearing securities that are purchased at a discount and have terms of one year or less. Multifamily MBS may be placed into Megas, REMICs, or other Structured Transactions mortgage-related securities.

Structured Transactions and Megas

Fannie Mae creates multiclass mortgage-backed securities including real estate mortgage investment conduits (REMICs) and stripped mortgage-backed securities (SMBS). REMICs permit an issuer to restructure cash flows on underlying mortgage assets into separately tradable securities. SMBS separate the principal and interest cash flows from underlying mortgage assets to create classes that pay only principal or only interest (known as principal only or interest only classes).

Fannie Mae also creates and guarantees a single-class MBS known as a Fannie Mega® security or Mega. Megas are single-class pass-through securities in which the underlying collateral are groups of existing Fannie Mae MBS or other Fannie Megas. The cash flows from the underlying MBS and/or Megas provide the cash flows for the Mega pool.

Federal Home Loan Mortgage Corporation

The **Federal Home Loan Mortgage Corporation (Freddie Mac)** is a stockholder-owned corporation chartered by Congress in 1970 to stabilize the mortgage markets and support homeownership and affordable rental housing. Freddie Mac stock is traded on the OTC Bulletin Board under FMCC.

Its mission is to provide liquidity, stability, and affordability by providing secondary mortgage support for conventional mortgages originated by thrift institutions. Since its inception, Freddie Mac has helped finance one out of every six homes in America.

Freddie Mac links Main Street to Wall Street by purchasing, securitizing, and investing in home mortgages. Freddie Mac conducts its business by buying mortgages that meet the company's underwriting and product standards from lenders. The loans are pooled, packaged into securities, guaranteed by Freddie Mac, and sold to investors such as insurance companies and pension funds. This provides homeowners and renters with lower housing costs and better access to home financing. The mortgage-backed securities that it issues tend to be very liquid and carry a credit rating close to that of U.S. Treasuries.

Mortgage Products

Freddie Mac offers a variety of mortgage-backed securities, such as the Gold Fixed-Rate PCs, ARM PCs, and Multifamily PCs.

Gold Fixed-Rate PCs

Gold Participation Certificate (PC) securities are the cornerstone of Freddie Mac's mortgage-backed securities program, offering an undivided interest in a pool of residential mortgages. Freddie Mac securitizes mortgages with various terms. In addition to traditional 30-year fixed-rate Gold PCs, Freddie Mac offers 40, 20, 15-year, and balloon Gold PCs. Freddie Mac offers Gold PCs backed either by fully amortizing mortgages or initial interest mortgages. Freddie Mac guarantees the timely payment of interest and scheduled principal on all Gold PCs.

ARM PCs

Freddie Mac's Adjustable Rate Mortgage (ARM) PCs are characterized by conventional first liens, with original maturities of 30 years or less. Freddie Mac offers ARM PCs backed either by fully amortizing mortgages or initial interest mortgages.

Multifamily PCs

Freddie Mac's Multifamily PCs are secured by structures with 5 or more units designed principally for residential use, with terms generally ranging from five to 30 years.

Freddie Mac's multifamily mortgage credit, appraisal, and underwriting guidelines generally require all multifamily mortgages it purchases to conform to the certain guidelines.

- Secured properties must have specified occupancy rates
- Specified debt coverage ratios
- Specified loan-to-value ratios (typically 80% to 85%)

For more information about Freddie Mac and the products if offers, go to http://www.freddiemac.com.

Government National Mortgage Association

The **Government National Mortgage Association** (**Ginnie Mae**) is a government-owned corporation within the Department of Housing and Urban Development (HUD). Ginnie Mae was created in 1968 when the Federal National Mortgage Association was split into Fannie Mae and Ginnie Mae. Fannie Mae's focus is to support the secondary market for conventional loans and Ginnie Mae's is to support the market for FHA, VA, and other loans.

Unlike Fannie Mae and Freddie Mac, Ginnie Mae does not buy or sell pools of loans. Ginnie Mae does not issue mortgage-backed securities (MBS). Instead, Ginnie Mae guarantees investors the timely payment of principal and interest on MBS backed by federally insured or guaranteed loans—mainly loans insured by the Federal Housing Administration (FHA) or guaranteed by the Department of Veterans Affairs (VA). Other guarantors or issuers of loans eligible as collateral for the Ginnie Mae guaranty include the Department of Agriculture's Rural Development (RD) and HUD's Office of Public and Indian Housing (PIH). In fact, the FHA insures approximately two-thirds of the loans backing Ginnie Mae securities.

Essentially Ginnie Mae is a government agency that provides payment guarantees on securities backed by FHA and VA loans. In fact, this guarantee is so important that the instruments are called "GNMAs" even though GNMA is not the issuer.

In contrast to the MBS issued by Fannie Mae and Freddie Mac, all Ginnie Mae securities are explicitly backed by the full faith and credit of the U.S. Government. This is because Ginnie Mae is a wholly owned government corporation.

Since Ginnie Mae does not actually issue the mortgage-backed securities, it works with approved issuers. **Approved issuers** are lenders that meet specific requirements and are approved to issue Ginnie Mae MBS. Approved issuers acquire or originate eligible FHA and VA loans. The loans are pooled and securitized into MBS, which are then guaranteed by Ginnie Mae. The Ginnie Mae guaranty allows approved issuers to obtain a better price for their MBSs in the secondary mortgage market.

Ginnie Mae's business model significantly limits the taxpayers' exposure to risk associated with secondary market transactions. Its strategy is to guarantee a simple pass-through security to lenders rather than buy loans and issue its own securities.

Ginnie Mae only guarantees securities created by approved issuers and backed by mortgages covered by other federal programs.

Federal Programs
- FHA's single-family and multifamily mortgage insurance programs
- VA's guarantee program
- HUD's Office of Public and Indian Housing loan guarantee program
- Department of Agriculture's Rural Housing Service loan guarantee programs

Because of this business model, Ginnie Mae is in the fourth loss position and only is at risk after the three preceding layers of risk protection are exhausted or fail.

If a borrower defaults, the bank can foreclose and collect from FHA or VA. However, the issuers of the securities bear primary responsibility for covering any losses resulting from borrower defaults. Because Ginnie Mae only guarantees securities backed by mortgages that are insured or guaranteed by other federal agencies, it can rely to some extent on their oversight of the underwriting, originating, and servicing of these loans and on their insurance/guarantees to limit the impacts on the issuers from borrower defaults. If loans default and federal agency insurance or guarantee does not cover the full amount, Ginnie Mae makes up the difference.

Ginnie Mae is in 4ᵗʰ Loss Position

1 Homeowner equity

2 Resources of issuer

3 Government agency insurance or guarantee

4 Ginnie Mae

Issuers also market and service the Ginnie Mae MBS. A lender may contract with a service bureau to service the loans in the pool. If approved lenders collect less from the pool of mortgages than is scheduled, they have to cover the shortfall with their own funds. For more information about Ginnie Mae go to http://www.ginniemae.gov/pages/default.aspx

FARMER MAC

The **Federal Agricultural Mortgage Corporation (Farmer Mac)** is a government-sponsored enterprise with the mission of providing a secondary market for agricultural real estate and rural housing mortgage loans. It was created by the Agricultural Credit Act of 1987 (Pub.L. 100–233) as a federally chartered, private corporation responsible for guaranteeing the timely repayment of principal and interest to investors in a new agricultural secondary market. The secondary market allows a lending institution to sell a qualified farm real estate loan to an agricultural mortgage marketing facility, or pooler, which packages these loans, and sells to investors securities that are backed by, or represent interests in, the pooled loans. Farmer Mac guarantees the timely repayment of principal and interest on these securities and can also serve as a loan pooler.

Farmer Mac is regulated by the Farm Credit Administration (FCA), an independent agency in the executive branch of the U.S. Government. FCA, acting through the Office of Secondary Market Oversight (OSMO), has general regulatory and enforcement authority over Farmer Mac and is responsible for an annual safety and soundness examination of Farmer Mac. Farmer Mac is required to file quarterly reports on its financial condition with FCA and is also required to comply with the periodic reporting requirements of the Securities Exchange Act of 1934.

Farmer Mac's Business Segments

Farmer Mac has four different business segments–Farm & Ranch, USDA Guarantees, Rural Utilities, and Institutional Credit.

Farm & Ranch Program

Under the Farm & Ranch Program, Farmer Mac operates a secondary market for mortgage loans on agricultural real estate. To be eligible, a loan must be secured by a first lien on agricultural property within the United States. The maximum original loan-to-value (LTV) on such loans is generally 70%. Under the Farm & Ranch Program, Farmer Mac also purchases or guarantees AgVantage securities, which represent secured debt obligations of agricultural lenders. These AgVantage securities are over-collateralized by eligible agricultural loans that must be current with respect to principal and interest payments.

Farmer Mac 2 USDA Guaranteed Loan Program

Under the Farmer Mac 2 USDA Guaranteed Loan Program, Farmer Mac's subsidiary, Farmer Mac 2, purchases in the secondary market, the USDA-guaranteed portion of private sector loans from an originating lender. Loan collateral for such loans includes farm real estate, farm equipment, rural business assets, and community facilities.

Rural Utilities Program

Under this Rural Utilities Program, Farmer Mac buys rural utility loans which are originated by a rural utility cooperative. Farmer Mac also issues AgVantage securities under the Rural Utilities program, where we purchase or guarantee obligations of rural utility cooperative lenders that are secured by eligible rural utility loans. Farmer Mac has never experienced a credit loss in its Rural Utilities program.

Institutional Credit

Under the Institutional Credit segment, Farmer Mac purchases or guarantees general obligations of lenders that are secured by pools of the types of loans eligible for purchase under Farmer Mac's Farm & Ranch, USDA Guarantees, or Rural Utilities lines of business. AgVantage® is a registered trademark of Farmer Mac used to designate Farmer Mac's guarantees of securities related to these general obligations of lenders that are secured by pools of eligible loans and that comprise the Institutional Credit line of business.

SUMMARY

The primary mortgage market is the market in which lenders make mortgage loans by lending directly to borrowers. In contrast to the primary mortgage market, the secondary mortgage market refers to the market that involves the buying and selling of existing mortgage loans from the primary mortgage market or from each other. The secondary mortgage market serves as a source of funds for the loan originators so they can continue to make loans and generate income.

The primary market lenders (banks, thrifts, or mortgage bankers) make real estate loans and then sell them to issuers (Fannie Mae, Freddie Mac, or other investors). The issuers package the loans into mortgage-backed securities (MBS), which are sold to investors in the secondary mortgage market. Farmer Mac is a government-sponsored enterprise with the mission of providing a secondary market for agricultural real estate and rural housing mortgage loans.

The issuer uses the money from the sale of the MBS to purchase more loans from lenders in the primary market. The loans are packaged and sold in order to get more money to make more loans, and the cycle continues.

Although Ginnie Mae is a participant in the secondary market, it does not issue mortgage-backed securities (MBS). Instead, Ginnie Mae guarantees investors the timely payment of principal and interest on MBS backed by federally insured or guaranteed loans.

This cycle and flow of capital has made the housing market in the U.S. one of the most robust in the world, as well as a model for other countries.

UNIT 4 REVIEW

Matching Exercise

Instructions: Write the letter of the matching term on the blank line before its definition. Answers are in Appendix A.

Terms

A. aggregator

B. approved issuers

C. CMO

D. default risk

E. Fannie Mae

F. Farm & Ranch Program

G. Farmer Mac

H. Freddie Mac

I. Ginnie Mae

J. loan origination fees

K. loan servicer

L. mortgage-backed security

M. mortgage banker

N. mortgage broker

O. mortgage yield

P. pass-through securities

Q. portfolio lender

R. primary mortgage market

S. REMIC

T. secondary mortgage market

U. securitization

V. subprime loans

W. tranche

X. zero coupon bond

Definitions

1. _____ Market in which originators provide loans to borrowers

2. _____ Channels liquidity into the primary market by purchasing loans from lenders

3. _____ Funding fees typically one to two points of the loan amount

4. _____ Amount returned from real estate loan portfolios expressed as a percentage

5. _____ A company that collects payments from borrowers, subtracts fees, and sends the balance of the money to investors who own the loans

6. _____ A direct lender that lends its own money, whose principal business is the origination and funding of loans secured by real property

7. _____ A lender that not only originates mortgage loans, but also holds a portfolio of their loans instead of selling them off in the secondary mortgage market

8. _____   A person who originates loans with the intention of brokering them to lending institutions

9. _____   A party involved within the secondary mortgage market that purchases mortgages from financial institutions and then securitizes them into mortgage-backed securities (MBS)

10. _____   Finance process that pools cash flow assets into securities that are sold to investors

11. _____   A type of asset-backed security that is protected by a collection of mortgages usually with similar characteristics

12. _____   Certificates that represent direct ownership in a pool of mortgages

13. _____   Type of MBS that represent claims to specific cash flows from large pools of home mortgages

14. _____   A mortgage securities vehicle authorized by the Tax Reform Act of 1986 that holds commercial and residential mortgages in trust, and issues securities representing an undivided interest in these mortgages

15. _____   Part or segment of a structured security

16. _____   Bond that pays no coupons, is sold at a deep discount to its face value, and matures to its face value

17. _____   Borrower's inability to meet interest payment obligations on time

18. _____   Loan comprised of a non-conforming mortgage, borrowers with weaker credit scores, and no documentation

19. _____   GSE created by Congress in 1938 to bolster the housing industry in the aftermath of the Great Depression

20. _____   GSE chartered by Congress in 1970 to stabilize mortgage markets, support homeownership, and support affordable rental housing

21. _____   Government-owned corporation within the Department of Housing and Urban Development (HUD)

22. _____   Lenders that are permitted to issue Ginnie Mae MBS because they meet specific requirements

23. _____   Government-sponsored enterprise with the mission of providing a secondary market for agricultural real estate and rural housing mortgage loans

24. _____   Program under which Farmer Mac operates a secondary market for mortgage loans on agricultural real estate

Multiple Choice Questions

Instructions: Circle your response and go to Appendix A to read the complete explanation for each question.

1. Which statement most clearly defines the purpose of the mortgage markets?
    a. They are irrelevant to originating and transferring loans.
    b. They are not a part of our national economic health.
    c. They create a continuous flow of money to borrowers.
    d. They impede the flow of funds for residential financing.

2. Participants in the mortgage market include:
    a. mortgage loan originators.
    b. securities dealers.
    c. investors.
    d. all of the above.

3. Pooling and repackaging cash flow producing financial assets and selling them to investors is known as:
    a. securitization.
    b. assetizing.
    c. liquidation.
    d. amortization.

4. The investments that are bought and sold in the secondary mortgage market are called:
    a. stock.
    b. insurance policies.
    c. mortgage-backed securities.
    d. commercial loans.

5. What is the simplest type of mortgage-backed securities?
    a. Collateralized mortgage obligations
    b. Pass-through securities
    c. Tranches
    d. REMICs

6. A _____ is a mortgage securities vehicle that holds commercial and residential mortgages in trust and issues securities representing an undivided interest in these mortgages.
    a. REMIC
    b. GSE
    c. tranche
    d. SMBS

7. The functions of Fannie Mae are to:
    a. support the secondary mortgage market by issuing mortgage-related securities and purchasing mortgages.
    b. buy loans from lenders who conform to Fannie Mae guidelines.
    c. put mortgage money back into the system so lenders can make more loans.
    d. do all of the above.

8. The mission of Freddie Mac is to:
    a. provide primary mortgage support for non-conventional mortgages originated by thrift institutions.
    b. buy mortgages that do not meet the company's underwriting and product standards from lenders.
    c. pool loans, packages them into securities, and sells them to investors such as insurance companies and pension funds.
    d. provide homeowners and renters with lower housing costs with minimum access to home financing.

9. Which statement most accurately describes the function of Ginnie Mae?
    a. Ginnie Mae buys and sells pools of loans.
    b. Ginnie Mae guarantees investors the timely payment of principal and interest on MBS loans issued by the FHA and the VA.
    c. Ginnie Mae issues mortgage-backed securities.
    d. Ginnie Mae's focus is to support the secondary market for conventional loans.

10. Which of the following provides a secondary market for agricultural real estate and rural housing mortgage loans?
    a. Fannie Mac
    b. Freddie Mac
    c. Ginnie Mae
    d. Farmer Mac

Sources of Funds

Unit 5

INTRODUCTION

When a person wanted a home loan in the old days, he or she would walk downtown to the neighborhood commercial bank or savings and loan (S&L). The banker would make the home loan if he or she considered the person a good credit risk. The loan was made from the funds of the bank's depositors and held in the bank's loan portfolio. A **loan portfolio** is the set of loans that a financial institution, or other lender, holds at any given time. In this scenario, there were no intermediaries between the borrower and the lender. This lender was considered a direct lender. A **direct lender** deals directly with its customers and funds its own loans. This loan was made in the primary mortgage market.

As we previously learned, the primary mortgage market is the market in which borrowers and loan originators meet to negotiate terms and make real estate loans. After being originated in the primary mortgage market, most residential loans are packaged and sold to buyers in the secondary mortgage market. The primary mortgage market has several types of real estate loan originators—each with its own strengths and weaknesses. Most loan originators perform similar tasks including finding, counseling, and qualifying borrowers, taking applications, checking credit, and verifying employment and assets. However, a **lender** is the person who or company that makes mortgage loans, such as a mortgage banker, credit union, bank, or a savings and loan. A lender underwrites and funds the loan. Those who originate but do not underwrite or fund loans are called **third party originators** (TPOs). This classification includes mortgage brokers and loan correspondents. TPOs package loans for lenders and are paid a commission when the loan is funded. This unit covers the loan originators in the primary market and their function in providing residential real estate financing.

Learning Objectives

After completing this Unit, you should be able to:

5A   differentiate between lenders and loan originators.

5B   recognize the types of fiduciary lenders and the loans they offer.

5C   recognize the types of semi-fiduciary lenders and the loans they offer.

5D   recognize the types of non-fiduciary lenders and the loans they offer.

5E   recognize types of third party originators.

5F   recall how loans are originated.

5G   identify the types of bonds used to finance real estate projects.

TYPES OF LENDERS

One method of classifying lenders is by their fiduciary responsibility toward their depositors and customers. The classifications are fiduciary, semi-fiduciary, or non-fiduciary. Lenders are regulated based on the fiduciary responsibilities the institution has for its customers. Therefore, some lenders must follow strict federal and state regulations, whereas others do not.

Fiduciary Lenders

A **financial fiduciary** is an institution that collects money from depositors, premium payers, or pension plan contributors and makes loans to borrowers. Financial fiduciaries include commercial banks, thrifts, credit unions, life insurance companies, and pension plans. These lenders have a fiduciary responsibility to the owners of the funds. As a result, lending practices are carefully regulated by law in order to protect the owners of the funds.

Most financial fiduciaries are depository institutions. A **depository institution** is a financial institution that is legally allowed to accept deposits from consumers. The main types of depository institutions in the United States are commercial banks, thrifts, and credit unions. Although they each offer similar banking services, they operate under different regulations. As time has passed, these three types of institutions have become more like each other and their unique identities have become less distinct.

A depository lender, such as a commercial bank, pools its deposits and invests them in various ways. These investments include extensions of credit in the form of real estate loans. Depository lenders receive most of their deposits from household savings (savings of individual investors). The main function of depository lenders is to transfer money from the people who deposit money to those who want to borrow it.

Financial fiduciaries set their own underwriting guidelines for the loans they originate unless they plan to sell the loans in the secondary mortgage market. In order to sell loans in the secondary market, they must follow the Fannie Mae/Freddie Mac guidelines.

Larger banks and thrifts that lend their own money and originate loans to keep in their own loan portfolio are called **portfolio lenders**. This is because they originate loans for their own portfolio and not for immediate resale in the secondary mortgage market. Because of this, they do not have to follow Fannie Mae/Freddie Mac guidelines and can create their own rules for determining creditworthiness.

Usually, only a few of the loans are held in the portfolio. A loan is considered seasoned once a borrower has made the payments on it for over a year without any late payments. Once a loan has a track history of timely payments, it becomes marketable even if it does not meet Fannie Mae/Freddie Mac guidelines. If the loans are sold, they are packaged into pools and sold in the secondary market. Selling these seasoned loans frees up money for the portfolio lender to make more loans.

Many commercial banks and thrifts have both retail and wholesale loan origination departments, which are discussed later in the unit.

Commercial Banks

Commercial banks are the all-purpose lenders. Commercial banks receive deposits and hold them in a variety of accounts, extend credit, and facilitate the movement of funds. Deposits held in checking accounts are called demand deposits. A **demand deposit** is a deposit that can be withdrawn at any time.

Commercial banks make the widest range of loans, including loans for buying real estate, home equity loans, business loans, and other short-term loans. Even though they make a variety of loans, a major type of lending activity funded by commercial banks is for short-term (6 to 36 month) construction loans. Commercial banks operate as retail lenders, wholesale lenders, or some combination of both.

Some banks require commercial borrowers to keep a certain amount of money on deposit as a requirement of the loan agreement. These deposits are called **compensating balances**. Deposits held as compensating balances by a bank do not earn interest. As a result, the lender's earnings on the loan are increased. Typically, compensating balances are 10% of the loan amount.

Commercial banks are generally stock corporations whose principal obligation is to make a profit for their shareholders. Their corporate charters and the powers granted to them under state and federal law determine the range of their activities. Banks can choose a state or a federal charter when starting their business and can convert from one charter to another after having been in business. State-chartered commercial banks are regulated by the responsible state agency but may be members of the Federal Reserve System. However, all federally chartered commercial banks must be members of the Federal Reserve System, which supervises member commercial banks.

Thrifts

Thrifts are the largest single resource for residential mortgage credit. A **thrift** is an organization formed to hold deposits for individuals.

Types of Thrift Institutions
- Savings and loan associations
- Savings banks
- Mutual savings banks

These institutions are referred to as thrifts because they originally offered only savings accounts or time deposits. Now, they offer checking accounts (demand deposits) and make business, consumer, and residential real estate loans.

Any thrift can be owned by the shareholders (stock ownership) or by their depositors (mutual ownership). **Mutual ownership** means that all the depositors share ownership in the savings and loan association, which is managed by a board of trustees. The depositors (investors) in S&Ls, savings banks, or mutual savings banks are paid dividends on their share of the organization's earnings. Mutual organizations issue no stock. On the other hand, if the institution is organized as a stock institution, investors can become **shareholders** by purchasing stock through their stockbroker. A stock institution is managed by a board of directors who represent the shareholders of the bank. Deposits for thrifts are insured by the FDIC, which was discussed earlier.

Thrifts count on short-term deposits from savers, and they loan that money to borrowers for long-term, fixed-rate mortgage loans. Their profit margins diminish in markets where they have to pay a higher interest rate to their depositors than they earn on their long-term loans. If thrifts cannot compete with the higher returns from other sources, depositors, and their money, drift away.

Savings and Loan Associations

Traditionally, **savings and loan associations (S&Ls)** have played a major role in the economy by pooling the savings of individuals to fund residential mortgages. The first customers of S&Ls were depositors and borrowers. As their customer base grew, the S&L associations became a primary source of loans for financing homebuilding.

Prior to 1992, S&Ls were the largest private holder of residential mortgage debt and the largest originator of residential mortgages in the country. Deregulation in the early 1980s allowed the S&Ls to participate in a wide range of investment opportunities. Within less than 10 years, 20% of S&Ls were insolvent, 20% were marginal, and only 60% were financially sound. This led to many S&L failures and caused others to change their charters to become savings banks.

Savings Banks

A **savings bank** has been described as a distinctive type of thrift institution because it can behave like a commercial bank or like an S&L. While savings banks are authorized to make mortgage loans, most specialize in consumer and commercial loans. However, they are active in purchasing low-risk FHA/VA and conventional mortgages from other mortgage lenders and mortgage companies. Since most savings banks are located primarily in the capital-surplus areas of the northeast and possess more funds than are needed locally, savings banks play an important part in the savings-investment cycle by purchasing loans from areas that are capital deficient. This flow of funds from areas with excess funds to areas with scarce resources helps to stimulate a healthy national financial environment.

Mutual Savings Banks

A **mutual savings bank** is a financial institution owned by depositors, each of whom has rights to net earnings of the bank in proportion to his or her deposits. The depositors' return on their investment is determined by how successful the bank is in managing its investment.

Initially, mutual savings banks were state-chartered, mutual organizations that relied on their customers' savings to provide all the capital they needed to be successful. They did not sell stock in the company to shareholders. Mutual savings banks were permitted to change their charter from mutual ownerships to federally chartered stock institutions that issue stock to raise capital. These institutions operate similarly to savings and loan associations and are located primarily in the northeastern section of the United States.

Credit Unions

A **credit union** is a cooperative, non-profit organization established for banking purposes. Credit unions are owned and operated by their members. Usually, members are people in associations who share a common affiliation such as teachers, workers in the same field, government employees, or union members.

Credit unions accept deposits in a variety of accounts. All credit unions offer savings accounts or time deposits. The larger institutions also offer checking and money market accounts. Credit unions' financial powers have expanded to include almost anything a bank or savings association can do, including making home loans, issuing credit cards, and even making some commercial loans. Credit unions are exempt from federal taxation and sometimes receive subsidies in the form of free space or supplies from their sponsoring organizations.

The members receive higher interest rates on savings and pay lower rates on loans. Both secured and unsecured loans are made at lower rates than other lenders can offer. Because of the low overhead and other costs of doing business, credit unions are a growing source of funds for consumers. The **National Credit Union Association Board** (NCUAB) supervises them and the federally insured National Credit Union Share Insurance Fund (NCUSIF) insures deposits.

National Credit Union Share Insurance Fund

The **National Credit Union Share Insurance Fund** (NCUSIF) insures the shares and deposits in a credit union. Share insurance is similar to the deposit insurance protection offered by the Federal Deposit Insurance Corporation (FDIC).

Most share accounts that have been established properly in federally insured credit unions are insured up to the Standard Maximum Share Insurance Amount (SMSIA), which is $250,000. Insurance coverage on certain retirement accounts such as IRAs and Keoghs is $250,000. Generally, if a credit union member has more than one account in the same credit union, the accounts are added together and insured in the aggregate. However, members may obtain additional separate coverage on multiple accounts if they have different ownership interests or rights in different types of accounts.

Members of an insured credit union do not pay directly for share insurance protection. Credit unions pay assessments into the NCUSIF based on the total amount of insured shares and deposits in the credit union. Insured credit unions are required to deposit and maintain 1 % of their insured shares and deposits in the NCUSIF. The NCUSIF is backed by the full faith and credit of the United States Government. For more information about the NCUSIF, go to www.ncua.gov.

Life Insurance Companies

Life insurance companies obtain their funds from insurance premiums. Unlike the demand deposits of depository institutions, the premiums invested in life insurance companies are not subject to early withdrawal and do not earn a high rate of interest. Therefore, life insurance companies have vast amounts of money to invest.

Life insurance companies do not usually originate individual loans in the single-family residential market. However, they are a major supplier of money for large commercial loans to developers and builders. Life insurance companies usually do not make construction loans but make takeout loans on large commercial properties. A **takeout loan** is the long-term permanent financing used to pay off a construction loan.

> Example: Developer David has a $5,000,000 interim construction loan from a local bank to build a small commercial center. Upon completion of construction, the permanent financing from a life insurance company pays off (takes out) the construction loan.

Loans made by life insurance companies have low interest rates and the lowest loan-to-value ratios (percentage of loan amount to appraised value). Life insurance companies also have stricter underwriting standards than other lenders. Even though they may deal directly with the borrower, they usually fund commercial loans through loan correspondents who negotiate and service the loans.

As previously described, life insurance companies have been major investors in the secondary mortgage market. Some life insurance companies have entered the primary mortgage market by creating wholly owned subsidiary mortgage companies.

Pension Funds

Pension funds have huge amounts of money to invest. In fact, it is in the trillions. Both employer and employees contribute to employee pension plans. A **pension plan** is a retirement fund reserved to pay money or benefits to workers upon retirement.

The contributions placed in a pension fund are used to purchase investments for the sole purpose of financing the pension plan benefits. The pension fund manager is responsible to invest the funds wisely and pay out a monthly income to retirees.

Like life insurance companies, pension funds are a direct source of funds for developers and large builders of commercial property. Pension funds also buy mortgages issued by banks. Large pension funds, such as those held by the state for the benefit of public employees, often guarantee the repayment of millions of dollars in bank loans used to build low-income and moderate-income housing. In exchange for the guarantee, these funds charge developers a percentage of the value of the loans they guarantee.

Additionally, they invest in blocks of mortgage-backed securities in the secondary mortgage market.

Semi-Fiduciary Lenders

Financial semi-fiduciaries are **non-depository lenders**. A semi-fiduciary institution is never directly accountable to depositors, premium payers, or pension plan contributors. Therefore, they are less strictly regulated and can take more risks than financial fiduciaries. These semi-fiduciary lenders invest their own funds or borrowed funds. Mortgage companies and real estate investment trusts (REITs) are semi-fiduciary lenders.

Mortgage Companies

A **mortgage company**, which is also known as a **mortgage banker**, is a company whose principal business is the origination, closing, funding, selling, and servicing of loans secured by real property. Mortgage companies originate a majority of all residential loans. They lend their own money or money borrowed from warehouse lenders to fund loans.

The biggest role of mortgage companies, however, is to originate and service loans that they package and sell. After loans are originated, a mortgage company might retain the loans in the lender's portfolio or may package and sell them to an investor. The sale of these loan packages provides added capital the mortgage company can use to make more loans to be packaged and sold, thus repeating the cycle. A mortgage company prefers to make loans that can be readily sold in the secondary market, such as FHA, VA, or conventional mortgages. Therefore, mortgage companies are careful to follow the required lending guidelines for these types of loans.

Warehouse Line of Credit

Since mortgage companies do not have depositors, they use short-term borrowing called a warehouse line or warehouse line of credit. A **warehouse line** is a revolving line of credit extended to a mortgage company from a warehouse lender to make loans to borrowers.

Both the mortgage company and the warehouse lender want to create a profitable business relationship. The mortgage company borrows money on the warehouse line to fund a loan. The warehouse lender wires the borrowed money directly to a closing agent to fund the loan. The closing agent closes the loan, sends the original promissory note to the warehouse lender, and sends the other closing documents to the mortgage company. Then the mortgage company gets the closed loan package ready for an investor to purchase. When an investor purchases the loan, the warehouse lender sends the original note to the investor. The investor wires the purchase funds directly to the warehouse lender and not to the mortgage company. The warehouse lender uses the purchase funds to repay the advance for that particular loan, less any fees. The balance of the purchase proceeds are deposited into the mortgage company's bank account, which is maintained by the warehouse lender. Each loan goes through this cycle.

Using a Warehouse Line to Fund Loans

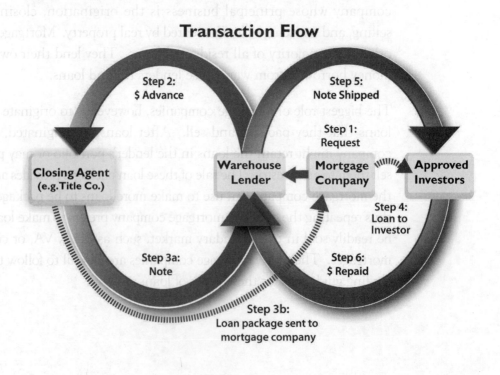

Transaction Flow

Steps in Using a Warehouse Line

1. A mortgage company submits a pre-funding loan package to the warehouse lender.

2. The mortgage company borrows money against its warehouse line for that loan and the money is wired to the closing agent to fund the loan.

3. When the loan is closed, the closing agent sends the warehouse lender the original promissory note (endorsed in blank) and a certified copy of the security instrument. The remaining loan documents are sent to the mortgage company.

4. The mortgage company prepares and sends the closed loan package to an investor for purchase.

5. At the same time, the mortgage company asks the warehouse lender to send the original promissory note to the investor.

6. The investor purchases the loan and wires the proceeds directly to the warehouse lender. This repays the warehouse lender for the advance on the line of credit for that particular loan. Any transaction fees due to the warehouse lender are subtracted from the proceeds and the balance is sent to the mortgage company.

Real Estate Investment Trusts

A share in a **real estate investment trust (REIT)** is a security that sells like a stock on the major exchanges. REITs invest in real estate or mortgages. REITs were designed to provide a similar structure for investment in real estate as mutual funds provide for investment in stocks. REITs are subject to a number of special requirements, one of which is that REITs must annually distribute at least 90% of their taxable income in the form of dividends to shareholders. REITs invest in equities, mortgages, or a combination of the two.

Equity REITs invest in property. A **mortgage REIT**, which is also called a **real estate mortgage trust (REMT)**, makes loans on commercial income property. Some REMTs specialize in buying and selling existing real estate loans. Their revenue is derived from the interest earned on the loans. A hybrid or **combination REIT** purchases equities and makes commercial loans.

Non-Fiduciary Lenders

Non-fiduciary lenders are **non-depository institutions**. In other words, they do not take deposits. Because they are relatively free from government regulations, these lenders follow their own underwriting guidelines and risk criteria.

They are private lenders that invest their own funds or borrowed funds. Some examples of non-fiduciary lenders are private loan companies, private investors, and foreign lenders.

Finance Companies

A **finance company** is a business that makes consumer loans for which household goods and other personal property serve as collateral. In addition, some private loan companies make home equity loans. The credit criteria may be more relaxed than the underwriting guidelines that traditional lenders follow, which allows those with poor credit to qualify.

Because these real estate loans are in a junior position, finance companies try to offset the risk by charging higher placement and origination fees. Usually, interest rates charged by a finance company are the maximum legally allowed.

Private Individuals

Private individuals are non-fiduciary lenders who offer an alternative source of financing. They participate in financing real estate by carrying back loans on their own property and by investing in security instruments (mortgages and deeds of trust).

Sellers are a major source of junior loans to buyers. Sellers may finance a portion of the purchase with a carryback loan. Sellers often require larger down payments than institutional lenders because of the higher risk normally associated with this type of loan.

Private investors who are looking for a higher rate of return than what is available in a bank certificate of deposit may buy and sell existing short-term junior loans through a mortgage company. Their main objectives are the safety of the loan and a high return on their investment.

Crowdfunding

Some people are investing in property or providing mortgage funds with crowdfunding. **Crowdfunding** is the practice of funding a project or venture by raising small amounts of money from a large number of people, typically via the Internet.

Although the industry is very young, it is rapidly reshaping the way individuals find and invest in properties. Real estate crowdfunding involves the pooling of funds by multiple investors in a real estate project.

Two Main Investment Types

- **Equity investments**

  Investors make investments in commercial or residential properties and in exchange, they hold an equity stake in the property. Each investor shares in a portion of the rental income the property generates.

- **Debt investments**

  People invest in a mortgage loan associated with a particular property. As the loan is repaid, the investor receives a share of the interest.

Foreign National Lenders

Due to the demand for real estate loans to people who are not American citizens, some niche lenders offer foreign national loans. Foreign national loans are similar to standard U.S. loans, except that the required down payment is generally larger—about 30%. A foreign national is not a U.S. citizen, but is temporarily residing in the United States. For tax reporting purposes, foreign nationals are issued individual tax identification numbers rather than social security numbers. Usually niche lenders work with foreign nationals because they do not have social security numbers and their American credit history may be minimal or nonexistent.

Review – Types of Lenders

Fiduciary Lenders

- Commercial banks
- Thrifts
- Credit unions
- Life insurance companies
- Pension fund

Semi-Fiduciary Lenders

- Mortgage companies
- REITs

Non-Fiduciary Lenders

- Finance companies
- Private investors
- Foreign lenders

THIRD PARTY ORIGINATORS

Third party originators (TPOs) originate but do not underwrite or fund loans. TPOs complete loan packages and act as the mediator between borrowers and lenders. TPOs include mortgage brokers and loan correspondents.

Mortgage Brokers

There is a niche for everyone in the mortgage loan business. A **mortgage broker** originates loans with the intention of brokering them to lending institutions that have a wholesale loan department. Mortgage brokers are third party originators (TPOs) and not lenders. Mortgage brokers qualify borrowers, take applications, and send completed loan packages to the wholesale lender. The lender approves and underwrites loans and funds them at closing. Usually, mortgage brokers are not authorized to provide final loan approval and they do not disburse money. The loan is funded in the name of the lender and not the mortgage broker. The mortgage broker does not service the loan and has no other concern with it once it is funded.

Mortgage brokers coordinate the loan process between the borrower and the wholesale lender and charge an origination fee to provide this service to the borrower. If the lender wants to make 2 points on the loan (2% of the loan amount), the lender charges the points to the borrower and discloses the amount as points on the Loan Estimate or Good Faith Estimate (GFE). A mortgage broker must disclose the same fee on the GFE as a broker fee.

Loan Correspondents

A **loan correspondent** is usually a third party originator who originates loans for a sponsor. However, the purchaser of the closed loan may make the underwriting decision in advance of closing. Alternatively, the purchaser may grant the authority to underwrite the loan according to its guidelines and allow the entire process to be undertaken by the correspondent who simply ships a funded loan. If the sponsor funds the loan, the process is called table funding. **Table funding** is the lender's ability to provide loan funds on the same day the transaction is signed by all parties, which is usually the same day as the closing. In the course of table funding, the correspondent closes a mortgage loan with funds belonging to the acquiring lender. Upon closing, the loan is assigned to the lender who supplied the funds.

However, some sponsors allow a correspondent to actually fund and close loans in the correspondent's name, providing the loans meet the sponsor's guidelines. The sponsor can force a correspondent to buy back a loan if it does not meet the sponsor's guidelines. Therefore, loan correspondents have a risk that mortgage brokers do not have.

The sponsor retains the loan in its portfolio or packages and resells the loan in the secondary mortgage market as part of a pool. Many insurance companies are sponsors for loan correspondents.

HOW LOANS ARE ORIGINATED

Loan origination is the lending process from application to closing. Historically, mortgage loans were offered directly to borrowers by a direct lender who completed the loan process during retail loan origination. Today, many loans are prepared by a third party originator and sold to a wholesale lender. The third party originator collects a fee from the lender when the borrower's loan is funded.

Since the mid-1980s, real estate lending has seen many changes that have brought desirable diversity to a conservative industry. Frequently, lenders such as commercial banks, thrifts, and mortgage companies have both retail and wholesale loan origination departments.

Retail Loan Origination

Retail loan origination refers to lenders (banks, thrifts, and mortgage bankers) that deal directly with the borrower and perform all of the steps necessary during the loan origination and funding process. This retail approach to loan origination is an outgrowth of early 20th century banks and savings and loans.

A retail lender employs loan officers and commissioned loan representatives to market the lender's mortgage loan products. While the loan officers may stay and work at the lending institution, loan representatives solicit business by talking to real estate agents at local real estate offices.

Normally, a retail lender is paid a commission of 1% or more of the loan amount, which is called the **origination fee** or **loan origination points**. This fee is payable upon funding of the loan, plus any negotiated settlement fees and premiums paid by the purchaser of the mortgage to the lender after funding.

As mentioned earlier, lenders may retain some loans in their own portfolios and sell others into the secondary market. These retail lenders often act as servicers when selling the loans into the secondary market. However, their retail presence is an important factor in the origination process.

Wholesale Loan Origination

When a lender buys a processed loan from a mortgage broker it is called wholesale mortgage lending. **Wholesale loan origination**, which is sometimes called third party origination, is the process in which mortgage brokers and loan correspondents originate loans. The third party originator completes the loan application with the borrower; verifies application information such as employment, income, and bank account information; and packages the file for underwriting. When the wholesale lender gets the loan package, the underwriting and funding is completed before the lender pays any premium due to the TPO.

Many retail lenders have a wholesale lending division that works with mortgage brokers and loan correspondents (TPOs) for loan origination. However, wholesale lenders that do not have any retail branches rely solely on TPOs for their loans. The lender takes completed loan packages from the TPOs and underwrites the loans.

If the lender has both retail and wholesale lending divisions, the TPO is given discounted pricing, which is lower than the rate the retail division offers to the public. Then the TPO adds his or her fee. The result for the borrower is that the loan costs about the same as if it were obtained directly from one of the wholesale lender's retail branches.

Lenders buy a loan or group of loans from the originating TPO because it is less expensive to buy loans than to originate, process, underwrite, and fund loans. In addition, it gives the wholesaler an opportunity to acquire loans in areas of the country or with methods that are too costly for the wholesaler to do on its own.

The TPO is interested in having the underwriting decision on any loan made quickly. If the loan is declined for some reason, the TPO will have to notify the borrower and attempt to resolve the problem. Then the TPO will submit the loan package to another wholesaler for loan approval.

Generally, the borrower pays the TPO an application fee and an origination fee. Either the borrower or the acquiring lender pays any points.

After the loan has been transferred to the wholesale lender, the lender will hold the loan in its portfolio or sell the loan in the secondary loan market.

Why Wholesale Lending?

Wholesale loan origination has pros and cons. The most important benefit to the wholesale lender is the large number of loans that may be purchased from TPOs. These loans may be acquired more economically than if the retail lender originated them. This is because the wholesale lender does not require a large staff to process the loans. Therefore, it can focus on other aspects of the transaction that fit its business model.

Another benefit to a wholesale lender is flexibility in the market. Money markets may change quickly and a wholesale lender can move its concentration to do business in other locations without as much concern about personnel or even a physical location. If a market declines rapidly, a wholesale lender can stop purchasing loans in one geographic area and buy loans in another location where the market is more profitable.

A lender who uses the wholesale approach can purchase more loans and have greater sources of revenue. After the loans are bought from correspondents or funded and closed for the mortgage brokers, they can be sold very quickly into the secondary mortgage market with the wholesale lender holding the servicing rights, or kept for interest earnings.

A loan is only as good as the originator makes it, and the issue of quality control is a major factor for a wholesale lender. **Quality control** refers to the procedures used to check loan quality throughout the application and funding process. Loan wholesalers must rely on the integrity of the correspondents and brokers with which they do business. The procedures used to perform appraisals, verify important employment and credit information, and gather other critical information must be done according to the highest standards to avoid the serious problems that come when a borrower defaults on a loan.

USING BONDS TO FINANCE REAL ESTATE

Issuing bonds is a way that the government (federal and state), corporations, and municipalities raise money to support spending. From a real estate perspective, bonds may be used to provide credit for the housing sector and to finance real estate projects. The types of debt instruments issued include U.S. Treasury securities, federal agency securities, mortgage- and asset-backed securities, corporate bonds, and municipal bonds.

Bond Basics

A **bond** is simply a contract between a lender (bondholder) and a borrower (issuer) by which the borrower promises to repay a loan with interest. An **issuer** is the entity obligated to pay principal and interest on a debt instrument it issues. A **bondholder** is a creditor; a shareholder is an owner.

Types of Bond Issuers

When investors purchase bonds, they are lending money to a government, municipality, corporation, federal agency, or other entity known as an issuer. In return for that money, the issuer provides investors with a bond, in which it promises to pay a specified rate of interest during the life of the bond and to repay the face value of the bond (the principal) when it matures, or comes due.

Bond Issuers

- U.S. Government and its Agencies
- Corporations
- State and municipal governments

There are significant differences between bonds issued by corporations and those issued by a state government/municipality or national government. The debt issuers follow different rules and, if applicable, varying state and municipal government-issued bond regulations.

Government Bonds

A government bond is a debt security issued by a government to support government spending. Federal government bonds in the United States include savings bonds, Treasury bonds and Treasury inflation-protected securities (TIPS).

Government bonds assist fund deficits in the federal budget and control the nation's money supply. When the government repurchases its own bonds, the money supply increases as sellers receive funds to utilize in the market. Eventually, when funds are deposited into a bank, financial institutions utilize the money multiplier to expand the money supply. Alternatively, the government can also sell bonds that reduce the money supply.

U.S. Treasury Securities

U.S. Treasury securities are debt obligations issued by the U.S. Department of the Treasury. Treasury securities are considered one of the safest investments because they are backed by the full faith and credit of the U.S. government. The income from Treasury securities is exempt from state and local taxes, but not from federal taxes. U.S. Treasury securities are all negotiable, meaning they can be traded freely.

U.S. Government Agency Securities

Not all federal government bonds are issued by the U.S. Treasury. Many federal agencies and Government Sponsored Enterprises (GSEs) raise money by issuing securities, called **agency bonds**. Issuers of agency bonds include Fannie Mae, Freddie Mac, Ginnie Mae, the Farm Credit System, Farmer Mac, and the Student Loan Marketing Association (Sallie Mae).

Some agency bonds carry a direct obligation of the Treasury, whereas others do not.

Bonds issued by GSEs, such as Freddie Mac, Fannie Mae, and the Federal Home Loan Banks, provide credit for the housing sector. Farmer Mac and the Farm Credit Banks do the same for the farming sector. GSEs are not backed by the full faith and credit of the U.S. government, unlike U.S. Treasury bonds. The yields of GSE agency bonds tend to be higher than the yields from Treasury securities.

Bonds issued or guaranteed by Federal Government agencies, such as the Small Business Administration (SBA), the Federal Housing Administration (FHA) and Ginnie Mae, are backed by the full faith and credit of the U.S. government just like U.S. Treasury bonds. **Full faith and credit** means that the U.S. government is committed to pay interest and principal back to the investor at maturity.

Corporate Bonds

Corporate bonds are debt instruments issued by industrial, financial, and service companies to finance capital investment and operating cash flow. Corporate bonds are usually issued in multiples of $1,000 or $5,000. Corporate bonds can generally be classified by the type of issuer. The five main classes of issuers that issue corporate bonds are: (1) public utilities, (2) transportation companies, (3) industrial corporations, (4) financial services companies, and (5) conglomerates. Such issuers may be U.S. companies or non-U.S. companies. Non-U.S. governments are also frequent issuers in the U.S. markets.

Secured or Unsecured Corporate Bonds

Corporate bonds are either secured or unsecured. Corporations often will issue both types of debt depending on their financial needs. For example, a corporation that wants to raise capital, but not pay too much interest to the investors, might issue secured debt. This is because the corporation can offer a lower interest rate on secured debt.

Secured Corporate Debt

A **secured debt** is a debt whose payment of interest and/or principal is secured, or backed by a specific pledged asset or other form of collateral. If the issuer defaults, bondholders have the right to liquidate its assets and recoup as much of their investment as they can. Examples of secured bonds include mortgage bonds, equipment trust certificates, and collateral trust bonds.

A **mortgage bond** provides the bondholders with a lien on corporate real property. A lien, in this case, gives the bondholders the right to sell the property if the corporation defaults on its payments. Mortgage bonds may be either first mortgage bonds or junior mortgage bonds. Should an issuer have to liquidate, first mortgage bonds are paid off before juniors are. Even if a corporation does default, the corporate trustee, who represents the interests of bondholders, rarely has to seize property and sell it for the benefit of bondholders. Most often, the company reorganizes and arranges other means of paying the bondholders, since the lien gives it a strong incentive to satisfy the claims of the bondholders.

Equipment trust certificates (ETCs) are issued primarily by railroad companies, although some airlines also issue this type of bond. These bonds are considered the safest of corporate bonds because of the way that the bonds are secured.

Collateral trust certificates are secured by other securities, such as stocks and bonds. These are often issued by companies that own little or no real estate, but own a significant amount of securities, such as holding companies. A **holding company** is a company that controls other companies, which are subsidiaries.

Unsecured Corporate Debt

Unsecured bonds, also called **debentures**, are not backed by equipment, revenue, or mortgages on real estate. Instead, they are backed only by the integrity (good faith and credit) of the issuer. As a general creditor, however, the holders of debentures have a claim over all of the property of the issuer.

Unsecured bonds naturally carry more risk than secured bonds; consequently, they usually pay higher interest rates than do secured bonds. If a company issuing debentures liquidates, it pays holders of secured bonds first, then debenture-holders, and then owners of subordinated debentures.

Municipal Securities

A **municipal security**, or **muni**, is a general term referring to securities issued by local governmental subdivisions, such as cities, towns, villages, counties, or special districts. When issuing munis, "local government" not only means a city, town, or county, but also school or water districts. Additionally, authorities dedicated to  public works projects, such as highway improvement, airport expansion, and hospital or low-income housing construction, may issue munis. The territorial possessions of the United States (Guam, Puerto Rico, and the U.S. Virgin Islands) are legally entitled to issue municipal securities, as well.

Beneficial Tax Treatment of Munis

The interest on munis is tax-exempt at the federal level and can be exempt at the state and local levels. A municipal bond may be **triple-tax exempt** if the interest payments are exempt from taxes at the municipal, state, and federal levels. Due to the triple-tax free status, these bonds may offer lower returns. However, munis are not exempt from capital gains taxes.

Types of Municipal Securities

Municipal bonds are classified into two categories based on the source of the money to pay bondholders. These are general obligation bonds and revenue bonds. The interest earned from general obligation and revenue bonds is exempt from Federal income tax.

General Obligation Bonds and Notes

A **general obligation bond** (GO) is a municipal bond that is backed by the issuer's good faith, credit, and taxing power only. In many cases, general obligation bonds are voter-approved.

Only entities with the ability to levy and collect taxes can issue GO bonds. They are usually issued to fund public properties or facilities that do not produce revenue, such as government buildings, schools, libraries, prisons, and police and fire stations. Local governments depend upon property taxes (ad valorem taxes) to pay the obligations of their debt securities, whereas state-issued GO bonds are paid from income, sales, and other taxes, as determined by the state legislature.

Limited tax GO bonds are issued by school districts, which have a legal limit on the amount of taxes they can impose. Other government units that have no legal limitation on their power to tax issue **unlimited tax GO bonds**.

The financial stability of the municipality that is issuing the bonds is usually based on four factors—tax burden, budget, existing debt, and overall economic health of the municipality.

Factors to Determine Creditworthiness of Issuer

1. Tax burden on and source of tax payments for the issuer

2. Budgetary structure and financial condition of the issuer

3. Existing issuer debt, as measured by net debt per capita and overlapping debt

4. Overall economic health of the community, including changes in property values, average household income, size of the employer pool, and other demographics

Revenue Bonds

A **revenue bond** is a municipal bond issued to finance public works, such as bridges or tunnels or sewer systems. The bond is supported directly by the revenues of the project, such as user fees and other charges generated by a particular public works project.

> Example: A state may issue revenue bonds to fund the construction of a new sports stadium and convention center. The revenue generated by the facility from sporting event ticket sales, parking fees, concert concessions, reservation fees for trade events, and so on will pay the interest and principal on the bonds.

Public Projects Typically Financed with Revenue Bonds

- Airports
- Toll roads and bridges
- Public power systems
- Sewer and water treatment systems
- Colleges and universities
- Hospitals
- Housing developments
- Sports facilities and convention centers

The quality of a revenue bond issue depends on whether the project that it funds can generate enough cash to pay the interest and principal on the bonds.

Factors to Determine the Quality of a Revenue Bond

- Can the issuer raise the rates that it charges without outside approval?
- Does the local government have the right to use the project's revenues for any other purpose?
- What circumstances would allow the project to issue new bonds that would take up a part of its revenues?

Industrial Revenue Bonds

Industrial development revenue bonds (IDRBs) are issued through a local governmental agency on behalf of a private business, and proceeds are intended to build or acquire factories or factory tools, which have the effect of improving the employment prospects in the local area. The debt service on the bonds is paid solely by the corporation.

Review – GO & Revenue Bonds

GO and revenue bonds are used much more often than the highly specialized IDRBs. All levels of municipal government use revenue bonds, but only states, counties, cities, and school districts put their full faith and credit behind GOs.

Issuer	Types of Debt Generally Issued
State governments	GO and revenue
Cities	GO and revenue
Counties	GO and revenue
Public school districts	GO and revenue
Colleges and universities	GO and revenue
Public power authorities	Revenue
Water/sewer authorities	Revenue
Transit authorities	Revenue
Health facilities	Revenue
Student loan agencies	Revenue
Housing authorities	Revenue
Water disposal districts	Revenue
Source: Federal Reserve Bank of Richmond (Va.)	

Special Types of Municipal Bonds

Sometimes munis are issued under special circumstances, such as special tax bonds, special assessment bonds, Public Housing Authority Bonds, and others.

Special Tax Bond. A special tax bond is a municipal bond secured by a sales or excise tax, such as a gasoline tax.

Special Assessment Bond. A special assessment bond is secured by the taxes on the properties benefiting from the bond-funded improvements, such as sidewalks, streets, and sewers.

Public Housing Authority Bonds. Public Housing Authority Bonds (PHAs), also called New Housing Authority Bonds (NHAs), are issued by a local housing authority to build and/or improve low-income housing. Sometimes, they are referred to as **Section 8 bonds**. They are backed by the U.S. government. If the local municipality cannot meet the entire obligation, the U.S. government will make up the difference. As a result, public housing authority bonds are the safest municipal bonds and receive a credit rating of AAA from Standard & Poor's.

Short-Term Municipal Notes

Municipal notes provide short-term (interim) financing. Maturities are 1 year or less—typically, 3 to 5 months. They are repaid when the municipality receives the anticipated funds.

Types of Municipal Notes

There are several classes of short-term muni obligations—BANs, RANs, PNs, CLNs, and others.

Bond Anticipation Notes (BANs). A BAN is a short-term note, usually but not always issued by a municipality, used to finance a project. BANs are often issued with a maturity of one year or less. The BAN is paid off with funds from a longer-term bond issue.

Revenue Anticipation Notes (RANs). A RAN is a short-term municipal bond that is repaid to bondholders with the expected revenues from the project the RAN intends to finance. For example, a RAN would be paid off with funds from such sources as turnpike tolls or stadium ticket sales.

Project Notes (PNs). A PN is a short-term debt security issued by a municipality. Usually they finance a federally sponsored real estate or urban renewal project. When project notes are issued for this purpose, they are guaranteed by the U.S. Department of Housing and Urban Development.

Construction Loan Notes (CLNs). A CLN is a short-term debt security issued by a municipality to fund construction of housing projects. They are repaid by permanent financing provided from bond proceeds or some other pre-arranged commitment, such as Ginnie Mae.

SUMMARY

Mortgage loans are originated through either direct or wholesale lending. Mortgage loans are offered directly to borrowers by a lender who completes the retail loan origination process. The retail loan origination process begins when the borrower completes an application and submits it to the lender. The lender verifies income, orders the appraisal, orders the credit report, completes the underwriting process, approves or rejects the loan, and funds the loan.

The wholesale side of lending, which is sometimes called third party origination, consists of a third party charging a fee to connect the borrower and the lender. Mortgage loan correspondents and loan brokers originate these loans and deliver them to acquiring wholesale mortgage lenders. Mortgage brokers deliver processed loans for lenders to close, while correspondent lenders sell closed loans to acquiring wholesale mortgage lenders. The practice of wholesale mortgage lending has grown out of borrowers' demands for a more efficient loan process and more variety in loan products.

The most important benefit to the wholesale lender is the large number of mortgage loans that may be provided by the loan broker and may be acquired more economically than if the lender originated the loans. Another benefit to a wholesale lender is flexibility in the market. A loan is only as good as the originator makes it, and the issue of quality control is a major factor for a wholesale lender.

Issuing bonds is a way that the government (federal and state), corporations, and municipalities raised money to support spending. From a real estate perspective, bonds may be used to provide credit for the housing sector and to finance real estate projects.

UNIT 5 REVIEW

Matching Exercise

Instructions: Write the letter of the matching term on the blank line before its definition. Answers are in Appendix A.

Terms

A. commercial bank	N. mortgage company	Y. retail loan origination
B. credit union	O. mutual ownership	Z. savings and loan association (S&L)
C. depository institution	P. mutual savings bank	
D. direct lender	Q. National Credit Union Share Insurance Fund (NCUSIF)	AA. savings bank
E. Federal Reserve System		BB. shareholders
F. finance company		CC. table funding
G. financial fiduciary	R. non-fiduciary lender	DD. takeout loan
H. financial semi-fiduciary	S. origination fee	EE. third party originator (TPO)
I. lender	T. pension fund	
J. loan correspondent	U. pension plan	FF. thrift
K. loan origination	V. portfolio lender	GG. warehouse line
L. loan portfolio	W. private individual	HH. wholesale loan
M. mortgage broker	X. real estate investment trust (REIT)	

Definitions

1. _____ Set of loans that a financial institution or other lender holds at any given time

2. _____ Deals directly with its customers and funds its own loans

3. _____ Person who or company that makes mortgage loans, such as a mortgage banker, credit union, bank, or a savings and loan

4. _____ One who originates but does not underwrite or fund loans

5. _____ Institution that collects money from depositors, premium payers, or pension plan contributors and makes loans to borrowers

6. _____ Financial institution that is legally allowed to accept deposits from consumers

7. _____ Larger bank or thrift that lends its own money and originates loans to keep in its own loan portfolio

8. _____ Lender that receives deposits and holds them in a variety of accounts, extends credit, and facilitates the movement of funds

9. _____ Federal agency that supervises member commercial banks

10. _____ Organization formed to hold deposits for individuals

11. _____ All the depositors share ownership in the savings and loan association, which is managed by a board of trustees

12. _____ Type of institution that played a major role in the economy by pooling the savings of individuals to fund residential mortgages

13. _____ Thrift institution that sometimes behaves like a commercial bank and sometimes like a savings and loan

14. _____ Cooperative, non-profit organization established for banking purposes

15. _____ Long-term permanent financing used to pay off a construction loan

16. _____ Retirement fund reserved to pay money or benefits to workers upon retirement

17. _____ Company whose principal business is the origination, closing, funding, selling, and servicing of loans secured by real property

18. _____ Revolving line of credit extended to a mortgage company from a warehouse lender to make loans to borrowers

19. _____ Security that sells like a stock on the major exchanges

20. _____ Business that makes consumer loans for which household goods and other personal property serve as collateral

21. _____ Person who carries back loans on his or her own property and invests in security instruments

22. _____ Originates loans with the intention of brokering them to lending institutions that have a wholesale loan department

23. _____ Usually a third party originator who originates loans for a sponsor

24. _____ Lender's ability to provide loan funds on the same day the transaction is signed by all parties, which is usually the same day as the closing

25. _____ Lending process from application to closing

26. _____ Refers to lenders (banks, thrifts, and mortgage bankers) who deal directly with the borrower and perform all of the steps necessary during the loan origination and funding process

Multiple Choice Questions

Instructions: Circle your response and go to Appendix A to read the complete explanation for each question.

1. Which statement is correct regarding lenders and third party originators?
   a. Lenders originate, underwrite, and fund loans.
   b. Third party originators originate and fund loans.
   c. Both lenders and third party originators originate and fund loans.
   d. Third party originators fund and service loans.

2. Larger banks and thrifts that lend their own money and originate loans to keep in their own loan portfolio are called _____ lenders.
   a. direct
   b. secondary
   c. wholesale
   d. portfolio

3. Which of the following specializes primarily in consumer and commercial loans?
   a. Savings banks
   b. Life insurance companies
   c. Credit unions
   d. Thrifts

4. A _____ is a type of semi-fiduciary lender whose principal business is the origination, closing, selling, and servicing of loans secured by real property.
   a. pension fund
   b. mortgage company
   c. life insurance company
   d. savings and loan

5. A _____ makes loans on commercial income property.
    a. mortgage REIT
    b. life insurance company
    c. mortgage broker
    d. All of the above

6. A warehouse line is a(n) _____ line of credit.
    a. fixed
    b. revolving
    c. adjustable
    d. long-term

7. _____ are third party originators.
    a. Mortgage brokers
    b. Direct lenders
    c. Loan correspondents
    d. Both (a) and (c)

8. During the loan origination process, a retail lender:
    a. completes the application with the borrower.
    b. orders employment, income, and deposit verifications.
    c. prepares the loan for underwriting.
    d. does all of the above.

9. When a lender acquires a processed loan from a mortgage loan originator, it is called _____ mortgage lending.
    a. consumer
    b. retail
    c. wholesale
    d. short-term

10. A concern for a wholesale lender is:
    a. that too many loans are sold to the wholesale dealer.
    b. flexibility in the mortgage loan marketplace.
    c. the lack of money to be made servicing loans.
    d. quality control.

Types of Loans

Unit 6

INTRODUCTION

What started out as a simple loan by a local bank—with an agreement that the borrower pay it all back in a timely manner—has become complex. The financing of property is a creative endeavor in which lenders analyze each individual situation and recommend the loan product most suited to the buyer. Lenders offer a variety of financing options designed to accommodate individual life situations.

In today's marketplace, lenders offer a variety of loan products. Thirty years ago, a borrower generally had a choice of a 30- or 15-year, fixed-rate loan, or a term loan at the local bank. Because of market-driven changes in the banking world during the 1980s, consumers have benefited from the creation of new types of loans.

Real estate loans can be classified in several ways. One of the most obvious ways to classify loans is by their purpose—purchase, refinance, or cash out. Lenders classify loans by the type of amortization—fixed-rate, ARM, or GPM. Any mortgage product other than a 30-year, fixed-rate mortgage is called a **nontraditional mortgage product**. Types of loans include conventional and government-backed (FHA and VA). Loans are further described by occupancy (residence or investment) and by priority (first or second loans).

Learning Objectives

After completing this Unit, you should be able to:

6A   specify the purpose of a real estate loan.

6B   recall the terms of a real estate loan.

6C   recognize loan amortization types.

6D   identify the features of fixed-rate loans.

6E   identify the features of adjustable-rate loans.

6F   identify the features of graduated payment loans.

LOAN PURPOSE, TYPE, AND TERMS

Most people must borrow money to purchase or refinance a property, so they go to banks (or other sources of available funds) that lend money. Lenders always ask about the purpose of the loan—the underlying reason an applicant is seeking a loan. The purpose of the loan is used by the lender to make decisions on the risk and may even affect the type of mortgage and loan terms that are offered.

Purpose of the Loan

Lenders offer a variety of loans to help people purchase a property, refinance an existing loan, or get cash out of a property. For example, loan products are available to assist first-time homebuyers who only have a small down payment, and to retired individuals who want to draw on the equity in their home. In  order to select the appropriate type of loan, a lender must know the purpose of the loan.

Is the loan to purchase a home or investment property? This is important because loans that are used to purchase owner-occupied properties have different underwriting guidelines than those used to finance investment properties. A loan that is used to purchase property is called a **purchase money loan.** It is used strictly for financing the purchase of real property. Any loan made at the time of a sale, as part of the sale, is a purchase money loan. Even seller carry back financing or a second loan that finances part of the purchase of a property are purchase money loans. Most loans used to purchase property are closed-end loans. A **closed-end loan** is one in which the borrower receives all loan proceeds in one lump sum at the time of closing. The borrower may not draw additional funds against the loan at a later date.

A borrower might refinance an existing loan. **Refinancing** replaces the old loan with a new one. A person may refinance to reduce the interest rate, lower monthly payments, or change from an adjustable-rate to a fixed-rate loan. The loan amount remains the same, but the terms change. Refinancing usually makes sense only when there has been a drop in interest rates and a person wants a new loan at a lower rate than the existing loan. Refinancing may also benefit those who want to refinance for a longer term to lower monthly payments.

If the borrower wants cash to make home repairs, pay for college tuition, pay off high-interest credit card debt, or take a vacation, he or she can get a cash-out refinance. **Cash-out refinancing** involves refinancing the loan for a larger amount than the current loan. Any loan used to take cash out of a property is a **hard money loan**. Hard money loans draw on the equity in property. This type of loan includes home equity loans, home equity lines-of-credit, and swing loans.

> Example: Homeowner Pat owes $90,000 on a house valued at $180,000 and wants $30,000 to add a family room. Pat can refinance the loan for $120,000, pay off the existing loan, and have $30,000 to add the family room.

Cash-out refinancing is not the same as a home equity loan. Cash-out refinancing replaces an existing loan with a new one. A home equity loan is a second loan against the equity in your home.

Type of Mortgage and Loan Terms

When a lender or loan originator talks to a borrower and begins the process of filling out the mortgage loan application, it is a very good idea to know what **types of mortgages** are available and the advantages and disadvantages for each of them. Typical residential mortgages include conventional loans, government loans (FHA, VA, and USDA), and other loans, such as secondary financing. These types of mortgage loans are discussed later in the course.

Regardless of the type of mortgage loan, most use the same basic **terms of the loan** to describe the transaction.

Terms of a Loan
- Principal (Loan Amount)
- Interest
- Interest Rate
- Loan Term (Number of Months)
- Repayment Schedule

Principal is the amount of money a person borrows from the lender.

Interest is the fee the lender charges for the use of their money. People pay for the privilege to borrow money. The interest charge on the loan depends on the amount of money that is borrowed, the interest rate, and the term of the loan. Interest is merely another name for the rent paid to use someone else's money. Interest as rent is a fascinating concept.

> Warren Buffet, who is the chairman of Berkshire Hathaway Inc. (and one of the wealthiest men in the world), has said that those who understand interest earn it and those who do not understand interest pay it. Therefore, interest is either (a) the income earned for lending money, or (b) the rent paid to borrow money.

Compound interest is the interest paid on original principal and on the accrued and unpaid interest that accumulates as the debt matures. It is the interest that interest earns.

> Example: If Kris invests $100 at 5% interest for 2 years, then she will have $105 at the end of the first year. Assuming she does not spend the interest, she will have $110.25 at the end of 2 years. Because she invests only $100 but gets back $110.25, her money is working for her.

The **interest rate** is a figure calculated as a percentage that is used to indicate the rate charged for use of money in a loan. Interest rates may be fixed or variable.

The **loan term** is the agreed period the borrower has to repay the loan. For some loans, this could be a year or less; however, for most home loans it is 25-30 years.

The **repayment schedule** shows the mortgage payments laid out over the life of the loan. Over the term of the loan, the borrower makes repayments on a regular basis—typically monthly. These **repayments** generally cover a portion of the principal and the interest charge (P & I). Some payments include the property taxes and insurance as well. A payment that includes the principal, interest, taxes, and insurance (**PITI**), represents the borrower's total monthly payment.

AMORTIZATION TYPE: FIXED, ARM, GPM

The lender's goal is to match the buyer's financial situation to the appropriate loan product. Buyers typically have some idea of the amount of loan payment they can afford. Many times, homebuyers and investors have already done preliminary research and have definite ideas about the type of loan product they intend to choose.

The interest rate and length of the loan help determine the payment the borrower will make. The other determining factor is the amortization. **Amortization** is the liquidation of a financial obligation on an installment basis. An amortization schedule details each payment, displays the specific amount applied to interest and principal, and shows the remaining principal balance after each payment.

A **fully amortizing loan** is fully repaid at maturity by periodic reduction of the principal. When a loan is fully amortized, the payments the borrower makes are equal over the duration of the loan. Any mortgage other than a 30-year, fully amortizing, fixed-rate mortgage is a nontraditional mortgage.

A **partially amortizing loan** has a repayment schedule that is not sufficient to pay off the loan over its term. This type of loan calls for regular, periodic payments of principal and interest for a specified period of time. At maturity, the remaining unpaid principal balance is due as a balloon payment. A **balloon payment** is substantially larger than any other payment and repays the debt in full.

A **straight loan** is not amortized. The borrower only makes periodic interest payments during the term of the loan. The entire principal balance is due in one lump sum upon maturity. These loans are also called interest-only loans. This type of loan is not commonly offered by institutional lenders but may be offered by a seller or a private lender to a buyer.

Loan products differ based on the terms of the loan, which include the amount borrowed, interest rate, length of the loan, and amortization type. **Amortization type** is the basis for how a loan will be repaid. The type of amortization influences changes in repayment terms during the life of the loan. The most common amortization types include fixed-rate loans, adjustable-rate mortgages (ARM), and graduated payment mortgages (GPM).

Fixed-Rate Loans

A **fixed-rate loan** has two distinct features—fixed interest for the life of the loan and level payments. The level payments of principal and interest are structured to repay the debt completely by the end of the loan term. The major advantage of fixed-rate loans is that they present predictable housing costs for the life of the loan. Fixed-rate loans are suitable for the majority of homebuyers. If the borrower plans to stay in his or her home for a long time and can afford the payments associated with a fully amortizing, fixed-rate loan, this type of loan offers level, predictable payments.

Fully Amortizing Fixed-Rate Loans

Maturity dates for fixed-rate loans range from 40, 30, 20, 15, to 10 years. A **maturity date** is the date on which a debt becomes due for payment. The longer the loan term, the smaller the payment and the more interest is paid over the term of the loan. During the early amortization period, a large percentage of the monthly payment is used to pay interest. As the loan is paid down, more of the monthly payment is applied to principal. The most popular maturity dates are 30 and 15 years.

The traditional **30-year fixed-rate loan** offers low monthly payments while providing for a never-changing monthly payment schedule. A typical 30-year, fixed-rate loan takes 22.5 years of level payments to pay half of the original loan amount.

A **15-year fixed-rate loan** is repaid twice as fast because the monthly payment is higher. More money is applied to the principal in the early months of the loan, which cuts the time it takes to reach free and clear ownership. Additionally, the borrower pays less than half the total interest costs of the traditional 30-year loan.

A **40-year fixed-rate loan** has the lowest monthly payments of fixed-rate loans but has a dramatically higher amount of interest costs.

Interest-Only Fixed-Rate Loans

Interest-only fixed-rate loans are short-term fixed-rate loans that have fixed monthly payments usually based on a 30-year fully amortizing schedule and a lump sum payment at the end of its term. They typically have terms of 3, 5, and 7 years.

The advantage of this type of loan is that the interest rate on balloon loans is generally lower than 30- or 15-year loans, which results in lower monthly payments. The disadvantage is that at the end of the term the borrower must make a lump sum payment to the lender. Additionally, with an interest-only fixed-rate loan, the borrower is not building equity. With this type of loan, the equity in the property can still increase if the market value of the property increases. However, during the term of the loan, the equity can decrease if the home's market value goes down.

Interest-only loans with a refinancing option allow borrowers to convert the mortgage at maturity to a fixed-rate loan if certain conditions are met. The interest rate on the new loan is a current rate at the time of conversion. There might be a minimal processing fee to obtain the new loan. The most popular terms are the 5/25 and 7/23.

> Example: A 30-year mortgage loan has a 5-year interest-only payment period. The borrower pays interest for five years and then pays both principal and interest over the next twenty-five years. Payments increase after the fifth year when the borrower begins to pay back the principal. However, the interest rate remains the same.

Biweekly Payment Plan

Loans with a **biweekly payment plan** call for payments every 2 weeks. Since there are 52 weeks in a year, the borrower makes 26 payments, which is equivalent to 13 months of payments, every year. The shortened loan term decreases the total interest costs. The interest costs for the biweekly mortgage are decreased even farther because a payment is applied to the principal (upon which the interest is calculated) every 14 days. The loan is repaid much faster. For example, a 30-year loan can be paid off within 21 to 23 years.

Comparison of Regular Monthly to Biweekly Payments		
	Regular Monthly Payments	**True Biweekly Payments**
Beginning Loan Amount:	$75,000	$75,000
Interest Rate:	10.0%	10.0%
Loan Term:	30 years	30 years
Monthly Payment:	$658	$658 (329 × 2)
Total Interest Paid:	$161,942	$104,331
Total Interest Saved:	0	$57,611
Loan will be paid off:	360 months	252 months

Adjustable-Rate Loans

When a fixed-rate loan is out of reach or impractical for the borrower, a nontraditional mortgage product, such as an ARM product may meet the borrower's specific financial situation. An adjustable-rate loan or **adjustable-rate mortgage (ARM)** is a loan with an interest rate that adjusts in accordance with a movable economic index. The interest rate on the loan varies upward or downward over the term of the loan depending on money market conditions and the agreed upon index. The interest rate on the ARM only changes if the chosen index changes. The borrower's payment stays the same for a specified time (for example, one year or two years) depending on the borrower's agreement with the lender. At the agreed upon time, the rate adjusts according to the current index rate.

ARMs are complex loans. They are very different from the traditional 30-year fixed-rate loan. An ARM may be the ideal home loan after all the variables are considered. In 2005, ARMs made up about 40% of all home loan originations; whereas, 10 years later they accounted for only 5.3%. ARM share data maintained by Freddie Mac records that ARM shares increased from 11% to 33% between 1998 and 2004. ARMs became more popular because of higher home prices and investor activity. However, the share of ARMs to total home loans changes relative to the cost of the product and the health of the economy. When fixed-rates decline, ARM products are not as attractive to borrowers. Mortgage loan originators and other real estate professionals need to understand the mechanics of ARMs and understand when this type of loan may be beneficial to buyers.

Basic Features of ARMs

A lender may offer a variety of ARMs, all of which share similar features— initial interest rate and payment, adjustment period, index, margin, and caps. These basic features are incorporated into every ARM loan.

Initial Interest Rate and Payment

For a limited period of time, every ARM has an initial interest rate and payment. These payments are usually lower than if the loan were a fixed-rate loan. In some ARMs, the initial rate and payment adjust after the first month. Other ARMs keep the initial rate and payment for several years before an adjustment is made.

Adjustment Period

For most ARMs, the interest rate and monthly payment change every month, quarter, year, 3 years, or 5 years. The period between rate changes is the **adjustment period**.

> Example: A loan with an adjustment period of 1 year is called a 1-year ARM. This means the interest rate and payment can change once every year. A loan with a 3-year adjustment period is called a 3-year ARM.

Interest Rate

The interest rate on an ARM changes periodically, usually in relation to an index, and payments may go up or down accordingly. The interest rate is made up of two parts: the index and the margin. The **index** is a measure of interest rates and the **margin** is an extra amount that the lender adds. The initial interest rate is determined by the current rate of the chosen index. Then, a margin, which might be anywhere from 1 to 3 percentage points, is added to the initial interest rate to determine the actual beginning rate (start rate) the borrower will pay.

There is usually a limit to how much the interest rate can change on an annual basis, as well as a lifetime cap, or limit, on changes to the interest rate. Some ARMS have an annual maximum increase (cap) of 1.0% to 2.0% and a lifetime cap of 5 or 6 points above the start rate on the loan. Many loans have caps that are greater or less than these caps.

Index

The **index** is a publicly published number that is used as the basis for adjusting the interest rates of adjustable-rate mortgages. The most common indices, or indexes, are the Constant Maturity Treasury (CMT), the 11th District Cost of Funds Index (COFI), the London Interbank Offering Rates (LIBOR), Certificate of Deposit Index (CODI), and the Bank Prime Loan (Prime Rate).

Each index has advantages and disadvantages. Each of these indices moves up or down based on conditions of the financial markets. Some indexes lag behind market changes. Generally, a loan tied to a lagging index, such as the COFI, is better for borrowers when interest rates are rising. Leading index loans, like those tied to the CMT, are best during periods of declining rates. The CMT, COFI, and LIBOR indexes are the most frequently used. Approximately 80% of ARMs are based on one of these three indexes.

In most circumstances, if the index rate moves up, so does the interest rate. On the other hand, if the index rate goes down, monthly payments can go down. Not all ARMs allow for a downward adjustment to the interest rate.

ARM loan products offer a variety of index options that accommodate individual borrower needs and lender risk tolerances. ARMs with different indexes are available for both purchases and refinances. When an ARM is tied to an index that reacts quickly to market changes, the borrower has the advantage of lower loan payments as interest rates fall. As rates rise, the reverse is true—loan payments suddenly increase.

CMT—Constant Maturity Treasury

The 1-year **Constant Maturity Treasury Index (CMT)** is the most widely used index. Nearly half of all ARMs are based on this index. It is used on ARMs with annual rate adjustments. The CMT index is a volatile index that responds quickly to market changes. The CMT index generally reacts more slowly than the CD index, but more quickly than the COFI.

COFI—11th District Cost of Funds Index

The **11th District Cost of Funds Index (COFI)** is more prevalent in the West. The COFI reflects the weighted-average interest rate paid by 11th Federal Home Loan Bank District savings institutions for savings and checking accounts and other sources of funds. Unlike the CMT and the LIBOR, this index tends to lag behind market interest rate adjustments. In fact, the COFI is the slowest moving and most stable of all ARM indexes. It smoothes out a lot of the volatility of the market. The COFI is one of the most widely used indexes for option ARMs.

LIBOR—London Interbank Offering Rate

The **London Interbank Offering Rate (LIBOR)** is the interest rate that major international banks are willing to offer term Eurodollar deposits to each other. A **Eurodollar** is a dollar deposited in a bank in a country in which the currency is not the dollar. The Eurodollar market has been around for over 40 years and is a major component of the international financial market. London is the center of the Eurodollar market in terms of volume.

The LIBOR rate quoted in the Wall Street Journal is an average of rate quotes from five major banks: Bank of America, Barclays, Bank of Tokyo, Deutsche Bank, and Swiss Bank. The LIBOR is an international index that tracks world market conditions. The LIBOR is similar to the CMT and less stable than the COFI. The LIBOR index is quoted for 1, 3, and 6 months, and 1 year. The 6-month LIBOR is the most common.

CODI—6 Month Certificate of Deposit Index

The 6-month Certificate of Deposit Index (CODI) is an average of the secondary market interest rates on nationally traded **Certificates of Deposit.** The 6-month Certificate of Deposit Index (CODI) generally reacts quickly to changes in the market.

MTA—Monthly Treasury Average

The **Monthly Treasury Average**, which is also known as the 12-Month Moving Average Treasury index (MAT), is relatively new. This index is the 12-month average of the monthly average yields of U.S. Treasury securities adjusted to a constant maturity of one year. The MAT index reacts more slowly in fluctuating markets, so adjustments in the ARM interest rate lag behind other market indicators.

Prime Rate

The **prime rate** refers to the interest rate that individual banks charge their most creditworthy customers for short-term loans. Because many large banks choose to set their prime rates based on the federal funds rate, the prime rates offered by different banks is similar. Banks use this rate as a base rate when determining the interest rates they charge on commercial loans and on some consumer loan products.

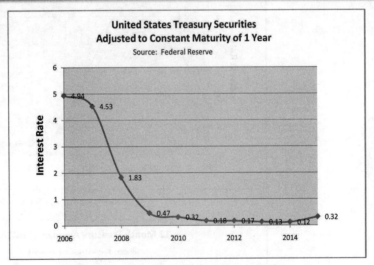

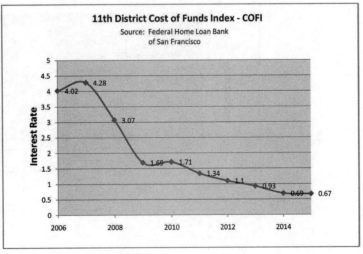

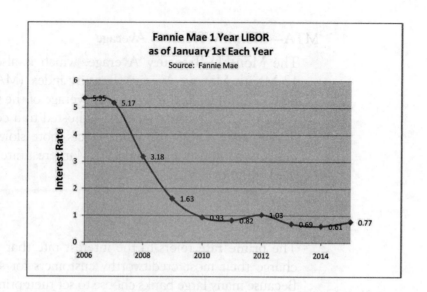

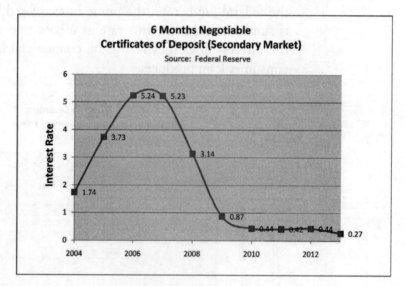

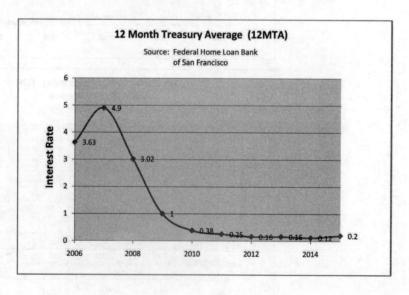

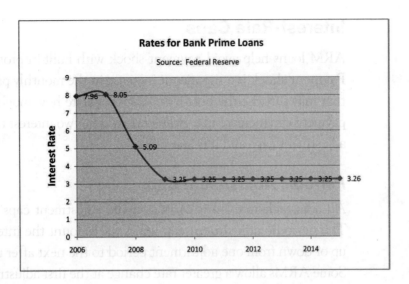

Margin

The lender adds a few percentage points, or **margin**, to the index to determine the interest rate that a borrower pays. The amount of the margin may differ from one lender to another, but it is constant over the life of the loan. Some lenders base the amount of the margin on the borrower's credit record—the better the credit, the lower the margin the lender adds and the lower the interest on the loan.

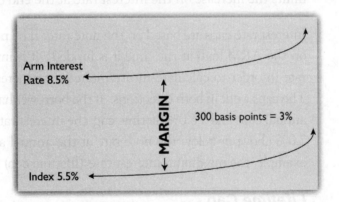

Margins on loans range from 1.75% to 3.5%, depending on the index and the total amount financed in relation to the property value. When the margin is added to the index, the result is known as the **fully indexed rate** on the loan.

> Example: The current index value is 5.5% and the loan has a margin of 2.5%.
> Therefore, the fully indexed rate is 8.0%.

Many adjustable-rate loans (ARMs) have a low **introductory rate** or **start rate**, sometimes as much as 5.0% below the current market rate of a fixed-rate loan. This start rate is usually good for 1 month to as long as 10 years. As a rule, the lower the start rate, the shorter the time before the lender makes the first adjustment to the loan.

Interest-Rate Caps

ARM loans help avoid payment shock with built-in protections called caps. **Payment shock** is a significant increase in the monthly payment on an ARM that may surprise the borrower. Caps regulate how much the interest rate or payment can increase in a given period. The two interest rate caps are periodic adjustment caps and lifetime caps.

Periodic Adjustment Cap

All adjustable-rate loans carry periodic adjustment caps (interim rate caps). The **periodic adjustment cap** limits the amount the interest rate can adjust up or down from one adjustment period to the next after the first adjustment. Some ARMs allow a greater rate change at the first adjustment and then apply an interim rate cap on all future adjustments.

The interim caps apply at the time the loan adjusts. For example, 1-year ARMs have annual caps, 3-year ARMs have 3-year caps, 5-year ARMs have 5-year caps, and so forth. Hybrid ARMs have two interim caps. A 5/1 ARM has a 5-year cap for the first adjustment period and an annual cap thereafter. An interest rate cap is beneficial to borrowers in a rising interest rate market. It limits the increase on the interest rate at the end of each adjustment period.

Interest rate caps are based on the note rate. The **note rate** is the interest rate on the ARM loan at the time it is funded. It is important to know the note rate in order to calculate future interest rate increases and future payments. The caps work in both directions. If the borrower has a 1-year ARM with 2.0% annual caps and a 6.0% lifetime cap, the interest rate cannot adjust more than 2.0% above or below the note rate at the annual adjustment period. In this example, the maximum interest rate (lifetime cap) is the note rate plus 6.0%.

Lifetime Cap

Almost all ARMs have a lifetime interest rate cap called a lifetime cap. The **lifetime cap** is the maximum interest rate that may be charged over the life of the loan. The lifetime cap varies from company to company and loan to loan. Loans with low lifetime caps usually have higher margins. Loans that carry low margins generally have higher lifetime caps.

> Example: An ARM has an initial interest rate of 5.5% with a 6.0% lifetime cap. This means that the interest rate can never exceed 11.5%. If the index increases 1.0% for 10 years, the interest rate on the loan will be 15.5% without the lifetime cap. However, with the lifetime cap it will be 11.5%.

Payment Caps

In addition to interest-rate caps, some ARMs have payment caps. A **payment cap** restricts a payment from increasing more than a specified percentage above the prior year's payment amount. These loans reduce payment shock in a rising interest rate market, but can also lead to negative amortization. **Negative amortization** is an increase in the principal balance caused by low monthly payments that do not pay all the interest due on the loan. This deferred interest is added to the principal on the loan. In some instances, the borrower can owe more than the amount of the original loan. Typically, the payment caps range between 5.0% and 8.0%. For example, if a loan has a 6.0% payment cap and the borrower's monthly payment in year 1 is $1,000, the payment cannot increase more than 6% ($60) in year 2, regardless of the actual interest rate increase.

Other Features of ARMs

The lender or mortgage broker may offer a choice of loans that include discount points, or prepayment penalties.

Discount Points

Discount points are a one-time charge paid by the borrower to lower the interest rate on the loan. A point is equal to one percent of the loan amount. If the fee paid only lowers the interest rate for a specified amount of time rather than for the entire loan term, it is called **limited discount points**. If borrowers choose to pay these points or fees in return for a lower interest rate, they should keep in mind that the lower interest rate may only last until the first adjustment.

If a lender offers a loan with a discounted rate, borrowers should not assume that this means the loan is a good one for them. The borrowers should carefully consider if they are able to afford higher payments that will come in later years when the discount expires and the rate is adjusted. When considering a discounted ARM, the borrower should compare future payments with those of a fully indexed ARM. If a deeply discounted initial rate is used to purchase or refinance a home, the borrower runs the risk of payment shock, negative amortization, prepayment penalties, or conversion fees.

> Example: Assume that the lender's fully indexed one-year ARM rate (index rate plus margin) is currently 6.0%. The monthly payment for the first year is $1,199.10. However, the lender is offering an ARM with a discounted initial rate of 4.0% for the first year. With the 4.0% rate, the first-year's monthly payment is $954.83.

With the discounted ARM, the initial payment probably remains at $954.83 for a limited time. Any savings during the discount period may be offset by higher payments over the remaining life of the mortgage.

Prepayment Penalties

Since January 10, 2014, prepayment penalties are not permitted on ARMS. However, some older ARM loans include a prepayment penalty clause in the promissory note. A **prepayment penalty** is a fee charged when the loan is paid off early. Prepayment penalties are  commonly in effect for three years, although the time may be longer or shorter. The penalty is typically equal to six months' interest on the loan. Borrowers should know how long the prepayment penalty clause is in effect and how the penalty is calculated.

If borrowers want to sell or refinance the property in 2 years and the prepayment penalty is in effect for 3 years, the amount of the penalty that is charged to the borrower may be significant. Depending on the loan term, interest rate, and loan balance, prepayment penalties can equal several thousand dollars.

Assumable Feature

Sometimes ARMs are assumable, which is important for borrowers who plan to resell the property within a short time. The **assumable feature** of a loan allows a borrower to transfer the loan to another borrower, usually with the same terms, if the new homebuyer qualifies for the loan.

Types of ARMs

Lenders offer a variety of ARMs, including interest-only ARMs, convertible ARMs, and payment-option ARMs.

Interest-Only ARM

An **interest-only ARM (IO)** loan allows payment of interest only for a specified number of years (typically between 3 and 10 years). This allows the borrower to have smaller monthly payments for a period of time. After that, monthly payments increase even if interest rates stay the same, because the borrower must start repaying the principal and the interest each month. Keep in mind that the longer the IO period, the higher the monthly payments are after the IO period ends. For some IO loans, the interest rate adjusts during the IO period as well.

Example: A person borrows $150,000 on a 6.0% 5/30 IO ARM. If the loan is fully amortizing over 30 years, the monthly payment will be $900. However, for the first 5 years, the borrower's monthly interest-only payment is $750. Over the next 25 years, the borrower repays both principal and interest. Therefore, the monthly payment increases even if the rate stays the same. Beginning in year 6, the new monthly payment will be $966.

If the borrower chose a 10/30 IO ARM instead of the 5/30 IO ARM, the monthly payment beginning in year 11 will be $1,075.

Convertible ARM

A **convertible ARM** is an ARM that can be converted to a fixed rate by the borrower at some point during the loan term. As an example, a lender may have a 1-year ARM with a feature that allows conversion from the ARM to a fixed–rate loan during the first 60 months of the loan. The lender may charge a one-time fee at the time the loan is converted to a fixed-rate. It is important for a borrower to know that the conversion fee may be large enough to take away all the benefits of the low interest rate charged at the beginning of the loan.

Some states prohibit the lender from charging a conversion fee if the convertibility option is included in the note. This convertibility feature is often accompanied by a higher interest rate than a lender's traditional non-convertible ARM and may have a higher margin as well. When the loan converts, it converts to the current prevailing rate, plus a margin of profit, which may increase the rate by an additional .5%.

Option ARM

An **option ARM** is a type of loan that allows the borrower to choose among several payment options each month. This provides flexibility for borrowers by allowing them to choose the payment that suits their current financial situation. Option ARMs offer a variety of payment options, such as a minimum payment (which can lead to negative amortization), a 15-year or 30-year fully-amortizing payment, or an interest-only payment.

Payment Choices

Payment choices can be made on a monthly basis, thereby enabling borrowers to manage their monthly cash flow. For obvious reasons, many refer to these types of loans as pick-a-payment ARMs. Managing the features of this type of loan requires expertise and vigilance on the part of the borrower because some payment choices may lead to negative amortization. Negative amortization on an option ARM can trigger sudden increases in payments.

Payment Cap

With an option ARM, the minimum payment is usually capped so that it cannot be increased more than 7.5% above the prior year's payment amount. Therefore, if the prior year payment was $1,000, the current year adjustment cannot increase the payment more than $75.

Low Initial Teaser Rate

Option ARMs are often 1-month adjustable loans and typically have low initial teaser rates with low initial payments that enable a borrower to qualify for a larger loan amount. A **teaser rate** is a low, short-term introductory interest rate designed to tempt a borrower to choose a loan. These low payments are usually guaranteed for 12-month periods although the rate may adjust every month. Teaser rates typically generate negative amortization on the loan and often produce payment shock when the interest rate adjusts.

> Example: The homebuyer knows he or she has a 1.25% teaser start rate, but does not understand how much the payments can increase when the loan rate changes to market rates. If the 1.25% teaser rate adjusts to 7.0% or more, the result is an almost 50% increase in payments. On a $100,000 loan amortized for 30 years at 1.25%, the monthly payment of principal and interest is $333.25. The payment for the same loan at a 4.25% market rate is $491.94.

Recasting

Option ARM payments are typically adjusted every 5 years. Lenders do this by amortizing the higher principal balance created by the addition of interest (negative amortization). This automatic payment adjustment is called **recasting**. It amortizes the loan so it can be paid in full by the end of the loan term.

If the option ARM is a 30-year loan, at the end of year 5 the payment is recalculated for the remaining 25 years. If the loan balance has increased because only minimum payments have been made, or if interest rates have risen faster than payments are made on the loan, payments increase each time the loan is recast. At each recast, the new minimum payment is a fully amortizing payment and any payment cap does not apply. This means that the monthly payment can increase significantly at each recast.

Lenders may recalculate loan payments before the recast period if the amount of principal owed grows beyond a set limit, say 110% or 125% of the original mortgage amount.

Example: Suppose only minimum payments are made on a $200,000 mortgage and any unpaid interest is added to the balance. If the balance grows to $250,000 (125% of $200,000), the lender recalculates payments so that the borrower will pay off the loan over the remaining term. It is likely that payments will go up substantially.

Hybrid Loans

While many consumers prefer the more familiar types of loans, a unique loan called a hybrid ARM may be suitable for some borrowers. A hybrid ARM may be desirable for borrowers who plan to sell their homes or pay off their loans within a few years.

A **hybrid ARM** combines the features of a fixed-rate loan with those of an adjustable-rate loan. The fixed-rate feature gives the borrower some security with fixed payments in the initial term of the loan. The adjustable-rate feature is that the initial interest rates on these loans are typically lower than a fixed-rate loan. Initially, a fixed interest rate exists for a period of 3, 5, 7, or 10 years.

At the end of the fixed-rate term of the loan, the interest rate adjusts periodically with an economic index. This adjustment period begins on what is called the reset date for the loan.

Hybrid ARMs are often advertised as 3/1, 5/1, 7/1, or 10/1 ARMs. These loans are a mix (hybrid) of a fixed-rate period and an adjustable-rate period. The interest rate is fixed for the first few years of these loans, for example, for 5 years in a 5/1 ARM. After that, the rate may adjust annually (the 1 in the 5/1 example) until the loan is paid off.

> ### 3/1, 5/1, 7/1, 10/1 ARMs
> - The first number tells how long the fixed interest-rate period will be.
> - The second number tells how often the rate will adjust after the initial period.

A 2/28 or 3/27 ARM is another type of hybrid ARM loan. For this type of ARM, the first number is how long the fixed interest-rate period will be and the second number is the number of years the rates on the loan will be adjustable. Some 2/28 and 3/27 mortgages adjust every 6 months, not annually.

Before the interest rate on the loan begins to adjust, the borrower can decide to sell the property or refinance the loan. The borrower takes a gamble with a hybrid loan by hoping that interest rates will be low when the note rate begins to adjust.

This chart compares all loans against the 30-year fixed-rate loan.

Loan Type	Monthly Payment	Interest Rate	Rate Changes	Total Interest Paid	Build Equity
30-Year Fixed-Rate	Average	Average	Never changes	Average	Average
40-Year Fixed-Rate	Notably lower	Slightly higher	Never changes	Higher	Slower
15-Year Fixed-Rate	Notably higher	Notably lower	Never changes	Notably lower	Notably faster
5/1 ARM	Lower for first 5 years (then may change once a year)	Lower	Fixed for the first 5 years (then may change once a year)	Varies depending on interest rates	Average
3/1 ARM	Lower for the first 3 years (then may change once a year)	Notably lower	Fixed for the first 3 years (then may change once a year)	Varies depending on interest rates	Average
NET 5® (5/1 Initial Interest-Only Payment) ARM	Notably lower for the first 5 years because only interest is required (then may adjust once a year)	Lower	Fixed for the first 5 years (then may change once a year)	Varies depending on interest rates	Does not build equity for the first 5 years

Graduated Payment Mortgage Loans

The graduated payment mortgage is another alternative to an adjustable-rate mortgage. A **graduated payment mortgage (GPM)** is a fixed-rate loan with initial payments that are lower than the later payments. The difference between the lower initial payment and the required amortizing payment is added to the unpaid principal balance. This loan is for the buyer who expects to be earning more after a few years and can make a higher payment at that time.

Unlike an ARM, GPMs are fixed-rate loans and have a fixed payment schedule. With a GPM, the payments are usually fixed for 1 year at a time. Each year for 5 years, the payments graduate from 7.5% to 12.5% of the previous year's payment.

GPMs are available in 30-year and 15-year amortization and for both conforming and jumbo loans. Because of the graduated payments and fixed interest rate, GPMs have scheduled negative amortization of approximately 10.0% to 12.0% of the loan amount depending on the note rate. The higher the note rate, the larger the negative amortization becomes. This is comparable to the potential negative amortization of a monthly adjusting ARM, which can amount to 10.0% of the loan amount.

Both GPMs and ARMs give the consumer the ability to pay the additional principal and avoid the negative amortization. However, in contrast to an ARM, the GPM has a fixed payment schedule so additional principal payments reduce the term of the loan. The ARM's additional payments avoid negative amortization and the payments decrease while the term of the loan remains constant.

The note rate of a GPM is traditionally .5% (half of a percent) to .75% (three-quarters of a percent) higher than the note rate of a straight fixed-rate loan. The higher note rate and scheduled negative amortization of the GPM make the cost of the mortgage more expensive to the borrower in the end. In addition, the borrower's monthly payment can increase by as much as 50% by the final payment adjustment.

The lower qualifying rate of the GPM helps borrowers maximize their purchasing power and can be useful in a market with rapid appreciation. In markets in which appreciation is moderate and a borrower needs to move during the scheduled negative amortization period, the property can be encumbered for more than it is worth.

SUMMARY

Lenders offer a variety of real estate loans and classify the loan products by their purpose for a property purchase, refinance, or cash out. The unique repayment terms of a loan help identify the associated loan product.

A purchase money loan finances the purchase of real property. Any loan used to take cash out of a property is a hard money loan, which draws on the equity of the property.

Amortization liquidates a financial obligation on an installment basis. The amortization schedule details each payment, displays the amount applied to interest and principal, and states the remaining principal balance after each payment. Amortization type is the basis for how a loan is repaid. The most common amortization types include fixed-rate loans, adjustable-rate mortgages (ARM), and graduated payment mortgages (GPM).

Fixed-rate loans have fixed interest and level payments for the life (15, 20, or 30 years) of the loan. The fully amortizing 30-year fixed-rate loan offers low monthly payments with a never-changing monthly payment schedule. An interest-only fixed-rate loan has a fixed rate, short term (3, 5, and 7 year), and fixed monthly payments based upon a 30-year amortizing schedule and a lump sum payment at the end of its term.

An adjustable-rate mortgage (ARM) is a loan with an interest rate that adjusts with a movable economic index. The interest rate varies upward or downward over the term depending on money market conditions and the agreed upon index. There are a variety of ARMs and all share key features—initial interest rate and payment, adjustment period, index, margin, and caps. The most familiar types include interest-only ARMs (IO ARM), convertible ARMs, option ARMs, and hybrid ARMs. Interest-only ARMs (IO ARM) allow payment of only the interest for a specified number of years. Convertible ARMs allow a borrower to convert to a fixed rate during the loan term. An option ARM offers the borrower choices of various payment plans. The unique hybrid ARM combines the features of a fixed-rate loan with those of an adjustable-rate loan.

An alternative to an adjustable-rate mortgage is a graduated payment mortgage (GPM) with a fixed-rate loan with initial payments that are lower than the later payments.

In contrast to an ARM, the GPM has a fixed payment schedule so additional principal payments reduce the term of the loan. The lower qualifying rate of the GPM helps borrowers maximize their purchasing power. However, the higher note rate and scheduled negative amortization of the GPM make the cost of the mortgage more expensive to the borrower in the end.

UNIT 6 REVIEW

▟ Matching Exercise

Instructions: Write the letter of the matching term on the blank line before its definition. Answers are in Appendix A.

Terms

A. adjustable-rate mortgage

B. adjustment period

C. amortization

D. biweekly payment

E. closed-end loan

F. COFI

G. fixed-rate loan

H. graduated payment mortgage

I. hard money loan

J. hybrid ARM

K. index

L. LIBOR

M. margin

N. negative amortization

O. option ARM

P. payment cap

Q. payment shock

R. prime rate

S. purchase money loan

T. teaser rate

Definitions

1. _____ Loan used to purchase property

2. _____ Loan in which the borrower receives all loan proceeds in one lump sum at the time of closing

3. _____ Loan that takes cash out of a property

4. _____ Liquidation of a financial obligation on an installment basis

5. _____ Loan with fixed interest and level payments for the life of the loan

6. _____ Loans with half the monthly payment due every 2 weeks

7. _____ Loan with an interest rate that adjusts with a movable economic index

8. _____ Period between rate changes on an ARM

9. _____ Publicly published number used as the basis for adjusting the interest rates of ARMs

10. _____ Extra amount lenders add to the index

11. _____ 11th District Cost of Funds Index

12. _____ London Interbank Offering Rate

13. _____ Interest rate that individual banks charge their most creditworthy
customers for short-term loans

14. _____ Significant increase in the monthly payment on an ARM that may
surprise the borrower

15. _____ Cap restricting increase in a payment on an ARM

16. _____ Increase in the principal balance caused by low monthly payments that do
not pay all the interest due on the loan

17. _____ Loan that allows the borrower to choose among several payment options
each month

18. _____ Low, short-term introductory interest rate designed to tempt a borrower to
choose a loan

19. _____ ARM with features of both fixed-rate and adjustable-rate loans

20. _____ Fixed-rate loan with initial payments that are lower than the later
payments

Multiple Choice Questions

Instructions: Circle your response and go to Appendix A to read the complete explanation
for each question.

1. Loan products are available to:
   a. purchase property.
   b. refinance an existing loan.
   c. get cash out of a property.
   d. do all of the above.

2. Pam has a loan in which she received all of the loan proceeds in one lump sum at the time of closing. This type of loan is a(n) _____ loan.

     a. closed-end
     b. open-end
     c. purchase money
     d. fixed-rate

3. Becky has purchased a new home with a fully amortizing loan. Her monthly payment schedule will have:

     a. periodic payments of principal and interest.
     b. interest payments only.
     c. periodic reduction of the principal.
     d. equal weekly payments of principal.

4. Which of the following is not commonly used by an institutional lender?

     a. Closed-end loan
     b. Fixed-rate loan
     c. Purchase money loan
     d. Straight loan

5. The most common amortization types include:

     a. fixed-rate loans.
     b. ARMs.
     c. GPMs.
     d. all of the above.

6. Sam wants a home loan with rates that will not change during the loan term. He just learned from the lender that he does not qualify for the $250,000 traditional 30-year fixed-rate loan for which he applied. However, the lender told Sam he does qualify for another fixed-rate loan with lower monthly payments. Based on this information, Sam qualifies for a _____ fixed-rate loan.

     a. 40-year
     b. 20-year
     c. 15-year
     d. 10-year

7. The adjustable-rate mortgage (ARM) loan has an interest rate that adjusts with a movable _____ index.
   a. economic
   b. lender
   c. price
   d. public

8. The interest rate of an ARM is comprised of the _____ and the _____.
   a. index / interest
   b. COFI / CMT
   c. index / margin
   d. indent / margin

9. Every ARM includes a(n):
   a. level payment plan.
   b. biweekly payment.
   c. index.
   d. capitalization rate.

10. A graduated payment mortgage:
    a. is a fixed-rate loan.
    b. has initial payments that are lower than the later payments.
    c. has scheduled negative amortization.
    d. is all of the above.

Conventional Loans

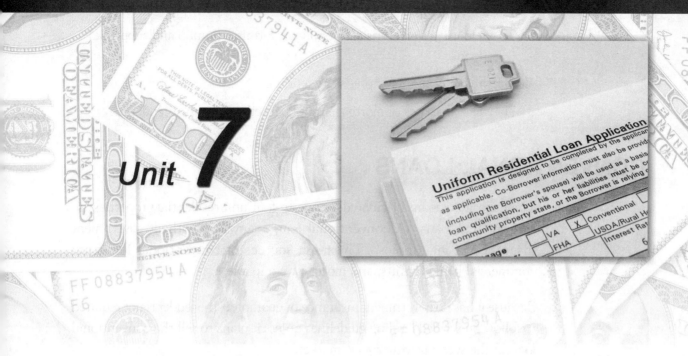

Unit 7

INTRODUCTION

Increased competition among lenders has forced them to be more dynamic and competitive, which results in lenders offering a wide variety of loan products. Some lenders offer nearly every variation of conventional and government-backed loans while others specialize in providing only fixed-rate loans or subprime loans. There are loans for nearly every borrower and lenders that specialize in providing those loans. This unit covers conforming and non-conforming conventional loans.

Learning Objectives

After completing this Unit, you should be able to:

7A   identify characteristics and terms of conventional loans.

7B   recall how conventional loans are used to purchase or refinance a primary residence, second home, or rental property.

7C   recall the purpose of private mortgage insurance.

7D   recall conforming loan guidelines.

7E   indicate the tax impact on income qualification in the mortgage lending process.

7F   calculate PITI.

7G   identify characteristics of non-conforming (jumbo and subprime) loans.

7H   recall elements of predatory lending.

7I   classify types of mortgage fraud perpetrated against lenders.

CONVENTIONAL LOANS

The majority of loans originated for one-to-four unit residential properties are conventional loans. A **conventional loan** is any loan without government insurance or guarantees. The main sources of conventional loans are commercial banks, thrifts, and mortgage companies.

Because it has no government insurance or guarantee, the lender is not required to follow prescribed lending guidelines unless it plans to sell the conventional loan in the secondary mortgage market.

Purpose of Conventional Loans

Conventional loans are used to buy a primary residence (detached or attached), second home, or rental property. Additionally, they are used to refinance existing conventional loans or other FHA/VA loans.

Many condominium projects across the country are eligible for conventional financing. Unlike government loan programs, conventional loans can be used to purchase a second home or a rental. However, the interest rates and down payment requirements are higher when financing a rental home.

As home values increase, many homeowners refinance their conventional home loans to reduce their monthly payments. However, before beginning the refinance, a homeowner should weigh the cost of the refinance versus the benefit of lower interest rates and/or payments. Typically, the lender or loan originator will help the borrower calculate how long it will take for the savings of the lower interest rate to make up for the cost of the refinance.

Conventional Loan Guidelines

Lenders who originate conventional loans set their own lending policies and underwriting standards on loans they keep. For these loans, the lenders are only subject to federal and state regulatory agencies. Lenders can establish the types of loans they originate and the types of acceptable properties.

They determine acceptable borrower qualifications, maximum loan limits, loan-to-value ratios, and loan fees. **Underwriting** is the practice of analyzing the degree of risk involved in a real estate loan.

Conventional lenders may change their loan guidelines at any time. Changes are usually based on market conditions. A lender may decide to stop lending on second homes or may require a larger down payment. If the lender wants to originate more loans, it loosens its underwriting and property guidelines by offering a low down payment, low interest rate, or no income qualification. Conversely, it tightens the standards to decrease lending activity. It can increase down payments and interest rates or only lend on newer single-family homes. No matter the guidelines, the underwriting criteria the lender follows must meet the fair housing and fair lending requirements.

Type of Amortization

As we previously learned, loans are fixed-rate, adjustable-rate, or have graduated payments. Conventional lenders may choose to offer all types of loans, or may specialize in ARMs or fixed-rate loans.

Type of Property

Lenders have preferences for the type and quality of property they will accept as security for a loan. For example, some lenders specialize in residential one-to-four unit properties and condominiums but do not lend on cooperatives. The lender determines the minimum property requirements for conventional loans. Frequently, they use the standardized Fannie Mae/Freddie Mac property guidelines in order to sell the loan in the secondary mortgage market at some point in the future.

Borrower Qualifications

Each conventional lender determines the criteria it uses to qualify borrowers for loans. Some have flexible guidelines and others are very strict. Many conventional lenders use the Fannie Mae/Freddie Mac guidelines discussed later in the unit. Loans that are underwritten using the Fannie Mae/Freddie Mac guidelines may be sold in the secondary mortgage market in the future.

Maximum Loan Limit

Conventional lenders set the maximum loan limits for loans that are not sold in the secondary market. Frequently, loan limits are based on property type or whether the property is owner occupied or for investment.

Interest Rate

Each lender measures risk through a process called risk-based pricing. **Risk-based pricing** is a process that lenders use to determine home loan rates and terms. Since each lender measures risk differently, interest rates vary from lender to lender. Conventional loans made to borrowers with excellent credit may have very low interest rates, while those made to borrowers with poor credit will have high interest rates.

Loan-to-Value Ratio

Conventional lenders set their own loan-to-value ratios. A **loan-to-value ratio (LTV)** is the ratio of the loan amount to the property's appraised value or selling price, whichever is less.

> Example: The lender has an 80% LTV ratio for its conventional loan. The property is appraised at $200,000. Therefore, the maximum loan amount is $160,000. ($200,000 x .80). Unless the lender will permit a second loan for part of the 20%, the borrower will need a 20% down payment of $40,000 to qualify for this loan. This LTV is written 80/20.

A common LTV ratio is 80%, but lenders often originate loans with LTVs of 90% or higher.

> Example: If someone is buying a $300,000 home and has $30,000 as a down payment, the buyer will borrow $270,000 (90% of the appraised value). This is referred to as a 90% LTV loan and is written 90/10.

Lenders may require low LTV ratios for certain property types or for borrowers with low credit scores. LTV loans in excess of 100% are risky and are seldom used.

Down Payment

The basic protection for a lender who makes conventional loans is the borrower's equity in the property. In a purchase transaction, this is the down payment. A **down payment** is the portion of the purchase price that is not financed.

If the borrower has 10% down, what type of loan can the lender structure? Obviously, the lender can structure a 90/10 loan, which gives the borrower a 90% first with a 10% down payment. An alternative might be an 80/10/10 loan. In this loan, the borrower has an 80% first, a 10% second, and the 10% down payment. Other variations include 80/15/5 (80% first, 15% second, 5% down payment) and 80/20/0 (80% first, 20% second, and zero down payment).

If the borrower makes a high down payment (20% or more), a lender has less risk and may offer a lower interest rate. Conversely, a low down payment means greater risk for the lender, who typically will charge the borrower a higher interest rate. Additionally, the lender will require the borrower to purchase private mortgage insurance on the loan.

Mortgage Insurance

Insurance in general is intended to spread any loss from a particular peril over a large insured group. **Mortgage insurance** is insurance that provides coverage for the top part of a residential loan in the event of default. The lender is insured against losses that result when a borrower defaults on a loan and the loan must be foreclosed by the lender. Mortgage insurance is used for loans with LTV ratios that are higher than 80%.

This insurance benefits both borrowers and lenders. Because lenders share the risk of default with the insurer, they are willing to take more risk. The insurance enables borrowers with less cash to have greater access to home ownership. With this type of insurance, it is possible for a borrower to buy a home with as little as a 3% to 5% down payment.

If a lender requires mortgage insurance, the insurance is a contingency of funding the loan. The costs to the borrower vary depending on the type of property and the amount and type of loan.

Types of mortgage insurance include private mortgage insurance (used for conventional loans) and mutual mortgage insurance (used for FHA loans).

Private Mortgage Insurance

Private mortgage insurance (PMI) is extra insurance that lenders require from most homebuyers who obtain conventional loans that are more than 80% of their new home's value. In other words, buyers with less than a 20% down payment are normally required to buy PMI.

Normally, the borrower pays the premium for PMI, not the lender. The borrower may pay the premium up front, but usually the lender collects monthly PMI payments. Since 2006, the IRS allows property owners to deduct qualified mortgage insurance (PMI and MMI) as an itemized deduction on their federal income tax returns.

When annual premiums are paid, a fee is due at the close of escrow and smaller payments are due monthly. When monthly premiums are utilized, there is no advance fee due at closing, just a monthly premium.

Many companies nationwide underwrite private mortgage insurance. Some of them include Mortgage Guaranty Insurance Corporation (mgic.com), The Radian Group (radian.biz), and Genworth Financial (mortgageinsurance.genworth.com).

Types of PMI Coverage

Private mortgage insurance companies set their rates and coverage parameters based on the type of property, loan amounts, loan type, LTV, credit scores, and other factors. Underwriting criteria and rates vary from company to company. The following examples are merely illustrative. Lenders get a specific quote from a PMI insurance provider for each loan.

Example: Borrower Bob lives in Texas and wants to buy a $200,000 home with a 30-year fixed-rate loan. He has verifiable income and a 700 FICO® score.

Loans between 95.1% and 97% LTV: With Bob's 3% ($6,000) down payment the loan is $194,000. The PMI insurance on loans between 95.1%-97% normally covers the top 35% of the loan. The coverage will be $67,900 ($194,000 x .35). The lender's actual exposure or risk is only $126,100 or 63%. Bob's PMI premium will be approximately $116 per month.

Loans between 90.1% and 95% LTV: With Bob's 5% ($10,000) down payment the loan is $190,000. The PMI insurance on loans between 90.1%-95% normally covers the top 30% of the loan. The coverage will be $57,000 ($190,000 x .30). The lender's actual exposure or risk is only $133,000 or 67%. Bob's PMI premium will be approximately $106 per month.

Loans between 85.1% and 90% LTV: With Bob's 10% ($20,000) down payment the loan is $180,000. The PMI insurance on loans between 85.1%-90% normally covers the top 25% of the loan. The coverage will be $45,000 ($180,000 x .25). The lender's actual exposure or risk is only $135,000 or 68%. Bob's PMI premium will be approximately $62 per month.

Loans between 80.1% and 85% LTV: With Bob's 15% ($30,000) down payment the loan is $170,000. The PMI insurance on loans between 80.1%-85% normally covers the top 12% of the loan. The coverage will be $20,400 ($170,000 x .12). The lender's actual exposure or risk is only $149,600 or 75%. Bob's PMI premium will be approximately $30 per month.

Canceling PMI

Effective July 29, 1999, the federal Homeowner's Protection Act (HPA) allows the cancellation of private mortgage insurance under certain circumstances.

Automatic Termination	Lenders or servicers must automatically cancel PMI coverage on most loans once a borrower pays down the mortgage to 78% of the value, providing payments are current.
Borrower Cancellation	By sending a written request, the borrower may ask for cancellation of PMI when the mortgage balance reaches 80% of the original value of the property. However, the borrower must have a good payment history and the value of the home must not have declined. The lender may require evidence that the value of the property has not declined below its original value and that the property does not have a second mortgage.

When the policy is cancelled, the borrower is entitled to a refund of the unearned portion of the mortgage insurance premium paid. The refund must be transferred to the borrower by the lender within 45 days of cancellation.

Types of Conventional Loans

Any conventional loans sold in the secondary mortgage market must conform to the Fannie Mae/Freddie Mac underwriting guidelines and are called **conforming loans**. Therefore, conventional loans that are kept by lenders are called **non-conforming loans** or portfolio loans.

A **portfolio loan** is a loan retained by the lender. Since these loans do not conform to Fannie Mae/Freddie Mac credit standards, they cannot be sold into the secondary market. They are either retained in the lender's portfolio or privately securitized for sale on Wall Street.

CONFORMING LOANS

The majority of loans originated by lenders for one-to-four unit residential properties are conventional loans and the majority of those are conforming loans. **Conforming loans** have terms and conditions that follow the guidelines set forth by Fannie Mae and Freddie Mac. These loans are called "A" paper loans, but are also known as prime loans or full documentation loans, for which the lender requires 2 years of tax returns, verification of income, deposits, employment, a high credit score, and a clean credit history. "A" paper loans can be made to purchase or refinance homes. Fannie Mae and Freddie Mac guidelines establish the maximum loan amount, borrower credit, income requirements, down payment, and property requirements.

It is important to note that any Fannie Mae or Freddie Mac loan product and loan guidelines are subject to change. However, an overview in this unit of some of their loan products provides a glimpse into the wide variety of properties for which conforming loans are available.

Conforming Loan Guidelines

As previously discussed, Fannie Mae and Freddie Mac play an important role in the secondary mortgage market by purchasing conforming loans from primary mortgage market lenders. In addition to that very important role, Fannie Mae and Freddie Mac provide the underwriting guidelines for conforming loans. **Underwriting guidelines** are principles lenders use to evaluate the risk of making real estate loans. The guidelines are just that—guidelines. They are flexible and vary according to the type of loan selected. If a borrower makes a small down payment or has marginal credit, the guidelines are more rigid. If a borrower makes a larger down payment or has sterling credit, the guidelines are less rigid. Lenders who expect to sell their loans to Fannie Mae or Freddie Mac use underwriting guidelines that adhere to the Fannie Mae/Freddie Mac standards.

Fannie Mae and Freddie Mac guidelines determine which properties are suitable, set maximum loan limits, and set debt-to-income ratios for conforming loans.

Suitable Property

Fannie Mae and Freddie Mac purchase loans used to finance a wide variety of one-to-four residential property types. Loans made on these properties that are within conforming loan guidelines can be sold to Fannie Mae.

Fannie Mae/Freddie Mac Suitable Property

- 1-4 family unit principal residences
- Single-family second homes
- 1-4 family investor properties (non-owner occupied)
- Co-ops, condos, PDs, and leaseholds

The location of the property near retail or office property does not necessarily make the property ineligible for Fannie Mae/Freddie Mac.

Loan Limits

In order to qualify for a conforming loan, the amount financed must not exceed the maximum loan limits established by Fannie Mae/Freddie Mac. Different loan limits apply according to the number of units. The limit is less for a single-family property and more for a fourplex.

Fannie Mae and Freddie Mac announce new loan limits every year or as market conditions change. To get the current loan limits, go to the Fannie Mae website at www.fanniemae.com or the Freddie Mac website at www.freddiemac.com. The maximum loan amount is 50% higher in Alaska, Guam, Hawaii, and the Virgin Islands. Properties with 5 or more units are considered commercial properties and are handled under different rules.

Conventional First Mortgage Loan Limits for 2017		
Units	Contiguous States, D.C., & Puerto Rico	Alaska, Guam, Hawaii, & U.S. Virgin Islands
1	$424,100	$636,150
2	$543,000	$814,500
3	$656,350	$984,525
4	$815,650	$1,223,475

Fannie Mae/Freddie Mac also have loan limits for second loans on residential property. A **second loan** is secured by either a mortgage or deed of trust and has a lien position that is subordinate to the first mortgage or deed of trust.

Debt-to-Income Ratios

To determine a consumer's maximum loan amount, lenders use a guideline called a debt-to-income ratio. A **debt-to-income ratio (DTI)** is a ratio derived by dividing the borrower's total monthly obligations (including housing expense) by his or her gross monthly income.

Components of a DTI Ratio

1. Total monthly obligations: This includes consumer debt and the total monthly payment for the mortgage loan. **Consumer debt** includes car payments, credit card debt, judgments, personal loans, child support, alimony, and similar obligations. The **mortgage payment** includes the principal, interest, property taxes, insurance and HOA fees (if applicable).

2. Total stable monthly income

Typically, the maximum DTI ratios for conforming loans range from 36% to 45%.

For loans **underwritten manually**, Fannie Mae's maximum total DTI ratio is 36% of the borrower's stable monthly income. The maximum can be extended up to 45% if the borrower meets the credit score and reserve requirements.

For loans **underwritten through Desktop Underwriter** (DU), the maximum allowable DTI ratio is based on the overall risk assessment of the loan casefile. DU applies a maximum allowable DTI of 45%, with flexibilities offered up to 50% for certain loan casefiles with strong compensating factors.

Example: Renter Rachel has a $4,500 gross monthly income. She currently pays $1,000 per month for her apartment and $400 for her car payment and credit cards. She is thinking of buying a small house using a conforming loan. Based on a debt-to-income ratio of 36%, what is the maximum monthly payment she will qualify for based on her salary and expenses?

$4,500 Monthly Income x .36 = $1,620 allowed for housing expense and recurring consumer debt.

Rachel qualifies for a $1,220 monthly PITI payment ($1,620 – $400).

A lender may require a lower ratio for low down payment loans. For example, if the down payment represents 5% of the home price, a 25% front ratio may be required.

Alternatively, a lender may use higher ratios for loans that have a large down payment or if the borrower makes timely rent payments that are close to the amount of the projected mortgage payment. Borrowers with a good credit history or a substantial net worth may get higher ratios.

Tax Implications in Lending

Lenders are risk averse and want to be sure the borrowers have enough income to repay the loan. Initially, they look at the borrower's W-2 and pay stubs to determine the income needed for loan qualification. Generally, lenders look at pretax income in calculating the debt-to-income ratio, so personal deductions that the applicant claims on his or her tax return are not a factor.

However, most lenders also want copies of the applicant's tax return as a part of reviewing the application package in its underwriting process. When reviewing the tax returns, the underwriter is looking for irregularities that could impact the borrower's income. For example, the income shown on the W-2 forms and paystubs could be negated by some types of tax deductions the borrower takes.

Obviously, people try to maximize their deductions when filing their income tax returns to avoid paying higher taxes. However, a type of deduction that can reduce income is writing off expenses that W-2 employees incur on the job that are not reimbursed by the employer.

Taxpayers use IRS Form 2106 "Employee Business Expense" to deduct ordinary and necessary expenses for the job. Filing this form allows the taxpayer to write off the job-related expenses against their gross income.

Commons expenses may include, but are not limited to:

- Tools
- Subscriptions
- Dues
- Uniforms
- Licensing

The result of subtracting deductions from the gross income is **adjusted gross income** (AGI). The AGI is less than the gross income. Using the adjusted gross income rather than the gross income reduces the applicant's ability to qualify for a loan. This changes the debt-to-income ratio (DTI) and the PITI calculation.

Calculating PITI

For loans with impound (escrow) accounts, lenders calculate the monthly payment that the borrower will make on the new loan consisting of principal (P), interest (I), property taxes (T), and insurance (I). It is known by its acronym **PITI**.

The principal and interest components of the monthly payment can be calculated using amortization tables or a financial calculator. To calculate the property tax component, divide the amount of the annual tax by 12 to get the monthly installment: $200. To calculate the monthly insurance payment, divide the total yearly premiums by 12. The combined sum of the above will equal the total PITI.

Automated Underwriting Systems

Automated underwriting (AU) is a technology-based tool that combines historical loan performance, statistical models, and mortgage lending factors to determine whether a loan can be sold into the secondary market. An **automated underwriting system (AUS)** can evaluate a loan application and deliver a credit risk assessment to the lender in a matter of minutes. It reduces costs and makes lending decisions more accurate and consistent. AUSs promote fair and consistent mortgage lending decisions because they are blind to an applicant's race and ethnicity. The most widely used automated underwriting systems are Fannie Mae's Desktop Underwriter® and Freddie Mac's Loan Prospector®. FHA-insured loan processing uses the FHA Total Scorecard AUS.

As useful as an AUS is, it is only as good as its inputs. If a lender inputs incorrect data (accidentally or intentionally), then the AUS results are invalid.

Desktop Underwriter®

Desktop Underwriter® (DU) is the automated underwriting system that Fannie Mae has developed to assist lenders in making informed credit decisions on conventional, conforming, and FHA/VA loans. Contrary to popular belief, DU does not approve loans. DU provides underwriting recommendations and underwriting reports to the lender, who uses these recommendations to approve or disapprove loans. DU supports most of the Fannie Mae loan products discussed here.

Loan Prospector®

Loan Prospector® (**LP**) is a risk assessment tool that gives lenders access to Freddie Mac's credit and pricing terms. Loan Prospector® uses statistical models based on traditional underwriting factors such as a person's capacity to repay a loan, a person's credit experience, the value of the property being financed, and the type of loan product. In accordance with federal fair housing laws, LP never uses factors such as a borrower's race, ethnicity, age, or any other factor prohibited by the nation's fair housing laws.

Loan Prospector® does not approve loans. It provides quick feedback as to the eligibility of the borrower and property for a particular Freddie Mac loan. The lender uses that information as a tool to approve the loan or fine-tune the application to meet Freddie Mac guidelines. LP supports most of the following Freddie Mac loan programs.

Fannie Mae Loan Products

Fannie Mae's traditional offerings are fixed-rate, conforming loans. Fannie Mae offers fixed-rate loans for 10, 15, 20, and 30-year terms. These **fixed-rate** loans lock in an interest rate and a stable, predictable monthly payment. They continue to be the mortgage of choice for the majority of borrowers. Fannie Mae's short-term fixed-rate loans allow the borrowers to build equity faster and carry a lower interest rate.

In addition to the conforming loans that Fannie Mae purchases, it also offers ARMs and other loan programs to ensure that working families have access to mortgage credit to buy homes they can afford over the long term.

A few of the Fannie Mae loan products are briefly described. Real estate professionals can assist homebuyers by directing them to Fannie Mae lenders who can provide a complete list of the loan products lenders are offering.

HomeReady® Mortgage

HomeReady is Fannie Mae's affordable lending product designed to help credit-worthy low to moderate income borrowers finance the purchase or refinance of their home. Some expanded flexibilities are available under the HomeReady product not available under other Fannie Mae loans.

As an affordable lending product, income restrictions may apply. Income restrictions will be based on the Area Median Income (AMI) amounts for the area in which the subject property is located. There is no income limit for properties located in a low-income census tract. Income limits of 100%

of the AMI will apply to properties located in high-minority census tracts or designated disaster areas. Income limits of 80% of the AMI will apply to all other locations.

Key Product Features
- Borrower is not required to be a first-time buyer
- 97% Loan to Value on purchase transactions
- Reduced mortgage insurance coverage requirement
- (25% coverage for 90.01 – 97% LTV)
- Underwriting Flexibilities
  - Allows non-occupant borrowers, such as a parent.
  - Permits rental income from an accessory dwelling unit (such as a basement apartment).
  - Allows boarder income (updated guidelines provide documentation flexibility).
  - Allows income from a non-borrower household member as a compensating factor
- No borrower required minimum contribution
- Allows gifts, grants, Community Seconds®, and cash-on-hand as a source of funds for down payment and closing costs.
- Supports manufactured housing up to 95% and HomeStyle® Renovation (approved lenders) to 95%.

97% LTV Program

The **97% LTV Program** allows homebuyers to purchase a single-family home, condo, co-op, or PUD without coming up with a full 5% down payment as previous guidelines mandated. The 3% down loan is similar to existing conventional loan programs.

Requirements for the 97% LTV Program
- The mortgage is a fixed rate loan with a term up to 30 years.
- The property is one-unit single-family home, co-op, PUD, or condo. Manufactured housing is not eligible.
- At least one buyer has not owned a home in the last three years.
- The property will be the owner's primary residence.
- The loan amount is at or below $424,100.
- According to Fannie Mae's Loan Level Price Adjustment (LLPA) chart, a borrower can have a score as low as 620 and still qualify.
- All loans must be underwritten through Desktop Underwriter (DU).

The 97% LTV Program allows home buyers to accept cash gifts for down payments. Monies may be 100% gifted from parents and relatives. The only requirement is that the gift is actually a gift—downpayment "loans" are not allowed.

Like other conventional loans, 97% LTV loans require borrowers to pay private mortgage insurance (PMI).

Community Seconds® Loan

Under the **Community Seconds®** loan program, a borrower can obtain a secured second loan that typically is funded by a federal, state, or local government agency, an employer, or a nonprofit organization. To qualify for this loan, borrowers must earn no more than 100% of the median income for their Metropolitan Statistical Area (MSA) or county and attend a homebuyer education session. According to the federal Office of Management and Budget, a **Metropolitan Statistical Area (MSA)** is an urban area that has at least one city with a population of 50,000 or more and has adjacent communities that share similar economic and social characteristics.

HomeStyle® Energy

HomeStyle® Energy helps homeowners finance new energy improvements or pay off debt they used to increase the energy or water efficiency of their homes. Energy improvements can involve added insulation, energy-efficient windows, or water saving devices. Solar panels and other innovative energy saving devices may also be eligible under HomeStyle Energy.

The program is available on one-to-four principal residences, one-unit second homes, and one-unit investment properties. It allows borrowers to use up to 15% of the "as completed" appraised value of the property for new energy improvements under either a refinance or a new purchase transaction.

Freddie Mac Loan Products

Like Fannie Mae, Freddie Mac's underwriting guidelines are flexible and vary according to loan program. The majority of Freddie Mac's home loans are fixed-rate, with 15, 20, and 30-year terms. These products enable the borrower to have the security of stable monthly payments throughout the life of the loan. The 15 and 20-year term loans allow the borrower to build equity faster and carry a lower interest rate. These fixed-rate loans can be combined with other Freddie Mac loan options to accommodate a wide variety of borrowers. In recent years, Freddie Mac has been more aggressive in serving the subprime market and has developed loan products to serve that market.

Affordable Merit Rate® Mortgage

Freddie Mac's **Affordable Merit Rate® Mortgage** offers borrowers who are credit challenged an initial interest rate that is closer to conventional rates. The program gives borrowers the opportunity to reduce their interest rate at no cost. If the borrowers make 24 consecutive on-time payments in a 4-year period, they qualify for an automatic one-time, 1% interest rate reduction. If a loan payment is made late in the first 24 months, borrowers are re-evaluated for an interest rate reduction on the 36-month or 48-month anniversary of the payment due date.

Home Possible® Mortgage

The **Home Possible® Mortgage** targets first-time homebuyers, move-up borrowers, retirees, families in underserved areas, new immigrants, and very low and low-to-moderate-income borrowers. This product features higher loan-to-value ratios, higher debt-payment-to-income ratios, and flexible credit terms to help borrowers qualify. For  borrowers without a readily verifiable credit history, noncredit payment references, such as a documented savings history of at least 12 months, may be included if the history shows periodic deposits (at least quarterly) resulting in a growing balance over the year. Temporary buy-downs offer the borrower an option to prepay interest up front and lower the overall interest rate.

A Mortgage Credit Certificate (MCC) issued by a state or local government agency is allowed on this loan, which helps borrowers qualify. The **Mortgage Credit Certificate** is a federal tax credit which entitles qualified homebuyers to reduce the amount of their federal income tax liability by an amount equal to a portion of the interest paid during the year on a home mortgage. A MCC worksheet is used to apply the tax benefit of the interest the borrower will pay on the loan, which results in a reduction of the calculated debt-payment-to-income ratio and monthly housing expense-to-income ratio. This allows buyers to qualify more easily for a loan by increasing their effective income.

Adjustable-Rate Mortgages

Freddie Mac's **adjustable-rate mortgages (ARMs)** help borrowers maximize their home buying power with lower interest rates. ARMs offer flexibility for borrowers who relocate frequently or expect their income to increase within the next couple of years. Borrowers using ARMs must understand that their payments can go up or down during the term of the loan.

Freddie Mac's **London Interbank Offered Rate (LIBOR)-Indexed ARMs** offer borrowers aggressive initial rates (lower than many other ARMs) and have proved to be competitive with other popular ARM indices.

Investment Property Mortgages

Freddie Mac's investment property mortgages offer a variety of mortgage options—fixed-rate mortgages, most ARMs, 5- and 7-year balloon/reset mortgages, and A-minus Mortgages. The loan-to-value ratio depends on the mortgage option chosen and the borrower must have sufficient funds for the down payment and closing costs. These loans are available to purchase or refinance 1- to 4-unit residential investment property.

NON-CONFORMING LOANS

A **non-conforming loan** is a loan that does not meet the Fannie Mae or Freddie Mac lending guidelines. This can be due to the type of property being financed or because the borrower's income is difficult to verify. Loans that exceed the maximum loan amount are called jumbo loans. Sometimes, subprime loans are an option for borrowers whose creditworthiness does not meet the guidelines.

Jumbo Loans

A **jumbo loan** exceeds the maximum conforming loan limit set by Fannie Mae and Freddie Mac. Because jumbo loans are bought and sold on a much smaller scale, these loans usually carry a higher interest rate and have additional underwriting requirements.

Subprime Loans

Loans that do not meet the borrower credit requirements of Fannie Mae and Freddie Mac are called **subprime loans** or "B" paper and "C" paper loans as opposed to "A" paper conforming loans. The purpose of "B" and

"C" paper loans is to offer financing to applicants who do not currently qualify for conforming "A" paper financing. Subprime loans are offered to borrowers who may have recently filed for bankruptcy or foreclosure, or have late payments on their credit reports.

Borrowers in the subprime category include those who have low credit scores or no credit score, income that is difficult or impossible to verify, an excessively high debt-to-income ratio, or a combination of these factors. Other factors, such as the purpose of the loan and the property type, may require the borrower to secure a subprime loan. For example, a borrower who is qualified to purchase a single-family home under standard Fannie Mae or Freddie Mac guidelines may have to use a subprime loan to finance the purchase of a non-owner occupied fourplex.

When Subprime Financing May Be Necessary
- Low credit scores
- No credit rating
- Good credit, but debt-to-income ratios exceeding limits allowable to qualify for a prime loan

Typical Subprime Terms

Subprime loans often include higher than market interest rates, higher than ordinary fees, prepayment penalties, and additional lender insurance.

Higher than Market Interest Rates

Subprime loans may carry interest rates anywhere from 1% to 7% above prime loan rates and are 4% above prime loan rates on average.

Higher than Ordinary Fees

Lenders charge higher fees on subprime loans due to their higher risk. Origination fees as high as 7% and various junk fees are common to subprime loans. A **junk fee** is a questionable fee charged in closing costs that may not bear any significant relationship to the actual loan transaction. In addition, mortgage broker yield-spread premiums increase loan costs to the borrower. **Yield-spread premiums** are points paid by lenders to mortgage brokers for delivering high interest rate loans.

Fees that May be Subject to Abuse

- **Processing fee:** The lender charges this fee for processing the loan. It is commonly charged in prime loans but may be excessive in subprime financing.

- **Loan origination fee:** The origination fee is the basic charge for executing the loan and, for a prime loan, is generally equal to 1% of the loan amount. The origination fee is typically higher for a subprime loan.

- **Credit report fee:** These should be the same with prime and subprime loans and the borrower should receive a copy of the credit report.

- **Warehouse fee:** A warehouse fee is a type of fee that mortgage brokers charge when they fund loans out of their own resources. The fee represents the cost the lender incurs to hold the loan until it is sold on the secondary market. The lender, not the borrower, should absorb this fee.

- **Consulting fee:** This is a junk fee. The lender should provide consulting services at no charge to the borrower.

- **Endorsement fee:** This fee relates to endorsements in title insurance policies that some lenders charge. Others include the fee in the cost of the lender's title insurance policy. This is a junk fee that lenders may inflate.

- **Document preparation fee:** This fee typically covers the cost to prepare the note and security instrument. Lenders can arbitrarily inflate this fee.

- **Underwriting fee:** The amount of this fee varies from lender to lender and loan to loan and represents the lender's expense for analyzing the borrower's ability to qualify for the loan.

If any of these fees appear on the HUD-1 or Good Faith Estimate, the borrower should ask the lender to explain them. If they seem inappropriate, the fee should be reduced or removed.

Prepayment Penalties

Many conventional non-conforming loans carry prepayment penalties. A typical prepayment penalty is equal to 6 months' interest on any prepayment that is greater than 20% of the loan balance. The prepayment penalty equals approximately 3% to 4% of the loan balance. Depending upon the amount, this penalty can effectively wipe out any equity gains the borrower might have realized in the first years of ownership. In addition, the prepayment penalty increases as the interest rate increases because this penalty is an interest-based fee.

Additional Lender Insurance

Packing is the practice of adding credit insurance or other extras to increase the lender's profit on a loan. Lenders can require the purchase of credit insurance provided the premiums are calculated and paid on a monthly basis. A lender may not finance a credit insurance premium. [12 CFR §1026.36(i)]. "CFR" stands for the "Code of Federal Regulations".

Typical Subprime Loans

Examples of "B" paper loans are the 2/28 ARM and 3/27 ARM. These ARMs have a fixed interest rate for the first 2 or 3 years of the loan. After that, the interest rate can change yearly according to the index plus the margin (subject to any caps). "B" paper loans allow borrowers with less-than-perfect credit to rebuild their credit and refinance the loan at a better rate. Usually 2/28 ARMs and 3/27 ARMs have a higher initial interest rate and a prepayment penalty during the first 3 years.

The **exploding ARM** is a notorious home loan product offered in the subprime industry. This adjustable-rate mortgage loan product features a low introductory teaser rate for which the borrower qualifies even with high debt-to-income ratios. When these rates adjust, typically in as little as 2 years, the new fully-indexed rate on this subprime home loan can increase debt-to-income ratios 20% or more. This dramatic rate increase causes the payments to jump to a level that is unmanageable for the majority of homeowners.

Predatory Lending

Predatory lending is the abusive practice of extending credit with the intent to deceive and take advantage of the borrower. Subprime borrowers pay higher rates and fees that make them more susceptible to predatory lending practices that can strip them of the equity in their homes and possibly lead to foreclosure.

The popularity of subprime loans, their explosive growth, and accompanying lending abuses brought the industry into Congressional focus.

Characteristics of Predatory Lenders

- Offer easy access to money but often use high-pressure sales tactics
- Inflate interest rates, charge outrageous fees, and have unaffordable repayment terms
- Use harassing collection tactics
- Trick buyers into taking out a loan they cannot afford to repay, knowing the homeowner is at a high risk of losing the home to foreclosure

Many states passed laws to protect consumers against predatory lending practices. The Dodd-Frank Wall Street Reform and Consumer Protection Act of 2010 has two titles that deal with predatory and abusive lending practices—Title X and Title XIV. Title X established the Consumer Financial Protection Bureau (CFPB) and authorized it to enforce laws that prohibit unfair, deceptive, or abusive acts and practices in connection with consumer financial products and services. Title XIV, the Mortgage Reform and Anti-Predatory Lending Act, regulates residential mortgage lending activities in a manner that is designed to remedy many of the abuses in the subprime mortgage lending market that helped cause the financial crisis of 2007.

Additionally, the Office of the Controller of the Currency (OCC), which regulates national banks, issues guidelines for these banks to tell them how to guard against abusive lending practices. These guidelines outline a number of abusive lending practices that often accompany predatory loans. These include packaging excessive or hidden fees in the amount financed, refinancing of subsidized mortgages that results in the loss of beneficial terms, and equity stripping.

Equity stripping is a predatory scheme in which unscrupulous investors take advantage of homeowners who are in financial trouble. Equity stripping occurs when these investors prey on people who are often uninformed and in need of help. In this scheme, the homeowner is promised an opportunity to buy back his or her home at some future time if the owner simply reconveys ownership of the property to the investor. In exchange, the investor promises the homeowner the right to continue to live in the home as a tenant. The agreement is often constructed in such a way that the individual is actually forfeiting all rights to the property along with any equity the property has accumulated over time.

MORTGAGE FRAUD

Just as some unethical loan originators and lenders take advantage of borrowers, there are borrowers that are motivated to commit mortgage fraud. The two most common types of mortgage fraud are fraud for housing and fraud for profit.

Fraud for housing is committed by borrowers who, often with the assistance of loan officers or other lender personnel, misrepresent or omit relevant details about employment and income, debt and credit, or property value and condition with the goal of buying real estate. Fraud for housing can be committed by individuals who intend to occupy a property as primary residence, or by investors who intend to rent the property or flip it.

Fraud for profit is committed by industry professionals who misstate, misrepresent, or omit relevant details about their personal or their clients' employment and income, debt and credit, or property value and condition with the goal of maximizing profits on a loan transaction. It is important to note here that fraud for profit can be committed by any professional in the loan transaction chain including the builder, real estate sales agent, loan officer, mortgage broker, real estate appraiser, property inspector, insurance agent, title company, attorney, and escrow agent. Industry professionals can also work in concert, as a network, to defraud underwriters, lenders and borrowers, and maximize fees and share profits on all mortgage related services. These actions are motivated either by the desire to gain extra sales commissions or simply increase an investment position.

SUMMARY

Loans are first classified by their amortization type—fixed-rate, ARM, and GPM. They are then classified by whether or not they have government backing. This unit covers conventional loans. A conventional loan is any loan made by lenders without any governmental guarantees. Conventional loans are either conforming or non-conforming.

Conforming loans have terms and conditions that follow the guidelines set forth by Fannie Mae and Freddie Mac. Sometimes the borrower's creditworthiness, or the size of the loan, does not meet conventional lending standards. In that case, a non-conforming loan product is used. Non-conforming loans include jumbo loans and subprime loans.

Subprime financing is the origination of loans for borrowers with less-than-perfect credit or other underwriting issues that do not allow them to qualify for market interest rates. Subprime lending involves elevated credit risk.

Predatory lending is the abusive practice of extending credit with the intent to deceive and take advantage of the borrower. Unscrupulous lenders instigate predatory lending. Predatory lending results in loans to borrowers that include inflated interest rates, outrageous fees, and unaffordable repayment terms.

The two most common types of mortgage fraud are fraud for housing and fraud for profit.

UNIT 7 REVIEW

Matching Exercise

Instructions: Write the letter of the matching term on the blank line before its definition. Answers are in Appendix A.

Terms

A. adjustable-rate mortgage (ARM)

B. Affordable Merit Rate® Mortgage

C. automated underwriting

D. consumer debt

E. conforming loan

F. conventional loan

G. debt-to-income ratio (DTI)

H. Desktop Underwriter®

I. down payment

J. equity stripping

K. exploding ARM

L. Fannie Mae's 7-year balloon loan

M. fixed-rate loan

N. Home Possible® Mortgage

O. interest rate

P. jumbo loan

Q. junk fee

R. Loan Prospector®

S. Metropolitan Statistical Area (MSA)

T. mortgage default insurance

U. HomeReady® Mortgage

V. non-conforming loan

W. packing

X. portfolio loan

Y. predatory lending

Z. private mortgage insurance (PMI)

AA. risk-based pricing

BB. second loan

CC. subprime loan

DD. underwriting guidelines

Definitions

1. _____ Any loan without government insurance or guarantees

2. _____ Process that lenders use to determine home loan rates and terms

3. _____ Insurance that provides coverage for the top part of a residential loan in the event of default

4. _____ Extra insurance that lenders require from most homebuyers who obtain conventional loans that are more than 80% of their new home's value

5. _____ Loan retained by the lender. Since these loans do not conform to Fannie Mae/Freddie Mac credit standards they cannot be sold into the secondary market

6. _____ Has terms and conditions that follow the guidelines set forth by Fannie Mae and Freddie Mac

7. _____ Principles lenders use to evaluate the risk of making real estate loans

8. _____ Secured by either a mortgage or deed of trust and has a lien position subordinate to the first mortgage or deed of trust

9. _____ The ratio derived by dividing the borrower's total monthly obligations (including housing expense) by his or her gross monthly income

10. _____ The debt that includes car payments, credit card debt, judgments, personal loans, child support, alimony, and similar obligations

11. _____ Technology-based tool that combines historical loan performance, statistical models, and mortgage lending factors to determine whether a loan can be sold into the secondary market

12. _____ The automated underwriting system that Fannie Mae has developed to assist lenders in making informed credit decisions on conventional, conforming, and FHA/VA loans

13. _____ Risk assessment tool that gives lenders access to Freddie Mac's credit and pricing terms

14. _____ Loan that locks in an interest rate and a stable, predictable monthly payment

15. _____ Loan that is targeted to help minority and other underserved markets

16. _____ The abusive practice of extending credit with the intent to deceive and take advantage of the borrower

17. _____ Freddie Mac mortgage targets first-time homebuyers, move-up borrowers, retirees, families in underserved areas, new immigrants, and very low and low-to-moderate-income borrowers

18. _____ Loan that helps borrowers maximize their home buying power with lower interest rates

19. _____ Loan that does not meet the Fannie Mae or Freddie Mac lending guidelines

20. _____ Loan that exceeds the maximum conforming loan limit set by Fannie Mae and Freddie Mac

21. _____ Loan that does not meet the borrower credit requirements of Fannie Mae and Freddie Mac

22. _____ Questionable fee charged in closing costs that may not bear any significant relationship to the actual loan transaction

23. _____ Practice of adding credit insurance or other extras to increase the lender's profit on a loan

24. _____ Adjustable-rate mortgage loan product with a low introductory teaser rate for which the borrower qualifies even with a high debt-to-income ratio

25. _____ Predatory scheme in which unscrupulous investors take advantage of homeowners who are in financial trouble

Multiple Choice Questions

Instructions: Circle your response and go to Appendix A to read the complete explanation for each question.

1. A lender who makes conventional loans has what basic protection against risk?
    a. Government backing
    b. Low down payments
    c. A borrower's home equity
    d. Fannie Mae insurance

2. Which of the following statements is true of private mortgage insurance? PMI is:
    a. extra insurance lenders require from most homebuyers who obtain jumbo loans.
    b. normally paid for by the lender.
    c. only provided by Freddie Mac.
    d. none of the above are true.

3. Fannie Mae purchases conforming loans made on which of the following single-family homes?
    a. Single-family second homes
    b. Mobile homes
    c. Timeshares
    d. Both (a) and (b)

4. Fannie Mae developed the Desktop Underwriter® system in order to:
    a. approve loans at a quicker rate to meet borrower demand.
    b. provide underwriting recommendations.
    c. help borrowers improve their credit scores.
    d. price a loan for purchase in the secondary market.

5. Sally is looking for a particular home loan product that offers a predictable monthly payment and a 30-year term to keep the payments low. What kind of loan product should she consider?
    a. Adjustable-rate mortgage
    b. Energy improvement loan
    c. Fixed-rate loan
    d. Interest only loan

6. The Community Seconds® loan program offers borrowers a second lien loan:
    a. with priority over the first lien.
    b. funded by Fannie Mae.
    c. funded by the local government.
    d. that may not be forgiven.

7. Which of the following is not true regarding Freddie Mac underwriting guidelines?
    a. Freddie Mac guidelines are the same for all products.
    b. Freddie Mac guidelines are flexible.
    c. Depending on the loan product, the guidelines vary.
    d. None of the above

8. Which of the following statements can be associated with jumbo loans? Jumbo loans:
    a. meet Fannie Mae guidelines.
    b. meet Freddie Mac guidelines.
    c. require additional underwriting conditions.
    d. have lower interest rates.

9. Lenders often suggest that borrowers obtain credit insurance. They can do this as long as:
    a. the price of the premium is included in the finance charge.
    b. the premiums are prepaid on an annual basis.
    c. the price of the premium is included in the APR.
    d. the premiums are calculated and paid on a monthly basis.

10. A federal law that was written specifically to combat predatory lending is the:
    a. Real Estate Settlement Procedures Act.
    b. Truth in Lending Act.
    c. Mortgage Reform and Anti-Predatory Lending Act.
    d. Fair Housing Act.

Alternative Financing

INTRODUCTION

Alternative financing offers a way for lenders and borrowers to respond to the realities of today's economy. In real estate transactions, traditional financing may not always be sufficient to complete a purchase; therefore, a borrower may opt for a nontraditional mortgage product. A borrower may not qualify for financing based on the lender's criteria, or the terms of the proposed financing are not favorable to the buyer. The changing needs of consumers have created an environment in which alternative financing is sometimes a necessity.

A borrower can seek alternative financing from a variety of sources in order to complete a real estate purchase. Alternative financing methods include seller financing, secondary financing, and other financing alternatives that are based on the type of property or the purpose of the loan. The secondary finance instruments and loan priority are discussed later in the course. This unit covers the different types of alternative financing as well as how the financing is beneficial to a prospective borrower in a real estate transaction.

Learning Objectives

After completing this Unit, you should be able to:

8A   identify the different types of alternative financing.

8B   recognize the advantages of seller financing.

8C   specify the types of seller financing available to borrowers.

8D   identify various types of secondary financing.

8E   distinguish the types of financing based on property type.

8F   recognize the type of financing based on the purpose of the loan.

8G   recall types of lender participation loans.

SELLER FINANCING

A common source for alternative financing is the seller. If the seller is going to be the lender, he or she agrees to provide the funds to the buyer for the amount required to close a real estate transaction. The funds are usually in the form of a loan that is secured by a trust deed in favor of the seller and recorded after the first trust deed. When a seller carries the paper on the sale of his or her home, it is also called a **purchase-money loan**, which is similar to the loan made by an outside lender. In a seller carryback loan, the seller acts as the beneficiary and the buyer is the trustor. Seller financing offers distinct advantages for both the buyer and seller when compared to traditional financing.

Advantages of Seller Financing

- Offers creative financing for buyers with a less than stellar credit rating, no down payment, or not enough cash to cover closing costs

- Buyers can avoid private mortgage insurance (PMI) associated with loan-to-value ratios above 80%

- Advertising the availability of seller financing attracts more prospective buyers to a property that is for sale

- Sellers can obtain a better return on investment by offering interest rates that are higher than market rates

- Helps to sell properties in times of tight money

Whenever seller financing is part of a real estate transaction, state laws may require the seller to complete a seller financing disclosure statement. It gives the buyer all the information necessary to make an informed decision about using seller financing to complete the sale. The buyer can see the existing loans as well as such things as due date and payments on existing loans that are senior to the loan in question.

In seller financing, options include carryback financing, contract for deed, and a wraparound mortgage (WRAP) or all-inclusive trust deed (AITD).

Carryback Financing

Carryback financing is the extension of credit by a seller who takes back a note for a portion or the entire purchase price of a property. A seller can choose to finance a significant portion of the real estate purchase by carrying back a first or second loan.

Example: Chad makes an offer on a house owned by John, who accepts an offer of $375,000. Chad is self-employed, but is currently unable to obtain a loan at favorable interest rates since his income fluctuates from year to year. John has no existing loans on the property and must sell as soon as possible, so he offers carryback financing on a new first loan for $300,000 with a favorable interest rate if Chad can put down $75,000. Chad agrees and the transaction is successful.

If a seller receives a substantial amount from the proceeds of a first loan, plus the buyer's down payment, it may be in the seller's interest to carry a second mortgage or trust deed—possibly for income or to reduce tax liability by accepting installment payments.

Example: Mark makes an offer on a house owned by Mike, who accepts an offer of $375,000 with $37,500 as the down payment. Mark, the buyer, qualifies for a new first loan for $318,750 and asks Mike, the seller, to carry a second loan for $18,750 to complete the purchase price. Mike agrees and the transaction is successful.

When the seller extends credit in the form of a loan secured by a second deed of trust (mortgage), the promissory note may be written as a straight note, with interest-only payments, or even no payments. Alternatively, it can be an installment note with a balloon payment at the end or a fully amortizing note with equal payments until it is paid off. A **balloon payment** is the final payment that is larger than the other installment payments provided under the terms of the note. The buyer and seller usually decide the terms of the loan. The instructions the buyer and seller give regarding the seller financing are usually carried out through escrow.

SELLER FINANCING ADDENDUM AND DISCLOSURE

(California Civil Code §§2956-2967)

(C.A.R. Form SFA, Revised 10/02)

This is an addendum to the ☐ Residential Purchase Agreement, ☐ Counter Offer, or ☐ Other _____

_____ , ("Agreement"), dated _____ ("Property"),

On property known as _____ ("Property"),

between _____ ("Buyer"),

and _____ ("Seller").

Seller agrees to extend credit to Buyer as follows:

1. **PRINCIPAL; INTEREST; PAYMENT; MATURITY TERMS:** ☐ Principal amount $ _____ , interest at _____ % per annum, payable at approximately $ _____ per ☐ month, ☐ year, or ☐ other _____ , remaining principal balance due in _____ years.

2. **LOAN APPLICATION; CREDIT REPORT:** Within 5 (or ☐ _____) Days After Acceptance: **(a)** Buyer shall provide Seller a completed loan application on a form acceptable to Seller (such as a FNMA/FHLMC Uniform Residential Loan Application for residential one to four unit properties); and **(b)** Buyer authorizes Seller and/or Agent to obtain, at Buyer's expense, a copy of Buyer's credit report. Buyer shall provide any supporting documentation reasonably requested by Seller. Seller, after first giving Buyer a Notice to Buyer to Perform, may cancel this Agreement in writing and authorize return of Buyer's deposit if Buyer fails to provide such documents within that time, or if Seller disapproves any above item within **5 (or** ☐ _____ **) Days** After receipt of each item.

3. **CREDIT DOCUMENTS:** This extension of credit by Seller will be evidenced by: ☐ Note and deed of trust; ☐ All-inclusive note and deed of trust; ☐ Installment land sale contract; ☐ Lease/option (when parties intend transfer of equitable title); OR ☐ Other (specify) _____
_____ .

THE FOLLOWING TERMS APPLY ONLY IF CHECKED. SELLER IS ADVISED TO READ ALL TERMS, EVEN THOSE NOT CHECKED, TO UNDERSTAND WHAT IS OR IS NOT INCLUDED, AND, IF NOT INCLUDED, THE CONSEQUENCES THEREOF.

4. ☐ **LATE CHARGE:** If any payment is not made within _____ **Days** After it is due, a late charge of either $ _____ , or _____ % of the installment due, may be charged to Buyer. **NOTE:** on single family residences that Buyer intends to occupy, California Civil Code §2954.4(a) limits the late charge to no more than 6% of the total monthly payment due and requires a grace period of no less than 10 days.

5. ☐ **BALLOON PAYMENT:** The extension of credit will provide for a balloon payment, in the amount of $ _____ , plus any accrued interest, which is due on _____ (date).

6. ☐ **PREPAYMENT:** If all or part of this extension of credit is paid early, Seller may charge a prepayment penalty as follows (if applicable): _____ . Caution: California Civil Code §2954.9 contains limitations on prepayment penalties for residential one-to-four unit properties.

7. ☐ **DUE ON SALE:** If any interest in the Property is sold or otherwise transferred, Seller has the option to require immediate payment of the entire unpaid principal balance, plus any accrued interest.

8.* ☐ **REQUEST FOR COPY OF NOTICE OF DEFAULT:** A Request for a copy of Notice of Default as defined in California Civil Code §2924(b) will be recorded. **If not,** Seller is advised to consider recording a Request for Notice of Default.

9.* ☐ **REQUEST FOR NOTICE OF DELINQUENCY:** A Request for Notice of Delinquency, as defined in California Civil Code §2924e, to be signed and paid for by Buyer, will be made to senior leinholders. **If not,** Seller is advised to consider making a Request for Notice of Delinquency. Seller is advised to check with senior leinholders to verify whether they will honor this request.

10.* ☐ **TAX SERVICE:**
A. If property taxes on the Property become delinquent, tax service will be arranged to report to Seller. **If not,** Seller is advised to consider retaining a tax service, or to otherwise determine that property taxes are paid.
B. ☐ Buyer, ☐ Seller, shall be responsible for the initial and continued retention of, and payment for, such tax service.

11. ☐ **TITLE INSURANCE:** Title insurance coverage will be provided to **both** Seller and Buyer, insuring their respective interests in the Property. **If not,** Buyer and Seller are advised to consider securing such title insurance coverage.

12. ☐ **HAZARD INSURANCE:**
A. The parties' escrow holder or insurance carrier will be directed to include a loss payee endorsement, adding Seller to the Property insurance policy. **If not,** Seller is advised to secure such an endorsement, or acquire a separate insurance policy.
B. Property insurance **does not** include earthquake or flood insurance coverage, unless checked: ☐ Earthquake insurance will be obtained; ☐ Flood insurance will be obtained.

13. ☐ **PROCEEDS TO BUYER:** Buyer will receive cash proceeds at the close of the sale transaction. The amount received will be approximately $ _____ , from _____ (indicate source of proceeds). Buyer represents that the purpose of such disbursement is as follows: _____

14. ☐ **NEGATIVE AMORTIZATION; DEFERRED INTEREST:** Negative amortization results when Buyer's periodic payments are less than the amount of interest earned on the obligation. Deferred interest also results when the obligation does not require periodic payments for a period of time. In either case, interest is not payable as it accrues. This accrued interest will have to be paid by Buyer at a later time, and may result in Buyer owing more on the obligation than at its origination. The credit being extended to Buyer by Seller will provide for negative amortization or deferred interest as indicated below. (Check A, B, or C. CHECK ONE ONLY.)
☐ A. All negative amortization or deferred interest shall be added to the principal _____ (e.g., annually, monthly, etc.), and thereafter shall bear interest at the rate specified in the credit documents (compound interest);
OR ☐ B. All deferred interest shall be due and payable, along with principal, at maturity;
OR ☐ C. Other _____ .

*(For Paragraph 8-10) In order to receive timely and continued notification, Seller is advised to record appropriate notices and/or to notify appropriate parties of any change in Seller's address.

SFA REVISED 10/02 (PAGE 1 OF 3)

Buyer's Initials (_____) (_____)
Seller's Initials (_____) (_____)

Reviewed by _____ Date _____

EQUAL HOUSING OPPORTUNITY

SELLER FINANCING ADDENDUM AND DISCLOSURE (SFA PAGE 1 OF 3)

Agent:
Broker:

Property Address: _____ Date: _____

15. ☐ **ALL-INCLUSIVE DEED OF TRUST; INSTALLMENT LAND SALE CONTRACT:** This transaction involves the use of an all-inclusive (or wraparound) deed of trust or an installment land sale contract. That deed of trust or contract shall provide as follows:
    A. In the event of an acceleration of any senior encumbrance, the responsibility for payment, or for legal defense is: _____
    _____ ; OR ☐ **Is not** specified in the credit or security documents.
    B. In the event of the prepayment of a senior encumbrance, the responsibilities and rights of Buyer and Seller regarding refinancing, prepayment penalties, and any prepayment discounts are: _____ ;
    OR ☐ **Are not** specified in the documents evidencing credit.
    C. Buyer will make periodic payments to _____ (Seller, collection agent, or any neutral third party), who will be responsible for disbursing payments to the payee(s) on the senior encumbrance(s) and to Seller.
    NOTE: The Parties are advised to designate a neutral third party for these purposes.
16. ☐ **TAX IDENTIFICATION NUMBERS:** Buyer and Seller shall each provide to each other their Social Security Numbers or Taxpayer Identification Numbers.
17. ☐ **OTHER CREDIT TERMS:** _____
18. ☐ **RECORDING:** The documents evidencing credit (paragraph 3) will be recorded with the county recorder where the Property is located. **If not,** Buyer and Seller are advised that their respective interests in the Property may be jeopardized by intervening liens, judgments, encumbrances, or subsequent transfers.
19. ☐ **JUNIOR FINANCING:** There will be additional financing, secured by the Property, junior to this Seller financing. Explain: _____
_____
20. **SENIOR LOANS AND ENCUMBRANCES:** The following information is provided on loans and/or encumbrances that will be **senior** to Seller financing. **NOTE:** The following are estimates, unless otherwise marked with an asterisk (*). If checked: ☐ A separate sheet with information on additional senior loans/encumbrances is attached.

	1st	2nd
A. Original Balance	$_____	$_____
B. Current Balance	$_____	$_____
C. Periodic Payment (e.g. $100/month):	$_____	$_____ / _____
Including Impounds of:	$_____	$_____ / _____
D. Interest Rate (per annum)	_____ %	_____ %
E. Fixed or Variable Rate:	_____	_____
If Variable Rate: Lifetime Cap (Ceiling)	_____	_____
Indicator (Underlying Index)	_____	_____
Margins	_____	_____
F. Maturity Date	_____	_____
G. Amount of Balloon Payment	$_____	$_____
H. Date Balloon Payment Due	_____	_____
I. Potential for Negative Amortization? (Yes, No, or Unknown)	_____	_____
J. Due on Sale? (Yes, No, or Unknown)	_____	_____
K. Pre-payment penalty? (Yes, No, or Unknown)	_____	_____
L. Are payments current? (Yes, No, or Unknown)	_____	_____

21. **BUYER'S CREDITWORTHINESS:** (CHECK EITHER A OR B. Do not check both.) In addition to the loan application, credit report and other information requested under paragraph 2:
    A. ☐ No other disclosure concerning Buyer's creditworthiness has been made to Seller;
OR **B.** ☐ The following representations concerning Buyer's creditworthiness are made by Buyer(s) to Seller:

Borrower _____	Co-Borrower _____
1. Occupation _____	1. Occupation _____
2. Employer _____	2. Employer _____
3. Length of Employment _____	3. Length of Employment _____
4. Monthly Gross Income _____	4. Monthly Gross Income _____
5. Other _____	5. Other _____

22. **ADDED, DELETED OR SUBSTITUTED BUYERS:** The addition, deletion or substitution of any person or entity under this Agreement or to title prior to close of escrow shall require Seller's written consent. Seller may grant or withhold consent in Seller's sole discretion. Any additional or substituted person or entity shall, if requested by Seller, submit to Seller the same documentation as required for the original named Buyer. Seller and/or Brokers may obtain a credit report, at Buyer's expense, on any such person or entity.

Copyright© 1997-2002, CALIFORNIA ASSOCIATION OF REALTORS®, INC.

SFA REVISED 10/02 (PAGE 2 OF 3)

Buyer's Initials (_____) (_____)
Seller's Initials (_____) (_____)

Reviewed by _____ Date _____

SELLER FINANCING ADDENDUM AND DISCLOSURE (SFA PAGE 2 OF 3)

Property Address: _____ Date: _____

23. CAUTION:
   A. If the Seller financing requires a balloon payment, Seller shall give Buyer written notice, according to the terms of Civil Code §2966, at least 90 and not more than 150 days before the balloon payment is due if the transaction is for the purchase of a dwelling for not more than four families.
   B. If **any** obligation secured by the Property calls for a balloon payment, Seller and Buyer are aware that refinancing of the balloon payment at maturity may be difficult or impossible, depending on conditions in the conventional mortgage marketplace at that time. There are no assurances that new financing or a loan extension will be available when the balloon prepayment, or any prepayment, is due.
   C. If **any** of the existing or proposed loans or extensions of credit would require refinancing as a result of a lack of full amortization, such refinancing might be difficult or impossible in the conventional mortgage marketplace.
   D. In the event of default by Buyer: (1) Seller may have to reinstate and/or make monthly payments on any and all senior encumbrances (including real property taxes) in order to protect Seller's secured interest; (2) Seller's rights are generally limited to foreclosure on the Property, pursuant to California Code of Civil Procedure §580b; and (3) the Property may lack sufficient equity to protect Seller's interests if the Property decreases in value.

If this three-page Addendum and Disclosure is used in a transaction for the purchase of a dwelling for not more than four families, it shall be prepared by an Arranger of Credit as defined in California Civil Code §2957(a). (The Arranger of Credit is usually the agent who obtained the offer.)

Arranger of Credit - (Print Firm Name) _____ By _____ Date _____

Address _____ City _____ State _____ Zip _____

Phone _____ Fax _____

BUYER AND SELLER ACKNOWLEDGE AND AGREE THAT BROKERS: (A) WILL NOT PROVIDE LEGAL OR TAX ADVICE; (B) WILL NOT PROVIDE OTHER ADVICE OR INFORMATION THAT EXCEEDS THE KNOWLEDGE, EDUCATION AND EXPERIENCE REQUIRED TO OBTAIN A REAL ESTATE LICENSE; OR (C) HAVE NOT AND WILL NOT VERIFY ANY INFORMATION PROVIDED BY EITHER BUYER OR SELLER. BUYER AND SELLER AGREE THAT THEY WILL SEEK LEGAL, TAX, AND OTHER DESIRED ASSISTANCE FROM APPROPRIATE PROFESSIONALS. BUYER AND SELLER ACKNOWLEDGE THAT THE INFORMATION EACH HAS PROVIDED TO THE ARRANGER OF CREDIT FOR INCLUSION IN THIS DISCLOSURE FORM IS ACCURATE. BUYER AND SELLER FURTHER ACKNOWLEDGE THAT EACH HAS RECEIVED A COMPLETED COPY OF THIS DISCLOSURE FORM.

Buyer _____ Date _____
                                 (signature)
Address _____ City _____ State _____ Zip _____
Phone _____ Fax _____ E-mail _____

Buyer _____ Date _____
                                 (signature)
Address _____ City _____ State _____ Zip _____
Phone _____ Fax _____ E-mail _____

Seller _____ Date _____
                                 (signature)
Address _____ City _____ State _____ Zip _____
Phone _____ Fax _____ E-mail _____

Seller _____ Date _____
                                 (signature)
Address _____ City _____ State _____ Zip _____
Phone _____ Fax _____ E-mail _____

THIS FORM HAS BEEN APPROVED BY THE CALIFORNIA ASSOCIATION OF REALTORS® (C.A.R.). NO REPRESENTATION IS MADE AS TO THE LEGAL VALIDITY OR ADEQUACY OF ANY PROVISION IN ANY SPECIFIC TRANSACTION. A REAL ESTATE BROKER IS THE PERSON QUALIFIED TO ADVISE ON REAL ESTATE TRANSACTIONS. IF YOU DESIRE LEGAL OR TAX ADVICE, CONSULT AN APPROPRIATE PROFESSIONAL.

This form is available for use by the entire real estate industry. It is not intended to identify the user as a REALTOR®. REALTOR® is a registered collective membership mark which may be used only by members of the NATIONAL ASSOCIATION OF REALTORS® who subscribe to its Code of Ethics.

SURE TRAC
The System for Success™

Published by the
California Association of REALTORS®

Reviewed by _____ Date _____

EQUAL HOUSING OPPORTUNITY

SFA REVISED 10/02 (PAGE 3 OF 3)

SELLER FINANCING ADDENDUM AND DISCLOSURE (SFA PAGE 3 OF 3)

Discounting Mortgages (Deeds of Trust)

If a mortgage or deed of trust held by the seller is sold to an outside party, usually a mortgage broker, the note and security instrument are discounted. **Discounting a note** is selling a note for less than the face amount or the current balance. Discounting a note increases the yield to the buyer, which makes the investment in the note more attractive. Even though the seller receives a reduction in value from the mortgage broker, it is one way a seller can cash out a trust deed that was carried back.

> Example: Bob and Todd own a house together as investors. After several years, they put the house on the market for $550,000 and hope to get a full-price offer so they can go their separate ways with the profit from the house.
>
> After a short time, they get a full-price offer. The buyer offers to put $110,000 down, get a $385,000 new first loan, and asks Bob and Todd to carry $55,000 for five years as a second trust deed. Bob and Todd want to turn down the offer but their agent suggests they accept and sell the second trust deed after the close of escrow. Even though it will be discounted, it is one way Bob and Todd can get most of the cash out of their investment.
>
> If the second trust deed is sold at a discounted 20%, or minus $11,000, Bob and Todd will end up with $55,000, less $11,000, or $44,000. In that way they will get the cash out of the sale even though they will net less than they originally planned because of the discount. They follow their agent's suggestion and are satisfied with the result.

Contract for Deed (Land Contract)

A **contract for deed** is a private financing contract held by the property seller. Instead of taking out a mortgage, the buyer agrees to make regular payments directly to the seller, who retains title to the property. A contract for deed is also known as a contract of sale, an agreement of sale, a conditional sales contract, or a land sales contract.

A primary difference between traditional mortgages and contracts for deed is the time that the buyer receives legal title to the property. At closing, with a mortgage, the seller receives his or her funds, the buyer receives title, and the seller's legal interest in the property terminates. However, with a contract for deed, the seller (**vendor**) becomes the lender to the buyer (**vendee**) and retains **legal title**. The buyer (vendee) has possession and use of the property (known as **equitable title**). Only when all the terms of the contract are met, does the vendor pass legal title to the vendee.

An owner-financed contract for deed provides buyers with an opportunity to buy property without having to qualify for a loan. Also, because there is no lender involved, the transaction is simply between the buyer and seller, without the involvement of a third party. This minimizes the amount of closing costs and can shorten the closing period as little as one day. Therefore, depending on the situation, a contract for deed may benefit both sellers and buyers.

Wraparound Loan

A **wraparound loan** is another type of seller financing. It is essentially a purchase-money loan that includes both the unpaid principal balance of the first loan and a new second loan against the property. This type of financing is commonly used when a seller acts as the lender in the sale of his or her own property.

In general, only assumable loans can be wrapped. **Assumable loans** are those on which existing borrowers can transfer their obligations to qualified homebuyers. Currently, only some FHA and VA loans are assumable without prior permission from the lender. Loans with "due on sale" clauses prohibits a homebuyer from assuming a seller's existing mortgage without the lender's permission. If permission is given, it will always be at the current market rate, which often defeats the purpose of using a wraparound loan.

The wraparound loan may be secured by a mortgage or deed of trust. When the security instrument is a mortgage, it is called a **wraparound mortgage (WRAP)** and when a deed of trust is used, it is an **all-inclusive trust deed (AITD)**.

A wraparound mortgage (WRAP) secures a wraparound loan. The WRAP is subordinate to existing encumbrances because the WRAP is created at a later date. This means any existing encumbrances have priority over the WRAP even though they are included, or wrapped, by the new wraparound mortgage. At the time of closing, the buyer receives title to the property.

Example: Art sells his house for $100,000. The existing first trust deed is for $50,000 at 8%, payable in payments of $377 monthly. The buyer's down payment is $20,000. Art agrees to carry a second trust deed of $30,000 for the buyer at 10%.

Sales price	$100,000
Less: Cash by buyer (down payment)	- 20,000
AITD carried by Art	$ 80,000
($50,000 existing loan plus $30,000 new loan)	

WRAPAROUND MORTGAGE RIDER

Rider and addendum to Security Instrument dated_____, _____

The attached security instrument is a wraparound mortgage/deed of trust subordinate to a certain mortgage/deed of trust dated _____, _____, executed in favor of _____ and currently held by_____ in the original principal amount of $_____, which was recorded on the _____ day of _____,_____ in the county records of _____ County, State_____ as follows:

Book:_____
Page: _____
Libor: _____
Reception: _____
Date: _____

Borrower agrees to comply with all the terms and conditions of the above described mortgage including, but not limited to, those concerning taxes and insurance, other than with respect to the payment of principal or interest due under said mortgage. If Borrower herein shall fail to comply with all the terms, provisions and conditions of said mortgage so as to result in a default thereunder (other than with respect to payments of principal or interest due), that failure on the part of Borrower herein shall constitute a default under this security instrument and shall entitle the lender, at its options, to exercise any and all rights and remedies given this security instrument in the event of a default under this security instrument.

If the lender hereunder shall default in making any required payment of principal or interest under the above described mortgage or deed of trust, the Borrower shall have the right to advance funds necessary to cure that default and all funds so advanced by Borrower shall be credited against the next installment of principal and interest due under the Note secured by this security instrument.

_____   _____
Borrower   Borrower

The buyer is to pay Art monthly payments of $702 on the AITD of $80,000 at 10%. Art must pay the original lender monthly payments of $377 on the existing first trust deed of $50,000 at 8%.

AITD payment to Art	$702
Existing First Trust Deed payment	- 377
Monthly difference to Art	$325

SECONDARY FINANCING

Borrowers obtain secondary financing to provide additional funds for the purchase of property or to take cash out of property. Second lien loans are available for these purposes. **Second lien** loans are subordinate (inferior) to the mortgage or deed of trust that secures a first lien. Secondary financing includes hard money loans from private lenders, swing loans, home equity loans (HEL), and home equity lines-of-credit (HELOC).

Private Lender Hard-Money Loan

As previously defined, a **hard money loan** is any loan used to take cash out of a property. Hard money loans are typically offered by private investors who are seeking to earn a higher return on their investment through the interest rates on the loan. These types of loans are beneficial when traditional bank financing is inadequate to complete a real estate transaction.

When a private lender extends credit to a borrower for a hard money loan, the property itself serves as collateral for the loan. If a borrower defaults on a hard money loan by a private lender, the lender can potentially take title to the property through foreclosure and obtain the property for significantly less than the original investment. As stated earlier, the private investor is also concerned with obtaining a reasonable return on his or her investment. This can be accomplished through the interest rates offered by the private lender. As a result, the interest rates on hard money loans from a private lender are typically higher than market rates. States establish usury laws to set a ceiling on how high the private lender can set the interest rates.

A lien recorded against the title of the borrower's property secures the investment by the private lender. The promissory note states the terms of the private loan and the procedures that take place in the event of a default.

Typical Information in a Promissory Note for a Private Loan

- A predetermined period for repayment of the loan

- The interest rate on the loan

- Statement confirming the transfer of conditional title to a third party in a deed of trust

- The power of the third party to reconvey the deed to the borrower after repayment of the loan

- The power of the third party to foreclose on the property in the event of a loan default

A private lender who invests in hard money loans must be aware of the potential risks, especially if the borrower defaults on the loan. While the lender can attempt to foreclose the property, the lender must realize that he or she may not receive steady income from the investment because of the default. In addition, the costs associated with foreclosure may also create a negative return on investment.

Swing Loan (Bridge Loan)

A **swing loan** or **bridge loan** is a temporary, short-term, hard money loan made on a borrower's equity in his or her present home. It is used when the borrower has purchased another property and the buyer needs cash to close the sale on the new home. The new loan is secured by a deed of trust or mortgage against the borrower's current home.

Borrowers can obtain a swing loan from a traditional lender such as a bank. The interest rate on a swing loan is about 2% higher than on a 30-year fixed-rate loan. There are usually no payments due until the home sells. Interest accrues during the term of the loan. Principal and interest are due in a balloon payment when the sale of the home closes.

The borrower's income must be sufficient to cover all loans on both properties. If the current home is unsold but is rented, the lender will include the rental income to help the borrower meet the income requirements. Some lenders may not give a swing loan unless the property that is for sale is already under contract.

Home Equity Loan

A **home equity loan (HEL)** is a hard money loan made against the equity in the borrower's home. The traditional home equity loan (HEL) is a one-time loan for a lump sum and is typically at a fixed-interest rate. The traditional home equity loan is repaid in equal monthly payments over a set period. Traditional lenders, such as banks, offer home equity loans at varying terms. The term of the loan for a fixed-rate second can extend up to 30 years.

A lender uses strict guidelines before loaning money against the equity in a property. The reason is simple. A lender who has to sell the property at a foreclosure sale must realize enough in the sale to pay off all outstanding liens. This is more likely if total liens equal no more than 75%-90% of the property value. Loan guidelines for home equity loans take into account all outstanding loans and set combined loan-to-value limits. An appraisal is used to determine market value.

Home equity loans provide homeowners cash for a number of reasons, but they also strip the equity out of the property. If homeowners need money to pay bills for home repairs, they may think a home equity loan is the answer. It may be. However, it is important to shop this type of loan and talk with several lenders.

With a home equity loan, as with any loan, the borrower should compare the annual percentage rate (APR) on the same loan with different lenders since the APR reflects total loan costs. If a home is used as security for a home equity loan, federal law gives the borrower 3 business days after signing the loan papers to cancel the deal for any reason, without penalty.

Home Equity Line-of-Credit Loan

A **home equity line-of-credit (HELOC)** is a typical open-end loan. An **open-end loan** is expandable by increments up to a maximum dollar amount. It is a line of credit that is secured by the borrower's home. The HELOC allows the homeowner to draw out cash up to a specified limit and use it at his or her discretion.

A HELOC is a type of second lien loan that taps into a property owner's equity and establishes a revolving credit line. By using the equity in their home, borrowers may qualify for a sizable amount of credit that is available for use when and how they please, at a relatively low interest rate. Furthermore, depending on each borrower's specific situation, tax laws may allow the borrower to deduct the interest because the debt is secured by the home. Both closed-end and open-end loans have a definite date by which the borrower must pay off the principal amount.

Since a home is generally a consumer's largest asset, many homeowners use their home equity credit lines for major items, such as education, home improvements, or medical bills. When a HELOC is used for these purposes, it is an open-end loan. With an open-end loan, an additional amount of money may be loaned to a borrower in the future under the same security instrument.

A number of traditional lenders, such as banks, can offer customers a HELOC. With a home equity line, a borrower is approved for a specific **credit limit**, which is the maximum amount he or she can borrow at any one time. Many lenders set the credit limit on a home equity line by taking a percentage (75%-90%) of the appraised value of the home and subtracting the balance owed on the existing mortgage.

Example:

Appraised value of home	$100,000
Percentage of appraised value	75%
	$75,000
Less balance owed on existing mortgage	40,000
Potential credit line	$35,000

When determining the borrower's actual credit line, the lender considers the borrower's ability to repay the loan by looking at income, debts, other financial obligations, and the borrower's credit history.

Home equity plans often set a fixed time during which a homeowner can borrow money (10 years, for example). When this period is up, the plan may allow the borrower to renew the credit line. With a plan that does not allow renewals, a borrower cannot borrow additional money once the time has expired.

The home equity plan outlines the method the borrower must use to repay the line of credit. Some plans may call for payment in full of any outstanding balance. Others may permit a borrower to repay over a fixed amount of time, such as 10 years.

Typically, a borrower is able to draw on the line by using special checks. Under some plans, borrowers use a credit card to make purchases using the line. However, the borrower may be limited in how he or she may use the line. Some plans require the homeowner to borrow a minimum amount each time he or she draws on the line (for example, $300) and to keep a minimum amount outstanding. Some lenders require that borrowers take an initial advance when the line is first set up.

Interest Rate Charges and Plan Features

Home equity plans typically have variable interest rates rather than fixed rates. A variable-rate HELOC is based on a published index, such as the prime rate or a U.S. Treasury bill rate. Interest rate changes coincide with the fluctuations in the chosen index. Most lenders add a margin of 1 or 2 percentage points to the index. Since the cost of borrowing is tied directly to the index rate, it is important to find out the index and margin each lender uses, how often the index changes, and how high it has risen in the past.

Sometimes lenders advertise a temporarily discounted teaser rate for home equity lines. A **teaser rate** is unusually low and often only lasts for an introductory period, such as 6 months. Variable-rate plans secured by a dwelling must have a ceiling (or lifetime cap) on the interest rate. Some variable-rate plans limit how much the payment may increase and how low the interest rate may fall if interest rates drop.

Lenders may permit a borrower to convert a variable interest rate to a fixed interest rate during the life of the plan or to convert all or a portion of the line-of-credit to a fixed-term installment loan. Agreements generally permit the lender to freeze or reduce a credit line under certain circumstances. For example, some variable-rate plans may not allow a borrower to receive additional funds during any period in which the interest rate reaches the cap.

Associated Costs

Many of the costs of setting up a home equity line-of-credit are similar to those borrowers pay when they buy a home.

Costs Associated with a HELOC

- A fee for a property appraisal, which estimates the value of the home

- An application fee, which may not be refundable if the borrower is turned down for credit

- Up-front charges, such as 1 "or more" point (1 point equals 1% of the credit limit)

- Other closing costs, which include fees for attorneys, title search, mortgage preparation and filing, property and title insurance, and taxes

- Certain fees during the plan. For example, some plans impose yearly membership or maintenance fees.

- Borrowers may be charged a transaction fee every time draws are made on the credit line

Repaying the HELOC

Before entering into a HELOC, a borrower should consider how he or she plans to repay the outstanding balance. Some plans set minimum payments that cover a portion of the principal (the amount borrowed) and accrued interest. Unlike a typical installment loan, the portion that goes toward principal may not be enough to repay the debt by the end of the term.

Other plans allow payments of interest only during the life of the plan, which means the borrower pays nothing toward the principal. If $10,000 is outstanding, the borrower owes the entire sum when the plan ends. If this is the case, the borrower must be prepared to make the balloon payment by refinancing with the lender, obtaining a loan from another lender, or obtaining the funds from another source.

Disclosures from Lenders

The Truth in Lending Act requires lenders to disclose the important terms and costs of their home equity plans, including the APR, miscellaneous charges, payment terms, and information about any variable-rate feature. The lender may not charge a fee until the borrower has received this information. Borrowers usually get these disclosures when they receive an application form and they receive additional disclosures before the plan is opened. If any term has changed before the plan is opened (other than a variable-rate feature), the lender must return all fees if the borrower decides not to enter into the plan as a result of the change.

Traditional Second Lien Loan vs. HELOC

A traditional second lien loan provides more predictable loan payments than a HELOC. A traditional second offers a fixed amount of money that is repayable over a fixed period. Usually, the payment schedule calls for equal payments that pay off the entire loan by the end of the loan term. A HELOC gives the borrower more flexibility while the traditional second gives the borrower a greater sense of security.

OTHER FINANCING

There are other types of financing available when traditional bank financing and seller financing are not enough to complete a real estate transaction. There are lenders who finance a specific type of property or offer a loan product for a particular loan purpose.

Financing by Property Type

There are different types of property available for purchase, whether the property serves as the buyer's primary residence or second home. As a result, there are different ways to finance real property and, quite often, the type of property dictates the type of financing that is available to the purchaser.

Financing Manufactured Housing

A **mobilehome** is a factory-built home manufactured prior to June 15, 1976, constructed on a chassis and wheels, and designed for permanent or semi-permanent attachment to land. In the past, mobilehomes were known as trailers and were used mainly as second, traveling homes. **Manufactured homes** are homes built in a factory after June 15, 1976 and must conform to the federal  Manufactured Home Construction and Safety Standards (HUD code). The federal standards regulate manufactured housing design and construction, strength and durability, transportability, fire resistance, energy efficiency, and quality.

A mobilehome is personal property unless it has been converted into real property. It is considered real property when it is attached to a permanent foundation.

Changing a Mobilehome from Personal to Real Property

- Permanent foundation
- Certificate of occupancy
- Building permit (where required)
- Recorded document stating that the mobilehome has been placed on a foundation

Financed as Personal Property

Traditionally, financing for manufactured homes required at least a 10% down payment, a term of up to 15 years, and higher than average interest rates. It was generally thought that the more mobile a home was, the less favorable the financing. There is still some truth to this notion, but changes in the lending industry have allowed for more favorable financing for owners of manufactured homes.

There are also companies that specialize in financial lending for mobile and manufactured homes. If the manufactured home is not permanently attached to the land, a borrower may obtain a personal property loan. A **personal property loan** is a loan for anything movable that is not real property. Another method borrowers use to finance manufactured homes is to obtain financing that is directly available from the retailer (**retailer financing**). The retailer who produces the home may offer in-store financing for qualified purchasers.

Financed as Real Property

If the manufactured home is permanently attached to the land, a borrower can obtain real property financing from a bank. As stated earlier, retailer financing is also available directly from the manufacturer. Owners of manufactured homes that meet the criteria for real property can obtain government assistance from the Federal Housing Administration (FHA) and the Department of Veterans Affairs (VA). Common features of government-backed loans include low down payments, low closing costs, and easy credit qualifications for borrowers. Like all other loans, the FHA or VA protect the lender against loss if the borrower defaults on the loan. There are government-backed home loans available for manufactured homes affixed to the land or located in a mobilehome park. Below are some features and requirements of FHA and VA loans for manufactured homes. For a complete list, visit www.hud.gov and www.va.gov.

Features and Requirements of FHA Manufactured Home Loans

- Maximum loan amounts
    - » $69,678 for the home or $92,904 for the home and the lot
- Maximum loans terms
    - » 20 years for the home or 25 years for the home and the lot
- 5% minimum down payment
- Adequate income for repaying the loan and other expenses
- Primary residence for borrowers

Features and Requirements of VA Manufactured Home Loans

- Maximum loan amounts
    - » 95% of the purchase price of the property securing the loan and the VA funding fee.
- Maximum loan terms
    - » Loan terms range from 15 years 32 days to 25 years 32 days depending on the type of unit and whether the lot is included in the purchase.
- Primary residence for borrowers
- Manufactured home property requirements
    - » Permanent frame built in one or more sections
    - » Permanent eating, cooking, sleeping, and sanitary facilities
    - » 10 feet wide (minimum 400 SF for a single-wide unit)
    - » 20 feet wide (minimum 700 SF for a double-wide unit)

Financing Co-ops

A **cooperative** or co-op is ownership of an apartment unit in which the owner has purchased shares in the corporation that holds title to the entire building. Members of a cooperative do not own their unit directly since the corporation officially owns or leases the real estate that the co-op member occupies. A  member of a cooperative possesses the right to live in the apartment unit through an occupancy agreement or a **proprietary lease**.

For prospective purchasers of a cooperative, there is financing available in the form of a co-op share loan. A **co-op share loan** is a type of loan that is made to finance the purchase or refinancing of the borrower's ownership interest in a residential unit in a co-op project owned by the co-op housing corporation. Co-op share loans are available from commercial banks that offer this specific type of loan product. Like mortgages, co-op share loans are secured loans. In addition to a promissory note, lenders also require a security agreement and file a lien against the borrower's property in public records. Most lenders also require the original stock certificate and a copy of the borrower's proprietary lease. A recognition agreement that prohibits the co-op corporation from canceling the stock or lease without the lender's permission is also demanded.

Different lenders that cater to co-op financing can offer loan programs for low-income properties to high-end buildings. In addition, funds are available for co-op improvement projects, the purchase of a co-op apartment, or the formation of a new housing cooperative.

Financing Vacation Homes

Individuals purchase vacation homes in order to relax and escape from the stresses of their lives. When someone decides to purchase a vacation home with a loan, he or she must be aware of the available financing options. A buyer can obtain a loan for a vacation home through a traditional lender, but there are certain nuances involved with the financing.

Since the prospective purchaser will not use the vacation home as his or her primary residence, lenders view the loan as a risky proposition. Their view is that borrowers will most likely default on the loan for a vacation home rather than the loan on the property that they occupy. As a result, the underwriting guidelines and qualifications are stricter in comparison to loans for primary residences. For example, a lender who offers loans for vacation homes may require that the borrower provide a 20% down payment. In addition, the loan products available to vacation home purchasers may contain more aggressive financing terms such as higher interest rates and shorter terms. Borrowers may need to explore other creative financing options such as seller carryback loans in order to complete the transaction.

Financing Timeshares

A **timeshare** is a real estate development in which a buyer can purchase the exclusive right to occupy a unit for a specified period of time each year. The time is usually in 1-week intervals and can be a fixed week or a floating week. In addition to the one-time purchase price, timeshare owners pay an annual fee for property management and maintenance. Timeshares are usually resort-type subdivisions that are created to be sold to people who want a retirement home or a second vacation home.

Prospective purchasers of this type of ownership can find unique financing arrangements. There are companies that specialize in making loans for purchasing timeshare properties. A timeshare company may work in tandem with a timeshare lender so that a prospective buyer can purchase the timeshare and obtain financing concurrently. Like a conventional loan, favorable financing terms for timeshares are available to borrowers with a good credit rating and sufficient income.

Financing Unimproved Land

Real estate buyers may express interest in purchasing unimproved land or raw land for building custom homes, investment purposes, or for other reasons. Financing options for raw land have their own unique characteristics. In general, the loans for raw land are riskier to a lender since the chance of default is higher for loans for land than loans for borrowers who are financing their primary residence. As a result, the interest rates for loans for raw land are generally higher than market rates and require larger down payments.

Along with a borrower's credit rating and income, lenders also examine the purpose for the raw land. If the borrower plans to build an improvement on the land, then a lender will be more disposed to lend money to finance the purchase than if the borrower has no plans for improving the land after acquiring it. Other considerations include whether the purpose of the land conforms to zoning laws, the existence of easements, and the availability of utilities.

Financing Rural Properties

Rural property is property located in the outlying region of an urban center. Rural property includes forests, national parks, farmland, lakeshores, mountains, riverbanks, and rural residential locations. Individuals may choose to live in a rural area to experience the peace and quiet enjoyment that they cannot realize in a busy metropolis or any other urban setting. Obtaining financing for rural property can be a challenge, especially since a majority of traditional lenders do not specialize in these types of properties.

A common financing tool is seller financing, which is provided by the owner of the rural property. Commonly, the purchaser will offer a down payment and the seller will carry back a loan for a specific term. Since there are no strict underwriting guidelines associated with seller financing, it is the easiest type of financing to obtain. Therefore, the seller may accept a smaller down payment than a bank would require. In addition, the seller may offer a favorable interest rate that is similar to or better than market rates with minimal or no origination fees.

A system that is particularly helpful in obtaining financing for agricultural property and other rural property is the Farm Credit System. The **Farm Credit System** is a national network of lenders that work together to provide funds to foster agricultural production and finance the purchase of rural property. Borrowers can obtain loan terms of up to 20 years with variable rates or fixed rates.

Another source of financing for rural properties is the **Farm Service Agency (FSA)**, which is part of the United States Department of Agriculture (USDA). The Farm Service Agency (FSA) encourages farm ownership and makes operating loans to borrowers who cannot obtain a loan from a bank or other Farm Credit System lender. The FSA assists beginning farmers that do not have sufficient income and current farmers that are experiencing financial difficulties. The FSA offers direct loan, guarantee loan, and land contract guarantee programs.

> **Direct Loan Program.** Direct loans are made and serviced by FSA using government money. FSA has the responsibility of providing credit counseling and supervision to its direct borrowers by helping applicants evaluate the adequacy of their real estate and facilities, machinery and equipment, financial and production management, and goals.

Guaranteed Loan Program. Guaranteed loans are made and serviced by commercial lenders, such as banks, the Farm Credit System, or credit unions. FSA guarantees the lender's loan against loss, up to 95%. FSA has the responsibility of approving all eligible loan guarantees and providing oversight of the lender's activities.

Land Contract Guarantee Program. Land contract guarantees are available to the owner of a farm or ranch who wishes to sell real estate through a land contract to a beginning or socially disadvantaged farmer or rancher.

Veterans who wish to obtain a farm loan can inquire with the VA. For a veteran to obtain financing for rural property, he or she must use the property as his or her primary residence. If the veteran also intends to use the property as a source of income through agricultural production, then the veteran must provide a business plan that shows how it will be profitable.

Financing Mixed-Use Properties

A **mixed-use property** is a property that combines residential living units and commercial space within the same building structure. Mixed-use properties are suitable for business owners who wish to have their residence located in the same building. In many communities, these are typically referred to as "live-work" units. This makes their business workspace readily accessible, especially in high-density, urban environments. A borrower may find that obtaining financing for a mixed-use property can be a challenge since the underwriting guidelines vary from lender to lender. The lender uses the mix of tenants on the property, the size of the loan, the borrower's intended use of the space, and other property characteristics to determine the type of loan product as well as the financing terms.

Financing by Loan Purpose

The loan purpose and the borrower's plans for the loan proceeds will determine other types of alternative financing. This includes loans for construction, pledged account mortgages, rollover mortgages, lender participation loans, and unsecured loans.

Construction Financing

Construction financing is comprised of two phases—the construction phase and completion. During the construction phase, an interim loan is necessary to fund the costs of the construction. Upon completion of the construction, the borrower must obtain permanent financing or pay the construction loan in full. The permanent loan that pays off a construction loan is a takeout loan.

Commercial banks can usually offer interim construction loans. Mortgage companies for large investors such as insurance companies arrange takeout loans and standby commitments. The lenders look at specific underwriting criteria prior to making a construction loan. Aside from the borrower's financial ability to repay the loan, construction lenders also look at the builder or developer's ability to complete and manage the construction project. For larger construction projects, borrowers must possess the skill and expertise necessary to complete the projects competently.

A construction loan may contain a subordination clause. A **subordination clause** is a statement in a financial instrument that is used to change its priority. The priority of a deed of trust is fixed by the date it is recorded—the earlier the date, the higher its priority. When a note and deed of trust includes a subordination clause, a new, later loan may be recorded and assume higher priority. This clause is used mainly when land is purchased with the intention of seeking future construction financing to build on the property. The lender giving the new construction financing expects to secure a first position interest in the property. If a deed of trust on the land includes a subordination clause, its priority becomes subordinate to the new construction loan once the new loan is funded and recorded.

Interim Financing

An **interim loan** is a short-term loan that finances construction costs such as the building of a new home. The lender advances funds to the borrower as needed while construction progresses. Lenders often include a contingency that states that after the project is completed, long-term financing must be secured. The lender and borrower agree on the terms of an interim loan. Interest rates can be fixed, variable, or interest only with terms that can range from 6 months to 5 years. Because construction loans have a higher risk, banks typically charge a higher interest rate.

Permanent Financing

After the construction is complete, a more permanent, long-term takeout loan is necessary. Takeout loans can be used to pay off any interim construction loans taken out prior to the construction project. Like an interim loan, the lender and borrower agree on the terms for the takeout loan. Interest rates vary and loan terms can go up to 25 years or more depending on the lender. A lender may also include a balloon payment that is due and payable after a certain number of years.

A takeout loan is different from a forward-takeout commitment, which may also be called a standby commitment. A **forward-takeout commitment** is a letter that promises to deliver a takeout loan in the future if the property is built according to plans and specifications and leased at the target rental rate. Typically, a forward-takeout commitment costs a developer 1 to 2 points plus at least 1 additional point if the loan is eventually funded. However, the borrower does not have to take the loan.

Blanket Loan

A **blanket loan** is a loan secured by several properties. The security instrument used can be a blanket deed of trust or a blanket mortgage. It is often used to secure construction financing. A blanket loan offers a convenient way to finance multiple properties under one security instrument.

Developers use blanket loans when they buy large tracts of land to be subdivided into parcels and sold separately. This type of loan allows the developer to sell the land a parcel at a time and receive cash from the sale. The lender releases a portion of the mortgage as each parcel is sold. This is possible because a blanket mortgage or blanket deed of trust contains a **release clause**. This clause enables the borrower to obtain partial release of specific parcels of land that are no longer required as security for the loan. The release occurs when the borrower partially repays the loan after the sale of each parcel.

Individuals can acquire a blanket loan when they have an existing home and are purchasing another one. In this case, the individual does not have to carry two separate mortgages. Once his or her existing home sells, the property is released from the blanket mortgage or blanket deed of trust so that it can be reconveyed to the new owner.

Pledged-Asset Mortgage Loan

A **pledged-asset mortgage** (PAM) is a loan that allows a borrower to give a security interest in other assets rather than having to liquidate them to pay a down payment. It allows the borrower to continue receiving income and other benefits from those assets. Additionally, it avoids the possibility of the borrower having to pay income taxes on sale proceeds if the assets had to be sold to make a down payment.

A relative can also pledge a savings account or certificate of deposit instead of giving a gift to assist a borrower with a down payment. This approach to financing with a PAM allows the borrower to get 100% financing. The lender releases the pledged account when the property has enough equity to qualify under normal loan-to-value ratios.

The advantage of a PAM is that the borrower or relative can keep the investment that is pledged. Generally, it also protects the borrower from having to purchase mortgage insurance on the loan. One of the disadvantages of a PAM is that the interest that is paid on the loan without the normal down payment is greater.

Lender Participation Loans

There are several types of participation loans. In some, the lender participates in the annual operating income as well as proceeds from the sale of the property. In others, the lender shares in the appreciation of the property.

Equity Participation Mortgage

An **equity participation mortgage** is a type of mortgage that allows the lender to share in part of the income or resale proceeds from a property owned by the borrower. The lender participates in the income of the mortgaged property beyond a fixed return, or receives a yield on the loan in addition to the straight interest rate.

Shared Appreciation Mortgage

Under a **shared appreciation mortgage (SAM)** loan, the lender and the borrower agree to share a certain percentage of the appreciation in the market value of the property that is security for the loan. In return for the shared equity, the borrower is offered beneficial loan terms.

For the lender, the money received from the appreciation of the property increases the effective yield on the investment. The borrower, by agreeing to share the interest rate, in turn reduces the monthly mortgage payment. A SAM is normally written so that at the end of the shared appreciation period, the property will be appraised and the amount due to the lender through appreciation is due at that time.

Unsecured Loan

Consumers who need a small loan to repair a car, buy a new appliance, or take a trip choose a closed-end, unsecured loan instead of using their credit cards or getting a home equity loan. An **unsecured loan** is one in which the lender receives a promissory note from the borrower without any security for payment of the debt, such as a trust deed or mortgage. The only recourse is a lengthy court action to force payment. This is truly the traditional IOU.

SUMMARY

In real estate transactions, traditional financing may not always be sufficient to complete a purchase. A borrower can seek alternative financing from a variety of sources in order to complete a real estate purchase. Alternative financing methods include seller financing, secondary financing, and other financing alternatives that are based on the type of property or the purpose of the loan.

A common source for secondary financing of a sale is the seller. If the seller agrees to be the lender, he or she gives the buyer the amount of funds required to close the real estate transaction. In seller financing, options include carryback financing, contract for deed, and a wraparound mortgage (WRAP) or all-inclusive trust deed (AITD). Carryback financing is the extension of credit by a seller who takes back a note for a portion or the entire purchase price of a property. A wraparound mortgage (WRAP) secures a wraparound loan. A wraparound loan is essentially a purchase-money loan that includes both the unpaid principal balance of the first loan and a new second loan against the property.

Borrowers obtain secondary financing to provide additional funds for the purchase of property or to take cash out of property. Secondary financing includes hard money loans from private lenders, swing loans, home equity loans (HEL), and home equity lines-of-credit (HELOC).

Other types of financing are available when traditional bank financing and seller financing are not enough to complete a real estate transaction. Financing is available based on the property type. Some lenders provide financing for manufactured housing, cooperatives, vacation homes, unimproved land, rural properties, and mixed-use properties. The loan purpose and the borrower's plans for the loan proceeds will determine other types of alternative financing. This includes loans for construction, pledged account mortgages, rollover mortgages, lender participation loans, and unsecured loans.

UNIT 8 REVIEW

Matching Exercise

Instructions: Write the letter of the matching term on the blank line before its definition. Answers are in Appendix A.

Terms

A. blanket loan
B. carryback financing
C. contract for deed
D. cooperative
E. Farm Credit System
F. Farm Service Agency
G. forward-takeout commitment
H. home equity line-of-credit
I. home equity loan
J. interim loan
K. manufactured home

L. mobilehome
M. participation loans
N. personal property loan
O. pledged-asset mortgage
P. retailer financing
Q. rural property
R. shared appreciation mortgage
S. swing loan
T. timeshare
U. unsecured loan
V. wraparound mortgage

Definitions

1. _____ Extension of credit by a seller who takes back a note for a portion or the entire purchase price of a property

2. _____ Contract in which the seller (vendor) becomes the lender to the buyer (vendee)

3. _____ Purchase-money loan that includes both the unpaid principal balance of the first loan and a new second loan against the property

4. _____ Temporary, short-term, hard money loan made on a borrower's equity in his or her present home

5. _____ Hard money loan made against the equity in the borrower's home

6. _____ Open-end loan that is a line of credit secured by the borrower's home

7. _____ Factory-built home manufactured prior to June 15, 1976, constructed on a chassis and wheels, and designed for permanent or semi-permanent attachment to land

8. _____ Homes built in a factory after June 15, 1976 that must conform to the federal Manufactured Home Construction and Safety Standards (HUD code)

9. _____ Loan for anything movable that is not real property

10. _____ Financing that is directly available from the retailer

11. _____ Ownership of an apartment unit in which the owner has purchased shares in the corporation that holds title to the entire building

12. _____ Property located in the outlying region of an urban center

13. _____ Federal agency that encourages farm ownership and makes operating loans to borrowers who cannot obtain a loan from a bank or other Farm Credit System lender

14. _____ Short-term loan that finances construction costs such as the building of a new home

15. _____ Letter that promises to deliver a takeout loan in the future if the property is built according to plans and specifications and leased at the target rental rate

16. _____ Loan secured by several properties

17. _____ Type of loan that allows a borrower to give a security interest in other assets rather than having to liquidate them to pay a down payment

18. _____ Loans that allow the lender to participate in the annual operating income and/or appreciation of the property

19. _____ Lender and borrower agree to share a certain percentage of the appreciation in the market value of the property that is security for the loan

20. _____ Loan in which the lender receives a promissory note from the borrower without any security for payment of the debt, such as a trust deed or mortgage

Multiple Choice Questions

Instructions: Circle your response and go to Appendix A to read the complete explanation for each question.

1. Which of the following is not a type of alternative financing?
    a. Seller financing
    b. Secondary financing
    c. Credit card financing
    d. Financing based on type of property and purpose of loan

2. An advantage of seller financing is that it helps a borrower with:
    a. no down payment.
    b. a damaged credit history.
    c. insufficient funds for closing costs.
    d. all of the above.

3. Which of the following is seller financing?
    a. Carryback financing
    b. Bank financing
    c. Contract for deed
    d. Both (a) and (c)

4. The contract for deed is also known as a(n):
    a. grant deed.
    b. installment sales contract.
    c. wraparound mortgage.
    d. all-inclusive trust deed.

5. Which of the following is a type of secondary financing?
    a. HELOC
    b. Swing loan
    c. Home equity loan
    d. All of the above

6. A home equity line-of-credit (HELOC) is a good example of a(n):
    a. wraparound mortgage.
    b. all-inclusive trust deed.
    c. open-end loan.
    d. contract for deed.

7. If a manufactured home is not permanently attached to the land, financing is available through a:

    a. grant deed.

    b. personal property loan.

    c. HELOC.

    d. interim loan.

8. What type of loan can a borrower get if he or she wants to purchase a cooperative unit?

    a. Shore loan

    b. Share loan

    c. Proprietary lease

    d. HELOC

9. A(n) _____ loan is a type of loan a borrower can get to finance the costs associated with construction.

    a. internal

    b. intermittent

    c. interim

    d. inherent

10. If a borrower wishes to purchase a new vehicle without having to use a credit card or obtain a loan secured against his or her home, which of the following options is best?

    a. HELOC

    b. Unsecured loan

    c. Interim loan

    d. Swing loan

Government-Backed Loans

Unit 9

INTRODUCTION

Although many state and local government programs help consumers purchase homes, this unit covers the two federal agencies that participate in real estate financing—the Federal Housing Administration (FHA) and the Department of Veterans Affairs (VA). Together, they make it possible for people to buy homes they would never be able to afford to purchase. The main differences between the two government programs are that only an eligible veteran may obtain a VA loan and that the VA does not require a down payment, up to a certain loan amount. Both programs were created to assist people in buying homes when conventional loan programs do not fit their needs.

Regulations change from time to time. Current information on loan programs is available for FHA requirements at http://portal.hud.gov and for VA programs at www.homeloans.va.gov.

Learning Objectives

After completing this Unit, you should be able to:

9A   recall the Federal Housing Administration and specify the FHA's contribution to real estate finance.

9B   indicate the benefits of the FHA-insured loan program.

9C   recall the Direct Endorsement program and identify FHA financing guidelines.

9D   recognize the most frequently used FHA loan programs.

9E   specify the VA's role in real estate financing.

9F   identify VA financing guidelines.

9G   recognize the most frequently used VA loan programs.

FEDERAL HOUSING ADMINISTRATION

The **Federal Housing Administration (FHA)** is a federal government agency that insures private home loans for financing homes and/or home repairs. Created by Congress in 1934, the FHA became part of the Department of Housing and Urban Development (HUD) in 1965. The FHA is not a tax burden on taxpayers because it operates from its own income. In fact, the FHA stimulates economic growth by its participation in the development of homes and communities.

FHA Contributions to Real Estate Finance

Originally created to stabilize the mortgage market, the FHA caused some of the greatest changes in the housing industry in the 20th century. It forever changed home mortgage lending by insuring long-term, amortized loans; creating standards for qualifying borrowers; and by establishing minimum property and construction standards for residential properties. Its efforts have been so influential that homeownership has increased from 40% in the 1930s to over 70% today. Backed by the full faith and credit of the Federal government, FHA-insured mortgages are some of the safest loans for lenders and are some of the most affordable types of loans available to homebuyers.

Long-Term, Amortized Loans

Today, we take long-term, fully amortized mortgages for granted. However, prior to the creation of the FHA, most home loans were short-term (3-5 years) with balloon payments and loan-to-value ratios (LTVs) of 50% or more. Many homeowners were unable to make the balloon payment and lost their homes through foreclosure.

In the 1930s, 25-year fixed-rate, fully amortized, FHA-insured loans were available for the first time. In addition, borrowers could get financing with only a 10% down payment. The FHA implemented standardized loan instruments and established standards lenders could use to qualify borrowers. These new standards combined with the FHA mortgage encouraged financial institutions to make affordable financing available. Now, borrowers can get 30-year amortized loans with 3.5% down.

Mutual Mortgage Insurance

The FHA does not make loans. It insures loans to protect the lenders who make the loans. On loans with less than a 20% down payment, the lender is protected in case of foreclosure by **mutual mortgage insurance (MMI)**. The borrower pays the mutual mortgage insurance premiums to the FHA Mutual Mortgage Insurance Fund. Money placed into the fund is used to pay lenders in the event of loss resulting from foreclosure. As long as FHA guidelines are used when the loan is financed, the FHA will pay the lender up to the established limit of the insurance upon default and foreclosure.

In most of the FHA mortgage insurance programs, the FHA collects two types of mortgage insurance premiums—upfront and annual.

Currently, the FHA charges an **upfront mortgage insurance premium (UFMIP)** of 1.75% of the base loan amount. The UFMIP must be either paid in cash at closing or financed in the mortgage amount. If financed, the UFMIP is added to the base loan amount to arrive at a greater "total" loan amount. The total FHA-insured first mortgage on a property is limited to 100% of the appraised value, and the UFMIP is required to be included within that limit. Any UFMIP amounts paid in cash are added to the total cash settlement amount.

In addition to the UFMIP, the FHA collects an annual insurance premium, on certain mortgages, which the borrower usually pays monthly. The percentage amount of the annual premium is based on the LTV and the term of the mortgage.

Effective January 27, 2017, on a less than 95% LTV, 30-year loan, the FHA would charge 0.55% per year of the loan amount. For LTVs equal to or greater than 95%, annual premiums are 0.60% [HUD Mortgagee Letter 2017-01].

Example: Pat plans to buy a new 3-bedroom, 2-bath home with a $250,000 purchase price. With a 3.5% down payment, she hopes to qualify for the $241,250 FHA loan, for which the FHA charges 1.75% UFMIP. If Pat decides to include the amount in the mortgage so that she can have some extra money for landscaping the front yard, the amount of the loan, including the $4,221.88 UFMIP, will be $245,471.88.

Because this is a 96.5% loan, Pat must pay the monthly MMI charge, which is 0.60% (0.0060) for this loan. In addition to the principal, interest, taxes, and insurance (PITI), Pat will pay an additional $122.74 per month for the MMI ($245,471.88 x 0.60% = $1,472.83 ÷ 12 months).

Refunds of UFMIP

The Consolidated Appropriations Act of 2005 eliminated refunds of the FHA's upfront mortgage insurance premiums for those mortgages endorsed for insurance on or after December 8, 2004, except when the borrower refinances to another mortgage to be insured by FHA.

MIP Cancellation Policy After April 1, 2013

Effective April 1, 2013, the FHA will remove annual MIP after 11 years provided that a homeowners' beginning LTV was 90% or less. For everyone else, including those making a 3.5 percent FHA down payment, the agency will assess MIP fees for so long as the loan is active.

For loans closed prior to April 1, 2013, the FHA will cancel the annual mortgage insurance requirement for homeowners who have paid mortgage insurance for at least 5 years, and whose loan size is less than 78% of the lower of a home's original purchase price or appraised value.

Minimum Property and Construction Standards

The FHA developed **minimum property standards (MPS)** and standards for new construction to reduce their mortgage risk and to improve housing standards and conditions. The MPS assured that the housing used as collateral for FHA-insured mortgages met minimum requirements for construction quality, safety, and durability.

Eventually, the MPS gained influence far beyond its originally intended role of reducing risks for FHA-insured properties. In fact, they served as a default standard if local building codes were of a lower standard or were non-existent. The minimum property standards have been a significant factor in the development of national building codes and their subsequent adoption by thousands of local communities. VA lenders rely on the VA's Minimum

Property Requirements, which are based on an early version of the MPS. Inclusion of the MPS in national and local building codes has been so successful that conventional lenders currently rely on local codes instead of the MPS.

FHA Home Inspection Notice

(b) Requirement for FHA-approved lenders

Each mortgagee approved for participation in the mortgage insurance programs under title II of the National Housing Act [12 U.S.C. 1707 et seq.] shall provide prospective homebuyers, at first contact, whether upon pre-qualification, pre-approval, or initial application, the materials specified in subparagraphs (A), (B), and (D) of subsection (a)(1).

A borrower who wants an FHA loan for any residential property of one to four units must receive and sign the notice called "The Importance of a Home Inspection".

Benefits of FHA-Insured Loans

FHA-insured loans allow low to moderate-income people to buy a home with lower initial costs. FHA-insured loans feature low down payments, competitive interest rates, easy qualifying requirements, and low closing costs. In addition, FHA loans are assumable and have no prepayment penalties.

Low Down Payment

The down payment (minimum required investment) on FHA loans varies with the amount of the loan. Typically, it is 3.5% of the appraised value of the property or of the sales price, whichever is less. [4000.1 II.A.2.C.ii.]. The FHA guidelines encourage home ownership by allowing 100% of the down payment to be a gift from family or friends and by allowing closing costs to be financed to reduce the up-front cost of buying a home.

Seller Contributions

The FHA currently allows the seller, or a third party, to contribute up to 6% of a home's sales price to pay for closing costs, discount points, upfront mortgage insurance premiums, or upfront interest. In this way, a purchaser with limited cash resources can purchase a new or pre-owned home.

Competitive Interest Rates

Since the FHA does not loan money, it does not set interest rates. Interest rates are negotiated between the borrower and the FHA-approved lender. However, FHA loans have competitive interest rates because the Federal Government insures the loans. This reduces the lender's risk.

Easy Qualifying Requirements

Because the FHA provides mortgage insurance, lenders are more willing to give loans with lower qualifying requirements. Even with less-than-perfect credit, it is easier to qualify for an FHA loan than a conventional loan.

Currently, borrowers must have a minimum FICO score of 580 to qualify for FHA's 3.5% down payment program. New borrowers with less than a 580 FICO score will be required to put down at least 10%.

Reasonable Loan Fees

HUD regulates the closing costs associated with FHA-insured loans. The FHA has reasonable and customary closing costs so that the FHA loan program remains affordable to home buyers.

Some loan fees may not be paid by the borrower and traditionally are paid by the seller. The FHA also allows the financing of closing costs, which are included in the loan amount and are amortized over 30 years.

Loan Origination Fee. Effective January 1, 2010, the 1% cap on the loan origination fee was eliminated, except for reverse mortgages and FHA 203(k) loans. However, the FHA expects lenders to charge fair and reasonable origination fees, and will monitor the lenders to ensure that FHA borrowers are not overcharged.

Loan Discount. A **loan discount** (also called points or discount points) is a one-time charge imposed by the lender to lower the rate at which the lender would otherwise offer the loan. This fee varies from lender to lender.

Appraisal Report Fee. The **appraisal report fee** ranges from $300 to $500 and pays for an appraisal report made by an independent FHA appraiser.

Credit Report Fee. A **credit report fee** ranges from $40 to $55 and pays for the credit report of the borrower's credit history. Many lenders use a tri-merge credit report. A **tri-merge credit report** takes the raw data from all of the major credit repositories—Trans Union, Experian and Equifax—and merges it into one easy-to-read credit report. The cost for this report can be $20 or less.

Mortgage Insurance Application Fee. The **mortgage insurance application fee** covers the processing of an application for mortgage insurance.

Assumption Fee. An **assumption fee** is charged when a buyer assumes the seller's existing real estate loan. FHA loans are fully assumable. Buyers must qualify under the FHA 203b income rules to assume the loan and release the seller from all liability.

Loan Processing Fee. The **loan processing fee** is not the same as the loan origination fee. This fee pays for preparing the paperwork in the loan files.

Underwriting Fee. An investor charges an **underwriting fee** for underwriting the submitted loan file and all of its paperwork.

Flood Certification. Mortgagees are required to obtain life-of-loan flood zone determination services for all properties that will be collateral for FHA-insured mortgages. If the property is in a flood zone, the borrower must obtain flood insurance as a condition of closing. Any property located within a designated Coastal Barrier Resource System unit is not eligible for an FHA-insured mortgage.

FHA Loan Limits

The FHA sets the maximum loan amounts. The loan limits are determined by the type of property—one-unit, two-unit, three-unit, and four-unit properties. The FHA national loan limit "floor" is $275,665, which is 65% of the national conforming loan limit (currently $424,100 for a 1-unit property). The FHA national "ceiling" loan limit is $636,150. The FHA maximum loan amounts vary from region to region and change annually. In addition, the FHA maximum loan limits may be changed according to market conditions.

The loan cap figure is derived from the median cost of a home in any given Metropolitan Statistical Area (MSA). While the largest FHA loan allowed for a single-family home in Nevada is $362,250, in Texas the largest loan available under the FHA's rules is $361,100. Even within states, the loan limits vary from county to county. In Florida for example, the largest loan for Gainesville is $275,665, compared to $450,800 for Naples and $277,150 in Orlando. The FHA Mortgage Limits page on HUD's website lets you look up the FHA mortgage limits by state, county, or Metropolitan Statistical Area.

Typically, loan limits for FHA-insured loans are less than the loan limits for conventional financing in most parts of the country. Borrowers who need a loan that exceeds the FHA loan limits for the area will have to put additional money down on the property or finance under a conventional mortgage.

Property Appraisal

The appraisal is a critical component of an FHA mortgage. The FHA requires an appraisal of the property, which is used to determine the market value and acceptability of the property for FHA mortgage insurance purposes. The loan amount that is approved for an FHA 203(b) loan is based on the appraised value of the property or the sales price, whichever is lowest.

The value of the property is the lender's best assurance that it will recover the money it lends. Therefore, appraisals are performed for the use and benefit of HUD and the lenders involved in FHA transactions, not the borrower.

The FHA allows only FHA-approved, licensed appraisers to perform the appraisals because they must check for required FHA items to confirm that the property does not contain any health or safety issues. The FHA emphasizes that an appraisal is not a home inspection and it does not guarantee that a home is without flaws.

FHA Repair Requirements

The FHA tries to make sure that the home is in a safe, sound, and sanitary condition. For that reason, the FHA appraiser is expected to require repair or replacement of anything that may affect the safe, sound, and sanitary habitation of the house. [4000.1 II.A.3.]. If repairs are required, the buyer will receive a list from the lender, and the seller (in most cases) may be responsible for seeing that the repairs are taken care of according to set local and FHA guidelines.

Typical Property Eligibility Criteria

Property

The property must be structurally sound, have adequate heating, electrical, and sanitary systems, have potable water, and have adequate space for healthful and comfortable living conditions.

The property must be free from environmental and safety hazards such as lead-based paint or methamphetamine contamination.

Site

The site cannot have any encroachments and onsite hazards or nuisances, such as abandoned gas, and oil wells must be reported. Any overhead electric power transmission lines cannot pass directly over any dwelling or property improvement, including pools. The site must have safe and adequate access from a public or private street.

Economic Life

The term of the mortgage must be less than or equal to the remaining economic life of the property.

As the on-site representative for the lender, appraisers verify that the property being appraised meets minimum property standards and must report all deficiencies.

Lenders can determine when a property's condition is a threat to safety or jeopardizes structural integrity. Some conditions affect the soundness of a property or may constitute a risk to the health and safety of occupants. These conditions still require repair by the owner before closing the loan. However, if defective conditions cannot be corrected, the lender must reject the property.

Partial List of Defective Conditions Requiring Repair

- Leaking or worn out roofs
- Foundation problems such as damage caused by settlement
- Standing water against the foundation or an excessively wet basement
- Hazardous materials on site
- Faulty mechanical systems (electrical, plumbing, or heating)
- Structural failure
- Evidence of possible pest infestation

At one time, the FHA required inspections for wood destroying organisms, private water wells, septic systems, and flat/unobservable roofs. Now, these inspections are required only if the appraiser observes possible infestation, well or septic problems, water damage attributed to the roof, or if an inspection for these issues is mandated by state or local jurisdiction.

Standardized Appraisal Reporting Forms

FHA-approved appraisers use the standardized Fannie Mae appraisal reporting forms. The appraisal reporting form used depends on the type of property that is being appraised.

Uniform Residential Appraisal Report (Form 1004). This report form is designed to report an appraisal of a one-unit property or a one-unit property with an accessory unit, including a unit in a planned development (PD).

Individual Condominium Unit Appraisal Report (Form 1073). This report form is designed to report an appraisal of a unit in a condominium project or a condominium unit in a planned development (PD).

Manufactured Home Appraisal Report (Form 1004C). This report form is designed to report an appraisal of a one-unit manufactured home, including a manufactured home in a planned development (PD).

Small Residential Income Property Appraisal (Form 1025). This report form is designed to report an appraisal of a two-to-four unit property, including a two-to-four unit property in a planned development (PD).

As of January 12, 2011, FHA does not accept the Master Appraisal Report (MAR) for valuing one- to four-unit, single-family residences. The FHA requires that each individual unit within a larger housing project, which is to be security for a FHA-insured mortgage, must be appraised on an individual basis. To see the types of appraisal reporting forms used for FHA loans, go to https://www.fanniemae.com/singlefamily/selling-servicing-guide-forms and choose the link for appraiser forms.

FHA Requirements

A borrower does not apply to the FHA for a home loan. Instead, the borrower applies for an FHA-insured loan through an approved lender, who processes the application and submits it for FHA approval.

Only an approved FHA lender can originate an FHA loan. Lenders who have met FHA standards are called **Direct Endorsement (DE) lenders**. Under the DE program, lenders may underwrite and close home loans without prior FHA review or approval. This includes all aspects of the loan application, the property analysis, and the borrower underwriting process.

Although the standards lenders use when evaluating applicants for FHA-insured loans are the most flexible of all loans that require less than a 5% down payment, there are still requirements. FHA-insured loans have borrower and property eligibility requirements and follow underwriting guidelines.

Borrower Eligibility

FHA-insured loans are available for individuals only, not partnerships or corporations. Therefore, almost anyone with decent (not perfect) credit who is a legal resident of the United States can qualify for an FHA-insured loan. U.S. citizenship is not a requirement, but the person must have a valid social security number.

Property Eligibility

The property must be the borrower's principal residence and located in the United States. The following property types are eligible for the FHA program.

Types of Eligible Property
- 1-4 family owner-occupied residences
- Row houses
- Multiplex and individual condominiums
- Eligible manufactured homes (must be real property)

HUD maintains a list of approved condominium projects that are eligible for FHA financing. The FHA website also contains specific guidelines for financing condominiums.

FHA Underwriting Guidelines

FHA guidelines are designed to promote homeownership. Additionally, helping people finance a home that is within their means promotes stability. When followed properly, lending guidelines help people purchase and keep their homes.

Basic Guidelines for an FHA-Insured Loan
- Borrower's income
- Employment history
- Credit history
- Debt-to-income ratios

Income

The FHA uses gross income when qualifying a borrower for a loan. Income includes salary, overtime, commissions, dividends, and any other source of income if the borrower can show a stable income for a minimum of 2 years.

The FHA does not require borrowers to have savings or checking accounts. Since the FHA allows the down payment for the purchase to be a gift, the money used for the down payment does not have to be seasoned like conventional loans. In this instance, **seasoned** means that the money has been in the bank for the previous 3 months. The FHA does not require the buyer to have any reserves or available cash on hand during the closing.

Employment

FHA underwriting guidelines do not impose a minimum length of time a borrower must have held a position of employment to be eligible. Typically, the lender must verify the borrower's employment for the most recent 2 full years. A borrower with a 25% or greater ownership interest in a business is considered self-employed for loan underwriting purposes.

If a borrower indicates that he or she was in school or in the military during any of this time, the borrower must provide evidence supporting this claim, such as college transcripts or discharge papers. Because of this rule, a new college graduate or recently discharged veteran can purchase a house immediately without first developing a 2-year job history as long as he or she meets the other underwriting requirements.

Credit History

Unlike Fannie Mae/Freddie Mac loans, FHA underwriting looks at the stability of income and the borrower's ability to make timely payments. An important aspect of FHA underwriting is that FHA loans are more flexible with credit scores. For example, to qualify for a 3.5% loan, a borrower must have at least a 580 FICO® score. Borrowers with less than a 580 FICO® score must have a down payment of at least 10%.

For those borrowers who do not use traditional credit, the lender may develop a credit history from utility payment records, rental payments, automobile insurance payments, or other means of direct access from the credit provider.

However, the FHA has certain credit history guidelines that generally play a role in qualifying for a loan. The FHA will allow for minor past credit issues as long as there is a reasonable explanation for the issue. A satisfactory reason can be the loss of a job, a serious illness, or a job transfer.

A person with a bankruptcy or foreclosure must re-establish good credit before applying for an FHA-insured loan. With re-established credit, applicants who filed Chapter 7 bankruptcy are eligible 2 years after the date of discharge and applicants who have gone through foreclosure are eligible 3 years from the foreclosure date. Any outstanding collection accounts, judgments, and charge offs must be paid off.

Debt-to-Income Ratios

FHA lenders look at the borrower's debt-to-income (DTI) ratios to determine the maximum loan amount. Currently, the FHA uses a 31% front ratio and a 43% back ratio, written 31/43. A more conservative back ratio is 41%, but FHA home loan guidelines allow up to 43%.

Front Ratio. The **front ratio** is the percentage of a borrower's monthly gross income that is used to pay the monthly housing expense. To calculate this percentage, divide the housing expense by the borrower's gross monthly income. The **monthly housing expense** for renters is the monthly rent payment. For homeowners, the monthly housing expense is the amount of principal, interest, taxes, and insurance (**PITI**). In addition, the front ratio for homeowners may include mutual mortgage insurance (MMI) and homeowners' association dues. The front ratio used in FHA loans is 31%.

Back Ratio. The **back ratio** is the percentage of income needed to pay for all recurring debt. To calculate this percentage, divide the housing expense and consumer debt by the borrower's gross monthly income. **Consumer debt** can be car payments, credit card debt, judgments, personal loans, child support, alimony, and similar expenses. Car or life insurance, utility bills, and cell phone bills are not used to calculate the ratio. The back ratio for FHA loans is 41%.

Stated differently, the borrower's housing-related expenses should add up to no more than 31% of his or her gross monthly income. And the borrower's total debt load (including the monthly mortgage payments, credit cards, car payments, etc.) should not exceed 43% of his or her gross monthly income.

Example: It has been 2 1/2 years since Bob's bankruptcy was discharged. Since then, he has re-established good credit and wants to buy a home. His gross monthly income is $4,000. He currently pays $1,400 per month for a 3-bedroom house and has no other obligations except a $300 car payment.

Bob spends the weekend with a real estate broker looking at houses and finds one that seems affordable. The broker tells Bob that with a 3.5% down payment, the monthly PITI will be about $1,300. Bob is excited because this is less than his monthly rent payment.

Although Bob is concerned he may not qualify for a loan because of the bankruptcy, he applies for an FHA-insured loan. The lender assures Bob that the bankruptcy should not be a problem since it was more than 2 years ago. Additionally, Bob has worked hard reestablishing good credit. However, the lender is concerned that Bob's income is not sufficient to meet both of the FHA front and back ratios.

The lender calculates both ratios as follows:

$1,300 ÷ $4,000 = 32.5% (front ratio)
$1,600 ($1,300 + $300) ÷ $4,000 = 40% (back ratio)

Unfortunately, Bob meets the back ratio, but exceeds the front ratio. He may need to consider a less-expensive home or a larger down payment.

An even higher ratio, the stretch ratio of 33/45, is available for loans on energy-efficient homes. Occasionally, certain compensating factors, such as good credit history and job stability, allow the lender to stretch debt-to-income ratios beyond FHA guidelines.

Selected FHA Loan Programs

The FHA offers several loan programs to meet the needs of borrowers—from first-time buyers to reverse mortgages for seniors. They even offer specially discounted loans for teachers and law enforcement officers. We will discuss some of the more common programs. The website http://portal.hud.gov describes all of the FHA loan programs.

FHA 203(b) Residential Loan

The basic FHA loan program is the **FHA 203(b) Loan** that offers financing on the purchase or construction of owner-occupied residences of one-to-four units. This program offers 30-year, fixed-rate, fully amortized loans with minimum upfront cash requirements. The loan is funded by a lending institution and insured by the FHA. The borrower must meet standard FHA credit qualifications and may be eligible for 96.5% financing. The borrower is also able to finance the upfront mortgage insurance premium into the loan and is responsible for paying an annual mortgage insurance premium that is included with the monthly loan payment. The majority of FHA loans made are Section 203(b) loans.

The **FHA 203(b)(2) Loan** is available to honorably discharged veterans. In certain circumstances, veterans are not required to make the 3.5% cash down payment required for the standard FHA 203(b) loans. This FHA program supplements but does not replace the VA entitlement programs. More information about this loan can be found at the FHA website.

FHA 251 Adjustable-Rate Mortgage

The FHA adjustable-rate mortgage provides a viable alternative to the Fannie Mae/Freddie Mac ARMs. The FHA administers a number of programs that are based on FHA Section 203(b) loans, but with special loan features. One of these programs, Section 251, insures ARMs. This type of program enables borrowers to obtain home loan financing that is more affordable because of its lower interest rate. The interest rate is adjusted annually based on market indices approved by the FHA, and therefore, may increase or decrease over the term of the loan. For adjustable-rate mortgages, the only index acceptable to the FHA is the 1-year Treasury bill interest rate. Annual increases are capped at 1% and the maximum interest rate can be no more than 5% greater than the original interest rate.

FHA 255 Home Equity Conversion Mortgage

Reverse mortgages are becoming popular in America. They can supplement retirement income and give older Americans greater financial security. A **reverse mortgage** is a loan that enables elderly homeowners to borrow against the equity in their homes and receive monthly payments and/or a line of credit from a lender. A retired couple can draw on their home's equity by increasing their loan balance each month.

The FHA-insured reverse mortgage, Home Equity Conversion Mortgage (HECM), is a loan program for homeowners who are 62 or older and who have paid off their existing home loan or have only a small balance remaining. The maximum loan amount depends on the age of the borrower, the expected interest rate, and the appraised value of the property. The older a borrower, the larger the percentage of the home's value that can be borrowed.

Payment Options of a Reverse Mortgage

- Lump sum payment
- Monthly payment for a fixed term or for as long as borrower lives in the home
- Line of credit

The borrower is not required to make payments as long as he or she lives in the home. The borrower is not required to repay the loan until a specified event, such as death or sale of the property, at which time the loan is paid off. If the property is sold, the borrower (or heir) receives any proceeds in excess of the amount needed to pay off the loan.

FHA 203(k) Rehabilitation Loan

A rehabilitation loan is a great option for buyers who are planning to improve their property immediately upon purchase. This home loan provides the funds to purchase a residential property and to complete an improvement project all in one loan, one application, one set of fees, one closing, and one convenient monthly payment. A rehabilitation loan can be used for a variety of improvements, such as adding a family room or bedroom, remodeling a kitchen or bathroom, performing general upgrades to an older property, or even completing a total teardown and rebuild. Minor or cosmetic repairs are unacceptable.

Title 1 Home Improvement Loan

Title 1 loans on single-family homes may be used for alterations, repairs, and for site improvements. The loan is available for single-family homes, manufactured homes, and multifamily structures. Title 1 loans may be used in connection with a 203(k) Rehabilitation Mortgage and are only available through an approved FHA Title 1 lender.

Title 1 Program Features		
Type of Property	**Loan Amount**	**Loan Term**
Single-family home	$25,000	20 years
Manufactured home (real property)	$25,090	15 years
Manufactured home (personal property)	$7,500	12 years
Multifamily structure	$12,000/unit (up to $60,000)	20 years

Energy Efficient Mortgage

The **Energy Efficient Mortgages Program** (EEM) helps homebuyers or homeowners save money on utility bills by enabling them to finance the cost for adding energy-efficient features to new or existing housing. The program provides mortgage insurance for the purchase or refinance of a principal residence that incorporates the cost of energy efficient improvements into the loan. Due to the anticipated energy conservation savings, lenders can be more flexible with underwriting guidelines.

DEPARTMENT OF VETERANS AFFAIRS

The United States **Department of Veterans Affairs** (**VA**) was created in 1989 to replace its predecessor, the Veterans Administration, which was established in 1930. It is a government-run military veteran benefit system with the responsibility of administering programs of veterans' benefits for veterans, their families, and survivors. In addition to home loan programs, the benefits provided include disability compensation, pension, education, life insurance, vocational rehabilitation, survivors' benefits, medical benefits, and burial benefits.

More than 63 million people are potentially eligible for VA benefits and services because they are veterans, family members, or survivors of veterans. Therefore, knowledge of VA home loan programs is very important for mortgage loan originators and other real estate professionals.

Contributions of the GI Bill to Real Estate

The GI Bill of Rights, which is officially called the Servicemen's Readjustment Act of 1944, was referred to as "a bill that made modern America" by historian Steve Ambrose. It was passed for two main reasons. The first was to compensate veterans of World War II for their services and sacrifices. The second was to reintegrate military personnel into the civilian economy. This helped the economy by preventing a flood of workers from creating a post-war depression as had happened after World War I.

The GI Bill of Rights helped elevate a generation of working-class veterans to the middle class. It opened the doors to higher education, fueled a housing boom, and turned renters into homeowners through low-interest, no-money-down home loans.

A better-educated population not only supplied the economy with skilled workers, but it also helped create a larger middle class that had a higher income. This led to a housing boom, as more and more Americans moved out of the cities and purchased homes with VA financing in the new suburban developments. In the 1950s, over 13 million homes were built, of which 11 million were financed with GI loans. Homeownership became a reality for millions of middle-class Americans.

Benefits of VA-Guaranteed Loans

VA-guaranteed home loans offer many benefits and advantages. The main benefit is that veterans may not need to make a down payment. Instead of the down payment from the borrower, lenders receive a certificate of guaranty from the VA. In appreciation for honorable military service, the VA vouches for the veteran's trustworthiness to repay the loan.

Advantages of VA-Guaranteed Loans
- No down payment (in most cases)
- Lenient qualifications
- Reasonable loan charges
- No PMI or MMI
- VA minimum property requirements. All new houses, regardless of when appraised, are covered by either a 1-year builder's warranty or a 10-year insured protection plan.
- Variety of loans—fixed-rate, adjustable-rate, GPM, Hybrids

Advantages of VA-Guaranteed Loans (continued)

- Assumable mortgage if VA approves the consumer's credit. VA loans that originated prior to March 1, 1988 are fully assumable with no prequalification for the new purchaser.

- No prepayment penalty

Although the VA requires that veterans only pay reasonable charges for the loan, law requires the VA funding fee. Veterans who obtain VA home loans pay the **funding fee**. This reduces the cost of the program to taxpayers. For loans made between November 22, 2011 and September 30, 2017, the funding fee for a less than 5% down payment loan is 2.15%. For second and subsequent use, the funding fee for a less than a 5% down payment loan is 3.30%. [VA Circular 26-11-19]. The fee is higher the second time because these veterans have already had a chance to use the benefit once.

In addition to the funding fee, the VA allows a lender to charge a 1% origination fee plus reasonable discount points and veterans to pay reasonable and customary charges. These costs are determined by each regional VA office. Any charges not considered reasonable and customary are generally paid by the seller when purchasing a new home or by the lender when refinancing an existing VA loan.

Reasonable and Customary Closing Charges

Appraisal and inspections	Prepaid items
Credit report	Recording fees
Flood zone determination	Survey
Hazard insurance	Title examination and insurance

Items That Cannot be Charged to the Veteran

Amortization schedules	Photographs
Attorney services other than title	Postage/mailing charges
Document preparation fees	Preparing loan papers
Escrow charges	Conveyance fees
Fees charged by brokers	Stationery
Finders or other third parties	Tax service fees
Interest rate lock-in fees	Telephone calls
Loan application/processing fees	Other overhead
Loan closing/settlement fees	Trustee's fees or charges
Notary fees	TILA disclosure fees

VA Loan Amounts

The VA's guaranty on the loan protects the lender against loss if payments are not made. This guaranty is intended to encourage lenders to offer veterans loans with more favorable terms.

The amount of guaranty on the loan depends on the amount of the loan and if the veteran previously used some of his or her entitlement. The **entitlement** is the maximum guaranty that the VA will provide for the veteran's home loan. With the current maximum guaranty, a veteran who has not previously used the benefit may be able to obtain a maximum VA loan with no down payment depending on the borrower's income level and the appraised value of the property. A local VA office can provide more details on specific guaranty and entitlement amounts.

The basic entitlement is $36,000 for loans up to $144,000. The Veterans Benefits Act of 2004 changed the maximum guaranty amount. For loans in excess of $144,000 that are used to purchase or construct a home, the entitlement increases up to an amount equal to 25% of the Freddie Mac conforming loan limit for a single-family home. Currently, the conforming loan limit is $424,100 ($636,150 for Hawaii, Alaska, Guam, and U.S. Virgin Islands). This means that qualified veterans can get a purchase loan for those amounts with no down payment. When this limit increases or decreases, the VA guaranty limits also go up or down. However, the maximum VA loan amount is dependent on the reasonable value of the property as indicated on the Certificate of Reasonable Value (CRV).

The lender orders an appraisal using the Request for Determination of Reasonable Value form. The appraisal for VA loans is known as a **Certificate of Reasonable Value (CRV)** and must be issued by a certified VA appraiser. A loan cannot exceed the value established by the CRV. If the value on the CRV is less than the purchase price, the veteran can make up the difference in cash, the seller may reduce the selling price of the home, or the transaction can be cancelled. The seller cannot carry back a second loan for the difference between the sales price and the value indicated on the CRV.

OMB Control No. 2900-0045
Respondent Burden: 12 minutes

Department of Veterans Affairs | **REQUEST FOR DETERMINATION OF REASONABLE VALUE (Real Estate)**

1. CASE NUMBER

4. TITLE LIMITATIONS AND RESTRICTIVE COVENANTS:

2. PROPERTY ADDRESS (Include ZIP Code and county) | 3. LEGAL DESCRIPTION

5. NAME AND ADDRESS OF FIRM OR PERSON MAKING REQUEST/APPLICATION (Include ZIP Code)

1. ☐ CONDOMINIUM   2. ☐ PLANNED UNIT DEVELOPMENT

6. LOT DIMENSIONS:

1. ☐ IRREGULAR: SQ/FT   2. ☐ ACRES:

7. UTILITIES (✓) | ELEC. | GAS | WATER | SAN. SEWER
1. PUBLIC
2. COMMUNITY
3. INDIVIDUAL

8. EQUIP. | 1. ☐ RANGE/OVEN | 4. ☐ CLOTHES WASHER | 7. ☐ VENT FAN
| 2. ☐ REFRIG. | 5. ☐ DRYER | 8. ☐ W/W CARPET
| 3. ☐ DISH WASHER | 6. ☐ GARBAGE DISPOSAL | 9. ☐

9. BUILDING STATUS
1. ☐ PROPOSED
2. ☐ UNDER CONSTRUCTION
3. ☐ EXISTING
4. ☐ ALTERATIONS, IMPROVEMENTS, OR REPAIRS

10. BUILDING TYPE
1. ☐ DETACHED   3. ☐ ROW APT.
2. ☐ SEMI-DETACHED   4. ☐ UNIT

11. FACTORY FABRICATED?
1. ☐ YES   2. ☐ NO

12A. NO. OF BUILDINGS

12B. NO. OF LIVING UNITS

13A. STREET ACCESS
1. ☐ PRIVATE
2. ☐ PUBLIC

13B. STREET MAINTENANCE
1. ☐ PRIVATE
2. ☐ PUBLIC

14A. CONSTRUCTION WARRANTY INCLUDED?
1. ☐ YES   2. ☐ NO   *(If "Yes," complete Items 14b and 14c also)*

14B. NAME OF WARRANTY PROGRAM

14C. EXPIRATION DATE (Month, day, year)

15. CONSTRUCTION COMPLETED (Mo.,yr.)

16. NAME OF OWNER

17. PROPERTY:
OCCUPIED BY OWNER ☐   NEVER OCCUPIED ☐   VACANT ☐   OCCUPIED BY TENANT (Complete Item 18 also) ☐

18. RENT (If applic.) $ / MONTH

19. NAME OF OCCUPANT

20. TELEPHONE NO.

21. NAME OF BROKER

22. TELEPHONE NO.

23. DATE AND TIME AVAILABLE FOR INSPECTION   ☐ AM ☐ PM

24. KEYS AT (Address)

25. ORIGINATOR'S IDENT. NO.

26. SPONSOR'S IDENT. NO.

27. INSTITUTION'S CASE NO.

28. PURCHASER'S NAME AND ADDRESS (Complete mailing address, Include ZIP Code)

EQUAL OPPORTUNITY IN HOUSING
NOTE: Federal laws and regulations prohibit discrimination because of race, color, religion, sex, or national origin in the sale or rental of residential property. Numerous State statutes and local ordinances also prohibit such discrimination. In addition, section 805 of the Civil Rights Act of 1968 prohibits discriminatory practices in connection with the financing of housing.

If VA finds there is noncompliance with any antidiscrimination laws or regulations, it may discontinue business with the violator.

29. NEW OR PROPOSED CONSTRUCTION - Complete Items 29A through 29G for new or proposed construction cases only

A. COMPLIANCE INSPECTIONS WILL BE OR WERE MADE BY:
☐ FHA   ☐ VA   ☐ NONE MADE

B. PLANS (Check one)
☐ FIRST SUBMISSION   ☐ REPEAT CASE (If checked complete Item 29C)

C. PLANS SUBMITTED PREVIOUSLY UNDER CASE NO.

D. NAME AND ADDRESS OF BUILDER

E. TELEPHONE NO.

F. NAME AND ADDRESS OF WARRANTOR

G. TELEPHONE NO.

30. COMMENTS ON SPECIAL ASSESSMENTS OR HOMEOWNERS ASSOCIATION CHARGES

31. ANNUAL REAL ESTATE TAXES $

32. MINERAL RIGHTS RESERVED?
☐ YES (Explain)
☐ NO

33. LEASEHOLD CASES (Complete if applicable)
A. LEASE IS: ☐ 99 YEARS   ☐ RENEWABLE
B. EXPIRES (Date)
C. ANNUAL GROUND RENT $

34A. SALE PRICE OF PROPERTY $

34B. IS BUYER PURCHASING LOT SEPARATELY?
☐ YES   ☐ NO   (If "Yes," see instruction page under "Sale Price")

35. REFINANCING-AMOUNT OF PROPOSED LOAN $

36. PROPOSED SALE CONTRACT ATTACHED   ☐ YES ☐ NO

37. CONTRACT NO. PREVIOUSLY APPROVED BY VA THAT WILL BE USED

CERTIFICATIONS FOR SUBMISSIONS TO VA

1. On receipt of "Certificate of Reasonable Value" or advice from the Department of Veterans Affairs that a "Certificate of Reasonable Value" will not be issued, we agree to forward to the appraiser the approved fee which we are holding for this purpose.

2. CERTIFICATION REQUIRED ON CONSTRUCTION UNDER FHA SUPERVISION (Strike out inappropriate phrases in parentheses)

I hereby certify that plans and specifications and related exhibits, including acceptable FHA Change Orders, if any, supplied to VA in this case, are identical to those (submitted to) (to be submitted to) (approved by) FHA inspections, and that FHA inspections (have been) (will be) made pursuant to FHA approval for mortgage insurance on this basis of proposed construction under Sec.

38. SIGNATURE OF PERSON AUTHORIZING THIS

39. TITLE

40. TELEPHONE NUMBER

41. DATE

42. DATE OF ASSIGNMENT

43. NAME OF APPRAISER

WARNING: Section 1010 of title 18, U.S.C. provides: "Whoever for the purpose of . . .influencing such Administration . . .makes, passes, utters or publishes any statement knowing the same to be false . . .shall be fined not more than $5,000 or imprisoned not more that two years or both."

VA FORM AUG 2004   **26-1805**   SUPERSEDES VA FORM 26-1805, JUN 2001, WHICH WILL NOT BE USED.

Department of Veterans Affairs

OMB Control No. 2900-0045
Respondent Burden: 12 minutes

INSTRUCTIONS FOR PREPARATION OF VA REQUEST FOR DETERMINATION OF REASONABLE VALUE

Respondent Burden: We need this information to request an appraisal on the property for which VA guarantee of the loan is requested (38 U.S.C. 3710(b)). Title 38, United States Code, allows us to ask for this information. We estimate that you will need an average of 12 minutes to review the instructions, find the information, and complete this form. VA cannot conduct or sponsor a collection of information unless a valid OMB control number is displayed. You are not required to respond to a collection of information if this number is not displayed. Valid OMB control numbers can be located on the OMB Internet Page at www.whitehouse.gov/omb/library/OMBINVC.html#VA. If desired, you can call 1-800-827-1000 and give your comments or ask for mailing information on where to send your comments.

NOTE: ALL ENTRIES MUST BE TYPED.

Complete the form following the instructions below. After completion forward the form, together with any necessary exhibits to the VA office having jurisdiction.

Since certain selected data from page 1 is transcribed onto VA NOV (Notice of Value), we request that this form be carefully prepared. Incomplete submissions impede timely processing at the expense of both the Government and the requester.

This report is authorized by law (38 U.S.C. 3704(a) and 3710(b)). Failure to provide the information requested can result in rejection of the property as security for a loan.

REQUIRED EXHIBITS TO BE SENT WITH APPLICATION

SALES CONTRACTS: In cases involving proposed construction or existing construction not previously occupied, a copy of the executed or proposed sales contract must be submitted or, if a previously approved form of contract is to be used, the approved contract code number may be shown in Item 37. In those cases in which a veteran is under contract, submission of the contract may be deferred until a loan application is received.

PROPOSED CONSTRUCTION: Complete working drawings, including plot plan, foundation or basement plans, plans of all floors, exterior elevations, grade levels, sectional wall details, heating layout, individual well and septic system layout, and specifications on VA Form 26-1852, Description of Materials. (Consult local VA office for number of exhibit sets required.) This information is subject to reproduction by VA under 38 U.S.C. 3705 (b) and for storage purposes.

EXISTING CONSTRUCTION: 1. ALTERATIONS, IMPROVEMENTS OR REPAIRS - Complete drawings and specifications indicating the work to be done and its relation to the house, in the quantity required by the local VA office. 2. NOT PREVIOUSLY OCCUPIED AND CONSTRUCTION COMPLETED WITHIN 12 CALENDAR MONTHS - Contact local VA office for eligibility criteria and required exhibits.

FORM ENTRIES

NAME, ADDRESS, AND ZIP CODE: Make sure to enter the ZIP code in all blocks which require an address entry.

LEGAL DESCRIPTION: Insert legal description. If necessary, attach 4 copies of a separate sheet showing the legal description.

TITLE LIMITATIONS: Enter known title exceptions. If none are known, enter "None." Include easements, special assessments, mandatory homeowners association membership, etc. Exceptions noted on this application will be considered in reasonable value. Attach separate sheet (4 copies) if necessary.

LOT DIMENSIONS: Show frontage X depth. If irregular, indicate dimensions of all perimeter lot lines.

REMOVABLE EQUIPMENT: Personal property, such as furniture, drapes and rugs, will not be valued and may not be included in the loan. However, wall-to-wall carpeting may be included in value and also included in the loan.

CONSTRUCTION COMPLETED: Insert both month and year when property has been completed less than two years. If over two years old, insert year completed only.

COMMENTS ON SPECIAL ASSESSMENTS AND/OR HOMEOWNER ASSOCIATION CHARGES: Indicate special assessments which are now a lien or will become a lien. In the case of a planned unit development, condominium, or a mandatory membership homeowner association, indicate the current monthly or other periodic assessment.

MINERAL RIGHTS: If reserved, explain either in space shown as title exceptions or by separate page.

LEASEHOLD CASES: (Usually Hawaii or Maryland.) If property involves a leasehold, insert the ground rent per year and show whether the lease is for 99 years or renewable, whether it has previously been VA approved, and its expiration date. Submit two copies of the lease agreement.

SALE PRICE: Enter proposed sale price except when application involves an individual owner-occupant building for himself/herself. In such cases, enter estimated cost of construction and the balance owned on the lot, if any. If refinancing, enter amount of proposed loan in Item 35.

NOTE: If title is not "fee simple," submit copies in duplicate of all pertinent legal data providing a full explanation of the title involved.

VA FORM AUG 2004 **26-1805**   SUPERSEDES VA FORM 26-1805, JUN 2001, WHICH WILL NOT BE USED.

Guaranty Amounts

The VA has limits for conforming loans and jumbo loans as described below.

Loans for $424,100 or Less

The guaranty amount for loans when the original principal loan amount is $424,100 or less is shown in the following chart.

Loan Amount	Guaranty Amount
$56,251 − $144,000	The lesser of $36,000 or 40% of the loan
$144,001 − $424,100	The lesser of $104,250 or 25% of the loan

Example: Tracy, a qualified veteran, applies to an approved VA lender for a zero-down loan on a house appraised for $285,000. The lender determines that the guaranty will be $71,250 ($285,000 x 25%). This meets the guidelines and Tracy will not be required to make a down payment.

Loans for More Than $424,100

Some lenders offer VA loans for more than $424,100. These are VA jumbo loans. Veterans pay a 25% down payment on the amount above the $424,100.

Example: Veteran Victor wants to use a VA loan for a home that costs $527,000. There is no down payment on the first $424,100 of the loan. Victor pays a 25% down payment only on the amount above $424,100, which is $102,900 ($527,000 - $424,100). $102,900 x 25% = $ 25,725. The entire down payment paid by Victor on a $527,000 loan is only $ 25,725, or 5.2%. The actual loan will be $501,275.

When compared to a conventional loan, Victor would have to provide a cash down payment of $105,400 (20%) or have a 5% down payment with a loan of $500,650 along with a monthly MMI payment. Obviously, the VA loan is a better choice.

VA Requirements

The Department of Veterans Affairs (VA) does not make loans. It guarantees loans made by approved lenders, much like the FHA. Only lenders who are VA-approved lenders can make VA loans. These lenders may underwrite and close home loans without prior VA review or approval. This includes all aspects of the loan application, the property analysis, and borrower underwriting.

Many VA-approved lenders originate these loans and have automatic authority to close VA-guaranteed loans. **Automatic authority** is the authority of a lender to close VA-guaranteed loans without the prior approval of the VA. VA-approved Lender Appraisal Processing Program (LAPP) lenders can process loans faster than other lenders. LAPP lenders do not need to send any paperwork to the VA until after the home sale is closed.

If a loan is eligible for automatic processing, VA automatic lenders are approved to use some automated underwriting systems. These systems incorporate the VA's credit standards and processing requirements. The approved systems are Freddie Mac's Loan Prospector®, Fannie Mae's Desktop Underwriter®, JP Morgan Chase's ZiPPY System (for JP Morgan Chase loans only), and Fannie Mae's Desktop/PMI AURA Underwriter.

These systems do not approve or disapprove loans, they merely assign a risk classification, which determines the level of underwriting and documentation needed. The lender must decide whether to approve the loan.

The loan process is not much different than any other type of real estate loan except that the borrower or the lender must obtain the veteran's Certificate of Eligibility.

Determine Eligibility

Like FHA loans, VA loans are available only for individuals and not partnerships or corporations, although co-borrowers are eligible. Unmarried surviving spouses of veterans who have died on active duty or from a service-connected disability are also eligible for VA loans.

Before lenders accept an application for a VA-guaranteed loan, they must be sure that the VA has determined that the applicant is eligible. The VA evaluates each applicant to see if the applicant meets the eligibility criteria established by law. **Eligibility** is the veteran's right to VA home loan benefits under the law and based on military service. However, an eligible veteran still must meet credit and income standards in order to qualify for a VA-guaranteed loan.

First, a veteran must request a **Certificate of Eligibility (COE)**, which is a document issued by the VA that provides evidence of an applicant's eligibility to obtain a VA loan. The applicant submits VA Form 26-1880 (Request for a Certificate of Eligibility) along with proof of service (DD Form 214) to a local VA Eligibility Center.

Based on the length and type of service, the VA issues a certificate for each person determined eligible to apply for a VA-guaranteed home loan. In general, veterans are eligible based on active wartime service and peacetime service. Additionally, a veteran who was discharged for a service-connected disability, for hardship, or at the convenience of the government is also eligible.

OMB Control No. 2900-0086
Respondent Burden: 15 minutes
Expiration Date: 10-31-2017

VA Department of Veterans Affairs	FOR VA USE ONLY COE REF. NO.	MAIL COMPLETED APPLICATION TO:
REQUEST FOR A CERTIFICATE OF ELIGIBILITY		Atlanta Regional Loan Center Attn: COE (262) P. O. Box 100034 Decatur, GA 30031

NOTE: Please read information on reverse before completing this form. If additional space is required, attach a separate sheet.

1. NAME OF VETERAN *(First, Middle, Last)*	2. DATE OF BIRTH	3. SOCIAL SECURITY NUMBER

4A. DID YOU SERVE UNDER ANOTHER NAME? ☐ YES ☐ NO *(If "Yes," complete Item 4B)*	4B. NAME(S) USED DURING MILITARY SERVICE *(If different from name in Item 1)*

5. DAYTIME TELEPHONE NUMBER	6. E-MAIL ADDRESS *(If applicable)*

7A. ADDRESS *(Number and street or rural route, city or P.O., State and ZIP Code)*	7B. MAIL CERTIFICATE OF ELIGIBILITY TO: *(Complete ONLY if the Certificate is to be mailed to an address different from the one listed in Item 7A.)*

8A. WERE YOU DISCHARGED, RETIRED, OR SEPARATED FROM SERVICE BECAUSE OF DISABILITY? ☐ YES ☐ NO	8B. VA CLAIM NUMBER *(If known)*

MILITARY SERVICE (SEE INSTRUCTIONS FOR PROOF OF SERVICE ON THE NEXT PAGE)

9A. ARE YOU CURRENTLY ON ACTIVE DUTY? *(If you currently serving on active duty, leave the "Date Separated" field blank.)*
☐ YES ☐ NO

IMPORTANT: Please provide your dates of service. In many cases eligibility can be established based on data in VA systems. However, it is recommended that proof of service be provided, if readily available. Proof of service is required for persons who entered service after September 7, 1980 and were discharged after serving less than 2 years.	BRANCH OF SERVICE	DATE ENTERED	DATE SEPARATED	OFFICER OR ENLISTED	SERVICE NUMBER *(if different from Social Security Number)*
9B. ACTIVE SERVICE - *Do not include any periods of Active Duty for Training or Active Guard Reserve service. Do include any activation for duty under Title 10 U.S.C. (e.g. Reserve or Guard unit mobilized.)*					
9C. RESERVE OR NATIONAL GUARD SERVICE Include any periods of Active Duty for Training (ADT) or Active Guard Reserve service. Do not include any activation for duty under Title 10 U.S.C. (e.g. Reserve or Guard unit mobilized.)*					

PREVIOUS VA LOANS (SEE INSTRUCTIONS ON THE NEXT PAGE - Attach a separate sheet if information for all homes will not fit in Item 10)

10A. DO YOU NOW OWN ANY HOME(S) PURCHASED OR REFINANCED WITH A VA-GUARANTEED LOAN? ☐ YES *(If "Yes," complete Items 10B through 10D)* ☐ NO *(If "No," skip to Item 14)* ☐ NOT APPLICABLE (NA) - I HAVE NEVER OBTAINED A VA-GUARANTEED HOME LOAN *(If "NA," skip to Item 14)*	10B. DATE OF LOAN *(Month and Year)*	10C. STREET ADDRESS	10D. CITY AND STATE

11A. ARE YOU APPLYING FOR THE **ONE-TIME ONLY RESTORATION** OF ENTITLEMENT TO PURCHASE ANOTHER HOME? ☐ YES ☐ NO *(If "Yes," complete Items 11B through 11D)*	11B. DATE OF LOAN *(Month and Year)*	11C. STREET ADDRESS	11D. CITY AND STATE

12A. ARE YOU APPLYING FOR A RESTORATION OF ENTITLEMENT TO OBTAIN A **REGULAR (CASH-OUT) REFINANCE** ON YOUR CURRENT HOME? ☐ YES ☐ NO *(If "Yes," complete Items 12B through 12D)*	12B. DATE OF LOAN *(Month and Year)*	12C. STREET ADDRESS	12D. CITY AND STATE

13A. ARE YOU REFINANCING AN EXISTING VA LOAN TO OBTAIN A LOWER INTEREST RATE **WITHOUT RECEIVING** ANY CASH PROCEEDS (IRRRL)? ☐ YES ☐ NO *(If "Yes," complete Items 13B through 13D)*	13B. DATE OF LOAN *(Month and Year)*	13C. STREET ADDRESS	13D. CITY AND STATE

I CERTIFY THAT the statements in this document are true and complete to the best of my knowledge.

14A. SIGNATURE OF VETERAN *(Do NOT print)*	14B. DATE SIGNED

FEDERAL STATUTES PROVIDE SEVERE PENALTIES FOR FRAUD, INTENTIONAL MISREPRESENTATION, CRIMINAL CONNIVANCE OR CONSPIRACY PURPOSED TO INFLUENCE THE ISSUANCE OF ANY GUARANTY OR INSURANCE BY THE SECRETARY OF VETERANS AFFAIRS

FOR VA USE ONLY *(Please do not write below this line)*	DATE RETURNED
REASON(S) FOR RETURN	

VA FORM
NOV 2014   **26-1880**   SUPERSEDES VA FORM 26-1880, MAR 2011, WHICH WILL NOT BE USED.

INSTRUCTIONS FOR VA FORM 26-1880

PRIVACY ACT NOTICE - VA will not disclose information collected on this form to any source other than what has been authorized under the Privacy Act of 1974 or Title 38, Code of Federal Regulations 1.576 for routine uses (for example: the authorized release of information to Congress when requested for statistical purposes) identified in the VA system of records, 55VA26, Loan Guaranty Home, Condominium and Manufactured Home Loan Applicant Records, Specially Adapted Housing Applicant Records, and Vendee Loan Applicant Records - VA, and published in the Federal Register. Your obligation to respond is required in order to determine the qualifications for a loan.

RESPONDENT BURDEN - This information is needed to help determine a veteran's qualifications for a VA guaranteed home loan. Title 38, U.S.C., section 3702, authorizes collection of this information. We estimate that you will need an average of 15 minutes to review the instructions, find the information, and complete this form. VA cannot conduct or sponsor a collection of information unless a valid OMB control number is displayed. You are not required to respond to a collection of information if this number is not displayed. Valid OMB control numbers can be located on the OMB Internet Page at www.reginfo.gov/public/do/PRAMain. If desired, you can call 1-800-827-1000 to get information on where to send comments or suggestions about this form.

A. YOUR IDENTIFYING INFORMATION

Item 1 - Tell us your complete name, *as you would like it to appear on your Certificate of Eligibility (COE).*

Item 4B - If you served under another name, provide the name as it appears on your discharge certificate (DD Form 214).

Item 7 - You can have your Certificate of Eligibility sent to you at your current mailing address, or directly to your lender, or to any mailing address you provide in Item 7B.

Item 8B - In most cases, your VA claim number is the same as your Social Security Number. If you are not sure of your VA claim number, leave this field blank.

B. MILITARY SERVICE

Item 9 - **NOTE** - Cases involving other than honorable discharges will usually require further development by VA. This is necessary to determine if the service was under other than dishonorable conditions.

Item 9A - If you are currently serving on regular active duty, eligibility can usually be established based on data in VA systems. However, in some situations you may be asked to provide a statement of service signed by, or by direction of, the adjutant, personnel officer, or commander of your unit or higher headquarters. The statement may be in any format; usually a standard or bulleted memo is sufficient. It should identify you by name and social security number, and provide: (1) your date of entry on your current active duty period and (2) the duration of any time lost (or a statement noting there has been no lost time). Generally this should be on military letterhead.

Item 9B - **Active Service** *(not including Active Duty Training or Active Guard Reserve service)* - the best evidence to show your service is your discharge certificate (DD Dorm 214) showing active duty dates and type of discharge. If you were separated after October 1, 1979, the DD214 was issued in several parts (copies). We are required to have a copy showing the character of service (Item 24) and the narrative reason for separation (Item 28). We prefer the MEMBER-4 copy, however, we can accept any copy that contains these items. The copy number is shown on the bottom right of the form. We don't need the original; a photocopy is acceptable. Any Veterans Services Representative in the nearest Department of Veterans Affairs office or center will assist you in securing necessary proof of military service.

Item 9C - **National Guard Service:** You may submit NGB Form 22, Report of Separation and Record of Service, or NGB Form 23, Retirement Points Accounting, or their equivalent. We are required to have a copy showing character of service.

Selected Reserve Service (Including Active Duty Training and Active Guard Reserve) - You may submit (Including Active Training and Active Guard Reserve) - You may submit a copy of your latest annual retirement points statement and evidence of honorable service. There is no single form used by the Reserves similar to the DD Form 214 or NGB Form 22. The following forms are commonly used, but others may be acceptable:

Army Reserve	DARP FM 249-2E
Naval Reserve	NRPC 1070-124
Air Force Reserve	AF 526
Marine Corps Reserve	NA VMC 798
Coast Guard Reserve	CG 4174 or 4175

If you are still serving in the Selected Reserves or the National Guard, you must include an original statement of service signed by, or by the direction of, the adjutant, personnel officer, or commander of your unit or higher headquarters showing your date of entry and the length of time that you have been a member of the Selected Reserves. At least 6 years of honorable service must be documented.

C. PREVIOUS LOANS

Items 10 through 14. Your eligibility is reusable depending on the circumstances. Normally, if you have paid off your prior VA loan and no longer own the home, you can have your used eligibility restored for additional use. Also, on a one-time only basis, you may have your eligibility restored if your prior VA loan has been paid in full but you still own the home. Normally VA receives notification that a loan has been paid. In some instances, it may be necessary to include evidence that a previous VA loan has been paid in full. Evidence can be in the form of a paid-in-full statement from the former lender, a satisfaction of mortgage from the clerk of court in the county where the home is located, or a copy of the HUD-1 settlement statement completed in connection with a sale of the home or refinance of the prior loan. Many counties post public documents (like the satisfaction of mortgage) online.

Item 11A. **One-Time Restoration.** If you have paid off your VA loan, but still own the home purchased with that loan, you may apply for a one-time only restoration of your entitlement in order to purchase another home that will be your primary residence. Once you have used your one-time restoration, you must sell all homes before any other entitlement can be restored.

Item 12A. **Regular (cash-out) Refinance.** You may refinance your current VA or non-VA loan in order to pay off the mortgage and/or other liens of record on the home. This type of refinance requires an appraisal and credit qualifying.

Item 13A. **Interest Rate Reduction Refinancing Loan (IRRRL).** You may refinance the balance of your current VA loan in order to obtain a lower interest rate, or convert a VA adjustable rate mortgage to a fixed rate. The new loan may not exceed the sum of the outstanding balance on the existing VA loan, plus allowable fees and closing costs, including VA funding fee and up to 2 discount points. You may also add up to $6,000 of energy efficiency improvements into the loan. **A certificate of eligibility is not required for IRRRL.** Instead, a Prior Loan Validation, obtained through our online system WebLGY can be used in lieu of COE. Presently, this application is only available to lenders. In WebLGY, a lender can select Eligibility from the tollbar and then Prior Loan Validation. Enter the veteran's Social Security Number and Last Name. The system will then, in most cases, pull up the veteran's active loan information. Print the prior Loan Validation screen and use it in lieu of the COE.

Wartime Service

Veterans with active duty service during World War II and later periods that were not dishonorable are eligible for VA loan benefits. Veterans who served during the following periods of active wartime service must have had at least 90 days of service.

World War II	09/16/1940 to 07/25/1947
Korean Conflict	06/27/1950 to 01/31/1955
Vietnam Era	08/05/1964 to 05/07/1975

Gulf War

Gulf War veterans must have completed 24 months of continuous active duty or the full period (at least 90 days) for which they were ordered to active duty. Individuals may also be eligible if they were released from active duty due to a service-connected disability, an involuntary reduction in force, certain medical conditions, or, in some instances, for the convenience of the Government.

08/02/1990 to TBD

Peacetime Service

Veterans with service during the following peacetime periods must have served at least 181 days of continuous active duty.

07/26/1947 to 06/26/1950

02/01/1955 to 08/04/1964

05/08/1975 to 09/07/1980 (Enlisted)

05/08/1975 to 10/16/1981 (Commissioned Officer)

Peacetime Service After 09/07/80 (enlisted) or 10/16/81 (officer)

In most cases, veterans of enlisted service that began after September 7, 1980 or officers with service beginning after October 16, 1981 must have served at least 2 years of continuous active duty.

Selected Reserve or National Guard

Members of the Selected Reserve, including the National Guard, who are not otherwise eligible and who have completed 6 years of service and have been honorably discharged or have completed 6 years of service and are still serving may be eligible.

Others Who May Be Eligible

An unremarried spouse of a serviceperson who died while in service, became missing in action, or became a prisoner of war may be eligible for VA home loan benefits. In addition, certain United States citizens who served in the armed forces of a government allied with the United States in WW II may be eligible. Others who may be eligible include public health service officers, cadets and midshipmen at the service academies, officers of the National Oceanic & Atmospheric Administration, and some merchant seaman with WW II service.

Certificate of Eligibility

The Certificate of Eligibility (COE) is important because the lender may rely on it as proof that a veteran is eligible for a VA home loan. The most important item on the COE is the amount of the entitlement, because the VA's guaranty on the loan generally cannot exceed the amount of the entitlement.

Until veterans use part of their entitlement, they have full entitlement. If the entire entitlement was not used, a veteran may be eligible for another VA loan with a partial entitlement. Veterans who have previously used their guaranty may use it repeatedly provided it is restored after each sale. If veterans allow their VA loan to be assumed, they may have partial entitlement available. This will enable them to secure another VA loan. A veteran may obtain a Reinstatement of Full Entitlement when the loan is fully repaid.

Qualifying Property

The VA has standards for the types of property that are eligible for the program.

Qualifying Property Types for VA Guaranty

- 1-4 family owner-occupied residences
- Condominium unit in a VA-approved housing development
- Manufactured home and lot
- Lots on which the veteran plans to place a manufactured home that he or she already owns and occupies
- Purchase of land on which the veteran's residence will be simultaneously constructed at the time the land purchase is completed

Minimum Property Requirements

The VA wants to make sure the home being purchased by the veteran is suitable and sanitary for living. In existing and new construction, the VA has minimum property requirements to determine the eligibility of the property. **Minimum property requirements (MPRs)** provide a basis for determining that the property is safe, structurally sound, sanitary, and meets the standards considered acceptable in a permanent home in its locality. The complete discussion of the VA MPRs can be found in Chapter 12 of VA Pamphlet 26-7, Revised.

Selected VA Minimum Property Requirements

- Each living unit must have the space necessary to provide suitable living, sleeping, cooking and dining accommodations, and sanitary facilities.

- Minimum standards are required for mechanical systems, heating, water supply, sanitary facilities, roof, crawlspace, ventilation, and electricity.

- Utilities must be separate for each living unit, or, at a minimum, have separate shut-off valves.

- There must be vehicular access to the property by means of an abutting public or private street surfaced with an all-weather material. For private streets, there must be a permanent easement and provisions for permanent maintenance, which means that there must be a written road maintenance agreement in place.

- Each living unit must be individually accessible for use and maintenance without trespass on adjoining properties.

- Each property must have access to its rear yard.

- The property must be free of hazards that may adversely affect the health and safety of the occupants, adversely affect the structure, or impair the use and enjoyment of the property by the occupants. Conditions that impair the safety, sanitation, or structural soundness of the dwelling will cause the property to be unacceptable until the defects or conditions have been remedied and the probability of further damage eliminated.

- If a property is not detached housing, the dwelling must be separated from an adjoining dwelling by a party or lot line wall extending the full height of the building.

- No part of any residential structure may be located within a high-pressure gas, a liquid petroleum pipeline, or a high-voltage electric transmission line easement.

VA Underwriting Guidelines

The VA Credit Standards are written as guidelines and lenders are encouraged to consider all factors when underwriting loan applications for qualified veterans. Although lenders use a debt-to-income ratio and residual income to qualify borrowers, no single factor is a determinant in any applicant's qualification.

For example, a veteran who has maintained an excellent credit history, (such as satisfactory rent payment comparable to the proposed PITI) may be approvable in spite of shortfall in the residual income. In such an instance, it might be appropriate to consider that the veteran has established a lifestyle that is substantially different from the average used in establishing the residual income tables in the credit standards.

Employment and Income Stability

The borrower's employment and income stability are central to underwriting a loan. He or she must show stable, reliable income over the most recent 2-year period even if he or she has worked for a variety of employers. In addition, the borrower's present and anticipated income should be sufficient to meet the repayment terms of the loan.

If a veteran is relying on rental income from the property to qualify for the loan, the veteran must show that he or she has the background or qualifications to be successful as a landlord. The veteran must also have enough cash reserves to make the loan payments for at least 6 months without relying on the rental income.

Two years' employment in the applicant's current position or line of work is a positive indicator of continued employment. Usually the lender uses a Verification of Employment (VOE) and a pay stub from the employer to verify income.

Credit History

The VA will analyze a borrower's past credit performance when determining whether to approve the loan. A borrower with timely payments for the last 12 months demonstrates his or her willingness to repay future credit obligations. On the opposite side, a borrower with continuous slow payments, judgments, and delinquent accounts is not a good candidate for loan approval.

As with FHA loans, if the borrower does not have an established credit history, a satisfactory payment history on items such as rent, utilities, phone bills, car payments, and the like may be used to establish a satisfactory credit history. Any outstanding collection accounts, judgments, and charge offs must be paid off.

A person with a Chapter 7 bankruptcy must re-establish good credit, qualify financially, and have good job stability before applying for a VA-guaranteed loan. The VA guidelines state that applicants who filed Chapter 7 bankruptcy are eligible 2 years after the date of discharge. A full explanation of the bankruptcy is required.

A borrower who gave a deed in lieu of foreclosure or whose previous residence was foreclosed is generally not eligible for a VA-guaranteed loan until 2 years after the disposition date. However, if the foreclosure was on a VA loan, the applicant may not have full entitlement available for the new loan.

Residual Income and Qualifying Ratio

The VA qualifies borrowers using the residual income method and one qualifying ratio.

Residual Income

Residual income is the amount of net income remaining after deducting debts, obligations, and monthly shelter expenses that is used to cover family living expenses, such as food, health care, clothing, and gasoline. The residual income method uses the veteran's net take-home pay. **Take-home pay** is the gross income less federal and state income taxes and any Social Security or retirement contributions. Housing expenses include the principal and interest on the loan (or rent), property taxes, homeowners' insurance, maintenance, and utilities. The amount used for maintenance and utilities varies with the type and location of the property. Regional VA offices have local guidelines. In addition, a deduction is made for alimony, long-term debt such as car payments, and job-related expenses such as childcare and uniforms. This final amount is the residual income.

The VA's minimum residual incomes are a guide and should not automatically trigger approval or rejection of a loan. Instead, consider residual income in conjunction with all other credit factors. Applicants with marginal residual income may still be approved if they prove they have previously handled similar housing expenses.

Using the residual income charts, the lender can determine if the borrower has sufficient residual income to qualify for the loan. An obviously inadequate residual income alone can be a basis for disapproving a loan.

Example: Bob is married and has two children. He wants to buy a single-family home with a back yard. Currently he earns $4,500 gross monthly salary. He pays $540 in federal income taxes, $90 in state income taxes, and $300 for Social Security. The sales price on the home he wants to buy is $240,000. The principal and interest on the home is $1,450, taxes are $250, and homeowners insurance is $60. The home is newer and well insulated, which keeps both maintenance and utility costs low. The average for this type of house is $300 a month. Bob's wife takes care of the children. They have two cars but only one $295 payment. The home is located in the South. Using this information, the lender calculates Bob's residual income.

Gross income		$ 4,500
Less:		
Federal income tax	$ 540	
State income tax	90	
Social security	300	
Net take-home pay		$ 3,570
Housing expense and fixed obligations		
Principal & interest	$1,450	
Property taxes	250	
Homeowners insurance	60	
Total PITI	1,760	
Maintenance & utilities	300	
Alimony	0	
Long-term debts (car payment)	295	
Job-related expenses	0	
Total housing and fixed obligations		$ 2,355
Residual income		$ 1,215

Based on the chart below, Bob's residual income must be $1,003 or more to qualify for the VA loan.

Table of Residual Incomes by Region				
For loan amounts of $79,999 and below				
Family Size	Northeast	Midwest	South	West
1	$390	$382	$382	$425
2	$654	$641	$641	$713
3	$788	$772	$772	$859
4	$888	$868	$868	$967
5	$921	$902	$902	$1,004
Over 5 add $75 for each additional member up to a family of 7.				

Table of Residual Incomes by Region				
For loan amounts of $80,000 and above				
Family Size	Northeast	Midwest	South	West
1	$450	$441	$441	$491
2	$755	$738	$738	$823
3	$909	$889	$889	$990
4	$1,025	$1,003	$1,003	$1,117
5	$1,062	$1,039	$1,039	$1,158
Over 5 add $80 for each additional member up to a family of 7.				

Debt-to-Income Ratio

The VA uses one debt-to-income ratio to qualify borrowers. The qualifying ratio is 41% and is calculated by dividing the monthly housing expense plus long-term debt by the gross monthly income. A ratio in excess of 41% requires scrutiny and compensating factors. A veteran with a good credit record who meets the residual income guideline may be approvable in spite of a high debt-to-income ratio.

Example: Using the information from the previous example, we can calculate Bob's debt-to-income ratio. First, add up the total PITI and all recurring monthly installment debt (car loans, personal loans, student loans, credit cards, etc.). Then, take that amount and divide it by the gross monthly income. The maximum ratio to qualify is 41%. In the event the number exceeds 41%, the VA has a residual income guideline that may allow approval.

Borrower's gross monthly income	$4,500
PITI	$1,760
Monthly revolving debt	$0
Monthly recurring installment debt	$ 295
Total PITI and debt	$2,055

Divide (PITI & Debt) by gross monthly income

Debt-to-income ratio   45.7% ($2,055 ÷ $4,500)

Selected VA Loan Programs

The VA offers a variety of loans with a choice of repayment plans—fixed-rate loans, adjustable-rate loans, and graduated payment loans. This text discusses some of the more common programs. The website, http://www.benefits.va.gov/homeloans describes all of the VA loan programs. These no-down payment loans have no prepayment penalty. Remember, all veterans, except those who are exempt because they are receiving disability compensation, must pay a funding fee. For all VA loans, the funding fee may be included in the loan or paid in cash.

If the borrower meets the eligibility requirements, the VA will guarantee loans involving temporary interest rate buydowns. A temporary interest rate buydown is acceptable for any type of VA-guaranteed loan except a graduated payment mortgage loan. Given certain circumstances, the veteran may be able to qualify at the buydown rate.

Traditional 30-year Fixed-Rate Loan

With a fixed-rate VA-guaranteed loan, a qualified veteran can purchase a home with no down payment depending on the appraised value of the property. The seller may give seller concessions of up to 4% of the reasonable value of the home. That 4% does not include the buyer's closing costs, which, when paid by the seller, can take the seller credits to the buyer for concessions and closing costs up to a maximum of 6% of the purchase price.

VA Adjustable-Rate Mortgage

The VA will guarantee an adjustable-rate mortgage. The VA offers various types of ARM products that are competitive with Fannie Mae and Freddie Mac products. The veteran must qualify at the initial note rate.

VA Graduated Payment Mortgage

A VA graduated payment mortgage (GPM) may only be used to acquire a single-family dwelling unit (not a manufactured home) and the loan can include funds for energy efficiency improvements. Since the principal balance increases during the initial years of a GPM, a down payment is required. For details on how the down payment is calculated, go to the VA website at www.va.gov.

Construction/Permanent Home Loan

The VA will guarantee a construction/permanent home loan, which is a loan to finance the construction and/or purchase of a residence. The loan is closed prior to the start of construction, at which time proceeds are disbursed to cover the cost of the land or the balance owed on the land. The remaining balance is placed into escrow. The escrowed monies are paid out to the builder during construction. The permanent loan interest rate is established at closing. The veteran begins making payments on this loan only after construction is complete. Therefore, the initial payment on principal may be postponed up to one year, if necessary. The loan must be amortized to achieve full repayment within its remaining term.

Interest Rate Reduction Refinancing Loan

A veteran with an existing VA loan may use an **Interest Rate Reduction Refinancing Loan (IRRRL)**, which may also be referred to as a streamlined loan, to lower his or her interest rate. Except when refinancing an existing VA-guaranteed ARM to a fixed-rate, the refinance must result in a lower interest rate. When refinancing from an existing VA ARM to a fixed-rate, the interest rate is allowed to increase. The VA does not require an appraisal or credit-underwriting package. However, the lenders may require an appraisal and a credit report.

Manufactured Home Loan

Private lenders such as finance companies make VA-guaranteed manufactured home loans. The VA will guarantee 40% of the loan amount or the veteran's available entitlement, up to a maximum amount of $20,000.

 **Department of
Veterans Affairs**

COUNSELING CHECKLIST FOR MILITARY HOMEBUYERS

1. Failure on the part of a borrower on active duty to disclose that he/she expects to leave the area within 12 months due to transfer orders or completion of his/her enlistment period may constitute "bad faith." If your loan is foreclosed under circumstances which include such bad faith, you may be required to repay VA for any loss suffered by the Government under the guaranty. (In ANY case in which VA suffers a loss under the guaranty, the loss must be repaid before your loan benefits can be restored to use in obtaining another VA loan.)

2. Although real estate values have historically risen in most areas, there is no assurance that the property for which you are seeking financing will increase in value or even retain its present value.

3. It is possible that you may encounter difficulty in selling your house, recovering your investment or making any profit, particularly if there is an active new home market in the area.

4. Receiving military orders for a permanent change of duty station or an unexpected early discharge due to a reduction in force will not relieve you of your obligation to make your mortgage payments on the first of each month.

5. "Letting the house go back" is **NOT** an acceptable option. A decision to do so may be considered "bad faith". A foreclosure will result in a bad credit record, a possible debt you will owe the government and difficulty in getting more credit in the future.

6. If unexpected circumstances lead to difficulty in making your payments, contact your mortgage company promptly. It will be easier to resolve any problems if you act quickly and be open and honest with the mortgage company.

7. **YOUR VA LOAN MAY NOT BE ASSUMED WITHOUT THE PRIOR APPROVAL OF VA OR YOUR LENDER.**

8. **DO NOT BE MISLED!** VA does not guarantee the **CONDITION** of the house which you are buying, whether it is new or previously occupied. VA guarantees only the **LOAN.** You may talk to many people when you are in the process of buying a house. Particularly with a previously occupied house, you may pick up the impression along the way that you need not be overly concerned about any needed repairs or hidden defects since VA will be sure to find them and require them to be repaired. This is **NOT TRUE!** In every case, ultimately, it is your responsibility to be an informed buyer and to assure yourself that what you are buying is satisfactory to you in all respects. Remember, VA guarantees only the loan - **NOT** the condition.

9. If you have any doubts about the condition of the house which you are buying, it is in your best interest to seek expert advice before you legally commit yourself in a purchase agreement. Particularly with a previously occupied house, most sellers and their real estate agents are willing to permit you, at your expense, to arrange for an inspection by a qualified residential inspection service. Also, most sellers and agents are willing to negotiate with you concerning what repairs are to be included in the purchase agreement. Steps of this kind can prevent many later problems, disagreements, and major disappointments.

10. Proper maintenance is the best way to protect your home and improve the chance that its value will increase.

11. If you are buying a previously owned house, you should look into making energy efficient improvements. You can add up to $6,000 to your VA loan to have energy efficient improvements installed. Consult your lender or the local VA office.

I HEREBY CERTIFY THAT the lender has counseled me and I fully understand the counseling items set forth above.

_____   _____
(Borrower's Signature)   (Date)

I HEREBY CERTIFY THAT the borrower has been counseled regarding the counseling items set forth above.

_____   _____
(Lender's Signature)   (Date)

VA Form
JUN 1995 **26-0592**   EXISTING STOCK OF VA FORM 26-0592, JUL 1990, WILL
                               BE USED.

OMB Control No. 2900-0406
Respondent Burden: 5 Minutes

| **VA** Department of Veterans Affairs | **VERIFICATION OF VA BENEFITS** |

PRIVACY ACT NOTICE: The VA will not disclose information collected on this form to any source other than what has been authorized under the Privacy Act of 1974 or Title 5, Code of Federal Regulations 1.576 for routine uses (i.e., information concerning a veteran's indebtedness to the United States by virtue of a person's participation in a benefits program administered by VA may be disclosed to any third party, except consumer reporting agencies) as identified in the VA system of records, 55VA26, Loan Guaranty Home, Condominium and Manufactured Home Loan Applicant Records, Specially Adapted Housing Applicant Records and Vendee Loan Applicant Records - VA, and published in the Federal Register. Your obligation to respond is required to obtain or retain benefits. Giving us your SSN account information is voluntary. Refusal to provide your SSN by itself will not result in the denial of benefits. The VA will not deny an individual benefits for refusing to provide his or her SSN unless the disclosure of the SSN is required by a Federal Statute of law in effect prior to January 1, 1975, and still in effect.

TO: NAME AND ADDRESS OF LENDER *(Complete mailing address including ZIP Code)*

INSTRUCTIONS TO LENDER

Complete this form ONLY if the veteran/applicant:
- is receiving VA disability payments; or
- has received VA disability payments; or
- would receive VA disability payments but for receipt of retired pay; or
- is surviving spouse of a veteran and in receipt of DIC payments
- has filed a claim for VA disability benefits prior to discharge from active duty service

Complete Items 1 through 10. Send the completed form to the appropriate VA Regional Loan Center where it will be processed and returned to the Lender. The completed form must be retained as part of the lender's loan origination package.

1. NAME OF VETERAN *(First, middle, last)*

2. CURRENT ADDRESS OF VETERAN

3. DATE OF BIRTH

4. VA CLAIM FOLDER NUMBER *(C-File No., if known)*

5. SOCIAL SECURITY NUMBER

6. SERVICE NUMBER *(If different from Social Security Number)*

7. I HEREBY CERTIFY THAT I ☐ DO ☐ DO NOT have a VA benefit-related indebtedness to my knowledge. I authorize VA to furnish the information listed below.

8. I HEREBY CERTIFY THAT I ☐ HAVE ☐ HAVE NOT filed a claim for VA disability benefits prior to discharge from active duty service (I am presently still on active duty.)

9. SIGNATURE OF VETERAN

10. DATE SIGNED

FOR VA USE ONLY

☐ The above named veteran does not have a VA benefit-related indebtedness
☐ The veteran has the following VA benefit-related indebtedness

VA BENEFIT-RELATED INDEBTEDNESS *(If any)*

TYPE OF DEBT(S)	AMOUNT OF DEBT(S)

TERM OF REPAYMENT PLAN *(If any)*

☐ Veteran is exempt from funding fee due to receipt of service-connected disability compensation of $_____ monthly. (Unless checked, the funding fee receipt must be remitted to VA with VA Form 26-1820, Report and Certification of Loan Disbursement)

☐ Veteran *is* exempt from funding fee due to entitlement to VA compensation benefits upon discharge from service.

☐ Veteran *is not* exempt from funding fee due to receipt of nonservice-connected pension of $_____ monthly. LOAN APPLICATION WILL REQUIRE PRIOR APPROVAL PROCESSING BY VA.

☐ Veteran has been rated incompetent by VA. LOAN APPLICATION WILL REQUIRE PRIOR APPROVAL PROCESSING BY VA.

☐ Insufficient information. VA cannot identify the veteran with the information given. Please furnish more complete information, or a copy of a DD Form 214 or discharge papers. If on active duty, furnish a statement of service written on official government letterhead, signed by the adjutant, personnel officer, or commanding officer. The statement should include name, birth date, service number, entry date and time lost.

| SIGNATURE OF AUTHORIZED AGENT | DATE SIGNED |

RESPONDENT BURDEN: We need this information to determine, establish, or verify your eligibility for VA Loan Guaranty Benefits and to determine if you are exempt from paying the VA Funding Fee. Title 38, United States Code, allows us to ask for this information. We estimate that you will need an average of 5 minutes to review the instructions, find the information, and complete this form. VA cannot conduct or sponsor a collection of information unless a valid OMB control number is displayed. You are not required to respond to a collection of information if this number is not displayed. Valid OMB control numbers can be located on the OMB Internet Page at http://www.reginfo.gov/public/do/PRAMain. If desired, you can call 1-800-827-1000 to get information on where to send comments or suggestions about this form.

VA FORM JAN 2013 **26-8937**

EXISTING STOCK OF VA FORM 26-8937, DEC 2012, WILL BE USED.

VA Department of Veterans Affairs	LOAN ANALYSIS	LOAN NUMBER

PRIVACY ACT INFORMATION: The VA will not disclose information collected on this form to any source other than what has been authorized under the Privacy Act of 1974 or Title 5, Code of Federal Regulations 1.526 for routine uses as (i.e., the record of an individual who is covered by this system may be disclosed to a member of Congress or staff person acting for the member when the request is made on behalf of the individual) identified in the VA system of records, 55VA26, Loan Guaranty Home, Condominium and Manufactured Home Loan Applicant Records, Specially Adapted Housing Applicant Records, and Vendee Loan Applicant Records - VA, published in the Federal Register. Your obligation to respond is required in order to determine the veteran's qualifications for the loan.

RESPONDENT BURDEN: This information is needed to help determine a veteran's qualifications for a VA guaranteed loan. Title 38, USC, section 3710 authorizes collection of this information. We estimate that you will need an average of 30 minutes to review the instructions, find the information, and complete this form. VA cannot conduct or sponsor a collection of information unless a valid OMB control number is displayed. You are not required to respond to a collection of information if this number is not displayed. Valid OMB control numbers can be located on the OMB Internet Page at: **www.reginfo.gov/public/do/PRASearch.** If desired, you can call 1-800-827-1000 to get information on where to send comments or suggestions about this form.

SECTION A - LOAN DATA

1. NAME OF BORROWER	2. AMOUNT OF LOAN	3. CASH DOWN PAYMENT ON PURCHASE PRICE
	$	$

SECTION B - BORROWER'S PERSONAL AND FINANCIAL STATUS

4. APPLICANT'S AGE	5. OCCUPATION OF APPLICANT	6. NUMBER OF YEARS AT PRESENT EMPLOYMENT	7. LIQUID ASSETS (Cash, savings, bonds, etc.)	8. CURRENT MONTHLY HOUSING EXPENSE
			$	$

9. UTILITIES INCLUDED	10. SPOUSE'S AGE	11. OCCUPATION OF SPOUSE	12. NUMBER OF YEARS AT PRESENT EMPLOYMENT	13. AGE OF DEPENDENTS
☐ YES ☐ NO				

NOTE: ROUND ALL DOLLAR AMOUNTS BELOW TO NEAREST WHOLE DOLLAR

SECTION C- ESTIMATED MONTHLY SHELTER EXPENSES (This Property)		SECTION D - DEBTS AND OBLIGATIONS (Itemize and indicate by (✓) which debts considered in Section E, Line 40) (If additional space is needed please use reverse or attach a separate sheet)			
ITEMS	AMOUNT	ITEMS	(✓)	MO. PAYMENT	UNPAID BAL.
14. TERM OF LOAN: YRS.		22.		$	$
15. MORTGAGE PAYMENT (Principal and Interest) @ _____ %	$	23.			
		24.			
16. REALTY TAXES		25.			
17. HAZARD INSURANCE		26.			
18. SPECIAL ASSESSMENTS		27.			
19. MAINTENANCE & UTILITIES		28.			
20. OTHER (HOA, Condo fees, etc.)		29. JOB RELATED EXPENSE (e.g., child care)			
21. TOTAL	$	30. TOTAL		$	$

SECTION E - MONTHLY INCOME AND DEDUCTIONS

	ITEMS		SPOUSE	BORROWER	TOTAL
31.	GROSS SALARY OR EARNINGS FROM EMPLOYMENT				$
32.	DEDUCTIONS	FEDERAL INCOME TAX	$	$	
33.		STATE INCOME TAX			
34.		RETIREMENT OR SOCIAL SECURITY			
35.		OTHER (Specify)			
36.		TOTAL DEDUCTIONS	$	$	$
37.	NET TAKE-HOME PAY				
38.	PENSION, COMPENSATION OR OTHER NET INCOME (Specify)				
39.	TOTAL (Sum of lines 37 and 38)		$	$	$
40.	LESS THOSE OBLIGATIONS LISTED IN SECTION D WHICH SHOULD BE DEDUCTED FROM INCOME				
41.	TOTAL NET EFFECTIVE INCOME				$
42.	LESS ESTIMATED MONTHLY SHELTER EXPENSE (Line 21)				
43.	BALANCE AVAILABLE FOR FAMILY SUPPORT			GUIDELINE $	$
44.	RATIO (Sum of Items 15, 16, 17, 18, 20 and 40 ÷ sum of Items 31 and 38)				%

45. PAST CREDIT RECORD	46. DOES LOAN MEET VA CREDIT STANDARDS? (Give reasons for decision under "Remarks," if necessary, e.g., borderline case)
☐ SATISFACTORY ☐ UNSATISFACTORY	☐ YES ☐ NO

47. REMARKS (Use reverse or attach a separate sheet, if necessary)

CRV DATA (VA USE)

48A. VALUE	48B. EXPIRATION DATE	48C. ECONOMIC LIFE YRS.

SECTION F - DISPOSITION OF APPLICATION AND UNDERWRITER CERTIFICATION

☐ Recommend that the application be approved since it meets all requirements of Chapter 37, Title 38, U.S. Code and applicable VA Regulations and directives.

☐ Recommend that the application be disapproved for the reasons stated under "Remarks" above.

The undersigned underwriter certifies that he/she personally reviewed and approved this loan. (Loan was closed on the automatic basis.)

49. DATE	50. SIGNATURE OF EXAMINER/UNDERWRITER

51. FINAL ACTION	52. DATE	53. SIGNATURE AND TITLE OF APPROVING OFFICIAL
☐ APPROVE APPLICATION ☐ REJECT APPLICATION		

VA FORM NOV 2012 **26-6393**   EXISTING STOCKS OF VA FORM 26-6393, SEP 2006, WILL BE USED.

SUMMARY

The two federal agencies that participate in real estate financing are the Federal Housing Administration (FHA) and the Department of Veterans Affairs (VA). The FHA is a federal government agency that insures loans made to individuals for financing homes and home repairs. The VA is a federal agency that guarantees approved lenders against financial loss on loans made to eligible veterans.

The FHA does not make loans. It insures loans made by authorized lending institutions, such as banks, savings banks, and independent mortgage companies. In case of foreclosure, the lender protects itself by charging the borrower a fee for an insurance policy called mutual mortgage insurance. The FHA uses the insurance premium requirement to finance its program. A borrower does not apply to the FHA for a home loan, but to an approved lender who processes the application and submits it for FHA approval. FHA-insured loans are available for purchases of property that qualify under FHA guidelines. Borrowers who wish to apply for selected FHA loan programs must meet specific qualifying conditions under FHA underwriting guidelines.

Like the FHA, the Department of Veterans Affairs (VA) does not make loans, but guarantees loans made by an approved institutional lender. Only an eligible veteran may obtain a VA loan. Up to a certain loan amount, the VA does not require a down payment. When a veteran wishes to purchase a home, a VA-approved lender takes the loan application and processes the loan according to VA underwriting guidelines. Before applying for a VA loan, a veteran must possess a Certificate of Eligibility, which is available from the Department of Veterans Affairs. The certificate shows the veteran's entitlement or right to obtain the loan. VA-insured loans are available for qualifying property types. Veterans who wish to apply for a VA loan must meet specific qualifying conditions under VA underwriting guidelines.

UNIT 9 REVIEW

Matching Exercise

Instructions: Write the letter of the matching term on the blank line before its definition. Answers are in Appendix A.

Terms

A. assumption fee

B. automatic authority

C. Certificate of Eligibility

D. Certificate of Reasonable Value

E. Department of Veterans Affairs

F. direct endorsement lender

G. eligibility

H. entitlement

I. Federal Housing Administration (FHA)

J. funding fee

K. loan origination fee

L. mortgage insurance premium

M. MPRs

N. mutual mortgage insurance

O. residual income

P. take-home pay

Definitions

1. _____ Federal government agency that insures loans made to individuals for the financing of homes and home repairs

2. _____ Mortgage default insurance sponsored by the FHA that protects the lender in the event of foreclosure

3. _____ Fee charged when a buyer assumes the seller's existing real estate loan

4. _____ Fee charged by the investor to cover the costs of underwriting a loan

5. _____ Approved FHA lender who meets FHA standards

6. _____ Federal agency that guarantees approved lenders against financial loss on loans made to eligible veterans

7. _____ Fee paid by veterans who obtain VA home loans to reduce the cost of the program to taxpayers

8. _____ Maximum guaranty provided by the VA for a veteran's home loan

9. _____ Department of Veterans Affairs' commitment of property value

10. _____ Authority for a lender to close VA-guaranteed loans without the prior approval of the VA

11. _____ Veteran's right to VA home loan benefits under the law, based on military service

12. _____ Document issued by the VA that provides evidence of eligibility to obtain a VA loan

13. _____ Property standards for VA loans that provide a basis for determining that the property is safe, structurally sound, and sanitary

14. _____ Net income remaining after deducting monthly housing expenses used to cover family living expenses

15. _____ Gross income less federal and state income taxes and any Social Security or retirement contributions

Multiple Choice Questions

Instructions: Circle your response and go to Appendix A to read the complete explanation for each question.

1. The FHA was established to:
   a. make loans to qualified borrowers.
   b. make loans to veterans.
   c. stabilize the mortgage market.
   d. set Fannie Mae/Freddie Mac lending standards.

2. FHA-insured loans are available for:
   a. corporations.
   b. LLCs.
   c. partnerships.
   d. individuals only.

3. Under FHA underwriting guidelines, what does a lender focus on when examining a borrower's ability to repay the loan?
   a. High credit scores
   b. Stability of income
   c. Ability to make timely payments
   d. Both (b) and (c)

4. Does the money for the down payment on an FHA-insured loan need to be seasoned?

   a. Yes, it needs to be seasoned for 3 months.

   b. No, seasoning is not required for any type of loan.

   c. Yes, because the FHA and conforming loans have identical requirements.

   d. No, the FHA does not require the money for a down payment to be seasoned.

5. Who is an ideal candidate for a reverse mortgage?

   a. First-time homebuyers with no down payment

   b. Individuals, age 62 or older, who want to purchase a home

   c. Homeowners, age 62 or older, with equity but little income

   d. Investors purchasing a duplex

6. Edward wants an FHA loan for a property he wants to improve immediately upon purchase. What type of FHA loan program should he consider?

   a. GPM

   b. Rehabilitation loan

   c. Reverse mortgage

   d. EEM

7. The main benefit of a VA-guaranteed home loan is:

   a. stringent qualifying criteria.

   b. no down payment.

   c. excessive loan charges.

   d. a prepayment penalty.

8. In real estate financing, the roll of the Department of Veterans Affairs is to:

   a. make loans to qualified veterans.

   b. guarantee loans made by an approved lender.

   c. make loans to any qualified resident of the United States.

   d. guarantee loans made to qualified veterans by an approved lender.

9. What is the first thing a veteran must do in order to apply for a VA-guaranteed loan?

   a. Apply at the VA office

   b. Obtain a certificate of value

   c. Close the loan and move in

   d. Apply for a Certificate of Eligibility

10. Which of the following is true regarding an Interest Rate Reduction Refinancing Loan (IRRRL)?

    a. Refinancing a VA ARM to a fixed-rate loan always results in a lower interest rate.

    b. Refinancing a VA ARM to a fixed-rate loan may increase the existing interest rate.

    c. To obtain an IRRRL loan, the VA requires a credit-underwriting package.

    d. Lenders are not allowed to request a credit report or appraisal for an IRRRL loan.

Instruments of Real Estate Finance

Unit 10

INTRODUCTION

Real estate finance instruments—promissory notes and security instruments—are legal documents that provide evidence of a debt and secure that debt with a collateral property. The lender holds the promissory note and the security instrument until the loan is repaid.

The promissory note is the evidence of the debt. It states the amount of money borrowed and the terms of repayment. A promissory note may stand alone (unsecured loan or note), but usually it is secured by a security instrument. The security instrument is a document—mortgage, deed of trust, security deed, or land contract—that is the evidence of the pledge of real estate as collateral for the loan. If there is a conflict between the terms of the promissory note and the security instrument, generally the terms of the note take precedence.

Learning Objectives

After completing this Unit, you should be able to:

10A   recall features and types of promissory notes.

10B   indicate special provisions and clauses of promissory notes.

10C   recall elements of negotiable instruments and the Uniform Commercial Code.

10D   review a promissory note and identify its sections.

10E   recall the purpose of a security instrument as a lien in real estate transactions.

10F   differentiate between senior and subordinate finance instruments.

10G   identify the elements of a mortgage.

10H   identify the elements of a deed of trust.

10I   review a deed of trust and identify its sections.

10J   recall the purpose of a contract for deed.

10K   recognize special provisions and uniform covenants in security instruments.

PROMISSORY NOTE

A **promissory note (note)** is a written legal contract that obligates the borrower to repay a loan. Even a note that is handwritten on a restaurant napkin and signed by both parties may be a binding promissory note. However, most lenders use a Fannie Mae/Freddie Mac Uniform Note. To see samples of these uniform notes, visit www.freddiemac.com/uniform.

Not only is a promissory note the evidence of the debt, but it describes the parties to the loan agreement and the specific terms of the loan. The parties involved are the maker (borrower) and the holder. The **maker** is the borrower who executes a note and becomes primarily liable for payment to the lender. The note states the personal obligation of the borrower and is a complete contract in itself between the borrower and lender. The lender is the party to whom a note is made payable. A subsequent owner of the note is a holder in due course and is called the **noteholder**.

When a borrower signs a note promising to repay a debt, the lender includes specific requirements in the note that define the terms of repayment. Standard clauses in a note include the parties to the note, amount of the original loan, interest rate, and the payment schedule. Usually it contains details about prepaying the loan and penalties for defaulting.

Types of Promissory Notes

Although many different types of notes are available in residential finance, most lenders use the Fannie Mae/Freddie Mac Uniform Promissory Notes. As we have seen, promissory notes have many similar or uniform clauses with the main difference being the repayment terms.

The different types of promissory notes are named based on the repayment terms of the loan. Some notes have a fixed interest rate, whereas others have an adjustable interest rate.

Basic Notes in General Use

Straight Note. This note calls for interest-only payments during the term of the note. The principal payment is due in one lump sum upon maturity. This type of note is not commonly used by institutional lenders but may be used between a buyer and seller or other private lenders.

Installment Note. This note requires periodic payments on the principal with payments of interest made separately.

Installment Note with Periodic Payments of Fixed Amounts. This fully amortized note consists of level, periodic payments of both interest and principal that pay off the debt completely at maturity.

Adjustable-Rate Note. This note has an interest rate that adjusts with a movable economic index.

Demand Note. This note does not become due until the noteholder makes a demand for its payment.

Fully Amortized Note. This note is fully repaid at maturity by periodic reduction of the principal.

Partially Amortized Installment Note. This note includes a repayment schedule that is not sufficient to pay off the loan over its term. This type of note calls for regular, periodic payments of principal and interest for a specified period of time. At maturity, the remaining unpaid principal balance is due as a balloon payment.

Typical Clauses Found in a Fixed-Rate Note

No matter the lender, there are certain clauses that must be included in promissory notes. These include but are not limited to all of the clauses mentioned in the following sections.

Date & Property Description

First, the note should include the date on which it is signed, as well as the address of the property. A legal description is not necessary in the note but usually is provided in the security instrument.

Parties to the Contract

The parties to the contract must be clearly identified. Some notes have the names of the borrower and lender written at the top of the form. Often in preprinted notes, the borrower is referred to as the undersigned and the lender's name is printed on the form.

1. Borrower's Promise to Pay

Next, the note should include the words "promise to pay" and the amount of the loan plus interest. In a note, the borrower receives the loan and the lender receives the borrower's promise to repay the loan as specified in the note. The note should state clearly the amount of the principal borrowed and the borrower's promise to repay it plus interest to the lender or noteholder.

2. Interest

Most lenders charge interest. Usually it is shown as an annual percentage. However, some notes show exactly how much interest is to be charged on a weekly, monthly, or yearly basis. If no interest will be charged on the loan, the note should state that clearly.

The interest charged on most real estate loans is **simple interest**, which is interest paid only on the principal owed. The interest rate stated in the note is called the **nominal** or **named** rate. The **effective interest rate** is the rate the borrower is actually paying and is commonly called the annual percentage rate (APR). Lenders are compensated for their risk in the form of interest rates. If the lender thinks the borrower is a high risk, the lender will charge a higher interest rate for the privilege of borrowing the money. The lower the risk, the lower the rate.

The amount of interest that can be legally charged may be subject to usury rate limits. **Usury** is the act of charging a rate of interest in excess of that permitted by law. Each state sets a rate that is the highest amount of simple interest that can be legally charged to an individual for a loan. National banks or other national lenders are governed by federal usury rules.

3. Payments

The note must show the date payments begin, when they are due, and when they stop. If a loan is to be repaid all in one lump sum, only the due date is necessary. There are several types of repayment plans, each with a different kind of obligation made clear by the terms of the note. Some notes are fixed-interest, fully amortized loans in which the interest rate and term do not change over the life of the loan. Others may include a fluctuating interest rate as well as changes in the payment over the life of the loan. The terms and conditions for repayment of a loan are varied and are expressed in the payment schedule of the note.

4. Borrower's Right to Prepay

The note usually includes a prepayment clause. A **prepayment clause**, which is also called an **or more clause**, allows a borrower to pay off a loan early or make higher payments without paying a prepayment penalty. The prepayment is applied first to any accrued or unpaid interest and then to principal.

A **prepayment penalty** allows a lender to collect a certain percentage of a loan as a penalty for early payoff. When lenders make loans, they calculate their return over the term of the loan. If a loan is paid off early, the lender receives less interest and the return on investment is lower than planned. This is especially true on loans that carry higher interest rates. The lender charges a prepayment penalty to offset lost revenues resulting from early payoff. Prepayment penalties are not allowed on conforming, FHA, and VA loans.

5. Loan Charges

The loan charges segment of the note explains the actions the noteholder must take if a law that sets a limit on the loan charges applies to the loan. If this is the case, the note states that the noteholder will reduce the charge as much as is necessary to comply with the legal limit. Usually, the note also states that if the noteholder has collected funds from the borrower that exceed the amount permitted, it must refund that amount to the borrower. The noteholder can do this either by refunding the borrower directly or by reducing the amount of principal still owed on the loan. If the noteholder chooses to reduce the principal, it is usually treated as a partial repayment.

6. Borrower's Failure to Pay as Required

The note includes a section that details the steps the noteholder will take if the borrower does not make a complete payment within an allotted number of days after it is due. This includes late charges and steps the noteholder will take if the borrower defaults on the loan.

a. Late Charges

Late charges can be a percentage of the payment of principal and interest due or a flat dollar amount. For a first mortgage lien, the late fee is assessed a specified number of calendar days—usually 15 —after the date the payment is due. [12 CFR §560.33].

b. Acceleration Clause

If the borrower defaults by not paying the payment as scheduled, the noteholder may accelerate the loan. An **acceleration clause** allows a noteholder to call the entire note due on occurrence of a specific event such as default in payment, taxes, insurance, or sale of the property. The borrower is responsible for paying all costs and expenses incurred by the noteholder for the collection of the note.

7. Giving of Notices

The note states that unless a law requires the noteholder to give notices to the borrower using a different method, the noteholder must deliver notices to the borrower by personal delivery or first class mail. All notices must be delivered or mailed to the address specified in the note or to a different address if the borrower has given notice of that address.

8. Joint and Several Liability

Each borrower who signs the promissory note agrees to be jointly and severally liable. **Joint and several liability** means that each debtor (borrower) is responsible for the entire amount of the loan.

9. Waivers

The waiver segment of the note mentions any rights the noteholder and borrower are waiving. This may include presentment and notice of dishonor. The right of **presentment** is the borrower's right to present the noteholder with a demand for payment of funds. The right of **notice of dishonor** is the right to require the noteholder to give notice that an amount has not been paid.

10. Reference to Security

A reference is made in the note that it is secured by a security instrument (mortgage, deed of trust, or security deed) upon real property. The security instrument protects the lender from possible loss. The lender formalizes the reference to the security instrument by attaching a copy of it to the note. Most security instruments have an alienation clause that allows the noteholder to accelerate the loan under certain situations.

An **alienation** or **due-on-sale clause** is a type of acceleration clause. A noteholder may call the entire note due if there is a transfer in property ownership from the original borrower to someone else. This clause protects the noteholder from an unqualified, unapproved buyer taking over a loan. Justifiably, the noteholder has the right to approve the party who is responsible for making the payments.

Under certain circumstances, a property owner may transfer responsibility on the current loan to someone who is buying the property. In other words, the buyer may assume the existing loan. If the security instrument has an **assumption clause**, a buyer may assume responsibility for the full payment of a loan after obtaining the lender's consent.

Signatures of the Borrowers

All of the borrowers who sign the note are jointly and severally liable for any debts secured by the note.

NOTE

_____, _____   _____, _____
[Date]   [City]   [State]

_____
[Property Address]

1. BORROWER'S PROMISE TO PAY

In return for a loan that I have received, I promise to pay U.S. $_____ (this amount is called "Principal"), plus interest, to the order of the Lender. The Lender is _____
_____. I will make all payments under this Note in the form of cash, check or money order.

I understand that the Lender may transfer this Note. The Lender or anyone who takes this Note by transfer and who is entitled to receive payments under this Note is called the "Note Holder."

2. INTEREST

Interest will be charged on unpaid principal until the full amount of Principal has been paid. I will pay interest at a yearly rate of _____%.

The interest rate required by this Section 2 is the rate I will pay both before and after any default described in Section 6(B) of this Note.

3. PAYMENTS

(A) Time and Place of Payments

I will pay principal and interest by making a payment every month.

I will make my monthly payment on the _____ day of each month beginning on _____, _____. I will make these payments every month until I have paid all of the principal and interest and any other charges described below that I may owe under this Note. Each monthly payment will be applied as of its scheduled due date and will be applied to interest before Principal. If, on _____, 20____, I still owe amounts under this Note, I will pay those amounts in full on that date, which is called the "Maturity Date."

I will make my monthly payments at _____
_____ or at a different place if required by the Note Holder.

(B) Amount of Monthly Payments

My monthly payment will be in the amount of U.S. $_____.

4. BORROWER'S RIGHT TO PREPAY

I have the right to make payments of Principal at any time before they are due. A payment of Principal only is known as a "Prepayment." When I make a Prepayment, I will tell the Note Holder in writing that I am doing so. I may not designate a payment as a Prepayment if I have not made all the monthly payments due under the Note.

I may make a full Prepayment or partial Prepayments without paying a Prepayment charge. The Note Holder will use my Prepayments to reduce the amount of Principal that I owe under this Note. However, the Note Holder may apply my Prepayment to the accrued and unpaid interest on the Prepayment amount, before applying my Prepayment to reduce the Principal amount of the Note. If I make a partial Prepayment, there will be no changes in the due date or in the amount of my monthly payment unless the Note Holder agrees in writing to those changes.

5. LOAN CHARGES

If a law, which applies to this loan and which sets maximum loan charges, is finally interpreted so that the interest or other loan charges collected or to be collected in connection with this loan exceed the permitted limits, then: (a) any such loan charge shall be reduced by the amount necessary to reduce the charge to the permitted limit; and (b) any sums already collected from me which exceeded permitted limits will be refunded to me. The Note Holder may choose to make this refund by reducing the Principal I owe under this Note or by making a direct payment to me. If a refund reduces Principal, the reduction will be treated as a partial Prepayment.

6. BORROWER'S FAILURE TO PAY AS REQUIRED

(A) Late Charge for Overdue Payments

If the Note Holder has not received the full amount of any monthly payment by the end of _____ calendar days after the date it is due, I will pay a late charge to the Note Holder. The amount of the charge will be _____ % of my overdue payment of principal and interest. I will pay this late charge promptly but only once on each late payment.

(B) Default

If I do not pay the full amount of each monthly payment on the date it is due, I will be in default.

(C) Notice of Default

If I am in default, the Note Holder may send me a written notice telling me that if I do not pay the overdue amount by a certain date, the Note Holder may require me to pay immediately the full amount of Principal which has not been paid and all the interest that I owe on that amount. That date must be at least 30 days after the date on which the notice is mailed to me or delivered by other means.

(D) No Waiver By Note Holder

Even if, at a time when I am in default, the Note Holder does not require me to pay immediately in full as described above, the Note Holder will still have the right to do so if I am in default at a later time.

(E) Payment of Note Holder's Costs and Expenses

If the Note Holder has required me to pay immediately in full as described above, the Note Holder will have the right to be paid back by me for all of its costs and expenses in enforcing this Note to the extent not prohibited by applicable law. Those expenses include, for example, reasonable attorneys' fees.

7. GIVING OF NOTICES

Unless applicable law requires a different method, any notice that must be given to me under this Note will be given by delivering it or by mailing it by first class mail to me at the Property Address above or at a different address if I give the Note Holder a notice of my different address.

Any notice that must be given to the Note Holder under this Note will be given by delivering it or by mailing it by first class mail to the Note Holder at the address stated in Section 3(A) above or at a different address if I am given a notice of that different address.

8. OBLIGATIONS OF PERSONS UNDER THIS NOTE

If more than one person signs this Note, each person is fully and personally obligated to keep all of the promises made in this Note, including the promise to pay the full amount owed. Any person who is a guarantor, surety or endorser of this Note is also obligated to do these things. Any person who takes over these obligations, including the obligations of a guarantor, surety or endorser of this Note, is also obligated to keep all of the promises made in this Note. The Note Holder may enforce its rights under this Note against each person individually or against all of us together. This means that any one of us may be required to pay all of the amounts owed under this Note.

9. WAIVERS

I and any other person who has obligations under this Note waive the rights of Presentment and Notice of Dishonor. "Presentment" means the right to require the Note Holder to demand payment of amounts due. "Notice of Dishonor" means the right to require the Note Holder to give notice to other persons that amounts due have not been paid.

10. UNIFORM SECURED NOTE

This Note is a uniform instrument with limited variations in some jurisdictions. In addition to the protections given to the Note Holder under this Note, a Mortgage, Deed of Trust, or Security Deed (the "Security Instrument"), dated the same date as this Note, protects the Note Holder from possible losses which might result if I do not keep the promises which I make in this Note. That Security Instrument describes how and under what conditions I may be required to make immediate payment in full of all amounts I owe under this Note. Some of those conditions are described as follows:

> If all or any part of the Property or any Interest in the Property is sold or transferred (or if Borrower is not a natural person and a beneficial interest in Borrower is sold or transferred) without Lender's prior written consent, Lender may require immediate payment in full of all sums secured by this Security Instrument. However, this option shall not be exercised by Lender if such exercise is prohibited by Applicable Law.

If Lender exercises this option, Lender shall give Borrower notice of acceleration. The notice shall provide a period of not less than 30 days from the date the notice is given in accordance with Section 15 within which Borrower must pay all sums secured by this Security Instrument. If Borrower fails to pay these sums prior to the expiration of this period, Lender may invoke any remedies permitted by this Security Instrument without further notice or demand on Borrower.

WITNESS THE HAND(S) AND SEAL(S) OF THE UNDERSIGNED.

_____(Seal)
                                                    - Borrower

_____(Seal)
                                                    - Borrower

_____(Seal)
                                                    - Borrower

[Sign Original Only]

MULTISTATE FIXED RATE NOTE—Single Family—Fannie Mae/Freddie Mac UNIFORM INSTRUMENT   Form 3200   1/01   *(page 3 of 3 pages)*

Negotiability of a Promissory Note

A note is considered personal property and is a negotiable instrument. A **negotiable instrument** is a written unconditional promise or order to pay a certain sum of money on demand or at a definite future date, payable either to order or to bearer and signed by the maker. Negotiable instruments are freely transferable and may be transferred by endorsement or delivery. **Freely transferable** means a bank or other creditor may sell the negotiable instrument (promissory note) for cash.

The most common type of negotiable instrument is an ordinary bank check. A **check** is an order to the bank to pay money to the person named. A note is the same thing. It can be transferred by **endorsement** (signature) just like a check. If correctly prepared, it is considered the same as cash.

However, in order to be considered a negotiable instrument, the document must be consistent with statutory definition.

> **Required Elements to Create a Negotiable Promissory Note**
> - Unconditional promise or order to pay a certain amount of money
> - Payable on demand or at a definite time
> - Payable to order or bearer
> - Signed by the maker (borrower)

The **Uniform Commercial Code (UCC)** governs negotiable instruments and is designed to give uniformity to commercial transactions across all 50 states. As we have seen, notes are negotiable instruments that are easily transferable from one person to another. However, the new buyer of a note (holder in due course) must be reasonably confident that the loan will be paid as agreed by the maker. The UCC defines a **holder in due course** as one who takes an instrument for value in good faith absent any notice that it is overdue, has been dishonored, or is subject to any defense against it or claim to it by any other person.

The holder in due course is a subsequent owner of a negotiable instrument such as a note. The holder in due course must have accepted possession of the financial instrument in good faith and given something of value for it. The holder in due course is presumed to be unaware that the financial instrument previously may have been overdue, been dishonored when presented for payment, or had a claim against it, if in fact such were the case. Because the holder in due course is a **bona fide purchaser**, he or she is entitled to payment by the maker of the note.

A holder in due course has a favored position with respect to the note because the maker (borrower) cannot raise certain personal defenses and refuse to pay. These personal defenses include lack of consideration, setoff, and fraud. **Setoff** is a claim that a person (or entity) who owes money to someone may reduce the amount he or she owes by the amount owed to him or her by the other person.

> Example: Sarah owes $30,000 to Joe. Joe owes $10,000 to Sarah. Joe cannot reduce the amount owed to Sarah to zero. Each is obligated to repay the original debt.

Protections for a Holder in Due Course

The favored position that the holder in due course enjoys is a greater claim to note payments than the original holder. If a court action is necessary to enforce payment on the note, the maker cannot use any of the following defenses to refuse payment to a holder in due course even though they can be used against the original lender.

Some defenses are good against any person, payee, or holder in due course. The defenses listed below may be used against the original payee, or lender, but cannot be used against a holder in due course.

Defenses Not Allowed by the Maker of a Note

- The maker cannot claim non-receipt of what was promised by the payee in exchange for the note.
- The maker cannot claim the debt has already been paid. Even if it was paid, the original maker may still be required to pay a holder in due course unless there is proof of payment such as a note that has been marked paid. The maker's only recourse is against the original payee.
- The maker cannot use fraud in the original making of the note as a defense.
- The maker cannot claim a setoff. For example, if the amount owed is $10,000 but the payee owes $15,000 to the holder, the difference cannot be used as a defense against paying the note.

Defenses Allowed Against Anyone

- Forgery, if the maker really did not sign the note
- Secret, material changes in the note
- Incapacity, if the maker is a minor or an incompetent
- Illegal object, if the note is connected to an illegal act or if the interest rate is usurious (higher than allowed by law)

These protections for a holder in due course offer assurances that it is safe to accept a negotiable instrument without checking the credit of the borrower or knowing the borrower.

SECURITY INSTRUMENTS

At the same time the promissory note is signed, the borrower is required to execute the security instrument. A security instrument is a separate agreement from the promissory note. A **security instrument** is a legal document given by the borrower to hypothecate (pledge) the property to the lender as collateral for the loan. **Hypothecation** is a legal arrangement that allows a borrower to remain in possession of a property secured by a loan. **Collateral** is something of value given as security for a debt. A loan secured by a lien on real property (whether a mortgage, deed of trust, or land contract) makes the real property the collateral for the loan.

Security instruments (deeds of trust, mortgages, and contracts of sale) do not have to be recorded to be valid. The security instrument legally is a lien (**monetary encumbrance**) that secures the loan whether it is recorded or not. A **lien** is the legal claim of one person upon the property of another person to secure the payment of a debt or financial obligation.

A lien uses real property as security or collateral for the payment of a debt. An owner may choose to borrow money, using the property as security for the loan, creating a **voluntary lien**. A voluntary lien does not have to be recorded, but if it is not recorded, then other parties (such as purchasers and lenders) may not be bound by it. Because the lien is placed against a specific property, it is a **specific lien**.

Although the lender retains a security interest in the property, the borrower retains right of possession as long as payments are made according to the loan agreement. If the borrower does not make payments per the agreement, he or she loses the rights of possession and ownership. The lender or subsequent noteholder holds the security instrument and the note until the loan is repaid. If the borrower defaults, the security instrument allows the lender to foreclose on the loan.

As you recall, the promissory note is the evidence of the debt. The promissory note can stand alone without the security instrument. It is a personal, unsecured note at that point. However, the security instrument needs the note to validate its existence.

If there is a conflict between the terms of a note and the security instrument, the provisions of the note prevail. If a note is unenforceable, the presence of a security instrument will not make it valid. However, if a note contains an acceleration clause (due on sale), the security instrument must also mention this clause or the acceleration clause in the note is not enforceable.

The security instrument includes the date of its execution and the names of the lender and borrower. The security instrument identifies the promissory note and the amount of the debt for which the instrument provides security. It also provides a description of the property to be used as security for the loan.

As part of the loan process, the borrower makes certain promises or covenants to the lender in the loan documents. The borrower promises to pay the taxes, not destroy or damage the improvements, keep sufficient insurance against the property, and maintain the property in good repair. There may or may not be an acceleration clause in the promissory note and security instrument that gives the lender the right to demand full payment of the debt.

Priority of Security Instruments

Recording gives public notice of the existence of a debt owed on the property. Generally, the priority of a lien is determined by its recording date. However, some liens, such as property tax liens, have automatic superiority over essentially all prior liens. First trust deeds or mortgages, as the name suggests, are recorded first and are in the "**superior**" or first lien position. Second trust deeds or mortgages, which are often recorded next, are usually in second or "**junior**" position.

The priority of liens establishes who gets paid first following a foreclosure. Senior liens are paid before junior liens because junior liens have lower priority. After the superior lien lender forecloses, any surplus funds from the foreclosure sale after the foreclosing lender's debt has been paid off will be distributed to creditors holding junior liens.

Senior (First) Liens

When a lender makes a home loan, it wants a security interest in the property that takes priority over all other liens. To secure its seniority, it obtains a **senior lien** (trust deed or mortgage) on the property. In the event of default on the loan, the senior lien status ensures the lender's priority during a foreclosure action, effectively eliminating all other junior liens that may exist. Although mortgages and deeds of trust do not have to be recorded to be valid, recording them perfects the lender's senior lien status.

From a lender's perspective, there is low risk associated with a senior lien, because there are virtually no other threats to its security position. The only exception to the priority of first lien mortgages or deeds of trust are delinquent real property taxes and IRS liens. Most liens that attach to a home after the senior lien is recorded become junior liens, and generally, a junior lienholder can only clear a senior lien from the property if they pay the debt secured by the senior lien in full.

Junior (Subordinate) Liens

A junior deed of trust (mortgage) is a lien that is **subordinate** to a first or prior (senior) deed of trust (mortgage). A **junior lien** often refers to a second trust deed (mortgage), but it could also be a third or fourth trust deed (mortgage). In the case of foreclosure, the senior mortgage will be paid down first.

Interest rates on junior lien loans tend to be higher than on senior loans. This is because, in the event of foreclosure, the holder of the junior lien is always second in line for any repayment. If no money is left after paying off the senior loan, the lender of the junior lien may not receive any money. This higher risk of loss for the junior lien lender is reflected in higher interest rates. Interest rates on junior liens may also vary with the amount of equity in the property. The more equity, the lower the risk of repayment for the junior lien

A junior lien is less risky for lenders than an unsecured loan, so it will likely have a lower interest rate than an unsecured loan. Junior liens are sometimes used in home purchases when the buyer cannot find financing for the entire cost of the home.

When a trust deed or mortgage is recorded against an property on which there already is an active senior lien, it automatically becomes a second trust deed (mortgage), if another happens it is a third trust deed (mortgage), and so on. They have the number because they are paid off in the order they are recorded.

Types of Security Instruments

Mortgages and deeds of trust are the most common types of security instruments used in real estate finance, whereas Georgia uses a security deed. A land contract is considered a security instrument and must be foreclosed like a mortgage, whether it is recorded or not.

Differences Between Mortgages and Deeds of Trust

Depending upon the state in which the financed property is located, a note is secured by either a mortgage or a deed of trust. The exception to this is Georgia, which uses a security deed.

Early distinctions between the legal and economic effects of the mortgage and deed of trust have diminished. Now, both security instruments basically are subject to the same reinstatement and redemption privileges before a foreclosure sale. They are also subject to the same judicial or nonjudicial procedures and restrictions for foreclosure. The same rules are generally applicable to both instruments, except when applying post foreclosure sale possession, redemption, and anti-deficiency limitations. Although mortgages and deeds of trust share many of the same covenants, they differ in number of parties, title, satisfaction, foreclosure, statutory redemption, deficiency judgment, and statute of limitations.

The principal advantage of the trust deed over the mortgage is that the trust deed's power of sale is not typically outlawed by time while a mortgage remains subject to the statute of limitations. Whether a mortgage or deed of trust is used to secure a promissory note, lenders have the full power of the law, depending on which state the property is in, to enforce their rights regarding repayment of a debt.

States Using Mortgages as the Primary Security Instrument		States Using Deeds of Trust as the Primary Security Instrument	
Alabama	Minnesota	Alaska	New Mexico
Arkansas	New Hampshire	Arizona	Nevada
Connecticut	New Jersey	California	North Carolina
Delaware	New York	Colorado	Oregon
Florida	North Dakota	District of Columbia	Tennessee
Hawaii	Ohio	Idaho	Texas
Illinois	Oklahoma	Maryland	Utah
Indiana	Pennsylvania	Mississippi	Virginia
Iowa	Rhode Island	Missouri	Washington
Kansas	South Carolina	Montana	West Virginia
Kentucky	South Dakota	Nebraska	
Louisiana	Vermont		
Maine	Wisconsin	**States Using Security Deeds as the Primary Security Instrument**	
Massachusetts	Wyoming		
Michigan		Georgia	

Trust Deed	Mortgage Contract
1. Number of Parties (3) **Trustor:** Borrower who conveys title to trustee who holds as a security for debt. **Beneficiary:** Lender who holds original note and trust deed during life of the debt. **Trustee:** Receiver of naked legal title who conveys it when debt is paid or will sell if foreclosure is necessary.	**1. Number of Parties (2)** **Mortgagor:** Borrower retains title but gives lender a lien on the property as security. **Mortgagee:** Lender who holds the mortgage.
2. Title: Conveyed to trustee with trustor retaining equitable possession of the property.	**2. Title:** Held by mortgagor together with possession.
3. Statute of Limitations: The security for debt is held by trustee, rights of creditor are not ended when statute runs out on the note.	**3. Statute of Limitations:** Foreclosure is barred if no action is taken within four (4) years of delinquency on the note.
4. Remedy for Default: Foreclosure can be instituted through trustee's sale or court foreclosure. (Court foreclosure follows mortgage foreclosure procedure #7.)	**4. Remedy for Default:** Court foreclosure is usually the only remedy.
5. Right of Redemption: When the title has been sold by trustee at trustee's sale no right of statutory redemption exists.	**5. Right of Redemption:** Mortgagor has up to one (1) year to redeem the property after court foreclosure called statutory redemption.
6. Satisfaction: The beneficiary sends a request for full reconveyance to the trustee with the original note and trust deed. Upon payment of fees, the trustee issues a reconveyance deed which must be recorded.	**6. Satisfaction:** Upon final payment and on demand, the mortgagee signs the certificate that the debt is satisfied. Then the certificate or release is recorded.

Trust Deed (cont.)	Mortgage Contract (cont.)
7. Foreclosure by Trustee's Sale:	**7. Foreclosure by Court:**
Beneficiary notifies the trustee of default. The trustee notifies the trustor and records the notice. Anyone who has recorded the Request for Notice for Default must also be notified.	Court action is commenced by the mortgagee. The court issues a decree of foreclosure and an order of sale. A court appointed commissioner sells to the highest bidder after the publication and posting of the sale notice.
The trustee waits at least three (3) months. During the three (3) month period, the trustor can reinstate the loan. Then the trustee advertises a notice of sale once a week for three weeks (21 days) and posts a notice on the property.	The certificate of sale is issued. Mortgagor has one (1) year to redeem the property and remains in possession for that year. If sale proceeds satisfy the debt, court costs, and interest then the mortgagor has only three (3) months to redeem the property.
Trustor can now invade the three (3) week advertising period and can reinstate the loan up to five (5) business days prior to the trustee's sale.	If a trust deed is foreclosed in court, it is treated like a mortgage contract, and trustor remains in possession during the redemption period.
The trustee conducts the sale and issues a trustee's deed to the highest bidder.	A sheriff's deed is issued after one (1) year.
8. Deficiency Judgment:	**8. Deficiency Judgment:**
No deficiency judgment is available if the foreclosure is by trustee's sale.	A deficiency judgment is available in a court foreclosure.

9. No deficiency judgment is available on a purchase-money trust deed or mortgage.

Mortgage

A **mortgage** is a security instrument that secures the payment of a promissory note. A mortgage is a two-party security instrument and is, in fact, a contract for a loan. The two parties are the **mortgagor** (borrower) and **mortgagee** (lender). This loan contract (mortgage) is commonly recorded to secure real property. A mortgage is held by the lender for the life of a loan or until the borrower pays it off.

Parties

A mortgage has two parties—mortgagor (borrower) and mortgagee (lender). The mortgagor (borrower) receives a loan from the mortgagee (lender) and signs a promissory note and mortgage.

Title

In a mortgage, who retains legal title to the property? Is it the borrower or the lender? A mortgage creates a lien on real property or gives actual title to the lender depending on the laws of the state in which the property is located. There are two theories of how title follows a mortgaged property—lien theory and title theory. In a **lien theory state**, title to real property is vested in the borrower. The borrower gives only a lien right to the lender during the term of the loan. In a **title theory state**, title to real property is vested in the lender. In a title theory state, the mortgage states that title reverts to the borrower once the loan is paid. Whether the state is a lien theory or title theory state, possession of the property remains with the borrower.

Some states are modified lien or intermediate theory states. A **modified lien theory state** is one in which the mortgage is a lien unless the borrower defaults. In this case, the title is automatically transferred to the lender. In any case, the borrower enjoys possession of the property during the full term of the mortgage no matter who holds title.

Satisfaction

A defeasance clause is included in the mortgage. A **defeasance clause** cancels the mortgage upon repayment of the debt in full. The title to the property transfers back to the mortgagor and the lender's interest in the property terminates. **Satisfaction of a mortgage,** or payment in full, requires that the lender deliver the original note and mortgage to the party making the request. This release should be recorded to give public notice that the mortgage encumbrance has been paid in full.

Remedy for Default

The common remedy for default of a mortgage is judicial foreclosure (court action). If the mortgage contains a power-of-sale clause, a non-judicial foreclosure is possible. The **power-of-sale clause** is a clause in a mortgage or deed of trust that gives the holder the right to sell the property in the event of default by the borrower.

Statutory Redemption

Some mortgages allow statutory redemption, which is the statutory right of a mortgagor to recover the property AFTER a foreclosure sale.

Deficiency Judgment

In some states, a lender who forecloses against a defaulted mortgage may obtain a deficiency judgment against the debtor. A **deficiency judgment** is a personal judgment against a borrower for the balance of a debt owed when the security for the loan is insufficient to repay the debt. If the proceeds of the foreclosure sale are insufficient to satisfy the debt, the lender may get a deficiency judgment against the borrower that will be effective for 10 years.

Statute of Limitations

In the case of nonpayment on a mortgage debt, creditors must be aware of how the statute of limitations affects their ability to bring legal action. The **statute of limitations** limits the period of time during which legal action may be taken on a certain issue.

It is interesting how widely the statute of limitations differs from state to state. After a mortgage has been foreclosed, judgments on mortgage notes can be sought for no more than two years in some states to over fifteen years in other states. There are websites that provide this information on a state-by-state basis, such as www.fair-debt-collection.com.

After Recording Return To:

_____

_____

_____

_____

_____[Space Above This Line For Recording Data]_____

MORTGAGE

DEFINITIONS

Words used in multiple sections of this document are defined below and other words are defined in Sections 3, 11, 13, 18, 20 and 21. Certain rules regarding the usage of words used in this document are also provided in Section 16.

(A)   **"Security Instrument"** means this document, which is dated _____, _____, together with all Riders to this document.

(B)   **"Borrower"** is _____. Borrower is the mortgagor under this Security Instrument.

(C)   **"Lender"** is _____. Lender is a _____ organized and existing under the laws of _____. Lender's address is _____ _____. Lender is the mortgagee under this Security Instrument.

(D)   **"Note"**   means   the   promissory   note   signed   by   Borrower   and   dated _____, _____. The Note states that Borrower owes Lender _____ Dollars (U.S. $_____) plus interest. Borrower has promised to pay this debt in regular Periodic Payments and to pay the debt in full not later than _____.

(E)   **"Property"** means the property that is described below under the heading "Transfer of Rights in the Property."

(F)   **"Loan"** means the debt evidenced by the Note, plus interest, any prepayment charges and late charges due under the Note, and all sums due under this Security Instrument, plus interest.

FLORIDA--Single Family--Fannie Mae/Freddie Mac UNIFORM INSTRUMENT   Form 3010   1/01   *(page 1 of 16 pages)*

(G) **"Riders"** means all Riders to this Security Instrument that are executed by Borrower. The following Riders are to be executed by Borrower [check box as applicable]:

☐ Adjustable Rate Rider   ☐ Condominium Rider   ☐ Second Home Rider
☐ Balloon Rider   ☐ Planned Unit Development Rider   ☐ Other(s) [specify]

☐ 1-4 Family Rider   ☐ Biweekly Payment Rider

(H) **"Applicable Law"** means all controlling applicable federal, state and local statutes, regulations, ordinances and administrative rules and orders (that have the effect of law) as well as all applicable final, non-appealable judicial opinions.

(I) **"Community Association Dues, Fees, and Assessments"** means all dues, fees, assessments and other charges that are imposed on Borrower or the Property by a condominium association, homeowners association or similar organization.

(J) **"Electronic Funds Transfer"** means any transfer of funds, other than a transaction originated by check, draft, or similar paper instrument, which is initiated through an electronic terminal, telephonic instrument, computer, or magnetic tape so as to order, instruct, or authorize a financial institution to debit or credit an account. Such term includes, but is not limited to, point-of-sale transfers, automated teller machine transactions, transfers initiated by telephone, wire transfers, and automated clearinghouse transfers.

(K) **"Escrow Items"** means those items that are described in Section 3.

(L) **"Miscellaneous Proceeds"** means any compensation, settlement, award of damages, or proceeds paid by any third party (other than insurance proceeds paid under the coverages described in Section 5) for: (i) damage to, or destruction of, the Property; (ii) condemnation or other taking of all or any part of the Property; (iii) conveyance in lieu of condemnation; or (iv) misrepresentations of, or omissions as to, the value and/or condition of the Property.

(M) **"Mortgage Insurance"** means insurance protecting Lender against the nonpayment of, or default on, the Loan.

(N) **"Periodic Payment"** means the regularly scheduled amount due for (i) principal and interest under the Note, plus (ii) any amounts under Section 3 of this Security Instrument.

(O) **"RESPA"** means the Real Estate Settlement Procedures Act (12 U.S.C. §2601 et seq.) and its implementing regulation, Regulation X (24 C.F.R. Part 3500), as they might be amended from time to time, or any additional or successor legislation or regulation that governs the same subject matter. As used in this Security Instrument, "RESPA" refers to all requirements and restrictions that are imposed in regard to a "federally related mortgage loan" even if the Loan does not qualify as a "federally related mortgage loan" under RESPA.

(P) **"Successor in Interest of Borrower"** means any party that has taken title to the Property, whether or not that party has assumed Borrower's obligations under the Note and/or this Security Instrument.

TRANSFER OF RIGHTS IN THE PROPERTY

This Security Instrument secures to Lender: (i) the repayment of the Loan, and all renewals, extensions and modifications of the Note; and (ii) the performance of Borrower's covenants and agreements under this Security Instrument and the Note. For this purpose, Borrower does hereby mortgage, grant and convey to Lender, the following described property located in the

_____ of _____:
   [Type of Recording Jurisdiction]   [Name of Recording Jurisdiction]

which currently has the address of _____
                                                                    [Street]

_____, Florida _____ ("Property Address"):
           [City]   [Zip Code]

   TOGETHER WITH all the improvements now or hereafter erected on the property, and all easements, appurtenances, and fixtures now or hereafter a part of the property. All replacements and additions shall also be covered by this Security Instrument. All of the foregoing is referred to in this Security Instrument as the "Property."

   BORROWER COVENANTS that Borrower is lawfully seised of the estate hereby conveyed and has the right to mortgage, grant and convey the Property and that the Property is unencumbered, except for encumbrances of record. Borrower warrants and will defend generally the title to the Property against all claims and demands, subject to any encumbrances of record.

   THIS SECURITY INSTRUMENT combines uniform covenants for national use and non-uniform covenants with limited variations by jurisdiction to constitute a uniform security instrument covering real property.

   UNIFORM COVENANTS. Borrower and Lender covenant and agree as follows:
   1.   **Payment of Principal, Interest, Escrow Items, Prepayment Charges, and Late Charges.** Borrower shall pay when due the principal of, and interest on, the debt evidenced by the Note and any prepayment charges and late charges due under the Note. Borrower shall also pay funds for Escrow Items pursuant to Section 3. Payments due under the Note and this Security Instrument shall be made in U.S. currency. However, if any check or other instrument received by Lender as payment under the Note or this Security Instrument is returned to Lender unpaid, Lender may require that any or all subsequent payments due under the Note and this Security Instrument be made in one or more of the following forms, as selected by Lender: (a)

cash; (b) money order; (c) certified check, bank check, treasurer's check or cashier's check, provided any such check is drawn upon an institution whose deposits are insured by a federal agency, instrumentality, or entity; or (d) Electronic Funds Transfer.

Payments are deemed received by Lender when received at the location designated in the Note or at such other location as may be designated by Lender in accordance with the notice provisions in Section 15. Lender may return any payment or partial payment if the payment or partial payments are insufficient to bring the Loan current. Lender may accept any payment or partial payment insufficient to bring the Loan current, without waiver of any rights hereunder or prejudice to its rights to refuse such payment or partial payments in the future, but Lender is not obligated to apply such payments at the time such payments are accepted. If each Periodic Payment is applied as of its scheduled due date, then Lender need not pay interest on unapplied funds. Lender may hold such unapplied funds until Borrower makes payment to bring the Loan current. If Borrower does not do so within a reasonable period of time, Lender shall either apply such funds or return them to Borrower. If not applied earlier, such funds will be applied to the outstanding principal balance under the Note immediately prior to foreclosure. No offset or claim which Borrower might have now or in the future against Lender shall relieve Borrower from making payments due under the Note and this Security Instrument or performing the covenants and agreements secured by this Security Instrument.

2. **Application of Payments or Proceeds.** Except as otherwise described in this Section 2, all payments accepted and applied by Lender shall be applied in the following order of priority: (a) interest due under the Note; (b) principal due under the Note; (c) amounts due under Section 3. Such payments shall be applied to each Periodic Payment in the order in which it became due. Any remaining amounts shall be applied first to late charges, second to any other amounts due under this Security Instrument, and then to reduce the principal balance of the Note.

If Lender receives a payment from Borrower for a delinquent Periodic Payment which includes a sufficient amount to pay any late charge due, the payment may be applied to the delinquent payment and the late charge. If more than one Periodic Payment is outstanding, Lender may apply any payment received from Borrower to the repayment of the Periodic Payments if, and to the extent that, each payment can be paid in full. To the extent that any excess exists after the payment is applied to the full payment of one or more Periodic Payments, such excess may be applied to any late charges due. Voluntary prepayments shall be applied first to any prepayment charges and then as described in the Note.

Any application of payments, insurance proceeds, or Miscellaneous Proceeds to principal due under the Note shall not extend or postpone the due date, or change the amount, of the Periodic Payments.

3. **Funds for Escrow Items.** Borrower shall pay to Lender on the day Periodic Payments are due under the Note, until the Note is paid in full, a sum (the "Funds") to provide for payment of amounts due for: (a) taxes and assessments and other items which can attain priority over this Security Instrument as a lien or encumbrance on the Property; (b) leasehold payments or ground rents on the Property, if any; (c) premiums for any and all insurance required by Lender under Section 5; and (d) Mortgage Insurance premiums, if any, or any sums payable by Borrower to Lender in lieu of the payment of Mortgage Insurance premiums in accordance with the provisions of Section 10. These items are called "Escrow Items." At origination or at any time during the term of the Loan, Lender may require that Community Association Dues, Fees, and Assessments, if any, be escrowed by Borrower, and such dues, fees and assessments shall be an Escrow Item. Borrower shall promptly furnish to Lender all notices

FLORIDA--Single Family--**Fannie Mae/Freddie Mac UNIFORM INSTRUMENT**   **Form 3010   1/01**   *(page 4 of 16 pages)*

of amounts to be paid under this Section. Borrower shall pay Lender the Funds for Escrow Items unless Lender waives Borrower's obligation to pay the Funds for any or all Escrow Items. Lender may waive Borrower's obligation to pay to Lender Funds for any or all Escrow Items at any time. Any such waiver may only be in writing. In the event of such waiver, Borrower shall pay directly, when and where payable, the amounts due for any Escrow Items for which payment of Funds has been waived by Lender and, if Lender requires, shall furnish to Lender receipts evidencing such payment within such time period as Lender may require. Borrower's obligation to make such payments and to provide receipts shall for all purposes be deemed to be a covenant and agreement contained in this Security Instrument, as the phrase "covenant and agreement" is used in Section 9. If Borrower is obligated to pay Escrow Items directly, pursuant to a waiver, and Borrower fails to pay the amount due for an Escrow Item, Lender may exercise its rights under Section 9 and pay such amount and Borrower shall then be obligated under Section 9 to repay to Lender any such amount. Lender may revoke the waiver as to any or all Escrow Items at any time by a notice given in accordance with Section 15 and, upon such revocation, Borrower shall pay to Lender all Funds, and in such amounts, that are then required under this Section 3.

Lender may, at any time, collect and hold Funds in an amount (a) sufficient to permit Lender to apply the Funds at the time specified under RESPA, and (b) not to exceed the maximum amount a lender can require under RESPA. Lender shall estimate the amount of Funds due on the basis of current data and reasonable estimates of expenditures of future Escrow Items or otherwise in accordance with Applicable Law.

The Funds shall be held in an institution whose deposits are insured by a federal agency, instrumentality, or entity (including Lender, if Lender is an institution whose deposits are so insured) or in any Federal Home Loan Bank. Lender shall apply the Funds to pay the Escrow Items no later than the time specified under RESPA. Lender shall not charge Borrower for holding and applying the Funds, annually analyzing the escrow account, or verifying the Escrow Items, unless Lender pays Borrower interest on the Funds and Applicable Law permits Lender to make such a charge. Unless an agreement is made in writing or Applicable Law requires interest to be paid on the Funds, Lender shall not be required to pay Borrower any interest or earnings on the Funds. Borrower and Lender can agree in writing, however, that interest shall be paid on the Funds. Lender shall give to Borrower, without charge, an annual accounting of the Funds as required by RESPA.

If there is a surplus of Funds held in escrow, as defined under RESPA, Lender shall account to Borrower for the excess funds in accordance with RESPA. If there is a shortage of Funds held in escrow, as defined under RESPA, Lender shall notify Borrower as required by RESPA, and Borrower shall pay to Lender the amount necessary to make up the shortage in accordance with RESPA, but in no more than 12 monthly payments. If there is a deficiency of Funds held in escrow, as defined under RESPA, Lender shall notify Borrower as required by RESPA, and Borrower shall pay to Lender the amount necessary to make up the deficiency in accordance with RESPA, but in no more than 12 monthly payments.

Upon payment in full of all sums secured by this Security Instrument, Lender shall promptly refund to Borrower any Funds held by Lender.

4.   Charges; Liens. Borrower shall pay all taxes, assessments, charges, fines, and impositions attributable to the Property which can attain priority over this Security Instrument, leasehold payments or ground rents on the Property, if any, and Community Association Dues, Fees, and Assessments, if any. To the extent that these items are Escrow Items, Borrower shall pay them in the manner provided in Section 3.

Borrower shall promptly discharge any lien which has priority over this Security Instrument unless Borrower: (a) agrees in writing to the payment of the obligation secured by the lien in a manner acceptable to Lender, but only so long as Borrower is performing such agreement; (b) contests the lien in good faith by, or defends against enforcement of the lien in, legal proceedings which in Lender's opinion operate to prevent the enforcement of the lien while those proceedings are pending, but only until such proceedings are concluded; or (c) secures from the holder of the lien an agreement satisfactory to Lender subordinating the lien to this Security Instrument. If Lender determines that any part of the Property is subject to a lien which can attain priority over this Security Instrument, Lender may give Borrower a notice identifying the lien. Within 10 days of the date on which that notice is given, Borrower shall satisfy the lien or take one or more of the actions set forth above in this Section 4.

Lender may require Borrower to pay a one-time charge for a real estate tax verification and/or reporting service used by Lender in connection with this Loan.

5.   Property Insurance. Borrower shall keep the improvements now existing or hereafter erected on the Property insured against loss by fire, hazards included within the term "extended coverage," and any other hazards including, but not limited to, earthquakes and floods, for which Lender requires insurance. This insurance shall be maintained in the amounts (including deductible levels) and for the periods that Lender requires. What Lender requires pursuant to the preceding sentences can change during the term of the Loan. The insurance carrier providing the insurance shall be chosen by Borrower subject to Lender's right to disapprove Borrower's choice, which right shall not be exercised unreasonably. Lender may require Borrower to pay, in connection with this Loan, either: (a) a one-time charge for flood zone determination, certification and tracking services; or (b) a one-time charge for flood zone determination and certification services and subsequent charges each time remappings or similar changes occur which reasonably might affect such determination or certification. Borrower shall also be responsible for the payment of any fees imposed by the Federal Emergency Management Agency in connection with the review of any flood zone determination resulting from an objection by Borrower.

If Borrower fails to maintain any of the coverages described above, Lender may obtain insurance coverage, at Lender's option and Borrower's expense. Lender is under no obligation to purchase any particular type or amount of coverage. Therefore, such coverage shall cover Lender, but might or might not protect Borrower, Borrower's equity in the Property, or the contents of the Property, against any risk, hazard or liability and might provide greater or lesser coverage than was previously in effect. Borrower acknowledges that the cost of the insurance coverage so obtained might significantly exceed the cost of insurance that Borrower could have obtained. Any amounts disbursed by Lender under this Section 5 shall become additional debt of Borrower secured by this Security Instrument. These amounts shall bear interest at the Note rate from the date of disbursement and shall be payable, with such interest, upon notice from Lender to Borrower requesting payment.

All insurance policies required by Lender and renewals of such policies shall be subject to Lender's right to disapprove such policies, shall include a standard mortgage clause, and shall name Lender as mortgagee and/or as an additional loss payee. Lender shall have the right to hold the policies and renewal certificates. If Lender requires, Borrower shall promptly give to Lender all receipts of paid premiums and renewal notices. If Borrower obtains any form of insurance coverage, not otherwise required by Lender, for damage to, or destruction of, the Property, such policy shall include a standard mortgage clause and shall name Lender as mortgagee and/or as an additional loss payee.

In the event of loss, Borrower shall give prompt notice to the insurance carrier and Lender. Lender may make proof of loss if not made promptly by Borrower. Unless Lender and Borrower otherwise agree in writing, any insurance proceeds, whether or not the underlying insurance was required by Lender, shall be applied to restoration or repair of the Property, if the restoration or repair is economically feasible and Lender's security is not lessened. During such repair and restoration period, Lender shall have the right to hold such insurance proceeds until Lender has had an opportunity to inspect such Property to ensure the work has been completed to Lender's satisfaction, provided that such inspection shall be undertaken promptly. Lender may disburse proceeds for the repairs and restoration in a single payment or in a series of progress payments as the work is completed. Unless an agreement is made in writing or Applicable Law requires interest to be paid on such insurance proceeds, Lender shall not be required to pay Borrower any interest or earnings on such proceeds. Fees for public adjusters, or other third parties, retained by Borrower shall not be paid out of the insurance proceeds and shall be the sole obligation of Borrower. If the restoration or repair is not economically feasible or Lender's security would be lessened, the insurance proceeds shall be applied to the sums secured by this Security Instrument, whether or not then due, with the excess, if any, paid to Borrower. Such insurance proceeds shall be applied in the order provided for in Section 2.

If Borrower abandons the Property, Lender may file, negotiate and settle any available insurance claim and related matters. If Borrower does not respond within 30 days to a notice from Lender that the insurance carrier has offered to settle a claim, then Lender may negotiate and settle the claim. The 30-day period will begin when the notice is given. In either event, or if Lender acquires the Property under Section 22 or otherwise, Borrower hereby assigns to Lender (a) Borrower's rights to any insurance proceeds in an amount not to exceed the amounts unpaid under the Note or this Security Instrument, and (b) any other of Borrower's rights (other than the right to any refund of unearned premiums paid by Borrower) under all insurance policies covering the Property, insofar as such rights are applicable to the coverage of the Property. Lender may use the insurance proceeds either to repair or restore the Property or to pay amounts unpaid under the Note or this Security Instrument, whether or not then due.

6.   Occupancy.   Borrower shall occupy, establish, and use the Property as Borrower's principal residence within 60 days after the execution of this Security Instrument and shall continue to occupy the Property as Borrower's principal residence for at least one year after the date of occupancy, unless Lender otherwise agrees in writing, which consent shall not be unreasonably withheld, or unless extenuating circumstances exist which are beyond Borrower's control.

7.   Preservation, Maintenance and Protection of the Property; Inspections. Borrower shall not destroy, damage or impair the Property, allow the Property to deteriorate or commit waste on the Property. Whether or not Borrower is residing in the Property, Borrower shall maintain the Property in order to prevent the Property from deteriorating or decreasing in value due to its condition. Unless it is determined pursuant to Section 5 that repair or restoration is not economically feasible, Borrower shall promptly repair the Property if damaged to avoid further deterioration or damage. If insurance or condemnation proceeds are paid in connection with damage to, or the taking of, the Property, Borrower shall be responsible for repairing or restoring the Property only if Lender has released proceeds for such purposes. Lender may disburse proceeds for the repairs and restoration in a single payment or in a series of progress payments as the work is completed. If the insurance or condemnation proceeds are not sufficient to repair or restore the Property, Borrower is not relieved of Borrower's obligation for the completion of such repair or restoration.

Lender or its agent may make reasonable entries upon and inspections of the Property. If it has reasonable cause, Lender may inspect the interior of the improvements on the Property. Lender shall give Borrower notice at the time of or prior to such an interior inspection specifying such reasonable cause.

8. Borrower's Loan Application. Borrower shall be in default if, during the Loan application process, Borrower or any persons or entities acting at the direction of Borrower or with Borrower's knowledge or consent gave materially false, misleading, or inaccurate information or statements to Lender (or failed to provide Lender with material information) in connection with the Loan. Material representations include, but are not limited to, representations concerning Borrower's occupancy of the Property as Borrower's principal residence.

9. Protection of Lender's Interest in the Property and Rights Under this Security Instrument. If (a) Borrower fails to perform the covenants and agreements contained in this Security Instrument, (b) there is a legal proceeding that might significantly affect Lender's interest in the Property and/or rights under this Security Instrument (such as a proceeding in bankruptcy, probate, for condemnation or forfeiture, for enforcement of a lien which may attain priority over this Security Instrument or to enforce laws or regulations), or (c) Borrower has abandoned the Property, then Lender may do and pay for whatever is reasonable or appropriate to protect Lender's interest in the Property and rights under this Security Instrument, including protecting and/or assessing the value of the Property, and securing and/or repairing the Property. Lender's actions can include, but are not limited to: (a) paying any sums secured by a lien which has priority over this Security Instrument; (b) appearing in court; and (c) paying reasonable attorneys' fees to protect its interest in the Property and/or rights under this Security Instrument, including its secured position in a bankruptcy proceeding. Securing the Property includes, but is not limited to, entering the Property to make repairs, change locks, replace or board up doors and windows, drain water from pipes, eliminate building or other code violations or dangerous conditions, and have utilities turned on or off. Although Lender may take action under this Section 9, Lender does not have to do so and is not under any duty or obligation to do so. It is agreed that Lender incurs no liability for not taking any or all actions authorized under this Section 9.

Any amounts disbursed by Lender under this Section 9 shall become additional debt of Borrower secured by this Security Instrument. These amounts shall bear interest at the Note rate from the date of disbursement and shall be payable, with such interest, upon notice from Lender to Borrower requesting payment.

If this Security Instrument is on a leasehold, Borrower shall comply with all the provisions of the lease. If Borrower acquires fee title to the Property, the leasehold and the fee title shall not merge unless Lender agrees to the merger in writing.

10. Mortgage Insurance. If Lender required Mortgage Insurance as a condition of making the Loan, Borrower shall pay the premiums required to maintain the Mortgage Insurance in effect. If, for any reason, the Mortgage Insurance coverage required by Lender ceases to be available from the mortgage insurer that previously provided such insurance and Borrower was required to make separately designated payments toward the premiums for Mortgage Insurance, Borrower shall pay the premiums required to obtain coverage substantially equivalent to the Mortgage Insurance previously in effect, at a cost substantially equivalent to the cost to

Borrower of the Mortgage Insurance previously in effect, from an alternate mortgage insurer selected by Lender. If substantially equivalent Mortgage Insurance coverage is not available, Borrower shall continue to pay to Lender the amount of the separately designated payments that were due when the insurance coverage ceased to be in effect. Lender will accept, use and retain these payments as a non-refundable loss reserve in lieu of Mortgage Insurance. Such loss reserve shall be non-refundable, notwithstanding the fact that the Loan is ultimately paid in full, and Lender shall not be required to pay Borrower any interest or earnings on such loss reserve. Lender can no longer require loss reserve payments if Mortgage Insurance coverage (in the amount and for the period that Lender requires) provided by an insurer selected by Lender again becomes available, is obtained, and Lender requires separately designated payments toward the premiums for Mortgage Insurance. If Lender required Mortgage Insurance as a condition of making the Loan and Borrower was required to make separately designated payments toward the premiums for Mortgage Insurance, Borrower shall pay the premiums required to maintain Mortgage Insurance in effect, or to provide a non-refundable loss reserve, until Lender's requirement for Mortgage Insurance ends in accordance with any written agreement between Borrower and Lender providing for such termination or until termination is required by Applicable Law. Nothing in this Section 10 affects Borrower's obligation to pay interest at the rate provided in the Note.

Mortgage Insurance reimburses Lender (or any entity that purchases the Note) for certain losses it may incur if Borrower does not repay the Loan as agreed. Borrower is not a party to the Mortgage Insurance.

Mortgage insurers evaluate their total risk on all such insurance in force from time to time, and may enter into agreements with other parties that share or modify their risk, or reduce losses. These agreements are on terms and conditions that are satisfactory to the mortgage insurer and the other party (or parties) to these agreements. These agreements may require the mortgage insurer to make payments using any source of funds that the mortgage insurer may have available (which may include funds obtained from Mortgage Insurance premiums).

As a result of these agreements, Lender, any purchaser of the Note, another insurer, any reinsurer, any other entity, or any affiliate of any of the foregoing, may receive (directly or indirectly) amounts that derive from (or might be characterized as) a portion of Borrower's payments for Mortgage Insurance, in exchange for sharing or modifying the mortgage insurer's risk, or reducing losses. If such agreement provides that an affiliate of Lender takes a share of the insurer's risk in exchange for a share of the premiums paid to the insurer, the arrangement is often termed "captive reinsurance." Further:

(a) **Any such agreements will not affect the amounts that Borrower has agreed to pay for Mortgage Insurance, or any other terms of the Loan. Such agreements will not increase the amount Borrower will owe for Mortgage Insurance, and they will not entitle Borrower to any refund.**

(b) **Any such agreements will not affect the rights Borrower has - if any - with respect to the Mortgage Insurance under the Homeowners Protection Act of 1998 or any other law. These rights may include the right to receive certain disclosures, to request and obtain cancellation of the Mortgage Insurance, to have the Mortgage Insurance terminated automatically, and/or to receive a refund of any Mortgage Insurance premiums that were unearned at the time of such cancellation or termination.**

11. **Assignment of Miscellaneous Proceeds; Forfeiture.** All Miscellaneous Proceeds are hereby assigned to and shall be paid to Lender.

FLORIDA--Single Family--**Fannie Mae/Freddie Mac** UNIFORM INSTRUMENT   Form 3010   1/01   *(page 9 of 16 pages)*

If the Property is damaged, such Miscellaneous Proceeds shall be applied to restoration or repair of the Property, if the restoration or repair is economically feasible and Lender's security is not lessened. During such repair and restoration period, Lender shall have the right to hold such Miscellaneous Proceeds until Lender has had an opportunity to inspect such Property to ensure the work has been completed to Lender's satisfaction, provided that such inspection shall be undertaken promptly. Lender may pay for the repairs and restoration in a single disbursement or in a series of progress payments as the work is completed. Unless an agreement is made in writing or Applicable Law requires interest to be paid on such Miscellaneous Proceeds, Lender shall not be required to pay Borrower any interest or earnings on such Miscellaneous Proceeds. If the restoration or repair is not economically feasible or Lender's security would be lessened, the Miscellaneous Proceeds shall be applied to the sums secured by this Security Instrument, whether or not then due, with the excess, if any, paid to Borrower. Such Miscellaneous Proceeds shall be applied in the order provided for in Section 2.

In the event of a total taking, destruction, or loss in value of the Property, the Miscellaneous Proceeds shall be applied to the sums secured by this Security Instrument, whether or not then due, with the excess, if any, paid to Borrower.

In the event of a partial taking, destruction, or loss in value of the Property in which the fair market value of the Property immediately before the partial taking, destruction, or loss in value is equal to or greater than the amount of the sums secured by this Security Instrument immediately before the partial taking, destruction, or loss in value, unless Borrower and Lender otherwise agree in writing, the sums secured by this Security Instrument shall be reduced by the amount of the Miscellaneous Proceeds multiplied by the following fraction: (a) the total amount of the sums secured immediately before the partial taking, destruction, or loss in value divided by (b) the fair market value of the Property immediately before the partial taking, destruction, or loss in value. Any balance shall be paid to Borrower.

In the event of a partial taking, destruction, or loss in value of the Property in which the fair market value of the Property immediately before the partial taking, destruction, or loss in value is less than the amount of the sums secured immediately before the partial taking, destruction, or loss in value, unless Borrower and Lender otherwise agree in writing, the Miscellaneous Proceeds shall be applied to the sums secured by this Security Instrument whether or not the sums are then due.

If the Property is abandoned by Borrower, or if, after notice by Lender to Borrower that the Opposing Party (as defined in the next sentence) offers to make an award to settle a claim for damages, Borrower fails to respond to Lender within 30 days after the date the notice is given, Lender is authorized to collect and apply the Miscellaneous Proceeds either to restoration or repair of the Property or to the sums secured by this Security Instrument, whether or not then due. "Opposing Party" means the third party that owes Borrower Miscellaneous Proceeds or the party against whom Borrower has a right of action in regard to Miscellaneous Proceeds.

Borrower shall be in default if any action or proceeding, whether civil or criminal, is begun that, in Lender's judgment, could result in forfeiture of the Property or other material impairment of Lender's interest in the Property or rights under this Security Instrument. Borrower can cure such a default and, if acceleration has occurred, reinstate as provided in Section 19, by causing the action or proceeding to be dismissed with a ruling that, in Lender's judgment, precludes forfeiture of the Property or other material impairment of Lender's interest in the Property or rights under this Security Instrument. The proceeds of any award or claim for damages that are attributable to the impairment of Lender's interest in the Property are hereby assigned and shall be paid to Lender.

All Miscellaneous Proceeds that are not applied to restoration or repair of the Property shall be applied in the order provided for in Section 2.

12.   Borrower Not Released; Forbearance By Lender Not a Waiver. Extension of the time for payment or modification of amortization of the sums secured by this Security Instrument granted by Lender to Borrower or any Successor in Interest of Borrower shall not operate to release the liability of Borrower or any Successors in Interest of Borrower. Lender shall not be required to commence proceedings against any Successor in Interest of Borrower or to refuse to extend time for payment or otherwise modify amortization of the sums secured by this Security Instrument by reason of any demand made by the original Borrower or any Successors in Interest of Borrower. Any forbearance by Lender in exercising any right or remedy including, without limitation, Lender's acceptance of payments from third persons, entities or Successors in Interest of Borrower or in amounts less than the amount then due, shall not be a waiver of or preclude the exercise of any right or remedy.

13.   Joint and Several Liability; Co-signers; Successors and Assigns Bound. Borrower covenants and agrees that Borrower's obligations and liability shall be joint and several. However, any Borrower who co-signs this Security Instrument but does not execute the Note (a "co-signer"): (a) is co-signing this Security Instrument only to mortgage, grant and convey the co-signer's interest in the Property under the terms of this Security Instrument; (b) is not personally obligated to pay the sums secured by this Security Instrument; and (c) agrees that Lender and any other Borrower can agree to extend, modify, forbear or make any accommodations with regard to the terms of this Security Instrument or the Note without the co-signer's consent.

Subject to the provisions of Section 18, any Successor in Interest of Borrower who assumes Borrower's obligations under this Security Instrument in writing, and is approved by Lender, shall obtain all of Borrower's rights and benefits under this Security Instrument. Borrower shall not be released from Borrower's obligations and liability under this Security Instrument unless Lender agrees to such release in writing. The covenants and agreements of this Security Instrument shall bind (except as provided in Section 20) and benefit the successors and assigns of Lender.

14.   Loan Charges. Lender may charge Borrower fees for services performed in connection with Borrower's default, for the purpose of protecting Lender's interest in the Property and rights under this Security Instrument, including, but not limited to, attorneys' fees, property inspection and valuation fees. In regard to any other fees, the absence of express authority in this Security Instrument to charge a specific fee to Borrower shall not be construed as a prohibition on the charging of such fee. Lender may not charge fees that are expressly prohibited by this Security Instrument or by Applicable Law.

If the Loan is subject to a law which sets maximum loan charges, and that law is finally interpreted so that the interest or other loan charges collected or to be collected in connection with the Loan exceed the permitted limits, then: (a) any such loan charge shall be reduced by the amount necessary to reduce the charge to the permitted limit; and (b) any sums already collected from Borrower which exceeded permitted limits will be refunded to Borrower. Lender may choose to make this refund by reducing the principal owed under the Note or by making a direct payment to Borrower. If a refund reduces principal, the reduction will be treated as a partial prepayment without any prepayment charge (whether or not a prepayment charge is provided for under the Note). Borrower's acceptance of any such refund made by direct payment to Borrower

FLORIDA--Single Family--**Fannie Mae/Freddie Mac UNIFORM INSTRUMENT**   Form 3010   1/01   *(page 11 of 16 pages)*

will constitute a waiver of any right of action Borrower might have arising out of such overcharge.

15. **Notices.** All notices given by Borrower or Lender in connection with this Security Instrument must be in writing. Any notice to Borrower in connection with this Security Instrument shall be deemed to have been given to Borrower when mailed by first class mail or when actually delivered to Borrower's notice address if sent by other means. Notice to any one Borrower shall constitute notice to all Borrowers unless Applicable Law expressly requires otherwise. The notice address shall be the Property Address unless Borrower has designated a substitute notice address by notice to Lender. Borrower shall promptly notify Lender of Borrower's change of address. If Lender specifies a procedure for reporting Borrower's change of address, then Borrower shall only report a change of address through that specified procedure. There may be only one designated notice address under this Security Instrument at any one time. Any notice to Lender shall be given by delivering it or by mailing it by first class mail to Lender's address stated herein unless Lender has designated another address by notice to Borrower. Any notice in connection with this Security Instrument shall not be deemed to have been given to Lender until actually received by Lender. If any notice required by this Security Instrument is also required under Applicable Law, the Applicable Law requirement will satisfy the corresponding requirement under this Security Instrument.

16. **Governing Law; Severability; Rules of Construction.** This Security Instrument shall be governed by federal law and the law of the jurisdiction in which the Property is located. All rights and obligations contained in this Security Instrument are subject to any requirements and limitations of Applicable Law. Applicable Law might explicitly or implicitly allow the parties to agree by contract or it might be silent, but such silence shall not be construed as a prohibition against agreement by contract. In the event that any provision or clause of this Security Instrument or the Note conflicts with Applicable Law, such conflict shall not affect other provisions of this Security Instrument or the Note which can be given effect without the conflicting provision.

As used in this Security Instrument: (a) words of the masculine gender shall mean and include corresponding neuter words or words of the feminine gender; (b) words in the singular shall mean and include the plural and vice versa; and (c) the word "may" gives sole discretion without any obligation to take any action.

17. **Borrower's Copy.** Borrower shall be given one copy of the Note and of this Security Instrument.

18. **Transfer of the Property or a Beneficial Interest in Borrower.** As used in this Section 18, "Interest in the Property" means any legal or beneficial interest in the Property, including, but not limited to, those beneficial interests transferred in a bond for deed, contract for deed, installment sales contract or escrow agreement, the intent of which is the transfer of title by Borrower at a future date to a purchaser.

If all or any part of the Property or any Interest in the Property is sold or transferred (or if Borrower is not a natural person and a beneficial interest in Borrower is sold or transferred) without Lender's prior written consent, Lender may require immediate payment in full of all sums secured by this Security Instrument. However, this option shall not be exercised by Lender if such exercise is prohibited Applicable Law.

If Lender exercises this option, Lender shall give Borrower notice of acceleration. The notice shall provide a period of not less than 30 days from the date the notice is given in accordance with Section 15 within which Borrower must pay all sums secured by this Security

Instrument. If Borrower fails to pay these sums prior to the expiration of this period, Lender may invoke any remedies permitted by this Security Instrument without further notice or demand on Borrower.

      19.   **Borrower's Right to Reinstate After Acceleration.** If Borrower meets certain conditions, Borrower shall have the right to have enforcement of this Security Instrument discontinued at any time prior to the earliest of: (a) five days before sale of the Property pursuant to any power of sale contained in this Security Instrument; (b) such other period as Applicable Law might specify for the termination of Borrower's right to reinstate; or (c) entry of a judgment enforcing this Security Instrument. Those conditions are that Borrower: (a) pays Lender all sums which then would be due under this Security Instrument and the Note as if no acceleration had occurred; (b) cures any default of any other covenants or agreements; (c) pays all expenses incurred in enforcing this Security Instrument, including, but not limited to, reasonable attorneys' fees, property inspection and valuation fees, and other fees incurred for the purpose of protecting Lender's interest in the Property and rights under this Security Instrument; and (d) takes such action as Lender may reasonably require to assure that Lender's interest in the Property and rights under this Security Instrument, and Borrower's obligation to pay the sums secured by this Security Instrument, shall continue unchanged. Lender may require that Borrower pay such reinstatement sums and expenses in one or more of the following forms, as selected by Lender: (a) cash; (b) money order; (c) certified check, bank check, treasurer's check or cashier's check, provided any such check is drawn upon an institution whose deposits are insured by a federal agency, instrumentality or entity; or (d) Electronic Funds Transfer. Upon reinstatement by Borrower, this Security Instrument and obligations secured hereby shall remain fully effective as if no acceleration had occurred. However, this right to reinstate shall not apply in the case of acceleration under Section 18.

      20.   **Sale of Note; Change of Loan Servicer; Notice of Grievance.** The Note or a partial interest in the Note (together with this Security Instrument) can be sold one or more times without prior notice to Borrower. A sale might result in a change in the entity (known as the "Loan Servicer") that collects Periodic Payments due under the Note and this Security Instrument and performs other mortgage loan servicing obligations under the Note, this Security Instrument, and Applicable Law. There also might be one or more changes of the Loan Servicer unrelated to a sale of the Note. If there is a change of the Loan Servicer, Borrower will be given written notice of the change which will state the name and address of the new Loan Servicer, the address to which payments should be made and any other information RESPA requires in connection with a notice of transfer of servicing. If the Note is sold and thereafter the Loan is serviced by a Loan Servicer other than the purchaser of the Note, the mortgage loan servicing obligations to Borrower will remain with the Loan Servicer or be transferred to a successor Loan Servicer and are not assumed by the Note purchaser unless otherwise provided by the Note purchaser.

      Neither Borrower nor Lender may commence, join, or be joined to any judicial action (as either an individual litigant or the member of a class) that arises from the other party's actions pursuant to this Security Instrument or that alleges that the other party has breached any provision of, or any duty owed by reason of, this Security Instrument, until such Borrower or Lender has notified the other party (with such notice given in compliance with the requirements of Section 15) of such alleged breach and afforded the other party hereto a reasonable period after the giving of such notice to take corrective action. If Applicable Law provides a time period which must elapse before certain action can be taken, that time period will be deemed to be reasonable for purposes of this paragraph. The notice of acceleration and opportunity to cure given to Borrower pursuant to Section 22 and the notice of acceleration given to Borrower pursuant to Section 18 shall be deemed to satisfy the notice and opportunity to take corrective action provisions of this Section 20.

21.   Hazardous Substances. As used in this Section 21: (a) "Hazardous Substances" are those substances defined as toxic or hazardous substances, pollutants, or wastes by Environmental Law and the following substances: gasoline, kerosene, other flammable or toxic petroleum products, toxic pesticides and herbicides, volatile solvents, materials containing asbestos or formaldehyde, and radioactive materials; (b) "Environmental Law" means federal laws and laws of the jurisdiction where the Property is located that relate to health, safety or environmental protection; (c) "Environmental Cleanup" includes any response action, remedial action, or removal action, as defined in Environmental Law; and (d) an "Environmental Condition" means a condition that can cause, contribute to, or otherwise trigger an Environmental Cleanup.

Borrower shall not cause or permit the presence, use, disposal, storage, or release of any Hazardous Substances, or threaten to release any Hazardous Substances, on or in the Property. Borrower shall not do, nor allow anyone else to do, anything affecting the Property (a) that is in violation of any Environmental Law, (b) which creates an Environmental Condition, or (c) which, due to the presence, use, or release of a Hazardous Substance, creates a condition that adversely affects the value of the Property. The preceding two sentences shall not apply to the presence, use, or storage on the Property of small quantities of Hazardous Substances that are generally recognized to be appropriate to normal residential uses and to maintenance of the Property (including, but not limited to, hazardous substances in consumer products).

Borrower shall promptly give Lender written notice of (a) any investigation, claim, demand, lawsuit or other action by any governmental or regulatory agency or private party involving the Property and any Hazardous Substance or Environmental Law of which Borrower has actual knowledge, (b) any Environmental Condition, including but not limited to, any spilling, leaking, discharge, release or threat of release of any Hazardous Substance, and (c) any condition caused by the presence, use or release of a Hazardous Substance which adversely affects the value of the Property. If Borrower learns, or is notified by any governmental or regulatory authority, or any private party, that any removal or other remediation of any Hazardous Substance affecting the Property is necessary, Borrower shall promptly take all necessary remedial actions in accordance with Environmental Law. Nothing herein shall create any obligation on Lender for an Environmental Cleanup.

NON-UNIFORM COVENANTS. Borrower and Lender further covenant and agree as follows:

22.   Acceleration; Remedies.   Lender shall give notice to Borrower prior to acceleration following Borrower's breach of any covenant or agreement in this Security Instrument (but not prior to acceleration under Section 18 unless Applicable Law provides otherwise).   The notice shall specify: (a) the default; (b) the action required to cure the default; (c) a date, not less than 30 days from the date the notice is given to Borrower, by which the default must be cured; and (d) that failure to cure the default on or before the date specified in the notice may result in acceleration of the sums secured by this Security Instrument, foreclosure by judicial proceeding and sale of the Property. The notice shall further inform Borrower of the right to reinstate after acceleration and the right to assert

in the foreclosure proceeding the non-existence of a default or any other defense of Borrower to acceleration and foreclosure. If the default is not cured on or before the date specified in the notice, Lender at its option may require immediate payment in full of all sums secured by this Security Instrument without further demand and may foreclose this Security Instrument by judicial proceeding. Lender shall be entitled to collect all expenses incurred in pursuing the remedies provided in this Section 22, including, but not limited to, reasonable attorneys' fees and costs of title evidence.

23. **Release.** Upon payment of all sums secured by this Security Instrument, Lender shall release this Security Instrument. Borrower shall pay any recordation costs. Lender may charge Borrower a fee for releasing this Security Instrument, but only if the fee is paid to a third party for services rendered and the charging of the fee is permitted under Applicable Law.

24. **Attorneys' Fees.** As used in this Security Instrument and the Note, attorneys' fees shall include those awarded by an appellate court and any attorneys' fees incurred in a bankruptcy proceeding.

25. **Jury Trial Waiver.** The Borrower hereby waives any right to a trial by jury in any action, proceeding, claim, or counterclaim, whether in contract or tort, at law or in equity, arising out of or in any way related to this Security Instrument or the Note.

BY SIGNING BELOW, Borrower accepts and agrees to the terms and covenants contained in this Security Instrument and in any Rider executed by Borrower and recorded with it.

Signed, sealed and delivered in the presence of:

_____   _____ (Seal)
                                                                    - Borrower

_____   _____ (Seal)
                                                                    - Borrower

_____**[Space Below This Line For Acknowledgment]**_____

Deed of Trust

A **deed of trust** (trust deed) is a security instrument that secures a loan on real property. When a promissory note is secured by a deed of trust, three parties are involved: the borrower (**trustor**), the lender (**beneficiary**), and a neutral third party (**trustee**).

After being signed by the trustor, the deed of trust (not the note) is recorded in the county where the property is located. The recorded deed of trust and the note are sent to the lender to hold for the life of the loan. Recording creates a lien against the property and gives public notice of the existence of a debt owed on the property. A **lien** is a claim on the property of another for the payment of a debt.

The deed of trust does not have to be recorded to be valid. It legally secures the loan whether it is recorded or not. In the case of foreclosure, the recording date establishes the order of lien priority for the deed of trust against other liens placed on the property.

Parties

The parties in a deed of trust are the borrower (trustor), the lender (beneficiary), and a neutral third party (trustee). The beneficiary (lender) holds the note and deed of trust until reconveyance or until the debt is paid in full. In most states, a title or trust company, escrow holder, or the trust department of a bank perform the duties of a trustee.

Title

In the deed of trust, the trustor (borrower) holds equitable title while paying off the loan. **Equitable title** is the right to obtain absolute ownership to property when legal title is held in another's name. As equitable owner, the borrower has all the usual rights that go with ownership, such as the right to possess, will, encumber, and transfer.

The borrower conveys bare legal title to the trustee, to be held in trust until the note is paid in full. **Bare legal title** is title that lacks the usual rights and privileges of ownership. The bare legal title held by the trustee allows the trustee to do only two things: reconvey the property to the borrower upon final payment of the debt or foreclose if the borrower defaults on the loan.

Reconveyance

Under a deed of trust, when the loan is paid off, the lender (beneficiary) sends the note and deed of trust to the trustee along with a request for reconveyance. The trustee cancels the note, signs a deed of reconveyance, and sends it to the borrower. The **deed of reconveyance** conveys title to the property from the trustee to the borrower (trustor). The deed of reconveyance should be recorded to give public notice that the lien has been paid in full, which removes the lien from the property.

Remedy for Default

Under a deed of trust, the lender has a choice of two types of foreclosure—trustee's sale or judicial foreclosure. The common remedy for default of a trust deed is a trustee's sale (non-judicial foreclosure). This is because a deed of trust has a power of sale clause. The power of sale clause gives the trustee the right to foreclose, sell, and convey ownership to a purchaser of the property if the borrower defaults on the loan. The trustee can start the sale without a court foreclosure order because the borrower has already given bare legal title to the trustee in the deed of trust. Additionally, the power of sale clause in the deed of trust gives the trustee the authority to sell the property.

Statutory Redemption

Under a deed of trust with a power of sale, there is no statutory redemption period after the trustee's sale. The sale is final.

Deficiency Judgment

In most cases, when a loan is secured by a deed of trust and the lender forecloses under a power of sale (trustee's sale), no deficiency judgment is available. In states in which deeds of trust are generally used to secure loans, the only security for a beneficiary is the property itself. Any other personal or real assets of the borrower are protected from judgment under the deed of trust.

Statute of Limitations

The rights of the lender (beneficiary) under a deed of trust do not end when the statute of limitations has run out on the note. The trustee is given both bare legal title and power of sale in the deed of trust. The power of sale in a deed of trust never expires.

After Recording Return To:

_____

_____

_____

_____

_____**[Space Above This Line For Recording Data]**_____

DEED OF TRUST

DEFINITIONS

Words used in multiple sections of this document are defined below and other words are defined in Sections 3, 11, 13, 18, 20 and 21. Certain rules regarding the usage of words used in this document are also provided in Section 16.

(A) **"Security Instrument"** means this document, which is dated _____, _____, together with all Riders to this document.

(B) **"Borrower"** is _____
Borrower is the trustor under this Security Instrument.

(C) **"Lender"** is _____
Lender is a _____ organized and existing under the laws of_____. Lender's address is _____
_____. Lender is the beneficiary under this Security Instrument.

(D) **"Trustee"** is _____.

(E) **"Note"** means the promissory note signed by Borrower and dated _____, _____. The Note states that Borrower owes Lender _____
Dollars (U.S. $_____) plus interest. Borrower has promised to pay this debt in regular Periodic Payments and to pay the debt in full not later than _____

(F) **"Property"** means the property that is described below under the heading "Transfer of Rights in the Property."

(G) **"Loan"** means the debt evidenced by the Note, plus interest, any prepayment charges and late charges due under the Note, and all sums due under this Security Instrument, plus interest.

(H) **"Riders"** means all Riders to this Security Instrument that are executed by Borrower. The following Riders are to be executed by Borrower [check box as applicable]:

☐ Adjustable Rate Rider ☐ Condominium Rider ☐ Second Home Rider
☐ Balloon Rider ☐ Planned Unit Development Rider ☐ Other(s) [specify]

☐ 1-4 Family Rider ☐ Biweekly Payment Rider

(I) **"Applicable Law"** means all controlling applicable federal, state and local statutes, regulations, ordinances and administrative rules and orders (that have the effect of law) as well as all applicable final, non-appealable judicial opinions.

(J) **"Community Association Dues, Fees, and Assessments"** means all dues, fees, assessments and other charges that are imposed on Borrower or the Property by a condominium association, homeowners association or similar organization.

(K) **"Electronic Funds Transfer"** means any transfer of funds, other than a transaction originated by check, draft, or similar paper instrument, which is initiated through an electronic terminal, telephonic instrument, computer, or magnetic tape so as to order, instruct, or authorize a financial institution to debit or credit an account. Such term includes, but is not limited to, point-of-sale transfers, automated teller machine transactions, transfers initiated by telephone, wire transfers, and automated clearinghouse transfers.

(L) **"Escrow Items"** means those items that are described in Section 3.

(M) **"Miscellaneous Proceeds"** means any compensation, settlement, award of damages, or proceeds paid by any third party (other than insurance proceeds paid under the coverages described in Section 5) for: (i) damage to, or destruction of, the Property; (ii) condemnation or other taking of all or any part of the Property; (iii) conveyance in lieu of condemnation; or (iv) misrepresentations of, or omissions as to, the value and/or condition of the Property.

(N) **"Mortgage Insurance"** means insurance protecting Lender against the nonpayment of, or default on, the Loan.

(O) **"Periodic Payment"** means the regularly scheduled amount due for (i) principal and interest under the Note, plus (ii) any amounts under Section 3 of this Security Instrument.

(P) **"RESPA"** means the Real Estate Settlement Procedures Act (12 U.S.C. §2601 et seq.) and its implementing regulation, Regulation X (24 C.F.R. Part 3500), as they might be amended from time to time, or any additional or successor legislation or regulation that governs the same subject matter. As used in this Security Instrument, "RESPA" refers to all requirements and restrictions that are imposed in regard to a "federally related mortgage loan" even if the Loan does not qualify as a "federally related mortgage loan" under RESPA.

(Q) **"Successor in Interest of Borrower"** means any party that has taken title to the Property, whether or not that party has assumed Borrower's obligations under the Note and/or this Security Instrument.

TRANSFER OF RIGHTS IN THE PROPERTY

This Security Instrument secures to Lender: (i) the repayment of the Loan, and all renewals, extensions and modifications of the Note; and (ii) the performance of Borrower's covenants and agreements under this Security Instrument and the Note. For this purpose, Borrower irrevocably grants and conveys to Trustee, in trust, with power of sale, the following described property located in the _____ of _____:

[Type of Recording Jurisdiction]   [Name of Recording Jurisdiction]

which currently has the address of _____

[Street]

_____, California _____ ("Property Address"):

[City]   [Zip Code]

TOGETHER WITH all the improvements now or hereafter erected on the property, and all easements, appurtenances, and fixtures now or hereafter a part of the property. All replacements and additions shall also be covered by this Security Instrument. All of the foregoing is referred to in this Security Instrument as the "Property."

BORROWER COVENANTS that Borrower is lawfully seised of the estate hereby conveyed and has the right to grant and convey the Property and that the Property is unencumbered, except for encumbrances of record. Borrower warrants and will defend generally the title to the Property against all claims and demands, subject to any encumbrances of record.

THIS SECURITY INSTRUMENT combines uniform covenants for national use and non-uniform covenants with limited variations by jurisdiction to constitute a uniform security instrument covering real property.

> *This Deed of Trust has the same Uniform Covenants as are in the Florida Single-Family Fannie Mae/Freddie Mac UNIFORM INSTRUMENT as shown on Page XX.*

NON-UNIFORM COVENANTS. Borrower and Lender further covenant and agree as follows:

22. Acceleration; Remedies. Lender shall give notice to Borrower prior to acceleration following Borrower's breach of any covenant or agreement in this Security Instrument (but not prior to acceleration under Section 18 unless Applicable Law provides otherwise). The notice shall specify: (a) the default; (b) the action required to cure the default; (c) a date, not less than 30 days from the date the notice is given to Borrower, by which the default must be cured; and (d) that failure to cure the default on or before the date specified in the notice may result in acceleration of the sums secured by this Security Instrument and sale of the Property. The notice shall further inform Borrower of the right to reinstate after acceleration and the right to bring a court action to assert the non-existence of a default or any other defense of Borrower to acceleration and sale. If the default is not cured on or before the date specified in the notice, Lender at its option may

require immediate payment in full of all sums secured by this Security Instrument without further demand and may invoke the power of sale and any other remedies permitted by Applicable Law. Lender shall be entitled to collect all expenses incurred in pursuing the remedies provided in this Section 22, including, but not limited to, reasonable attorneys' fees and costs of title evidence.

If Lender invokes the power of sale, Lender shall execute or cause Trustee to execute a written notice of the occurrence of an event of default and of Lender's election to cause the Property to be sold. Trustee shall cause this notice to be recorded in each county in which any part of the Property is located. Lender or Trustee shall mail copies of the notice as prescribed by Applicable Law to Borrower and to the other persons prescribed by Applicable Law. Trustee shall give public notice of sale to the persons and in the manner prescribed by Applicable Law. After the time required by Applicable Law, Trustee, without demand on Borrower, shall sell the Property at public auction to the highest bidder at the time and place and under the terms designated in the notice of sale in one or more parcels and in any order Trustee determines. Trustee may postpone sale of all or any parcel of the Property by public announcement at the time and place of any previously scheduled sale. Lender or its designee may purchase the Property at any sale.

Trustee shall deliver to the purchaser Trustee's deed conveying the Property without any covenant or warranty, expressed or implied. The recitals in the Trustee's deed shall be prima facie evidence of the truth of the statements made therein. Trustee shall apply the proceeds of the sale in the following order: (a) to all expenses of the sale, including, but not limited to, reasonable Trustee's and attorneys' fees; (b) to all sums secured by this Security Instrument; and (c) any excess to the person or persons legally entitled to it.

23.   **Reconveyance.** Upon payment of all sums secured by this Security Instrument, Lender shall request Trustee to reconvey the Property and shall surrender this Security Instrument and all notes evidencing debt secured by this Security Instrument to Trustee. Trustee shall reconvey the Property without warranty to the person or persons legally entitled to it. Lender may charge such person or persons a reasonable fee for reconveying the Property, but only if the fee is paid to a third party (such as the Trustee) for services rendered and the charging of the fee is permitted under Applicable Law. If the fee charged does not exceed the fee set by Applicable Law, the fee is conclusively presumed to be reasonable.

24.   **Substitute Trustee.** Lender, at its option, may from time to time appoint a successor trustee to any Trustee appointed hereunder by an instrument executed and acknowledged by Lender and recorded in the office of the Recorder of the county in which the Property is located. The instrument shall contain the name of the original Lender, Trustee and Borrower, the book and page where this Security Instrument is recorded and the name and address of the successor trustee. Without conveyance of the Property, the successor trustee shall succeed to all the title, powers and duties conferred upon the Trustee herein and by Applicable Law. This procedure for substitution of trustee shall govern to the exclusion of all other provisions for substitution.

25.   **Statement of Obligation Fee.** Lender may collect a fee not to exceed the maximum amount permitted by Applicable Law for furnishing the statement of obligation as provided by Section 2943 of the Civil Code of California.

BY SIGNING BELOW, Borrower accepts and agrees to the terms and covenants contained in this Security Instrument and in any Rider executed by Borrower and recorded with it.

Witnesses:

_____ _____ (Seal)
                                                              - Borrower

_____ _____ (Seal)
                                                              - Borrower

_____**[Space Below This Line for Acknowledgment]**_____

Contract for Deed (Land Contract)

A **contract for deed** is a financing instrument with many names. It may be called an installment sales contract, a contract of sale, an agreement of sale, a conditional sales contract, or a land sales contract.

This is a contract in which the seller (**vendor**) becomes the lender to the buyer (**vendee**). The vendor pays off the original financing while receiving payments from the vendee on the contract of sale. The vendor and vendee's relationship is like that of a beneficiary and a trustor in a trust deed. The vendor in a land contract may not use the vendee's impound money for any other purpose without the consent of the payor (vendee).

The buyer (**vendee**) has possession and use of the property even though the seller (**vendor**) holds legal title. In a contract of sale, the vendor retains legal ownership of the property and the vendee holds what is known as equitable title. **Equitable title** is the interest held by the buyer under a contract for deed that gives the buyer the equitable right to obtain absolute ownership to the property when the seller holds legal title. When all the terms of the contract are met, the vendor passes title to the vendee.

Standardized Forms

Lenders are encouraged to use the **Fannie Mae/Freddie Mac Uniform Security Instruments** (mortgage, deed of trust, or security deed) when originating single-family residential loans. However, any residential loans sold to Freddie Mac must use the applicable single-family security instrument. To see these uniform security instruments, visit www.freddiemac.com/uniform.

The Fannie Mae/Freddie Mac Uniform Security Instruments use standard terms and uniform covenants (promises) in all security instruments whether they are mortgages or deeds of trust. Additionally, each state security instrument has non-uniform covenants that are specific to the state in which the security instrument is used.

Standard Terms Used in Uniform Security Instruments

Whether the security instrument used is a mortgage, deed of trust, or security deed, it will use certain identical terms and clauses.

Items in Security Instruments

- Date of its execution
- Name(s) of borrower(s)
- Name of lender
- Reference to the promissory note including amount of loan
- Description of property securing loan

Parties to a Security Instrument

Every security instrument describes the parties to the security instrument. The type of security instrument dictates the parties.

> **Borrower.** Depending on the type of security instrument, the borrower is called the mortgagor, trustor, or grantor.

> **Lender.** Depending on the type of security instrument, the lender is called the mortgagee, beneficiary, or grantee.

> **Trustee.** Only a deed of trust has a trustee.

Type of Security Instrument	Borrower	Lender	Trustee
Mortgage	Mortgagor	Mortgagee	N/A
Deed of Trust	Trustor	Beneficiary	Trustee
Security Deed	Grantor	Grantee	N/A

Note

The note is the promissory note signed and dated by the borrower. The dollar amount, promise to make regular periodic payments, and due date are shown. **Periodic payment** is the regularly scheduled amount due for principal and interest under the note plus escrow amounts, if any.

Loan

The loan refers to the debt evidenced by the note plus interest, any prepayment charges, and late charges due under the note.

Riders

Many security instruments have riders. A **rider** is an addition or amendment separate from but attached to the original document. Typical riders to security instruments include the Adjustable Rate Rider, Balloon Rider, Condominium Rider, and Biweekly Payment Rider.

Covenant of Seisin

The **covenant of seisin** is the borrower's promise that he or she has the right to grant and convey the property and that the property is unencumbered except for encumbrances of record.

Uniform Covenants

The uniform covenants discussed in the following sections are identical in all of the Fannie Mae/Freddie Mac Uniform Security Instruments.

Periodic Payments

The borrower promises to pay the principal and interest on the note when due. If the note requires items to be paid in an escrow account, the borrower promises to pay those when due as well. **Escrow items** include fees or assessments that must be paid in addition to the periodic payment of principal and interest. These include taxes, assessments, leasehold payments, ground rents, insurance premiums, and mortgage insurance premiums, if any. **Mortgage insurance** is insurance that protects the lender against the nonpayment of, or default on, the loan.

Charges and Liens

The borrower promises to pay all taxes, assessments, charges, and fines that can attain priority over the security instrument.

Property Insurance

The borrower must provide adequate homeowner and hazard (i.e., fire, flood, and earthquake) insurance coverage for improvements on the property. The lender may require the amount (including deductible levels) of the insurance and has the right to approve the insurance carrier providing the insurance. This coverage is called force placed insurance.

Occupancy

If the loan is for the borrower's personal residence, the borrower must occupy the property for at least one year unless the lender agrees otherwise in writing. If the borrower states on the loan application that the property will be the principal residence but the statement is false, the borrower is in default.

Preservation and Maintenance of the Property

The borrower will not destroy or damage the property and promises to maintain the property to prevent it from deteriorating or decreasing in value due to its condition. The lender (or its agent) has the right to inspect the property.

Lender's Right to Protect its Interest in the Property

The lender may do whatever is reasonable to protect its interest in the property. The lender may protect itself if the borrower fails to perform the covenants contained in this security instrument, or abandons the property, or if a legal proceeding (i.e., bankruptcy, probate, condemnation) threatens the lender's interest.

The lender may secure the property and change the locks. The lender may (but is not required to) make repairs, replace or board up doors and windows, drain water from pipes, eliminate building or other code violations or dangerous conditions, and have the utilities turned on or off.

Any money spent by the lender to protect its interest in the property will be added to the borrower's debt that is secured by the security instrument. The borrower must repay these amounts plus interest when asked to do so by the lender.

Mortgage Insurance

The borrower promises to pay mortgage insurance premiums if the lender requires mortgage insurance as a condition of making the loan.

Joint and Several Liability

Each borrower who signs the security instrument agrees to be jointly and severally liable. However, a borrower who co-signs the security instrument but not the note only conveys his or her interest in the property under the terms of this security instrument and is not personally obligated to pay the sums in the note.

Borrower's Copy

The borrower is given one copy of the note and of the security instrument. The lender keeps the originals.

Transfer of the Property

An acceleration or **due on sale clause** gives the lender the right to demand full payment of the loan secured by the security instrument if the borrower transfers the property without the lender's permission. If the lender exercises this option, the lender sends a notice of acceleration to the borrower. The notice states the time within which the borrower must pay the loan and any other charges. If the borrower does not pay the amount before the allotted time expires, the lender may employ any remedies permitted by the security instrument.

Borrower's Right to Reinstate

The borrower has the right to reinstate the loan after acceleration if he or she meets certain conditions. To **reinstate** means to bring current or to restore. Borrowers in default can avoid foreclosure by bringing the loan to a current status. **Foreclosure** is a legal procedure in which the borrower's property is sold to satisfy the debt. In order to reinstate the loan the borrower must pay the lender all sums due under the note as if no acceleration occurred. In addition, the borrower must cure any default of any other covenants and pay all expenses incurred by the lender in enforcing the security instrument (i.e., attorneys' fees, property inspection, valuation fees, etc.). Under a mortgage, the right of a mortgagor who is in default on the loan to recover the property BEFORE a foreclosure sale is called **equity of redemption**. A mortgagor may not waive his or her right to the equity of redemption.

Sale of Note

The lender can sell the note (together with the security instrument) one or more times without giving prior notice to the borrower.

Change of Loan Servicer

The lender may retain or sell the servicing rights to the note. Any time the loan servicer changes, the borrower must be given written notice of the change. The notice will state the name and address of the new loan servicer, the address to which payments should be made, and any other information the Real Estate Settlement Procedures Act (RESPA) requires in connection with a notice of transfer of servicing.

Hazardous Substances

The borrower shall not use, dispose of, store, or release any hazardous substances on the property that can create a condition that adversely affects the value of the property. **Hazardous substances** include gasoline, kerosene, other flammable or toxic petroleum products, toxic pesticides and herbicides, volatile solvents, materials containing asbestos or formaldehyde, and radioactive materials. This does not apply to small quantities of cleaning supplies, paint, and materials used to maintain residential property.

Non-Uniform Covenants

The non-uniform covenants vary due to the type of instrument—mortgage, deed of trust, and security deed. The non-uniform covenants pertain primarily to the remedies for default. These remedies are discussed under mortgages and deeds of trust later in this unit.

SUMMARY

When a loan is made for the purchase of real property, the borrower signs a promissory note. The promissory note is the evidence of the debt. It states the amount of money borrowed and the terms of repayment.

No matter the lender, there are certain clauses that must be included in fixed-rate promissory notes. These include clauses such as the date and property description, parties to the contract, borrower's promise to pay, and so forth.

Different types of notes include straight, installment, installment with periodic payments of fixed amounts, adjustable-rate, demand, and fully and partially amortized notes.

The interest of a lender in the property of a borrower is called the security interest. The security instrument (mortgage, deed of trust, security deed, or contract of sale) is evidence of that security interest. A security instrument is a legal document given by the borrower to hypothecate (pledge) the property to the lender as collateral for the loan.

A mortgage is a two-party instrument and is, in fact, a contract for a loan. The two parties in a mortgage are the mortgagor (borrower) and mortgagee (lender). A deed of trust has three parties—the trustor (borrower), the beneficiary (lender), and the trustee (neutral third party).

A contract for deed is a financing contract in which the seller (vendor) becomes the lender to the buyer (vendee).

Recording a security instrument (mortgage, deed of trust, security deed, or contract of sale) creates a lien against the property and gives public notice of the existence of a debt owed on the property. Generally, the priority of a lien is determined by its recording date.

UNIT 10 REVIEW

Matching Exercise

Instructions: Write the letter of the matching term on the blank line before its definition. Answers are in Appendix A.

Terms

A. acceleration clause
B. assumption clause
C. covenant of seisin
D. deed of reconveyance
E. defeasance clause
F. deficiency judgment
G. equitable title
H. foreclosure
I. holder in due course
J. hypothecation

K. installment note
L. maker
M. mortgage
N. negotiable instrument
O. noteholder
P. power of sale clause
Q. prepayment penalty
R. promissory note
S. security instrument
T. Uniform Commercial Code

Definitions

1. _____ Written legal contract that obligates the borrower to repay a loan

2. _____ The borrower who executes a note and becomes primarily liable for payment to the lender

3. _____ Subsequent owner of the note who is called a holder in due course

4. _____ This note requires periodic payments on the principal with payments of interest made separately

5. _____ Allows a lender to collect a certain percentage of a loan as a penalty for early payoff

6. _____ Allows a noteholder to call the entire note due on occurrence of a specific event such as default in payment, taxes, or insurance, or sale of the property

7. _____ Allows a buyer to assume responsibility for the full payment of a loan after obtaining the lender's consent

8. _____ Written unconditional promise or order to pay a certain sum of money on demand or at a definite future date, payable either to order or to bearer and signed by the maker

9. _____ Governs negotiable instruments and is designed to give uniformity to commercial transactions across all 50 states

10. _____ One who takes an instrument for value in good faith absent any notice that it is overdue, has been dishonored, or is subject to any defense against it or claim to it by any other person

11. _____ Legal document given by the borrower to pledge the property to the lender as collateral for the loan

12. _____ Legal arrangement allowing a borrower to remain in possession of a property secured by a loan

13. _____ A two-party security instrument (contract for a loan)

14. _____ Clause that cancels the mortgage upon repayment of the debt in full

15. _____ Clause giving the holder the right to sell the property in the event of default by the borrower

16. _____ Personal judgment against a borrower for the balance of a debt owed when the security for the loan is insufficient to repay the debt

17. _____ Right to obtain absolute ownership to property when legal title is held in another's name

18. _____ Deed transferring title to the property from the trustee to the borrower

19. _____ Borrower promises that he or she has the right to convey the property and that it is unencumbered

20. _____ Legal procedure to sell borrower's property to satisfy a debt

Multiple Choice Questions

Instructions: Circle your response and go to Appendix A to read the complete explanation for each question.

1. Which of the following is the evidence of a debt?
   a. Mortgage
   b. Promissory note
   c. Financing statement
   d. Grant deed

2. The note with a repayment schedule that is not sufficient to pay off the loan over its term is a _____ note.
   a. fixed-rate
   b. fully amortized
   c. partially amortized
   d. adjustable-rate mortgage

3. _____ interest is the rate the borrower is actually paying.
   a. Simple
   b. Nominal
   c. Named
   d. Effective

4. A _____ clause allows a borrower to pay off a loan early or make higher payments without paying a penalty.
   a. borrower's promise to pay
   b. borrower's right to prepay
   c. prepayment
   d. due-on-sale

5. All of the following are elements of a negotiable promissory note, except:
   a. the signature of the maker.
   b. an unconditional promise to pay a certain amount of money.
   c. the signature of the lender.
   d. its payability to order or bearer.

6. The Uniform Commercial Code:
   a. governs negotiable instruments.
   b. is designed to give uniformity to commercial transactions across all 50 states.
   c. Both (a) and (b)
   d. Neither (a) or (b)

7.   Someone who obtains an existing negotiable promissory note is known as the:
   a. maker.
   b. noteholder.
   c. holder in due course.
   d. trustee.

8.   If a court action is begun by the holder in due course, which of the following defenses can the maker use to refuse payment?
   a. Claim non-receipt of what was promised by the payee in exchange for the note
   b. Claim the debt has already been paid
   c. Accuse the original lender of fraud in the process of making the original note
   d. Accuse the holder in due course of making secret, material changes to the note

9.   The legal document given by the borrower to hypothecate (pledge) the property to the lender as collateral for the loan is the:
   a. promissory note.
   b. security instrument.
   c. debt.
   d. collateral.

10.   Every security instrument includes:
   a. the date of its execution.
   b. a reference to the promissory note.
   c. a description of property securing the loan.
   d. all of the above

11.   In the event of default on the loan, the _____ status ensures the lender's priority during a foreclosure action, effectively eliminating all other _____ that may exist.
   a. senior lien; junior liens
   b. junior lien; senior liens
   c. subordinate lien; insubordinate liens
   d. none of the above

12. What is the principal advantage of a trust deed over a mortgage?

    a. A trust deed's power of sale is not typically outlawed by time, whereas a mortgage remains subject to the statute of limitations.

    b. A trust deed's power of sale is outlawed by time, whereas a mortgage remains is not.

    c. A trust deed's power of sale is outlawed by the statute of limitations, whereas a mortgage remains is subject to time.

    d. A trust deed's power of sale is outlawed by no limitation, whereas a mortgage remains is subject to time.

13. One difference between a mortgage and a deed of trust is that a mortgage has _____ parties.

    a. two

    b. three

    c. four

    d. five

14. In a _____ theory state, title to real property is vested in the lender.

    a. title

    b. lien

    c. intermediate

    d. advanced

15. Statutory redemption allows a defaulted mortgagor to:

    a. borrow against the property.

    b. recover the property for a specified time period after the foreclosure sale.

    c. sell the property.

    d. convey title to the property to a third party.

16. In a deed of trust, the lender is the:

    a. trustee.

    b. trustor.

    c. holder in due course.

    d. beneficiary.

17. A deed of trust may be foreclosed through:

    a. judicial foreclosure.

    b. a trustee's sale.

    c. reinstatement.

    d. either (a) or (b).

18. In a contract for deed, the _____ is the interest held by the buyer that gives the buyer the equitable right to obtain absolute ownership to the property when the seller holds legal title.
    a. bare legal title
    b. deed of reconveyance
    c. equitable title
    d. none of the above

19. In order to reinstate a loan the borrower must:
    a. pay the lender all sums due under the note.
    b. cure any default of any other covenants.
    c. pay all expenses incurred by the lender in enforcing the security instrument.
    d. do all of the above.

20. The note together with the security instrument can be sold:
    a. by giving prior notice to the borrower.
    b. only one time.
    c. one or more times without giving prior notice to the borrower.
    d. one or more times after giving prior notice to the borrower.

The Loan Package

INTRODUCTION

From the time a borrower submits a loan application through the time the request is presented to an underwriter, who decides whether the package meets required loan standards, the lender takes certain actions and follows certain procedures. The careful, thoughtful, lawful, and professional processing of the loan is critical to the success of a real estate lender.

The professional lender's job is to guide the borrower through the loan origination process. This includes helping the customer complete a loan application and explaining what documents or verifications, such as credit card numbers, evidence of employment, tax returns, or bank account references, should be included in the loan package. Many prospective borrowers do not understand the lending process and require understanding and patience as they learn. A lender who is helpful, fair, and respectful toward the loan applicant builds a base of business that grows.

Processing a loan is probably the most time consuming and most important part of the loan procedure. The processor must gather important information and evaluate it to determine if a loan fits specific loan guidelines.

Usually, a loan processor follows a checklist to make sure that the borrower has provided all necessary documentation. A thorough analysis of this information lowers the risk of loss to investors.

385

This unit discusses the first two steps in the loan process: completing the application and processing the application.

Learning Objectives

After completing this Unit, you should be able to:

11A   recognize steps involved in obtaining a real estate loan.

11B   recall the definition of application as used for most real estate loans.

11C   identify information included in sections of the Uniform Residential Loan Application.

11D   recall the purpose of a loan estimate.

11E   designate loan packaging procedures.

11F   distinguish between the VOD, VOE, and other types of documentation.

STEPS IN THE LOAN PROCESS

Someone has to gather information about a prospective borrower from a loan application, analyze the financial and personal data, and decide if the applicant is a qualified candidate for the loan. The decision to make the loan rests with a lender's loan committee or a single person whose job it is to approve loan applications based on the capacity of the borrower to qualify under the lender's guidelines.

After the lender's underwriter gives loan approval, the paperwork is prepared and the loan is closed. The four basic steps in the loan process are 1) completing the application, 2) processing, 3) underwriting, and 4) closing. The application and processing steps are discussed in this unit.

> **Review – Four Steps in Obtaining a Real Estate Loan**
> 1. Completing the Loan Application
> 2. Processing
> 3. Underwriting (risk analysis)
> 4. Closing

COMPLETING THE LOAN APPLICATION

As the level of sophistication, distance, and relationship changed between banker and borrower, so did the process for obtaining the loan. Lenders began requiring borrowers to complete a written application and sign a written promise to repay the loan. At first, these forms varied from lender to lender. Since there was no standardized form, approval requirements varied as well. Because lenders asked different questions of potential borrowers, it was reasonable to believe that a borrower might be accepted by one lender and turned down by another.

Today, a standardized form called the **Fannie Mae/Freddie Mac Uniform Residential Loan Application (URLA or Form 1003)** is used for most residential home loans. This form is called either the Freddie Mac Form 65 or Fannie Mae Form 1003, which is its more common name. Use of the standardized form makes it possible for lenders to sell their loans in the secondary mortgage market (to Fannie Mae, Freddie Mac, and Ginnie Mae) because the approval requirements are consistent and conforming. In 1992, the Departments of Housing and Urban Development (HUD) and Veterans Affairs (VA) also approved the form for use in processing FHA and VA loans. Because of the adoption of the URLA, lenders and borrowers have to complete a HUD/VA Addendum to the Uniform Residential Loan Application (Form HUD-92900-A). This addendum to the URLA is necessary because HUD and VA have certain statutory and regulatory requirements that must be satisfied for insured or guaranteed loans. Nearly all portfolio lenders (lenders who want to keep their real estate loans within their own house) have adopted the Uniform Residential Loan Application to make sure the loans conform to the standards required in the secondary market in case they decide to sell the loans at a future time.

The first thing a borrower does when applying for a loan is to complete the application and other documents in the loan package. A **loan package** is the file of documents the lender needs to determine whether to fund a loan. The documents in the loan package include the loan application; verifications of employment, income, and bank accounts; and information on the property. The loan application asks for detailed information about the borrower, his or her employment record, and the property. In addition, the lender needs documentation pertaining to the borrower's personal finances—earnings, monthly expenses, and debts. This information helps the lender gauge the borrower's willingness and ability to repay the loan.

Since every borrower supplies the same required information, the buyers of these loans can presume the borrowers and the loan security are reported consistently and are creditworthy. Therefore, buyers in the secondary market are able to assess risk based on their analysis of a standardized loan application.

Definition of Application

The TILA-RESPA Rule (TRID Rule) defines "**application**" as the submission of a borrower's financial information for the purposes of obtaining an extension of credit. For loan applications submitted in the anticipation of obtaining a federally related mortgage loan, six elements are required.

Elements in the Reg. Z Definition of Application
1. Borrower's name
2. Borrower's monthly income
3. Borrower's social security number to obtain a credit report
4. Property address
5. Estimate of the value of the property
6. Mortgage loan amount

A lender is free to collect additional information, but once it has received the six pieces of required information, it has received an application. [12 CFR §1026.2(a)(3)].

Uniform Residential Loan Application

The lender may help the borrower complete the following sections in the Uniform Residential Loan Application (Fannie Mae/Freddie Mac Form 1003).

Sections in the Uniform Residential Loan Application
I. Type of Mortgage and Terms of Loan
II. Property Information and Purpose of Loan
III. Borrower Information
IV. Employment Information
V. Monthly Income and Combined Housing Expense Information
VI. Assets and Liabilities
VII. Details of Transaction
VIII. Declarations
IX. Acknowledgment and Agreement
X. Information for Government Monitoring Purposes

I. Type of Mortgage and Terms of Loan

The first section of the loan application is a request for a specific type of home loan. It includes the borrower's name and the requested loan amount and repayment terms.

II. Property Information and Purpose of Loan

Collateral is something of value given as security for a debt. Real property is the primary collateral for a real estate loan and acts as the security for repayment of the loan in case the borrower defaults. The second section of the application describes the property used as collateral for the loan and states the purpose of the loan.

The lender usually requests a copy of the original offer to purchase if the sale is conditioned on the funding of the loan. If the property is income producing (apartment or commercial buildings), the lender will want information about operating expenses and income for several years, as well as how any negative cash flow will be covered. This is commonly referred to as the annual property operating data and/or rent rolls.

Property Information Required

- Specific identification of the property, including legal description and common address (street address)

- Title information, such as vesting, claims, encumbrances, liens, and real estate loans. As you may recall, an **encumbrance** is a claim, charge, or liability that attaches to and is binding on real property. Encumbrances fall into two categories—**financial encumbrances** that affect title such as a lien and **non-financial encumbrances** that affect use such as an easement or restriction.

- Description of the land and type of improvements, including work that might be subject to mechanics' liens

- Purchase price and terms, such as date purchased, taxes, zoning, and assessments

- Present value, which might be different from the purchase price

III. Borrower Information

The lender uses information about the borrower to decide if he or she has the ability and willingness to repay the loan. This section asks for the borrower's name, social security number and/or Taxpayer Identification Number (TIN), date of birth, marital status, number of dependents, and address/former addresses. Most lenders require the borrower to provide information on previous addresses if the borrower has not lived at his or her current address for 2 years.

IV. Employment Information

Evidence that a borrower can pay back the loan is supported by his or her employment. This section asks for the name and address of the borrower's employer, the borrower's position, and length of employment. If the borrower has less than 2 years of employment at the current site, the lender will require more information about past employment.

V. Monthly Income and Combined Housing Expense Information

This section informs the lender about the borrower's current income and proposed housing expense (if the loan is funded). It includes other income, such as rents, annuities, and royalties. This section shows the lender how much of the gross income is available for loan payments, taxes, and insurance. It also shows the lender the borrower's other debt obligations and liabilities.

If the borrower has an investment property that produces a positive net cash flow that is listed on the Operating Income Statement, the borrower should enter this number in the box labeled Net Rental Income.

In the Present column of the Combined Monthly Housing Expense section, the borrower should list the present combined expenses of the borrower and co-borrower. This should be based on the borrower's principal residence.

In the Proposed column, the borrower should give the PITI for the property that is the subject of the loan if the subject property is a 2-4 unit property in which the borrower will use one unit as his or her principal residence.

VI. Assets and Liabilities

The borrower's assets include checking and savings accounts, CDs, stocks and bonds, life insurance, real estate owned, retirement funds, net worth of a business owned (the lender may require an audited financial statement of the business), automobiles owned, personal property, valuable collections, and any other items of value. If the borrower or co-borrower owns individual investments, he or she should include a current brokerage statement with the application. This statement should detail the names of the stocks, amount per share, and the number of shares owned.

Some borrowers own other property. This information is included in the section called Schedule of Real Estate Owned. The form has space to write the address of the property, the type, current value, loan amount (if any), and real estate loan payments. If the property is income property, include the encumbrances and repayment obligations for other real property the applicant owns. The borrower should include the name and contact information for the mortgage company that owns the loan if it is not completely paid off. If the property is rented, the borrower should include the current lease.

Credit card accounts, pledged assets, alimony or child support owed, job-related expenses, and any other amounts owed are listed as liabilities.

If including a combined statement of the assets and liabilities of the borrower and co-borrower is not a meaningful representation of their assets and liabilities, the co-borrower must complete a Statement of Assets and Liabilities (Form 1003A) to be included with the loan application.

VII. Details of Transaction

Detailed listings of the purchase price, the loan amount, and other costs of obtaining the loan are included in this section for the benefit of borrower and lender. The borrower should not include any discounts, rebates, or other allowances in line a. Purchase Price.

When the loan is for a refinance, the borrower does not use lines a., b., and c. The borrower should show the amount of the refinance on line d. Refinance. This number includes all liens in addition to the cost of improvements that are complete or will be completed.

VIII. Declarations

The Declaration section asks questions that the borrower must answer. They include questions regarding judgments, bankruptcies, foreclosures, lawsuits, or any other voluntary or involuntary legal obligations. If the applicant answers "Yes" to any of them, he or she will need to write a detailed explanation.

If the borrower states that he or she is not a U.S. citizen or a permanent resident alien, the lender has the right to ask if the borrower is lawfully present in the United States. Fannie Mae does purchase loans made to borrowers who are not citizens as long as they have proof that their presence in the U.S. is lawful. Please note that presenting an Individual Tax Identification Number (ITIN) is not sufficient proof of the borrower's legal or illegal presence.

IX. Acknowledgment and Agreement

This is a final declaration by the borrower regarding the statements and information made in the application, as well as an acknowledgment of the borrower's awareness of his or her obligation regarding the loan. This form states that it is a federal crime punishable by fine or imprisonment, or both, knowingly to make any false statements concerning any of the facts on the application. The borrower and co-borrower must sign and date this section.

X. Information for Government Monitoring Purposes

Regulation C, which implements the Home Mortgage Disclosure Act (HMDA), requires lenders to collect certain information (ethnicity, race, and sex) when making loans to purchase or refinance homes. The borrower does not have to give the information and can check a box stating, "I do not wish to furnish this information." However, if the borrower completes the application in the presence of the lender, but decides not to complete this section, the lender must indicate the borrower's ethnicity, race, and gender based on the lender's visual observations or the borrower's surname.

Retaining the Loan Application

The Uniform Residential Loan Application is an important document because it is used to prove compliance with various federal regulations. Therefore, it should be kept with the loan file for as long as the loan is outstanding. For cancelled, declined, or withdrawn loans, the loan application should be kept for at least 25 months after the date when the decline notice was sent.

Uniform Residential Loan Application

This application is designed to be completed by the applicant(s) with the Lender's assistance. Applicants should complete this form as "Borrower" or "Co-Borrower," as applicable. Co-Borrower information must also be provided (and the appropriate box checked) when ☐ the income or assets of a person other than the Borrower (including the Borrower's spouse) will be used as a basis for loan qualification or ☐ the income or assets of the Borrower's spouse or other person who has community property rights pursuant to state law will not be used as a basis for loan qualification, but his or her liabilities must be considered because the spouse or other person has community property rights pursuant to applicable law and Borrower resides in a community property state, the security property is located in a community property state, or the Borrower is relying on other property located in a community property state as a basis for repayment of the loan.

If this is an application for joint credit, Borrower and Co-Borrower each agree that we intend to apply for joint credit (sign below):

Borrower _____   Co-Borrower _____

I. TYPE OF MORTGAGE AND TERMS OF LOAN

Mortgage Applied for:	☐ VA ☐ FHA	☐ Conventional ☐ USDA/Rural Housing Service	☐ Other (explain):	Agency Case Number	Lender Case Number

Amount $	Interest Rate %	No. of Months	Amortization Type:	☐ Fixed Rate ☐ GPM	☐ Other (explain): ☐ ARM (type):

II. PROPERTY INFORMATION AND PURPOSE OF LOAN

Subject Property Address (street, city, state & ZIP)	No. of Units

Legal Description of Subject Property (attach description if necessary)	Year Built

Purpose of Loan	☐ Purchase ☐ Construction ☐ Refinance ☐ Construction-Permanent	☐ Other (explain):	Property will be: ☐ Primary Residence ☐ Secondary Residence ☐ Investment

Complete this line if construction or construction-permanent loan.

Year Lot Acquired	Original Cost $	Amount Existing Liens $	(a) Present Value of Lot $	(b) Cost of Improvements $	Total (a + b) $

Complete this line if this is a refinance loan.

Year Acquired	Original Cost $	Amount Existing Liens $	Purpose of Refinance	Describe Improvements ☐ made ☐ to be made Cost: $

Title will be held in what Name(s)	Manner in which Title will be held	Estate will be held in: ☐ Fee Simple ☐ Leasehold (show expiration date)

Source of Down Payment, Settlement Charges, and/or Subordinate Financing (explain)

III. BORROWER INFORMATION

Borrower	Co-Borrower
Borrower's Name (include Jr. or Sr. if applicable)	Co-Borrower's Name (include Jr. or Sr. if applicable)

Social Security Number	Home Phone (incl. area code)	DOB (mm/dd/yyyy)	Yrs. School	Social Security Number	Home Phone (incl. area code)	DOB (mm/dd/yyyy)	Yrs. School

☐ Married ☐ Separated ☐ Unmarried (include single, divorced, widowed)	Dependents (not listed by Co-Borrower) no. ages	☐ Married ☐ Separated ☐ Unmarried (include single, divorced, widowed)	Dependents (not listed by Borrower) no. ages

Present Address (street, city, state, ZIP) ☐ Own ☐ Rent ___ No. Yrs.	Present Address (street, city, state, ZIP) ☐ Own ☐ Rent ___ No. Yrs.

Mailing Address, if different from Present Address	Mailing Address, if different from Present Address

If residing at present address for less than two years, complete the following:

Former Address (street, city, state, ZIP) ☐ Own ☐ Rent ___ No. Yrs.	Former Address (street, city, state, ZIP) ☐ Own ☐ Rent ___ No. Yrs.

IV. EMPLOYMENT INFORMATION

Borrower	Co-Borrower

Name & Address of Employer	☐ Self Employed	Yrs. on this job	Name & Address of Employer	☐ Self Employed	Yrs. on this job
		Yrs. employed in this line of work/profession			Yrs. employed in this line of work/profession

Position/Title/Type of Business	Business Phone (incl. area code)	Position/Title/Type of Business	Business Phone (incl. area code)

If employed in current position for less than two years or if currently employed in more than one position, complete the following:

Borrower			IV. EMPLOYMENT INFORMATION (cont'd)		Co-Borrower	
Name & Address of Employer	☐ Self Employed	Dates (from – to)	Name & Address of Employer	☐ Self Employed	Dates (from – to)	
		Monthly Income $			Monthly Income $	
Position/Title/Type of Business		Business Phone (incl. area code)	Position/Title/Type of Business		Business Phone (incl. area code)	
Name & Address of Employer	☐ Self Employed	Dates (from – to)	Name & Address of Employer	☐ Self Employed	Dates (from – to)	
		Monthly Income $			Monthly Income $	
Position/Title/Type of Business		Business Phone (incl. area code)	Position/Title/Type of Business		Business Phone (incl. area code)	

V. MONTHLY INCOME AND COMBINED HOUSING EXPENSE INFORMATION

Gross Monthly Income	Borrower	Co-Borrower	Total	Combined Monthly Housing Expense	Present	Proposed
Base Empl. Income*	$	$	$	Rent	$	
Overtime				First Mortgage (P&I)		$
Bonuses				Other Financing (P&I)		
Commissions				Hazard Insurance		
Dividends/Interest				Real Estate Taxes		
Net Rental Income				Mortgage Insurance		
Other (before completing, see the notice in "describe other income," below)				Homeowner Assn. Dues		
				Other:		
Total	$	$	$	Total	$	$

* Self Employed Borrower(s) may be required to provide additional documentation such as tax returns and financial statements.

Describe Other Income   *Notice:* Alimony, child support, or separate maintenance income need not be revealed if the Borrower (B) or Co-Borrower (C) does not choose to have it considered for repaying this loan.

B/C		Monthly Amount
		$

VI. ASSETS AND LIABILITIES

This Statement and any applicable supporting schedules may be completed jointly by both married and unmarried Co-Borrowers if their assets and liabilities are sufficiently joined so that the Statement can be meaningfully and fairly presented on a combined basis; otherwise, separate Statements and Schedules are required. If the Co-Borrower section was completed about a non-applicant spouse or other person, this Statement and supporting schedules must be completed about that spouse or other person also.

Completed ☐ Jointly ☐ Not Jointly

ASSETS Description	Cash or Market Value	Liabilities and Pledged Assets. List the creditor's name, address, and account number for all outstanding debts, including automobile loans, revolving charge accounts, real estate loans, alimony, child support, stock pledges, etc. Use continuation sheet, if necessary. Indicate by (*) those liabilities, which will be satisfied upon sale of real estate owned or upon refinancing of the subject property.		
Cash deposit toward purchase held by:	$			
List checking and savings accounts below		LIABILITIES	Monthly Payment & Months Left to Pay	Unpaid Balance
Name and address of Bank, S&L, or Credit Union		Name and address of Company	$ Payment/Months	$
Acct. no.	$	Acct. no.		
Name and address of Bank, S&L, or Credit Union		Name and address of Company	$ Payment/Months	$
Acct. no.	$	Acct. no.		
Name and address of Bank, S&L, or Credit Union		Name and address of Company	$ Payment/Months	$
Acct. no.	$	Acct. no.		

Uniform Residential Loan Application
Freddie Mac Form 65 7/05 (rev. 6/09)   Page 2 of 5   Fannie Mae Form 1003 7/05 (rev.6/09)

VI. ASSETS AND LIABILITIES (cont'd)

Name and address of Bank, S&L, or Credit Union	Name and address of Company	$ Payment/Months	$

Acct. no.	$	Acct. no.			
Stocks & Bonds (Company name/ number & description)	$	Name and address of Company		$ Payment/Months	$

		Acct. no.	
Life insurance net cash value	$	Name and address of Company	$ Payment/Months	$
Face amount: $				

Subtotal Liquid Assets	$
Real estate owned (enter market value from schedule of real estate owned)	$
Vested interest in retirement fund	$
Net worth of business(es) owned (attach financial statement)	$

Automobiles owned (make and year)	$	Acct. no.	
		Alimony/Child Support/Separate Maintenance Payments Owed to:	$
Other Assets (itemize)	$	Job-Related Expense (child care, union dues, etc.)	$

		Total Monthly Payments	$
Total Assets a.	$	Net Worth (a minus b)	$	**Total Liabilities b.**	$

Schedule of Real Estate Owned (If additional properties are owned, use continuation sheet.)

Property Address (enter S if sold, PS if pending sale or R if rental being held for income) ▼	Type of Property	Present Market Value	Amount of Mortgages & Liens	Gross Rental Income	Mortgage Payments	Insurance, Maintenance, Taxes & Misc.	Net Rental Income
		$	$	$	$	$	$
Totals		$	$	$	$	$	$

List any additional names under which credit has previously been received and indicate appropriate creditor name(s) and account number(s):

Alternate Name	Creditor Name	Account Number

VII. DETAILS OF TRANSACTION		VIII. DECLARATIONS		
a. Purchase price	$	If you answer "Yes" to any questions a through i, please use continuation sheet for explanation.	Borrower	Co-Borrower
			Yes No	Yes No
b. Alterations, improvements, repairs		a. Are there any outstanding judgments against you?	☐ ☐	☐ ☐
c. Land (if acquired separately)		b. Have you been declared bankrupt within the past 7 years?	☐ ☐	☐ ☐
d. Refinance (incl. debts to be paid off)		c. Have you had property foreclosed upon or given title or deed in lieu thereof in the last 7 years?	☐ ☐	☐ ☐
e. Estimated prepaid items		d. Are you a party to a lawsuit?	☐ ☐	☐ ☐
f. Estimated closing costs		e. Have you directly or indirectly been obligated on any loan which resulted in foreclosure, transfer of title in lieu of foreclosure, or judgment?	☐ ☐	☐ ☐
g. PMI, MIP, Funding Fee		(This would include such loans as home mortgage loans, SBA loans, home improvement loans, educational loans, manufactured (mobile) home loans, any mortgage, financial obligation, bond, or loan guarantee. If "Yes," provide details, including date, name, and address of Lender, FHA or VA case number, if any, and reasons for the action.)		
h. Discount (if Borrower will pay)				
i. Total costs (add items a through h)				

Uniform Residential Loan Application
Freddie Mac Form 65 7/05 (rev.6/09)

Page 3 of 5

Fannie Mae Form 1003 7/05 (rev.6/09)

VII. DETAILS OF TRANSACTION			VIII. DECLARATIONS					
				Borrower		Co-Borrower		
				Yes	No	Yes	No	
j.	Subordinate financing		If you answer "Yes" to any question a through i, please use continuation sheet for explanation.					
			f. Are you presently delinquent or in default on any Federal debt or any other loan, mortgage, financial obligation, bond, or loan guarantee?	☐	☐	☐	☐	
k.	Borrower's closing costs paid by Seller		g. Are you obligated to pay alimony, child support, or separate maintenance?	☐	☐	☐	☐	
			h. Is any part of the down payment borrowed?	☐	☐	☐	☐	
l.	Other Credits (explain)		i. Are you a co-maker or endorser on a note?	☐	☐	☐	☐	
m.	Loan amount (exclude PMI, MIP, Funding Fee financed)		j. Are you a U.S. citizen?	☐	☐	☐	☐	
n.	PMI, MIP, Funding Fee financed		k. Are you a permanent resident alien?	☐	☐	☐	☐	
o.	Loan amount (add m & n)		l. **Do you intend to occupy the property as your primary residence?** If Yes," complete question m below.	☐	☐	☐	☐	
p.	Cash from/to Borrower (subtract j, k, l & o from i)		m. Have you had an ownership interest in a property in the last three years?	☐	☐	☐	☐	
			(1) What type of property did you own—principal residence (PR), second home (SH), or investment property (IP)?					
			(2) How did you hold title to the home—by yourself (S), jointly with your spouse (SP), or jointly with another person (O)?					

IX. ACKNOWLEDGEMENT AND AGREEMENT

Each of the undersigned specifically represents to Lender and to Lender's actual or potential agents, brokers, processors, attorneys, insurers, servicers, successors and assigns and agrees and acknowledges that: (1) the information provided in this application is true and correct as of the date set forth opposite my signature and that any intentional or negligent misrepresentation of this information contained in this application may result in civil liability, including monetary damages, to any person who may suffer any loss due to reliance upon any misrepresentation that I have made on this application, and/or in criminal penalties including, but not limited to, fine or imprisonment or both under the provisions of Title 18, United States Code, Sec. 1001, et seq.; (2) the loan requested pursuant to this application (the "Loan") will be secured by a mortgage or deed of trust on the property described in this application; (3) the property will not be used for any illegal or prohibited purpose or use; (4) all statements made in this application are made for the purpose of obtaining a residential mortgage loan; (5) the property will be occupied as indicated in this application; (6) the Lender, its servicers, successors or assigns may retain the original and/or an electronic record of this application, whether or not the Loan is approved; (7) the Lender and its agents, brokers, insurers, servicers, successors and assigns may continuously rely on the information contained in the application, and I am obligated to amend and/or supplement the information provided in this application if any of the material facts that I have represented herein should change prior to closing of the Loan; (8) in the event that my payments on the Loan become delinquent, the Lender, its servicers, successors or assigns may, in addition to any other rights and remedies that it may have relating to such delinquency, report my name and account information to one or more consumer reporting agencies; (9) ownership of the Loan and/or administration of the Loan account may be transferred with such notice as may be required by law; (10) neither Lender nor its agents, brokers, insurers, servicers, successors or assigns has made any representation or warranty, express or implied, to me regarding the property or the condition or value of the property; and (11) my transmission of this application as an "electronic record" containing my "electronic signature," as those terms are defined in applicable federal and/or state laws (excluding audio and video recordings), or my facsimile transmission of this application containing a facsimile of my signature, shall be as effective, enforceable and valid as if a paper version of this application were delivered containing my original written signature.

Acknowledgement. Each of the undersigned hereby acknowledges that any owner of the Loan, its servicers, successors and assigns, may verify or reverify any information contained in this application or obtain any information or data relating to the Loan, for any legitimate business purpose through any source, including a source named in this application or a consumer reporting agency.

Borrower's Signature X	Date	Co-Borrower's Signature X	Date

X. INFORMATION FOR GOVERNMENT MONITORING PURPOSES

The following information is requested by the Federal Government for certain types of loans related to a dwelling in order to monitor the lender's compliance with equal credit opportunity, fair housing and home mortgage disclosure laws. You are not required to furnish this information, but are encouraged to do so. The law provides that a lender may not discriminate either on the basis of this information, or on whether you choose to furnish it. If you furnish the information, please provide both ethnicity and race. For race, you may check more than one designation. If you do not furnish ethnicity, race, or sex, under Federal regulations, this lender is required to note the information on the basis of visual observation and surname if you have made this application in person. If you do not wish to furnish the information, please check the box below. (Lender must review the above material to assure that the disclosures satisfy all requirements to which the lender is subject under applicable state law for the particular type of loan applied for.)

BORROWER ☐ I do not wish to furnish this information	CO-BORROWER ☐ I do not wish to furnish this information
Ethnicity: ☐ Hispanic or Latino ☐ Not Hispanic or Latino	**Ethnicity:** ☐ Hispanic or Latino ☐ Not Hispanic or Latino
Race: ☐ American Indian or Alaska Native ☐ Asian ☐ Black or African American ☐ Native Hawaiian or Other Pacific Islander ☐ White	**Race:** ☐ American Indian or Alaska Native ☐ Asian ☐ Black or African American ☐ Native Hawaiian or Other Pacific Islander ☐ White
Sex: ☐ Female ☐ Male	**Sex:** ☐ Female ☐ Male

To be Completed by Loan Originator:
This information was provided:
☐ In a face-to-face interview
☐ In a telephone interview
☐ By the applicant and submitted by fax or mail
☐ By the applicant and submitted via e-mail or the Internet

Loan Originator's Signature X		Date
Loan Originator's Name (print or type)	Loan Originator Identifier	Loan Originator's Phone Number (including area code)
Loan Origination Company's Name	Loan Origination Company Identifier	Loan Origination Company's Address

Uniform Residential Loan Application

CONTINUATION SHEET/RESIDENTIAL LOAN APPLICATION		
Use this continuation sheet if you need more space to complete the Residential Loan Application. Mark **B** f or Borrower or **C** for Co-Borrower.	Borrower:	Agency Case Number:
	Co-Borrower:	Lender Case Number:

I/We fully understand that it is a Federal crime punishable by fine or imprisonment, or both, to knowingly make any false statements concerning any of the above facts as applicable under the provisions of Title 18, United States Code, Section 1001, et seq.

Borrower's Signature	Date	Co-Borrower's Signature	Date
X		X	

Uniform Residential Loan Application
Freddie Mac Form 65   7/05 (rev.6/09)

Fannie Mae Form 1003   7/05 (rev.6/09)

STATEMENT OF ASSETS AND LIABILITIES
(Supplement to Residential Loan Application)

Name _____

The following information is provided to complete and become a part of the application for a mortgage in the amount of $ _____

with interest at ____%, for a term of _____ months and to be secured by property known as: _____

Subject Property Address (street, city, state, & ZIP)

Legal Description of Subject Property (attach description if necessary)

ASSETS AND LIABILITIES

This Statement and any applicable supporting schedules may be completed jointly by both married and unmarried Co-Borrowers if their assets and liabilities are sufficiently joined so that the Statement can be meaningfully and fairly presented on a combined basis; otherwise, separate Statements and Schedules are required. If the Co-Borrower section was completed about a non-applicant spouse or other person, this Statement and supporting schedules must be completed about that spouse or other person also.

Completed ☐ Jointly ☐ Not Jointly

ASSETS Description	Cash or Market Value	Liabilities and Pledged Assets. List the creditor's name, address, and account number for all outstanding debts, including automobile loans, revolving charge accounts, real estate loans, alimony, child support, stock pledges, etc. Use continuation sheet, if necessary. Indicate by (*) those liabilities, which will be satisfied upon sale of real estate owned or upon refinancing of the subject property.		
Cash deposit toward purchase held by:	$			
		LIABILITIES	Monthly Payment & Months Left to Pay	Unpaid Balance
List checking and savings accounts below		Name and address of Company	$ Payment/Months	$
Name and address of Bank, S&L, or Credit Union				
		Acct. no.		
Acct. no.	$	Name and address of Company	$ Payment/Months	$
Name and address of Bank, S&L, or Credit Union				
		Acct. no.		
Acct. no.	$	Name and address of Company	$ Payment/Months	$
Name and address of Bank, S&L, or Credit Union				
		Acct. no.		
Acct. no.	$	Name and address of Company	$ Payment/Months	$
Name and address of Bank, S&L, or Credit Union				
		Acct. no.		
Acct. no.	$	Name and address of Company	$ Payment/Months	$
Stocks & Bonds (Company name/number description)	$			
		Acct. no.		
Life insurance net cash value	$	Name and address of Company	$ Payment/Months	$
Face amount: $				
Subtotal Liquid Assets	$			
Real estate owned (enter market value from schedule of real estate owned)	$			
Vested interest in retirement fund	$			

ASSETS AND LIABILITIES (cont'd)

Net worth of business(es) owned (attach financial statement)	$	Acct. no.			
Automobiles owned (make and year)	$	Alimony/Child Support/Separate Maintenance Payments Owed to:	$		
Other Assets (itemize)	$	Job-Related Expense (child care, union dues, etc.)	$		
		Total Monthly Payments	$		
Total Assets a.	$	Net Worth (a minus b) ▶	$	Total Liabilities b.	$

Schedule of Real Estate Owned (If additional properties are owned, use continuation sheet.)

Property Address (enter S if sold, PS if pending sale or R if rental being held for income)		Type of Property	Present Market Value	Amount of Mortgages & Liens	Gross Rental Income	Mortgage Payments	Insurance, Maintenance, Taxes & Misc.	Net Rental Income
	▼		$	$	$	$	$	$
		Totals	$	$	$	$	$	$

List any additional names under which credit has previously been received and indicate appropriate creditor name(s) and account number(s):

Alternate Name	Creditor Name	Account Number

ACKNOWLEDGEMENT AND AGREEMENT

Each of the undersigned specifically represents to Lender and to Lender's actual or potential agents, brokers, processors, attorneys, insurers, servicers, successors and assigns and agrees and acknowledges that: (1) the information provided in this application is true and correct as of the date set forth opposite my signature and that any intentional or negligent misrepresentation of this information contained in this application may result in civil liability, including monetary damages, to any person who may suffer any loss due to reliance upon any misrepresentation that I have made on this application, and/or in criminal penalties including, but not limited to, fine or imprisonment or both under the provisions of Title 18, United States Code, Sec. 1001, et seq.; (2) the loan requested pursuant to this application (the "Loan") will be secured by a mortgage or deed of trust on the property described in this application; (3) the property will not be used for any illegal or prohibited purpose or use; (4) all statements made in this application are made for the purpose of obtaining a residential mortgage loan; (5) the property will be occupied as indicated in this application; (6) the Lender, its servicers, successors or assigns may retain the original and/or an electronic record of this application, whether or not the Loan is approved; (7) the Lender and its agents, brokers, insurers, servicers, successors, and assigns may continuously rely on the information contained in the application, and I am obligated to amend and/or supplement the information provided in this application if any of the material facts that I have represented herein should change prior to closing of the Loan; (8) in the event that my payments on the Loan become delinquent, the Lender, its servicers, successors or assigns may, in addition to any other rights and remedies that it may have relating to such delinquency, report my name and account information to one or more consumer reporting agencies; (9) ownership of the Loan and/or administration of the Loan account may be transferred with such notice as may be required by law; (10) neither Lender nor its agents, brokers, insurers, servicers, successors or assigns has made any representation or warranty, express or implied, to me regarding the property or the condition or value of the property; and (11) my transmission of this application as an "electronic record" containing my "electronic signature," as those terms are defined in applicable federal and/or state laws (excluding audio and video recordings), or my facsimile transmission of this application containing a facsimile of my signature, shall be as effective, enforceable and valid as if a paper version of this application were delivered containing my original written signature.

Acknowledgement. Each of the undersigned hereby acknowledges that any owner of the Loan, its servicers, successors and assigns, may verify or reverify any information contained in this application or obtain any information or data relating to the Loan, for any legitimate business purpose through any source, including a source named in this application or a consumer reporting agency.

Borrower's Signature	Date	Co-Borrower's Signature	Date
X		X	

TO BE COMPLETED BY INTERVIEWER

This application was taken by: ☐ Face-to-face interview ☐ Mail ☐ Telephone ☐ Internet	Interviewer's Name (print or type)	Name and Address of Interviewer's Employer
	Interviewer's Signature Date	
	Interviewer's Phone Number (incl. area code)	

Instructions

Statement of Assets & Liabilities

The lender uses this form to record relevant financial information regarding a co-borrower's assets and liabilities in any instance in which the borrower's and co-borrower's assets and liabilities are not sufficiently joined to make a combined statement meaningful.

Lenders must use this form on and after 1/1/06.

Copies
Original, plus one.

Printing Instructions
We provide Form 1003A in an electronic format that prints as a letter size document. However, lenders may print Form 1003A as a legal size document or with different fonts or margins that may affect pagination; we have no specific standards for the number or size of pages the form may have. Consequently, the number and size of pages will not affect compliance with Fannie Mae requirements pertaining to use of the Uniform Residential Loan Application, provided that the content of the form has not been materially altered. When printing this form, you must use the "shrink to fit" option in the Adobe Acrobat print dialogue box.

Instructions
When a Form 1003A is completed, it should be attached to the Uniform Residential Loan Application (Form 1003) to assure that the co-borrower's assets and liabilities are considered along with those of the borrower.

All instructions for completing the "Assets and Liabilities," "Acknowledgment and Agreement," and "To Be Completed By Reviewer" portions of Form 1003 also apply to Form 1003A.

Instructions Page

PROVIDING THE LOAN ESTIMATE

The **Loan Estimate** is a good-faith estimate of credit costs and transaction terms that replaces the HUD Good Faith Estimate (GFE) and the "early" Truth in Lending disclosure. The Loan Estimate form is designed to highlight the most important information that borrowers need on the first page (e.g., interest rate, monthly payment, and the closing costs). This will make it easier for borrowers to compare loans and choose the one that is right for them.

The lender is generally required to provide the Loan Estimate within 3 business days of the receipt of the borrower's loan application. However, if a lender determines within the 3-business-day period the borrower's application will not or cannot be approved on the terms requested by the borrower, or if it the application is withdrawn within that period, the lender does not have to provide the Loan Estimate.

Business Day

The definition of "**business day**" varies from form to form, and from use to use. Sometimes Saturday is counted as a business day, but sometimes it is not. For purposes of timing the delivery of the Loan Estimate, the general definition of business day is used. However, the specific definition of business day applies to the right of rescission and for counting both the 3- and 7-day waiting periods.

General Definition. A business day is a day on which the lender's offices are open to the public for carrying out substantially all of its business functions.

Specific Definition. A business day means all calendar days except Sundays and the Federal legal public holidays. [12 CFR §1026.2(a)(6)]. The ten legal holidays specified in 5 U.S.C. 6103(a)) include New Year's Day, the birthdays of George Washington and Martin Luther King, Jr., Memorial Day, Independence Day, Labor Day, Columbus Day, Veterans Day, Thanksgiving Day, and Christmas Day.

Rate Lock

Borrowers may choose to lock in their interest rate with a rate lock or rate commitment. A **rate lock** is a lender's promise to hold a certain interest rate and a certain number of points for the applicant, usually for a specified period of time, while the loan application is processed. This may be done at the same time they file the application, during processing of the loan, when the loan is approved, or later.

Borrower's Intention to Proceed

Before actual loan processing can begin, borrowers must communicate their intention to proceed with the loan. After the Loan Estimate has been delivered, borrowers indicate their intention to proceed with the transaction by communicating that intention to the lender or other person, such as a mortgage loan originator. The communication can be made in person, over the phone, via email, or by signing a pre-printed form after receipt of the Loan Estimate. However, a borrower's silence does not indicate an intention to proceed.

Once the Loan Estimate is delivered and the borrower has agreed to proceed with the loan, the next phase—loan processing—may begin.

PREPARING THE LOAN PACKAGE

Once the borrower completes the application, the loan processing begins. **Loan processing** is described as the steps taken by a lender from the time the application is received to the time the loan is approved. The person in charge of processing the loan is known as a loan processor. The **loan processor** performs clerical or support duties as an employee under the direction of a licensed mortgage loan originator or an exempt lender. The first step in the loan process is to gather information and prepare the loan package.

Just as the escrow officer monitors escrow deadlines, the loan processor makes sure that the all of the financing deadlines are met. As long as the processor and borrower stay in touch, and are both committed to creating and processing the loan package quickly, it can often be done quite efficiently.

Order Reports and Services

An important duty of the loan processor is to order a credit report and contact service professionals needed to close the loan, such as an appraiser and a title company.

Credit History

The first thing the processor usually does is to order a credit report and review the potential borrower's credit history to ensure that he or she is a good credit risk.

A loan processor is in charge of checking the credit history of potential borrowers. If any credit issues are found, such as bankruptcies, late payments, or problems with property, the processor usually notifies the applicant. The applicant can provide an explanation of the credit issues or dispute them if they are incorrect.

Order Appraisal

The loan processor orders an appraisal of the property to verify the value of the home. The processor requires the borrower to contact the appraiser to schedule a convenient date and time for the home appraisal.

Order Title Search

If not already ordered by the escrow officer, the processor orders a title search through a title company in the area, which verifies that the property is free of liens that could hold up the closing.

Gather Documents

The loan processor also must gather important documentation from the borrowers in order to process the loan. That includes pay stubs, W-2s, past tax returns, bank statements and lists of assets. Borrowers must also provide proof of all other sources of income, like retirement or rental income to support their income statements on the loan.

Verification Letters

The processor also sends out the necessary verification letters to confirm the borrower's employment, income, bank accounts and other liquid assets, and any other claims made by the borrower that must be verified. Typical verification letters include the Verification of Deposit (VOD) and Verification of Employment (VOE).

The **VOD** is a form completed by the borrower's bank to confirm the status and balance of the borrower's bank accounts.

The **VOE** is a form completed by the borrower's employer to confirm the borrower's employment and employment history.

The processor who is confirming information regarding the borrower of a VA loan must send out a Request for Certificate of Eligibility (COE) in addition to the aforementioned verification letters. The **COE** is a form completed by the VA that confirms the borrower is sufficiently entitled to a VA loan.

The processor then compares the information on the returned verifications with the borrower's loan application to make sure they are the same. If not, the borrower is asked to explain the differences.

◢ FannieMae

Request for Verification of Deposit

Privacy Act Notice: This information is to be used by the agency collecting it or its assignees in determining whether you qualify as a prospective mortgagor under its program. It will not be disclosed outside the agency except as required and permitted by law. You do not have to provide this information, but if you do not your application for approval as a prospective mortgagor or borrower may be delayed or rejected. The information requested in this form is authorized by Title 38, USC, Chapter 37 (If VA); by 12 USC, Section 1701 et.seq. (If HUD/FHA); by 42 USC, Section 1452b (if HUD/CPD); and Title 42 USC, 1471 et.seq. or 7 USC, 1921 et.seq. (If USDA/FmHA).

Instructions: Lender — Complete Items 1 through 8. Have applicant(s) complete Item 9. Forward directly to depository named in Item 1.
Depository — Please complete Items 10 through 18 and return DIRECTLY to lender named in Item 2.
The form is to be transmitted directly to the lender and is not to be transmitted through the applicant(s) or any other party.

Part I — Request

1. To (Name and address of depository)	2. From (Name and address of lender)

I certify that this verification has been sent directly to the bank or depository and has not passed through the hands of the applicant or any other party.

3. Signature of lender	4. Title	5. Date	6. Lender's No. (Optional)

7. Information To Be Verified

Type of Account	Account in Name of	Account Number	Balance
			$
			$
			$

To Depository: I/We have applied for a mortgage loan and stated in my financial statement that the balance on deposit with you is as shown above. You are authorized to verify this information and to supply the lender identified above with the information requested in Items 10 through 13. Your response is solely a matter of courtesy for which no responsibility is attached to your institution or any of your officers.

8. Name and Address of Applicant(s)	9. Signature of Applicant(s)

To Be Completed by Depository
Part II — Verification of Depository

10. Deposit Accounts of Applicant(s)

Type of Account	Account Number	Current Balance	Average Balance For Previous Two Months	Date Opened
		$	$	
		$	$	
		$	$	

11. Loans Outstanding To Applicant(s)

Loan Number	Date of Loan	Original Amount	Current Balance	Installments (Monthly/Quarterly)		Secured By	Number of Late Payments
		$	$	$	per		
		$	$	$	per		
		$	$	$	per		

12. Please include any additional information which may be of assistance in determination of credit worthiness. (Please include information on loans paid-in-full in Item 11 above.)

13. If the name(s) on the account(s) differ from those listed in Item 7, please supply the name(s) on the account(s) as reflected by your records.

Part III — Authorized Signature - Federal statutes provide severe penalties for any fraud, intentional misrepresentation, or criminal connivance or conspiracy purposed to influence the issuance of any guaranty or insurance by the VA Secretary, the U.S.D.A., FmHA/FHA Commissioner, or the HUD/CPD Assistant Secretary.

14. Signature of Depository Representative	15. Title (Please print or type)	16. Date

17. Please print or type name signed in item 14	18. Phone No.

Fannie Mae
Form 1006   July 96

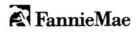 **FannieMae**

Request for Verification of Employment

Privacy Act Notice: This information is to be used by the agency collecting it or its assignees in determining whether you qualify as a prospective mortgagor under its program. It will not be disclosed outside the agency except as required and permitted by law. You do not have to provide this information, but if you do not your application for approval as a prospective mortgagor or borrower may be delayed or rejected. The information requested in this form is authorized by Title 38, USC, Chapter 37 (if VA); by 12 USC, Section 1701 et. seq. (if HUD/FHA); by 42 USC, Section 1452b (if HUD/CPD); and Title 42 USC, 1471 et. seq., or 7 USC, 1921 et. seq. (if USDA/FmHA).

Instructions: **Lender** — Complete items 1 through 7. Have applicant complete item 8. Forward directly to employer named in item 1.
Employer — Please complete either Part II or Part III as applicable. Complete Part IV and return directly to lender named in item 2.
The form is to be transmitted directly to the lender and is not to be transmitted through the applicant or any other party.

Part I — Request

1. To (Name and address of employer)	2. From (Name and address of lender)

I certify that this verification has been sent directly to the employer and has not passed through the hands of the applicant or any other interested party.

3. Signature of Lender	4. Title	5. Date	6. Lender's Number (Optional)

I have applied for a mortgage loan and stated that I am now or was formerly employed by you. My signature below authorizes verification of this information.

7. Name and Address of Applicant (include employee or badge number)	8. Signature of Applicant

Part II — Verification of Present Employment

9. Applicant's Date of Employment	10. Present Position	11. Probability of Continued Employment

12A. Current Gross Base Pay (Enter Amount and Check Period)
☐ Annual ☐ Hourly ☐ Monthly ☐ Other (Specify) $ _____ ☐ Weekly

13. For Military Personnel Only Pay Grade

Type	Monthly Amount
Base Pay	$
Rations	$
Flight or Hazard	$
Clothing	$
Quarters	$
Pro Pay	$
Overseas or Combat	$
Variable Housing Allowance	$

14. If Overtime or Bonus is Applicable, Is Its Continuance Likely?
Overtime ☐ Yes ☐ No   Bonus ☐ Yes ☐ No

15. If paid hourly — average hours per week

16. Date of applicant's next pay increase

17. Projected amount of next pay increase

18. Date of applicant's last pay increase

19. Amount of last pay increase

12B. Gross Earnings

Type	Year To Date	Past Year	Past Year
Base Pay	Thru _____ $	$	$
Overtime	$	$	$
Commissions	$	$	$
Bonus	$	$	$
Total	$ 0.00	$ 0.00	$ 0.00

20. Remarks (If employee was off work for any length of time, please indicate time period and reason)

Part III — Verification of Previous Employment

21. Date Hired	23. Salary/Wage at Termination Per (Year) (Month) (Week)
22. Date Terminated	Base _____ Overtime _____ Commissions _____ Bonus _____
24. Reason for Leaving	25. Position Held

Part IV — Authorized Signature
Federal statutes provide severe penalties for any fraud, intentional misrepresentation, or criminal connivance or conspiracy purposed to influence the issuance of any guaranty or insurance by the VA Secretary, the U.S.D.A., FmHA/FHA Commissioner, or the HUD/CPD Assistant Secretary.

26. Signature of Employer	27. Title (Please print or type)	28. Date
29. Print or type name signed in Item 26	30. Phone No.	

Fannie Mae
Form 1005   July 96

OMB Control No. 2900-0086
Respondent Burden: 15 minutes
Expiration Date: 10-31-2017

VA Department of Veterans Affairs	**FOR VA USE ONLY** **COE REF. NO.**	**MAIL COMPLETED APPLICATION TO:** **Atlanta Regional Loan Center** **Attn: COE (262)** **P. O. Box 100034** **Decatur, GA 30031**
REQUEST FOR A CERTIFICATE OF ELIGIBILITY		

NOTE: Please read information on reverse before completing this form. If additional space is required, attach a separate sheet.

1. NAME OF VETERAN *(First, Middle, Last)*	2. DATE OF BIRTH	3. SOCIAL SECURITY NUMBER

4A. DID YOU SERVE UNDER ANOTHER NAME? ☐ YES ☐ NO *(If "Yes," complete Item 4B)*	4B. NAME(S) USED DURING MILITARY SERVICE *(If different from name in Item 1)*

5. DAYTIME TELEPHONE NUMBER	6. E-MAIL ADDRESS *(If applicable)*

7A. ADDRESS *(Number and street or rural route, city or P.O., State and ZIP Code)*	7B. MAIL CERTIFICATE OF ELIGIBILITY TO: *(Complete ONLY if the Certificate is to be mailed to an address different from the one listed in Item 7A.)*

8A. WERE YOU DISCHARGED, RETIRED, OR SEPARATED FROM SERVICE BECAUSE OF DISABILITY? ☐ YES ☐ NO	8B. VA CLAIM NUMBER *(If known)*

MILITARY SERVICE (SEE INSTRUCTIONS FOR PROOF OF SERVICE ON THE NEXT PAGE)

9A. ARE YOU CURRENTLY ON ACTIVE DUTY? *(If you currently serving on active duty, leave the "Date Separated" field blank.)*
☐ YES ☐ NO

	BRANCH OF SERVICE	DATE ENTERED	DATE SEPARATED	OFFICER OR ENLISTED	SERVICE NUMBER *(if different from Social Security Number)*
IMPORTANT: Please provide your dates of service. In many cases eligibility can be established based on data in VA systems. However, it is recommended that proof of service be provided, if readily available. Proof of service is required for persons who entered service after September 7, 1980 and were discharged after serving less than 2 years.					
9B. ACTIVE SERVICE - *Do not include any periods of Active Duty for Training or Active Guard Reserve service. Do include any activation for duty under Title 10 U.S.C. (e.g. Reserve or Guard unit mobilized.)*					
9C. RESERVE OR NATIONAL GUARD SERVICE *Include any periods of Active Duty for Training (ADT) or Active Guard Reserve service. Do not include any activation for duty under Title 10 U.S.C. (e.g. Reserve or Guard unit mobilized.)*					

PREVIOUS VA LOANS (SEE INSTRUCTIONS ON THE NEXT PAGE - Attach a separate sheet if information for all homes will not fit in Item 10)

10A. DO YOU NOW OWN ANY HOME(S) PURCHASED OR REFINANCED WITH A VA-GUARANTEED LOAN? ☐ YES *(If "Yes," complete Items 10B through 10D)* ☐ NO *(If "No," skip to Item 14)* ☐ NOT APPLICABLE (NA) - I HAVE NEVER OBTAINED A VA-GUARANTEED HOME LOAN *(If "NA," skip to Item 14)*	10B. DATE OF LOAN *(Month and Year)*	10C. STREET ADDRESS	10D. CITY AND STATE
11A. ARE YOU APPLYING FOR THE **ONE-TIME ONLY RESTORATION** OF ENTITLEMENT TO PURCHASE ANOTHER HOME? ☐ YES ☐ NO *(If "Yes," complete Items 11B through 11D)*	11B. DATE OF LOAN *(Month and Year)*	11C. STREET ADDRESS	11D. CITY AND STATE
12A. ARE YOU APPLYING FOR A RESTORATION OF ENTITLEMENT TO OBTAIN A **REGULAR (CASH-OUT) REFINANCE** ON YOUR CURRENT HOME? ☐ YES ☐ NO *(If "Yes," complete Items 12B through 12D)*	12B. DATE OF LOAN *(Month and Year)*	12C. STREET ADDRESS	12D. CITY AND STATE
13A. ARE YOU REFINANCING AN EXISTING VA LOAN TO OBTAIN A LOWER INTEREST RATE **WITHOUT RECEIVING** ANY CASH PROCEEDS (IRRRL)? ☐ YES ☐ NO *(If "Yes," complete Items 13B through 13D)*	13B. DATE OF LOAN *(Month and Year)*	13C. STREET ADDRESS	13D. CITY AND STATE

I CERTIFY THAT the statements in this document are true and complete to the best of my knowledge.

14A. SIGNATURE OF VETERAN *(Do NOT print)*	14B. DATE SIGNED

FEDERAL STATUTES PROVIDE SEVERE PENALTIES FOR FRAUD, INTENTIONAL MISREPRESENTATION, CRIMINAL CONNIVANCE OR CONSPIRACY PURPOSED TO INFLUENCE THE ISSUANCE OF ANY GUARANTY OR INSURANCE BY THE SECRETARY OF VETERANS AFFAIRS

FOR VA USE ONLY *(Please do not write below this line)*	DATE RETURNED
REASON(S) FOR RETURN	

VA FORM
NOV 2014   **26-1880**   SUPERSEDES VA FORM 26-1880, MAR 2011,
                              WHICH WILL NOT BE USED.

INSTRUCTIONS FOR VA FORM 26-1880

PRIVACY ACT NOTICE: VA will not disclose information collected on this form to any source other than what has been authorized under the Privacy Act of 1974 or Title 38, Code of Federal Regulations 1.576 for routine uses (i.e., to a member of Congress inquiring on your behalf) identified in the VA system of records, 55VA26, Loan Guaranty Home, Condominium and Manufactured Home Loan Applicant Records, Specially Adapted Housing Applicant Records, and Vendee Loan Applicant Records - VA, and published in the Federal Register. Your obligation to respond is required in order to determine the veteran's qualifications for a loan.

RESPONDENT BURDEN: This information is needed to help determine a veteran's qualifications for a VA -guaranteed home loan. Title 38, U.S.C., section 3702, authorizes collection of this information. We estimate that you will need an average of 15 minutes to review the instructions, find the information, and complete this form. VA cannot conduct or sponsor a collection of information unless a valid OMB control number is displayed. You are not required to respond to a collection of information if this number is not displayed. Valid OMB control numbers can be located on the OMB Internet Page at www.whitehouse.gov/omb/library/OMBINV.VA.EPA.html#VA. If desired, you can call 1-800-827-1000 to get information on where to send your comments or suggestions about this form.

A. Mail this completed form, along with proof of service, to the Eligibility Center at P.O. Box 20729, Winston-Salem, NC 27120.

B. Military Service Requirements for VA Loan Eligibility: (NOTE: Cases involving other than honorable discharges will usually require further development by VA. This is necessary to determine if the service was under other than dishonorable conditions.)

1. Wartime Service. If you served anytime during World War II (September 16, 1940 to July 25, 1947), Korean Conflict (June 27, 1950 to January 31, 1955), or Vietnam Era (August 5, 1964 to May 7, 1975) you must have served at least 90 days on active duty and have been discharged or released under other than . dishonorable conditions. If you served less than 90 days, you may be eligible if discharged because of service-connected disability.

2. Peacetime Service. If your service fell entirely within one of the following periods: July 26, 1947 to June 26, 1950, or February 1, 1955 to August 4, 1964, you must have served at least 181 days of continuous active duty and have been discharged or released under conditions other than dishonorable. If you entered service after May 7, 1975 but prior to September 8, 1980 (enlisted) or October 17, 1981 (officer) and completed your service before August 2, 1990, 181 days service is also required. If you served less than 181 days, you may be eligible if discharged for a service-connected disability.

3. Service after September 7, 1980 (enlisted) or October 16, 1981 (officer) and prior to August 2, 1990. If you were separated from service which began after these dates, you must have: (a) Completed 24 months of continuous active duty for the full period (at least 181 days) for which you were called or ordered to active duty, and been discharged or released under conditions other than dishonorable; or (b) Completed at least 181 days of active duty and been discharged under the specific authority of 10 U.S.C. 1173 (hardship discharge) or 10 U.S.C. 1171 (early out discharge), or have been determined to have a compensable service-connected disability; or (c) Been discharged with less than 181 days of service for a service-connected disability. Individuals may also be eligible if they were released from active duty due to an involuntary reduction in force, certain medical conditions, or, in some instances for the convenience of the Government.

4. Gulf War. If you served on active duty during the Gulf War (August 2, 1990 to a date yet to be determined), you must have: (a) Completed 24 months of continuous active duty or the full period (at least 90 days) for which you were called or ordered to active duty, and been discharged or released under conditions other than dishonorable; or (b) Completed at least 90 days of active duty and been discharged under the specific authority of 10 U.S.C. 1173 (hardship discharge), or 10 U.S.C. 1171 (early out discharge), or have been determined to have a compensable service-connected disability; or (c) Been discharged with less than 90 days of service for a service-connected disability. Individuals may also be eligible if they were released from active duty due to an involuntary reduction in force, certain medical conditions, or, in some instances, for the convenience of the Government.

5. Active Duty Service Personnel. If you are now on active duty, you are eligible after having served on continuous active duty for at least 181 days (90 days during the Persian Gulf War) unless discharged or separated from a previous qualifying period of active duty service.

6. Selected Reserve Requirements for VA Loan Eligibility. If you are not otherwise eligible and you have completed a total of 6 years in the Selected Reserves or National Guard (member of an active unit, attended required weekend drills and 2-week active duty training) and (a) Were discharged with an honorable discharge; or (b) Were placed on the retired list or (c) Were transferred to the Standby Reserve or an element of the Ready Reserve other than the Selected Reserve after service characterized as honorable service; or (d) Continue to serve in the Selected Reserve. Individuals who completed less than 6 years may be eligible if discharged for a service-connected disability.

C. Unmarried surviving spouses of eligible veterans seeking determination of basic eligibility for VA Loan Guaranty benefits are NOT required to complete this form, but are required to complete VA Form 26-1817, Request for Determination of Loan Guaranty Eligibility-Unmarried Surviving Spouse.

D. Proof of Military Service

1. "Regular" Veterans. Attach to this request your most recent discharge or separation papers from active military duty since September 16, 1940, which show active duty dates and type of discharge. If you were separated after January 1, 1950, DD Form 214 must be submitted. If you were separated after October 1, 1979, and you received DD Form 214, Certificate of Release or Discharge From Active Duty, 1 July edition, VA must be furnished Copy 4 of the form. You may submit either original papers or legible copies. In addition, if you are now on active duty submit a statement of service signed by, or by direction of, the adjutant, personnel officer, or commander of your unit or higher headquarters showing date of entry on your current active duty period and the duration of any time lost. Any Veterans Services Representative in the nearest Department of Veterans Affairs office or center will assist you in securing necessary proof of military service.

2. Selected Reserves/National Guard. If you are a discharged member of the Army or Air Force National Guard you may submit a NGB Form 22, Report of Separation and Record of Service, or NGB Form 23, Retirement Points Accounting, or it's equivalent (this is similar to a retirement points summary). If you are a discharged member of the Selected Reserve you may submit a copy of your latest annual point statement and evidence of honorable service. You may submit either your original papers or legible copies. Since there is no single form used by the Reserves or National Guard similar to the DD Form 214, it is your responsibility to furnish adequate documentation of at least 6 years of honorable service. In addition, if you are currently serving in the Selected Reserve you must submit a statement of service signed by, or by the direction of, the adjutant, personnel officer or commander of your unit or higher headquarters showing the length of time that you have been a member of the unit.

VA FORM 26-1880, APR 2008

> ### Review – Preparing the Loan Package
> - Order the appraisal
> - Order the credit report
> - Send out employment, income, and bank account verifications
> - Verify information

Automatic Underwriting

Lenders may automate some of the steps of the lending process using automated underwriting (AU). Lenders use AU systems to evaluate quickly a wide range of information such as consumer credit history, property information, and loan type to determine the probability that the borrower will repay the loan. Credit bureau scores are used in AU to indicate consumer credit history, and, therefore, are a primary factor in the evaluation of real estate loan applications.

Check Accuracy of the Loan Package

The loan processor must be sure that all of the documents required for the loan package are present and in proper order. It is the loan processor's job to ensure that all of the information in the loan package is correct and verified. The loan processor also needs to double-check all numbers to make sure that there are no accounting mistakes.

Most processors use a loan application checklist to be sure that all of the documents in the loan package are complete. Once everything is in order, the loan application is ready for loan underwriting, which is a process to determine if the loan will be approved or denied.

FORM 9

REQUEST FOR VERIFICATION OF RENT OR MORTGAGE

We have received an application for a loan from the applicant listed below, to whom we understand you rent or have extended a loan.

INSTRUCTIONS: LENDER- Complete items 1 thru 8. Have applicant(s) complete item 9. Forward directly to lender named in item 1.
LANDLORD/CREDITOR- Please complete Part II as applicable. Sign and return directly to the lender named in item 2.

PART I - REQUEST

1.TO (Name and address of Landlord/Creditor)	2. FROM (Name and address of lender)

3.SIGNATURE OF LENDER	4. TITLE	5.DATE	6.LENDERS NUMBER

7. INFORMATION TO BE VERIFIED

	PROPERTY ADDRESS	ACCOUNT IN THE NAME OF:	ACCOUNT NO.
_____MORTGAGE			
_____LAND CONTRACT			
_____RENTAL			
_____OTHER			

8.NAME AND ADDRESS OF APPLICANT(S)	9. SIGNATURE OF APPLICANT(S)

PART II – TO BE COMPLETED BY LANDLORD/CREDITOR

RENTAL ACCOUNT

Tenant has rented since _____

To _____

Amount of rent $ _____ per _____

Is rent in arrears ? Yes _____ No _____

Number of times 30 days past due* _____

Is account satisfactory ? Yes _____ No_____

_____

_____MORTGAGE ACCOUNT   _____ LAND CONTRACT

Date mortgage originated _____   Interest rate _____

Original mortgage amount $ _____   FIXED_____ ARM_____

Current mortgage balance $ _____   FHA_____ VA_____

Monthly Payment P & I only $ _____   FNMA_____ CONV_____

Payment with taxes and ins. $ _____   Next pay date _____

Is mortgage current ? Yes_____ No_____   No of late payments*_____

Is mortgage assumable ? Yes_____ No _____   Insurance agent: _____

Satisfactory account ? Yes _____ No _____   _____

* Number of times account has been 30 days overdue in the last 12 months

ADDITIONAL INFORMATION WHICH MAY BE OF ASSISTANCE IN DETERMINING APPLICANT(S) CREDIT WORTHINESS

SIGNATURE OF CREDITOR	TITLE	DATE

The confidentiality of the information you have furnished will be preserved except where disclosure of this information is requires by applicable law. The form is to be transmitted directly to the lender and is not to be transmitted through the applicant or any other party.

GFI- form VOM rev. 6-5-2002

1

AUTHORIZATION FOR THE SOCIAL SECURITY ADMINISTRATION TO RELEASE SOCIAL SECURITY NUMBER VERIFICATION

Printed Name: _____ SSN: _____

Date of Birth: _____

I authorize the Social Security Administration to verify my social security number to

_____ through their agent, _____.

I understand that my consent allows no additional information from my Social Security records

to be provided to _____ and that the verification of my Social Security

Number may not be used for any other purpose other than the one stated above, including

resale or redisclosure to other parties.   The only other redisclosure permitted by this

authorization is for review purposes to insure that _____ complies

with SSA's consent requirements.

I am the individual to whom the Social Security Number was issued or that person's legal

guardian.   I declare and affirm under the penalty of perjury that the information contained

herein is true and correct.   I know that if I make any representation that I know is false to

obtain information from Social Security records, I could be found guilty of a misdemeanor and

fined up to $5,000.

Signature: _____ Date Signed: _____

This consent is valid only for 90 days from the date signed, unless indicated otherwise by the individual named above.

Contact information of individual signing authorization:

Address: _____

_____

Phone Number: _____

If consent is signed other than by the individual named above, indicate relationship:

_____

Form **4506**

(Rev. September 2013)

Department of the Treasury
Internal Revenue Service

Request for Copy of Tax Return

▶ **Request may be rejected if the form is incomplete or illegible.**

OMB No. 1545-0429

Tip. You may be able to get your tax return or return information from other sources. If you had your tax return completed by a paid preparer, they should be able to provide you a copy of the return. The IRS can provide a **Tax Return Transcript** for many returns free of charge. The transcript provides most of the line entries from the original tax return and usually contains the information that a third party (such as a mortgage company) requires. See **Form 4506-T, Request for Transcript of Tax Return**, or you can quickly request transcripts by using our automated self-help service tools. Please visit us at IRS.gov and click on "Order a Return or Account Transcript" or call 1-800-908-9946.

1a Name shown on tax return. If a joint return, enter the name shown first.	**1b** First social security number on tax return, individual taxpayer identification number, or employer identification number (see instructions)
2a If a joint return, enter spouse's name shown on tax return.	**2b** Second social security number or individual taxpayer identification number if joint tax return

3 Current name, address (including apt., room, or suite no.), city, state, and ZIP code (see instructions)

4 Previous address shown on the last return filed if different from line 3 (see instructions)

5 If the tax return is to be mailed to a third party (such as a mortgage company), enter the third party's name, address, and telephone number.

Caution. If the tax return is being mailed to a third party, ensure that you have filled in lines 6 and 7 before signing. Sign and date the form once you have filled in these lines. Completing these steps helps to protect your privacy. Once the IRS discloses your tax return to the third party listed on line 5, the IRS has no control over what the third party does with the information. If you would like to limit the third party's authority to disclose your return information, you can specify this limitation in your written agreement with the third party.

6 **Tax return requested.** Form 1040, 1120, 941, etc. and all attachments as originally submitted to the IRS, including Form(s) W-2, schedules, or amended returns. Copies of Forms 1040, 1040A, and 1040EZ are generally available for 7 years from filing before they are destroyed by law. Other returns may be available for a longer period of time. Enter only one return number. If you need more than one type of return, you must complete another Form 4506. ▶ _____

Note. If the copies must be certified for court or administrative proceedings, check here . . . . ☐

7 **Year or period requested.** Enter the ending date of the year or period, using the mm/dd/yyyy format. If you are requesting more than eight years or periods, you must attach another Form 4506.

_____   _____   _____   _____

_____   _____   _____   _____

8 **Fee.** There is a $50 fee for each return requested. **Full payment must be included with your request or it will be rejected. Make your check or money order payable to "United States Treasury." Enter your SSN, ITIN, or EIN and "Form 4506 request" on your check or money order.**

a	Cost for each return	$	**50.00**
b	Number of returns requested on line 7		
c	Total cost. Multiply line 8a by line 8b	$	

9 If we cannot find the tax return, we will refund the fee. If the refund should go to the third party listed on line 5, check here . . . . . ☐

Caution. Do not sign this form unless all applicable lines have been completed.

Signature of taxpayer(s). I declare that I am either the taxpayer whose name is shown on line 1a or 2a, or a person authorized to obtain the tax return requested. If the request applies to a joint return, at least one spouse must sign. If signed by a corporate officer, partner, guardian, tax matters partner, executor, receiver, administrator, trustee, or party other than the taxpayer, I certify that I have the authority to execute Form 4506 on behalf of the taxpayer. **Note.** For tax returns being sent to a third party, this form must be received within 120 days of the signature date.

Phone number of taxpayer on line 1a or 2a

Sign Here

▶ Signature (see instructions)   Date

▶ Title (if line 1a above is a corporation, partnership, estate, or trust)

▶ Spouse's signature   Date

For Privacy Act and Paperwork Reduction Act Notice, see page 2.   Cat. No. 41721E   Form **4506** (Rev. 9-2013)

Form 4506 (Rev. 9-2013)

Section references are to the Internal Revenue Code unless otherwise noted.

Future Developments

For the latest information about Form 4506 and its instructions, go to *www.irs.gov/form4506*. Information about any recent developments affecting Form 4506, Form 4506T and Form 4506T-EZ will be posted on that page.

General Instructions

Caution. Do not sign this form unless all applicable lines have been completed.

Purpose of form. Use Form 4506 to request a copy of your tax return. You can also designate (on line 5) a third party to receive the tax return.

How long will it take? It may take up to 75 calendar days for us to process your request.

Tip. Use Form 4506-T, Request for Transcript of Tax Return, to request tax return transcripts, tax account information, W-2 information, 1099 information, verification of non-filing, and records of account.

Automated transcript request. You can quickly request transcripts by using our automated self-help service tools. Please visit us at IRS.gov and click on "Order a Return or Account Transcript" or call 1-800-908-9946.

Where to file. Attach payment and mail Form 4506 to the address below for the state you lived in, or the state your business was in, when that return was filed. There are two address charts: one for individual returns (Form 1040 series) and one for all other returns.

If you are requesting a return for more than one year and the chart below shows two different addresses, send your request to the address based on the address of your most recent return.

Chart for individual returns (Form 1040 series)

If you filed an individual return and lived in:	Mail to:
Alabama, Kentucky, Louisiana, Mississippi, Tennessee, Texas, a foreign country, American Samoa, Puerto Rico, Guam, the Commonwealth of the Northern Mariana Islands, the U.S. Virgin Islands, or A.P.O. or F.P.O. address	Internal Revenue Service RAIVS Team Stop 6716 AUSC Austin, TX 73301
Alaska, Arizona, Arkansas, California, Colorado, Hawaii, Idaho, Illinois, Indiana, Iowa, Kansas, Michigan, Minnesota, Montana, Nebraska, Nevada, New Mexico, North Dakota, Oklahoma, Oregon, South Dakota, Utah, Washington, Wisconsin, Wyoming	Internal Revenue Service RAIVS Team Stop 37106 Fresno, CA 93888
Connecticut, Delaware, District of Columbia, Florida, Georgia, Maine, Maryland, Massachusetts, Missouri, New Hampshire, New Jersey, New York, North Carolina, Ohio, Pennsylvania, Rhode Island, South Carolina, Vermont, Virginia, West Virginia	Internal Revenue Service RAIVS Team Stop 6705 P-6 Kansas City, MO 64999

Chart for all other returns

If you lived in or your business was in:	Mail to:
Alabama, Alaska, Arizona, Arkansas, California, Colorado, Florida, Hawaii, Idaho, Iowa, Kansas, Louisiana, Minnesota, Mississippi, Missouri, Montana, Nebraska, Nevada, New Mexico, North Dakota, Oklahoma, Oregon, South Dakota, Texas, Utah, Washington, Wyoming, a foreign country, or A.P.O. or F.P.O. address	Internal Revenue Service RAIVS Team P.O. Box 9941 Mail Stop 6734 Ogden, UT 84409
Connecticut, Delaware, District of Columbia, Georgia, Illinois, Indiana, Kentucky, Maine, Maryland, Massachusetts, Michigan, New Hampshire, New Jersey, New York, North Carolina, Ohio, Pennsylvania, Rhode Island, South Carolina, Tennessee, Vermont, Virginia, West Virginia, Wisconsin	Internal Revenue Service RAIVS Team P.O. Box 145500 Stop 2800 F Cincinnati, OH 45250

Specific Instructions

Line 1b. Enter your employer identification number (EIN) if you are requesting a copy of a business return. Otherwise, enter the first social security number (SSN) or your individual taxpayer identification number (ITIN) shown on the return. For example, if you are requesting Form 1040 that includes Schedule C (Form 1040), enter your SSN.

Line 3. Enter your current address. If you use a P.O. box, please include it on this line 3.

Line 4. Enter the address shown on the last return filed if different from the address entered on line 3.

Note. If the address on Lines 3 and 4 are different and you have not changed your address with the IRS, file Form 8822, Change of Address. For a business address, file Form 8822-B, Change of Address or Responsible Party — Business.

Signature and date. Form 4506 must be signed and dated by the taxpayer listed on line 1a or 2a. If you completed line 5 requesting the return be sent to a third party, the IRS must receive Form 4506 within 120 days of the date signed by the taxpayer or it will be rejected. Ensure that all applicable lines are completed before signing.

Individuals. Copies of jointly filed tax returns may be furnished to either spouse. Only one signature is required. Sign Form 4506 exactly as your name appeared on the original return. If you changed your name, also sign your current name.

Corporations. Generally, Form 4506 can be signed by: (1) an officer having legal authority to bind the corporation, (2) any person designated by the board of directors or other governing body, or (3) any officer or employee on written request by any principal officer and attested to by the secretary or other officer.

Partnerships. Generally, Form 4506 can be signed by any person who was a member of the partnership during any part of the tax period requested on line 7.

All others. See section 6103(e) if the taxpayer has died, is insolvent, is a dissolved corporation, or if a trustee, guardian, executor, receiver, or administrator is acting for the taxpayer.

Documentation. For entities other than individuals, you must attach the authorization document. For example, this could be the letter from the principal officer authorizing an employee of the corporation or the letters testamentary authorizing an individual to act for an estate.

Signature by a representative. A representative can sign Form 4506 for a taxpayer only if this authority has been specifically delegated to the representative on Form 2848, line 5. Form 2848 showing the delegation must be attached to Form 4506.

Privacy Act and Paperwork Reduction Act Notice. We ask for the information on this form to establish your right to gain access to the requested return(s) under the Internal Revenue Code. We need this information to properly identify the return(s) and respond to your request. If you request a copy of a tax return, sections 6103 and 6109 require you to provide this information, including your SSN or EIN, to process your request. If you do not provide this information, we may not be able to process your request. Providing false or fraudulent information may subject you to penalties.

Routine uses of this information include giving it to the Department of Justice for civil and criminal litigation, and cities, states, the District of Columbia, and U.S. commonwealths and possessions for use in administering their tax laws. We may also disclose this information to other countries under a tax treaty, to federal and state agencies to enforce federal nontax criminal laws, or to federal law enforcement and intelligence agencies to combat terrorism.

You are not required to provide the information requested on a form that is subject to the Paperwork Reduction Act unless the form displays a valid OMB control number. Books or records relating to a form or its instructions must be retained as long as their contents may become material in the administration of any Internal Revenue law. Generally, tax returns and return information are confidential, as required by section 6103.

The time needed to complete and file Form 4506 will vary depending on individual circumstances. The estimated average time is: **Learning about the law or the form,** 10 min.; **Preparing the form,** 16 min.; and **Copying, assembling, and sending the form to the IRS,** 20 min.

If you have comments concerning the accuracy of these time estimates or suggestions for making Form 4506 simpler, we would be happy to hear from you. You can write to:

Internal Revenue Service
Tax Forms and Publications Division
1111 Constitution Ave. NW, IR-6526
Washington, DC 20224.

Do not send the form to this address. Instead, see *Where to file* on this page.

GIFT LETTER

Date: _____

To Whom It May Concern:

I, _____ of _____
        (Donor's Name)   (Donor's Address)

_____ , _____
     (Donor's Address Continued)   (Donor's Phone Number)

do hereby certify that I have given/will give a gift of $_____ to my

_____ , to be applied toward the purchase of the property located at

_____ .

I further certify that there is no repayment expected or implied on this gift either in the form of cash or future service from the recipient. The funds given were not made available to me from any person or entity with an interest in the sale of the property including the seller, real estate agent or broker, builder, loan officer or any entity associated with them.

NOTE: **Provide verification that the donor has withdrawn the funds from a personal account and transferred the money to the recipient (i.e.: cancelled gift check or other withdrawal document along with a copy of the check). Also show the money deposited into recipient's account.**

WARNING: **Section 1010 of title 18, U.S.C. Department of Housing and Urban Development Transactions provides. "Whoever for the purpose of influencing in any way the action of such department makes, passes, utters or published any statement knowing the same to be false shall be fined not more than $5,000.00 or imprisoned not more than two years, or both."**

Signed: _____
                    (Donor's Signature)

Notary: _____
                (Veteran's Administration Loans Only)

Signed: _____
                    (Recipient's Signature)

_____
            (Donor's Signature)

Processor's Final Checklist

☐ **Residential Loan Application—Fannie Mae/Freddie Mac form or other approved equivalent**

- Typed copy preferred
- Completed in full, including borrower's signature
- Occupancy status indicated
- Application matches verification documents

☐ **Residential Mortgage Credit Report**

- All supplements, including public records examination
- All open credit accounts listed on the loan application

☐ **Additional credit documentation**

- Direct verification included for any accounts not listed on the credit report
- Letter of explanation included for adverse items

☐ **Verification of Income, Verification of Employment (VOE)**

- VOEs covering the past 2 years' work history
- School transcripts or diploma if borrower does not have 2 years of work history
- Overtime and bonuses verified (if needed to qualify)
- Year-to-date and last year's earnings sections completed
- If borrower is relying on commission income, include 2 years' signed tax returns with schedules
- Employment gaps explained, self-employed documentation
- If borrower is self-employed, 2 years of profit and loss statements and balance sheets
- 2 years of signed tax returns with schedules
- Current and past 2 years' financial and income statements
- Income analysis forms

☐ **Verification of Deposit (VOD)**

- Verified sufficient funds for closing
- Average balance for past 2 months listed—if not, last 2 monthly statements
- Source of funds: explanation of any significant changes in account balances or any recently opened accounts or gift letter, if applicable
- Gift letter with verification of gift funds
- Gift donor must be a member of the borrower's immediate family
- Completed in full, including borrower's signature

☐ **Residential Appraisal Report—Fannie Mae/Freddie Mac form or other approved equivalent**

- Photos of subject property, street scene, and comparables
- Review appraisal included (if available)
- All addendums and explanations

☐ **Sales Contract and/or Escrow Instructions**

- Document includes all addendums and is signed by all parties
- If earnest money is equal to 50% or more of the ultimate down payment, include proof of payment, such as canceled checks or the deposit receipt

☐ **Additional documents that may be required**

- Divorce decree/separation agreement (if applicable)
- Verification of child support/alimony, if such income is being used to qualify or if borrower is obligated to pay support/alimony
- Signed construction cost breakdown (if applicable)
- Most recent 12-month payment history on previous home loans
- Rental agreements or leases (if applicable)
- Any other clarifying documents
- Bankruptcy filing statement, schedule of debt, discharge, and explanation (if applicable)

Documents must not be over 120 days old unless the property is new construction—then documents may be up to 180 days old.

Eligible alternative documentation

☐ **Verification of Employment alternatives**

- Pay stub or salary voucher for the most recent 30-day period with year-to-date earnings indicated, and

- IRS W-2 forms for the previous 2 years, and

- Documented telephone verification

☐ **Verification of Deposit alternative**

- The most recent 3 months' depository institution statements. Borrowers must, at a minimum, report the ending balance and all transactions (deposits and withdrawals)

☐ **Verification of Home Loan Payment alternatives**

- Credit report reference for the last 12 months, or

- Home loan payment history for the last 12 months, or

- Copy of all canceled checks for the most recent 12-month period

Once the loan package is complete, the lender's underwriter begins the next step in the loan approval process. The underwriter analyzes the borrower's financial and personal data and approves or disapproves the loan. If the loan is approved, it is funded and closed.

Submit Loan Package to Underwriter

When the loan processor is satisfied that the loan package is complete, he or she submits everything to an underwriter. The underwriter analyzes the borrower's financial and personal data and approves or disapproves the loan. If there is an issue with any of the paperwork or information listed, the underwriter informs the processor, who then communicates with the borrower to resolve the issue. Keep in mind that in some cases, the processor communicates all needs to the originator rather than speaking directly to the borrower.

Once the loan is approved, the processor can schedule a closing date with the borrower.

SUMMARY

The lender takes certain actions and follows certain procedures when a borrower applies for a real estate loan. The careful, lawful, and professional processing of the loan is critical to the success of a real estate lender. Processing a loan is probably the most time consuming and most important part of the loan procedure. Important information must be gathered and evaluated to determine if a loan fits the lender's required loan guidelines. A thorough analysis of this information lowers the risk of loss to investors.

Today, a standardized form called the Fannie Mae/Freddie Mac Uniform Residential Loan Application (URLA or Form 1003) is used for most residential home loans. The first thing a borrower does when applying for a loan is to complete the application and the other documents in the loan package. The lender prepares the loan package for underwriting. This package provides specific details regarding the loan.

Once the loan package is complete, the lender's underwriter begins the next step in the loan approval process. The underwriter analyzes the borrower's financial and personal data and approves or disapproves the loan.

UNIT 11 REVIEW

Matching Exercise

Instructions: Write the letter of the matching term on the blank line before its definition. Answers are in Appendix A.

Terms

A. COE
B. collateral
C. loan package
D. loan processing

E. rate lock
F. Uniform Residential Loan Application
G. VOD
H. VOE

Definitions

1. _____ Standardized form used for most residential home loans

2. _____ The file of documents the lender needs to determine whether to fund a loan

3. _____ Something of value given as security for a debt

4. _____ Lender's promise to hold a certain interest rate and a certain number of points for the applicant, usually for a specified period of time, while the loan is processed

5. _____ The steps taken by a lender from the time the application is received to the time the loan is approved

6. _____ Form completed by the borrower's bank to confirm the status and balance of the borrower's bank accounts

7. _____ Form completed by the borrower's employer to confirm the borrower's employment and employment history

8. _____ Form completed by the VA that confirms the borrower is sufficiently entitled to a VA loan

Multiple Choice Questions

Instructions: Circle your response and go to Appendix A to read the complete explanation for each question.

1. Which is not one of the four steps in obtaining a real estate loan?
    a. Underwriting
    b. Servicing
    c. Processing
    d. Completing the application

2. Typically, a loan package includes:
    a. the loan application.
    b. RESPA disclosures.
    c. verifications.
    d. both (a) and (c).

3. Which of the following is the lender's primary security for repayment of a real estate loan if the borrower defaults?
    a. Borrower's personal assets
    b. Property
    c. Borrower's promise to pay
    d. Promissory note

4. Of the following items, which is not included in the Property Information and Purpose of Loan section of Form 1003?
    a. Legal description of property
    b. Title information
    c. Photograph of property from the street
    d. Description of the land and type of improvements

5. Which section of the Uniform Residential Loan Application gives evidence that the borrower can repay the loan?
    a. Borrower Information
    b. Assets and Liabilities
    c. Employment Information
    d. Property Information and Purpose of Loan

6.   Which of the following is not included in the Monthly Income and Combined Housing Expense Information section of the Uniform Residential Loan Application?
   a. Intangible Assets
   b. Income
   c. Rents
   d. Royalties

7.   A borrower may use a rate commitment to lock in an interest rate and number of points:
   a. when the borrower files the application.
   b. during the processing of the loan.
   c. only during the lender's office hours.
   d. Both (a) and (b)

8.   The reason for inclusion of the Verification of Deposit (VOD) in the loan package is to confirm the:
   a. borrower's credit score.
   b. status and balance of the borrower's bank accounts.
   c. borrower has a stable job.
   d. borrower pays revolving accounts on time.

9.   To evaluate loan applications quickly, real estate lenders use:
   a. redlining.
   b. automated underwriting.
   c. automatic funding.
   d. distance funding.

10. Which of the following items can be used as an alternate form of documentation?
   a. Most recent 3 months' depository institution statements
   b. Average balance for past 2 months listed
   c. 2 years of signed tax returns with schedules
   d. None of the above

Underwriting

Unit 12

INTRODUCTION

The loan processor collects all the paperwork and presents the complete loan package to the underwriter. The underwriter analyzes the information in the loan package to determine if the loan will be funded.

Good underwriting is the foundation of performing loans. A **performing loan** is a loan on which the agreed-upon payments of principal and interest are current. Accurate risk assessment is basic and vital to buying affordable housing. Mistakes in risk assessment that lead to foreclosure can be devastating to borrowers, the neighborhoods in which they live, and the lenders.

All mortgage underwriting, whether traditional or automated, is based on the factors known as the three Cs. These are capacity, character, and collateral. Consistently, research has shown that a borrower with a significant financial stake in the property is less likely to default.

Learning Objectives

After completing this Unit, you should be able to:

12A   recall the underwriting process.

12B   recognize the three Cs of underwriting.

12C   recognize underwriting guidelines.

12D   recall the underwriting requirements for qualifying borrowers.

12E   specify features of credit reporting.

12F   apply the conventional, FHA, and VA underwriting guidelines to a borrower looking for a loan.

12G   recall the underwriting requirements for qualifying the collateral.

12H   identify the sections of the URAR.

WHAT LENDERS LOOK FOR

Upon receiving the loan package, the underwriter analyzes the risk factors associated with the borrower and the property before making the loan. **Underwriting** is the practice of analyzing the degree of risk involved in a real estate loan. The underwriter determines whether the borrower has the ability and willingness to repay the debt and if the property to be pledged as collateral is adequate security for the debt.

The underwriter also examines the loan package to see if it conforms to the guidelines for selling in the secondary mortgage market or directly to another permanent investor. In any case, the loan must be attractive to an investor from the perspectives of risk and profitability. If any part of the loan process is poorly done (the processing or underwriting is subpar, for example), the lender might find it difficult to sell the loan. In addition, if the borrower defaults on a carelessly underwritten loan, the loss to the real estate lender can be considerable. For example, if the appraisal is too high and the borrower defaults, the lender may sustain a loss. The probability of a loss is higher when the house is appraised at more than its actual worth because it is likely that the property will sell for less than the loan amount plus other costs of default.

The "Three Cs" of Underwriting

Lenders look for the borrower's ability and willingness to repay debt. They speak of the three Cs of underwriting: capacity, character, and collateral. If one of these components is not acceptable or if there is excessive layering of risk across components, the mortgage may not be acceptable for sale to Fannie Mae or Freddie Mac.

Lenders use different combinations of the three Cs to reach their decisions. Some set unusually high standards while others simply do not make certain kinds of loans. Lenders also use different rating systems. Some strictly rely on their own instinct and experience. Others use a credit scoring or statistical system to predict whether the borrower is a good credit risk. They assign a certain number of points to each of the various characteristics that have been proven to be reliable signs that a borrower will pay his or her debts. Then they rate the borrower on this scale.

Once the components of a mortgage application have been analyzed, a lender must determine whether the risks associated with capacity, character, and collateral combine to make an investment-quality mortgage. The probability that the borrower will default grows when there are multiple risk factors present. This is known as layering risk. Layering also can appear within one of the three Cs. In terms of capacity, for example, a borrower may possess both a high debt-to-income ratio and minimal reserves.

To complicate the lending decision further, an underwriter must analyze not only the layers of risk, but must identify the strengths that offset those risks. Different lenders may reach different conclusions based on the same set of facts. One may find the applicant an acceptable risk, but another may deny the loan.

Capacity

A borrower's financial ability to repay a mortgage is one of the three determining factors of credit. In other words, can the borrower repay the debt? In general, lenders assess capacity by using the debt-to-income ratios. This expresses the percentage of income necessary to cover monthly debt, including the mortgage payment. Lenders ask for employment information such as the borrower's occupation, how long the borrower has worked for his or her current employer, and the borrower's earnings. Lenders may also consider the borrower's savings or cash reserves as income and use them to assess capacity. Lenders want to know the borrower's expenses, how many dependents there are, if the borrower pays alimony or child support, and the amount of any other obligations.

Capacity

- Debt ratios: Qualifying monthly housing expense-to-income ratio or monthly debt payment-to-income ratio
- Salaried versus self-employed borrower
- Cash reserves
- Number of borrowers
- Loan Characteristics:
  - Product: a 15-, 20-, and 30-year fixed rate, an adjustable rate mortgage
  - Purpose of Loan: purchase or refinance (cash-out or no cash-out)

Character

Lenders ask if the borrower will repay the debt. Lenders look at the borrower's credit history, including the amount of money owed, the frequency of borrowing, the timeliness of bill payment, and a pattern of living within one's means.

The credit information compiled by national credit bureaus (Experian®, TransUnion™, and Equifax®) reveals a borrower's history of handling credit. A **credit bureau** is an agency that collects and maintains up-to-date credit and public record information about consumers. A credit bureau may also be called a credit-reporting agency.

In addition to detailed financial information, credit bureaus give lenders a numerical score or a credit summary that projects a borrower's expected credit performance. Credit bureau scores are based on the statistical relationship between information in a borrower's credit files and his or her repayment practices. These scores accurately summarize a borrower's likelihood of repayment. A FICO® score is one example of a credit bureau score. FICO® scores range in value from about 300, which denotes the highest risk, to about 850, which indicates the lowest risk. Another example of a credit bureau score is the MDS bankruptcy score, for which a lower score indicates lower risk. Lenders look for signs of stability such as how long the borrower has lived at the present address, if he or she owns or rents the home, and the length of current employment. For more information about FICO scores, go to www.fico.com.

Credit files also document the number and nature of recent credit inquiries and information from public records, such as declarations of bankruptcy and unpaid judgments. Because there is such an assortment of information the lender must consider, it is difficult to make an accurate assessment of a borrower's credit profile.

Credit Reputation

- Credit Score
- Foreclosures, bankruptcies, liens and/or judgments
- Mortgage delinquencies
- Credit delinquencies, repossessions, collections, or charge-offs
- Credit accounts: type, age, limits, usage and status of revolving accounts
- Borrower's request for new credit in last 12 months

Collateral

When money is loaned for financing real property, the borrower gives the promise to repay the loan and gives collateral as security for the loan. **Collateral** is something of value given as security for a debt. This is because the lender wants to be fully protected in case the borrower fails to repay the debt. Borrowers have many types of assets that may be used to back up or secure a loan. These assets include any resources other than income the borrower has for repaying debt, such as savings, investments, or real property.

Collateral

- Borrower's total equity or down payment
- Property type: a 1-unit or 2- to 4- unit detached property, condominium unit or manufactured home
- Property use: primary residence, second home, or investment property

The Three Cs of Mortgage Underwriting

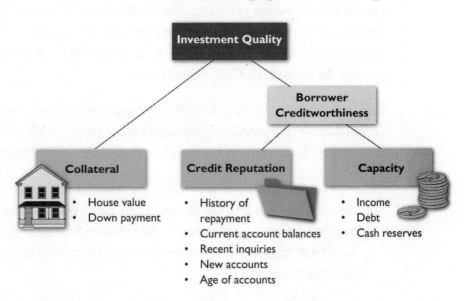

Underwriting Guidelines

Guidelines are a set of general principles or instructions used to direct an action. **Underwriting guidelines** are principles lenders use to evaluate the risk of making real estate loans. The guidelines are just that—guidelines. They are flexible and vary according to loan program. If a borrower makes a small down payment, or has marginal credit, the guidelines are more rigid. If a borrower makes a larger down payment or has sterling credit, the guidelines are less rigid. Lenders who expect to sell their loans in the secondary market use underwriting guidelines that adhere to Fannie Mae and/or Freddie Mac standards. During the underwriting process, underwriters use loan-to-value ratios and debt-to-income ratios, among other economic considerations, to qualify the borrower.

Loan-to-Value Ratios

To calculate the payment, the lender begins by asking for the loan amount. The **maximum loan amount** is determined by the value of the property and the borrower's personal financial condition. To estimate the value of the property, the lender asks a real estate appraiser to give an opinion about its value.

Real estate appraisers are regulated by state law and must meet federal appraisal guidelines. The appraiser is a neutral party who appraises property without bias toward the lender or borrower. The appraiser's opinion can be an important factor in determining if the borrower qualifies for the loan size he or she wants.

Lenders usually lend borrowers up to a certain percentage of the appraised value of the property, such as 80 or 90%, and expect the down payment to cover the difference. If the appraisal is below the asking price of the home, the down payment the borrower plans to make and the amount the lender is willing to lend may not be enough to cover the purchase price. In that case, the lender may suggest a larger down payment to make up the difference between the price of the house and its appraised value.

Evaluating the loan-to-value ratio (LTV) is probably the most important aspect of the underwriting process. The **loan-to-value ratio** (**LTV**) is the relationship between the loan (amount borrowed) and the value of the property.

> For example, if the property in question is valued at $100,000 and the loan amount requested is $80,000, the loan-to-value ratio is 80%. The down payment from the borrower is equal to the difference between the amount borrowed and the value of the property. The **down payment** is the initial equity the borrower has in the property.

Some borrowers have more than one loan on the property. In this case, the lender uses a **CLTV ratio**. The **combined loan-to-value ratio** (CLTV) is used by lenders to determine the risk of default by prospective homebuyers when more than one loan is used. The higher the CLTV ratio, the lower the property's attractiveness as collateral. It is calculated by dividing the sum of the unpaid loan balances on the property by the property's appraised value.

There is a distinct relationship between borrower equity and loan default. Borrowers with a sizable down payment are less likely to default. In one 5-year period for loans purchased by Freddie Mac, borrowers who put down 5% to 9% were 5 times more likely to enter foreclosure than those who made down payments of 20% or more.

Example: Freddie Mac found that borrowers with both smaller down payments (collateral) and riskier credit profiles experience a dramatically higher probability of default than borrowers with only one of these two risk factors present.

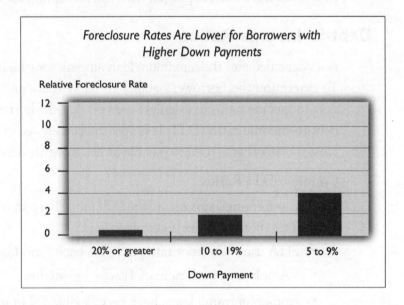

Larger down payments lower the LTV ratio on the loan and reduce risk to the lender. The risk to the lender is the risk that the borrower will default on loan payments, thereby causing the property to go into foreclosure. In that event, the lender either receives the property at the foreclosure sale or receives a deficient amount at the sale. A **deficiency** occurs when the amount for which the property sells is less than the total amount due to the lender. Neither is desirable from the point of view of the lender or investor. Therefore, it is important for the underwriter to determine if the LTV falls within the guidelines for that particular loan.

Down Payment Guidelines

Most lenders require the borrower to pay some kind of down payment to show that he or she does have a monetary or equitable interest in the property. The belief is that the borrower protects his or her interest to a greater degree if there is some personal money invested in the purchase. The loan processor has already verified the down payment during loan processing by checking the borrower's bank account to confirm the money is currently on deposit. As previously mentioned, the Verification of Deposit (VOD) is the documentation that establishes the existence and history of funds to be used for a down payment and determines how long the funds have been in the account. The loan processor determines the length of time funds have been on deposit to make sure the applicant has not recently borrowed the money from a friend or relative. If borrowed money is deposited, the lender's concern is that the borrower is not investing any personal money in the purchase. Lenders verify that funds have been deposited with the institution for at least 3 months.

Debt-to-Income Ratios

A lender calculates the maximum loan amount for which a borrower qualifies. To determine the borrower's ability to repay the loan, the underwriter uses debt-to-income ratios to calculate the risk that the borrower will default. The **debt-to-income ratio (DTI)** is simply the percentage of a borrower's monthly gross income that is used to pay his or her monthly debts.

Common DTI Ratios

- Conforming loans use a 36% DTI ratio that can be extended up to 45% if the borrower meets certain criteria
- FHA uses 31% front ratio and 43% back ratio (31/43)
- VA only uses back ratio of 41% as a guideline
- Non-conforming loans have very flexible DTI ratios

The **front ratio** is the percentage of the borrower's monthly gross income (before taxes) that is used to pay housing costs, including principal, interest, taxes, and insurance (**PITI**). When applicable, it also includes mortgage insurance and homeowners' association fees.

PITI is calculated by determining the monthly principal and interest payment for a loan and adding the monthly amount for property taxes and hazard insurance. For example, the sales price of the home is $200,000 and the buyers are putting 20% down. The monthly principal and interest (p&i) payment for a $160,000 loan, for 30 years at a 4% interest rate is $763.86. If, in our example, the property tax is 0.75% of the sales price ($75 per month) and hazard insurance is $50 per month, the total monthly PITI is $938.86.

You may use a financial calculator or go online to a website such as http://www.piticalc.com to calculate the principal and interest payment for a mortgage loan.

The **back ratio** is the total monthly PITI and consumer debt divided by the gross monthly income. **Consumer debt** can be car payments, credit card debt, installment loans, and similar expenses. Auto or life insurance is not considered a debt. When the maximum DTI ratio is 36%, it means that total debt (housing and consumer) should not be more than 36% of the gross monthly income. There is a distinct relationship between total-debt-to-income ratios and foreclosure rates.

Case Study

Becky earns $3,600 monthly and wants to purchase a 2-bedroom bungalow in an urban neighborhood that is close to work. She has saved $45,000 for the down payment and has paid off all of her debts with the exception of a $375 car payment. She found the perfect property listed for $180,000 and wants to put in an offer, but is not sure if she will qualify for an 80/20 conventional loan. Since the current interest rate is 4%, her monthly principal and interest payment is $687.48. For homes in the area, monthly property taxes are 1% of the sales price and monthly hazard insurance is $40.

Does Becky qualify for the loan?

Yes, her DTI is 35%, which meets the debt-to-income ratio.

No, DTI is 35%, which does not meet the debt-to-income ratio.

Yes, her DTI is 38%, which meets the debt-to-income ratio. .

No, she does not meet the DTI ratio.

Solution:

Determine the PITI. The monthly principal and interest payment is $687.48. The monthly property tax payment is $150.00 ($180,000 x 1% = $1,800 / 12 months). The PITI is $877.48 ($687.48, $150.00 property tax, and $40 hazard insurance.)

Calculate the debt-to-income: $3,600 monthly income x .36 = $1,296 allowed for housing expense and recurring debt. Becky's total PITI ($877.48) and recurring debt is ($375) is $1,252.48, which is 35% DTI ($1,252.48/$3,600 = 34.8%). **This meets the 36% DTI ratio.**

While capacity is an important underwriting component, debt-to-income ratios generally are less powerful predictors of loan performance than other factors. The Relative Foreclosure Rate chart shows the relationship between debt-to-income ratios and foreclosure rates among borrowers.

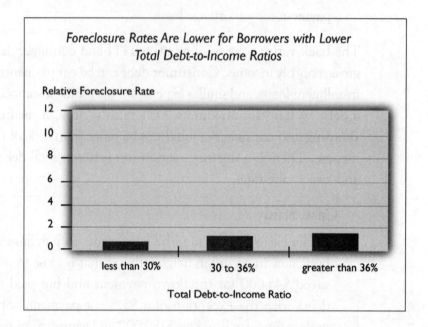

FHA guidelines state that a 31/43 qualifying ratio is acceptable. VA guidelines do not have a front ratio at all, but the guideline for the back ratio is 41.

> Example: If Borrower Brenda makes $5,000 a month, to meet 31/43 qualifying ratio guidelines, her maximum monthly housing cost should be around $1,550. Including Brenda's consumer debt, her monthly housing and credit expenditures should not exceed about $2,150.

Lenders who do not provide FHA or VA loans commonly use the guideline that suggests the total of all debt should not be more than 36% of the borrower's gross monthly income. However, the lender may consider other factors and allow a higher debt-to-income ratio. These factors include a larger down payment than normal, a large amount of cash in savings, a large net worth, or an especially solid credit rating. A **credit rating** is a formal evaluation given by credit bureaus of a borrower's ability to handle new credit based on past performance. Typically, credit ratings are provided in the form of a credit score.

UNDERWRITING THE BORROWER

The risk factors associated with the borrower include employment history, income, assets, credit history, and credit score. The amount of income indicates the borrower's ability to repay the loan, whereas the credit history reflects the borrower's willingness to repay the loan.

Ability-to-Repay Rule

What is meant by **repayment ability**? The **Ability-to-Repay Rule**, Regulation Z Section 1026.43, requires that a lender make a "reasonable and good faith determination at or before consummation that the borrower will have a reasonable ability to repay the loan according to its terms." [§1026.43(c)(1)]. The lender must follow underwriting requirements and verify the information by using reasonably relied upon third-party records.

The rule applies to all residential mortgages including purchase loans, refinances, home equity loans, first liens, and subordinate liens. In short, if the lender is making a loan secured by a principal residence, second or vacation home, condominium, or mobile or manufactured home, the lender must verify the borrowers' ability to repay the loan. The section does not apply to commercial or business loans, even if secured by a personal dwelling. It also does not apply to loans for timeshares, reverse mortgages, loan modifications, and temporary bridge loans.

However, the Ability-to-Repay Rule does not apply to every loan. Principally, the rule does not apply where a **non-standard mortgage** (such as an adjustable rate loan, interest-only loan, or negative amortization loan) is refinanced into a standard mortgage, where the current lender provides the refinance, the new payment will be materially (10 percent) lower, and most of the previous payments were timely. However, the ability-to-repay analysis implicitly applies to the new loan.

Ability to Repay Underwriting Factors

When making the ability-to-repay determination, lenders must use third-party records to verify all information on which they rely, and consider at least eight ATR underwriting factors to use as the basis for determining a borrower's ability to repay the loan. When evaluating these eight factors, lenders may rely on their own definitions and underwriting standards except for the underwriting standards the rule provides for calculating monthly payments on the loan and debt-to-income ratios.

Eight Underwriting Factors Used to Determine a Borrower's ATR

1. Current or reasonably expected income or assets, other than those used to secure the loan.
2. Current employment status, if "income" is used as a basis for determination.
3. Expected monthly payment on the covered transaction.
4. Monthly payment on any simultaneous loans.
5. Monthly payment of mortgage related obligations.
6. Current debt obligations, alimony, and child support.
7. Debt-to-income ratio or residual income.
8. Credit history.

Current or Reasonably Expected Income or Assets

The lender may consider any type of current or reasonably expected income, such as earned income (wages or salary), unearned income (interest and dividends), and other regular payments to the consumer such as alimony, child support, or government benefits. If a borrower has more income than is needed to repay the loan, the extra income does not have to be verified.

> Example: If a borrower has a full-time job and a part-time job and only uses the income from the full-time job to pay the loan, a lender does not need to verify the income from the part-time job.

Income does not have to be full-time or salaried for it to be considered in the ATR determination. A lender may also consider a joint applicant's income and assets. However, if the income or assets of one applicant are sufficient to support the lender's repayment ability determination, the lender is not required to consider the income or assets of the other applicant.

The lender may consider any of the borrower's assets (other than the value of the dwelling that secures the covered transaction).

Current Employment Status

Employment status can be full-time, part-time, seasonal, irregular, or self-employment. The lender must consider borrowers' current employment status to the extent that the lender relies on the employment income to repay the loan. However, if borrowers intend to repay the loan with investment income, employment need not be considered.

Monthly Payments on the Covered Transaction

A lender must determine a borrower's ability to make the monthly payment based on the "full" payment—not based on a teaser rate. The payment must be considered on a monthly basis, and be at the fully adjusted indexed rate or the introductory rate, whichever is higher. The **fully indexed rate** is the interest rate calculated using the index or formula that will apply after recast, as determined at the time of consummation, and the maximum margin that can apply at any time during the loan term.

Monthly Payments on a Simultaneous Loans

The lender must consider the "full" monthly payments on any simultaneous loan that the lender knows or has reason to know will be made on or before consummation when secured by the same dwelling. This includes piggy-back loans, concurrent loans, and open-ended home equity loans, even if made by another lender. The rule applies to purchases and refinances.

Monthly Payments for Mortgage-Related Obligations

The lender must consider payments for mortgage-related obligations. **Mortgage-related obligations** are property taxes and premiums (mortgage insurance, credit life, accident, health, or hazard insurance) that are required by the lender and certain other costs related to the property such as homeowners association fees or ground rent. The lender must consider these amounts whether or not an escrow is established. When these charges are paid on an annual or periodic basis, they are to be calculated as if paid monthly. However, when the charge is a onetime, up-front fee, it need not be considered in the ability-to-repay calculation.

Current Debt Obligations, Alimony, Child Support

The lender must consider a borrower's other debt obligations that are actually owed. Each applicant's obligations are to be evaluated, but the lender does not need to consider other obligations of sureties or guarantors. Lenders are given significant flexibility in this area and may use reasonable means to consider other debt obligations.

Monthly Debt-To-Income Ratio or Residual Income

The ATR rule requires lenders to consider DTI or residual income, but does not contain specific DTI or residual income thresholds. The rule also gives the lender flexibility in evaluating the appropriate debt-to-income ratio in light of residual income.

Example: When the debt-to-income ratio is high and the borrowers have a large income, the borrowers should have sufficient remaining income to satisfy living expenses and therefore justify the loan. The determination would be subject to a reasonable and good faith standard.

Credit History Information

The lender is particularly interested in how likely the borrower is to repay the loan. Although the ATR Rule requires a lender to examine the borrower's credit history, it does not have to review a specific credit report or have a minimum credit score. Most lenders use credit reports to determine credit history, but may also use nontraditional credit references such as rental payment history or utility payments.

Verification Using Third-Party Records

Lenders must verify the borrower's information by using reasonably reliable third-party records. A **third-party record** is a document or other record prepared or reviewed by an appropriate person other than the borrower, the lender, or the mortgage broker (any loan originator that is not an employee of the lender), or an agent of the lender or mortgage broker. [§1026.43(c)(3)].

Reasonably Reliable Third-Party Records

- Records from government organizations such as a tax authority or local government
- Federal, state, or local government agency letters detailing the borrower's income, benefits, or entitlements
- Statements provided by a cooperative, condominium, or homeowners association
- A ground rent or lease agreement
- Credit reports
- Statements for student loans, auto loans, credit cards, or existing mortgages
- Court orders for alimony or child support
- Copies of the borrower's federal or state tax returns
- W-2 forms or other IRS forms for reporting wages or tax withholding
- Payroll statements
- Military leave and earnings statements

Reasonably Reliable Third-Party Records (continued)

- Financial institution records, such as bank account statements or investment account statements reflecting the value of particular assets
- Records from the borrower's employer or a third party that obtained borrower- specific income information from the employer
- Receipts from the borrower's use of check cashing services
- Receipts from the borrower's use of a funds transfer service

The ATR Rule requires that the lender retain evidence of the ability to repay for 3 years. However, because of possible challenges by borrowers to the ability-to-repay determination, it is recommended that lenders and their successors maintain these records for the life of the loan.

Verifying Income and Assets

A lender must verify the amounts of income or assets that the lender relies on under to determine a borrower's ability to repay a covered transaction. Typical third-party records used to verify a borrower's income to determine ATR include documents such as W-2s or payroll statements. In addition to a W-2 or payroll statement, income may be verified using tax returns, bank statements, receipts from check-cashing or funds-transfer services, benefits-program documentation, or records from an employer. Copies of tax-return transcripts or payroll statements can be obtained directly from the borrower or from a service provider, and do not need to be obtained directly from a government agency or employer, as long as the records are reasonably reliable and specific to the individual borrower.

Verifying Employment Status

Lenders use the **Verification of Employment** (VOE) form as part of the process of documenting the borrower's employment history. Alternatively, a borrower's employment status may be documented by calling the employer and getting oral verification, provided the record of the information received on the call is maintained.

Verifying Mortgage-Related Obligations

Lenders can obtain third-party records for the borrower's mortgage-related obligations from many sources.

- Property Taxes: Government entities or the amount listed on the title report (if the source of the information was a local taxing authority)
- Cooperative, Condominium, or Homeowners Associations: A billing statement from the association
- Levies and Assessments: Statement from the assessing entity (for example, a water district bill)
- Ground Rent: The current ground rent agreement
- Lease Payments: The existing lease agreement
- Other Records: Can be reasonably reliable if they come from a third party

Verifying Debts

A credit report may be used to verify a borrower's debt obligations—individual statements for every debt are not required. If a borrower does not have a credit history from a credit bureau, credit history can be verified by using documents that show nontraditional credit references, such as rental payment history or utility payments.

A **credit report** generally is considered a reasonably reliable third-party record for purposes of verifying items customarily found on it, such as the borrower's current debt obligations, monthly debts, and credit history. A credit report includes four categories of data that have been collected and reported to the credit bureaus. They are (1) personal information, (2) credit information, (3) public record information, and (4) inquiries. According to the Equal Credit Opportunity Act (ECOA), the credit report does not include certain factors such as gender, income, race, religion, marital status, and national origin.

The report should show the borrower's credit patterns over the last 7 years and must be less than 90 days old. Credit reports should include credit information from two national credit bureaus, as well as information gathered from public records, such as judgments, divorces, tax liens, foreclosures, bankruptcies, or any other potentially damaging information that may indicate a credit risk. The credit report should include information on the borrower's employment and reflect any credit inquiries made by any lender within the last 90 days.

When the underwriter analyzes the borrower's credit, he or she reviews the overall pattern of credit behavior rather than isolated cases of slow payments. A period of financial difficulty does not disqualify the borrower if a good payment pattern has been maintained since then. Sometimes the lender will ask the borrower to write a letter of explanation for adverse items in his or her credit report.

The credit report includes a **credit score**, which is a statistical summary of the information contained in the report. Lenders use credit scores to rank borrower risk and determine loan amounts. The quality of the credit score also affects the interest rate the lender charges the borrower. Borrowers with high credit scores are usually offered the lowest rates on loans. The lower the credit score, the less likely the lender is to extend credit. However, if the lender does extend credit, borrowers with low credit scores pay higher interest rates. The higher interest rate reflects the higher risk involved in making such a loan. The following chart illustrates this concept for a $225,000, 30-year, fixed-rate loan.

Credit Scores Affect the Interest Rates and Monthly Payments		
FICO® Score	**APR**	**Monthly Payment**
760-850	6.146%	$1,370
700-759	6.368%	$1,403
660-699	6.652%	$1,445
620-659	7.462%	$1,567
580-619	9.451%	$1,884
500-579	10.310%	$2,026
*Estimated average over the life of the loan. Payments may vary.		

The best-known type of credit score is the Fair Isaac or **FICO®** score, which is calculated by the Fair Isaac Corporation. FICO® scores run from 300 to 850 and are generated using complex statistical models. The models are based on computer analyses of millions of borrowers' credit histories.

Qualified Mortgages

A **qualified mortgage** is a mortgage that meets certain requirements specified under the Dodd-Frank Act and clarified by the Bureau.

If a mortgage satisfies the requirements of a qualified mortgage, and is NOT a higher-priced mortgage, then the lender is deemed to have complied with the ability-to-pay requirement and is entitled to the safe harbor provided by Section 1026.43(e) of Regulation Z.

Alternatively, if the mortgage satisfies the requirements of a qualified mortgage and is a higher-priced mortgage, then there is a rebuttable presumption that the creditor complied with the ability-to-repay requirement. Borrowers may overcome the presumption when they can show that after making all mortgage related payments, debt obligations, alimony, and child support there is insufficient income left over to meet living expenses. The longer it takes for borrowers to default, the more difficult it is to overcome the presumption.

The CFPB defines a **Qualified Mortgage** as a credit transaction secured by a dwelling:

1. that has regular substantially equal periodic payments. The mortgage cannot have negative amortization, interest only payments, or balloon payments. If the loan does not require monthly payments, the payments are to be calculated as if paid monthly.

2. that has a term of 30 years or less.

3. that has total points and fees that do NOT exceed 3% of the loan amount. The **loan amount** is the amount stated in the promissory note.

   Points and fees are broadly interpreted. The 3% cap is adjusted as the loan balance falls below $101,749. Points and fees include all items in the finance charge as defined in the Truth in Lending Act, other than interest. The points and fees include loan originator compensation paid by the borrower or lender, as known at the time the interest rate is set, if attributable to the transaction, whether paid to the individual loan officer or a broker. The points and fees include charges paid to the lender, originator, or affiliate, even if the same fees would not be included if charged by an independent third party.

For example, title charges by an affiliated title company are included in the 3% calculation, but similar charges by an independent title company are not. The points and fees included other charges as detailed by the rule.

4. in which the monthly payment is calculated based on the highest expected payment in the first 5 years. The lender must underwrite the loan based on a fully amortized payment schedule taking into account the highest adjustment of any loan payment, and all other mortgage-related payments, including taxes and insurance, whether or not impounded by the lender.

5. in which the lender considers and verifies the borrower's current and reasonably expected income and expenses. This includes debt obligations, alimony, and child support. This eliminates low-document and no-document loans from being qualified mortgages.

6. in which the borrower's debt-to-income ratio does not exceed 43%. The debt includes all mortgage-related expenses, and simultaneous mortgage-related expenses that the lender knows or has reason to know.

If these criteria are met and the loan is underwritten with good faith and reasonable reliance on verified third-party provided documentation, then the loan is a qualified mortgage entitled to a conclusive presumption that the loan meets the ability-to-pay requirements.

These requirements are similar to the ability-to-repay factors but establish a higher threshold of compliance to justify both the safe harbor and presumption of compliance provisions. Essentially, lenders must meet a higher underwriting standard for qualified mortgages than those needed to satisfy the ability-to-repay requirement. For example, qualified mortgages have a specific DTI ratio, 30-year term limit, and a cap on the points and fees assessed. Additionally, qualified mortgages exclude negative amortization loans, interest-only loans, and non-rural balloon-payment loans.

PRACTICAL APPLICATION

Fred and Jan Spring, a young married couple, want to purchase a single-family detached home located at 1652 Hill Street, Any City, Any County, USA. The sellers, Sam and Cindy Winter, have the home listed at $189,000. Fred and Jan put an offer to purchase the property for $180,000 with a 1% deposit, which the seller quickly accepts. The agreed upon closing date is June 30, 20xx.

Fred and Jan have a net combined income of $6,000 per month. Fred's credit was marred by some delinquencies with credit cards during college, but he is on the path to raising his credit score. After college, Fred served in the armed forces as an officer and was able to pay off a good majority of his debt. As it stands, his current FICO® is 640 based on a tri-merged report from all the major credit bureaus. Jan was more fiscally responsible than Fred was, and as a result, has a stellar credit rating of 710.

Currently, their total credit card expenses equal $200 per month. Fred and Jan both commute to work using their own separate vehicles, both of which still have monthly payments. The combined monthly payment for both vehicles is $500. Jan has a school loan amounting to $100 per month that she took out while she attended Best University. When Fred and Jan got married a year ago, the couple received cash gifts that totaled $25,000, which they put into an interest bearing account. Since then, they have contributed 10% of their monthly income and any other extra cash they received throughout the past year (bonuses, part-time work, etc.) to the account. The total savings in their account is now $40,000. Fred and Jan only want to put 5% down so that they have extra cash on hand as reserve funds.

Based on their financial criteria, are Fred and Jan able to qualify for conventional, FHA, or VA financing?

Do the Springs Qualify for a Conventional Loan?

One particular lender offers the Springs a conventional loan that requires at least a 95% LTV, or a maximum loan amount of $171,000 (.95 × 180,000). With a $171,000 loan at 6% interest rate for 30 years, the monthly payment comes to about $1,300 per month with taxes, insurance, and PMI. Will the Springs be able to make this payment?

Most conventional lenders require that the prospective borrower must meet a debt-to-income ratio of 36% of their monthly income for all debts. The maximum monthly payment that the Springs can qualify for is $2,160.

DTI Ratio Calculation
DTI: $6,000 x .36 = $2,160

The Springs meet the DTI ratio of 36%. The $1,300 monthly housing payment plus their total recurring debt of $800 is $2,100. They are under the $2,160 requirement for the back end ratio so they qualify for the conventional loan.

Do the Springs Qualify for an FHA Loan?

The Springs also inquire about getting an FHA loan just in case they do not qualify for conventional financing. FHA lenders also look at the borrower's debt-to-income ratios to qualify a borrower for a loan. The FHA usually uses a 31% front ratio and a 43% back ratio or a 31/43 ratio. After hearing these qualifying ratios, the Springs decide that they would rather put down only 3.5% or $6,300 to keep more cash in their account.

The FHA lender can offer the Springs the same loan terms as the conventional lender. For a $173,700 loan with a 6% interest for 30 years, the payment amounts to about $1,325 per month including taxes, insurance, and MMI.

DTI Ratio Calculations
Front Ratio: $6,000 x .31 = $1,860
Back Ratio: $6,000 x .43 = $2,580

Once again, the Springs meet the front-end ratio since the $1,325 monthly housing expense is well below $1,860. As for the back-end ratio, their recurring debt plus the loan payment is $2,125 ($1,325 + $800). This means that the Springs can also qualify for an FHA loan with a smaller down payment.

Do the Springs Qualify for a VA Loan?

Since Fred Spring is also a veteran, the couple decide to inquire about a VA loan. A VA lender uses a 41% qualifying ratio and residual income. They use specific charts to determine if a borrower has sufficient residual income to qualify for a loan. The Springs decide to try for a no money down loan to see if they can take advantage of Fred's veteran status. Below are the calculations for a VA loan with a $180,000 amount and a 6% interest rate for 30 years.

Residual Income

Gross income		$ 6,000
Less:		
Federal income tax	$ 900	
State income tax	90	
Social security	450	
Net take-home pay		$ 4,560
Housing expense and fixed obligations		
Principal & interest	$1,080	
Property taxes	150	
Homeowners insurance	50	
Total PITI	1,280	
Maintenance & utilities	500	
Alimony	0	
Recurring monthly debts	800	
Job-related expenses	0	
Total housing and fixed obligations		$ 2,580
Residual income		$ 1,980

The Springs live in the West. Based on the Table of Residual Incomes by Region, the Springs' residual income must be $823 or more to qualify for the VA loan. In this case, they are able to qualify for the no money down VA loan.

Table of Residual Incomes by Region				
For loan amounts of $80,000 and above				
Family Size	**Northeast**	**Midwest**	**South**	**West**
1	$450	$441	$441	$491
2	$755	$738	$738	$823
3	$909	$889	$889	$990
4	$1,025	$1,003	$1,003	$1,117
5	$1,062	$1,039	$1,039	$1,158
Over 5 add $80 for each additional member up to a family of 7.				

Qualifying Ratio Calculations

DTI = (housing expense + recurring debt) ÷ gross monthly income

DTI = ($1,280 + $800) ÷ $6,000

DTI = $2,080 ÷ $6,000

DTI = 35%

The Springs' DTI is 35% so they meet the VA DTI 41% ratio.

The Springs qualify for all three loans—conventional loan with a 5% down payment, FHA loan with 3.5% down payment, and VA loan with zero down.

UNDERWRITING THE PROPERTY

One of the risk factors associated with approving a real estate loan is the type and value of the collateral (single-family, condominium, duplex, or rental) used as security for the loan. The property itself is the lender's primary security for repayment of the loan if the borrower defaults. The secondary security is the promissory note, which is the borrower's personal promise to pay. The property must be structurally sound and in good repair. The lender's decision to fund the loan is dependent as much on the value of the property as it is on the borrower's ability to pay off the loan.

The underwriter wants to make sure that the lender is protected from loss as a result of default and foreclosure by establishing the value of the property to which the loan-to-value ratio is applied. For example, if the lender's loan-to-value ratio for making the loan is 80%, the loan cannot be more than 80% of the value of the property.

Example:

$100,000.00	Value of Property
X .80	Loan-to-Value Ratio
$80,000.00	Loan Amount

As far as risk of loss goes, if the property goes into foreclosure the lender can feel reasonably safe if there is a 20% cushion between the loan amount and the value of the property. Lenders do make loans with higher ratios, but these loans inherently involve more risk for the lender. The cost for 80%, 90%, or even 100% loans goes up according to the perceived risk to the lender. Interest rates and points are increased to offset this risk and the buyer is normally required to purchase mortgage insurance on most loans that exceed an 80% LTV.

After reviewing the loan-to-value ratios, loan amount, down payment, income ratios, employment, and credit history in the loan package, the underwriter must determine the adequacy of the security for the loan. Since a real estate loan is secured by the property, the value of the property must be determined to validate the loan-to-value ratio.

Appraising the Property

The value of a property is determined by an appraisal. An **appraisal** is an unbiased estimate or opinion of the property value on a given date. The purpose of the appraisal is to analyze the current market value of the property and determine if there are any adverse factors that might affect value in the near future. Each property is appraised to determine if it has sufficient fair market value to serve as reasonable security for a loan.

The basic principles of establishing value for property include the interconnected characteristics of the property itself and the real estate market in general. These include physical condition, location, and market conditions. Any deterioration of the physical condition of the property relates to its uses, construction materials, and maintenance. The location of the property can neutralize a number of other faults in the property and is one characteristic of the property that cannot be substituted. Market conditions play a major role in establishing value. The obvious considerations are the current and future market conditions. A soft market indicates a greater supply than demand, whereas a tight market reflects the opposite condition—a greater demand than supply.

Elements That Influence Value

- Current use of the subject and neighboring properties

- Type of improvements on the subject property and neighboring properties

- Whether or not the land size and land-value to total-value ratio are typical for the area

- Degree, amount, and type of development occurring in the area

- Pending zoning changes or changes in use of the properties in the area

- Whether the subject property and neighboring properties are residential and marketable

Appraisal Approaches to Value

The three appraisal approaches used to analyze property value are the sales comparison approach, the cost approach, and the income approach. Each approach analyzes the property from a different perspective.

The **sales comparison approach**, or market approach, is the one most easily and commonly used by real estate associates. The sales approach depends on recent sales and listings of similar properties in the area that the appraiser evaluates to form an opinion of value. It is best for single-family homes or condominiums and vacant lots because sales information is readily available and easily compared. This approach uses the principle of substitution to compare similar properties.

The **cost approach** is used to look at the value of the appraised parcel as the combination of two elements. These elements are: (1) the value of the land as if vacant and (2) the cost to rebuild the appraised building as new on the date of valuation, less the accrued depreciation. Appraisers use the cost approach to evaluate construction costs, developer profits, and land costs, and make a downward adjustment for physical depreciation of the subject property.

The **income approach** is used to estimate the present worth of future benefits from ownership of a property. The value of the property is based on its capacity to continue producing an income. This method is used to estimate the value of income-producing property (rentals), usually in combination with one or both of the other methods. This approach is based mainly on the appraisal principles of comparison, substitution, and anticipation.

Reporting Options

The Uniform Standards of Professional Appraisal Practice (USPAP) lists the type of reports an appraiser can use. They are the Appraisal Report and the Restricted Appraisal Report. Regardless of the type, each written appraisal report must be prepared according to the Uniform Standards of Professional Appraisal Practice (USPAP). Each report includes the identity of the client and any intended users (by name or type), the intended use of the appraisal, the real estate involved, the real property interest appraised, the purpose of the appraisal, and the dates of the appraisal and the report. Each report also describes the work used to develop the appraisal, including the assumptions and limiting conditions applied, information analyzed, procedures followed, and conclusions supported by appropriate reasoning.

Because an **Appraisal Report** must be used when the intended users include parties other than the client, the Appraisal Report is the most commonly used report option. The Uniform Residential Appraisal Report (URAR) is an example of an Appraisal Report. It contains many fields of information in organized categories, and allows for proper summarizing statements and even an addendum to support and clarify concepts when necessary. Most residential appraisals are completed on this standardized form, and are considered Appraisal Reports.

An Appraisal Report includes the identity of the client and any intended users (by name or type), the intended use of the appraisal, the real estate involved, the real property interest appraised, the purpose of the appraisal, and dates of the appraisal and of the report. It also describes work used to develop the appraisal, the assumptions, and limiting conditions, the information that was analyzed, the procedures followed, and the reasoning that supports the conclusions. The report states the current use of the real estate and the use reflected in the appraisal, the support for an appraiser's opinion of the highest and best use, and any departures from the Standards. It also includes a signed certification.

The **Restricted Appraisal Report** is the briefest presentation of an appraisal and contains the least detail. This type of report is restricted because there can only be one intended user of the report, not any other party. This type of report is not appropriate for most appraisal situations due to the fact that it contains minimal details and content. This is the least common appraisal report type because it does not satisfy the needs of most lenders or appraisal users.

Uniform Residential Appraisal Report   File

The purpose of this summary appraisal report is to provide the lender/client with an accurate, and adequately supported, opinion of the market value of the subject property.

Property Address		City	State	Zip Code
Borrower		Owner of Public Record	County	

Legal Description

Assessor's Parcel #		Tax Year	R.E. Taxes $
Neighborhood Name		Map Reference	Census Tract

Occupant ☐ Owner ☐ Tenant ☐ Vacant   Special Assessments $ ☐ PUD   HOA $ ☐ per year ☐ per month

Property Rights Appraised ☐ Fee Simple ☐ Leasehold ☐ Other (describe)

Assignment Type ☐ Purchase Transaction ☐ Refinance Transaction ☐ Other (describe)

Lender/Client   Address

Is the subject property currently offered for sale or has it been offered for sale in the twelve months prior to the effective date of this appraisal? ☐ Yes ☐ No

Report data source(s) used, offering price(s), and date(s).

I ☐ did ☐ did not analyze the contract for sale for the subject purchase transaction. Explain the results of the analysis of the contract for sale or why the analysis was not performed.

Contract Price $ Date of Contract   Is the property seller the owner of public record? ☐ Yes ☐ No Data Source(s)

Is there any financial assistance (loan charges, sale concessions, gift or downpayment assistance, etc.) to be paid by any party on behalf of the borrower? ☐ Yes ☐ No
If Yes, report the total dollar amount and describe the items to be paid.

Note: Race and the racial composition of the neighborhood are not appraisal factors.

Neighborhood Characteristics			One-Unit Housing Trends				One-Unit Housing		Present Land Use %	
Location ☐ Urban	☐ Suburban	☐ Rural	Property Values ☐ Increasing	☐ Stable	☐ Declining		PRICE	AGE	One-Unit	%
Built-Up ☐ Over 75%	☐ 25-75%	☐ Under 25%	Demand/Supply ☐ Shortage	☐ In Balance	☐ Over Supply		$ (000)	(yrs)	2-4 Unit	%
Growth ☐ Rapid	☐ Stable	☐ Slow	Marketing Time ☐ Under 3 mths	☐ 3-6 mths	☐ Over 6 mths		Low		Multi-Family	%
Neighborhood Boundaries							High		Commercial	%
							Pred.		Other	%

Neighborhood Description

Market Conditions (including support for the above conclusions)

Dimensions		Area	Shape	View
Specific Zoning Classification		Zoning Description		

Zoning Compliance ☐ Legal ☐ Legal Nonconforming (Grandfathered Use) ☐ No Zoning ☐ Illegal (describe)

Is the highest and best use of the subject property as improved (or as proposed per plans and specifications) the present use? ☐ Yes ☐ No If No, describe

Utilities	Public	Other (describe)		Public	Other (describe)	Off-site Improvements—Type	Public	Private
Electricity	☐	☐	Water	☐	☐	Street	☐	☐
Gas	☐	☐	Sanitary Sewer	☐	☐	Alley	☐	☐

FEMA Special Flood Hazard Area ☐ Yes ☐ No FEMA Flood Zone   FEMA Map #   FEMA Map Date

Are the utilities and off-site improvements typical for the market area? ☐ Yes ☐ No If No, describe

Are there any adverse site conditions or external factors (easements, encroachments, environmental conditions, land uses, etc.)? ☐ Yes ☐ No If Yes, describe

General Description		Foundation		Exterior Description	materials/condition	Interior	materials/condition
Units ☐ One ☐ One with Accessory Unit		☐ Concrete Slab ☐ Crawl Space		Foundation Walls		Floors	
# of Stories		☐ Full Basement ☐ Partial Basement		Exterior Walls		Walls	
Type ☐ Det. ☐ Att. ☐ S-Det./End Unit		Basement Area sq. ft.		Roof Surface		Trim/Finish	
☐ Existing ☐ Proposed ☐ Under Const.		Basement Finish %		Gutters & Downspouts		Bath Floor	
Design (Style)		☐ Outside Entry/Exit ☐ Sump Pump		Window Type		Bath Wainscot	
Year Built		Evidence of ☐ Infestation		Storm Sash/Insulated		Car Storage ☐ None	
Effective Age (Yrs)		☐ Dampness ☐ Settlement		Screens		☐ Driveway # of Cars	
Attic ☐ None		Heating ☐ FWA ☐ HWBB ☐ Radiant		Amenities	☐ Woodstove(s) #	Driveway Surface	
☐ Drop Stair ☐ Stairs		☐ Other Fuel		☐ Fireplace(s) #	☐ Fence	☐ Garage # of Cars	
☐ Floor ☐ Scuttle		Cooling ☐ Central Air Conditioning		☐ Patio/Deck	☐ Porch	☐ Carport # of Cars	
☐ Finished ☐ Heated		☐ Individual ☐ Other		☐ Pool	☐ Other	☐ Att. ☐ Det. ☐ Built-in	

Appliances ☐ Refrigerator ☐ Range/Oven ☐ Dishwasher ☐ Disposal ☐ Microwave ☐ Washer/Dryer ☐ Other (describe)

Finished area above grade contains: Rooms   Bedrooms   Bath(s)   Square Feet of Gross Living Area Above Grade

Additional features (special energy efficient items, etc.)

Describe the condition of the property (including needed repairs, deterioration, renovations, remodeling, etc.).

Are there any physical deficiencies or adverse conditions that affect the livability, soundness, or structural integrity of the property? ☐ Yes ☐ No If Yes, describe

Does the property generally conform to the neighborhood (functional utility, style, condition, use, construction, etc.)? ☐ Yes ☐ No If No, describe

Uniform Residential Appraisal Report   File

There are _____ comparable properties currently offered for sale in the subject neighborhood ranging in price from $ _____ to $ _____ .
There are _____ comparable sales in the subject neighborhood within the past twelve months ranging in sale price from $ _____ to $ _____ .

FEATURE	SUBJECT	COMPARABLE SALE # 1		COMPARABLE SALE # 2		COMPARABLE SALE # 3	
Address							
Proximity to Subject							
Sale Price	$		$		$		$
Sale Price/Gross Liv. Area	$ sq. ft.	$ sq. ft.		$ sq. ft.		$ sq. ft.	
Data Source(s)							
Verification Source(s)							
VALUE ADJUSTMENTS	DESCRIPTION	DESCRIPTION	+(-) $ Adjustment	DESCRIPTION	+(-) $ Adjustment	DESCRIPTION	+(-) $ Adjustment
Sale or Financing Concessions							
Date of Sale/Time							
Location							
Leasehold/Fee Simple							
Site							
View							
Design (Style)							
Quality of Construction							
Actual Age							
Condition							
Above Grade	Total Bdrms. Baths	Total Bdrms. Baths		Total Bdrms. Baths		Total Bdrms. Baths	
Room Count							
Gross Living Area	sq. ft.	sq. ft.		sq. ft.		sq. ft.	
Basement & Finished Rooms Below Grade							
Functional Utility							
Heating/Cooling							
Energy Efficient Items							
Garage/Carport							
Porch/Patio/Deck							
Net Adjustment (Total)		☐ + ☐ -	$	☐ + ☐ -	$	☐ + ☐ -	$
Adjusted Sale Price of Comparables		Net Adj. % Gross Adj. %	$	Net Adj. % Gross Adj. %	$	Net Adj. % Gross Adj. %	$

I ☐ did ☐ did not research the sale or transfer history of the subject property and comparable sales. If not, explain

My research ☐ did ☐ did not reveal any prior sales or transfers of the subject property for the three years prior to the effective date of this appraisal.
Data source(s)
My research ☐ did ☐ did not reveal any prior sales or transfers of the comparable sales for the year prior to the date of sale of the comparable sale.
Data source(s)
Report the results of the research and analysis of the prior sale or transfer history of the subject property and comparable sales (report additional prior sales on page 3).

ITEM	SUBJECT	COMPARABLE SALE # 1	COMPARABLE SALE # 2	COMPARABLE SALE # 3
Date of Prior Sale/Transfer				
Price of Prior Sale/Transfer				
Data Source(s)				
Effective Date of Data Source(s)				

Analysis of prior sale or transfer history of the subject property and comparable sales

Summary of Sales Comparison Approach

Indicated Value by Sales Comparison Approach $

Indicated Value by: Sales Comparison Approach $ Cost Approach (if developed) $ Income Approach (if developed) $

This appraisal is made ☐ "as is", ☐ subject to completion per plans and specifications on the basis of a hypothetical condition that the improvements have been completed, ☐ subject to the following repairs or alterations on the basis of a hypothetical condition that the repairs or alterations have been completed, or ☐ subject to the following required inspection based on the extraordinary assumption that the condition or deficiency does not require alteration or repair:

Based on a complete visual inspection of the interior and exterior areas of the subject property, defined scope of work, statement of assumptions and limiting conditions, and appraiser's certification, my (our) opinion of the market value, as defined, of the real property that is the subject of this report is
$ _____ , as of _____ , which is the date of inspection and the effective date of this appraisal.

Uniform Residential Appraisal Report

File #

ADDITIONAL COMMENTS

SAMPLE

COST APPROACH TO VALUE (not required by Fannie Mae)

Provide adequate information for the lender/client to replicate the below cost figures and calculations.

Support for the opinion of site value (summary of comparable land sales or other methods for estimating site value)

ESTIMATED ☐ REPRODUCTION OR ☐ REPLACEMENT COST NEW	OPINION OF SITE VALUE .... = $
Source of cost data	Dwelling Sq. Ft. @ $ .... =$
Quality rating from cost service Effective date of cost data	Sq. Ft. @ $ .... =$
Comments on Cost Approach (gross living area calculations, depreciation, etc.)	Garage/Carport Sq. Ft. @ $ .... =$
	Total Estimate of Cost-New .... = $
	Less Physical Functional External
	Depreciation =$( )
	Depreciated Cost of Improvements .... =$
	"As-is" Value of Site Improvements .... =$
Estimated Remaining Economic Life (HUD and VA only) Years	Indicated Value By Cost Approach .... =$

INCOME APPROACH TO VALUE (not required by Fannie Mae)

Estimated Monthly Market Rent $ X Gross Rent Multiplier   = $ Indicated Value by Income Approach

Summary of Income Approach (including support for market rent and GRM)

PROJECT INFORMATION FOR PUDs (if applicable)

Is the developer/builder in control of the Homeowners' Association (HOA)? ☐ Yes ☐ No Unit type(s) ☐ Detached ☐ Attached

Provide the following information for PUDs ONLY if the developer/builder is in control of the HOA and the subject property is an attached dwelling unit.

Legal name of project

Total number of phases	Total number of units	Total number of units sold
Total number of units rented	Total number of units for sale	Data source(s)

Was the project created by the conversion of an existing building(s) into a PUD? ☐ Yes ☐ No If Yes, date of conversion

Does the project contain any multi-dwelling units? ☐ Yes ☐ No Data source(s)

Are the units, common elements, and recreation facilities complete? ☐ Yes ☐ No If No, describe the status of completion.

Are the common elements leased to or by the Homeowners' Association? ☐ Yes ☐ No If Yes, describe the rental terms and options.

Describe common elements and recreational facilities

Freddie Mac Form 70 March 2005   Page 3 of 6   Fannie Mae Form 1004 March 2005

Uniform Residential Appraisal Report   File

This report form is designed to report an appraisal of a one-unit property or a one-unit property with an accessory unit; including a unit in a planned unit development (PUD). This report form is not designed to report an appraisal of a manufactured home or a unit in a condominium or cooperative project.

This appraisal report is subject to the following scope of work, intended use, intended user, definition of market value, statement of assumptions and limiting conditions, and certifications. Modifications, additions, or deletions to the intended use, intended user, definition of market value, or assumptions and limiting conditions are not permitted. The appraiser may expand the scope of work to include any additional research or analysis necessary based on the complexity of this appraisal assignment. Modifications or deletions to the certifications are also not permitted. However, additional certifications that do not constitute material alterations to this appraisal report, such as those required by law or those related to the appraiser's continuing education or membership in an appraisal organization, are permitted.

SCOPE OF WORK: The scope of work for this appraisal is defined by the complexity of this appraisal assignment and the reporting requirements of this appraisal report form, including the following definition of market value, statement of assumptions and limiting conditions, and certifications. The appraiser must, at a minimum: (1) perform a complete visual inspection of the interior and exterior areas of the subject property, (2) inspect the neighborhood, (3) inspect each of the comparable sales from at least the street, (4) research, verify, and analyze data from reliable public and/or private sources, and (5) report his or her analysis, opinions, and conclusions in this appraisal report.

INTENDED USE: The intended use of this appraisal report is for the lender/client to evaluate the property that is the subject of this appraisal for a mortgage finance transaction.

INTENDED USER: The intended user of this appraisal report is the lender/client.

DEFINITION OF MARKET VALUE: The most probable price which a property should bring in a competitive and open market under all conditions requisite to a fair sale, the buyer and seller, each acting prudently, knowledgeably and assuming the price is not affected by undue stimulus. Implicit in this definition is the consummation of a sale as of a specified date and the passing of title from seller to buyer under conditions whereby: (1) buyer and seller are typically motivated; (2) both parties are well informed or well advised, and each acting in what he or she considers his or her own best interest; (3) a reasonable time is allowed for exposure in the open market; (4) payment is made in terms of cash in U. S. dollars or in terms of financial arrangements comparable thereto; and (5) the price represents the normal consideration for the property sold unaffected by special or creative financing or sales concessions* granted by anyone associated with the sale.

*Adjustments to the comparables must be made for special or creative financing or sales concessions. No adjustments are necessary for those costs which are normally paid by sellers as a result of tradition or law in a market area; these costs are readily identifiable since the seller pays these costs in virtually all sales transactions. Special or creative financing adjustments can be made to the comparable property by comparisons to financing terms offered by a third party institutional lender that is not already involved in the property or transaction. Any adjustment should not be calculated on a mechanical dollar for dollar cost of the financing or concession but the dollar amount of any adjustment should approximate the market's reaction to the financing or concessions based on the appraiser's judgment.

STATEMENT OF ASSUMPTIONS AND LIMITING CONDITIONS: The appraiser's certification in this report is subject to the following assumptions and limiting conditions:

1. The appraiser will not be responsible for matters of a legal nature that affect either the property being appraised or the title to it, except for information that he or she became aware of during the research involved in performing this appraisal. The appraiser assumes that the title is good and marketable and will not render any opinions about the title.

2. The appraiser has provided a sketch in this appraisal report to show the approximate dimensions of the improvements. The sketch is included only to assist the reader in visualizing the property and understanding the appraiser's determination of its size.

3. The appraiser has examined the available flood maps that are provided by the Federal Emergency Management Agency (or other data sources) and has noted in this appraisal report whether any portion of the subject site is located in an identified Special Flood Hazard Area. Because the appraiser is not a surveyor, he or she makes no guarantees, express or implied, regarding this determination.

4. The appraiser will not give testimony or appear in court because he or she made an appraisal of the property in question, unless specific arrangements to do so have been made beforehand, or as otherwise required by law.

5. The appraiser has noted in this appraisal report any adverse conditions (such as needed repairs, deterioration, the presence of hazardous wastes, toxic substances, etc.) observed during the inspection of the subject property or that he or she became aware of during the research involved in performing this appraisal. Unless otherwise stated in this appraisal report, the appraiser has no knowledge of any hidden or unapparent physical deficiencies or adverse conditions of the property (such as, but not limited to, needed repairs, deterioration, the presence of hazardous wastes, toxic substances, adverse environmental conditions, etc.) that would make the property less valuable, and has assumed that there are no such conditions and makes no guarantees or warranties, express or implied. The appraiser will not be responsible for any such conditions that do exist or for any engineering or testing that might be required to discover whether such conditions exist. Because the appraiser is not an expert in the field of environmental hazards, this appraisal report must not be considered as an environmental assessment of the property.

6. The appraiser has based his or her appraisal report and valuation conclusion for an appraisal that is subject to satisfactory completion, repairs, or alterations on the assumption that the completion, repairs, or alterations of the subject property will be performed in a professional manner.

Uniform Residential Appraisal Report   File

APPRAISER'S CERTIFICATION: The Appraiser certifies and agrees that:

1. I have, at a minimum, developed and reported this appraisal in accordance with the scope of work requirements stated in this appraisal report.

2. I performed a complete visual inspection of the interior and exterior areas of the subject property. I reported the condition of the improvements in factual, specific terms. I identified and reported the physical deficiencies that could affect the livability, soundness, or structural integrity of the property.

3. I performed this appraisal in accordance with the requirements of the Uniform Standards of Professional Appraisal Practice that were adopted and promulgated by the Appraisal Standards Board of The Appraisal Foundation and that were in place at the time this appraisal report was prepared.

4. I developed my opinion of the market value of the real property that is the subject of this report based on the sales comparison approach to value. I have adequate comparable market data to develop a reliable sales comparison approach for this appraisal assignment. I further certify that I considered the cost and income approaches to value but did not develop them, unless otherwise indicated in this report.

5. I researched, verified, analyzed, and reported on any current agreement for sale for the subject property, any offering for sale of the subject property in the twelve months prior to the effective date of this appraisal, and the prior sales of the subject property for a minimum of three years prior to the effective date of this appraisal, unless otherwise indicated in this report.

6. I researched, verified, analyzed, and reported on the prior sales of the comparable sales for a minimum of one year prior to the date of sale of the comparable sale, unless otherwise indicated in this report.

7. I selected and used comparable sales that are locationally, physically, and functionally the most similar to the subject property.

8. I have not used comparable sales that were the result of combining a land sale with the contract purchase price of a home that has been built or will be built on the land.

9. I have reported adjustments to the comparable sales that reflect the market's reaction to the differences between the subject property and the comparable sales.

10. I verified, from a disinterested source, all information in this report that was provided by parties who have a financial interest in the sale or financing of the subject property.

11. I have knowledge and experience in appraising this type of property in this market area.

12. I am aware of, and have access to, the necessary and appropriate public and private data sources, such as multiple listing services, tax assessment records, public land records and other such data sources for the area in which the property is located.

13. I obtained the information, estimates, and opinions furnished by other parties and expressed in this appraisal report from reliable sources that I believe to be true and correct.

14. I have taken into consideration the factors that have an impact on value with respect to the subject neighborhood, subject property, and the proximity of the subject property to adverse influences in the development of my opinion of market value. I have noted in this appraisal report any adverse conditions (such as, but not limited to, needed repairs, deterioration, the presence of hazardous wastes, toxic substances, adverse environmental conditions, etc.) observed during the inspection of the subject property or that I became aware of during the research involved in performing this appraisal. I have considered these adverse conditions in my analysis of the property value, and have reported on the effect of the conditions on the value and marketability of the subject property.

15. I have not knowingly withheld any significant information from this appraisal report and, to the best of my knowledge, all statements and information in this appraisal report are true and correct.

16. I stated in this appraisal report my own personal, unbiased, and professional analysis, opinions, and conclusions, which are subject only to the assumptions and limiting conditions in this appraisal report.

17. I have no present or prospective interest in the property that is the subject of this report, and I have no present or prospective personal interest or bias with respect to the participants in the transaction. I did not base, either partially or completely, my analysis and/or opinion of market value in this appraisal report on the race, color, religion, sex, age, marital status, handicap, familial status, or national origin of either the prospective owners or occupants of the subject property or of the present owners or occupants of the properties in the vicinity of the subject property or on any other basis prohibited by law.

18. My employment and/or compensation for performing this appraisal or any future or anticipated appraisals was not conditioned on any agreement or understanding, written or otherwise, that I would report (or present analysis supporting) a predetermined specific value, a predetermined minimum value, a range or direction in value, a value that favors the cause of any party, or the attainment of a specific result or occurrence of a specific subsequent event (such as approval of a pending mortgage loan application).

19. I personally prepared all conclusions and opinions about the real estate that were set forth in this appraisal report. If I relied on significant real property appraisal assistance from any individual or individuals in the performance of this appraisal or the preparation of this appraisal report, I have named such individual(s) and disclosed the specific tasks performed in this appraisal report. I certify that any individual so named is qualified to perform the tasks. I have not authorized anyone to make a change to any item in this appraisal report; therefore, any change made to this appraisal is unauthorized and I will take no responsibility for it.

20. I identified the lender/client in this appraisal report who is the individual, organization, or agent for the organization that ordered and will receive this appraisal report.

Uniform Residential Appraisal Report

File #

21. The lender/client may disclose or distribute this appraisal report to: the borrower; another lender at the request of the borrower; the mortgagee or its successors and assigns; mortgage insurers; government sponsored enterprises; other secondary market participants; data collection or reporting services; professional appraisal organizations; any department, agency, or instrumentality of the United States; and any state, the District of Columbia, or other jurisdictions; without having to obtain the appraiser's or supervisory appraiser's (if applicable) consent. Such consent must be obtained before this appraisal report may be disclosed or distributed to any other party (including, but not limited to, the public through advertising, public relations, news, sales, or other media).

22. I am aware that any disclosure or distribution of this appraisal report by me or the lender/client may be subject to certain laws and regulations. Further, I am also subject to the provisions of the Uniform Standards of Professional Appraisal Practice that pertain to disclosure or distribution by me.

23. The borrower, another lender at the request of the borrower, the mortgagee or its successors and assigns, mortgage insurers, government sponsored enterprises, and other secondary market participants may rely on this appraisal report as part of any mortgage finance transaction that involves any one or more of these parties.

24. If this appraisal report was transmitted as an "electronic record" containing my "electronic signature," as those terms are defined in applicable federal and/or state laws (excluding audio and video recordings), or a facsimile transmission of this appraisal report containing a copy or representation of my signature, the appraisal report shall be as effective, enforceable and valid as if a paper version of this appraisal report were delivered containing my original hand written signature.

25. Any intentional or negligent misrepresentation(s) contained in this appraisal report may result in civil liability and/or criminal penalties including, but not limited to, fine or imprisonment or both under the provisions of Title 18, United States Code, Section 1001, et seq., or similar state laws.

SUPERVISORY APPRAISER'S CERTIFICATION: The Supervisory Appraiser certifies and agrees that:

1. I directly supervised the appraiser for this appraisal assignment, have read the appraisal report, and agree with the appraiser's analysis, opinions, statements, conclusions, and the appraiser's certification.

2. I accept full responsibility for the contents of this appraisal report including, but not limited to, the appraiser's analysis, opinions, statements, conclusions, and the appraiser's certification.

3. The appraiser identified in this appraisal report is either a sub-contractor or an employee of the supervisory appraiser (or the appraisal firm), is qualified to perform this appraisal, and is acceptable to perform this appraisal under the applicable state law.

4. This appraisal report complies with the Uniform Standards of Professional Appraisal Practice that were adopted and promulgated by the Appraisal Standards Board of The Appraisal Foundation and that were in place at the time this appraisal report was prepared.

5. If this appraisal report was transmitted as an "electronic record" containing my "electronic signature," as those terms are defined in applicable federal and/or state laws (excluding audio and video recordings), or a facsimile transmission of this appraisal report containing a copy or representation of my signature, the appraisal report shall be as effective, enforceable and valid as if a paper version of this appraisal report were delivered containing my original hand written signature.

APPRAISER

Signature _____
Name _____
Company Name _____
Company Address _____
_____
Telephone Number _____
Email Address _____
Date of Signature and Report _____
Effective Date of Appraisal _____
State Certification # _____
or State License # _____
or Other (describe) _____ State # _____
State _____
Expiration Date of Certification or License _____

ADDRESS OF PROPERTY APPRAISED
_____
_____
APPRAISED VALUE OF SUBJECT PROPERTY $ _____
LENDER/CLIENT
Name _____
Company Name _____
Company Address _____
_____
Email Address _____

SUPERVISORY APPRAISER (ONLY IF REQUIRED)

Signature _____
Name _____
Company Name _____
Company Address _____
_____
Telephone Number _____
Email Address _____
Date of Signature _____
State Certification # _____
or State License # _____
State _____
Expiration Date of Certification or License _____

SUBJECT PROPERTY
☐ Did not inspect subject property
☐ Did inspect exterior of subject property from street
  Date of Inspection _____
☐ Did inspect interior and exterior of subject property
  Date of Inspection _____

COMPARABLE SALES
☐ Did not inspect exterior of comparable sales from street
☐ Did inspect exterior of comparable sales from street
  Date of Inspection _____

HUD/VA Addendum to Uniform Residential Loan Application

OMB Approval No.   VA: 2900-0144
HUD: 2502-0059 (exp. 9/30/2007)

Part I - Identifying Information (mark the type of application)

1. ☐ **VA** Application for Home Loan Guaranty ☐ **HUD/FHA** Application for Insurance under the National Housing Act	2. Agency Case No. (include any suffix)	3. Lender's Case No.	4. Section of the Act (for HUD cases)

5. Borrower's Name & Present Address (Include zip code)

7. Loan Amount (include the UFMIP if for HUD or Funding Fee if for VA) $	8. Interest Rate %	9. Proposed Maturity yrs. mos.
10. Discount Amount (only if borrower is permitted to pay)	11. Amount of Up Front Premium $	12a. Amount of Monthly Premium $ / mo. 12b. Term of Monthly Premium months

6. Property Address (including name of subdivision, lot & block no. & zip code)

13. Lender's I.D. Code	14. Sponsor / Agent I.D. Code

15. Lender's Name & Address (include zip code)	16. Name & Address of Sponsor / Agent
	17. Lender's Telephone Number

Type or Print all entries clearly

VA: The veteran and the lender hereby apply to the Secretary of Veterans Affairs for Guaranty of the loan described here under Section 3710, Chapter 37, Title 38, United States Code, to the full extent permitted by the veteran's entitlement and severally agree that the Regulations promulgated pursuant to Chapter 37, and in effect on the date of the loan shall govern the rights, duties, and liabilities of the parties.

18. First Time Homebuyer?	19. **VA Only** Title will be Vested in:	20. Purpose of Loan (blocks 9 - 12 are for VA loans only)
a. ☐ Yes b. ☐ No	☐ Veteran ☐ Veteran & Spouse ☐ Other (specify)	1) ☐ Purchase Existing Home Previously Occupied 7) ☐ Construct Home (proceeds to be paid out during construction) 2) ☐ Finance Improvements to Existing Property 8) ☐ Finance Co-op Purchase 3) ☐ Refinance (Refi.) 9) ☐ Purchase Permanently Sited Manufactured Home 4) ☐ Purchase New Condo. Unit 10) ☐ Purchase Permanently Sited Manufactured Home & Lot 5) ☐ Purchase Existing Condo. Unit 11) ☐ Refi. Permanently Sited Manufactured Home to Buy Lot 6) ☐ Purchase Existing Home Not Previously Occupied 12) ☐ Refi. Permanently Sited Manufactured Home/Lot Loan

Part II - Lender's Certification

21. The undersigned lender makes the following certifications to induce the Department of Veterans Affairs to issue a certificate of commitment to guarantee the subject loan or a Loan Guaranty Certificate under Title 38, U.S. Code, or to induce the Department of Housing and Urban Development - Federal Housing Commissioner to issue a firm commitment for mortgage insurance or a Mortgage Insurance Certificate under the National Housing Act.

A. The loan terms furnished in the Uniform Residential Loan Application and this Addendum are true, accurate and complete.

B. The information contained in the Uniform Residential Loan Application and this Addendum was obtained directly from the borrower by an employee of the undersigned lender or its duly authorized agent and is true to the best of the lender's knowledge and belief.

C. The credit report submitted on the subject borrower (and co-borrower , if any) was ordered by the undersigned lender or its duly authorized agent directly from the credit bureau which prepared the report and was received directly from said credit bureau.

D. The verification of employment and verification of deposits were requested and received by the lender or its duly authorized agent without passing through the hands of any third persons and are true to the best of the lender's knowledge and belief.

Items "H" through "J" are to be completed as applicable for VA loans only.

H. The names and functions of any duly authorized agents who developed on behalf of the lender any of the information or supporting credit data submitted are as follows:

E. The Uniform Residential Loan Application and this Addendum were signed by the borrower after all sections were completed.

F. This proposed loan to the named borrower meets the income and credit requirements of the governing law in the judgment of the undersigned.

G. To the best of my knowledge and belief, I and my firm and its principals: **(1)** are not presently debarred, suspended, proposed for debarment, declared ineligible, or voluntarily excluded from covered transactions by any Federal department or agency; **(2)** have not, within a three-year period preceding this proposal, been convicted of or had a civil judgment rendered against them for (a) commission of fraud or a criminal offense in connection with obtaining, attempting to obtain, or performing a public (Federal, State or local) transaction or contract under a public transaction; (b) violation of Federal or State antitrust statutes or commission of embezzlement, theft, forgery, bribery, falsification or destruction of records, making false statements, or receiving stolen property; **(3)** are not presently indicted for or otherwise criminally or civilly charged by a governmental entity (Federal, State or local) with commission of any of the offenses enumerated in paragraph G(2) of this certification; and **(4)** have not, within a three-year period preceding this application/proposal, had one or more public transactions (Federal, State or local) terminated for cause or default.

Name & Address	Function (e.g., obtained information on the Uniform Residential Loan Application, ordered credit report, verifications of employment, deposits, etc.)

I. If no agent is shown above, the undersigned lender affirmatively certifies that all information and supporting credit data were obtained directly by the lender. The undersigned lender understands and agrees that it is responsible for the omissions, errors, or acts of agents identified in item H as to the functions with which they are identified.

J. The proposed loan conforms otherwise with the applicable provisions of Title 38, U.S. Code, and of the regulations concerning guaranty or insurance of loans to veterans.

Signature of Officer of Lender	Title of Officer of Lender	Date (mm/dd/yyyy)

Part III - Notices to Borrowers. Public reporting burden for this collection of information is estimated to average 6 minutes per response, including the time for reviewing instructions, searching existing data sources, gathering and maintaining the data needed, and completing and reviewing the collection of information. This agency may not conduct or sponsor, and a person is not required to respond to, a collection information unless that collection displays a valid OMB control number. **Privacy Act Information.** The information requested on the Uniform Residential Loan Application and this Addendum is authorized by 38 U.S.C. 3710 (if for DVA) and 12 U.S.C. 1701 et seq. (if for HUD/FHA). The Debt Collection Act of 1982, Pub. Law 97-365, and HUD's Housing and Community Development Act of 1987, 42 U.S.C. 3543, require persons applying for a federally insured or guaranteed loan to furnish his/her social security number (SSN). You must provide all the requested information, including your SSN. HUD and/or VA may conduct a computer match to verify the information you provide. HUD and/or VA may disclose certain information to Federal, State and local agencies when relevant to civil, criminal, or regulatory investigations and prosecutions. It will not otherwise be disclosed or released outside of HUD or VA, except as required and permitted by law. The information will be used to determine whether you qualify as a mortgagor. Any disclosure of information outside VA or HUD/FHA will be made only as permitted by law. Failure to provide any of the requested information, including SSN, may

VA Form **26-1802a** (3/98)   page 1   form **HUD-92900-A** (06/2005)

result in disapproval of your loan application. This is notice to you as required by the Right to Financial Privacy Act of 1978 that VA or HUD/FHA has a right of access to financial records held by financial institutions in connection with the consideration or administration of assistance to you. Financial records involving your transaction will be available to VA and HUD/FHA without further notice or authorization but will not be disclosed or released by this institution to another Government Agency or Department without your consent except as required or permitted by law.

Caution. Delinquencies, defaults, foreclosures and abuses of mortgage loans involving programs of the Federal Government can be costly and detrimental to your credit, now and in the future. The lender in this transaction, its agents and assigns as well as the Federal Government, its agencies, agents and assigns, are authorized to take any and all of the following actions in the event loan payments become delinquent on the mortgage loan described in the attached application: (1) Report your name and account information to a credit bureau; (2) Assess additional interest and penalty charges for the period of time that payment is not made; (3) Assess charges to cover additional administrative costs incurred by the Government to service your account; (4) Offset amounts owed to you under other Federal programs; (5) Refer your account to a private attorney, collection agency or mortgage servicing agency to collect the amount due, foreclose the mortgage, sell the property and seek judgment against you for any deficiency; (6) Refer your account to the Department of Justice for litigation in the courts; (7) If you are a current or retired Federal employee, take action to offset your salary, or civil service retirement benefits; (8) Refer your debt to the Internal Revenue Service for offset against any amount owed to you as an income tax refund; and (9) Report any resulting written-off debt of yours to the Internal Revenue Service as your taxable income. All of these actions can and will be used to recover any debts owed when it is determined to be in the interest of the lender and/or the Federal Government to do so.

Part IV - Borrower Consent for Social Security Administration to Verify Social Security Number

I authorize the Social Security Administration to verify my Social Security number to the Lender identified in this document and HUD/FHA, through a computer match conducted by HUD/FHA.

I understand that my consent allows no additional information from my Social Security records to be provided to the Lender, and HUD/FHA and that verification of my Social Security number does not constitute confirmation of my identity. I also understand that my Social Security number may not be used for any other purpose than the one stated above, including resale or redisclosure to other parties. The only other redisclosure permitted by this authorization is for review purposes to ensure that HUD/FHA complies with SSA's consent requirements.

I am the individual to whom the Social Security number was issued or that person's legal guardian. I declare and affirm under the penalty of perjury that the information contained herein is true and correct. I know that if I make any representation that I know is false to obtain information from Social Security records, I could be punished by a fine or imprisonment or both.

This consent is valid for 180 days from the date signed, unless indicated otherwise by the individual(s) named in this loan application.

Signature(s) of Borrower(s) - Read consent carefully. Review accuracy of social security number(s) and birth dates provided on this application.

Date signed

Part V - Borrower Certification

22. Complete the following for a HUD/FHA Mortgage .

	Is it to be sold?	**22b.** Sales Price	**22c.** Original Mortgage Amt
22a. Do you own or have you sold **other** real estate within the ☐ Yes ☐ No	☐ Yes ☐ No	$	$
past 60 months on which there was a HUD/FHA mortgage?			

22d.Address

22e. If the dwelling to be covered by this mortgage is to be rented, is it a part of, adjacent or contiguous to any project subdivision or group of concentrated rental properties involving eight or more dwelling units in which you have any financial interest? ☐ Yes ☐ No If "Yes" give details.

22f. Do you own more than four dwellings ? ☐ Yes ☐ No If "Yes" submit form HUD-92561.

23. Complete for VA-Guaranteed Mortgage . Have you ever had a VA home Loan? ☐ Yes ☐ No

24. Applicable for Both VA & HUD. As a home loan borrower, you will be legally obligated to make the mortgage payments called for by your mortgage loan contract. The fact that you dispose of your property after the loan has been made **will not relieve you of liability for making these payments. Payment of the loan in full is ordinarily the way liability on a mortgage note is ended.** Some home buyers have the mistaken impression that if they sell their homes when they move to another locality, or dispose of it for any other reasons, they are no longer liable for the mortgage payments and that liability for these payments is solely that of the new owners. Even though the new owners may agree in writing to assume liability for your mortgage payments, this assumption agreement will not relieve you from liability to the holder of the note which you signed when you obtained the loan to buy the property. Unless you are able to sell the property to a buyer who is acceptable to VA or to HUD/FHA and who will assume the payment of your obligation to the lender, you will not be relieved from liability to repay any claim which VA or HUD/FHA may be required to pay your lender on account of default in your loan payments. **The amount of any such claim payment will be a debt owed by you to the Federal Government.** This debt will be the object of established collection procedures.

25. I, the Undersigned Borrower(s) Certify that:

(1) I have read and understand the foregoing concerning my liability on the loan and Part III Notices to Borrowers.

(2) **Occupancy:** (for VA only -- mark the applicable box)

☐ **(a)** I now actually occupy the above-described property as my home or intend to move into and occupy said property as my home within a reasonable period of time or intend to reoccupy it after the completion of major alterations, repairs or improvements.

☐ **(b)** My spouse is on active military duty and in his or her absence, I occupy or intend to occupy the property securing this loan as my home.

☐ **(c)** I previously occupied the property securing this loan as my home. (for interest rate reductions)

☐ **(d)** While my spouse was on active military duty and unable to occupy the property securing this loan, I previously occupied the property that is securing this loan as my home. (for interest rate reduction loans)

Note: If box **2b** or **2d** is checked, the veteran's spouse must also sign below.

(3) Mark the applicable box (not applicable for Home Improvement or Refinancing Loan) I have been informed that ($) is :

☐ the reasonable value of the property as determined by VA or;

☐ the statement of appraised value as determined by HUD / FHA.

Note: If the contract price or cost exceeds the VA "Reasonable Value" or HUD/FHA "Statement of Appraised Value", mark either item (a) or item (b), whichever is applicable.

☐ **(a)** I was aware of this valuation when I signed my contract and I have paid or will pay in cash from my own resources at or prior to loan closing a sum equal to the difference between contract purchase price or cost and the VA or HUD/FHA established value. I do not and will not have outstanding after loan closing any unpaid contractual obligation on account of such cash payment;

☐ **(b)** I was not aware of this valuation when I signed my contract but have elected to complete the transaction at the contract purchase price or cost. I have paid or will pay in cash from my own resources at or prior to loan closing a sum equal to the difference between contract purchase price or cost and the VA or HUD/FHA established value. I do not and will not have outstanding after loan closing any unpaid contractual obligation on account of such cash payment.

(4) Neither I, nor anyone authorized to act for me, will refuse to sell or rent, after the making of a bona fide offer, or refuse to negotiate for the sale or rental of, or otherwise make unavailable or deny the dwelling or property covered by his/her loan to any person because of race, color, religion, sex, handicap, familial status or national origin. I recognize that any restrictive covenant on this property relating to race, color, religion, sex, handicap, familial status or national origin is illegal and void and civil action for preventive relief may be brought by the Attorney General of the United States in any appropriate U.S. District Court against any person responsible for the violation of the applicable law.

(5) All information in this application is given for the purpose of obtaining a loan to be insured under the National Housing Act or guaranteed by the Department of Veterans Affairs and the information in the Uniform Residential Loan Application and this Addendum is true and complete to the best of my knowledge and belief. Verification may be obtained from any source named herein.

(6) **For HUD Only** (for properties constructed prior to 1978) I have received information on lead paint poisoning. ☐ Yes ☐ Not Applicable

(7) I am aware that neither HUD / FHA nor VA warrants the condition or value of the property

Signature(s) of Borrower(s) -- **Do not sign** unless this application is fully completed. Read the certifications carefully & review accuracy of this application. Date

Federal statutes provide severe penalties for any fraud, intentional misrepresentation, or criminal connivance or conspiracy purposed to influence the issuance of any guaranty or insurance by the VA Secretary or the HUD/FHA Commissioner.

VA Form **26-1802a** (3/98)   page 2   form **HUD-92900-A** (06/2005)

Direct Endorsement Approval for a HUD/FHA-Insured Mortgage

U.S. Department of Housing and Urban Development

Part I - Identifying Information (mark the type of application)

1. ☐ **HUD/FHA** Application for Insurance under the National Housing Act

2. Agency Case No. (include any suffix)
3. Lender's Case No.
4. Section of the Act (for HUD cases)

5. Borrower's Name & Present Address (Include zip code)

7. Loan Amount (include the UFMIP) $
8. Interest Rate %
9. Proposed Maturity yrs. mos.

6. Property Address (including name of subdivision, lot & block no. & zip code)

10. Discount Amount (only if borrower is permitted to pay) $
11. Amount of Up Front Premium $
12a. Amount of Monthly Premium $ / mo.
12b. Term of Monthly Premium months

13. Lender's I.D. Code
14. Sponsor / Agent I.D. Code

15. Lender's Name & Address (include zip code)

16. Name & Address of Sponsor / Agent

17. Lender's Telephone Number

Type or Print all entries clearly

☐ **Approved:** Approved subject to the additional conditions stated below, if any.

Date Mortgage Approved _____   Date Approval Expires _____

☐ **Modified & Approved as follows:**

Loan Amount (include UFMIP)	Interest Rate	Proposed Maturity	Monthly Payment	Amount of Up Front Premium	Amount of Monthly Premium	Term of Monthly Premium
$	%	Yrs. Mos	$	$	$	months

Additional Conditions:

☐ If this is proposed construction, the builder has certified compliance with HUD requirements on form HUD-92541.

☐ If this is new construction, the lender certifies that the property is 100% complete (both on site and off site improvements) **and** the property meets HUD's minimum property standards and local building codes.

☐ Form HUD-92544, Builder's Warranty is required.

☐ The property has a 10-year warranty.

☐ Owner-Occupancy **Not** required (item (b) of the Borrower's Certificate does not apply).

☐ The mortgage is a high loan-to-value ratio for non-occupant mortgagor in military.

☐ Other: (specify)

☐ This mortgage was rated as an "accept" or "approve" by FHA's Total Mortgage Scorecard. As such, the undersigned representative of the mortgagee certifies to the integrity of the data supplied by the lender used to determine the quality of the loan, that a Direct Endorsement Underwriter reviewed the appraisal (if applicable) and further certifies that this mortgage is eligible for HUD mortgage insurance under the Direct Endorsement program. I hereby make all certifications required for this mortgage as set forth in HUD Handbook 4000.4

Mortgagee Representative _____

☐ This mortgage was rated as a "refer" by a FHA's Total Mortgage Scorecard, and/or was manually underwritten by a Direct Endorsement underwriter. As such, the undersigned Direct Endorsement underwriter certifies that I have personally reviewed the appraisal report (if applicable), credit application, and all associated documents and have used due diligence in underwriting this mortgage. I find that this mortgage is eligible for HUD mortgage insurance under the Direct Endorsement program and I hereby make all certifications required for this mortgage as set forth in HUD Handbook 4000.4

Direct Endorsement Underwriter _____   DE's CHUMS ID Number _____

The Mortgagee, its owners, officers, employees or directors ☐ **do** ☐ **do not have a financial interest in or a relationship, by affiliation or ownership, with the builder or seller involved in this transaction.**

Borrower's Certificate:

The undersigned certifies that:

(a) I will not have outstanding any other unpaid obligations contracted in connection with the mortgage transaction or the purchase of the said property except obligations which are secured by property or collateral owned by me independently of the said mortgaged property, or obligations approved by the Commissioner;

(b) One of the undersigned intends to occupy the subject property, (note: this item does not apply if owner-occupancy is not required by the commitment);

(c) All charges and fees collected from me as shown in the settlement statement have been paid by my own funds, and no other charges have been or will be paid by me in respect to this transaction;

(d) Neither I, nor anyone authorized to act for me, will refuse to sell or rent, after the making of a bona fide offer, or refuse to negotiate for the sale or rental of or otherwise make unavailable or deny the dwelling or property covered by this loan to any person because of race, color, religion, sex, handicap, familial status or national origin. I recognize that any restrictive covenant on this property relating to race, color, religion, sex, handicap, familial status or national origin is illegal and void and any such covenant is hereby specifically disclaimed. I understand that civil action for preventative relief may be brought by the Attorney General of the United States in any appropriate U.S. District Court against any person responsible for a violation of this certificate.

Borrower'(s) Signature(s) & Date

Lender's Certificate:

The undersigned certifies that to the best of its knowledge:

(a) The statements made in its application for insurance and in this Certificate are true and correct;

(b) The conditions listed above or appearing in any outstanding commitment issued under the above case number have been fulfilled;

(c) Complete disbursement of the loan has been made to the borrower, or to his/her creditors for his/her account and with his/her consent;

(d) The security instrument has been recorded and is a good and valid first lien on the property described;

(e) No charge has been made to or paid by the borrower except as permitted under HUD regulations;

(f) The copies of the credit and security instruments which are submitted herewith are true and exact copies as executed and filed for record;

(g) It has not paid any kickbacks, fee or consideration of any type, directly or indirectly, to any party in connection with this transaction except as permitted under HUD regulations and administrative instructions.

I, the undersigned, as authorized representative of
mortgagee at this time of closing of this mortgage loan, certify that I have personally reviewed the mortgage loan documents, closing statements, application for insurance endorsement, and all accompanying documents. I hereby make all certifications required for this mortgage as set forth in HUD Handbook 4000.4.

Lender's Name		
	Note: If the approval is executed by an agent in the name of lender, the agent must enter the lender's code number and type.	
Title of Lender's Officer		
	Code Number (5 digits)	Type
Signature of Lender's Officer	Date	

SUMMARY

Underwriting is the practice of analyzing the degree of risk involved in a real estate loan and is a method used to evaluate a borrower's eligibility (degree of risk) to receive a loan. The underwriter determines if a borrower is willing and able to repay a loan and if the property used as collateral is adequate security for the debt. Using underwriting guidelines and the information in a complete loan package, the underwriter decides whether the loan will be funded. He or she also examines the loan package to see if it conforms to the guidelines for selling in the secondary mortgage market or directly to another permanent investor. Lenders also examine the borrower's credit report to see if the borrower pays bills in full and on time.

Upon receiving the loan package, the underwriter evaluates the risk factor of certain elements in the loan application such as the loan-to-value ratios, loan amount, down payment, debt-to-income ratios, employment, credit history, and the appraisal of the property.

The loan payment is based on the loan amount, interest, and term of the loan. The lender uses the value of the property and the borrower's personal financial condition to determine the maximum loan amount. To estimate the value of the property, the lender asks an appraiser to prepare an appraisal (opinion about its value). The appraiser's opinion is an important factor in determining the amount of the loan for which the borrower qualifies.

The credit score affects the interest rate the lender charges the consumer. Generally, consumers with higher credit scores qualify for lower interest rates and lower payments, whereas borrowers with low credit scores qualify for higher interest rates and higher payments.

After all the required information in the underwriting process is received, processed, and analyzed and the security for the loan is determined to be sufficient, the lender makes the decision to accept or reject the loan.

One of the risk facts associated with approving a real estate loan is the type and value of the collateral used as security for the loan. The property itself is the lender's primary security for repayment of the loan if the borrower defaults.

UNIT 12 REVIEW

Matching Exercise

Instructions: Write the letter of the matching term on the blank line before its definition. Answers are in Appendix A.

Terms

A. appraisal

B. back ratio

C. collateral

D. consumer debt

E. credit rating

F. credit report

G. credit score

H. debt-to-income ratio

I. deficiency

J. down payment

K. FICO®

L. front ratio

M. loan-to-value ratio

N. maximum loan amount

O. performing loan

P. PITI

Q. underwriting

R. underwriting guidelines

Definitions

1. _____ Loan on which the agreed-upon payments of principal and interest are current

2. _____ Something of value given as security for a debt

3. _____ Practice of analyzing the degree of risk involved in a real estate loan

4. _____ Principles lenders use to evaluate the risk of making real estate loans

5. _____ Relationship between the amount borrowed and the value of the property

6. _____ Initial equity the borrower has in the property

7. _____ Negative amount of money when a property sells for less than the mortgage

8. _____ Percentage of the borrower's monthly gross income (before taxes) that is used to pay housing costs, including principal, interest, taxes, and insurance

9. _____ Principal, interest, taxes, and insurance

10. _____ The percentage of a consumer's monthly gross income (before taxes) that is used to pay his or her monthly debts

11. _____ Car payments, credit card debt, installment loans, and similar expenses

12. _____ Document that lists the credit history of an individual

13. _____ Statistical summary of the information contained in a consumer's credit report

14. _____ Best known type of credit score

15. _____ Unbiased estimate or opinion of the property value on a given date

Multiple Choice Questions

Instructions: Circle your response and go to Appendix A to read the complete explanation for each question.

1. Lenders speak of and use what three components to determine the borrower's ability and the willingness to repay debt?
    a. Cash, class, and carry-over
    b. Capacity, credit, and collateral
    c. Capacity, character, and collateral
    d. Classification, capacity, and cash

2. Upon receiving the loan package, the underwriter begins the process of:
    a. evaluating the risk factors of certain elements of the application.
    b. closing the loan.
    c. gathering information about the borrower.
    d. gathering information about the property.

3. The greater the borrower's _____, which lowers the LTV ratio, the less risk the loan is to the lender.
    a. income
    b. down payment
    c. mortgage insurance
    d. collateral

4. To determine a borrower's ability to repay a maximum loan amount, the underwriter uses _____ ratios to calculate the risk of default on the part of the borrower.
    a. income-to-value
    b. upside-down
    c. debt-to-income
    d. borrower-lender

5. The percentage of the borrower's monthly gross income that is used to pay housing costs, including principal, interest, taxes, insurance, and mortgage insurance is the _____ ratio.

    a. back

    b. forward

    c. front

    d. end

6. Which is a common debt-to-income ratio?

    a. DTI 36%

    b. Front 31% / Back 43%

    c. Back 41%

    d. All of the choices are debt-to-income ratios.

7. An underwriter reviews the borrower's _____ to see if the borrower makes payments in a timely manner according to contract terms.

    a. bank account

    b. employment

    c. credit history

    d. personal verifications

8. Experian®, TransUnion™, and Equifax® are:

    a. real estate lenders.

    b. title companies.

    c. credit bureaus.

    d. software programs.

9. The Ability-to-Repay Rule does not apply to:

    a. a residential loan to purchase a principal residence.

    b. the refinance of a condominium.

    c. a business loan secured by a personal dwelling.

    d. a residential loan to purchase a vacation home.

10. Substantially equal periodic payments, 30-year or less term, and a back-end ratio not to exceed 43% are all criteria for a(n):

    a. open end loan.

    b. qualified mortgage.

    c. adjustable rate mortgage.

    d. graduated payment mortgage.

Settlement & Closing

Unit 13

INTRODUCTION

The closing of a real estate transaction is the final milestone on the path that began with making the sale. The closing process includes signing documents that transfer the title of the property from the seller to the buyer and the distribution of funds. Closing and settlement are interchangeable terms.

Once a lender approves the loan, it goes to the final stage of the real estate loan approval process—the loan closing—at which time necessary documents are prepared and executed. At the closing or settlement table, the borrower receives the package of closing documents, some of which must be signed before a notary. The borrower signs the note and security instruments (deed of trust or mortgage) and various accompanying disclosures. Once the borrower has executed all documents, the loan is funded and the deed of trust or mortgage (as applicable) is recorded.

In this unit, you will learn about title insurance, property taxes, and basic closing and funding procedures.

Learning Objectives

After completing this Unit, you should be able to:

13A   recall the process of closing (settlement).

13B   recall the purpose of qualifying the title and identify the elements of a commitment and title policy.

13C   identify property tax issues.

13D   categorize the various closing costs.

13E   recognize elements of the loan closing process.

13F   identify various RESPA-required disclosures and notices.

SETTLEMENT

Settlement, or closing, is the final meeting of the parties involved in the real estate transaction at which the transaction documents are signed and the deed and money are transferred. The closing process is sometimes called passing papers because, to the casual observer, that is primarily what happens at this meeting. In some states, primarily west of the Rocky Mountains, the closing or settlement procedure is handled through escrow. **Escrow** is a short-lived trust arrangement. If escrow is used, sellers and buyers usually do not meet face to face.

Steps to Closing

The settlement agent (closing agent or escrow officer) follows instructions and holds the documents and money until all of the terms, conditions, and contingencies have been met. If all is in order, the lender funds the loan and sends the proceeds to the closing agent. Buyers send their money to the closing agent as well. After that, closing statements are prepared and delivered, deeds are recorded, and money is paid to the proper parties.

The goal of the closing meeting is to transfer ownership of the property to the buyer and pay the seller for the property. To accomplish this goal, the paperwork brought to the meeting must be prepared, inspected, corrected if needed, approved, signed if necessary, and exchanged as required.

Preparation

In preparation for closing, the closing agent conducts a title search and obtains certificates of estoppel to verify outstanding balances on loans, liens, and encumbrances. The closing agent uses the sales contract, invoices submitted by various third parties (appraisers and inspectors), and instructions from the lender to prepare the documents. In escrow states, escrow instructions are prepared based on these documents. **Escrow instructions** are the written authorization to the escrow holder or title company to carry out the direction of the parties involved in the transaction. Prior to closing, buyers and sellers approve the estimated settlement statement, which details the allocation of the money.

Inspection

At the closing, each party reviews the documents that are of interest to his or her side. For instance, the buyer's side examines the long list of documents that the seller's side brings and the lender's representative reviews the documents that assure the security of the title.

Approval & Exchange

Approval and the exchange of the documents and checks are interwoven. This is because, for legal reasons, certain events need to take place before others. For instance, the buyer must be in possession of the property in order to pledge it for the new mortgage. The relevant documents are recorded to ensure that the sale is legally documented. The seller gives the buyer the deed, keys to the property, and any other relevant items such as garage door openers.

Roles of Closing Participants

The people who are present at a closing meeting vary from state to state. Sometimes it even varies from one region of a state to another. The closing agent, seller, buyer, and real estate agents generally attend the real estate closing. Sometimes the title officer, loan officer, and attorneys for the buyer and/or seller also attend. When the principals' agents and attorneys attend, they are not neutral third parties. Agents and attorneys attend the closing meeting to represent their client's interests.

Real Estate Agents

The real estate agent's role at closing is to be as prepared as possible to represent the client's best interests. An agent must understand the roles of the various players and the documents that are required.

The agent or agents must be sure the buyer and seller are aware of what may occur in the closing meeting and what roles they will play. The real estate agent for each party must also see that the closing agent has access to all needed information so the transaction can close without problems.

Seller & Seller's Attorney

In states that "pass papers" or have closing meetings rather than closing escrow, the seller or the seller's attorney must prepare the paperwork that ensures a smooth transfer of ownership and answer questions regarding the status of the property.

Documents Needed for the Closing Meeting

✓ **Deed**: A warranty deed is the most common deed used for this purpose, but others (such as a grant deed) are also used to transfer ownership.

✓ **Survey**: A survey shows the property's boundaries, improvements, and any encroachments. The buyer will likely require that major encroachments be corrected before closing.

✓ **Property Tax Bill**: By bringing both the bill (if available) and a receipt to show any payment, the new owner will be able to see how much is owed. If the tax bill is not yet available, the taxes are estimated to close the transaction. Usually both parties agree that if the actual taxes are significantly different than the estimated taxes, then an adjustment can be made after the actual figures become available.

✓ **Homeowner's Insurance Policy**: Lenders often require that this type of insurance be carried.

✓ **Title Insurance Policy**: Lenders typically require this type of insurance to protect them from claims of ownership by people other than the buyer. It is highly recommended that buyers obtain an owner's title insurance policy.

✓ **Abstract of Title**: If title insurance is not used, the seller is responsible for either bringing the **abstract of title**, which is a compilation of all the documents that affect the title to a property, or inviting the abstracter to the meeting.

✓ **Flood Insurance Policy**: Lenders may request this type of insurance for properties that are located on flood plains.

✓ **Termite Inspection Certificate**: Some lenders require this certificate. It is also legally required in certain areas.

✓ **Water and Sewer Certification**: Properties that are not connected to public facilities must have a certificate that indicates that they have a private water source and sewage disposal system.

✓ **Building Code Compliance Certificate**: Some areas require that a property be inspected before sale to ensure that it conforms to all current building codes.

✓ **Certificate of Occupancy**: New homes must have a certificate of occupancy that the city supplies to the builder.

✓ **Offset Statement**: If there is an existing lien against the property, this statement indicates the balance due.

✓ **Beneficiary Statement**: This lender's statement cites important information about the trust deed, including the unpaid balance, monthly payment, and interest rate.

✓ **Bill of Sale for Personal Property**: If any personal property is being sold with the property, the seller should supply this document to show that the item is being included with the sale of the property.

Specific documents are needed if the property being sold is a shared ownership property such as a condominium or an income-producing property.

Homeowners' Association Documents
- Restrictions
- Bylaws
- Articles of Incorporation
- Reserve Fund Report
- Management company contract or name

Documents Needed for an Income Property

- Current leases
- Rent schedules
- Lists of current expenditures
- Letter to be sent to current tenants to inform them of the upcoming change in ownership

Buyer & Buyer's Attorney

The buyer's primary responsibility is to have the money available to pay for the property at closing. The buyer must also inform the lender of when and where the closing meeting will occur. The buyer and his or her agent must complete certain obligations before the meeting.

Tasks That Must Be Complete Prior to the Meeting

- Complete any major contingencies that are present in the contract of sale and are the responsibility of the buyer. These might include arranging for new financing or getting approval to assume a loan.
- Inform the lending institution of the name of the closing agent and give approval to have borrowed funds delivered there upon request.
- If needed, deposit additional funds required to pay for property and closing costs with the closing agent.

Lender

When buyers obtain financing to purchase the property, the lender wire transfers the amount of the loan or prepares a cashier's check to be presented at the meeting. In addition, the lender creates a note and mortgage for the buyer to sign.

Title Insurer or Title Abstracter

If a title insurance policy is being issued, the representative from the title company must bring information that provides the status of the property's title to the closing meeting. If title insurance is not being issued, a title abstracter attends the meeting to provide information about the property's chain of title and any liens against the property.

Review – Participants at a Closing		
Seller's Side	**Buyer's Side**	**Neutral**
Seller	Buyer	Representative from each lending institution
Seller's Attorney	Buyer's Attorney	Representative from the title insurance company or escrow company
Seller's Agent	Buyer's Agent	

QUALIFYING THE TITLE

When a home is being purchased, a thorough search of the title must be completed to see if there are any liens, claims of ownership, or other outstanding judgments against the property, such as back taxes. Under the old doctrine of **caveat emptor**, "let the buyer beware", the buyer had the final responsibility to verify title of a property prior to purchasing it. As a result, many buyers lost their investment. Buyers, sellers, lenders, and real estate brokers all rely on title insurance companies for chain of title information and policies of title insurance. The goal of title insurance companies is to insure good title to the property. **Good title** is a title that is legally valid or effective, which can be sold to a reasonable purchaser, or mortgaged to a person of reasonable prudence as security for the loan of money.

Several states, such as California and Florida require the seller to convey "good and marketable" title to the buyer. **Marketable title** is a saleable title that is reasonably free from risk of litigation over possible defects. Other states, like Texas, require the seller to convey "good and indefeasible" title to the buyer. **Indefeasible title** is a slightly lesser degree of title that states that one's title is better than anyone else claiming it. The distinction between marketable and indefeasible goes back to the Great Depression when many properties were sold at sheriff's sales. Issues of marketability were raised, and this led to Texas adopting the "good and indefeasible" title rule.

Evidence of Title

Evidence of title is the means by which the ownership of land is satisfactorily demonstrated within a given jurisdiction. There are four kinds of evidence of title: abstract and opinion, certificate of title, title insurance and Torrens certificate of title. In farm areas, the abstract and opinion method is common. The certificate of title is used extensively in the Eastern states, and some

Southern states. In urban centers in a great many sections of the country, title insurance occupies a dominant position in real estate transactions. Some states, such as Iowa, still use the Torrens system. To a great extent, the acceptability of a particular kind of evidence of title depends on the local custom.

Abstract and Legal Opinion

Before reliable histories of properties came into existence, abstractors investigated the status of title to property. They searched available records and pertinent documents to review the chain of title and then prepared an abstract of title. The **chain of title** is the public record of prior transfers and encumbrances that affect the title of a parcel of land. The **abstract and legal opinion** is an abstract of title prepared by an abstract company or individual engaged in the business of preparing abstracts of title and accompanied by the legal opinion as to the quality of such title signed by an attorney at law experienced in examination of titles. If title evidence consists of an Abstract and an Attorney's Certificate of Title, the search shall extend for at least forty years prior to the date of the certificate to a well-recognized source of good title.

Certificate of Title

Over time, the abstracts and references to the recorded information were accumulated. Information regarding the property was organized in lot books and information affecting titles was organized in general indices. In time, these records became known as **title plants**. The abstract company used these title plants to supply interested parties with a certificate of title. A **certificate of title** is a legal written document that is used to establish the ownership of a piece of property. In addition to identifying the ownership, the certificate of title has other information relevant to the property. This may include easements and buildings.

Title Insurance Policy

An **owner policy of title insurance** is a contract of indemnity that imposes a duty on the insurance company to indemnify the insured against losses caused by defects in title. A title insurance policy insures **"good and indefeasible"** title.

Torrens Certificate of Title

A Torrens certificate of title is a certificate showing the ownership of property based on the Torrens method of registering property ownership. The Torrens system differs from traditional recording systems because it uses a legal procedure whereby the state **guarantees** the owner's title. This system is similar to state registration of motor vehicles.

Title Insurance

Title insurance was created in response to the need for reliable assurance of title combined with an insurance against loss caused by errors in searching records and reporting the status of title. The title insurance company uses the title plant to conduct the most accurate search of the public records possible (county recorder, county assessor, county clerk, and the federal land office) to make sure the chain of title is correct. If there is a missing connection in a property's history or ownership (i.e., if a deed was recorded in error or is incomplete), it clouds the title.

Title Commitment (Preliminary Report)

Before homebuyers receive their owner policy of title insurance, they receive a title commitment from the title company. Depending on the state, the title commitment is called a preliminary title report (prelim), or a title binder. A **title commitment (preliminary title report)** is not a policy of title insurance but is only an offer to issue a policy of title insurance in the future for a specific fee. It shows encumbrances, liens or any other items of record that might affect ownership and it is used as the basis for the final title insurance policy. In addition, it describes the various conditions, exclusions, and exceptions that will apply to that particular policy.

Any problems that arise may be corrected during the transaction period so the new owner gets a clear title. The title company must determine insurability of the title as part of the search process that leads to issuance of a title policy. A good title is guaranteed because of title insurance and a new owner is protected against recorded and unrecorded matters. If someone challenges the title, the title insurance company defends the title and pays the losses covered under the policy.

Types of Title Insurance Policies

The main benefit of title insurance is that it provides protection against matters of record and many non-recorded types of risks, depending on the coverage purchased. Policies for lenders and owners are the main types of title insurance policies. Each policy is designed to suit the needs of the purchaser.

Lender's Title Insurance Policy

The lender's policy is designed to benefit the lender. Some lenders require a title company to provide them with a 24-month chain of title in order to see if the property has been subject to flipping. Lenders look at the flipping of properties very closely. If a property is flipped too many times, the lender may decline the loan.

> Example: There are reported cases of properties being sold to buyer A, then to buyer B, then to buyer C, then "flipped" back to buyer A, and then to buyer D. All the parties were related in some manner and this fraudulently drove the price and demand up for the property.

Lender's policies generally have extended coverage. Lender's policies cover only the amount of money still owed on the loan. Therefore, lender's policies decline in coverage as the buyer pays off the mortgage. If the buyer completely pays off the mortgage, the lender's title insurance policy ceases to exist. If the lender sells the loan to another institution, the lender's title insurance can be assigned to the new holder of the loan. At closing, the buyer typically pays for the lender's title insurance policy.

Owner's Title Insurance Policy

The owner's title insurance policy is designed to benefit the owner and his or her heirs. The coverage is usually a standard policy but owners can purchase an extended coverage policy at extra cost. The coverage cited in an owner's policy is in force for the duration of the policy. Owner's policies cannot be assigned. Typically, the seller of a property pays for the new owner's title insurance policy at closing.

Types of Title Insurance Coverage

The **American Land Title Association (ALTA)** is the national trade association for title insurance companies and title insurance agents. The American Land Title Association (ALTA) forms are used almost universally throughout the nation. The two types of title insurance coverage are (1) standard and (2) extended.

Standard Coverage Policy

A standard title insurance policy is usually issued to homebuyers. No physical inspection of the property is required and the buyer is protected against all recorded matters and certain risks such as forgery and incompetence. The title company does not do a survey or check boundary lines when preparing a standard title insurance policy.

Losses Protected by Standard Title Policies

- Matters of record
- Off-record hazards such as forgery, impersonation, or failure of a party to be legally competent to make a contract
- The possibility that a deed of record was not delivered with intent to convey title
- Losses that might arise from the lien of federal estate taxes, which becomes effective without notice upon death
- Expenses incurred in defending the title

Losses Not Protected by Standard Title Policies

- Defects in the title known to the holder to exist at the date of the policy but not previously disclosed to the title insurance company
- Easements and liens that are not shown by public records
- Rights or claims of persons in physical possession of the land but whose claims are not shown by the public records
- Rights or claims not shown by public records but which can be discovered by physical inspection of the land
- Mining claims
- Reservations in patents or water rights
- Zoning ordinances

Extended Coverage Policy

All risks covered by a standard policy are covered by an extended coverage policy. An extended coverage policy also covers other unrecorded hazards such as outstanding mechanics' liens, tax liens, encumbrances, encroachments, unrecorded physical easements, facts shown by a correct survey, and certain water claims. Also covered are rights of parties in possession, including tenants and owners under unrecorded deeds.

PROPERTY TAX ISSUES

Most people have questions about taxes in a real estate transaction. Taxation is an indirect, yet important, factor that affects the value of property.

In this section, we will see how taxes affect buying and selling real estate. As a student, use this unit for general knowledge about real estate taxation. However, always refer your clients to an expert for their own tax information as well as current tax laws.

Property Taxes

The idea of land taxation began in 1086 in England when all land and resources were compiled into the *Domesday Book* that William the Conqueror commissioned. Taxation was based on the notion that taxes should be assessed according to an owner's ability to pay. At that time, since most people's income came almost entirely from products of their land, ability was reliably determined by how much and how good the owner's agricultural holdings were. Therefore, land became the basis for determining the amount of tax imposed.

Property taxes are paid in arrears (at the end of each tax period). Paying in **arrears** is payment at the end of a period for which payment is due. It is the opposite of paying in advance.

When a property tax is assessed against a property, a property tax lien for that amount is placed on the property. This type of lien is superior to all other liens and cannot be cleared by a foreclosure. Property taxes are assessed differently in each state.

Assessment & Collection of Taxes

Real property is taxed at the local level through ad valorem property taxes, special assessments, and transfer taxes. **Ad valorem** means according to value.

A **taxing authority** is any organization that is legally able to set (levy) and collect a tax. The first taxing authority that most real estate owners think of is their local government, but a piece of real estate may also be within districts that belong to other taxing authorities.

Other Taxing Authorities

- Local governments — taxes to pay for schools, police and fire departments, street maintenance, public parks, and libraries, among other expenses
- School districts— taxes to support schools
- Drainage districts — taxes for drainage infrastructure construction and maintenance
- Sanitary districts — taxes for the construction, maintenance, and operation of sewage treatment plants
- Recreational districts — taxes for the construction, maintenance, and operation of parks, playgrounds, baseball diamonds, tennis courts, recreation centers, marinas, and trails

Immune & Exempt Property

All property within the locality of the taxing authority, whether state or local government, is taxed unless specifically immune or exempt. **Immune properties** typically include those owned by governments, such as schools, parks, military bases, and government buildings. **Exempt properties** include hospitals, homesteads, and property that belongs to religious organizations such as churches or synagogues. Property tax exemptions are discussed in detail later in this unit.

Review – Immune Property
- Governments are typically exempt from paying property tax on their own property. No property taxes are paid on military bases, public water treatment plants, public dumps, public roads, city halls, public schools, libraries, or parks.

Review – Exempt Property
- Most states offer a property tax exemption to religious or charitable organizations.
- Cemeteries and hospitals are often exempt from property taxes.
- Owners of homesteaded property are partially exempt. The taxable value of a property is determined by the assessed value minus any exemptions.

Special Assessments

When specific improvements are needed to benefit a certain area—such as underground utilities, sewers, or streets—special assessments are levied to pay for the improvements. **Special assessments** are taxes used for specific, local purposes. In contrast, property taxes are used to operate the government in general.

Special assessment liens are placed on the properties involved and are usually paid at the same time as property taxes. The liens created by special assessments are equal in priority to general tax liens.

Additionally, a public agency or a group of homeowners can initiate improvements that result in special assessments. The costs of the improvements are divided equally or proportionally (often on a per-front-foot basis) among the homeowners. When computing using the front foot method, consider that the burden is shared with the neighbor across the street.

CLOSING COSTS AND STATEMENTS

Closing costs are the expenses buyers and sellers normally incur in the transfer of ownership of real property that are over and above the cost of the property. These costs appear on the seller's and buyer's closing statements. The **closing statement** is an accounting of funds made to the sellers and buyers individually. It shows how all closing costs, including prepaid and prorated expenses, are allocated between the buyer and seller. In most transactions, the seller pays for title insurance and any delinquent assessment liens that show up as debits.

A real estate agent should be able to compute the costs and competently explain all costs and expenses to his or her clients. These costs do not include the cost of the property.

In order to complete the real estate transaction, closing costs must be paid. The buyer and seller give the closing agent instructions regarding prorations and other accounting that must be done at the close of the transaction.

Closing costs are either prorated or allocated. Do not confuse allocation with proration. **Allocation** assigns a cost (generally one not yet spent) to either the seller or the buyer. **Proration** divides a cost (most often one that has already been paid) between the two parties. It is up to the parties to determine if a cost is allocated or prorated. Usually, property tax and interest are prorated at closing.

Prorated Costs

Proration is the division and distribution of expenses and/or income between the buyer and seller of property as of the date of closing. Prorations are typically calculated using the seller's last full day of ownership and the buyer is charged for the closing day. Prorations are typically based on one of two methods: a 365-day year method or a 30-day month method. Frequently, the method that is used is stated in the purchase contract.

> **Proration Calculations**
> - Using the 365-day method, the annual cost is divided by 365 days. This gives a daily rate. The daily rate is then multiplied by the number of days. This equals the amount due.
> - Using the 30-day month method, divide the annual cost by 12 months then by 30 days. This gives a daily rate. The daily rate is then multiplied by the number of buyer or seller days, which then equals the amount due.

Property Tax

Property tax is the money owed to the local or state government for services used by the homeowner. Property taxes are often prorated. If the seller prepaid property taxes, he or she expects to get the unused portion back. This shows up as a credit.

> Example: Closing is October 31 and the seller has not paid the property tax of $3,650, which is due November 1. To calculate the amount owed, prorate the tax according to the number of days in the tax year each party owned the property. In this example, the buyer is responsible for the taxes as of the closing date.
>
> 1. Calculate the cost of taxes per day.
> $3,650 ÷ 365 days = $10.00 daily
>
> 2. Count the days during the tax period in question when seller owned the property.
>   January 1 – October 30 = 303 days
>
> 3. Multiply the number of days the seller owned the property by the cost of taxes per day.
>   303 x $10.00 = $3,030 owed by seller
>
> 4. Subtract $3,030 from the total tax charged to buyer.
> $3,650 – $3,030 = $620 owed by buyer

Interest on Loan Assumption

When a buyer assumes an existing loan, the interest is shown on the closing statement as a debit to the seller and a credit to the buyer.

Assumable loans are not very common in today's market. However, it is important to understand how to calculate prorated interest on an assumed loan. Because mortgage interest is paid in arrears—at the end of a time period—the seller credits the buyer for his or her share of the interest.

Escrow (Impound) Account

An **escrow account**, which is sometimes referred to as an **impound account**, is a trust account for funds set aside for future, recurring costs relating to a property, such as payment of property taxes and hazard insurance. Usually the lender determines whether there will be an impound account, but sometimes the buyer decides on the use of an impound account and the closing agent is given instructions regarding how to handle the credits and debits.

Allocated Costs

The list of costs to be allocated can become quite long. Generally, the costs fall into the categories of inspections, required retrofits, and fees. Some items that may be on the list include transfer taxes, recording fees, and hazard and title insurance.

Transfer Taxes

Transfer taxes are paid to state or local governments to transfer the ownership of property from one owner to another. Transfer taxes allow the government to assess property values. Transfer tax may also be known as **documentary stamp tax** or **conveyance tax**. Most of the time, it is paid by the seller. The buyer normally pays the state taxes associated with the financing.

A transfer of property can involve three transfer taxes, each with its own set of calculations. The three taxes are the documentary stamp tax on deeds, the documentary stamp tax on notes, and the intangible tax on new mortgages.

Stamp Tax on Deeds

The **stamp tax on deeds** is required whenever real property is transferred from one owner to another. In order to establish accurate tax assessments, this tax allows governments to secure data about the fair market value of real properties in their jurisdictions.

Many transactions are exempt from this tax. Some exempted transactions include transfers between a husband and wife or parent and child, gift deeds, and tax deeds.

Recording Fees

Recording fees are monies paid to government agencies, typically the county, to legally record documents that concern the property. The buyer often pays the recording fees.

Title & Hazard Insurance

Title insurance protects the policyholder from losses due to a problem in the chain of title. Typically, both the owner and the lender take out separate policies. Often, the previous owner pays for a new owner's policy and the buyer pays for the lender's policy.

Hazard insurance is a property insurance policy that protects both owner and lender against physical hazards to property such as fire and windstorm damage. Lenders require hazard insurance that covers the lesser of 100% of the insurable value of the improvements (established by the property insurer) or the outstanding loan on the property provided it is at least 80% of the insurable value of the improvements.

Many casualty insurance companies provide hazard insurance. In most cases, the lender is the loss payee on the policy and receives the proceeds on a claim. The proceeds are then used to pay for the repairs. In addition, depending on the location of the property, the lender may require flood insurance.

What Are Credits & Debits?

A **credit** is the reduction or elimination of an asset or expense. A credit is usually recorded on the right side of a column on a closing statement. A **debit** shows the amount owed.

Typically, the buyer and seller negotiate the allocation of these costs in the sale contract. Usually, the person who must sign the document is the one who pays the fee for its preparation. Therefore, the seller pays for the preparation of the deed and the buyer pays for the preparation of the loan documents. A particular cost may be paid in full by either the buyer or the seller, split evenly, negotiated between the two parties, or prorated. The closing agent assigns the credits and debits according to the principal's instructions.

Seller's Statement

The seller's statement is a record of the financial proceeds the sellers receive upon the transaction's closing.

> ### Seller's Credits
> - Amount of the total consideration or sales price
> - Any prepaid property taxes
> - Prepaid monthly property owner's association dues
> - interest on loan seller owes will reduce payoff if prepaid

---

Seller's Debits (only if contracted to be paid by seller)

- Loan payoff on existing loan plus any interest charges
- Broker's commission
- Title insurance (owner's policy)
- Abstract or title search
- Settlement or escrow fee (seller's share)
- Legal fees

- Documentary transfer tax (deed)
- Prepayment penalty
- Pest control inspection fee
- Pest control work
- FHA or VA points
- Pest inspection report
- Home warranty plan

Buyer's Statement

The buyer's statement is a record of costs and credits incurred for the purchase of the property.

Buyer's Credits

- Down payment
- Binder deposit (good faith deposit)
- Amount of new loan
- Asumed loan

- Prorated taxes
- Prorated rents
- Security deposits held by sellers
- Balance from buyer needed to close

Buyer's Debits for Non-Recurring Costs

- Purchase price
- Title insurance (lender's policy)
- Settlement or escrow fee (buyer's share)
- Legal fees
- Loan application fee
- Underwriting fee
- Loan fee/points
- Appraisal fee

- Tax service
- Credit report
- Notary fee
- Recording fees
- Assumption fee
- Documentary transfer tax (note, mortgage)
- Pest control inspection (according to agreement with sellers)
- Survey

> **Buyer's Debits for Recurring Costs**
> - Hazard insurance
> - Trust fund or impound account
> - Prorated taxes (if prepaid by sellers beyond recordation)
> - Prorated interest (if charged in arrears)

Types of Settlement Statements

The **closing statement** is an accounting of funds made to the sellers and buyers individually. The closing agent must complete closing statements for every real estate transaction. The sellers and buyers are both credited and debited for their agreed-upon share of costs. Generally, a real estate agent attends the closing meeting. As a sales agent, you should understand closing statement calculations because you may be required to explain the costs outlined on these statements.

Some of the settlement statements used for residential real estate transaction are the CFPB Closing Disclosure, a standardized ALTA settlement statement, the HUD-1 Settlement Statement, or a generic settlement statement prepared by the escrow company. Since an all-cash sale is not covered by the CFPB, an escrow officer may use any settlement statement he or she chooses—including the CFPB Closing Disclosure.

TILA-RESPA (TRID) Closing Disclosure

The Closing Disclosure created by the Consumer Financial Protection Bureau (CFPB) must be used for real estate transactions financed using closed-end residential loans, construction-only loans, vacant-land loans, and 25-acre loans. Additionally, the Closing Disclosure must be used for any federally related residential mortgage loans subject to RESPA (which will include most mortgages).

> RESPA defines **federally related mortgage loans** as loans (or refinances) secured by a first or subordinate lien on a one-to four-family residential real property. The definition also includes loans made by or insured by an agency of the federal government and any loans made by lenders that are regulated by or whose deposits or accounts are insured by any agency of the federal government. [12 CFR §1024.2].

As you can see, this definition covers nearly all residential real estate loans obtained from a lender. Obviously, the Closing Disclosure will be the most frequently used settlement statement for 1-4 residential transactions. (An example of the Closing Disclosure is provided in Unit 3.)

ALTA Settlement Statements

The American Land Title Association (ALTA) developed four standardized ALTA Settlement Statements for title insurance and settlement companies to use to itemize all the fees and charges that both the homebuyer and seller must pay during the settlement process of a housing transaction.

If a residential transaction does not involve a lender, the ALTA Settlement Statement Cash, could be used for an all-cash sale.

HUD-1 Settlement Statement

The HUD-1 Settlement Statement is still used for transactions involving home-equity lines of credit (HELOCs), reverse mortgages, mortgages secured by a mobile home or a dwelling that is not attached to real property.

LOAN CLOSING PROCEDURES

Below is a brief explanation of a typical funding process. In order to start the funding process with the mortgage company, proper documentation must be sent to the lender or underwriter before each individual loan is funded.

1. Request for purchase summary of transaction from mortgage company

2. Required documents to fund

    - Completed loan application (Form 1003)
    - Appraisal - first two pages
    - Firm Commitment by D.E. Underwriter (FHA), VA Loan Analysis by VA Automatic Underwriter (VA), Investor Underwriter, LP or DU approvals from authorized channels (Fannie Mae, Freddie Mac)
    - Copy of Borrower's credit report
    - Insured closing letter in name of originator from title company
    - Wiring instructions
    - Copy of hazard insurance policy or binder of coverage
    - Flood certification
    - Mortgage insurance (MMI or PMI) or VA mortgage guaranty
    - VA certificate of eligibility (if applicable)
    - Purchase commitment from investor — investor lock

3. Funds are wired to closing agent along with specific funding instructions

4. Closing agent faxes a copy of signed note on the date of the closing and overnights the following documents within 1 business day immediately preceding settlement.

   - Original signed note
   - Certified copy of deed of trust
   - Copy of title commitment
   - Copy of the Closing Disclosure or the HUD-1
   - Copy of Truth In Lending Act

Endorsement & Flow of Documents

1. Original signed note is to be sent directly from closing agent back to bank; note is to be endorsed in blank

2. Original Assignment of Deed of Trust in blank, plus assignment to investor is sent with the note to closing agent

Collection of the Note

3. Upon receipt of note, a bailee letter is prepared and sent with note to the investor for payment

4. Loan is booked at the negotiated rate

Payoff Procedures

5. Funds wired to the closing agent from the investor

6. Borrower sent payoff information

7. Payoff calculated from date of closing to date of receipt of wire

8. Loan for payoff amount credited at the negotiated rate

9. Appropriate fees deducted from the wire and deposited into the mortgage company loan income account

10. Mortgage company account credited for the remainder of the wire

11. Copies of the transaction are faxed or e-mailed to the mortgage company

After all information that is required in the underwriting process is received, processed, and analyzed, and the security for the loan is determined to be sufficient, the decision is made to accept or reject the loan. This decision is made by the person or loan committee whose job is to decide which loans to fund. Once approved, the loan goes to the final stage of the real estate loan approval process, the loan closing, at which time necessary documents are prepared and executed.

At closing, the borrower receives the package of closing documents, some of which must be signed before a notary. The borrower signs the note and security instruments (deed of trust or mortgage) and various accompanying disclosures. Once the borrower has executed all documents, the loan is funded and the deed of trust or mortgage (as applicable) is recorded.

RESPA Settlement Disclosures

Lenders who make real estate loans and brokers who arrange these loans must comply with various federal and state disclosure laws and regulations. Underwriters must be aware of these laws and act in accordance with them.

Certain disclosures that protect consumers from unfair lending practices are required at different times during a loan transaction. They are the **Special Information Booklet** (not necessary for refinances), the **Loan Estimate** and the **Mortgage Servicing Disclosure Statement**. After October 3, 2015, the Good Faith Estimate and the Truth-in-Lending Disclosure Statement will only be used for certain transactions, such as reverse mortgages.

Disclosures at Settlement/Closing

The Closing Disclosure or the HUD-1 Settlement Statement shows the actual settlement costs of the loan transaction. Lenders must ensure that BORROWERS receive the Closing Disclosure no later than 3 business days before consummation (the day the loan closes). [12 CFR §1026.19(f)(1)(ii)]. The settlement agent is responsible for preparing and providing the Closing Disclosure to the SELLER at or before consummation. [12 CFR §1026.19(f) (4)(ii)]. If the HUD-1 is used, the settlement statement should be available for inspection by the borrower/buyer and seller at or before the closing. [12 USC §2603(b)].

Separate forms may be prepared for the borrower and the seller. When it is not standard practice for both the borrower and seller to attend the settlement, the final Closing Disclosure or the HUD-1 is mailed or delivered as soon as is practical after settlement.

The lender may require a borrower to maintain an escrow account with the lender to ensure the payment of taxes, insurance, and other items. This typically occurs when the borrower's first loan exceeds 80%. HUD regulations limit the maximum amount that a lender can require a borrower to maintain in the escrow account. If the lender does require it, the **Initial Escrow Statement** or **Estimated Closing Statement** itemizes the estimated taxes, insurance premiums, and other charges to be paid from the escrow account during the first 12 months of the loan. It lists the escrow payment amount and any required cushion. Although the statement is usually given at settlement, the lender has 45 days from settlement to deliver it.

Disclosures After Settlement

Loan servicers must deliver an Annual Escrow Statement to borrowers once a year. The **Annual Escrow Statement** summarizes all escrow account deposits and payments during the servicer's 12-month computation year. It also notifies borrowers of any shortages or surpluses in the account and advises them of the course of action taken to correct the overage or shortage. A shortage in an escrow account can occur if insurance rates or tax rates increase on the property. If the account is short, the lender may increase the borrower's monthly home loan payment to accommodate the shortage. Under RESPA statutes, the lender is allowed to maintain a cushion equal to one-sixth of the amount of items paid out of the account, or approximately 2 months of escrow payments. If state law or loan documents allow for a lesser amount, the lesser amount prevails.

A **Servicing Transfer Statement** is required if the loan servicer sells or assigns the servicing rights to a borrower's loan to another loan servicer. Generally, the loan servicer must notify the borrower 15 days before the effective date of the loan transfer. As long as the borrower makes a timely payment to the old servicer within 60 days of the loan transfer, the borrower cannot be penalized. The notice must include the name and address of the new servicer, toll-free telephone numbers, and the date the new servicer will begin accepting payments.

SUMMARY

Settlement, or closing, is the final meeting of the parties involved in the real estate transaction at which the transaction documents are signed and the deed and money are transferred. In some states, primarily west of the Rocky Mountains, the closing or settlement procedure is handled through escrow. Escrow is a short-lived trust arrangement. The goal of the closing meeting is to transfer ownership of the property to the buyer and pay the seller for the property. To accomplish this goal, the paperwork brought to the meeting must be prepared, inspected, corrected if needed, approved, signed if necessary, and exchanged as required.

The people who are present at a closing meeting vary from state to state. Sometimes it even varies from one region of a state to another. The closing agent, seller, buyer, and real estate agents generally attend the real estate closing.

Sometimes the title officer, loan officer, and attorneys for the buyer or seller also attend. When the principals' agents and attorneys attend, they are not neutral third parties. Agents and attorneys attend the closing meeting to represent their client's interests.

Buyers, sellers, lenders, and real estate brokers all rely on title insurance companies for chain of title information and policies of title insurance. The goal of title insurance companies is to ensure good title to the property. Title insurance is insurance that protects the policyholder from losses due to a problem in the chain of title. Typically, both the owner and the lender take out separate policies. The American Land Title Association (ALTA) is the national trade association for title insurance companies and title insurance agents. The two types of title insurance coverage are (1) standard and (2) extended.

Property tax is the money owed to the local or state government for services used by the homeowner. Property taxes are often prorated. If the seller prepaid property taxes, he or she will expect to get the unused portion back. This shows up as a credit. Property taxes are paid in arrears (at the end of each tax period). Paying in arrears is payment at the end of a period for which payment is due. It is the opposite of paying in advance.

Closing costs are the expenses buyers and sellers normally incur in the transfer of ownership of real property that are over and above the cost of the property. These costs appear on the seller's and buyer's closing statements. The closing statement is an accounting of funds made to the seller and buyer individually. It shows how all closing costs, including prepaid and prorated expenses, are divided between the buyer and seller. In most transactions, the seller pays for title insurance and any delinquent assessment liens that show up as debits. Closing costs are either prorated or allocated. Allocation assigns a cost (generally one not yet spent) to either the seller or the buyer. Proration divides a cost (most often one that has already been paid) between the two parties.

In order to start the funding process with the mortgage company, proper documentation must be sent to the closing agent before each individual loan is funded. After all required information in the underwriting process is received, processed, and analyzed, and the security for the loan is determined to be sufficient, the decision is made to accept or reject the loan.

UNIT 13 REVIEW

Matching Exercise

Instructions: Write the letter of the matching term on the blank line before its definition. Answers are in Appendix A.

Terms

A. allocation

B. annual escrow statement

C. chain of title

D. closing costs

E. Closing Disclosure

F. closing statement

G. escrow

H. escrow account

I. escrow instructions

J. evidence of title

K. good title

L. hazard insurance

M. indefeasible title

N. marketable title

O. proration

P. recording fees

Q. settlement

R. special assessments

S. title commitment

T. title insurance policy

Definitions

1. _____ Final meeting of the parties involved in the real estate transaction at which the transaction documents are signed and the deed and money are transferred

2. _____ Short-lived trust arrangement

3. _____ Written authorization to the escrow holder or title company to carry out the direction of the parties involved in the transaction

4. _____ A title that is legally valid or effective, which can be sold to a reasonable purchaser, or mortgaged to a person of reasonable prudence as security for the loan of money

5. _____ A saleable title that is reasonably free from risk of litigation over possible defects

6. _____ A slightly lesser degree of title that states that one's title is better than anyone else claiming it

7. _____ The means by which the ownership of land is satisfactorily demonstrated within a given jurisdiction

8. _____ Public record of prior transfers and encumbrances that affect the title of a parcel of land

9. _____ A contract of indemnity that imposes a duty on the insurance company to indemnify the insured against losses caused by defects in title

10. _____ An offer to issue a policy of title insurance in the future for a specific fee

11. _____ Taxes used for specific, local purposes

12. _____ Expenses buyers and sellers normally incur in the transfer of ownership of real property that are over and above the cost of the property

13. _____ Accounting of funds made to the sellers and buyers individually

14. _____ Assigning a cost (generally one not yet spent) to either the seller or the buyer

15. _____ Dividing a cost (most often one that has already been paid) between the two parties

16. _____ Trust account for funds set aside for future, recurring costs relating to a property, such as payment of property taxes and insurance

17. _____ Monies paid to government agencies, typically the county, to legally record documents that concern the property

18. _____ Property insurance policy that protects both owner and lender against physical hazards to property such as fire and windstorm damage

19. _____ The settlement statement that must be used for any federally related residential mortgage loans subject to RESPA

20. _____ Statement that summarizes all escrow account deposits and payments during the servicer's 12-month computation year

◻ **Multiple Choice Questions**

Instructions: Circle your response and go to Appendix A to read the complete explanation for each question.

1. The goal of the closing meeting is to:
    a. transfer ownership of the property to the buyer.
    b. pay the seller for the property.
    c. fund the loan.
    d. do both (a) and (b).

2. Which of the following is not a neutral party at a closing meeting?
    a. Attorney
    b. Representative from the title company
    c. Title abstractor
    d. Representative from each lending institution

3. Evidence of title is the means by which the ownership of land is satisfactorily demonstrated within a given jurisdiction. Which of the following is not one of the four kinds of evidence of title?
    a. Abstract and opinion
    b. Certified title assurance
    c. Certificate of title
    d. Title insurance

4. The _____ is the public record of prior transfers and encumbrances affecting the title of a parcel of land.
    a. abstract of title
    b. chain of title
    c. opinion of title
    d. assessment of title

5. Property taxes are paid in:
    a. advance.
    b. installments.
    c. arrears.
    d. collections.

6. How do special property tax assessments differ from annual property tax assessments?

    a. Special assessments provide for local improvements.

    b. Annual assessments have priority over special assessments.

    c. Judicial foreclosure is required for unpaid special assessments.

    d. Special assessments are imposed only by local authorities.

7. Which of the following is a credit on the seller's closing statement?

    a. Sales price

    b. Broker's commission

    c. Loan payoff on existing loan plus any interest charges

    d. Recording fee

8. Which is a recurring cost in a closing statement?

    a. Attorney fees

    b. Recording fees

    c. Escrow account

    d. Title insurance

9. The settlement statement shows the:

    a. borrower's credit history.

    b. borrower's employment history.

    c. costs for the buyer to maintain their property.

    d. settlement costs for the loan transaction.

10. Which statement summarizes all escrow account deposits and payments during the servicer's 12-month computation year?

    a. Annual Escrow Statement

    b. Initial Escrow Statement

    c. HUD-1 Settlement Statement

    d. Itemization of Escrow Statement

Loan Servicing

Unit **14**

INTRODUCTION

Loan servicing is the act of supervising and administering a loan after it has been made. Normally, the servicing function begins at the point of funding. Loan servicing is required for most real estate loans and for all real estate loans that are subject to RESPA.

The lender who originated the loan may perform this function, or the servicing may be sold to a loan servicing company. When a borrower takes out a real estate loan with a mortgage company or a bank, there is always a possibility that the lender will sell or transfer the note to another institution with or without the servicing of the loan. This may happen right after the borrower closes the loan or several years later. In cases in which the lender sells the note but keeps the opportunity to continue to collect and disburse payments, the originating lender remains the servicer. In today's market, real estate loans and loan servicing rights are bought and sold often.

Learning Objectives

After completing this Unit, you should be able to:

14A   identify characteristics of loan servicing.

14B   specify how a change in servicer affects loan terms.

14C   recognize procedures for loan servicing transfers.

14D   recall the responsibilities of real estate loan administrators.

14E   identify the purpose of an escrow (impound) account.

14F   select the elements in a payoff demand statement.

TRANSFER OF REAL ESTATE LOAN SERVICING

A promissory note is a negotiable instrument that may be bought and sold. The loan servicing may be retained or transferred. The **transfer of loan servicing** is a process in which the servicing is sold to a third party who will service the loan in the future. A lender may sell both the promissory and servicing, retain the note and sell the servicing, or sell the note and retain the servicing. Real estate lenders involved in the origination of loans usually transfer the servicing of their loans soon after closing and funding. Since the servicing of a loan is a paid service, the originating lender receives a fee, which is called a **servicing release premium (SRP)**, from the loan servicing company (servicer) who buys the loan. The new loan administrator takes the payments, handles the escrow accounts, pays the insurance and/or taxes, and answers questions about the loan.

The practice of selling or transferring the servicing of a loan is a very common and necessary part of the mortgage loan industry. In fact, the real estate loan servicing may be transferred more than once during the life of a loan.

When the servicing is sold, it is usually packaged (pooled) in a bundle with other loans. Many of the larger loan servicing companies set up servicing centers in order to consolidate loan servicing and keep costs as low as possible.

Changes to Terms and Conditions

The transfer of servicing should not affect the borrower or the real estate loan adversely. The original terms and conditions of the real estate loan stay the same. The interest rate and duration of the loan do not change on fixed-rate loans. The payment amount and payment schedule stay the same. However, the payments on loans with escrow accounts may change due to increases or decreases in real property taxes or insurance requirements.

If the borrower has an adjustable-rate mortgage (ARM) loan, the original conditions of the ARM note stay in effect and the rate changes according to the adjustment period (i.e., every 6 months, annually, every 3 years). This information is contained in the note and any riders to the note. The subsequent servicer(s) must honor all the terms of the original agreements contained in the note and its riders.

Although the ability to sell and transfer the rights in a real estate loan is standard practice in our national mortgage industry, the process is not always without incident. Human and computer errors sometimes interfere with the orderly transfer of the servicing. As a result, the Real Estate Settlement Procedures Act (RESPA) requires disclosures to protect borrowers during the **loan-servicing period** (life of the loan).

Notification of Loan Servicing Transfer

The originating lender and subsequent noteholder holding a loan do not have to ask the borrower's permission to transfer the servicing, but they do have to inform the borrower of the transfer. If the loan servicing is going to be sold, the borrower should receive two notices—one from the current servicer and one from the new loan servicer.

Servicing Transfer Statement

If the loan servicer sells the servicing rights to a borrower's loan to another loan servicer, a **Servicing Transfer Statement** must be sent to the borrower. The loan servicer must notify the borrower 15 days before the effective date of the loan transfer.

This letter states that the transfer will not affect any terms or conditions of the loan documents except the terms directly related to the servicing of the loan.

BEST MORTGAGE SERVICING COMPANY

SERVICING TRANSFER DISCLOSURE STATEMENT

NOTICE TO MORTGAGE LOAN APPLICANTS: THE RIGHT TO COLLECT YOUR MORTGAGE LOAN PAYMENTS MAY BE TRANSFERRED. FEDERAL LAW GIVES YOU CERTAIN RIGHTS. READ THIS STATEMENT AND SIGN IT ONLY IF YOU UNDERSTAND ITS CONTENTS.

Because you are applying for a mortgage loan covered by the Real Estate Settlement Procedures Act (RESPA) (12 U.S.C. 2601 et seq.) you have certain rights under Federal law. This statement tells you about those rights. It also tells you what the chances are that the servicing for this loan may be transferred to a different loan servicer. "Servicing" refers to collecting your principal, interest and escrow account payments. If the loan servicer changes, there are certain procedures that must be followed. This statement generally explains those procedures.

Transfer Practices and Requirements:

If the servicing of your loan is assigned, sold, or transferred to a new servicer, you must be given written notice of that transfer. The present loan servicer must send you notice in writing of the assignment, sale or transfer of the servicing not less than 15 days before the effective date of the transfer. The new loan servicer must also send you notice within 15 days after the effective date of the transfer. The present servicer and the new servicer may combine this information in one notice, so long as the notice is sent to you 15 days before the effective date of transfer. The 15 day period is not applicable if a notice of prospective transfer is provided to you at settlement. The law allows a delay in the time (not more than 30 days after a transfer) for servicers to notify you under certain limited circumstances, when your servicer is changed abruptly. This exception applies only if your servicer is fired for cause, is in bankruptcy proceedings, or is involved in a conservatorship or receivership initiated by a Federal Agency.

Notices must contain certain information. They must contain the effective date of the transfer of the servicing of your loan to the new servicer, the name, address, and toll-free or collect-call telephone number of the new servicer, and toll free or collect call telephone numbers of a person or department for both your present servicer and your new servicer to answer your questions about the transfer of servicing. During the 60-day period following the effective date of the transfer of the loan servicing, a loan payment received by your old servicer before its due date may not be treated by the new loan servicer as late, and a late fee may not be imposed on you.

Complaint Resolution:

Section 6 of RESPA(1 U.S.C. 2605) gives you certain rights, whether or not your loan servicing is transferred. If you send a "qualified written request" to your loan servicer concerning the servicing of your loan, your servicer must provide you with a written acknowledgment within 20 Business Days of receipt of your request. A "qualified written request" is a written correspondence, other than notice on a payment coupon or other payment medium supplied by the servicer, which includes your name and account number, and your reasons for the request. Not later than 60 Business Days after receiving your request, your servicer must make any appropriate corrections to your account, or must provide you with a written clarification regarding any dispute. During this 60-Business Day period, your servicer may not provide information to a consumer reporting agency concerning any overdue payment related to such period or qualified written request.

A Business Day is any day, excluding public holidays (State or Federal), Saturday and Sunday.

Damages and Costs:

Section 6 of RESPA also provides for damages and costs for individuals or classes of individuals in circumstances where servicers are shown to have violated the requirements of that section.

Servicing Transfer Estimated by Lender:

[1]   The following is the best estimate of what will happen to the servicing of your mortgage loan:

We may assign, sell or transfer the servicing of your loan sometime while the loan is outstanding. _____ We are able to service your loan and we _____ will/ _____ will not/ _____ haven't decided whether to service your loan.   **or**

___XXX___ We do not service mortgage loans, and we presently intend to assign, sell or transfer the servicing of your mortgage loan. You will be informed about your servicer.

[2]   For all the mortgage loans that we make in the 12 month period after your mortgage loan is funded, we estimate that the percentage of mortgage loans for which we will transfer servicing is between:

_____ 0 to 25%   _____ 26 to 50%   _____ 51 to 75%   __X__ 76 to 100%

This is only our best estimate and it is not binding. Business conditions or other circumstances may affect our future transferring decisions.

[3]   This is our record of transferring the servicing of the loans we have made in the past:

Year   Percentage of Loans Transferred (Rounded to Nearest Quartile)
20
20 } _____ 0 to 25%   _____ 26 to 50%   _____ 51 to 75%   __XX__ 76 to 100%
20

ACKNOWLEDGEMENT OF MORTGAGE LOAN APPLICANT

I/we have read this disclosure form, and understand its contents, as evidenced by my/our signature(s) below.

_____   _____   _____
APPLICANT'S SIGNATURE   CO-APPLICANT'S SIGNATURE   DATE

Items Included in a Servicing Transfer Statement
- Name and address of new servicer
- Toll-free telephone number
- Contact information for new servicing company
- Date and location to which borrower should send next payment

It should state if a borrower can continue any option insurance, such as mortgage life or disability insurance, and what action, if any, a borrower must take to maintain coverage.

> Example: If the contract states the borrower is allowed to pay property taxes and insurance premiums on his or her own, the new servicer cannot demand that the borrower establish an escrow account. However, if the contract is neutral on this issue or merely limits the actions of the originating lender, the new servicer may be able to require such an account.

Welcome Letter

The borrower should also receive a **welcome letter** from the new servicer that outlines the same information. This letter should give the same information that was given in the Servicing Transfer Statement such as the name of the new institution, a contact, phone number (toll-free if available), the new servicer's address, and instructions for making the next payment. The welcome letter from the new servicer informs the borrower that new payment coupons will be mailed. However, if the payment is due before the coupons arrive, the borrower should write the loan number on the check and mail it to the address provided in the welcome letter. If the borrower has coupons from the previous servicer, one of the coupons can be included with the payment.

The borrower should read the welcome letter carefully for payment instructions. The payment date will not change since it is determined in the original loan documents. If the loan is paid through electronic funds transfer or automatic draft each month, the borrower needs to cancel that arrangement and fill out new forms for the payment to be sent to the new servicer. Since this can take time, the borrower may need to pay by check until changes in electronic funds transfer are completed. The new servicer cannot take the payment from the borrower's savings or checking account without his or her signature.

It is very important that the borrower receive both letters. If the borrower receives only one of the two letters, he or she should be sure to call the original servicer to verify that the loan has actually been transferred. It is extremely important that the borrower keep the servicer informed of his or her current mailing address so that all relevant correspondence will be received on time.

BEST MORTGAGE
SERVICING COMPANY

August 6, 20XX

45678 Mountain View Road
Any City, Any State USA

Fred and Jan Spring
1652 Hill Street
Any City, Any State USA

RE: NOTICE OF ASSIGNMENT, SALE OR TRANSFER OF SERVICING RIGHTS

Prior Account Number: 12345678900
New Account Number: 98765432100
Effective Date of Transfer: 9/1/20XX
Original Loan Amount: $171,000.00

Dear Valued Customer:

Welcome to Best Mortgage Servicing Company. We are pleased to inform you that your mortgage loan has been purchased and the servcing of your account, i.e. the right to collect payments, will now be conducted by Best Mortgage Servicing.

Please be assured that the assignment, sale or transfer of the servicing of your mortgage loan does not affect any term condition of the mortgage instruments, other than the terms directly related to the servicing of your loan.

Except in limited circumstances, the law requires that your new servicer must send you this notice no later than 15 days after the effective date of transfer or at closing. Your prior servicer is ABC Mortgage Company. If you have any questions relating to the transfer of servicing from your prior servicer, please call (555) 555- 1234.

Your new servicer is Best Mortgage Servicing Company. The business address is 45678 Mountain View Road, Any City, Any State 90000. If you have any questions relating to the transfer of servicing, please call our customer service center at (555) 555-7890, Monday – Friday, between 8 a.m. and 9 p.m., PST.

Your prior servicer will stop accepting payments from you on 06/07/XX. Please send all payments due on or after that date to the address above. Please include your account number on your payment.

You will receive a billing statement from Best Mortgage Servicing each month. If you do not receive your first billing statement, please mail your payment to Best Mortgage Servicing with the temporary payment coupon attached to this letter. If your monthly payment includes escrow for taxes and insurance, this will continue without interruption.

If you enrolled in an automatic debit program through your prior servicer, this service will not continue upon the transfer to Best Mortgage Servicing. If you are interested in automatic debit of your monthly payment from your checking or savings account, plead contact our Customer Care department after the effective date of transfer to enroll in EZ Pay Plus, our automatic payment plan.

Mortgage life, accidental death, or other optional products billed and collected with your mortgage payment will not continue upon the transfer to Best Mortgage Servicing. Please contact your insurance carrier or prior servicer to maintain your coverage by direct billing, if available.

Once again, Welcome to Best Mortgage Servicing Company. We are proud to offer premium customer service and we encourage you to contact us to confirm your current account information so we can provide the quality service you expect. Our customer service staff is available at (555) 555-7890, Monday – Friday, between 8 a.m. and 9 p.m., PST.

Sincerely,

Best Mortgage Servicing Company

Mailing Payments to New Servicer

If the borrower has received both letters or has verified the transfer of the real estate loans with the previous servicer, he or she should be sure to send all payments to the new servicer from that point forward. If the payment is sent to the previous servicer, the borrower runs the risk of the payment not reaching the correct noteholder in time, paying a late charge, or increasing the chance that the payment is lost. It is the borrower's responsibility to send the payment to the new servicer once the borrower has been informed of the transfer. Regardless of who holds the note, the borrower must fulfill his or her responsibilities under the deed of trust or mortgage. These include making loan payments, keeping property taxes and insurance premiums current, and maintaining the property. If a servicing transfer occurs during a grace period, late charges cannot be assessed on a payment that is received beyond the usual grace period.

If a borrower accidentally sends the payment to the previous servicer, the company will usually forward the first payment to the new servicer, but this will not continue after the first month. In some instances, such as a merger or takeover, the previous servicer no longer exists. In this case, the payment may not be returned by the postal service for several weeks, which can result in the servicer assessing a late charge to the borrower's account. If this occurs, the borrower should request a refund of the late charge as soon as new servicer information is provided.

After transfer, it is the previous servicing company's responsibility to provide the insurance agent or company with a notice of transfer. The servicing company may change the beneficiary on the hazard insurance policy from one company to the other. The borrower should make sure this occurs so that if there is a claim, the check will be written and sent to the appropriate servicing company.

Grace Period

After the transfer, there is a grace period of 60 days. The **grace period** is a time period provided by the noteholder during which the borrower makes payments without penalty. A borrower cannot be charged a late fee for mistakenly sending a loan payment to the previous real estate loan servicer instead of to the new one. In addition, during the grace period, the new servicer cannot report late payments to a credit bureau.

RESPONSIBILITIES OF A LOAN ADMINISTRATOR

A **loan administrator** is an employee of a loan servicing company. He or she performs the day-to-day management of individual loans and services entire loan portfolios while protecting the interests of both the borrower and the investor. In addition, the loan administrator must establish effective lines of communication with borrowers and investors and maintain them throughout the life of the loan. Loan administrators process payments and pay real estate taxes, insurance premiums, and other assessments from escrow accounts. In addition, they handle loan assumptions, payoff requests, defaults, and foreclosures.

Payment Processing

The collection and processing of payments is the primary responsibility of real estate loan administrators. This includes collecting both principal and interest on the loan. If an escrow account is set up, loan payments may also include amounts for hazard insurance premiums, property taxes, and, in some instances, mortgage default insurance. An **escrow account (impound account)** is a fund the lender may require the borrower to establish in order to pay mortgage default insurance, property taxes, and/or hazard insurance as they become due on the property during the year. This account protects the lenders' and any subsequent noteholders' interests because the loan administrator controls the remittance of these payments.

The loan administrator sets up a billing process, which can be by coupon book or direct billing. If the monthly payment is fixed, the administrator may provide a coupon book. However, with an ARM or option-ARM loan, the administrator may prefer direct billing.

Items the Bill Should Show
- Total payment due
- Due date
- Date after which payment is considered late
- Amount of late charge
- Remaining principle balance
- Escrow amounts

Whether a coupon book or direct billing is used, most noteholders allow borrowers to make the payments online.

BEST MORTGAGE
SERVICING COMPANY

STATEMENT DATE: 11/16/20XX   LOAN NUMBER: 98765432100

IF YOU HAVE ANY QUESTIONS REGARDING YOUR LOAN
OR THIS STATEMENT, PLEASE CONTACT:

Lisa Summers, Loan Officer
Any City Branch Office
(555) 555-6345

BALANCES PRIOR TO BILLING TRANSACTIONS ARE SHOWN BELOW:
PRINCIPAL: $170,313.95

Account Name: Fred Spring

Account Name: Jan Spring

Address: 1652 Hill Street
                 Any City, Any County, USA

EXP DATE	DESCRIPTION	INTEREST	PRINCIPAL	TOTAL AMOUNT DUE
11/1/20XX	Amount Due	$852.43	$172.80	$1,023.25
11/5/20XX	Amount Received			$1,023.25
	Interest Paid	[$852.43]		
	Principal Paid		[$172.80]	
	TOTAL AMOUNT DUE	$0.00	$0.00	$0.00

Add if Payment Recieved at Office After:	12/15/20XX	$50.00

IF YOU HAVE QUESTIONS AFTER CONTACTING THE ABOVE OFFICE, PLEASE CONTACT THE DISTRICT INTERNAL AUDITOR AT: 45678 Mountain View Rd., Any City, Any State, USA (555) 555- 2345

- -

KEEP THIS PORTION FOR YOUR RECORDS

(DETACH ON PERFORATION AND FORWARD THE BOTTOM PORTION WITH YOUR PAYMENT TO THE BELOW REFERENCED ADDRESS)

BEST MORTGAGE
SERVICING COMPANY

STMT DATE	BRANCH	LOAN NUMBER	FREQUENCY
11/16/20XX	ANY CITY	98765432100	MONTHLY

DUE ON OR BEFORE	TOTAL AMOUNT DUE
12/01/20XX	1,023.25

$ _____ $ _____   SPECIAL PRINCIPAL PMT
AMOUNT ENCLOSED

$ _____   PREPAID INTEREST

☐ ADDRESS CHANGED MARKED

MAKE CHECK PAYABLE
AND MAIL TO:

FRED SPRING
JAN SPRING
1652 HILL STREET
ANY CITY, ANY COUNTY USA

Best Mortgage Servicing Company
45678 Mountain View Road
Any City, Any State 90000

Late Payments

If a payment is not received when due, a computer-generated reminder notice should be sent. In states where a late charge is allowed, the reminder states that a late charge will be assessed unless the payment is received before the end of the grace period. The late charge encourages prompt payment and helps offset any collection expenses. The late fee is stated in the promissory note as a percentage or a flat amount.

The loan administrator should never waive late charges without the knowledge and consent of the investor. If the loan becomes 30 or more days delinquent, the loan administrator drafts a formal demand for payment and forwards a copy to the investor. Sometimes, mentioning the possibility of accelerating the entire loan balance encourages the borrower to make timely payments.

Default and Foreclosure

If the borrower's delinquency is caused by circumstances beyond his or her control, the loan administrator may need to work out a loan modification plan or foreclose. Loan servicers must let borrowers know about any loss mitigation options to retain their home after borrowers have missed two consecutive payments. **Loss mitigation option** means an alternative to foreclosure offered by the owner or assignee of a mortgage loan that is made available through the servicer to the borrower. [§1024.31]. Servicers must provide borrowers a written notice that includes examples of available alternatives to foreclosure and instructions how to obtain more information.

Servicers cannot start a foreclosure proceeding if a borrower has already submitted a complete application for a loan modification or other alternative and that application is still pending review. To give borrowers reasonable time to submit such applications, servicers cannot make the first notice required for the foreclosure process until a mortgage loan account is delinquent more than 120 days.

Escrow Account

The loan administrator is responsible for managing the borrower's escrow account. When the escrow (impound) account is first established, the lender determines the estimated taxes, insurance premiums, and other charges that are anticipated over the next 12 months, along with the expected totals for these payments. These amounts are shown on the **Initial Escrow Statement**. Although the statement is usually given at settlement, the lender has 45 days from settlement to deliver it.

APPENDIX G–1: *INITIAL* ESCROW ACCOUNT DISCLOSURE STATEMENT — FORMAT

[Servicer's name, address, and toll-free number.]

INITIAL ESCROW ACCOUNT DISCLOSURE STATEMENT

THIS IS AN ESTIMATE OF ACTIVITY IN YOUR ESCROW ACCOUNT DURING THE COMING YEAR BASED ON PAYMENTS ANTICIPATED TO BE MADE FROM YOUR ACCOUNT.

Month	Payments to Escrow Account	Payments from Escrow Account	Description	Escrow Account Balance

Initial deposit: .... $_____

[A filled-out format follows.]

(PLEASE KEEP THIS STATEMENT FOR COMPARISON WITH THE ACTUAL ACTIVITY IN YOUR ACCOUNT AT THE END OF THE ESCROW ACCOUNTING COMPUTATION YEAR.)

Cushion selected by servicer: $_____.

YOUR MONTHLY MORTGAGE PAYMENT FOR THE COMING YEAR WILL BE $_____, OF WHICH $_____ WILL BE FOR PRINCIPAL AND INTEREST, $_____ WILL GO INTO YOUR ESCROW ACCOUNT, AND $_____ WILL BE FOR DISCRETIONARY ITEMS (SUCH AS LIFE INSURANCE, DISABILITY INSURANCE) THAT YOU CHOSE TO BE INCLUDED WITH YOUR MONTHLY PAYMENT.]

[YOUR FIRST MONTHLY MORTGAGE PAYMENT FOR THE COMING YEAR WILL BE $_____, OF WHICH $_____ WILL BE FOR PRINCIPAL AND INTEREST, $_____ WILL GO INTO YOUR ESCROW ACCOUNT, AND $_____ WILL BE FOR DISCRETIONARY ITEMS (SUCH AS LIFE INSURANCE, DISABILITY INSURANCE) THAT YOU CHOSE TO BE INCLUDED WITH YOUR MONTHLY PAYMENT. THE TERMS OF YOUR LOAN MAY RESULT IN CHANGES TO THE MONTHLY PRINCIPAL AND INTEREST PAYMENTS DURING THE YEAR.]

[INSTRUCTIONS TO PREPARER: The servicer is to use the appropriate option above describing the principal and interest payments for the coming year. The reference to payments for discretionary items should be omitted if there are no such payments included with the monthly payment. This instruction paragraph should not appear on the form.]

At closing, the borrower deposits money into the escrow account and then makes monthly deposits to accumulate funds to pay real estate taxes, insurance premiums, and other assessments. The loan administrator pays these items from the account when they become due and payable. If the lender's estimates were correct, there will be enough money in the account to pay the taxes and insurance. However, if the funds are insufficient, the administrator must collect the extra money from the borrower.

The loan administrator does an annual analysis of the escrow account. During the analysis, the administrator reviews the escrow amount and determines if it is adequate to cover the fees for the insurance, taxes, and any other premiums paid through the escrow account. If the amount is insufficient, the servicer may ask the borrower to increase the regular monthly deposit.

Sometimes the borrower receives a notice that either the insurance or taxes are due. The borrower should call the servicing company to make sure the company has information on file that funds have been escrowed for the premium.

Annual Statements

The loan administrator is required to give the borrower an **Annual Escrow Statement** that details the activity in the escrow account. This statement shows deposits into the account and the account balance. It also reflects remittances of property taxes and homeowners insurance. It accounts for any shortages or surpluses in the account and helps advise the borrower about the course of action being taken.

Items on the Annual Escrow Account Reconciliation

- Balance of account at beginning of year

- Total amount deposited by borrower

- Amount, date, and nature of disbursements

- Balance of account at end of year

APPENDIX I–1: ANNUAL ESCROW ACCOUNT DISCLOSURE STATEMENT — FORMAT

[Account history of pre-rule accounts computed using single-item analysis.]

[Servicer's name, address, and toll-free number.]

ANNUAL ESCROW ACCOUNT DISCLOSURE STATEMENT — *ACCOUNT HISTORY*

THIS IS A STATEMENT OF ACTUAL ACTIVITY IN YOUR ESCROW ACCOUNT FROM _____ THROUGH _____. {COMPARE IT TO THE ANNUAL ESCROW ACCOUNT DISCLOSURE STATEMENT — *PROJECTIONS FOR COMING YEAR*—WHICH WAS SENT TO YOU LAST YEAR ON _____ (ANOTHER COPY ENCLOSED).}

[INSTRUCTIONS TO PREPARER: Delete material in brackets {} if initial escrow account disclosure statement or annual disclosure payment history was not delivered in previous year. Also, if the servicer elects to provide a side-by-side comparison of last year's projection to the account history, delete "{COMPARE . . . ENCLOSED.}". This instruction paragraph should not be included in the form.]

[Your monthly mortgage payment for the past year was $_____, of which $_____ was for principal and interest, $_____ went into your escrow account, and $_____ was for discretionary items (such as life insurance, disability insurance) that you chose to have included with your monthly mortgage payment.]

[INSTRUCTIONS TO PREPARER: The reference to the discretionary items should be omitted if there are no payments for such items included in the monthly mortgage payment. This instruction paragraph should not appear on the form.]

Month	Payments to Escrow Account	Payments from Escrow Account	Description	Escrow Account Balance
Starting balance: .... $_____				

[A filled-out example follows.]

An asterisk (*) indicates a difference from a previous estimate either in the date or the amount.

Last year, we anticipated that payments from your account would be made during this period equaling $_____. Under Federal law, your lowest monthly balance should not have exceeded $_____, unless your mortgage contract or State law specifies a lower amount. (Your mortgage contract and State law are silent on this issue.) (Under your mortgage contract and State law, your lowest monthly balance should not have exceeded $_____.)

[INSTRUCTIONS TO PREPARER: The servicer is to use the appropriate sentence above describing the mortgage contract. This instruction paragraph should not appear in the form.]

Your actual lowest monthly balance was greater than $_____. The items with an asterisk on your Account History may explain this. If you want a further explanation, please call our toll-free number.

[INSTRUCTIONS TO PREPARER: The servicer is to use the paragraph above if the lowest month-end balance exceeds either the Federal or the contract/State law limit. Put the lower of the two in the blank. This instruction paragraph should not appear in the form.]

APPENDIX I–2: ANNUAL ESCROW ACCOUNT DISCLOSURE STATEMENT — FORMAT

[Projections for pre-rule accounts computed using single-item analysis.]

[Servicer's name, address, and toll-free number.]

ANNUAL ESCROW ACCOUNT DISCLOSURE STATEMENT — *PROJECTIONS FOR COMING YEAR*

THIS IS AN ESTIMATE OF ACTIVITY IN YOUR ESCROW ACCOUNT DURING THE COMING YEAR BASED ON PAYMENTS ANTICIPATED TO BE MADE FROM YOUR ACCOUNT.

Month	Payments to Escrow Account	Payments from Escrow Account	Description	Escrow Account Balance

Starting balance: .... $_____

[A filled-out format follows.]

Your ending balance, from the last month of the account history, is $_____. Your starting balance according to this analysis should be $_____.

[This means you have a surplus of $_____. This surplus must be returned to you unless it is less than $50, in which case we have the additional option of keeping it and lowering your monthly payments accordingly. (We are sending you a check for the surplus.) (We are keeping the surplus and lowering your monthly payments.)]

[This means you have a shortage of $_____. This shortage may be collected from you over a period of 12 months or more unless the shortage is less than 1 month's deposit, in which case we have the additional option of requesting payment within 30 days. (We have decided to collect it over _____ months.) (We have decided to collect it within 30 days.) (We have decided to do nothing.)]

[This means you have a deficiency of $_____. This deficiency may be collected from you over a period of 2 months or more unless the deficiency is less than 1 month's deposit, in which case we have the additional option of requesting payment within 30 days. (We have decided to collect it over _____ months.) (We have decided to collect it within 30 days.) (We have decided to do nothing.)]

[INSTRUCTIONS TO PREPARER: The servicer is to use the appropriate paragraph above if there is a surplus, shortage, or deficiency. The servicer should then print the response selected from the choices given. If the deficiency and shortage paragraphs are to be used on the same form, appropriate explanatory language may be used. This instruction paragraph should not be included in the form.]

(PLEASE KEEP THIS STATEMENT FOR COMPARISON WITH THE ACTUAL ACTIVITY IN YOUR AC-COUNT AT THE END OF THE NEXT ESCROW ACCOUNTING COMPUTATION YEAR.)

[YOUR MONTHLY MORTGAGE PAYMENT FOR THE COMING YEAR WILL BE $_____, OF WHICH $_____ WILL BE FOR PRINCIPAL AND INTEREST, $_____ WILL GO INTO YOUR ESCROW ACCOUNT, AND $_____ WILL BE FOR DISCRETIONARY ITEMS (SUCH AS LIFE INSURANCE, DISABILITY INSURANCE) THAT YOU CHOSE TO BE INCLUDED WITH YOUR MONTHLY PAYMENT.]

[YOUR FIRST MONTHLY MORTGAGE PAYMENT FOR THE COMING YEAR WILL BE $_____, OF WHICH $_____ WILL BE FOR PRINCIPAL AND INTEREST, $_____ WILL GO INTO YOUR ESCROW ACCOUNT, AND $_____ WILL BE FOR DISCRETIONARY ITEMS (SUCH AS LIFE INSURANCE, DISABILITY INSURANCE) THAT YOU CHOSE TO BE INCLUDED WITH YOUR MONTHLY PAYMENT. THE TERMS OF YOUR LOAN MAY RESULT IN CHANGES TO THE MONTHLY PRINCIPAL AND INTEREST PAYMENTS DURING THE YEAR.]

[INSTRUCTIONS TO PREPARER: The servicer is to use the appropriate option above describing the principal and interest payments for the coming year. The reference to payments for discretionary items should be omitted if there are no such payments included with the monthly payment. This instruction paragraph should not appear on the form.]

The loan administrator prepares annual statements for noteholders and borrowers. At the end of the year, the borrower will receive a 1098 Mortgage Interest Statement that shows how much interest was paid. If the loan had two or more servicers over the course of the year, the borrower may receive more than one statement. Sometimes, the interest paid to the noteholders is combined into one report from the final servicing company, which sends the borrower one tax statement at the end of the year that covers the entire year.

The loan administrator also forwards the proceeds to investors who have purchased real estate loans and acts as the investors' representative when any problems arise with the loan.

Insurance Requirements

Noteholders always require evidence of property insurance coverage for building(s) on which a loan is made before they disburse money on the loan. As set out in the loan documents, borrowers must have fire and hazard insurance on the property. If the borrower does not maintain insurance coverage, the noteholder may take out **force-placed insurance** to cover the property until the borrower provides a new insurance policy.

However, an initial notice must be sent to a borrower at least 45 days before charging a borrower for force-placed insurance coverage, and a second reminder notice must be sent no earlier than 30 days after the first notice and at least 15 days before charging a borrower for force-placed insurance coverage. All costs for installing the necessary insurance will be added to the loan balance at the time of installation of the borrower's new insurance. If a borrower provides proof of hazard insurance coverage, the servicer must cancel any force-placed insurance policy and refund any premiums paid for overlapping periods in which the borrower's coverage was in place. [§1024.37].

The loan administrator is responsible for protecting the investor from liability by making sure that all properties in the portfolio are adequately insured against loss or liability. Each insurance policy should describe the coverage terms, the policy limits, effective/expiration dates, and have a mortgagee's clause. The **mortgagee's clause** gives the full name and address of the noteholder and provides that any loss be paid to the noteholder.

The loan administrator should keep copies of the policies and create a tracking system with the expiration dates. This system will help avoid any lapse in policy coverage. Records of expired policies should be kept for 5 years. When a property is properly insured, the element of risk is shared with, or partly transferred to, the insurer.

Types of Insurance Coverage

There is a broad range of types of insurance offered to protect the noteholder and borrower. Typically, a noteholder requires homeowners and hazard insurance. In areas subject to flooding, flood insurance is required as well.

Homeowners Insurance

Homeowners insurance is property insurance that covers the building or structure, any completed additions, and the possessions inside from serious loss such as theft or fire. Homeowners insurance is required by all lenders to protect their residential loan investment and must be obtained before the loan closes. In most cases, coverage must be at least equal to the loan balance or the value of the home.

Policy coverage for property insurance is written to cover either the replacement value or actual cash value of the building. **Replacement value** covers a structure for the amount it will cost to rebuild the same structure if it is built today. **Actual cash value** covers a structure at the depreciated value of the loss. If a building is 10 years old, the structure is considered to have depreciated to a lesser value over the last 10 years. When the building is insured for actual cash value, the amount paid is equal to today's cost to replace the structure minus depreciation.

The noteholder must be named as a loss payee on the required policy. A **loss payee** is a party named to receive benefits when a claim on an insurance policy is filed. The insurance company provides a copy of the loss payee endorsement to the noteholder.

Fire, Extended Coverage, & Vandalism

Basic property insurance can be customized with additional coverage. This coverage insures against direct loss to property caused by fire or lightning, windstorm or hail, explosions, riot or civil commotion, theft, aircraft, vehicles, smoke, vandalism, and malicious mischief.

Earthquake Insurance

In states like California, where earthquakes are common, owners of property can obtain earthquake insurance. **Earthquake insurance** policies cover damage to the structure during an earthquake, but can vary greatly in terms of exclusions and deductibles. Deductibles are much higher than those on property insurance policies. Some earthquake insurance policies have extensive exclusions—patios, decks, detached garages, fences, swimming pools, satellite dishes, and sprinkler systems, to name a few.

Flood Insurance

Property located in areas that tend to flood should be covered with flood insurance. In fact, federal law requires mortgage lenders to assure that all properties within designated flood prone areas have flood insurance before the lenders provide a mortgage on the property. **Flood insurance** covers losses from flooding, including structural

damage; damage to furnace, water heater, and air conditioner units; flood debris clean up; and the replacement of floor surfaces.

For more information, visit http://www.fema.gov. Flood insurance is provided almost exclusively by the **National Flood Insurance Program** (NFIP), which is operated by the **Federal Emergency Management Agency** (FEMA). The National Flood Insurance Program requires that all new and substantially improved structures must have (at a minimum) the lowest floor elevated to or above the Base Flood Elevation (BFE).

Insurer Eligibility

The loan administrator determines whether an insurance policy is acceptable and meets the investor's requirements. The insurance carrier must have financial strength and be licensed to transact business in the state where the property is located. Another important consideration the loan administrator has is to verify the carrier's rating. Only policies from insurance carriers with a rating of A or better should be accepted.

Independent firms such as **A.M. Best** rate insurance companies. A.M. Best can be found at www.ambest.com. A.M. Best ratings of A++ or A+(superior), A or A– (excellent), or B++ or B+ (good) are given to companies that are considered financially secure. Companies considered financially vulnerable are rated B, B–, and lower.

A.M. BEST		STANDARD & POOR'S	
A++ A+	(Superior) (Superior)	AAA	(Extremely Strong)
A A-	(Excellent) (Excellent)	AA+ AA AA-	(Very Strong) (Very Strong) (Very Strong)
B++ B+ B B-	(Very Good) (Very Good) (Fair) (Fair)	A+ A A-	(Strong) (Strong) (Strong)
C++ C+	(Marginal) (Marginal)	BBB+ BBB BBB-	(Good) (Good) (Good)
C C-	(Weak) (Weak)	BB+ BB BB-	(Marginal) (Marginal) (Marginal)
D	(Poor)	B+ B B-	(Weak) (Weak) (Weak)
E F S	(Under Regulatory Supervision) (In Liquidation) (Rating Suspended)	CCC CC R	(Very Weak) (Extremely Weak) (Regulatory Action)

Real Estate Taxes

Property taxes must be kept current during the term of the loan. The loan administrator is responsible for making sure that the real estate taxes and other assessments are paid promptly whether they are paid out of an established escrow (impound) account or paid directly by the borrower. Before releasing funds from an escrow account, the loan administrator should review the property tax bill to determine its accuracy. The bill should have the correct property description and assessment.

If the borrower pays the property tax directly, he or she must submit proof of payment to the loan administrator. Some administrators use a tax service bureau to ensure that the property taxes have been paid.

Non-payment of property taxes puts the noteholder at risk. At the least, the property will be subject to a tax lien. This is critical because tax liens are superior to mortgage liens. If left unpaid, the property may be sold at a tax sale with insufficient proceeds remaining to satisfy the noteholder's lien.

If the borrower fails to maintain payment of property taxes, the noteholder may choose to advance funds to pay the delinquent property taxes to prevent the property from being sold at a tax sale. The amount advanced (tax payment plus any penalties) is added to the loan balance.

At this point, the loan administrator will continue to monitor the account. If any delinquencies occur—in loan payments, insurance premiums, or property taxes—the loan administrator should recommend foreclosure proceedings to protect the investor's interest.

Loan Assumption and Payoff Procedures

The loan administrator must be notified whenever ownership of the property is transferred. The administrator needs to know if the loan is to be assumed or paid off.

Assumption Request

When a property is sold, the buyer may want to assume the existing loan. Under an assumption, the buyer takes over primary liability for the loan and the original borrower becomes secondarily liable. In the event of a default by the new borrower, the original borrower may still be held responsible for the note based on state laws.

The original borrower (seller) can avoid any responsibility for the loan by asking the noteholder for a substitution of liability. The **substitution of liability (novation)** relieves the seller of all liability for repayment of the loan.

Before approving the assumption, the loan administrator must determine if the loan documents have an alienation (due-on-sale) clause. A due-on-sale clause in the note prevents a buyer from assuming the loan. If the note does not have an alienation clause, many noteholders allow an assumption, but only after the buyer pays an assumption fee. The noteholder may also require a credit report and other information from the new borrower.

The settlement agent requests that the noteholder prepare a document called a **statement of condition**. This document acknowledges the current balance, interest rate, amount and due date for monthly payments, late fees, and the date of maturity for a loan. The statement of condition is used when property subject to a real estate loan is sold and the buyer wants to assume the debt. The statement of condition is called a **reduction certificate** when a mortgage is being assumed and a **beneficiary statement** in deed of trust situations.

NOVATION AGREEMENT

This AGREEMENT made as of _____ **BETWEEN**: _____
                                    Date   Name of Debtor

of _____ (the "Debtor") - and - _____
              Address of Debtor

_____ , of _____ (the "New Debtor")
   Name of New Debtor   Address of New Debtor

- and - _____ , of _____ (the "Creditor")
           Name of Creditor   Address of Creditor

WHEREAS:

(A)   The debtor is indebted to the Creditor in the amount of [Amount of Indebtedness owning by Debtor to Creditor] Pursuant to the terms and conditions of a [Name of Agreement Creating Indebtedness (i.e., Loan Agreement)] (the "Loan Agreement") dated [Date of Agreement Creating Indebtedness] (the "Indebtedness"); and

(B)   The New Debtor has agreed with the Debtor and the Creditor to assume the Indebtedness;

(C)   In consideration of the foregoing, the Creditor hereby consents to the assumption of the Indebtedness by the New Debtor and hereby forever releases and discharges the Debtor in respect of any and all claims which the Creditor has or may have, now or in the future, whether arising in respect of the Obligations and the Loan Agreement.

IN WITNESS WHEREOF the parties hereto have executed this Agreement as of the date first above written.

_____   _____
Witness   [NAME OF DEBTOR]

_____   _____
Witness   [NAME OF NEW DEBTOR]

_____   _____
Witness   [NAME OF CREDITOR]

STATEMENT OF CONDITION

Date:

Lender of Record
P.O. Box 3768
Any Town, Any City USA

ATTN: Loan Status Department   RE: Loan # XX-00000-XX

Property Address:

Title Vested as:

Legal description:

Current unpaid balance: $_____ Interest rate on the loan _____%

The monthly payment is $ _____ Due on the _____ day of each month.

The next date a payment is due is _____ The amount of the late fee is $ _____

The late fee is assessed and due on what day of each month _____

The impound account status is:
   There is no impound connected with this loan _____
   There is an impound shortage of $ _____
   The impound account contains $ _____

The loan terms for assumption are: _____
_____

The loan terms for taking title subject to the existing title are: _____
_____

Pat Green, Closing Officer   Ed Baker, Title Officer
No. MBS-100   Title Order No. 1-123456
Any State Escrow Company   Any State Title Company
980 Riverview Road
Any City, Any State USA

Payoff Request

When the loan administrator receives a request for a payoff demand statement (typically from a settlement or escrow officer), he or she must determine if the loan has a lock-in provision or prepayment penalty. This must be determined before he or she prepares the payoff demand statement.

A **lock-in clause** in the promissory note prohibits prepayment of the loan prior to a specified date. Typically, the lock-in period is for the first 2-3 years of the loan. Some promissory notes have a prepayment penalty clause. However, prepayment penalties are not allowed on conforming, FHA, or VA loans. If the note has a prepayment penalty clause, the loan administrator should calculate the amount of the premium and send it, along with the payoff figure, to the noteholder for approval.

The loan administrator prepares the payoff demand statement. The **payoff demand statement** is a written statement that details the current principal balance, interest, and any other amounts to satisfy the debt. The noteholder's approval must be obtained unless there are specific instructions to the contrary.

The payoff demand statement requires payoff funds to be sent by wire transfer or certified funds. A **wire transfer** is the electronic transfer of funds from one bank to another. **Certified funds** refer to a payment that is guaranteed to clear by the company certifying the funds. Types of certified funds include cashier's checks, certified bank checks, and money orders. Personal checks and credit cards are not allowed. This is because the personal checking account may have insufficient funds and the credit card transaction may be disputed and reversed.

Once the loan is **satisfied** (paid in full), the loan administrator prepares and records loan release documents. A **satisfaction of mortgage** is the recorded instrument used to evidence payment in full of a mortgage debt. When a loan secured by a deed of trust is paid in full, a deed of reconveyance is recorded. The **deed of reconveyance** transfers title from the trustee to the trustor (borrower).

The loan administrator should do a final review of the file to be sure everything is complete. The loan servicing company should archive the paid-in-full files. The length of time required varies by state.

Any State Home Loans, Inc.
Payoff Department
123 Main Street
Any City, Any State USA
1-800-555-5555
Fax: 1-555-555-555

PAYOFF DEMAND STATEMENT
Statement Date: April 6, 20XX
Statement Void After: April 16, 20XX

(CV- JMB-ARM)

Mailed to:	Property Address:
Attn:	
X	321 Any Drive
X	Any City, Any State USA
X 99999	

Faxed to: 1-555-432-5678

Escrow# 1234

Payoff Loan No.: 4444
Case # CA

Principal Balance as of 03/01/20XX	$ 370,260.30
Interest from 03/01/20XX to 3/10/20XX	502.13
*Statement Fees	30.00
County Recording Fee	16.00
Reconveyance Fee	45.00
Total Payoff Due on Loan No. 44440000	$ 370,853.43

Total Due	$ 370,853.43

PLUS ADDITIONAL
INTEREST SHOWN BELOW

*Please refer to important information about this fee on the next page of this statement.

Daily Interest[1]	From	To	Interest Rate
55.7926	3/10/20XX		5.50%

[1]Daily Interest Daily interest = Principal Balance x Interest Rate ÷ 365.

AMENDED DEMAND STATEMENTS ARE SENT AUTOMATICALLY IF THE TOTAL AMOUNT DUE INCREASES BEFORE APRIL 16, 20XX.

Payoff funds must be made payable to **Any State Home Loans, Inc.** and will be accepted by **WIRE** or **CERTIFIED FUNDS ONLY.** They **MUST** reference the **Any State loan number, property address** and **borrower's name** in the OBI (Originator Beneficiary Information) field of the wire transfer or on the face of the check and must be sent per the instructions below. Failure to do so may cause delays resulting in additional interest due or the return of the funds to the remitter. Funds received after 3:00 p.m. Pacific Time may be posted the following business day.

<table>
<tr><td><u>Wire</u> funds to:</td><td><u>Mail</u> funds to:</td></tr>
<tr><td>All State Bank</td><td>Any State Home Loans, Inc.</td></tr>
<tr><td>ABA Routing # 123400000</td><td>Attn: Payoff Department, Mail Stop AC-12</td></tr>
<tr><td>MRC Account # 56789-4321</td><td>123 Main Street</td></tr>
<tr><td></td><td>Any City, Any State USA</td></tr>
</table>

This communication is from a debt collector

SATISFACTION OF MORTGAGE

THIS DOCUMENT is signed by _____ ("Mortgagee"), who is the owner and holder of, and has not transferred, assigned, pledged, or otherwise encumbered any interest in, the following described mortgage ("Mortgage"):

Mortgage dated _____, from ("Mortgagor") to _____ securing that certain promissory note ("Note") in the original principal amount of _____ and _____/100 DOLLARS ($_____) which mortgage is recorded in Official Records Book _____, Page _____, Public Records of _____ County, Florida, encumbering certain property situate in _____ County, Florida, as more particularly described in the Mortgage ("Property"); AND

THAT Mortgagee hereby acknowledges full payment and satisfaction of the Note and Mortgage, does hereby surrender the Note and Mortgage as cancelled, releases the Property from the lien of the Mortgage, and directs the Clerk of the Circuit Court in and for _____ County to cancel the same of record.

IN WITNESS WHEREOF, the Mortgagee has executed these presents this _____ day of _____, A.D. _____ (year).

Signed, sealed and delivered in the presence of:

_____   _____

_____   _____

Acknowledged before me on _____, by _____, who _____ is personally known to me/_____ produced _____ as identification, and who _____ did/_____ did not take an oath.

_____

NOTARY PUBLIC – STATE OF FLORIDA

Name: _____

Commission No.: _____

My Commission Expires: _____

THIS INSTRUMENT PREPARED BY:

NAME _____

ADDR. _____

_____

RECORDING REQUESTED BY

_____

AND WHEN RECORDED, MAIL THIS DEED AND, UNLESS
OTHERWISE SHOWN BELOW, MAIL TAX STATEMENT TO:

Name: _____

Street
Address: _____

City, State &
Zip code   : _____

TITLE ORDER NO. _____ ESCROW NO _____

_____   SPACE ABOVE THIS LINE FOR RECORDER'S USE

DEED OF FULL RECONVEYANCE

Whereas, _____, the Trustee ___ under the Deed
of Trust dated _____, made and executed by _____ as Trustor(s)
to _____ as beneficiary and recorded as Instrument No. _____,
on _____, in Book _____ at Page _____ of the Office Records in the Office of the
Recorder of _____ County, State of _____
having received from Beneficiary ___ under said Deed of Trust a written request to reconvey, reciting that
all sums secured by said Deed of Trust have been fully paid, and said Deed of Trust and the note or
notes secured thereby having been surrendered to the Trustee ___ for cancellation, do ___ hereby
reconvey, without warranty, to the person or persons legally entitled thereto, all right, title and interest
heretofore acquired and now held by said Trustee under said Deed of Trust, in the real property
commonly know as _____ situated in the County
of _____, State of _____, and more particularly
described as follows:

_____
_____
_____

Date: _____   _____

_____

_____, as Trustee ___

STATE OF _____
COUNTY OF _____

On _____ before me, _____, a Notary Public,
personally appeared _____ who proved to me on the basis of
satisfactory evidence to be the person(s) whose name(s) is/are subscribed to the within instrument and
acknowledged to me that he/she/they executed the same in his/her/their authorized capacity(ies), and
that by his/her/their signature(s) on the instrument the person(s), or the entity upon behalf of which the
person(s) acted, executed the instrument. I certify under PENALTY OF PERJURY under the laws of
the State of California that the foregoing paragraph is true and correct.

Witness my hand and official seal.

Signature _____ (SEAL)

CAPACITY CLAIMED BY SIGNER(S)
☐ INDIVIDUAL(S) _____
☐ CORPORATE _____
OFFICER(S) _____
                                          (TITLES)
☐ PARTNER(S)   ☐ LIMITED
                ☐ GENERAL
☐ ATTORNEY IN FACT
☐ TRUSTEE(S)
☐ GUARDIAN/CONSERVATOR
☐ OTHER: _____

SIGNER IS REPRESENTING:
Name of Person(s) or Entity(ies)

_____
_____

SUMMARY

At closing, the lender must tell the borrower who will be servicing (administering) the real estate loan. In other words, to whom does the borrower send loan payments? When a borrower takes out a real estate loan with a mortgage company or a bank, there is always a possibility that the lender will sell or transfer the note to another institution with or without servicing the loan. In other words, the loan servicing may be handled by a third party instead of the lender who originated and approved the loan. The loan servicing may be sold once or several times.

UNIT 14 REVIEW

Matching Exercise

Instructions: Write the letter of the matching term on the blank line before its definition. Answers are in Appendix A.

Terms

A. deed of reconveyance
B. escrow account
C. flood insurance
D. grace period
E. homeowners insurance
F. loan servicing
G. loan-servicing period
H. lock-in clause
I. loss payee

J. mortgagee clause
K. payoff demand statement
L. replacement value
M. satisfaction of mortgage
N. servicing release premium
O. statement of condition
P. substitution of liability
Q. transfer of loan servicing
R. wire transfer

Definitions

1. _____ Act of supervising and administering a loan after it has been made

2. _____ Process in which a loan is sold to a third party who will service the loan in the future

3. _____ Fee paid to the originating lender from the servicer who buys the loan

4. _____ Time provided by the lender in which the borrower makes payments without penalty

5. _____ Fund the lender may require the borrower to establish in order to pay property taxes and/or hazard insurance as they become due on the property during the year. Also called impound account

6. _____ Insurance clause that names the full name and address of the noteholder and provides that any loss is paid to the noteholder

7. _____ Insurance that covers buildings or structures and any completed additions from serious loss such as theft or fire

8. _____ Insurance that covers a structure for the amount it will cost to rebuild the same structure if it is built today

9. _____ Party named to receive benefits when a claim on an insurance policy is filed

10. _____ Seller is relieved of all liability for repayment of the loan

11. _____ Document that acknowledges the current balance, interest rate, amount and due date for monthly payments, late fees, and date of maturity for a loan

12. _____ Clause in promissory note prohibiting prepayment of the loan prior to a specified date

13. _____ A written statement detailing the current principal balance, interest, and any other amounts to satisfy the debt

14. _____ Electronic transfer of funds from one bank to another

15. _____ Recorded instrument used to evidence payment in full of a mortgage debt

16. _____ Recorded instrument used to transfer title from the trustee to the trustor (borrower) when a loan secured by a deed of trust is paid in full

Multiple Choice Questions

Instructions: Circle your response and go to Appendix A to read the complete explanation for each question.

1.   Of the following statements, which is not characteristic of loan servicing?
   a. Loan servicing is required for all real estate loans.
   b. Loan servicing is the act of supervising and administering a loan after it has been made.
   c. Loan servicing always stays with the originating lender.
   d. Loan servicing rights and real estate loans are often bought and sold.

2. Which statement is true regarding the transfer of loan servicing?

    a. The original terms and conditions of the real estate loan change each time the loan servicing is transferred.

    b. The transfer of servicing should not affect the borrower or the real estate loan adversely.

    c. Both the interest rate and duration of the loan change on fixed-rate loans.

    d. Depending on the last loan servicing company providing the service, the payment amount and payment schedule change.

3. How does a transfer of service affect a borrower with an adjustable-rate mortgage (ARM) loan?

    a. The ARM will adjust to a different index.

    b. The terms of the ARM will not change.

    c. The borrower has the option of changing to a fixed-rate loan.

    d. The servicer can change the ARM terms to favor the borrower.

4. If the current servicer plans to sell the loan servicing, the borrower must be notified at least _____ days before the effective date of the transfer.

    a. 15

    b. 30

    c. 45

    d. 60

5. Once proper notification of transfer of service has been sent by both servicers, who is responsible if a payment is sent to the previous servicer instead of to the new servicer?

    a. Borrower

    b. Noteholder

    c. Previous Servicer

    d. Current Servicer

6. In a loan servicing company, who performs the day-to-day management of individual loans?

    a. Loan processor

    b. Loan administrator

    c. Loan originator

    d. Loan officer

7. What is the name of the fund established by the lender to pay the property taxes and/or hazard insurance during the year?

    a. Adjustable-rate mortgage

    b. Escrow account

    c. Impound account

    d. Both (b) and (c)

8. If an escrow account is established, the real estate loan administrator is required to give the borrower a(n):

    a. annual statement reflecting account activity.

    b. monthly update on average interest rates.

    c. accounting of foreclosure costs in the event of default.

    d. weekly statement reflecting account activity.

9. In addition to detailing _____, the payoff demand statement requires payoff funds be sent by wire transfer or certified funds.

    a. current principal balance and interest

    b. statement fees

    c. recording and reconveyance fees

    d. all of the above

10. When a loan secured by a deed of trust is paid in full, a deed of reconveyance is recorded that transfers title from the:

    a. lender to the lendee.

    b. trustee to the borrower.

    c. mortgagor to the mortgagee.

    d. lessor to the lessee.

Default & Foreclosure

Unit **15**

INTRODUCTION

When it comes to paying a loan on time, uncertainty can affect even the most creditworthy borrowers. A sudden job loss, terminal illness, or other life-changing catastrophe can bring turmoil to an individual's personal finances. When a borrower faces financial difficulties, he or she can fall behind on loan payments, which can result in default and possibly foreclosure. While borrowers usually do not intend to be behind on their loan payments, certain life situations are beyond their control and can turn their financial world upside down.

Fortunately, there are methods borrowers can use to avoid foreclosure, keep their credit intact, and, most importantly, stay in their home. In addition, lenders can work with borrowers and offer remedies to assist them during a financial crisis. However, when foreclosure is inevitable, certain steps must take place, depending on the type of foreclosure.

This unit covers loan default, the different types of foreclosure, the processes that occur during foreclosure, and other ways that lenders can recover their investment.

Learning Objectives

After completing this Unit, you should be able to:

15A   recall the definition of default.

15B   identify borrower options during a loan default.

15C   identify lender options during a loan default.

15D   recall the different types of foreclosure.

15E   recall the tax implications of default and foreclosure.

15F   indicate how a lender sues on the promissory note to obtain a deficiency judgment.

DEFAULT

When a borrower fails to pay a contractual debt, the situation is known as a **default**. A default can occur in a number of debt obligations such as car payments, home loans, credit card payments, and other recurring monthly payments. A borrower may default on his or her payments for a number of reasons such as job loss, divorce, medical expenses, and insurmountable debts. In real estate finance, a default can signal the beginning of the foreclosure process. However, the borrower has options and can take certain measures to save his or her property. In addition, the lender will also work with the borrower to prevent the foreclosure process, which can be costly.

Borrower's Options – Adjustments & Modifications

When a borrower is in default, there are options the borrower can use to salvage his or her credit and, more importantly, stay in the home. The borrower must be proactive in his or her efforts, which can include refinancing the existing loan, obtaining a loan modification, or selling the property when necessary.

Refinance

Refinancing the existing loan is a possible solution especially if the borrower has enough equity in the property and qualifying credit according to the lender's guidelines. The borrower can seek a new loan with a lower interest rate or longer term that will effectively lower the payments and the risk of default or foreclosure. This is especially beneficial for borrowers who have adjustable-rate loans that will reset or have already done so. In addition, government agencies such as the Federal Housing Administration (FHA) may have refinancing programs for borrowers who are in default.

Loan Modification

A **loan modification** is a permanent change in one or more of the terms of a borrower's loan, allows the loan to be reinstated, and results in a payment the borrower can afford.

Loan Terms that May be Changed
- Reduce interest rate
- Change from an adjustable rate to a fixed rate
- Reduce principal amount
- Reduce or waive late fees or other penalties
- Lengthen the loan term

Since the modifications are made at the discretion of the lender, they use specific financial analysis criteria when determining which modifications to offer a borrower. The goal in providing a borrower with a loan modification is to bring the delinquent mortgage current and give the borrower a new start.

Sell the Property

If the borrower is in default and knows that sustaining payments in the future will be difficult, he or she can opt to sell the property. Although selling the property is difficult, especially if the borrower is emotionally attached, the proceeds of the sale can cover the delinquent amount and help the borrower start fresh.

If the borrower owes more on the loan than the property's fair market value, the borrower can attempt to negotiate a short sale. A **short sale** is a sale of encumbered real property that produces less money than is owed to the lender. The lender essentially decides to accept a loss on the loan and release the property from the mortgage or deed of trust. In a short sale, the lender can either accept or reject the proposed sale. The defaulting borrower's financial status and the current conditions of the real estate market influence the lender's decision to consider a short sale. A lender also takes into account whether the financial loss incurred in accepting a short sale is less than pursuing foreclosure. The short sale is a quicker transaction and less costly than a foreclosure.

For the borrower, the negative impact on his or her credit report is not as severe as a foreclosure although there might be certain tax implications involved with the short sale. In addition, short sales spare homeowners the embarrassment of having their name(s) published in the local newspaper for trustee sales.

Lender's Options – Adjustments & Modifications

While borrowers can be proactive in their attempts to cure loan defaults, lenders can also actively protect their investment. The lender can work with a borrower who is experiencing financial difficulties by offering forbearance, recasting the existing loan on the property, or accepting a deed in lieu of foreclosure.

Forbearance

The lender can work with the defaulting borrower by offering a forbearance or moratorium. **Forbearance** is the forgiving of a debt or obligation. During the forbearance, a lender can waive payments or allow reduced payments until the borrower is economically sound.

The forbearance usually lasts for a specific amount of time as negotiated by both the lender and the borrower. During that time, the borrower can attempt to remedy his or her financial crisis. Some examples of actions the borrower can take include obtaining employment after a job loss, securing funds from an alternate source, or selling the property.

Depending on the agreement between the lender and the borrower, any interest accrued during the forbearance period may be added to the existing loan payments when the borrower is economically stable again.

Recasting

When a borrower is delinquent with payments, recasting is another option a lender can seek. **Recasting** is the act of redesigning an existing loan balance in order to avoid default or foreclosure. The loan period may be extended, payments reduced, or the interest rate periodically adjusted to assist the distressed borrower.

During a recasting, a title company performs a title search in order to discover any existing liens on the property that may have been recorded after the funding of the initial loan. During the recasting process, the lender may request additional contingencies such as more collateral or co-signers prior to giving the borrower the new loan terms.

Deed in Lieu of Foreclosure

If the previously mentioned remedies do not help the borrower, a last resort is to exercise a deed in lieu of foreclosure. A **deed in lieu of foreclosure** is a voluntary transfer of the property back to the lender. When this occurs, the lender avoids a lengthy and costly foreclosure proceeding. Typically, a lender

DEED IN LIEU OF FORECLOSURE

WHEN RECORDED MAIL TO:

|

|

| ID_____

|

|

_____

The undersigned

_____

GRANTOR(s) declare(s): _____

FOR VALUABLE CONSIDERATION, receipt of which is hereby acknowledged,
hereby GRANT(S) to

_____

the following described real property in the

County of_____, State of _____:

This deed is an absolute conveyance, the GRANTOR(s) having sold the above-described real
property to the GRANTEE for a fair and adequate consideration, such consideration being full
satisfaction of all obligations secured by the deed of trust heretofore executed by GRANTOR(s).
GRANTOR(s) declare(s) that this conveyance is freely and fairly made and that there are no
agreements, oral or written, other than this deed between GRANTOR(s) and GRANTEE with
respect to the above-described real property.

_____ Dated: _____
     signature

_____ Dated: _____
     signature

(NOTARY)

resists a deed in lieu of foreclosure when the total debt exceeds the fair market value for the property. Negotiations between the borrower and lender must occur and both parties must voluntarily agree to a deed in lieu of foreclosure.

FORECLOSURE

Foreclosure is the legal procedure lenders use to terminate the trustor or mortgagor's rights, title, and interest in real property by selling the property and using the sale proceeds to satisfy the liens of creditors. Deeds of trust or mortgages that contain a **power-of-sale clause** allow the lender to initiate the foreclosure process.

Types of Foreclosure

Foreclosure laws vary in each state, but there are three general types of foreclosure proceedings. When the promissory note conveys a power of sale to the lender, a non-judicial foreclosure is allowed. In states that recognize judicial foreclosure, a lender must request a court-ordered sale of the property once the lender proves that the borrower has defaulted on the terms of the loan. Strict foreclosure, which is much less common, allows a lender to obtain title to the property immediately upon default by the borrower and either sell the property or keep it to satisfy the debt.

Three Methods of Foreclosure

1. Non-judicial foreclosure—requires power of sale

2. Judicial foreclosure—requires court-ordered sale

3. Strict foreclosure—no judicial sale, not commonly used

The lender must give the borrower any proceeds from the sale in excess of the loan amount and certain fees. Currently, a few more than two-thirds of the states that use mortgages instead of deeds of trust conduct judicial foreclosures except for Connecticut, which uses strict foreclosure to acquire the property. The states that use a deed of trust as a security instrument conduct non-judicial foreclosures.

Non-Judicial Foreclosure

A **non-judicial foreclosure** is the procedure a lender uses to sell a property without the involvement of a court. This is also known as **foreclosure by power of sale**. A **trustee's sale** is the part of a non-judicial foreclosure process in which the forced sale of real property is held through public auction. The opening bids usually start at the amount of the current outstanding debt. A trustee's sale is allowed only when there is a power-of-sale clause included in the deed of trust, which is common practice. In most states, deficiency judgments are not allowed in a trustee's sale, nor does the debtor have any rights of redemption after the sale. More information on deficiency judgments is set forth in a later section.

A non-judicial foreclosure is a relatively uncomplicated process that does not involve attorneys or courts. The trustee's fees on a deed of trust are hundreds of dollars instead of the multi-thousand dollar fees used in judicial foreclosure. While the process may vary from state to state, the total length of the foreclosure process is approximately 4 months. The lender declaring the default is cured, paid off, or becomes the owner of the property during the 4-month process.

The debtor, or any other party with a junior lien, may **reinstate** (bring current and restore) the defaulted loan during the statutory reinstatement period. During this time, the debtor may still redeem the property and stop the foreclosure sale by paying off the entire debt, plus interest, costs, and fees, prior to the date of the sale.

Foreclosure procedures under a deed of trust are different from one state to the next. The process of giving initial notice and/or notice of sale and the requirement to advertise before the foreclosure sale are unique to each state. The foreclosure process typically begins with an initial notice.

Notice of Default

In many states, the foreclosure procedure begins when the lender asks the trustee to file (record) a **notice of default**.

> **Items Stated in a Notice of Default**
> - Legal description of the property
> - Borrower's name
> - Lender's name

A typical default might state, "The borrower is in default for non-payment of the installment of principal and interest which became due January 15, 20xx. Borrower is also responsible for all subsequent installments of principal and interest, plus late fees, plus delinquent real estate taxes, plus fees and costs."

Some states require that a **preliminary hearing** take place before a court clerk to determine if the foreclosure should proceed. Notice of the hearing must be sent by certified mail (return receipt requested). If the process of giving notice of the hearing does not result in finding the borrower, the notice can be posted at the property in a conspicuous place.

Notice of Default and Election to Sell Under Deed of Trust
IMPORTANT NOTICE
IF YOUR PROPERTY IS IN FORECLOSURE BECAUSE YOU ARE BEHIND IN YOUR PAYMENTS, IT MAY BE SOLD WITHOUT ANY COURT ACTION, and you may have the legal right to bring your account in good standing by paying all of your past due payments plus permitted costs and expenses within the time permitted by law for reinstatement of your account, which is normally five business days prior to the date set for the sale of your property. No sale date may be set until three months from the date this notice of default may be recorded (which date of recordation appears on this notice). This amount is _____
as of _____, and will increase until your account becomes current.
        (Date)

You may not have to pay the entire unpaid portion of your account, even though full payment was demanded, but you must pay the amount stated above. However, you and your beneficiary or mortgagee may mutually agree in writing prior to the time the notice of sale is posted (which may not be earlier than the end of the three-month period stated above) to, among other things, (1) provide additional time in which to cure the default by transfer of the property or otherwise: (2) establish a schedule of payments in order to cure your default; or both (1) and (2).

Following the expiration of the time period referred to in the first paragraph of this notice, unless the obligation being foreclosed upon or a separate written agreement between you and your creditor permits a longer period, you have only the legal right to stop the sale of your property by paying the entire amount demanded by your creditor.

To find the amount you must pay, or to arrange for payment to stop the foreclosure, or if your property is in foreclosure for any other reason, contact:

_____
(Name of beneficiary or mortgagee)

_____
(Mailing address)

_____
(Telephone)

If you have any questions, you should contact a lawyer or the government agency which may have insured your loan.

Notwithstanding the fact that your property is in foreclosure, you may offer your property for sale, provided the sale is concluded prior to the conclusion of the foreclosure.

Remember, **YOU MAY LOSE LEGAL RIGHTS IF YOU DO NOT TAKE PROMPT ACTION.**

NOTICE IS HEREBY GIVEN, THAT_____ a corporation, is duly appointed Trustee under a Deed of Trust dated _____ executed by _____
_____ as Trustor, to secure certain obligations
in favor of_____
_____ , as beneficiary,
recorded _____ , as instrument no. ___ , in book _____ , page _____ , of Official Records
                                        in the Office of the
Recorder of _____ County, California, describing land
therein as: _____
_____ said obligations
including_____ note _____ for the _____ sum of $ _____

that the beneficial interest under such Deed of Trust and the obligations secured thereby are presently held by the undersigned; that a breach of, and default in, the obligations for which such Deed of Trust is security has occurred in that payment has not been made of:

that by reason thereof, the undersigned, present beneficiary under such Deed of Trust, has executed and delivered to said duly appointed Trustee, a written Declaration of Default and Demand for Sale, and has deposited with said duly appointed Trustee, such Deed of Trust and all documents evidencing obligations secured thereby, and has declared and does hereby declare all sums secured thereby immediately due and payable and has elected and does hereby elect to cause the trust property to be sold to satisfy the obligations secured thereby.

_____

_____

Dated _____

Advertising

Some states do not require **preliminary advertising** or the publishing of a foreclosure sale in a newspaper or other advertising media. However, the majority of states do. When the state requires that notice of the sale be posted in a newspaper, the deed of trust specifies the requirements for the ad. The ad notice includes the time, place, and terms of the sale. It should also include the name of the trustee and his or her contact information so that readers know how to obtain additional information regarding the foreclosure sale. In addition to the advertising requirements stated in the deed of trust, different states or legal jurisdictions may require more information in the advertisement. The number of days the ad must run and the timing of the ad vary by state.

Some states actually permit foreclosure by advertisement and include language in the deed of trust to that effect. In this case, the deed of trust names the trustee conducting the foreclosure. Notice of the advertisement must be mailed or delivered to concerned parties according to statute.

Notice of Sale

From the default date, the borrower has a certain number of days (specified by state or jurisdiction) to cure the default by paying all payments due, including the trustee's foreclosure charges and any unpaid real estate taxes. In some instances, the note's maturity date has passed, which means the entire principal, accrued interest, late fees, and any other fees are due and payable.

In some states, the initial step to begin foreclosure proceedings is to file a notice of sale rather than a notice of default. However, in states in which the initial step in a foreclosure is to file a notice of default, the next step is for the trustee to record a **notice of sale** if the borrower has not paid the debt within the allotted time. This notice sets forth the date of a public auction of the property.

Original - Court
1st copy - Plaintiff
2nd copy - Defendant

Approved, SCAO		
ANY STATE **JUDICIAL CIRCUIT** **COUNTY**	**NOTICE OF FORECLOSURE SALE**	**CASE NO.**

Court address
Court telephone no.

Plaintiff name(s) and address(es)		Defendant name(s) and address(es)
	v	

Plaintiff attorney, bar no., address, and telephone no.	Defendant attorney, bar no., address, and telephone no.

NOTICE OF FORECLOSURE SALE

1. On _____ the _____ Circuit Court of _____ County
   Date

   entered judgment in favor of the plaintiff(s),_____ ,

   and against the defendant(s), _____ .

2. On _____ at public auction to be held at _____
   Date and time   Place and city

   _____ in this county, I shall offer for sale to the highest bidder all of the right,

   title and interest of defendant(s) in and to the following property:

_____ , County Clerk

Date   Signature

CC 115 (6/04) **NOTICE OF FORECLOSURE SALE**   MCL 600.3125, MCL 600.6052, MCL 600.6091, MCR 3.410

AFFIDAVIT OF PUBLISHING

Name of ☐ publisher ☐ agent of publisher		Attach copy of publication here
Name of newspaper	County where published	

This newspaper is a qualified newspaper. The attached copy of notice of foreclosure sale was published in this newspaper at least once each week for six successive weeks, from

_____ to _____ .

_____
Affiant signature

Subscribed and sworn to before me on _____ , _____ County, Any State.
Date

My commission expires: _____ Signature: _____
Date   Court clerk/Notary public

Notary public, Any State, County of _____

AFFIDAVIT OF POSTING

As deputy sheriff of this county, on _____ I posted a true copy of the notice of foreclosure
Date

sale on the front of this form in the following three public places in _____ Township,

_____ County:

1. _____
2. _____
3. _____

I also posted a true copy in the following three public places in the City of _____ :

1. _____
2. _____
3. _____

_____
Affiant signature

Subscribed and sworn to before me on _____ , _____ County, Any State.
Date

My commission expires: _____ Signature: _____
Date   Court clerk/Notary public

Notary public, Any State, County of _____

Public Auction

The terms of the sale, or auction, are generally all cash. The sale is held a specified number of days after the notice of sale is filed and is held at a stated date, time, and place. Auction sales often occur at the county courthouse. At the sale, the trustee collects the winning bid price from the successful bidder

and issues a **trustee's deed**, which grants title to the property. If there are no outside bidders at the sale, the property reverts to the beneficiary (lender). In this instance, the trustee issues a trustee's deed to the original lender, who now owns the property.

The sale is subject to certain liens of record that are not eliminated by a foreclosure sale. These include federal tax liens and real property assessments and taxes. That means the new owner is responsible for payment of those liens. The non-judicial foreclosure process eliminates any junior liens.

Judicial Foreclosure

A beneficiary (lender) may choose a judicial foreclosure instead of a trustee sale under a deed of trust. A **judicial foreclosure** is the procedure a lender uses to sell a mortgaged property with the involvement of a court. Judicial foreclosures are not typical with deeds of trust. Of the two common methods of foreclosure, the judicial foreclosure is more costly and time consuming. The length of time from the initial default to the public auction of the property is long and tedious. The process of judicial foreclosure is commonly used when foreclosing a mortgage.

The reason a beneficiary may decide to choose a judicial foreclosure under a deed of trust is that a deficiency judgment is allowable. If a deficiency judgment comes from the court, the lender has the right to collect any unpaid amounts on the loan from the borrower.

To foreclose in accordance with judicial procedure, a lender must prove that the mortgagor is in default. Once the lender has exhausted its attempts to resolve the default with the homeowner, the next step is to contact an attorney to pursue court action.

State Bar of Wisconsin Form 7-2003
TRUSTEE'S DEED

Document Number   Document Name

THIS DEED, made between _____
as Trustee of _____
_____ ("Grantor," whether one or more),
and _____

_____ ("Grantee," whether one or more).
Grantor conveys to Grantee, without warranty, the following described real estate,
together with the rents, profits, fixtures and other appurtenant interests, in
_____ County, State of Wisconsin ("Property") (if more space is
needed, please attach addendum):

Recording Area

Name and Return Address

Parcel Identification Number (PIN)

Dated _____.

_____(SEAL)   _____(SEAL)
*   *

_____(SEAL)   _____(SEAL)
*   *

AUTHENTICATION   **ACKNOWLEDGMENT**

Signature(s) _____   STATE OF WISCONSIN   )
) ss.
authenticated on _____ .   _____ COUNTY)

*_____   Personally came before me on _____,
_____   the above-named _____
TITLE: MEMBER STATE BAR OF WISCONSIN
    (If not, _____   _____
    authorized by Wis. Stat. § 706.06)   to me known to be the person(s) who executed the foregoing
                                                instrument and acknowledged the same.
THIS INSTRUMENT DRAFTED BY:
                                                _____
_____   *
_____   Notary Public, State of Wisconsin
                                                My Commission (is permanent) (expires: _____)

(Signatures may be authenticated or acknowledged.   Both are not necessary.)
NOTE: THIS IS A STANDARD FORM. ANY MODIFICATIONS TO THIS FORM SHOULD BE CLEARLY IDENTIFIED.
TRUSTEE'S DEED   © 2003 STATE BAR OF WISCONSIN   FORM NO. 7-2003
* Type name below signatures.

The attorney for the lender contacts the mortgagor to try to resolve the default. If no resolution occurs, the attorney files a **lis pendens** (action pending) with the court. The lis pendens gives notice to the public that a pending action has been filed against the title to real property or some interest in that real property. Any prospective buyer for the property is then notified of the cloud on title.

The purpose of the court action is to provide evidence of default and get the court's approval to initiate foreclosure. Once the case goes to an attorney, the impending foreclosure must be advertised as required by state law.

After advertisement of the public sale, the property is sold through a public auction and the successful bidder at the foreclosure sale owns the property. The lender may get the property back to hold or sell later as it chooses. The property is then bank-owned and the lender bears the burdens of upkeep and selling the property.

Depending on which state the property is located in, the new owner receives a **referee's deed in foreclosure, sheriff's deed**, or a **certificate of sale**. The first two are special warranty deeds that give the buyer title the borrower had at the time of the original loan. Referee's deeds and sheriff's deeds are used primarily in states with no statutory redemption laws. The buyer gets immediate possession of the property after the sale, which is final.

In states with statutory redemption laws, a certificate of sale is issued to the buyer at a foreclosure sale. **Redemption** is the legal right of a borrower to make good on a defaulted loan within a statutory period of time and thus regain the property. The **redemption period** is a period of time established by state law during which a property owner has the right to recover real estate after a foreclosure or tax sale by paying the sales price plus interest and costs. Depending on the state, the borrower may have between no time and 1 year or more after foreclosure to redeem the property by paying off the judgment and reclaiming title to the property. In some states, the buyer does not receive possession of the property until the redemption period is over.

> **Steps in a Judicial Foreclosure**
> - Public notice is given of impending foreclosure
> - Lender files lawsuit against borrower and anyone else who has acquired an interest in the property after the mortgage being foreclosed on was recorded
> - Lender's attorney shows evidence of default of loan to court
> - Lender's attorney asks for judgment instructing that the borrower's interest in the property be severed, the property be sold at a public auction, and includes the lender's demand to be paid from the sale
> - Copy of complaint and summons is delivered to defendants
> - Lis pendens is filed, informing public of pending litigation
> - Court orders sale of property
> - Public sale is advertised and public auction sells property to highest bidder
> - Highest bidder receives sheriff's deed or certificate of sale
> - Statutory redemption is allowed in some states

Strict Foreclosure

In Connecticut, and under certain circumstances in other states, strict foreclosure can also occur. **Strict foreclosure** is a type of foreclosure in which the mortgagee initiates a lawsuit on the defaulting mortgagor, who must pay the mortgage within a specific time frame as ordered by the court. If the defaulting mortgagor is unable to pay back the mortgage, the title to the property involuntarily transfers to the mortgagee.

During the initial suit, the lender petitions the court to eliminate the defaulting mortgagor's right of redemption. If the mortgagee is successful in lobbying for the petition, the court orders the mortgagor to relinquish the rights to the property if the mortgage is not paid back after a certain time period. Once the time period passes and the defaulting mortgagor has not paid back the mortgagee, he or she surrenders any interests associated with the property.

STATE	TYPE OF FORECLOSURE		
	Non-Judicial	Judicial	Comment
Alabama	X	X	Non-judicial mostly
Alaska	X	X	Non-judicial mostly
Arizona	X	X	Non-judicial mostly
Arkansas	X	X	Non-judicial mostly
California	X	X	Non-judicial mostly
Colorado	X	X	Non-judicial mostly
Connecticut		X	Judicial only
Delaware		X	Judicial only
District of Columbia	X		Non-judicial mostly
Florida		X	Judicial only
Georgia	X	X	Non-judicial mostly
Hawaii	X	X	Non-judicial mostly
Idaho	X	X	Non-judicial mostly
Illinois		X	Judicial only
Indiana		X	Judicial only
Iowa	X	X	Judicial mostly
Kansas		X	Judicial only
Kentucky		X	Judicial only
Louisiana		X	Judicial only
Maine		X	Judicial only
Maryland	X	X	Non-judicial mostly
Massachusetts	X	X	Non-judicial mostly
Michigan	X	X	Non-judicial mostly
Minnesota	X	X	Non-judicial mostly
Mississippi	X	X	Non-judicial mostly
Missouri	X	X	Non-judicial mostly
Montana	X	X	Non-judicial mostly
Nebraska	X	X	Non-judicial mostly
Nevada	X	X	Non-judicial mostly
New Hampshire	X		Non-judicial only
New Jersey		X	Judicial only
New Mexico	X	X	Non-judicial mostly
New York		X	Judicial only
North Carolina	X	X	Non-judicial mostly
North Dakota		X	Judicial only
Ohio		X	Judicial only
Oklahoma	X	X	Non-judicial mostly
Oregon	X	X	Non-judicial mostly
Pennsylvania		X	Judicial only
Rhode Island	X	X	Non-judicial mostly

STATE	TYPE OF FORECLOSURE (Continued)		
	Non-Judicial	**Judicial**	**Comment**
South Carolina		X	Judicial only
South Dakota	X	X	Non-judicial mostly
Tennessee	X	X	Non-judicial mostly
Texas	X	X	Non-judicial mostly
Utah	X		Non-judicial only
Vermont		X	Judicial only
Virginia	X	X	Non-judicial mostly
Washington	X	X	Non-judicial mostly
West Virginia	X		Non-judicial mostly
Wisconsin	X	X	Judicial mostly
Wyoming	X	X	Non-judicial mostly

Disbursing the Proceeds of the Sale

A property may be used as the security for more than one loan. There may be second or even third loans against a property. These are known as junior loans. Junior loans pose no difficulty for the original lender as long as the borrower is willing and able to make the payments on all the loans. It becomes more than a nuisance, however, when a default occurs on one or more of the loans and the property does not sell for an amount that covers all of the loans against it at the foreclosure sale.

In many foreclosures, the proceeds of the sale do not pay all the debt. Therefore, a fair system of priorities for paying off lenders was created. The proceeds of the sale are used to satisfy the debt with the highest priority first, and then the next highest priority debt is paid, then the next, and so on until either the sale proceeds have faded to nothing or all holders of debt relating to the property have been repaid.

Lenders prefer to have the highest priority of recording possible, for obvious reasons. Since the time of recording determines the priority of a loan, the one that is recorded first will be in the first position for payment if the borrower defaults. After that, the second loan recorded will receive payment, and so on. The loan itself is not identified as first, second, or third. The county recorder stamps the date and time of recording on the document and the imprint is used to determine priority.

The logical outcome of this priority system of paying off lenders in case of foreclosure is that, sometimes, the property does not bring enough money at the foreclosure sale to satisfy all the creditors who have loans against the property. In those cases, the loans that are not paid off are eliminated. In some cases, there is not even enough money to pay off the first loan completely. That lender must decide if it is worthwhile to pursue a deficiency judgment. If the amount is small enough, the lender may decide recovering the deficiency is not worth the costs associated with the lawsuit. In addition, if the defaulting borrower's financial condition is already in a crisis, there is no guarantee the lender will receive a timely repayment.

A majority of states allow the lender to obtain a deficiency judgment for any amount that is not recovered at the foreclosure sale. The judgment, if you recall, allows a lender to proceed against the borrower's other unsecured assets if he or she has any.

Foreclosure by Junior Lienholders

Most junior lienholders record a Request for Notice of Default (or Delinquency) to protect themselves in the event the borrowers default on senior loans. Upon learning of the impending foreclosure by a senior lienholder, the junior lienholder has three choices.

Actions Available to Junior Lienholders

- Stay silent and hope the proceeds from the foreclosure sale are enough to pay off the loan balance
- Bid for the property in order to protect his or her investment
- Start its own foreclosure proceedings

If the junior lienholder chooses to pursue foreclosure, the junior lienholder has the right to claim the property after the statutory time period has passed without having to bid against other buyers at the foreclosure sale. The junior lienholder acquires the property subject to all senior loans and must keep them current or face foreclosure. The junior lienholder now owns the property and may either keep it until the property has regained its former value or try to sell it on the open market.

The sale of a property at the trustee's sale extinguishes the deed of trust lien securing the debt for the beneficiary (lender) and extinguishes any junior liens. In order to protect his or her interest, the holder of a junior lien must make a bid for the property or possibly lose the right to collect on the loan if the sale amount is not enough to pay off all secured notes on the property.

RECORDING REQUESTED BY

WHEN RECORDED MAIL TO

NAME

ADDRESS

CITY

STATE&ZIP

Title Order No.   Escrow No.

SPACE ABOVE THIS LINE FOR RECORDER'S USE

REQUEST FOR NOTICE OF DELINQUENCIES
UNDER SECTION 2924e CIVIL CODE

In accordance with Section 2924e. California Civil Code. request is hereby made that a written notice of any or all delinquencies of four months or more. in payments of principal or interest on any obligation secured under the Deed of Trust recorded as Instrument Number: _____ on: _____
Official Records of _____ County, California, loan number _____
Wherein _____ is the trustor, and describing land therein as:
_____

1. The ownership or security interest of the requester, is the beneficial interest under that certain deed of trust recorded as instrument Number: _____ on _____ of the Official Records of:
_____ County, California. _____
Wherein _____ is the trustor.
2. _____ is the date on which the interest of the requester will terminate as evidenced by the maturity date of the note of the trustor in favor of the requester.
3. _____ is the name of the current owner of the security property described above.
4. The street address of the security property as described above is: _____

5. Said notice of delinquency and the amount thereof shall be sent to: _____
(Requester Beneficiary)
at _____
(Address)   (City)
_____
(State)   (Zip)

Dated _____
(Requester Beneficiary)

CONSENT BY TRUSTOR/OWNER

I _____ AUTHORIZE _____
(Trustee)   (Senior Lienholder)
TO DISCLOSE IN WRITING TO _____
(Requesting Beneficiary)
NOTICE OF ANY AND ALL DELINQUENCIES OF FOUR MONTHS OR MORE, IN PAYMENT OF PRINCIPAL OR INTEREST ON ANY OBLIGATION SECURED BY THAT SENIOR LIEN MORE PARTICULARLY DESCRIBED AS INSTRUMENT NUMBER _____ RECORDED ON _____
IN OFFICIAL RECORDS OF _____ COUNTY. CALIFORNIA.
DATED _____

Foreclosing Government-Backed Loans

Government-backed loans are not immune to foreclosure. A lender can file a default claim with the government agency that is guaranteeing the loan.

Foreclosing FHA Loans

If a borrower defaults on a loan backed by the Federal Housing Administration (FHA), a lender can file Form 2068 – Notice of Default with a local FHA office. The filing must take place within 60 days of the default and must contain a detailed account of the borrower's delinquency. In order to curb theforeclosure process, FHA counselors may ask the lender to recast the loan terms to reduce the borrower's payment or offer forbearance in order for borrowers to work out their financial situation.

If the borrower resolves the conditions leading to the default within 1 year, the lender must notify the FHA of the solvency. However, if financial problems persist, a form disclosing the default status is filed, which gives the lender the right to proceed with the foreclosure process. If auction bids for the property are less than the outstanding debt, the lender can bid for the total amount of the debt and take title to the property. The lender can then file an insurance claim with the FHA for the unpaid balance.

In certain instances, the lender can assign the defaulted loan to the FHA prior to the auction and obtain insurance benefits in return. If the property can sell for the amount to pay the balance, then the extra insurance benefits do not apply. However, if the FHA takes ownership of the property it may refurbish the home and sell it for a higher price to cover any losses. These properties are known as HUD homes.

Foreclosing VA Loans

If the Department of Veterans Affairs (VA) insures the defaulted loan, the lender can file a claim with the local VA office. Delinquency claims must occur after the borrower has defaulted for more than 3 months. After the VA office is notified of the default, the VA has subrogation rights to bring the loan current. **Subrogation** refers to the substitution of one party's entitlement of debt obligations to another party. In this case, the VA has priority when it comes to making a claim against the defaulting veteran for the amount owed in the default.

A lender with a loan secured by the VA must also work with the borrower in order to prevent foreclosure proceedings as much as possible. If foreclosure is inevitable, then, like the FHA foreclosure process, the lender can bid up to the amount of the balance owed at the foreclosure auction and submit a claim for losses to the VA. The VA must then decide whether it wants to pay the balance and any costs incurred during the foreclosure proceedings, take title to the property, or have the defaulting veteran stay in the home while the VA covers the difference of the property's fair market value and unpaid balance.

Tax Impacts of Default and Foreclosure

Default and foreclosure may have tax consequences for the borrower. When a borrower is in default, the lender may foreclose on the loan or repossess the property. The IRS treats a foreclosure or repossession as a sale from which the

Mortgagee Notice
of Foreclosure Sale

Single Family Housing

**U.S. Department of Housing
and Urban Development**
Office of Housing
Federal Housing Commissioner

Public reporting burden for this collection of information is estimated to average 1 hour per response, including the time for reviewing instructions, searching existing data sources, gathering and maintaining the data needed, and completing and reviewing the collection of information. Send comments regarding this burden estimate or any other aspect of this collection of information, including suggestions for reducing this burden, to the Reports Management Officer, Office of Information Policies and Systems, U.S. Department of Housing and Urban Development, Washington, D.C. 20410-3600 and to the Office of Management and Budget, Paperwork Reduction Project (2502-0347), Washington, D.C. 20503. Do not send this completed form to either of these addressees.

Privacy Act Statement: The Department of Housing and Urban Development (HUD) is authorized to collect this information, including Social Security Numbers (SSN), by the U.S. Housing Act of 1937, as amended, and by the Housing and Community Development Act of 1987, 42 U.S.C. 3543. The information is being collected by HUD for use in expediting the foreclosure process or alternatives to foreclosure that HUD may authorize. The SSN is used as a unique identifier. HUD may disclose this information to Federal, State and local agencies when relevant to civil, criminal, or regulatory investigations and prosecutions. It will not be otherwise disclosed or released outside of HUD, except as permitted or required by law. Providing the SSN is mandatory.

Part A. Mortgagee's Instructions: When authorized by the Department, the Mortgagee must complete Part A of this form when foreclosure of an FHA insured mortgage is begun. Mail the form to the local HUD Office (Single Family Loan Management) that has jurisdiction over the mortgaged property. The form must be delivered to HUD at least 45 days before the estimated foreclosure sale date, but no later than on or before the date of the first publication, posting, or other standard legal notice of sale, whichever is earlier. HUD may return the Commissioner's Adjusted Fair Market Value (CAFMV) of the property to the mortgagee no later than five (5) days prior to the foreclosure sale.

1. Mortgagee's Name & Address :	3a. Name of Mortgagee Contact Person :
	3b. Signature of Authorized Mortgagee Official : X
2. Telephone No. (include area code) :	
4. Mortgagor's Name & Property Address :	6. Mortgagor's Last Known Mailing Address :
5. Mortgagor's Last Known Telephone No. :	7. Mortgagor's Social Security No. :

8. Original Mortgage : $	9. Mortgage Interest Rate : %	14. Full Name of Selected Appraiser (or check appropriate box) :
10a. Unpaid Principal Balance (as of the date shown in block A16.)	$	☐ Pre-Foreclosure Appraisal Attached ☐ HUD Staff Assigned
10b. Unpaid Mortgage Interest (as of the date shown in block A16)	$	15. Estimated Date of Foreclosure Sale: (at least 45 days from date form is mailed to HUD) / 16. Date this Form was Completed:
10c. Other Costs Incurred to Date (Itemize these in block 21 on the back of this form)	$	17a. The Property Is : ☐ Occupied ☐ Vacant / 17b. The Owner Is : ☐ Occupant ☐ Non-Occupant / 18. Check this block if entry to the property is a problem. ☐
10d. Estimated Outstanding Indebtedness (enter the total of blocks 10a + 10b + 10c)	$	
11. FHA Case No.	12. Mortgage Loan No.	19. ☐ Check here if Default/Foreclosure Action was reported to Credit Bureau.
13. Conditional Commitment or Property Appraisal Date		20. Check one of the following: ☐ Deficiency Judgment ☐ Pre-Foreclosure Sale ☐ Other (Specify)

Part B. HUD Data to Mortgagee	
1. HUD Field Office (name & address) :	3. ☐ Check here if additional advertising is required.
	4. Estimated Outstanding Indebtedness (enter as indicated in Part A, 10d.) $
	5. Fair Market Value (FMV) of Property (enter FMV determined by Valuation Division) $
	6. Less Adjustments (estimate post-acquisition & property disposition costs) $
2. Mortgagee's Name & Address :	7. Commissioner's Adjusted Fair Market Value of Property (CAFMV) (subtract B6 from B5) $
	8. Actual Foreclosure Sale Date: (if applicable, from a copy of the Notice of Sale or other legal notice furnished by the Mortgagee)
Name & Signature of HUD Personnel Completing this form : X	Name, Title & Signature of Authorized HUD Official : X Date Signed :

Previous editions are obsolete.

form **HUD-91022** (08/2002)
ref. Handbook 4330.1

OMB Approved No. 2900-0021
Respondent Burden: 20 minutes

VA Department of Veterans Affairs	**NOTICE OF DEFAULT AND INTENTION TO FORECLOSE**

INSTRUCTIONS: See Privacy Act Information on reverse. Type or print. Note the special instructions for Items 2, 7, 10 and 14. For 38 CFR 36.4600 loans use VA Form 26-6850, NOTICE OF DEFAULT. Return copy 1 to VA. Copy 2 may be retained.

1. DATE OF THIS NOTICE	NOTE: VA LIN (loan identification number) must be numeric 12 digits.	2. VA LIN	3. PURPOSE OF LOAN (*Check one*)
			☐ HOME (1) ☐ HOME REFINANCING (5) ☐ HOME CONDO (0) ☐ MANUFACTURED HOME (8)

To (*Complete Regional Office/Center Address*)
**DEPARTMENT OF VETERANS AFFAIRS
LOAN GUARANTY DIVISION**

5. HOLDER'S NAME, ADDRESS AND TELEPHONE NUMBER

6A. SERVICING AGENT'S NAME, ADDRESS AND TELEPHONE NUMBER (*Complete only if different from holder shown above*)	6B. SERVICER CODE (*6 Digits*)

DESCRIPTION OF DELINQUENT LOAN

NOTE: Enter number only without spaces, dashes, etc. **DO NOT ENTER MORE THAN 14 CHARACTERS** ▶	1. SERVICER LOAN NUMBER	8. DATE OF FIRST UNCURED DEFAULT (*Example: enter 02 01 86 for February 1, 1986*)		9. SOCIAL SECURITY NO. (*Present Owners*)

NOTE: In item 10A enter last name, comma, first name, and middle initial. Limit entries in Items 10A, 10B and 10C to not more than 25 characters.	10A. NAME OF PRESENT OWNER	11. COUNTY OR PARISH (*Property Location*)
	10B. NUMBER AND STREET OR RURAL ROUTE	12. PROPERTY ADDRESS (*If different than 11B and 11C*)
	10C. CITY AND STATE	10D. ZIP CODE	13. AMOUNT OF EACH INSTALLMENT

14. DATE OF FIRST PAYMENT (*Per loan instruments*)	15. ORIGINAL VETERAN'S NAME AND PRESENT ADDRESS (*If different than Items 3B and 4 above*).	PRINCIPAL AND INTEREST	
EXAMPLE: Enter 02 01 86 for February 1, 1986 ▶		TAX AND INSURANCE	
		OTHER	
		TOTAL	

18. OUTSTANDING LOAN BALANCE

16. OTHER DEFAULT (*Specify, real estate, taxes, insurance, special assessments, etc.*)	17. AMOUNT OF DEFAULT	PRINCIPAL		A. AS OF: (*Date*)	B. AMOUNT
		INTEREST			
		TAX AND INSURANCE			
		TOTAL			$

19. OCCUPANCY DATA

A. IS PROPERTY OCCUPIED? ☐ YES ☐ NO	B. OCCUPANT IS (*Check One*) ☐ TENANT ☐ ORIGINAL BORROWER ☐ TRANSFEREE	☐ OTHER (*Specify*)	C. KEYS TO PROPERTY MAY BE OBTAINED FROM: (*If vacant*)

D. IF VACANT, HAVE STEPS BEEN TAKEN TO PROTECT PROPERTY?	E. POSSIBILITIES OF CURING DEFAULT HAVE BEEN EXHAUSTED?	F. WERE OTHER TRANSFEREES ☐ YES ☐ NO (*If "Yes," complete Item 20*)

20. OTHER TRANSFEREE DATA	A. NAME	B. LAST KNOWN ADDRESS	C. NAME	D. LAST KNOWN ADDRESS

21. REPOSSESSION AND/OR FORECLOSURE	A. PROCEEDINGS WILL BE INSTITUTED ON OR AFTER (*Date*)	B. PROCEEDINGS UNDER EMERGENCY PROVISIONS OF 38 CFR 36.4280(e) or 36.4317(A) WERE INSTITUTED ON (*Date*)	C. ESTIMATED COST OF FORECLOSURE AND/OR REPOSSESSION	22. VOLUNTARY CONVEYANCE DATA

HOLDERS LOAN SERVICING

23. CONTACT(S) WITH MORTGAGE OWNER	TYPE	NUMBER	24. DATES OF PROPERTY INSPECTIONS	25. CONDITION OF PROPERTY
	LETTER/WIRE			
	FACE TO FACE			
	TELEPHONE			

26.	A. MONTHLY INCOME	B. MONTHLY OBLIGATIONS	C. ATTITUDE TOWARD DEFAULT	D. PLACE OF EMPLOYMENT	E. WORK TELEPHONE NO.	F. HOME TELEPHONE NO.
BORROWER						
SPOUSE						

27. REASON FOR DEFAULT AND SUMMARY OF LOAN SERVICING (*Must give complete details to support conclusion that forbearance is not warranted. Include description of broken repayment schedules's or other arrangements, etc.*) (*If additional space is needed, continue on reverse*)

28. NAME AND TITLE OF AUTHORIZED OFFICIAL	☐ HOLDER ☐ SERVICING AGENT	29. SIGNATURE OF AUTHORIZED OFFICIAL

VA FORM JUL 1996 **26-6850a**   EXISTING STOCKS OF VA FORM 26-6850, FEB 1995, WILL BE USED.   **VA COPY 1**

borrower may realize gain or loss. This is true even if the borrower voluntarily returns the property to the lender. If a lender cancels or forgives the debt, the borrower also may realize ordinary income from the cancellation of debt, which must be reported on the borrower's income tax return, depending on the circumstances. However, the cancellation of debt is not always taxable because there are some exceptions.

Common Situations when Cancellation of Debt is not Taxable

Bankruptcy: Debts discharged through bankruptcy are not considered taxable income.

Non-recourse loans: A **non-recourse loan** is a loan for which the lender's only remedy in case of default is to repossess the property being financed or used as collateral. That is, the lender cannot pursue the borrower personally in case of default.

Insolvency: If a person is insolvent when the debt is cancelled, some or all of the cancelled debt may not be taxable. A person is considered **insolvent** when his or her total debts are more than the fair market value of his or her total assets.

As with all complex tax issues, a person should obtain the assistance of a tax professional.

SUE ON PROMISSORY NOTE – DEFICIENCY JUDGMENT

For a lender, sometimes the proceeds of the sale are not sufficient to satisfy the foreclosed debt. In addition, the expenses incurred while pursuing a foreclosure can be costly and the lender may want to recover those expenses as well. If that happens, the lender may try to sue on the promissory note and obtain a deficiency judgment against the borrower to recover the money owed on the defaulting balance of the loan.

A **deficiency judgment** is a personal judgment against a borrower for the balance of a debt owed when the security for the loan is not sufficient to pay the debt. In a deed of trust, the lender must decide whether to sue on the promissory note or pursue foreclosure. DEPENDING ON STATE LAW, once the lender decides to pursue foreclosure in a deed of trust, the lender cannot obtain a deficiency judgment against the trustor after the trustee sale.

The lender's ability to sue for a deficiency judgment against the borrower is dependent on the particular state's foreclosure laws. Some states do not allow a deficiency judgment after a property is foreclosed; others do allow it if certain conditions apply. In certain instances, a state with an anti-deficiency statute does not allow a deficiency judgment on purchase money loans.

In a deed of trust, the anti-deficiency statute applies to all loans secured by residential property. Therefore, if a defaulting loan is on a residential property, the lender may not be able to obtain a deficiency judgment. However, if the lender initiates a judicial foreclosure, the lender can seek a deficiency judgment whether the secured property is residential or not. It is best to consult with an attorney to obtain specific information regarding a particular state's foreclosure laws.

SUMMARY

When a borrower faces financial difficulties, he or she can fall behind on loan payments. This can result in default and possibly foreclosure. While borrowers usually do not intend to get behind on their loan payments, certain life situations are beyond their control and can create problems for their personal finances.

When a borrower fails to pay a contractual debt, the situation is known as a default. However, the borrower has options and can take certain measures to save his or her property. The borrower can attempt to refinance the property or sell the property to pay the balance on the loan. In addition, the lender will work with the borrower to prevent the foreclosure process, which can be costly. Lenders can offer forbearance, recasting, or accept a deed in lieu of foreclosure.

When the lender allows a borrower to use funds to purchase a property, the lender is making an investment on the interest earned back from the loan. However, a loan default causes a negative return on investment and lenders must take the necessary steps to recover their funds through foreclosure or by suing on the promissory note. Foreclosure is the legal procedure used by lenders to terminate the trustor or mortgagor's rights, title, and interest in real property by selling the property and using the sale proceeds to satisfy the liens of creditors. The three types of foreclosure are non-judicial foreclosure, judicial foreclosure, and strict foreclosure. Foreclosure proceedings can also apply to junior loans as well as government-backed loans.

For a lender, sometimes the proceeds of the sale are not sufficient to satisfy the foreclosed debt. If that happens, the lender may try to sue on the promissory note and obtain a deficiency judgment against the borrower to recover the money owed on the defaulting balance of the loan. A deficiency judgment is a personal judgment against a borrower for the balance of a debt owed when the security for the loan is not sufficient to pay the debt.

UNIT 15 REVIEW

◖ Matching Exercise

Instructions: Write the letter of the matching term on the blank line before its definition. Answers are in Appendix A.

Terms

A. certificate of sale

B. deed in lieu of foreclosure

C. default

D. deficiency judgment

E. forbearance

F. foreclosure

G. judicial foreclosure

H. lis pendens

I. non-judicial foreclosure

J. notice of default

K. notice of sale

L. power-of-sale clause

M. preliminary advertising

N. preliminary hearing

O. recasting

P. reinstate

Q. sheriff's deed

R. short sale

S. strict foreclosure

T. subrogation

U. trustee's deed

V. trustee's sale

Definitions

1. _____ Situation that occurs when a borrower fails to pay a contractual debt

2. _____ Sale of encumbered real property that produces less money than is owed to the lender

3. _____ Forgiving of a debt or obligation

4. _____ Redesigning an existing loan balance in order to avoid default or foreclosure

5. _____ Voluntary transfer of the property back to the lender

6. _____ Legal procedure used by lenders to terminate the trustor or mortgagor's rights, title, and interest in real property by selling the property and using the sale proceeds to satisfy the liens of creditors

7. _____ Clause that allows the lender to initiate the foreclosure process

8. _____ Procedure a lender uses to sell a property without the involvement of a court

9. _____ Part of a non-judicial foreclosure process in which the forced sale of real property is held through public auction

10. _____ Bring current and restore

11. _____ Notice that states the legal description of the property, borrower's name, lender's name, the amount of the default, and the reason for the default

12. _____ Hearing that determines if a lender should proceed with the foreclosure process

13. _____ Publishing of a foreclosure sale in a newspaper or other advertising media

14. _____ Notice that sets forth the date of a public auction of the property

15. _____ Deed that grants title to property during a public auction in a trustee's sale

16. _____ Procedure a lender uses to sell a mortgaged property with the involvement of a court

17. _____ Action pending

18. _____ Type of foreclosure in which the mortgagee initiates a lawsuit on the defaulting mortgagor who must pay the mortgage within a specific time frame as ordered by the court

19. _____ Substitution of one party's entitlement of debt obligations to another party

20. _____ Personal judgment against a borrower for the balance of a debt owed when the security for the loan is not sufficient to pay the debt

Multiple Choice Questions

Instructions: Circle your response and go to Appendix A to read the complete explanation for each question.

1. Default may be described as:
   a. failure to pay a contractual debt.
   b. failure to meet a financial obligation.
   c. failure to perform a legal or contractual duty.
   d. any of the above.

2. When a borrower is in default, he or she may choose to:
   a. refinance the existing loan for a lower monthly payment.
   b. sue the lender for violations of the promissory note.
   c. sell the property and pay the balance with the proceeds.
   d. Both (a) and (c)

3. In order to assist the borrower during difficult financial times, the lender can:
   a. redesign the current loan.
   b. waive the borrower's payments temporarily.
   c. have the borrower give title to the property back to the lender.
   d. All of the above

4. Which of the following is a type of foreclosure procedure?
   a. Judicial
   b. Administrative
   c. Governmental
   d. Local

5. When does the non-judicial foreclosure process usually begin?
   a. After issuing a notice of sale
   b. When a notice of default is filed
   c. During the public auction
   d. When the property is advertised for sale in a newspaper

6. A property is foreclosed and it is time to disburse the proceeds. If there are three liens securing the property, which lien is satisfied first?
   a. Debt with the highest priority
   b. Defiant investment lien
   c. Lowest deficiency lien
   d. Selective default lien

7. What can a junior lienholder do when a senior lienholder initiates the foreclosure process?

    a. Do nothing and hope the auction proceeds cover the junior lien

    b. Begin the foreclosure process

    c. Add an additional lien on the property

    d. Both (a) and (b)

8. _____ homes are refurbished properties that are sold for a higher price by the FHA after it obtains title to those properties through foreclosure.

    a. HUB

    b. HUD

    c. VA

    d. Subrogation

9. If a borrower defaults on a VA loan, the VA has _____ rights to bring the loan current.

    a. subrogation

    b. substantiation

    c. severance

    d. standardization

10. How can a lender recover the money owed on a defaulting loan if the proceeds of the sale are less than the actual debt?

    a. File a recovery suit with the local government

    b. Place a lien on the defaulting borrower's new property

    c. Garnish the defaulting borrower's wages

    d. Sue on the note and seek a deficiency judgment

APPENDIX A: ANSWER KEY

Unit 1 – The Nature & Cycle of the Economy and Real Estate Finance

Answers Matching

1.	L	9.	BB	17.	K	25.	M
2.	Z	10.	A	18.	E	26.	S
3.	AA	11.	X	19.	Y	27.	B
4.	I	12.	DD	20.	P	28.	T
5.	U	13.	Q	21.	J	29.	V
6.	D	14.	O	22.	W	30.	N
7.	F	15.	G	23.	R		
8.	CC	16.	H	24.	C		

Answers Multiple Choice

1. **b** Real estate is the single largest component of wealth for individuals.

2. **c** This function is carried out in the primary mortgage market, in which lenders originate mortgages by lending to homeowners and purchasers

3. **d** The economy speeds up during expansion and then peaks. During expansions, the economy, measured by indicators like jobs, industrial production, and retail sales, is growing. Unfortunately, if the economic activity is too fast, inflation may rise.

4. **a** The NBER defines a recession as "a significant decline in economic activity spread across the economy, lasting more than two quarters, which is 6 months, normally visible in real gross domestic product (GDP), real income, employment, industrial production, and wholesale-retail sales".

5. **d** The peak phase of the market occurs when real estate supply growth slowly begins to exceed demand growth. Real estate prices enter a period of stabilization after a period of expansion.

6. **d** Cycles are periodic, irregular up and down movements of economic activity that take place over a period of 2 to 6 years. Real estate markets are cyclical due to the relationship between demand and supply for particular types of property.

7. **d** The real estate cycle has two phases and two turning points: (1) expansion, (2) peak, (3) contraction, and (4) trough.

8. **b** The National Bureau of Economic Research defines business cycles as two phases and two turning points. The two phases are expansion (recovery or boom) and contraction (recession or bust). The two turning points are peaks and troughs.

9. **d** An efficient market is one with a large number of buyers and sellers in which easily produced goods and services are readily transferable, and market prices adjust rapidly to reflect new information.

10. **d** Financial markets are further subdivided into money, capital, commodity, and mortgage markets.

Unit 2 – Money & The Monetary System

Answers Matching

1. N	6. M	11. Q	16. P
2. C	7. J	12. I	17. T
3. O	8. E	13. A	18. G
4. L	9. B	14. F	19. K
5. R	10. D	15. S	20. H

Answers Multiple Choice

1. **b** Collateral is something of value given as security for a debt. A good example of this is mortgage debt or a car loan.

2. **d** Currently, there is over $930 billion dollars of U.S. currency in circulation. The amount of cash in circulation has risen rapidly in recent decades and much of the increase has been caused by demand from abroad. This supply comes from governments, private investors, banks, and other similar sources.

3. **a** Demand has two components: (1) the desire for something and (2) the ability to pay for it.

4. **b** The federal budget shows fiscal policy and budget priorities not only for the coming year but also for the next five years or more.

5. **d** The two main ways to calculate gross domestic product (GDP) are the expenditure approach and the income approach.

6. **a** When the total operating cost of the federal government exceeds available funds, the Treasury Department's Bureau of the Public Debt borrows money by selling U.S. Treasury Securities (treasuries) to the public, institutional investors, and authorized government agencies.

7. **b** Proponents of a tight fiscal policy argue that government acts best when it acts least; they promote low taxes and spending and ideally limit government involvement to the setting of prevailing interest rates.

8. **d** An expansionary fiscal policy expands the amount of money available for consumers and businesses to spend and speeds up the rate of GDP growth. The purpose of an expansionary fiscal policy is to reduce unemployment, increase consumer demand, and avoid a recession.

9. **b** The goals of monetary policy are to promote maximum employment, stable prices and moderate long-term interest rates.

10. **c** To carry out its monetary policy, the Fed uses the discount rate, open market operations, and reserve requirements.

11. **a** The Fed increases or decreases the amount of money in circulation by raising or lowering reserve requirements for member banks.

12. **c** Functions of the Federal Reserve System including acting as the banker for the U.S. Treasury, supervising and regulating banking institutions and certain consumer protection laws, acting as a lender of last resort to nation's banks, and determining monetary policy.

13. **a** The Board of Governors (BOG) is an independent agency of the federal government that reports to and is directly accountable to Congress. The Federal Reserve System consists of twelve Federal Reserve Banks (Reserve Banks), which are under the supervision of the Board of Governors in Washington, D.C.

14. **b** The Federal Reserve System consists of twelve Federal Reserve Banks (Reserve Banks) located in major cities throughout the United States.

15. **d** The automated clearinghouse (ACH) provides a nationwide network to exchange paperless payments among financial institutions and government agencies. The ACH accommodates a wide range of recurring corporate and consumer transactions, such as payroll deposits, electronic bill payments, insurance payments, and Social Security disbursements.

16. **b** The U.S. Department of the Treasury was created in 1789 to manage the government finances, and Alexander Hamilton was the first Secretary of the Treasury.

17. **a** The Secretary of the Treasury serves as a major policy advisor to the President and has primary responsibility for participating in the formulation of broad fiscal policies that have general significance for the economy.

18. **b** The FDIC has three major program areas or lines of business: insurance, supervision of financial institutions, and receivership management.

19. **d** Currently, FHFA establishes, monitors, and enforces the affordable housing goals for Fannie Mae and Freddie Mac that are mandated by the Housing and Economic Recovery Act of 2008 (HERA).

20. **d** FHLBanks provide stable, on-demand, low-cost funding to financial institutions (not individuals) for home mortgage loans, small business, rural, agricultural, and economic development lending.

ANSWER KEY

Unit 3 – Government Influence on Lending

Answers Matching

1.	C	6.	P	11.	N	16.	R
2.	G	7.	F	12.	A	17.	O
3.	Q	8.	L	13.	E	18.	S
4.	D	9.	J	14.	H	19.	K
5.	T	10.	M	15.	I	20.	B

Answers Multiple Choice

1. **a**   The Depository Institutions Deregulation and Monetary Control Act of 1980 had sweeping changes, one of which was to allow savings and loan associations to enter the business of commercial lending, trust services, and non-mortgage consumer lending.

2. **d**   A loan originator is defined as an individual who "takes a residential mortgage loan application and also offers or negotiates terms of a residential mortgage loan for compensation or gain". A person who performs only administrative or clerical tasks in connection with loan origination is not considered a loan originator.

3. **c**   The primary purpose of the ECOA, as implemented by Regulation B, is to prevent banks and other creditors from discriminating when granting credit by requiring them to make extensions of credit equally available to all creditworthy applicants with fairness, impartiality, and without discrimination on any prohibited basis. The regulation applies to consumer and other types of credit transactions.

4. **c**   The Fair Credit Reporting Act establishes procedures for correcting mistakes on a person's credit record and requires that a consumer's record only be provided for legitimate business needs.

5. **d**   The purposes of RESPA are to help consumers get fair settlement services by requiring that key service costs be disclosed in advance, to protect consumers by eliminating kickbacks and referral fees that unnecessarily increase the costs of settlement services, and to further protect consumers by prohibiting certain practices that increase the cost of settlement services.

6. **a**   The federal Truth in Lending Act (TILA) is Title 1 of the Consumer Credit Protection Act of 1968. The CFPB implements TILA through Regulation Z.

7. **c**   The finance charge includes interest, loan fees, finder fees, credit report fees, insurance fees, and mortgage insurance fees (PMI or MMI). In real estate, the finance charge does not include appraisal fees or credit report fees.

8. **a**   Beginning October 3, 2015, lenders must use the Loan Estimate and Closing Disclosure for most closed-end federally related residential mortgages that are covered by RESPA. Additionally, the integrated disclosure requirements apply to construction-only loans, vacant-land loans, and 25-acre loans, all of which are currently exempt from RESPA coverage. However, some home loans (reverse mortgages, HELOCs, and manufactured home loans) are exempt from the TRID rule.

9. **b** The lender is generally required to provide the Loan Estimate within 3 business days of the receipt of the borrower's loan application.

10. **b** Lenders must ensure that borrowers receive the Closing Disclosure at least 3 business days before consummation (the day the loan closes). The seller's Closing Disclosure must be provided to the seller at or before consummation.

Unit 4 – The Mortgage Markets

Answers Matching

1. R	7. Q	13. C	20. H
2. T	8. N	14. S	21. I
3. J	9. A	15. X	22. B
4. O	10. U	17. D	23. G
5. K	11. L	18. V	24. F
6. M	12. P	19. E	

Answers Multiple Choice

1. **c** The purpose of the mortgage markets is to create a continuous flow of money to borrowers. This stimulates the real estate industry and financial markets.

2. **d** The participants in the mortgage markets are the mortgage loan originators, aggregators, securities dealers (brokerage firms and investment banks), and investors.

3. **a** Securitization is the pooling and repackaging of cash flow producing financial assets into securities that are then sold to investors. Any asset that has a cash flow can be securitized.

4. **c** The investment that is bought and sold in the secondary mortgage market is an asset called a mortgage-backed security.

5. **b** The simplest mortgage-backed securities are pass-through securities.

6. **a** A Real Estate Mortgage Investment Conduit (REMIC) is a mortgage securities vehicle that holds commercial and residential mortgages in trust and issues securities representing an undivided interest in these mortgages.

7. **d** Fannie Mae supports the secondary mortgage market by issuing mortgage-related securities and purchasing mortgages. Fannie Mae buys loans from lenders who conform to Fannie Mae guidelines and, by doing so, puts mortgage money back into the system so lenders can make more loans. Fannie Mae is the largest investor in the secondary market.

8. **c** Freddie Mac links Main Street to Wall Street by purchasing, securitizing, and investing in home mortgages. Freddie Mac conducts its business by buying mortgages that meet the company's underwriting and product standards from lenders. The loans are pooled, packaged into securities, guaranteed by Freddie Mac, and sold to investors such as insurance companies and pension funds. This provides homeowners and renters with lower housing costs with better access to home financing

9. **b** Ginnie Mae's focus was to support the market for FHA, VA, RD, and PIH loans. Unlike Fannie Mae and Freddie Mac, Ginnie Mae does not buy or sell pools of loans. Ginnie Mae does not issue mortgage-backed securities (MBS). Instead, Ginnie Mae guarantees investors the timely payment of principal and interest on MBS backed by federally insured or guaranteed loans—mainly loans issued by the FHA and the DVA. In fact, FHA insures approximately two-thirds of the loans backing Ginnie Mae securities.

10. **d** The Federal Agricultural Mortgage Corporation (Farmer Mac) is a government-sponsored enterprise with the mission of providing a secondary market for agricultural real estate and rural housing mortgage loans.

Unit 5 – Sources of Funds

Answers Matching

1. L	8. A	15. DD	22. M
2. D	9. E	16. U	23. J
3. I	10. FF	17. N	24. CC
4. EE	11. O	18. GG	25. K
5. G	12. Z	19. X	26. Y
6. C	13. AA	20. F	
7. V	14. B	21. W	

Answers Multiple Choice

1. **a** A lender is the person who or company that makes mortgage loans, such as a mortgage banker, credit union, bank, or a savings and loan. A lender underwrites and funds the loan.

2. **d** Larger banks and thrifts that lend their own money and originate loans to keep in their own loan portfolio are called portfolio lenders. This is because they originate loans for their own portfolio and not for immediate resale in the secondary mortgage market.

3. **a** While savings banks are authorized to make mortgage loans, most specialize in consumer and commercial loans.

4. **b** A mortgage company, which is also known as a mortgage banker, is a company whose principal business is the origination, closing, funding, selling, and servicing of loans secured by real property.

5. **a** A mortgage REITs, also called a real estate mortgage trust (REMT), makes loans on commercial income property.

6. **b** Since mortgage companies do not have depositors, they use short-term borrowing called a warehouse line or warehouse line of credit. A warehouse line is a revolving line of credit extended to a mortgage company from a warehouse lender to make loans to borrowers.

7. **d**   Third party originators (TPOs) originate but do not underwrite or fund loans. TPOs complete loan packages and act as the mediator between the borrowers and lenders. TPOs include mortgage brokers and loan correspondents.

8. **d**   Retail loan origination refers to lenders (banks, thrifts, and mortgage bankers) that deal directly with the borrower and perform all of the steps necessary during the loan origination and funding process.

9. **c**   When a lender buys a processed loan from a mortgage broker it is called wholesale mortgage lending.

10. **d**   A loan is only as good as the originator makes it, and the issue of quality control is a major factor for a wholesale lender. Quality control refers to the procedures used to check loan quality throughout the application and funding process. Loan wholesalers must rely on the integrity of the correspondents and brokers with which they do business.

Unit 6 – Types of Loans

Answers Matching

1. S	6. D	11. F	16. N
2. E	7. A	12. L	17. O
3. I	8. B	13. R	18. T
4. C	9. K	14. Q	19. J
5. G	10. M	15. P	20. H

Answers Multiple Choice

1. **d**   Lenders offer a variety of loans to help people purchase a property, refinance an existing loan, or get cash out of a property.

2. **a**   A closed-end loan is one in which the borrower receives all of the loan proceeds in one lump sum at the time of closing.

3. **c**   A fully amortizing loan is fully repaid at maturity by periodic reduction of the principal. When a loan is fully amortizing, the payments the borrower makes are equal over the duration of the loan.

4. **d**   A straight loan is not amortized. The borrower only makes periodic interest payments during the term of the loan. The entire principal balance is due in one lump sum upon maturity. These loans are also called interest-only loans. This type of loan is not commonly offered by institutional lenders but may be offered by a seller or a private lender to a buyer.

5. **d**   The most common amortization types include fixed-rate loans, adjustable-rate mortgages (ARMs), and graduated payment mortgages (GPMs).

6. **a**   A 40-year fixed-rate loan extends the repayment term of a fixed-rate mortgage, which results in smaller monthly payments. This longer-term fixed-rate loan product provides another way to put a more expensive home within the reach of buyers.

7. **a**   An adjustable-rate loan or adjustable-rate mortgage (ARM) is a loan with an interest rate that adjusts with a movable economic index. The interest rate on the loan varies upward or downward over the term of the loan depending on money market conditions and the agreed upon index.

8. **c**   The interest rate on an ARM changes periodically, usually in relation to an index, and payments may go up or down accordingly. The interest rate is made up of two parts: the index and the margin.

9. **c**   A lender may offer a variety of ARMS, but they all share similar features—initial interest rate and payment, adjustment period, index, margin, and caps. These basic features are incorporated into every ARM loan.

10. **d**   A graduated payment mortgage (GPM) is a fixed-rate loan with initial payments that are lower than the later payments. The difference between the lower initial payment and the required amortizing payment is added to the unpaid principal balance.

Unit 7 – Conventional Loans

Answers Matching

1. F	8. BB	15. U	22. Q
2. AA	9. G	16. Y	23. W
3. T	10. D	17. N	24. K
4. Z	11. C	18. A	25. J
5. X	12. H	19. V	
6. E	13. R	20. P	
7. DD	14. M	21. CC	

Answers Multiple Choice

1. **c**   The basic protection for a lender who makes conventional loans is the borrower's equity in the property. Therefore, a low down payment means greater risk for the lender, who typically will charge the borrower a higher interest rate.

2. **d**   Private mortgage insurance (PMI) is extra insurance that lenders require from most homebuyers who obtain conventional loans that are more than 80% of their new home's value. Normally, the borrower pays the premium for PMI, not the lender. Many companies nationwide underwrite private mortgage insurance.

3. **a**   Fannie Mae purchases conforming loans made on 1-4 family unit residences (both owner and non-owner occupied), single family second homes, co-ops, condos, PDs, and leaseholds.

4. **b** Contrary to popular belief, DU does not approve loans. DU provides underwriting recommendations and underwriting reports to the lender, who uses these recommendations to approve or disapprove loans.

5. **c** Fannie Mae's traditional offerings consist of fixed-rate loans. Fannie Mae offers them in 10, 15, 20, and 30-year terms. These fixed-rate loans lock in an interest rate and stable, predictable monthly payments.

6. **c** Under the Community Seconds® loan program, a borrower can obtain a secured second loan that typically is funded by a federal, state, or local government agency, an employer, or a nonprofit organization.

7. **a** Like Fannie Mae, Freddie Mac's underwriting guidelines are flexible and vary according to loan program.

8. **c** A jumbo loan exceeds the maximum conforming loan limit set by Fannie Mae and Freddie Mac. Because jumbo loans are bought and sold on a much smaller scale, these loans usually carry a higher interest rate and have additional underwriting requirements.

9. **d** Packing is the practice of adding credit insurance or other extras to increase the lender's profit on a loan. Lenders can require the purchase of credit insurance provided the premiums are calculated and paid on a monthly basis. A lender may not finance a credit insurance premium. [12 CFR §1026.36(i)]. "CFR" stands for the "Code of Federal Regulations".

10. **c** While only one federal law—the Home Ownership and Equity Protection Act—is specifically designed to combat predatory lending, federal agencies have taken actions, sometimes jointly, under various federal consumer protection laws.

Unit 8 – Alternative Financing

Answers Matching

1. B	6. H	11. D	16. A
2. C	7. L	12. Q	17. O
3. V	8. K	13. F	18. M
4. S	9. N	14. J	19. R
5. I	10. P	15. G	20. U

Answers Multiple Choice

1. **c** Alternative financing methods include seller financing, secondary financing, and other financing alternatives that are based on the type of property or the purpose of the loan.

2. **d** Seller financing offers creative financing for buyers with a less than stellar credit rating, no down payment, or not enough cash to cover closing costs.

3. **d**   In seller financing, options include carryback financing, contract for deed, and a wraparound mortgage (WRAP) or all-inclusive trust deed (AITD).

4. **b**   The contract for deed is a financing instrument with many names. It may be called an installment sales contract, a contract of sale, an agreement of sale, a conditional sales contract, or a land sales contract.

5. **d**   Secondary financing includes hard money loans from private lenders, swing loans, home equity loans (HEL), and home equity lines of credit (HELOC).

6. **c**   A home equity line of credit (HELOC) is a typical open-end loan. An open-end loan is expandable by increments up to a maximum dollar amount. It is a line of credit secured by the borrower's home.

7. **b**   If the manufactured home is not permanently attached to the land, a borrower may obtain a personal property loan, which is a loan for anything movable that is not real property.

8. **b**   For prospective purchasers of a cooperative, there is financing available in the form of a share loan. A share loan is a type of loan that is made to finance the purchase of shares in a corporation.

9. **c**   An interim loan is a short-term loan that finances construction costs, such as the building of a new home.

10. **b**   Consumers who need a small loan to repair a car, buy a new appliance, or take a trip choose a closed-end, unsecured loan instead of using their credit cards or getting a home equity loan.

Unit 9 – Government-Backed Loans

Answers Matching

1.	I	5.	F	9.	D	13.	M
2.	N	6.	E	10.	B	14.	O
3.	A	7.	J	11.	G	15.	P
4.	K	8.	H	12.	C		

Answers Multiple Choice

1. **c**   Originally created to stabilize the mortgage market, the FHA caused the some of the greatest changes in the housing industry in the 20th century. It forever changed home mortgage lending by insuring long-term, amortized loans; creating standards for qualifying borrowers; and by establishing minimum property and construction standards for residential properties.

2. **d**   FHA-insured loans are available for individuals only, not LLCs, partnerships or corporations.

3. **d**   Unlike Fannie Mae/Freddie Mac loans, FHA underwriting looks at the stability of income and the borrower's ability to make timely payments. An important aspect of FHA underwriting is that FHA loans are not credit score driven.

4. **d**   The FHA does not require the buyer to have any reserves or available cash on hand during the closing.

5. **c**   The reverse mortgage is a loan program for homeowners who are 62 or older and who have paid off their existing home loan or have only a small balance remaining.

6. **b**   A rehabilitation loan is a great option for buyers who are planning to improve their property immediately upon purchase. This home loan provides the funds to purchase a residential property and the funds to complete an improvement project all in one loan, one application, one set of fees, one closing, and one convenient monthly payment.

7. **b**   VA-guaranteed home loans offer many benefits and advantages. The main benefit is that veterans may not need to make a down payment.

8. **d**   The Department of Veterans Affairs (DVA or VA) does not make loans. It guarantees loans made by approved lenders, much like the FHA.

9. **d**   First, a veteran must request a Certificate of Eligibility (COE), which is a document issued by the DVA that provides evidence of an applicant's eligibility to obtain a VA loan.

10. **b**   Except when refinancing an existing VA-guaranteed ARM to a fixed rate, an IRRRL loan must result in a lower interest rate. When refinancing from an existing VA ARM to a fixed-rate, the interest rate is allowed to increase. The DVA does not require an appraisal or credit-underwriting package. However, the lenders may require an appraisal and a credit report.

Unit 10 – Instruments of Real Estate Finance

Answers Matching

1. R	6. A	11. S	16. F
2. L	7. B	12. J	17. G
3. O	8. N	13. M	18. D
4. K	9. T	14. E	19. C
5. Q	10. I	15. P	20. H

Answers Multiple Choice

1. **b**   The promissory note is the evidence of the debt. It states the amount of money borrowed and the terms of repayment.

2. **c**   A partially amortized installment note is a note with a repayment schedule that is not sufficient to pay off the loan over its term. This type of note calls for regular, periodic payments of principal and interest for a specified period of time. At maturity, the remaining unpaid principal balance is due as a balloon payment.

3. **d** The effective interest rate is the rate the borrower is actually paying and is commonly called the annual percentage rate (APR).

4. **c** A prepayment clause, which is also called an or more clause, allows a borrower to pay off a loan early or make higher payments without paying a prepayment penalty.

5. **c** Required elements to create a negotiable promissory note include the unconditional promise or order to pay a certain amount of money, its payability on demand or at a definite time, its payability to order or bearer, and the signature of the borrower.

6. **c** The Uniform Commercial Code (UCC) governs negotiable instruments and is designed to give uniformity to commercial transactions across all 50 states.

7. **c** The UCC defines a holder in due course as one who takes an instrument for value in good faith absent any notice that it is overdue, has been dishonored, or is subject to any defense against it or claim to it by any other person.

8. **d** The maker can use certain defenses against anyone in a court action. These include forgery if the maker really did not sign the note; accusing the plaintiff of making secret, material changes to the note; claiming incapacity if the maker is a minor or is incompetent; and claiming illegal object if the note is connected to an illegal act or if the interest rate is usurious.

9. **b** A security instrument is a legal document given by the borrower to hypothecate (pledge) the property to the lender as collateral for the loan.

10. **d** Every security instrument includes the date of its execution, the name(s) of the borrower(s), the name of the lender, a reference to the promissory note including the amount of the loan, and a description of the property securing the loan.

11. **a** In the event of default on the loan, the senior lien status ensures the lender's priority during a foreclosure action, effectively eliminating all other junior liens that may exist.

12. **a** The principal advantage of the trust deed over the mortgage is that the trust deed's power of sale is not typically outlawed by time, whereas a mortgage remains subject to the statute of limitations.

13. **a** The two parties are the mortgagor (borrower) and mortgagee (lender).

14. **a** In a lien theory state, title to real property is vested in the borrower. The borrower gives only a lien right to the lender during the term of the loan. In a title theory state, title to real property is vested in the lender. In a title theory state, the mortgage states that title reverts to the borrower once the loan is paid.

15. **b** Statutory redemption is the right of a mortgagor to recover the property AFTER a foreclosure sale.

16. **d** When a promissory note is secured by a deed of trust, three parties are involved: the borrower (trustor), the lender (beneficiary), and a neutral third party (trustee).

17. **d**   Under a deed of trust, the lender has a choice of two types of foreclosure. The lender may choose between foreclosure under the power of sale clause, which is an auction type sale held by the trustee, with the property going to the highest bidder, or judicial foreclosure, in which the property is foreclosed through court action.

18. **c**   Equitable title is the interest held by the buyer under a contract for deed that gives the buyer the equitable right to obtain absolute ownership to the property when the seller holds legal title.

19. **d**   In order to reinstate the loan the borrower must pay the lender all sums due under the note as if no acceleration occurred. In addition, the borrower must cure any default of any other covenants and pay all expenses incurred by the lender in enforcing the security instrument (i.e., attorneys' fees, property inspection, valuation fees, etc.).

20. **c**   The lender can sell the note (together with the security instrument) one or more times without giving prior notice to the borrower.

Unit 11 – The Loan Package

Answers Matching

1. F	4. E	7. H
2. C	5. D	8. A
3. B	6. G	

Answers Multiple Choice

1. **b**   The four basic steps in the loan process are 1) completing the application, 2) processing, 3) underwriting, and 4) closing.

2. **d**   A loan package is the file of documents the lender needs to determine whether to fund a loan. The documents in the loan package include the loan application; verifications of employment, income, and bank accounts; and information on the property.

3. **b**   Real property is the primary collateral for a real estate loan and acts as the security for repayment of the loan in case the borrower defaults. The second section of the application describes the property used as collateral for the loan and states the purpose of the loan.

4. **c**   The borrower is required to include: 1) specific identification of the property, including legal description and common address (street address); 2) title information, such as vesting, claims, encumbrances, liens, and real estate loans; 3) description of the land and type of improvements, including work that might be subject to mechanics' liens; 4) purchase price and terms, such as date purchased, taxes, zoning, and assessments; and 5) present value, which might be different from the purchase price.

5. **c**   Evidence that a borrower can pay back the loan is shown by his or her employment. The Employment Verification section of the application asks for the name and address of the borrower's employer, the borrower's position, and length of employment.

6. **a**   The Monthly Income and Combined Housing Expense Information section of the Uniform Residential Loan Application informs the lender about the borrower's current income and proposed housing expense. It includes other income such as rents, annuities, and royalties.

7. **d**   Depending on the lender, borrowers may be able to lock in the interest rate and number of points charged on the loan. This may be done at the same time they file the application, during the processing of the loan, when the loan is approved, or later.

8. **b**   The Verification of Deposit (VOD) is a form completed by the borrower's bank to confirm the status and balance of the borrower's bank accounts.

9. **b**   Real estate lenders using AU systems quickly evaluate a wide range of information, including consumer credit history, property information, and loan type to determine the probability that the borrower will repay the loan.

10. **a**   The borrower may provide the most recent 3 months' statements from the depository institution the borrower uses as an alternative way to document the Verification of Deposit.

Unit 12 – Underwriting

Answers Matching

1.	O	5.	M	9.	P	13.	G
2.	C	6.	J	10.	H	14.	K
3.	Q	7.	I	11.	D	15.	A
4.	R	8.	L	12.	F		

Answers Multiple Choice

1. **c**   Lenders look for the borrower's ability and willingness to repay debt. They speak of the three Cs of credit: capacity, character, and collateral. Lenders use different combinations of the three Cs to reach their decisions.

2. **a**   The underwriter evaluates the risk based on the information in the loan package. Choices (c) and (d) are used to create the loan package. Choice (b) only occurs after the loan is evaluated and approved.

3. **b**   Larger down payments lower the LTV ratio on the loan and reduce risk to the lender.

4. **c**   A lender calculates the maximum loan amount for which a borrower qualifies. To determine the borrower's ability to repay the loan, the underwriter uses debt-to-income ratios to calculate the risk that the borrower will default.

5. **c**   The front ratio is the percentage of the borrower's monthly gross income (before taxes) that is used to pay housing costs, including principal, interest, taxes, and insurance (PITI). When applicable, it also includes mortgage insurance and homeowner's association fees.

6. **d** Common DTI Ratios include: conforming loans – 36% DTI, FHA - 31% front ratio and 43% back ratio (31/43), and VA only uses back ratio of 41% as a guideline.

7. **c** An underwriter reviews the borrower's history to see it the borrower makes payments in a timely manner according to contract terms.

8. **c** Experian®, TransUnion™, and Equifax® are the three major credit bureaus that collect data independently and use the data to create consumer credit reports.

9. **c** The rule applies to all residential mortgages including purchase loans, refinances, home equity loans, first liens, and subordinate liens. In short, if the lender is making a loan secured by a principal residence, second or vacation home, condominium, or mobile or manufactured home, the lender must verify the borrowers' ability to repay the loan. The section does not apply to commercial or business loans, even if secured by a personal dwelling. It also does not apply to loans for timeshares, reverse mortgages, loan modifications, and temporary bridge loans.

10. **b** The CFPB defines a Qualified Mortgage as a credit transaction secured by a dwelling that meets six specific criteria.

Unit 13 – Settlement & Closing

Answers Matching

1.	Q	6.	M	11.	R	16.	H
2.	G	7.	J	12.	D	17.	P
3.	I	8.	C	13.	F	18.	L
4.	K	9.	T	14.	A	19.	E
5.	N	10.	S	15.	O	20.	B

Answers Multiple Choice

1. **d** The goal of the closing meeting is to transfer ownership of the property to the buyer and pay the seller for the property. To accomplish this goal, the paperwork brought to the meeting must be prepared, inspected, corrected if needed, approved, signed if necessary, and exchanged as required.

2. **a** When the principals' agents and attorneys attend the closing, they are not neutral third parties. Agents and attorneys attend the closing meeting to represent their client's interests.

3. **b** There are four kinds of evidence of title: abstract and opinion, certificate of title, title insurance and Torrens certificate of title.

4. **b** The chain of title is the public record of prior transfers and encumbrances that affect the title of a parcel of land.

5.   **c**   Property taxes are paid in arrears (at the end of each tax period). Paying in arrears is payment at the end of a period for which payment is due. It is the opposite of paying in advance.

6.   **a**   When specific improvements are needed to benefit a certain area—such as underground utilities, sewers, or streets—special assessments are levied to pay for the improvements. The difference between special assessments and property taxes is that property taxes are used to operate the government in general, whereas special assessments are used for specific, local purposes.

7.   **a**   The amount of the total consideration, or the sales price, is a credit on the seller's closing statement. It appears as a debit to the buyer.

8.   **c**   An escrow (impound) account is a trust account for funds set aside for future, recurring costs relating to a property, such as payment of property taxes and hazard insurance.

9.   **d**   The settlement statement shows the actual settlement costs of the loan transaction.

10. **a**   The Annual Escrow Statement summarizes all escrow account deposits and payments during the servicer's 12-month computation year.

Unit 14 – Loan Servicing

Answers Matching

1. F	5. B	9. I	13. K
2. Q	6. J	10. P	14. R
3. N	7. E	11. O	15. M
4. D	8. L	12. H	16. A

Answers Multiple Choice

1.   **c**   The lender who originated the loan may service the loan, or the servicing may be sold to a loan servicing company.

2.   **b**   The transfer of servicing should not affect the borrower or the real estate loan adversely. The original terms and conditions of the real estate loan stay the same. The interest rate and duration of the loan do not change on fixed-rate loans. The payment amount and payment schedule stay the same. However, the payments on loans with escrow accounts may change due to increases or decreases in real property taxes or insurance requirements.

3.   **b**   If the borrower has an adjustable-rate mortgage (ARM) loan, the original conditions of the loan note stay in effect and the rate will change according to the adjustment periods (i.e. every 6 months, annually, every 3 years).

4.   **a**   The current servicer must notify the borrower no less than 15 days before the effective date of the transfer.

5. **a** If the borrower has received both letters or has verified the transfer of the real estate loans with the previous servicer, he or she should be sure to send all payments to the new servicer from that point on.

6. **b** The loan administrator performs the day-to-day management of individual loans and services entire loan portfolios while protecting the interests of both the borrower and investor.

7. **d** An escrow account (impound account) is a fund the lender may require the borrower to establish in order to pay property taxes and/or hazard insurance as they become due on the property during the year.

8. **a** The real estate loan administrator also is required to give the borrower an annual statement that details the activity of the escrow account. This statement shows the deposits and account balance and reflects payments for property taxes and homeowners insurance.

9. **d** The payoff demand statement details the current principal balance, interest, statement fees, and recording and reconveyance fees. The payoff demand statement requires payoff funds to be sent by wire transfer or certified funds.

10. **b** When a loan secured by a deed of trust is paid in full, a deed of reconveyance is recorded. The deed of reconveyance transfers title from the trustee to the trustor (borrower).

Unit 15 – Default & Foreclosure

Answers Matching

1. C		6. F		11. J		16. G	
2. R		7. L		12. N		17. H	
3. E		8. I		13. M		18. S	
4. O		9. V		14. K		19. T	
5. B		10. P		15. U		20. D	

Answers Multiple Choice

1. **d** When a borrower fails to perform a legal or contractual duty, such as paying a contractual debt, the situation is known as a default. In real estate finance, a default can signal the beginning of the foreclosure process.

2. **d** When a borrower is in default, there are options the borrower can use to salvage his or her credit and, more importantly, stay in the home. Borrowers must be proactive in their efforts, which can include refinancing the existing loan and selling the property when necessary.

3. **d**   The lender can work with a borrower who is experiencing financial difficulties by offering forbearance, recasting the existing loan on the property, or by accepting a deed in lieu of foreclosure.

4. **a**   Foreclosure laws vary in each state, but there are three general types of foreclosure proceedings: non-judicial foreclosure, judicial foreclosure, and strict foreclosure.

5. **b**   In many states, the foreclosure procedure begins when the lender asks the trustee to file (record) a notice of default.

6. **a**   The proceeds of the sale are used to satisfy the debt with the highest priority first, and then the next highest priority debt is paid, then the next, and so on until either the sale proceeds have faded to nothing or all holders of debt relating to the property have been repaid.

7. **d**   Upon learning of the impending foreclosure by a senior lienholder, the junior lienholder has two choices. Junior lienholders may stay silent and hope the proceeds from the foreclosure sale are enough to pay off the loan balance, or the lienholder may start its own foreclosure proceedings.

8. **b**   If the FHA takes ownership of a property after a foreclosure, it may refurbish the home and sell it for a higher price to cover any losses. These properties are known as HUD homes.

9. **a**   After notifying the VA office of the default, the VA has subrogation rights to bring the loan current.

10. **d**   For a lender, sometimes the proceeds of the sale are not sufficient to satisfy the foreclosed debt. If that happens, the lender may try to sue on the promissory note and obtain a deficiency judgment against the borrower to recover the money owed on the defaulting balance of the loan.

GLOSSARY

A

acceleration clause
A clause in a loan document that would cause the entire loan to be due, under certain circumstances—sale of the property or failure to repay the debt.

adjustable-rate mortgage (ARM)
A loan whose interest rate is periodically adjusted according to the terms of the promissory note.

adjustment period
Period between rate changes on an adjustable-rate mortgage

alienation clause
A clause in a contract giving the lender certain rights in the event of the sale or transfer of a mortgaged property.

all-inclusive trust deed (AITD)
A method of financing in which a new junior loan is created that includes both the unpaid principal balance of the first loan and whatever new sums are loaned by the lender.

allocation
Assigning a cost (generally one not yet spent) to either the seller or the buyer

amortize
The reduction of a debt through regular payments of both interest and principal.

annual percentage rate (APR)
The cost of a mortgage stated as a yearly rate; includes such items as interest, mortgage insurance and loan origination fee (points). Use of the APR permits a standard expression of credit costs, which facilitates easy comparison of lenders.

appreciation
An increase in value as a result of economic or other related changes.

assume
A term used in real estate transactions where the buyer may take over, or assume, responsibility for a pre-existing mortgage.

assumption clause
A clause in loan contracts that allows a buyer to take over the existing loan from the seller and become liable for repayment of the loan.

automated clearinghouse (ACH)
A nationwide network to exchange paperless payments among financial institutions and government agencies.

automated underwriting
Technology-based tool that combines historical loan performance, statistical models, and mortgage lending factors to determine whether a loan can be sold into the secondary market.

B

back ratio
In underwriting, the percentage of income needed to pay for all recurring debt.

balloon payment
A final loan payment that is substantially larger than the other payments and repays the debt in full.

bare legal title
Refers to the title held by a trustee to a trust deed.

biweekly payment
A loan with a payment due every 2 weeks

blanket loan
A loan often used in construction financing secured by several properties.

Board of Governors (BOG)
The BOG regulates the banking system and supervises certain types of financial institutions, overseeing a network of 12 Federal Reserve Banks (FRBs) and 25 branches of the Federal Reserve System.

bond
A debt instrument

C

capacity
Legitimate legal status to enter into a contract (mentally competent and of legal age), one of the legal essentials of a valid contract.

capital
Equity (one's own money) and debt (borrowed money)

capital market
The market in which long-term or intermediate-term securities are traded.

capitalization
The process of converting the future income stream into an indication of the property's present worth.

closed-end loan
Loan in which the borrower receives all loan proceeds in one lump sum at the time of closing.

GLOSSARY

Closing Disclosure

A settlement statement designed by the Consumer Financial Protection Bureau that discloses the final settlement charges paid by the buyer and/or the seller in a real estate transaction.

closing statement

Accounting of funds made to the sellers and buyers individually.

collateral

Something of value given as security for a debt.

collateralized mortgage obligation (CMO)

A type of MBS, CMOs are bonds that represent claims to specific cash flows from large pools of home mortgages. The streams of principal and interest payments on the mortgages are distributed to the different classes of CMO interests, known as tranches.

compound interest

The interest paid on original principal and on the accrued and unpaid interest that accumulates as the debt matures.

conforming loan

Loan with terms and conditions that follow the guidelines set forth by Fannie Mae and Freddie Mac.

constructive notice

Knowledge of a fact that is a matter of public record.

Consumer Financial Protection Bureau (CFPB)

An independent bureau within the Federal Reserve Board. The CFPB enforces federal consumer financial laws, promotes consumer financial education, and handles consumer complaints and inquiries.

contract of sale

A contract to purchase real property in which the seller agrees to defer all or part of the purchase price for a specified period of time.

conventional loan

Any loan without government insurance or guarantees.

credit bureau

Agency that collects and maintains up-to-date credit and public record information about consumers.

credit report

Document that lists the credit history of an individual.

credit score

Statistical summary of the information contained in a consumer's credit report.

currency

A country's official unit of monetary exchange.

cycles

Periodic, irregular up and down movements of economic activity that take place over a period of 2 to 6 years.

debt

Dollar amount that is borrowed from another party, usually under specific terms.

debt-to-income ratio

A ratio derived by dividing the borrower's total monthly obligations (including housing expense) by his or her gross monthly income.

debtor

One who owes debt; a borrower.

deed in lieu of foreclosure

Voluntary transfer of the property back to the lender

deed of reconveyance

A document used to transfer legal title from the trustee back to the borrower (trustor) after a debt secured by a deed of trust has been paid to the lender (beneficiary).

default

Failure to pay a contractual debt. Also a failure to appear in court.

default risk

The borrower's inability to meet interest payment obligations on time.

deficiency judgment

A judgment against a borrower for the balance of a debt owed when the security for the loan is not sufficient to pay the debt.

demand

A desire to buy or obtain a commodity

demand deposit

A deposit that can be withdrawn at any time.

Department of Veterans Affairs (VA)

The federal agency that provides benefits including VA loans to qualified veterans.

depository institution

A financial institution that is legally allowed to accept deposits from consumers.

deregulation

A process by which financial institutions that were legally restrained in their lending activities are allowed to compete freely for profits in the marketplace.

direct lender

Lender that deals directly with its customers and funds its own loans.

discharge of the loan

Cancellation or termination of a loan contract.

discount rates
The interest rate charged by the Federal Reserve Bank to its member banks for loans.

disintermediation
The process of a depositor removing funds from savings.

down payment
The initial equity the borrower has in the property.

due-on-sale clause
A provision in a mortgage that states that the balance of the loan is due if the property is subsequently sold.

eligibility
Veteran's right to VA home loan benefits under the law, based on military service.

entitlement
The maximum guaranty provided by the VA for a veteran's home loan.

equitable right of redemption
The right of a debtor before a foreclosure sale to reclaim property that had been given up due to mortgage default.

equitable title
The right to obtain absolute ownership to property when legal title is held in another's name.

equity
An owner's financial interest in real or personal property at a specific moment in time.

equity of redemption
The right of a debtor, before a foreclosure sale, to reclaim property that had been given up due to mortgage default. Also known as the right of redemption.

execute
To perform, to sign, or to complete.

fed funds rate
The rate at which depository institutions trade balances at the Federal Reserve.

Federal Home Loan Mortgage Corporation
This government-sponsored enterprise (GSE) is a stockholder-owned corporation charted by Congress in 1970 to stabilize the mortgage markets and support homeownership and affordable rental housing. Also called Freddie Mac.

Federal Housing Administration (FHA)
A federal agency established in 1934 that encourages improvements in housing standards and conditions, provides an adequate home-financing system, and exerts a stabilizing influence on the mortgage market.

Federal Housing Finance Agency (FHFA)
An independent agency, established by the Federal Housing Finance Reform Act of 2007, to regulate the government sponsored enterprises.

Federal National Mortgage Association
This government-sponsored enterprise (GSE) was created by Congress in 1938 to bolster the housing industry in the aftermath of the Great Depression. Also called Fannie Mae.

Federal Reserve Bank
The twelve Federal Reserve Banks are the operating arms of the central bank. The Federal Reserve Banks handle the Treasury's payments, assist with the Treasury's cash management and investment activities, and sell government securities.

finance
The commercial activity of providing funds and capital to a borrower.

finance company
A business that makes consumer loans for which household goods and other personal property serve as collateral.

financial fiduciary
An institution that collects money from depositors, premium payers, or pension plan contributors and makes loans to borrowers.

financial intermediaries
An organization (commercial bank or credit union) that obtains funds through deposits and then lends those funds to earn a return.

financial market
A market in which financial securities and commodities are bought and sold.

fiscal policy
Government policy on taxes and government spending.

fiscal year
The financial year that starts on July 1 and runs through June 30 of the following year; used for real property tax purposes.

fixed-rate loan
Loan with fixed interest and level payments for the life of the loan

forbearance
Forgiving of a debt or obligation

foreclose

The legal process by which a borrower in default under a mortgage is deprived of his or her interest in the mortgaged property.

foreclosure with power of sale

A forced sale when property is sold to satisfy a debt secured by a trust deed or mortgage where the security instrument allows the property to be sold at auction by a trustee or mortgagee.

front ratio

In underwriting, the percentage of a borrower's monthly gross income that is used to pay the monthly housing expense.

fully amortized note

A note that is fully repaid at maturity through periodic reduction of the principal.

Government National Mortgage Association

A government-owned corporation within the Department of Housing and Urban Development (HUD). Also called Ginnie Mae.

government sponsored enterprises

Financial services corporations created by the United States Congress.

graduated payment mortgage

A loan in which the monthly payment graduates by a certain percentage each year for a specific number of years, then levels off for the remaining term of the loan.

hard money loan

Loan that takes cash out of a property.

holder

The party to whom a promissory note is payable.

home equity line-of-credit (HELOC)

A form of revolving credit in which a borrower's home serves as collateral.

hypothecation

To pledge property as security for a debt without actually giving up possession or title.

index

Publicly published number used as the basis for adjusting the interest rates of ARMs.

interest

In real estate finance, the cost of borrowing money.

interim financing

A short-term loan usually made to finance the cost of construction.

intermediate title theory

Some states follow the intermediate theory that says a mortgage is a lien unless the borrower defaults. The title then is automatically transferred to the lender.

intermediation

The process of transferring capital from those who invest funds to those who wish to borrow.

judicial foreclosure

Foreclosure by court action.

junior lien

An encumbrance second in priority to a previously recorded lien or to a lien to which the encumbrance has been subordinated.

junior trust deed

Any trust that is recorded after a first trust deed, and whose priority is less than the first.

lender

Person who or company that originates and funds loans, such as a mortgage banker, credit union, bank, or a savings and loan.

leverage

The utilization of borrowed funds to increase purchasing power, or using a smaller, borrowed investment to generate a larger rate of return.

lien

A form of encumbrance that holds property as security for the payment of a debt.

liquid assets

Securities and financial instruments that are converted easily and quickly into cash.

loan correspondent

A third party originator who originates loans for a sponsor.

Loan Estimate

A form designed by the Consumer Financial Protection Bureau to provide borrowers with good-faith estimates of credit costs of real estate transactions.

loan origination
The lending process from application to closing.

loan package
The file of documents the lender needs to determine whether to fund a loan.

loan portfolio
Set of loans that a financial institution, or other lender, holds at any given time.

loan processing
The steps taken by a lender from the time the application is received to the time the loan is approved.

loan servicer
Company that collects payments from borrowers, subtracts fees, and sends the balance of the money to investors who own the loans.

loan servicing
The act of supervising and administering a loan after it has been made.

loan-to-value ratio (LTV)
The ratio of the amount borrowed to the appraised value or sales price of a parcel of real property; generally expressed as a percentage.

maker
The borrower who executes a promissory note and becomes primarily liable for payment to the lender.

margin
In an adjustable-rate loan, the amount added to the index rate that represents the lender's cost of doing business (includes costs, profits, and risk of loss of the loan).

market economy
An economy that relies primarily on interactions between buyers and sellers to allocate resources.

monetary policy
Policy carried out by the Federal Reserve System to influence the cost and availability of credit to promote economic growth, full employment, and price stability.

money
Any generally accepted medium of exchange and unit of account.

money market
The interaction of buyers and sellers of short-term money market instruments such as short-term financing and securities.

money supply
The total amount of money available for transactions and investment in the economy.

mortgage
The use of property as security for the payment of a debt; also the document used to establish a mortgage lien.

mortgage banker
A lender who originates new mortgage loans, and services and sells existing loans in the secondary mortgage market.

mortgage broker
A person who brings borrowers and lenders together.

mortgage default insurance
The insurance that provides coverage for the top part of a residential loan in the event of default.

mortgage pool
Group of mortgages that usually have the same interest rate and term.

mortgage yield
The amount received or returned from real estate loan portfolios expressed as a percentage.

mortgage-backed securities
Debt issues collateralized by mortgages.

mortgagee
The lender under a mortgage.

mortgagor
A borrower who pledges property through a mortgage to secure a loan.

negative amortization
A condition created when a loan payment is less than the interest payment due.

negotiable instrument
Any written instrument that may be transferred by endorsement or delivery.

net operating income (NOI)
The annual gross income of an investment, which includes all revenues generated by the property, including rent, laundry income, late fees and parking charges (less an annual vacancy factor or any rental losses), less operating expenses to calculate the net operating income (NOI).

net worth
The value of all assets minus all liabilities.

non-amortizing loan
A loan with no payments; principal and interest due at the end of the term.

non-conforming loan
A loan that does not meet the Fannie Mae or Freddie Mac lending guidelines.

non-judicial foreclosure
The power to foreclose on a property without court approval. Also called a strict foreclosure or forfeiture.

noteholder
A subsequent owner of the note is a holder in due course.

notice of default
A notice to a defaulting party that there has been non-payment of the debt.

novation
The substitution of a new obligation for an old one; substitution of new parties to an existing obligation, as where the parties to an agreement accept a new debtor in place of an old one.

open-end loan
A loan that is expandable by increments up to a certain amount.

open-market operations
The process where the Fed buys and sells government securities to influence the amount of available credit.

or more clause
A clause in a promissory note that allows a borrower to pay it off early with no penalty.

origination fee
A fee payable upon funding of a real estate loan

package loan
A loan on real property that can be secured by land, structure, or personal property.

partially amortized installment note
A promissory note with a repayment schedule that is not sufficient to pay off the loan over its term. At maturity, the remaining principal balance is due in full.

pass-through securities
The proceeds from the sale of securities in the secondary market that are passed on to the securities buyer.

payment cap
Cap restricting increase in a payment on an ARM.

performing loan
Loan on which the agreed-upon payments of principal and interest are current.

pledge account
The transfer of property to a lender to be held as security for repayment of a debt.

power of sale
A clause in a trust deed or mortgage that gives the mortgage holder the right to sell the property in the event of default by the borrower.

prepayment penalty clause
A clause in a trust deed that allows a lender to collect a certain percentage of a loan as a penalty for an early payoff.

price
The amount of money, or other consideration, paid for specific goods or services.

primary mortgage market
The market in which mortgage originators provide loans to borrowers.

prime rate
The rate the bank charges its strongest customers (those with the highest credit ratings), is heavily influenced by the discount rate.

promissory note
A written legal contract that obligates the borrower to repay a loan.

proration
Dividing a cost (most often one that has already been paid) between the two parties.

purchase-money loan
Loan used to purchase real property.

Real Estate Settlement Procedures Act (RESPA)
A federal law enacted in 1974 and later revised, that ensures that the buyer and seller in a real estate transaction have knowledge of all settlement costs when the purchase of one-to-four family residential dwelling is financed by a federally related mortgage loan.

reconvey
The act of transferring title of property back to the original owner.

redemption
The legal right of a borrower to make good on a defaulted loan within a statutory period of time and thus regain the property.

reinstate
To bring current and restore.

remedy
Selection from several alternative courses of action to cure a breach of contract.

request for notice
Notice to be sent to any parties interested in a trust deed, informing them of a default.

reserve requirements
The amount of money (usually a percentage of deposits) and liquid assets the Federal Reserve requires member banks to set aside as a safety measure.

residual income
In VA underwriting, the net income remaining after deducting monthly housing expenses used to cover family living expenses.

retail loan origination
Lenders (banks, thrifts, and mortgage bankers) that deal directly with the borrower and perform all of the steps necessary during the loan origination and funding process.

reverse annuity mortgage
A loan that enables elderly homeowners to borrow against the equity in their homes by receiving monthly payments from a lender to help meet living costs.

risk analysis
A study made, usually by a lender, of the various factors that might affect the repayment of a loan.

risk rating
A process used by a lender to decide on the soundness of making a loan and to reduce all the factors affecting the repayment of the loan to a qualified rating of some kind.

rollover mortgage
A loan that allows the rewriting of a new loan at the termination of a prior loan.

satisfaction
Full payment of a debt.

secondary mortgage market
Market in which mortgages as bought and sold to provide liquidity into the lenders in the primary mortgage market.

secured debt
Debt owed to a creditor that is secured by collateral.

securitization
The pooling and repackaging of cash flow producing financial assets into securities that are then sold to investors. Any asset that has a cash flow can be securitized.

security instrument
An instrument of finance, such as a mortgage or trust deed, used as security for a loan.

settlement
Final meeting of the parties involved in the real estate transaction at which the transaction documents are signed and the deed and money are transferred.

shared appreciation mortgage
A mortgage in which the lender and borrower agree to share a certain percentage of the increase in market value of the property.

sheriff's deed
A deed given to a buyer when property is sold through court action in order to satisfy a judgment for money or foreclosure of a mortgage.

Special Information Booklet
When a potential homebuyer applies for a mortgage loan, the lender must give the buyer a *Special Information Booklet*, which contains consumer information on various real estate settlement services.

statute of limitations
A statute limiting the period of time during which legal action may be taken on a certain issue.

statutory foreclosure
The legal process of terminating a debtor's right to a property as a result of default on a mortgage or other lien.

strict foreclosure
A foreclosure proceeding in which the debtor has a limited amount of time, once appropriate notice has been given, to repay the debt before their equitable and statutory redemption rights are waived and full legal title to the property is granted to the lender. This type of foreclosure is rarely used in contemporary markets.

subject to clause
Clause in a security instrument that states the buyer will take over payments on an existing loan, but assumes no personal liability for the loan.

subordination clause
A clause in a contract in which the holder of a trust deed permits a subsequent loan to take priority.

supply
The quantity of a product on the market that is available for consumption at a particular time at a particular price.

swing loan or bridge loan
A short-term loan that allows a buyer to purchase property before selling another property, and receiving the money from the sale.

takeout financing
Long term, permanent loan used primarily in construction financing.

third party originator (TPOs)
Those who originate but do not underwrite or fund loans.

thrift
An organization formed to hold deposits for individuals.

title
Evidence of the ownership of land, publicly recorded in the county where the property is located.

title theory
In some states, the lender has the title to a mortgaged property until the loan is fully repaid. The borrower holds equitable title, or the right to use and possess the property.

trust deed
A written security instrument that legally conveys property to a trustee. Also called a deed of trust.

trustee's deed
A deed given to a buyer of real property at a trustee's sale.

underwriting
The process of determining a borrower's financial strength, so that the loan amount and terms can be established.

underwriting guidelines
Principles lenders use to evaluate the risk of making real estate loan.

unsecured debt
Debt that is not connected to any specific piece of property.

value
The significance placed on goods or services, current or future.

vendee
The buyer under a contract of sale.

vendor
The seller under a contract of sale (land contract).

warehouse line
A revolving line of credit extended to a mortgage company from a warehouse lender to make loans to borrowers.

warehousing
The process of assembling a number of mortgage loans into one package and holding them for a period of time prior to selling them to an investor.

wholesale loan origination
The process in which mortgage brokers and loan correspondents originate loans.

wraparound mortgage
A method of financing in which a new loan is placed in a secondary position. The new loan includes both the unpaid principal balance of the first loan and whatever sums are loaned by the lender. Also known as an all-inclusive trust deed.

yield
The return on investment stated as a percentage.

INDEX

S